Andalucía

Córdoba Province (p195)

Jaén Province (p219)

Huelva & Sevilla Provinces (p79)

⊙ **Seville** (p48)

Granada Province (p246)

Almería Province (p285)

Málaga Province (p156)

Cádiz Province & Gibraltar (p108)

THIS EDITION WRITTEN AND RESEARCHED BY
Isabella Noble, John Noble,
Josephine Quintero, Brendan Sainsbury

PLAN YOUR TRIP

Welcome to
Andalucía 4

Andalucía Map 6

Andalucía's Top 17 8

Need to Know 18

What's New 20

If You Like.... 21

Month by Month 23

Itineraries 26

Eat Like a Local 30

Outdoor Activities 36

Travel with Children.....41

Regions at a Glance.... 44

FERIA DE ABRIL,
SEVILLE P70

ALAN COPSON / GETTY IMAGES ©

HORSE RIDING, TARIFA P143

JOCHEM D WIJNANDS / GETTY IMAGES ©

ON THE ROAD

SEVILLE 48

HUELVA & SEVILLA
PROVINCES. 79
Huelva 82
Lugares Colombinos . . . 84
La Rábida. 84
Palos de la Frontera. 84
Moguer. 85
Huelva's
Costa de la Luz. 86
Flecha del Rompido. 86
Isla Cristina. 86
Ayamonte 87
East of Huelva. 87
Matalascañas 87
Parque Nacional
de Doñana 87
El Rocío 90
North of Huelva 92
Minas de Riotinto. 92
Aracena 93
Sierra de Aracena. 95
Sevilla Province 98
Santiponce 98
Carmona 99
Osuna. 102
Écija 103
Parque Natural Sierra
Norte de Sevilla 105

CÁDIZ PROVINCE
& GIBRALTAR 108
Cádiz. 109
The Sherry Triangle 118
Jerez de la Frontera. 119
El Puerto
de Santa María 125
Sanlúcar
de Barrameda. 129
The White Towns. 131
Arcos de la Frontera 131

Grazalema 135
Zahara de la Sierra 136
Parque Natural Sierra
de Grazalema 137
Olvera. 138
Costa de la Luz
& the Southeast 139
Vejer de la Frontera 139
Los Caños de Meca 141
Zahara de los Atunes. . . . 142
Tarifa. 142
Bolonia. 148
Parque Natural Los
Alcornocales 148
Gibraltar. 150

MÁLAGA
PROVINCE. 156
Málaga 157
Costa del Sol. 170
Torremolinos
& Benalmádena 170
Fuengirola 172
Marbella. 173
Estepona 175
Mijas. 177
The Interior 178
Ronda. 178
Serranía de Ronda 184
Ardales & El Chorro 185
Antequera 185
Paraje Natural Torcal
de Antequera 188
Laguna de Fuente
de Piedra 189
East of Málaga 189
La Axarquía 189
Nerja. 191

CÓRDOBA
PROVINCE. 195
Córdoba 198
Southern
Córdoba Province 211

Contents

Baena............... 211
Parque Natural
Sierras Subbéticas...... 211
**Western
Córdoba Province.....** **216**
Almodóvar del Río...... 216
Parque Natural Sierra
de Hornachuelos....... 216

JAÉN PROVINCE... 219
Jaén 222
**Northwest
Jaén Province 225**
Desfiladero de
Despeñaperros
& Santa Elena.......... 225
Parque Natural Sierra
de Andújar............. 226
**Eastern Jaén
Province............. 227**
Baeza 227
Úbeda................. 231
Cazorla............... 237
Parque Natural Sierras
de Cazorla, Segura
y Las Villas............. 239

**GRANADA
PROVINCE........ 246**
Granada 247
**La Vega
& El Altiplano 271**
Guadix 271
**Sierra Nevada
& Las Alpujarras...... 272**
Sierra Nevada......... 273
Las Alpujarras......... 275
Costa Tropical....... 282
Salobreña 282
Almuñécar
& La Herradura........ 283

**ALMERÍA
PROVINCE........ 285**
Almería............. 288
North of Almería...... 294
Desierto de Tabernas ...294
Níjar 295
**Las Alpujarras
de Almería.......... 296**
Laujar de Andarax...... 297
Costa de Almería 298
Parque Natural de
Cabo de Gata-Níjar 298
Mojácar 303
Los Vélez 307

UNDERSTAND

Andalucía
Today 310
History 312
Andalucian
Architecture 325
Landscape & Wildlife... 332
Flamenco 338
Andalucian Arts 344
Bullfighting 348
Andalucian Kitchen 351

SURVIVAL GUIDE

Directory A–Z 358
Transport 367
Language............. 373
Index................ 383
Map Legend.......... 391

SPECIAL FEATURES

**Seville Cathedral
3D Illustration.........** 52
**Flamenco
Colour Feature ....** 62
**Mezquita
3D Illustration........** 200
**Teterías & Hammams
Colour Feature ....** 244
**Alhambra
3D Illustration........** 252

Welcome to Andalucía

The scent of orange blossom, the thrash of a flamenco guitar, the glimpse of a white village perched spectacularly atop a crag: memories of Andalucía stay with you like collected souvenirs.

The Essence of Spain

Immortalised in operas and vividly depicted in 19th-century artworks, Andalucía often acts as a synonym for Spain as a whole: a sun-dappled, fiesta-loving land of guitar-wielding troubadours, reckless bullfighters, feisty operatic heroines and roguish Roma singers wailing sad laments. While this simplistic portrait might be outdated and overly romantic, it carries an element of truth. Andalucía, despite creeping modernisation, remains a spirited and passionate place where the atmosphere – rather like a good flamenco performance – creeps up and taps you on the shoulder when you least expect it.

A Cultural Marinade

Part of the fascination Andalucía holds for people springs from its peculiar history. For eight centuries the region sat on a porous frontier between two different faiths and ideologies, Christianity and Islam. Left to ferment like a barrel of the bone-dry local sherry, the ongoing cross-fertilisation has thrown up a slew of cultural colossi: ancient mosques transformed into churches; vast palace complexes replete with stucco; a cuisine infused with dashes of North African spices; and a chain of lofty white towns that dominates the arid, craggy landscape, from the tightly knotted lanes of Granada's Albayzín to the hilltop settlements of Cádiz province.

Wild Andalucía

It takes more than a few thirsty Costa del Sol golf courses to steamroller Andalucía's diverse ecology. Significant pockets of the region's southern coast remain relatively unblemished, while inland you'll stumble into bucolic, agriculturally dependent villages where life doesn't seem to have changed much since playwright Federico Lorca envisioned *Bodas de sangre* (Blood Wedding). Twenty percent of Andalucía's land is sheltered in natural and national parks, and the protective measures are showing dividends. The Iberian lynx is no longer impossibly elusive, while the handsome ibex is positively flourishing. Another laudable reclamation project is the region's *vía verdes,* old railway lines reborn as biking and hiking greenways.

Duende

One of Andalucía's most intriguing attractions is the notion of *duende,* the elusive spirit that douses much of Spanish art, especially flamenco. *Duende* loosely translates as a moment of heightened emotion experienced during an artistic performance, and it can be soulfully evoked in Andalucía if you mingle in the right places. Seek it out in a Lorca play at a municipal theatre, an organ recital in a Gothic church, the hit-or-miss spontaneity of a flamenco *peña* (club) or the remarkable art renaissance currently gripping Málaga.

ALAN COPSON / GETTY IMAGES ©

Why I Love Andalucía

By Brendan Sainsbury, Author

Andalucía is where I met my wife, developed an incurable infatuation with flamenco and worked for several halcyon seasons as a travel guide. No small wonder that the region ranks so highly in my hit parade of 'favourite places on the planet'. Its crowning glory for me will always be Granada, though I also admire Seville and Málaga, and have a typically British affection for Gibraltar. For rural satisfaction, I love running along the region's *vía verdes*, trying to keep up with the cyclists.

For more about our authors, see page 392

Above: Albayzín neighbourhood (p256), Granada

Andalucía

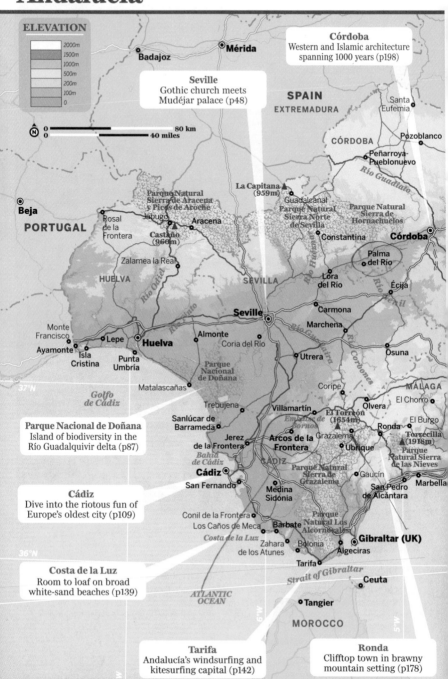

ELEVATION

2000m
1500m
1000m
500m
200m
100m
0

0 — 80 km
0 — 40 miles

Córdoba
Western and Islamic architecture
spanning 1000 years (p198)

Seville
Gothic church meets
Mudéjar palace (p48)

SPAIN
EXTREMADURA

Badajoz
Mérida
Santa
Eufemia
Pozoblanco
CÓRDOBA
Peñarroya-
Pueblonuevo

Río Guadiato

Beja
La Capitana▲
(959m)
Guadalcanal
Parque Natural
Sierra de Aracena
y Picos de Aroche
Jabugo
Aracena
Parque Natural
Sierra Norte
de Sevilla
Parque Natural
Sierra de
Hornachuelos

PORTUGAL
Rosal
de la
Frontera
Castaño
(960m)
Constantina
Córdoba
Palma
del Rio
Zalamea la Real
Río Odiel
SEVILLA
Lora
del Río
Écija
Río Huelva
Río Genil

HUELVA
Monte
Francisco
Lepe
Huelva
Almonte
Coria del Río
Seville
Carmona
Marchena
Río Corbones
MÁLAGA
Ayamonte
Isla
Cristina
Punta
Umbría
Utrera
Osuna
El Chorro
37°N
Golfo
de Cádiz
Matalascañas
Parque
Nacional
de Doñana
Coripe
El Burgo

Parque Nacional de Doñana
Island of biodiversity in the
Río Guadalquivir delta (p87)

Trebujena
Villamartín
El Torreón▲
(1654m)
Olvera
Ronda
Torrecilla
▲(1918m)
Sanlúcar de
Barrameda
Embalse de
Bornos
Grazalema
Parque
Natural Sierra
de las Nieves
Jerez
de la Frontera
Ubrique
Arcos de la
Frontera
Bahía
de Cádiz
CÁDIZ
Parque Natural
Sierra de
Grazalema
Gaucín
San Pedro
de Alcántara
Marbella
Cádiz
San Fernando

Cádiz
Dive into the riotous fun of
Europe's oldest city (p109)

Medina
Sidonia
Parque
Natural Los
Alcornocales
Conil de la Frontera
Los Caños de Meca
Barbate
Gibraltar (UK)
Costa de la Luz
Zahara
de los Atunes
Bolonia
Algeciras
36°N
Tarifa
Ceuta
Strait of Gibraltar

Costa de la Luz
Room to loaf on broad
white-sand beaches (p139)

ATLANTIC
OCEAN
Tangier
MOROCCO

Tarifa
Andalucía's windsurfing and
kitesurfing capital (p142)

Ronda
Clifftop town in brawny
mountain setting (p178)

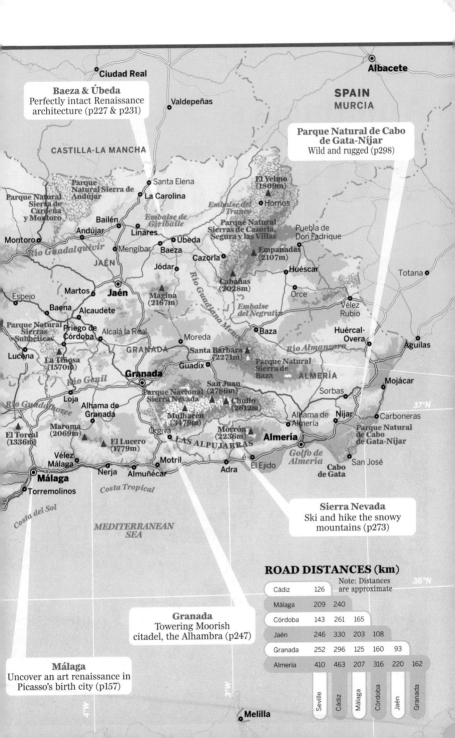

Baeza & Úbeda
Perfectly intact Renaissance architecture (p227 & p231)

Parque Natural de Cabo de Gata-Níjar
Wild and rugged (p298)

SPAIN
MURCIA

Ciudad Real
Albacete
Valdepeñas

CASTILLA-LA MANCHA

Parque Natural Sierra de Andújar
Santa Elena
La Carolina
El Yelmo (1809m)
Hornos

Embalse del Tranco

Parque Natural Sierra de Cardeña y Montoro

Parque Natural Sierras de Cazorla, Segura y las Villas
Puebla de Don Fadrique
Totana

Bailén
Embalse de Giribaile
Andújar
Linares
Úbeda
Empanadas (2107m)
Montoro
Río Guadalquivir
Mengíbar
Baeza
Cazorla
JAÉN
Jódar
Huéscar
Río Guadiana Menor
Cabañas (2028m)
Orce

Martos
Jaén
Magina (2167m)
Espejo
Embalse del Negratín
Vélez Rubio

Baena
Alcaudete
Río Almanzora
Aguilas
Parque Natural Sierras Subbéticas
Priego de Córdoba
Alcalá la Real
Moreda
Baza
Huércal-Overa
Lucena
La Tiñosa (1570m)
GRANADA
Santa Bárbara (2271m)
Parque Natural Sierra de Baza
ALMERÍA
Mojácar
Guadix
Río Genil
Granada
San Juan (2786m)
Sorbas
Loja
Parque Nacional Sierra Nevada
Chullo (2612m)
Níjar
Carboneras
Alhama de Granada
Mulhacén (3479m)
Alhama de Almería
Parque Natural de Cabo de Gata-Níjar
Río Guadalhorce
Órgiva
Motrón (2236m)
Almería
El Toreal (1336m)
Maroma (2069m)
El Lucero (1779m)
LAS ALPUJARRAS
Golfo de Almería
San José
Vélez Málaga
Motril
Adra
El Ejido
Cabo de Gata
Nerja
Almuñécar
Málaga
Torremolinos
Costa Tropical

Costa del Sol

MEDITERRANEAN SEA

37°N

Sierra Nevada
Ski and hike the snowy mountains (p273)

ROAD DISTANCES (km)
Note: Distances are approximate

36°N

	Cádiz	Málaga	Córdoba	Jaén	Granada
Cádiz	126				
Málaga	209	240			
Córdoba	143	261	165		
Jaén	246	330	203	108	
Granada	252	296	125	160	93
Almería	410	463	207	316	220	162

| Seville | Cádiz | Málaga | Córdoba | Jaén | Granada |

Granada
Towering Moorish citadel, the Alhambra (p247)

Málaga
Uncover an art renaissance in Picasso's birth city (p157)

3°W

4°W

Melilla

Andalucía's
Top 17

Alhambra

1 What is there to say? If the Nasrid builders of the Alhambra (p250) proved one thing, it was that – given the right blend of talent and foresight – art and architecture can speak far more eloquently than words. Perched on a hill with the snow-dusted Sierra Nevada as a backdrop, Granada's towering Moorish citadel has been rendering visitors speechless for nigh on 1000 years. The reason: a harmonious architectural balance between humankind and the natural environment. Fear not the dense crowds and the snaking queues; this is an essential pilgrimage.

Seville's Catedral & Alcázar

2 The 13th-century builders of Seville's cathedral (p50) wanted to construct a church so big that future generations would think they were mad. They gloriously succeeded. Only a bunch of loco architectural geniuses could have built a Gothic masterpiece this humongous. Offering greater subtlety and more intricate beauty is the adjacent Alcázar (p56), still a palace for the Spanish Royals and an identikit of Mudéjar architecture. The two buildings sit either side of the Plaza del Triunfo in ironic juxtaposition.

Bottom right: Seville cathedral

WILL SALREP / GETTY IMAGES ©

GONZALO AZUMENDI / GETTY IMAGES ©

DAVID C TOMLINSON / GETTY IMAGES ©

Ronda

3 For Ronda (p178), read 'rugged'. First, there's the brawny mountain setting in the Serranía de Ronda, where the town sits atop sheer cliffs. Second, there's the embattled history infested with bandits, smugglers, warriors and rebels. Third, there's the local penchant for bullfighting – Spain's modern bullfighting tradition was carved out here by the hardbitten Romero and Ordóñez families. And fourth, there are the famous artistic connections with self-styled 'rugged' Hollywood types, namely Ernest Hemingway and Orson Welles. Dust off your mountain boots and pay it a visit. Top left: Puente Nuevo, Ronda

Córdoba's Mezquita

4 A church that became a mosque before reverting back to being a church, Córdoba's Mezquita (p198) charts the evolution of Western and Islamic architecture over a 1000-year trajectory. Its most innovative features include some early horseshoe arches, an intricate mihrab (prayer niche) and a veritable forest of 856 columns, many of them recycled from Roman ruins. The sheer scale of the Mezquita reflects Córdoba's erstwhile power as the most cultured city in 10th-century Europe. It was also the inspiration for even greater buildings to come, most notably in Seville and Granada.

Sherry Tasting

5 A very Spanish product made for very British tastes, sherry is often considered a drink for mildly inebriated English grannies sitting down to discuss blue rinses before Sunday lunch. But wine lovers can dig deeper. Here in the sun-dappled vineyards of Cádiz province, fortified white wine has been produced since Phoenician times, and enjoyed by everyone from Christopher Columbus to Francis Drake. To get a sniff of its oaky essence, head to the historic 'sherry triangle' towns of Jerez de la Frontera (p119) and El Puerto de Santa María (p125). Bottom right: Sherry, Bodegas González Byass (p120), Jerez de la Frontera

Sierra Nevada & Las Alpujarras

6 Snow in Andalucía is a rarity, a factor that adds more exoticism to the Sierra Nevada (literally 'snowy mountains'), the mountain range that forms a lofty backdrop to one of the most striking cityscapes in Europe: Granada. There are other rarities here too, such as Andalucía's only ski station (p273), and mainland Spain's highest peak. The scattered white villages that beautify the mountains' southern slopes, known communally as Las Alpujarras, are well-known for their ancient craft-making and agricultural fertility. Below: Sierra Nevada ski station (p273)

Flamenco

7 Like all great anguished music, flamenco (p338) has the power to lift you out of the doldrums and stir your soul. It's as if by sharing in the pain of innumerable generations of dispossessed misfits you open a door to a secret world of musical ghosts and ancient Andalucian spirits. On the other side of the coin, flamenco culture can also be surprisingly jolly, jokey and tongue-in-cheek. There's only one real proviso: you have to hear it live, preferably in its Seville-Jerez-Cádiz heartland.

ALFREDO MAIQUEZ / GETTY IMAGES ©

ANDREA PISTOLESI / GETTY IMAGES ©

Cabo de Gata

8 For a cherished memory of what the Spanish coastline used to look like before mega-resorts gatecrashed the Costa del Sol, come to Cabo de Gata (p298) in Almería province, a wild, rugged, golf-course-free zone, where fishing boats still reel in the day's catch and bold cliffs clash with the azure Mediterranean. Considering it's one of the driest areas of Europe, the Cabo is abundant with feathered fauna and scrubby vegetation. It's also a protected area and ideal for hassle-free hiking and biking. Top left: Playa de los Muertos, Parque Natural de Cabo de Gata-Níjar (p298)

Tapas

9 Spanish cuisine might have gone molecular in recent years but there's no getting away from the basics. Tapas (p34) define Spain's *style* of eating as much as its *type* of cuisine – a long, drawn-out smorgasbord of tasting and savouring that can go on well into the night. Seville claims the most creative tapas, although *malagueños* (people from Málaga) might agree to differ. Granada is one of few places in Spain that still serves up recession-busting free tapas with every drink you order at the bar.

Cádiz

10 The *gaditanos* (citizens of Cádiz) are Spain's great laughers and jokers. Here in the city of ancient *barrios* (districts) and the nation's greatest Carnaval (p112), nothing is taken too seriously. Even the locally concocted brand of flamenco, known as *alegrías*, is uncharacteristically joyful and upbeat. Sitting like a great unlaunched ship on a peninsula that juts out into the Atlantic, Cádiz also sports the region's most romantic sea drive, its most expansive municipal beaches and an unbelievable stash of ancient sights.

Parque Nacional de Doñana

11 A figurative 'island' of biodiversity in the delta of the Río Guadalquivir, Parque Nacional de Doñana (p87) is one of Europe's most important wetland sites, and one of only two national parks in Andalucía (and 14 in Spain). Long a blueprint for eco-management, the park's assertive environmental policies have set precedents on how to balance conservation with the demands of tourism and agriculture. Aside from offering multiple nature excursions, the region is a precious landfall for migrating waterfowl and home to the rare Iberian lynx. Bottom: Iberian lynx (p335)

Costa de la Luz Beaches

12 Habitual Costa del Sol–goers may not have heard of Tarifa, Bolonia or Zahara de los Atunes, but Andalucía's west-facing Atlantic coast is wilder, windier and far less crowded than the southern Mediterranean littoral. For those in the know, what the Costa de la Luz (p86) lacks – theme parks, fish-and-chip shops and a massive hotel infrastructure – is actually its main draw. Beach loafers are outnumbered by windsurfers and happy wanderers here, though there's plenty of room to loaf on broad sweeps of fine white sand should you desire. Top right: Zahara de los Atunes (p142), Costa de la Luz

RICHARD KEMP / GETTY IMAGES ©

12

WITOLD SKRYPCZAK / GETTY IMAGES ©

13

HILARY MORGAN / ALAMY ©

Málaga's Art Renaissance

13 There's no stopping Málaga (p157) at the moment. Until 2003 the city lacked even a museum devoted to legendary native son Picasso; now it's becoming an art heavyweight to rival Madrid or Barcelona. Recent gallery openings include the modernist Centre Pompidou and an evocative museum of Russian art. They join over 20 established art nooks, anchored by the distinguished Museo Picasso Málaga. Moving with the times, Málaga is also developing its own arts district, Soho, transforming a formerly rundown area near the port with giant murals and groovy cafes. Left: Museo Picasso Málaga (p157)

Renaissance Baeza & Úbeda

14 These two little-visited outposts etched in the olive groves of Jaén province look more Italian than Spanish; it's the perfectly intact Renaissance architecture that deceives you. The towns' monumental palaces and symmetrical civic buildings introduced Renaissance ideas to Spain, and ultimately provoked the style's assimilation into Latin America. In 2003 Baeza (p227) and Úbeda (p231) joined the Alhambra, Córdoba's Mezquita and Seville's cathedral as Andalucian Unesco World Heritage Sites, yet they get far less foot traffic. Top left: Baeza

Touring the White Villages

15 Choosing your favourite white village is like choosing your favourite Beatles album. They're all so damned good it's hard to make a definitive decision. Pressured for an answer, most people tend to look out for the classic calling cards: a thrillingly sited location, a soporific old town, a fancy *parador* (luxurious state-owned hotel), and a volatile frontier history. The best examples lie dotted all over the region with two heavy concentrations: one in eastern Cádiz province (p134) and the other in the mountainous Alpujarras. Middle: Vejer de la Frontera (p139)

Kitesurfing in Tarifa

16 If Andalucía has a hallmark outdoor activity, it is kitesurfing, a daring white-knuckle sport given extra oomph by the stiff winds that enliven the choppy waters off the Strait of Gibraltar. The activity has lent a hip vibe to the Costa de la Luz and its windy southern nexus Tarifa (p142), a whitewashed coastal town that often feels more Moroccan than Spanish. Cool windsurfing and kitesurfing outlets proliferate along the nearby beachfronts, tempting the adventurous to take to the water.

BEN WELSH / DESIGN PICS / GETTY IMAGES ©

16

Semana Santa in Seville

17 Only the *sevillanos* could take the themes of grief and death and make them into a jaw-dropping spectacle. Many cities around the world mark the Catholic feast of Holy Week (p69), but none approach it with the verve and outright passion of Seville. Watch ancient processions led by various *hermanadades* (brotherhoods; the oldest dating back to 1340) shoulder elaborately decorated floats through the city streets in an atmosphere doused in emotion and religious significance.

Bottom right: Marching penitents

HARRY ENGELS / GETTY IMAGES ©

17

Need to Know

For more information, see Survival Guide (p357)

Currency
Euro (€); Gibraltar pound (£)

Language
Spanish (Castilian); English in Gibraltar

Visas
Generally not required for stays of up to 90 days, and not at all for members of EU or Schengen countries; some nationalities need a Schengen visa.

Money
ATMs widely available. Credit cards accepted in most hotels, restaurants and shops.

Mobile Phones
Local SIM cards widely available and can be used in European and Australian mobile phones. Not compatible with many North American or Japanese systems.

Time
Central European Time (GMT/UTC plus one hour).

When to Go

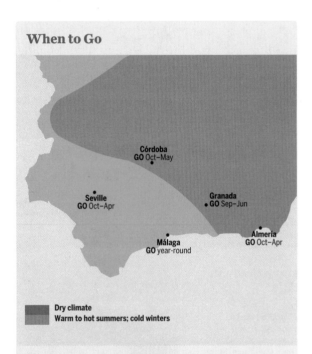

Córdoba
GO Oct–May

Seville
GO Oct–Apr

Granada
GO Sep–Jun

Málaga
GO year-round

Almería
GO Oct–Apr

■ Dry climate
Warm to hot summers; cold winters

High Season
(Jun–Aug)

➡ The sun is boiling hot in summer and the climate very dry.

➡ Most Spaniards holiday in July and, in particular, August; expect traffic jams and heavy crowds.

➡ Most (though not all) hotels hike up their prices.

Shoulder
(Mar–May, Sep–Oct)

➡ Hotel prices can triple during Semana Santa and the various city and town ferias.

➡ Ideal weather – warm, but not too hot.

➡ In spring there is a colourful cavalcade of Andalucian festivals to choose from.

Low Season
(Nov–Feb)

➡ The climate remains warm and relatively dry on the Costa del Sol, but cooler and wetter inland.

➡ Skiing is possible in the Sierra Nevada.

➡ The best time for hotel bargains.

➡ Some sights close up for the winter.

Useful Websites

Turismo Andalucía (www. andalucia.org) Encyclopedic official tourism site.

Holiday in Spain (www.spain. info) Useful official site.

Andalucia.com (www. andalucia.com) One of the most interesting and comprehensive guides to the region.

Lonely Planet (lonelyplanet. com/spain/andalucia) Build your own itinerary.

Iberianature (www.iberia nature.com) Devoted to Spain's natural world.

Important Numbers

Telephone numbers in Spain don't use area codes; simply dial the nine-digit number.

Country code	✆34
International access code	✆00
Ambulance	✆061
Emergency	✆112
National police	✆091

Exchange Rates

Australia	A$1	€0.67
Canada	C$1	€0.71
Japan	¥100	€0.73
Morocco	Dh1	€0.09
New Zealand	NZ$1	€0.60
UK	UK£1	€1.44
US	US$1	€0.91

For current exchange rates see www.xe.com.

Daily Costs

Budget:
Less than €75

➡ *Hostales* and *pensiones*: €25–50

➡ Traditional tapas bars: €2–3 per tapa

➡ Make the most of free sights

Midrange:
€75–€150

➡ Room at a midrange hotel: €65–140

➡ Flamenco show in cultural centre: €18

➡ Use buses to get around: €22 (Seville–Granada)

Top End:
Over €150

➡ Stay at *paradores* or boutique hotels: €140+

➡ Meal in a high-end restaurant: €40

➡ Evening flamenco show with dinner: €76

Opening Hours

Opening hours have some local and seasonal variations.

Banks 8.30am to 2pm Monday to Friday, 9am to 1pm Saturday

Cafes 8am to 11pm

Night-time bars & clubs 10pm to 4am

Post offices 8.30am to 8.30pm Monday to Friday, 9am to 1.30pm Saturday

Restaurants 1pm to 4pm and 8pm to midnight

Shops 9am to 1.30pm and 5pm to 9pm Monday to Saturday

Supermarkets 9am to 9pm Monday to Saturday

Gibraltar businesses don't take a siesta. Restaurants tend to open 8am to 8pm and shops 10am to 6pm; most shops close after lunch on Saturday and reopen Monday morning.

Arriving in Andalucía

Seville Airport (p367) A bus (€4) leaves every 15 minutes at peak times to the city centre (every 30 minutes off-peak and Sundays). Taxis cost €21 to €25 and take about 15 to 20 minutes.

Málaga Airport (p367) A train (€1.80–€2.70) leaves every 20 minutes and takes 15 minutes to the city centre. Bus A75 leaves for the city centre (€3, 20 minutes) every 20 minutes from outside the main arrivals hall at Terminal 3. There are also direct buses from the airport to Granada, Marbella and Torremolinos. A taxi from the airport to the city centre costs €15 to €19.

Getting Around

Car Andalucía has an excellent road system. Though public transport is good, some visitors elect to opt for the greater freedom offered with a hire (or private) car. If you're renting, you'll save time organising the details before you leave.

Bus With a more extensive network than trains, buses in Andalucía travel to even the smallest villages. Alsa runs the best intercity routes. Various other companies reach out to remoter areas. Buses are usually cheaper than trains over equivalent distances.

Train High-speed AVE trains serve Seville, Córdoba and Málaga. Slower but cheaper regional trains link most of Andalucía's other main towns and cities. Reserve ahead on AVE trains.

For much more on **getting around**, see p369

PLAN YOUR TRIP NEED TO KNOW

What's New

Centre Pompidou Málaga

A new art nook situated below a giant glass cube in Málaga's resurgent port, with 70 artworks including sculpture, videos and installations. A-listers include Francis Bacon, Frida Kahlo and René Magritte. (p160)

Palacio de los Olvidados

A new museum that explores Granada's oft-forgotten Jewish past, and also acts as a performance space hosting nightly music shows that meld themes from Lorca and flamenco. (p256)

Museo Ruso de Málaga

Housed in the evocative setting of a 1920s former tobacco factory, with over 200 works dedicated to Russian art from the 16th to 20th centuries. (p161)

Caminito del Rey

This lofty, vertigo-inducing walkway, halfway up the sheer El Chorro gorge north of Málaga, reopened in March 2015 after a €4-million renovation. (p187)

Centro Lorca

After years of delay, Granada's Centro Lorca finally opened in July 2015. Debate still surrounds the full details of how it will function, but the bold modernist form will ultimately host a theatre, expo space and library in the city of the writer's birth. (p270)

Mezquita Belltower

The belltower of Córdoba's Mezquita reopened for visits in 2014 after being closed for 25 years. You can now climb up inside the city's tallest building (54m) for spectacular panoramas. (p198)

Vejer de la Frontera

No one's quite sure when it happened: magical 'white town' Vejer de la Frontera has transformed itself into a culinary highlight of Andalucía, triumphing with both traditional recipes and contemporary flair. (p139)

GR247 Footpath

A new 479km long-distance footpath in the beautiful Parque Natural Sierras de Cazorla, Segura y Las Villas in Jaén province, designed in 21 stages with accommodation in village hotels or basic refuges. (p241)

Centro de Interpretación Olivar y Aceite

Jaén province produces about 17% of the world's olive oil and this new centre explains all about how that extra virgin gets from the tree to your table, with the chance to taste a few varieties. (p230)

Gourmet Aracena: Jesús Carrión

From wild mushroom risotto to Iberian ham carpaccio, this fabulous new family-run restaurant is throwing exquisite, contemporary creativity into traditional Sierra de Aracena flavours. (p95)

For more recommendations and reviews, see lonelyplanet.com/spain/andalucia

If You Like...

Hiking

Grazalema Guided-only hikes or vigorous solo stints through brawny mountain ruggedness among flying vultures and delicate orchids. (p137)

Sierra de Aracena The lost world of Huelva is a jigsaw of pastoral paths punctuated by tiny time-warped villages. (p95)

Cabo de Gata Sixty kilometres of wild coastal paths provide breathing space on this part of Andalucía's much-maligned *costa* (coast). (p298)

Sierra Nevada Tick off mainland Spain's highest peak, Mulhacén, or the easier and slighter lower Veleta, both doable as day hikes if you're fit. (p272)

GR7 Hop onto one of Spain's best long-distance footpaths, which bisects Andalucía from Tarifa to the mountains of Cazorla. (p146)

Vía Verdes Old railway lines converted into 'greenways' for bikers and hikers; Andalucía has over a dozen of these flat, well-signposted routes. (p37)

Las Alpujarras On the south-facing slopes of the Sierra Nevada, white villages and canyons are linked by an ancient web of paths. (p275)

Beaches

Cabo de Gata You can pretend you're living in the 1950s in the sheltered sandy coves of the Costa de Almería's protected littoral. (p300)

Cádiz The grand Playa de la Victoria is large enough to accommodate most of Cádiz' population on hot weekends in summer. (p113)

Nerja A cute Málaga-province beach town that has found the right balance between tourism and authenticity. (p191)

Zahara de los Atunes Run marathons on the wide empty beaches of the Costa de la Luz, with Africa shimmering on the horizon. (p142)

Mojácar Broad sands with dozens of easygoing beach bars, backed by low-rise buildings. (p303)

Moorish Architecture

Alhambra The high point of Moorish (nay, all!) architecture was reached in the 1350s under Sultan Muhammad V. (p250)

Alcázar (Seville) Only the Alhambra can overshadow the Alcázar, which is just a few smidgens down on the brilliance scale. (p56)

Mezquita (Córdoba) One of the greatest mosques ever built is today a Christian church and a historical manual of early Al-Andalus architecture. (p198)

Alcazaba (Almería) A magnificent fort in an equally magnificent coastal setting from where it once rivalled the Alhambra. (p288)

Giralda Formerly a minaret, now a belfry; this Moorish remnant blends harmoniously into the Gothic mass of Seville's cathedral. (p50)

Great Local Food

Sanlúcar de Barrameda Fantastic fish moulded into highly inventive tapas is washed down with subtly salty *manzanilla* (sherry with a chamomile-like flavour). (p129)

Sierra de Aracena Created from black pigs fattened on acorns, Spain's luxury ham is best sampled in rural Huelva province. (p95)

Granada Free tapas, Moroccan-influenced food, and fresh vegetables plucked straight out of the nearby *vega* (agricultural land). (p247)

Cádiz *Pescaito frito* (fried fish) is Andalucía's stand-out offering; it's ubiquitous here, within sight of the boats that caught it. (p109)

Las Alpujarras Scale the local mountains to work up an appetite for *plato alpujarreño*, a heavy mix of meat, eggs and more meat. (p275)

Málaga Bypass the Michelin stars and head for a *chiringuito* (beach bar) for grilled sardines and a cold beer. (p157)

Hilltop Towns

Arcos de la Frontera The quintessential white town with a castle, church and dazzling Moorish houses, all clinging to a steep crag. (p131)

Vejer de la Frontera Cavernous Moorish restaurants, ornate tiled fountains, esoteric festivals, luxury boutique hotels and an indescribable timelessness. (p139)

Olvera A Cádiz-province white town from which you can gain immediate access to others on the Vía Verde de la Sierra 'greenway'. (p138)

Capileira A white village in Las Alpujarras where crafts are hewn and hikers strike out for the Sierra Nevada. (p278)

Zuheros Lesser-known white town in Córdoba province overlooking endless fields striped with olive trees. (p211)

Segura de la Sierra Steeply stacked village with medieval castle amid the mountains of Andalucía's largest protected area. (p242)

Fine Arts

Málaga A museum to native son Picasso plus a score of other galleries, including the Centre Pompidou Málaga (p160), now embellish Andalucía's fast-growing cultural powerhouse. (p157)

Seville The Museo de Bellas Artes is the obvious draw, but there are also fine Golden Age works hanging in Seville's cathedral. (p48)

Cádiz Great art can be seen for free upstairs at the Museo de Cádiz, including important work by the Andalucian masters. (p109)

Granada Lots of art hides in Granada's holy buildings, including the Capilla Real and the intricately painted Monasterio de San Jerónimo. (p247)

Top: View over the hilltop town of Olvera (p138)
Bottom: Fresco, Monasterio de San Jerónimo (p259), Granada

Month by Month

TOP EVENTS

Semana Santa,
March–April

Feria de Abril, April

Carnaval, February

Festival de Jerez,
February

Feria del Caballo, May

January

The year starts quietly – well, relatively quietly. Various *romerías* (religious pilgrimages and celebrations) and saints' days have upped the ante by the end of the month, including San Sebastián Day (20 January). Average temperatures in Málaga remain an unfrigid 12°C.

Día de los Reyes Magos

To celebrate the Feast of the Epiphany on 6 January, effigies of the three kings are carried through myriad Andalucian towns and villages. The accompanying bearers traditionally throw sweets into the amassed crowds, a practice largely aimed at children.

February

Enter the big guns. Cádiz' carnival and Jerez' flamenco festival lure people from far and wide in February. It's also the best month for skiing in the Sierra Nevada, while the coast gauges a balmy 13°C.

Festival de Jerez

The self-styled *cuna* (cradle) of flamenco hosts what is claimed to be the world's most esteemed flamenco festival, with every great artist this side of Camarón de la Isla stepping up to perform. Unlike Seville's biennial, it's an annual fixture spread over two weeks. (p122)

Carnaval

February is carnival season around the globe and Cádiz hosts mainland Spain's biggest with a spectacle that draws more on humour and satire than Rio de Janeiro–style grandeur. The party continues for 10 days. Anyone left standing can pitch into the Festival de Jerez. (p112)

March

The best time to visit Andalucía starts now, especially in years when Easter falls early. Sombre Semana Santa parades usher in a season of ebullient festivals that heat up as the weather gets warmer.

Semana Santa (Holy Week)

The calm before the storm, the woe before the re-birth; there are few more elaborate manifestations of Catholic Holy Week than in Seville, where hooded *nazarenos* (penitents) carry huge floats through the streets in ghostly solemnity. Often falls in April. (p69)

April

Possibly the best month of all to visit, April promises fine (but not boiling) weather and exuberant festivals headlined by the big one in Seville. Hotel prices can go through the roof, rooms fill up early.

Feria de Abril

Seville's legendary spring fair proceeds something like this: drink sherry, ride a horse, dance *sevillanas* (folk dances), hit the bumper cars, drink more sherry, and stumble home at 2am-ish. It's the blueprint for spring fairs everywhere. A full bullfighting program runs alongside it. (p70)

🏃 Moto GP

Jerez' horse, flamenco and sherry aficionados also harbour a subtler motorcycle obsession: the yearly Spanish Motorcycle Grand Prix takes place here. Supporters arrive in convoy from all over Spain, and many camp near the circuit in scenes resembling a giant HOG get-together. (p122)

May

The mountain slopes are strewn with wild blooms, the sunflowers are out, and everyone in Andalucía seems to be getting on their horses to take part in *romerías* or summer fiestas.

🎊 Feria del Caballo

Jerez hogs many of the region's best festivals, including the famous horse fair that dates back to medieval times and involves plenty of parades, bullfights, fair rides and makeshift bars serving the best local sherry. (p122)

🎊 Romería del Rocío

The mother of all pilgrimages attracts over one million people to the obscure village of El Rocío in Huelva province to venerate the Virgin of El Rocío. They come from all directions by foot, horseback, carriage and boat. Dates: 15 May 2016, 4 June 2017 and 20 May 2018. (p90)

🎊 Fiesta de los Patios de Córdoba

Everything happens in Córdoba in May, from a flower festival to a spring fair. Sandwiched in between is this homage to the city's gorgeous patios, where home-

Top: Riders in the annual Feria del Caballo (p122), Jerez de la Frontera
Bottom: Women in traditional dress, Semana Santa (p69), Seville

ROBIN SMITH / GETTY IMAGES ©

THOMAS DRESSLER / GETTY IMAGES ©

owners open up their courtyards to compete for the title of 'best patio'. (p206)

June

The summer fiesta season is in full swing, with every town and village in Andalucía hosting their own particular shindig. If Easter's late, Pentecost and the Romería del Rocío (second day of Pentecost) can fall in June.

 Corpus Christi

Another movable Catholic feast, celebrated eight-and-a-half weeks after Easter, Corpus Christi is particularly significant in Granada where, despite the underlying solemnity, it has long been fused with the annual feria. Lush greenery traditionally carpets the streets. (p260)

July

Exiles from Northern Europe hit the Mediterranean beaches. You can stay and converse with them, or escape to the smaller mountain towns and villages for some (slightly) cooler air. The Spanish holiday season starts midmonth, raising crowds and prices.

Festival Internacional de la Guitarra

Flamenco is the highlight of this two-week guitar festival held in late June or early July in the (by then) sizzling city of Córdoba, but you'll also hear live classical, rock and blues performances. (p206)

August

It's hot. Seriously hot. Hit the beaches for some sea breezes and Málaga's feria answer to Seville. If you're on the *costas*, bear in mind that half of Spain will be joining you. Book ahead!

Feria de Málaga

Trying hard to emulate Seville's festival and nearly succeeding, Málaga hosts Andalucía's second-most-famous party and is awash with all of the usual calling cards: sherry, lights, dancing and fireworks. Mysteriously, relatively few Costa del Sol tourists show up. (p163)

September

At last, some relief from the heat. September promises good hiking weather, and is harvest time for grapes. Jerez and Montilla both have wine festivals.

Bienal de Flamenco

Seville shares this biennial flamenco festival with Málaga; Seville hosts in even-numbered years. Top-notch artists have been gracing the stages since 1980 to perform at the 30-day event. (p70)

Feria de Pedro Romero

Old-fashioned costumes and fighting bulls combine in the mountain town of Ronda, where elaborate Goya-era attire is donned in an attempt to add historical significance to the 'ballet' of bullfighting. A full program of events ensues. (p181)

Fiestas de Otoño

Even extravagant rock stars would have a tough time keeping pace in the fiesta-packed city of Jerez. This shindig uses the grape harvest as an excuse to tread on grapes, drink sherry and play *bulerías*-oriented flamenco.

October

Autumn brings the harvest and an alluring stash of food festivals. Look out for cheese tastings, soup days and ham-cutting contests.

Feria de la Tapa

Head to unheralded Sanlúcar de Barrameda for some alfresco tapa tasting in this great, fish-biased culinary town. You can wash down the best plates with *copas* (glasses) of the local *manzanilla* sherry. Late October.

December

You think they'd be wiped out after a year of nonstop merrymaking, but the Andalucians save enough energy for one last hurrah – Christmas. Otherwise, December is low-key unless you're going skiing.

Fiesta Mayor de Verdiales

On 28 December the village of Almogía in Málaga province organises a competition of fandango-like folk dances known as *verdiales*. Groups of singers and dancers called *pandas* dress in ribboned costumes and play an obscure type of flamenco with guitars and violins. (p163)

Itineraries

 Highlights

You'd need months to poke into every corner of Andalucía, but two weeks can bag you the well-known highlights. This greatest hits itinerary is ideal for first-timers or those with a strict time ration.

The best starting point is unmissable **Seville**, deserving of three days, where the famous cathedral and Alcázar stand side by side in surreal juxtaposition. Head 150km east by train and a few centuries back in time to explore **Córdoba**, site of the ancient Mezquita and guarder of hidden patios. Free tapas, shadowy tea rooms and the incomparable Alhambra beckon in **Granada**, where you could fill at least three days reclining in Moorish bathhouses and deciphering the Lorca paraphernalia. Easily reached by bus, **Málaga** is understated by comparison. Spend a day absorbing the Picasso museum and sample fresh-from-the-Med seafood. **Ronda** is a dramatic contrast, surrounded by mountains and doused in bullfighting and rebel-rousing history. You'll be unlucky to hit **Jerez de la Frontera** and not take in a festival; the city is also famous for its horses, sherry bodegas and flamenco. Forty-five minutes away by train, **Cádiz** has an abundance of free sights, including a fine city museum and an aficionado's flamenco club. You can contemplate your trip's achievements while walking its romantic *malecón* (sea drive).

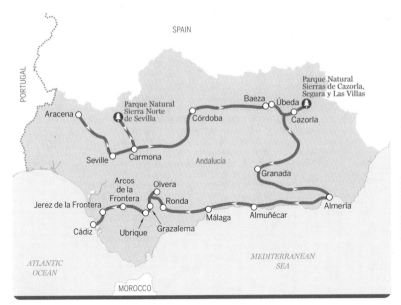

4 WEEKS Grand Tour

To understand every nuance of Andalucía, you need to put aside at least a month and undertake a 'grand tour' of all eight provinces. This expansive itinerary is busy and detailed, and will see you staggering home with a virtual PhD in Andalucian culture.

Start in **Seville**, visiting the obvious sights (the cathedral, Alcázar) and the less obvious ones (Casa de Pilatos, Triana). Sorties to the west lead to Huelva province; there's prime hiking country in the province's north, where the gentle pastoral hills around **Aracena** promise legendary walks between sleepy villages. Passing back through Seville, head east, stopping for a day in gentle **Carmona** before a serendipitous escape to the serially overlooked **Parque Natural Sierra Norte de Sevilla**. On week two, head to **Córdoba**, long a historical foil to Seville, where you can map Andalucian history in its whitewashed streets, Roman relics and Islamic architecture. Tracking east to Jaén province delivers you to the land of olive groves and weighty Renaissance architecture. The former can be seen pretty much everywhere you look. The latter is concentrated in the twin towns of **Baeza** and **Úbeda**. Further east, **Cazorla** is the gateway to Andalucía's largest protected area, but one visited only by a small minority, **Parque Natural Sierras de Cazorla, Segura y Las Villas**.

Granada, at the start of week three, is a more mainstream sight, loaded with exotic majesty. To check out all the provinces you'll now need to circumnavigate the Sierra Nevada to **Almería**, the dry east that once hosted spaghetti western films. Hit the coast at the unadulterated Spanish town of **Almuñécar** and follow it west through ever-growing resorts to **Málaga**, the Costa del Sol city that is actually nothing like the Costa del Sol. Start your last week in white town 'capital', **Ronda**; with its bullfighting museum and plunging gorge, it's been on most itineraries since Hemingway visited. The white towns continue across the border in Cádiz province; pick and choose between **Olvera**, **Grazalema** and **Ubrique**, and enjoy the surrounding natural parks. Attempts to bypass **Arcos de la Frontera** are normally futile – the sight of the spectacular hilltop settlement practically drags you off the bus. Your final week can be spent tying up the threads of Andalucía's culture in **Jerez de la Frontera** and **Cádiz**, two ancient yet quintessential cities that contain all the ingredients that have made this region so great.

 ## 1 WEEK — The Cultural Triangle

If you had to pick a smaller region-within-a-region that best sums up Andalucía's essence it would lie in the triangle of territory between Seville, Cádiz and Jerez de la Frontera.

With excellent air, rail and bus connections, **Seville** is the best starting point for this sojourn. Lap up the Moorish-meets-Gothic architecture and seemingly limitless festivals for a day or two. Fast trains now forge south to **Jerez de la Frontera**, first stop on the 'sherry triangle', where you can spend two days mixing bodega tours with horse shows, authentic flamenco and perhaps a *hammam*. Continuing west by bus to **Sanlúcar de Barrameda** gives you the option to compare *fino* with *manzanilla* and bag some of the best seafood tapas in Spain. This is also a good base for forays into the biodiverse **Parque Nacional de Doñana**. Spend the evening in **El Puerto de Santa María**, home of more bodegas, festivals and fish restaurants. Surrounded by sea, **Cádiz** feels like the edge of Europe, and the home of something mystical and old. The beaches here are famously broad and they continue south along the Costa de la Luz. Explore them from a base in **Vejer de la Frontera**, a dramatically perched white town with a refined air.

 ## 2 WEEKS — The West in Detail

Already seen the Alhambra and hiked the Sierra Nevada? Then go west to the proverbial cradle of Andalucian culture.

Start in Huelva province's **Parque Nacional de Doñana**, possibly Andalucía's finest natural attraction and a rare European wetland replete with bird life. **Seville** broadcasts a litany of well-known sights, but its provincial hinterland is less heralded. Visit the tranquil towns of **Carmona**, with its Alcázar, and **Osuna**, with its grand palaces. Rugged **Ronda** is well on the tourist map, though if you stay overnight you'll wave goodbye to 80% of them. Recommended stops on the way to Málaga include **El Chorro** gorge and ancient **Antequera**. **Málaga** is a ballsy yet arty city that offers great seafood and a decent August feria. With time to linger you can visit some of Cádiz province's less trodden jewels: **Jimena de la Frontera** demands a detour, as does hiking in the **Parque Natural Los Alcornocales**. **Gibraltar** lures expat Brits missing roast beef and warm beer. Ply the Costa de la Luz next, spending at least one night in the white village of **Vejer de la Frontera**. A final few days can be devoted to the culturally intense city of **Cádiz**, with a detour for sherry and flamenco in **Jerez de la Frontera**.

 The Coast <small>3 WEEKS</small>

 The East in Detail <small>2 WEEKS</small>

The Coast

The coast looms large in Andalucía, lapping five of its eight provinces. Empires were once built here, although more recently resorts have colonised the littoral. Most coastal towns are linked by bus.

Start in underdeveloped **Cabo de Gata**, a spectacular combination of cliffs and salt flats. Tracking west you'll dock in **Almería**, worth a stop for its Moorish Alcazaba and winding streets. Granada's Costa Tropical is precipitous and authentic; **Almuñécar** is a great base for exploring and **La Herradura** offers good diving. A short bus ride west, **Nerja** has tempered its development better than other resorts, while excellent hiking beckons in **La Axarquía**. **Málaga** deserves three days of this trip; its international reputation has skyrocketed in recent years thanks to its fine art and inventive gastronomy. **Marbella** is possibly the most interesting stop on the busy Costa del Sol, though **Mijas** merits a day trip. Further west, **Gibraltar** guards the jaws of Europe with British pubs and fascinating military history. Starting in windsurfing mecca **Tarifa**, the Costa de la Luz harbours a variety of flavours and different food. While away three days in **Barbate** and **Los Caños de Meca**, then it's a grand two-day finale in **Cádiz**.

The East in Detail

The east is Andalucía's less obvious itinerary, filled with more obscure attractions. Spend three days each in the two big-hitter cities and then branch out.

Córdoba is a must-see – a one-time Iberian capital with one of the finest Islamic mosques ever built. **Granada** showcases the later Nasrid era in its Alhambra, Albayzín and Moorish-style bathhouses. You can use both cities as a base for rural forays into nearby mountainous regions. Córdoba province's ample wilderness includes the **Parque Natural Sierras Subbéticas**. Granada has the **Parque Nacional Sierra Nevada** and Las Alpujarras, the valleys that embellish the sierra's southern slopes. Detours from here can include **Guadix**, with its unusual inhabited caves, and coastal **Almuñécar**, a bit of domestic seaside bliss detached from the Costa resorts. **Jaén** is olive-oil heaven and guardian of fine tapas bars, while **Baeza** and **Úbeda** are unique for their Renaissance architecture. Almería province is Andalucía's far east: **Mojácar** promises a sometimes boho, sometimes glitzy taste of the Levant; **Cabo de Gata** is the region's most unspoiled coastal enclave; and **Almería** city is a kind of Granada-on-the-sea, with plenty of mystic Moorish relics.

Plan Your Trip

Eat Like a Local

Dining in Andalucía isn't just about what you eat; it's about how you eat too. True to the Mediterranean spirit, the culinary culture is less about fast food, takeaway lunches and half-litre measures of coffee, and more about light breakfasts, leisurely lunches and late dinners spent grazing slowly from a selection of small tapas plates in a traditional bar. If you're a visitor, adjust your time-clock to a quintessentially Spanish groove, otherwise you'll miss out on half of what Andalucía is all about.

The Year in Food

Andalucía is unusual in Europe in that, due to the balmy climate and extensive use of giant greenhouses, fruit and vegetables can be grown year-round, especially in Almería province and on the Costa Tropical.

April to August

Spring and summer mean gazpacho, Andalucía's signature chilled soup, which is accompanied by its regional variations such as *salmorejo* (Córdoba) and *ajo blanco* (Málaga).

August to September

The grape harvest ushers in a number of wine festivals, most notably Jerez de la Frontera's Vendimia incorporated into the Fiestas de Otoño in September – an excellent opportunity to pair your *finos* and *manzanillas* with tapas.

November to January

November is the start of the pig *matanza* (slaughter) and its accompanying feasts, which are heavy on pork. The olive-tree harvest is also under way. Winter is the time for hot roast chestnuts plied by street vendors, especially in the more mountainous areas.

Food Experiences

Meals of a Lifetime

➡ **La Brunilda** (p73) Seville's best tapas bar, bar none.

➡ **La Fábula Restaurante** (p266) Service, food, atmosphere and decor; this is far and away Granada's best fine-dining experience.

➡ **Café Azul** (p146) Best breakfasts in Andalucía.

➡ **El Jardín del Califa** (p140) Delicious Moroccan food in a beautiful Moroccan-styled maze of a restaurant.

➡ **Misa de 12** (p235) Small bar with a big food reputation in Úbeda.

➡ **Restaurante La Fuente** (p215) Home-style cooking in the small village of Zagrilla Alta in Córdoba province.

➡ **Óleo** (p165) The result of a partnership between a *malagueño* chef and a Japanese sushi master.

Cheap Treats

➡ **Free tapas** – That old adage about there being no such thing as a free lunch comes a cropper in Granada, Jaén and Almería provinces, Spain's last bastions of free tapas. Watch as small gratis snack plates arrive with every drink you order.

➡ **Chiringuitos** – Semipermanent beach shacks/restaurants that specialise in fried seafood. The staples – *espeto de sardinas* (sardine skewers) and *boquerones fritos* (fried anchovies) – are best washed down with a bottle of beer. Most *chiringuitos* only operate in summer.

➡ **Casetas** – Temporary tents set up at Andalucía's seemingly endless round of festivals and parties. Many of them sell cheap snack-oriented food and drink.

➡ **Desayuno** – A typical Andalucian *desayuno* (breakfast) consisting of a small cup of strong coffee and a toasted bun topped with olive oil and/or crushed tomato should rarely cost more than €2.50.

➡ **Menú del día** – Three-course lunchtime restaurant meal usually served with bread and wine. Prices start at €10, all included. It's not nouveau cuisine, but if you're on a budget...

Dare to Try

➡ **Rabo de toro** – Stewed bull's tail cut from the toppled bull from the local *corrida de toros* (bullfight), preferably eaten the same day.

➡ **Mollete** – Toasted bread roll usually drizzled with olive oil and topped with crushed tomato (though there are other toppings) – the standard savoury Andalucian breakfast.

➡ **Ortiguillas** – Croquette-sized sea anemone deep-fried in olive oil. Their intense seafood flavour is considered a delicacy in the Cádiz area.

➡ **Partridge** – Game meat best enjoyed in mountain villages in areas such as the Sierra de Grazalema and the Sierra de Cazorla.

➡ **Tripe stew** – A traditionally cheap leftover dish particularly popular in Seville that has recently been given a modern makeover by some of Andalucía's cutting-edge chefs.

➡ **Jabalí** – Wild boar is fairly common on menus throughout rural parts of Jaén and Córdoba provinces. It can come plain-grilled or in sauces or stews and tastes like a slightly coarser version of pork.

Cooking Courses

➡ **All Ways Spain** (www.allwaysspain.com) Offers three different seven- to eight-day gourmet-food tours with cooking classes.

➡ **Annie B's Spanish Kitchen** (p140) Popular cooking courses in Vejer de la Frontera, often incorporating sherry tours and tastings.

➡ **Cooking Holiday Spain** (⏲637 802743; www.cookingholidayspain.com) Offers, among

---

HAY CHURROS

Supposedly invented by Spanish shepherds centuries ago, churros are long, thin, doughnut-like strips deep-fried in olive oil and then eaten as a snack dipped in coffee, or – even better – thick hot chocolate. In Andalucía churros are enjoyed for breakfast or during the early-evening *merienda* (snack). Good churro cafes or *churrerías* are legion in the region, although Granada is often held up as the churros capital, in particular Plaza Bib-Rambla and its eponymous cafe (p263). Casa Aranda (p165) in Málaga is another legendary churros spot. The *tejerngo* is a distinctively Andalucian version of the churro, a lighter, fluffier doughnut strip rolled into a large wheel.

---

other things, a six-hour cooking class in the mountains near Ronda.

➡ **Taller Andaluz de Cocina** (p69) Combines cooking courses and food-market tours in Seville's Triana district.

➡ **Al-Andalus Spanish School** (www.alandalustarifa.com) Combines Spanish classes with optional cooking courses at a language school in Tarifa.

Local Specialities
Sevilla Province

As well as its extraordinarily varied tapas, Seville also produces some excellent sweets. *Polvorones* are small crumbly shortbreads that traditionally come from the town of Estepa. *Tortas de aceite* are sweet biscuits made from olive oil. *Huevos a la flamenco* is an ancient savoury dish made with *morcilla* (blood sausage), garlic, onions and tomatoes topped with baked eggs. Seville's bitter oranges are primarily used to make marmalade, the breakfast spread so loved by the English.

Huelva Province

Two gastronomic words define Huelva province: strawberries (the region grows 90% of the Spanish crop) and *jamón ibérico*. The famous *jamón* (ham) is the

VEGETARIANS & VEGANS

Throughout Andalucía fruit and vegetables are delicious and fresh, and eaten in season, but unfortunately there are only a handful of avowedly vegetarian restaurants in the region. A word of warning: 'vegetable' dishes may contain more than just vegetables (eg beans with bits of ham). Vegetarians will find that salads in most restaurants are a good bet, as are gazpacho (chilled tomato soup) and *ajo blanco* (a white gazpacho made from a blend of almonds and garlic, served with grapes floating on top). Another reliable dish is *pisto* (ratatouille), especially good when eaten with bread dipped in the sauce; or try *espárragos trigueros* (thin wild asparagus), either grilled or in *revueltos* (scrambled eggs cooked with slices of fried garlic). Tapas without meat include *pimientos asados* (roasted red peppers), *alcachofas* (artichokes), *garbanzos con espinacas* (chickpeas with spinach) and, of course, *queso* (cheese). A plate of Andalucian *aceitunas* (olives) is another staple of the region's tapas.

champagne of Spain's cured meats, produced from black Iberian pigs that roam freely in the Sierra de Aracena feeding mainly on acorns. Sweeter and nuttier than the more ubiquitous *jamón serrano,* it is served sliced wafer thin and is notoriously expensive.

Cádiz Province

Cádiz' Atlantic coast and river estuaries support different types of fish from the Mediterranean. Tuna headlines on the Costa de la Luz, and the village of Barbate claims the best catches. Prawns are similarly fabulous along the coast. In Sanlúcar de Barrameda they are put in fried pancakes called *tortillitas de camerones* and served as tapas. Cádiz is also the home of sherry (fortified wine). Jerez de la Frontera and El Puerto de Santa María produce the best *fino* (dry) and *oloroso* (sweet and dark) varieties. Sanlúcar de Barrameda makes its own unique *manzanilla.*

Málaga Province

The Med is all about fish, most notably the *boquerones* (anchovies) and *sardinas* (sardines) from Málaga. *Espeto de sardinas* are sardines grilled on a skewer, best eaten on the beach at a *chiringuito. Ajo blanco* is Málaga's take on cold gazpacho soup. It's the same basic recipe but with the tomatoes replaced by almonds, giving it a creamy white colour, and fresh grapes floating on top. The local grapes have a long history of producing sweet dessert wines (white and red), which have recently come back into fashion.

Córdoba Province

Landlocked Córdoba grows copious chickpeas and olives, while its grapes are made into Montilla wines from which comes the name *amontillado,* an unfortified sherry. Pedroches is a strong semicured sheep's milk cheese from the Pedroches-Alcudia Valley. Córdoba menu specialities include *salmorejo* (a thick gazpacho-like soup usually topped with boiled eggs and cured ham) and *flamenquín* (a pork loin wrapped in *jamón serrano,* then coated in breadcrumbs and deep-fried).

Jaén Province

Jaén is the olive-oil capital of the world, the province alone accounting for 17% of global production. Quality is understandably high; classic Jaén oils are bitter but fruity. The mountainous area of Parque Natural Sierras de Cazorla, Segura y Las Villas has a strong hunting fraternity and is famous for its game, including partridge, venison and wild boar.

Granada Province

Few cuts of *jamón serrano* are better than those left to mature in the fresh mountain air of the village of Trevélez in Las Alpujarras. The mountains are also home to rabbit stews and the classic *plato alpujarreño,* a meat-heavy stomach-filler not dissimilar to a full English breakfast. Meanwhile, down on the flat plains of La Vega, beans and asparagus grow in abundance. Granada is Spain's most strongly Arabic-influenced city with some fine tagines, couscous and *teterías* (Moroccan-style teahouses).

Almería Province

There are more coastal fish here but rather than deep-frying them, Almeríans tend to cook theirs *a la plancha* (on a metal grill). Then there's those ubiquitous greenhouses filled with fruit and vegetables soaking up the equally ubiquitous sunrays. Almería is rightly famous for its plump year-round tomatoes.

How to Eat & Drink Like a Local

In Andalucía it's easy to spot an unversed tourist. It's the dog-tired, confused-looking, hypoglycemic street wanderer who rolls into the local tapas bar at 6pm and tries to order full roast chicken with a 2L jug of sangria. It doesn't have to be this way. Like a lot of things in life, eating in Andalucía is all about timing, etiquette and a little insider knowledge.

When to Eat

Tip number one: get into the groove and feast on Spanish time. A typical Andalucian eating day transpires something like this. Wake up to a strong coffee accompanied by a light, sweet pastry, preferably taken standing up in a cafe. A more substantial *desayuno* (breakfast) can be

procured at around 10am; the standard is a *mollete* (a bread roll, sliced in half, lightly toasted, drizzled with olive oil and topped with crushed tomatoes). Your first *tapa* window comes at 1pm when you can *picar* (graze) your way through a few small plates as a prelude to a larger *almuerzo* (lunch) at around 2pm. Some favour a full-blown meal with starter and main, others just up the ante at the bar and order a selection of *medias raciones* (larger tapas servings) or *raciones* (full-plate servings).

Next comes the siesta. Find somewhere you can lie down for an hour or two and close your eyes – you'll feel a lot better for it. If you're vertical by 5pm consider having a revitalising *merienda,* a quick round of coffee and cakes (preferably in a cafe) to fill the hole between lunch and dinner. It is not impolite to start on tapas again around 8pm, or closer to 9pm in summer. Elbow your way to the bar and claim your *platillos* (small plates) as you sip on a beer or perhaps a *tinto de verano* (red wine with lemonade and ice). *Cena* (dinner) never happens before 9pm and is usually less substantial than lunch, especially if you've warmed up with some tapas first. It's almost a faux pas to hit the sack before midnight. At weekends many party until dawn. Enterprising churro (deep-fried doughnut) vendors ply their sweet treats to insomniacs in the small hours. Why resist?

SHERRY & FOOD PAIRINGS

Wine novices are in luck. Sherry, aside from being one of the world's most unappreciated wines, is also one of its most versatile, particularly the *fino* and *manzanilla* varietals, so you don't need a degree in oenology to pair it. Here are some pointers:

TYPE OF SHERRY	SERVING TEMPERATURE	QUALITIES	FOOD PAIRINGS
Manzanilla	well-chilled	dry, fresh, delicate, slightly salty essence	tapas, almonds, sushi, olives
Fino	chilled	very dry & pale	aperitif, tapas, soup, white fish, shellfish, prawns, oysters, a counterpoint for cheeses
Amontillado	cool, but not chilled	off dry	aperitif, blue cheeses, chicken & white meat, cured cheese, foie gras, organs, rabbit, consommé
Oloroso	cool, but not chilled	dry, nutty, dark	red meat & game, cheese sauces
Pale Cream	room temperature	sweetened *fino*	fresh fruit, blue cheese
Cream	room temperature	sweet	dried fruit, cheesecake
Pedro Ximénez	room temperature	very sweet	dark chocolate, biscotti

ORDERING TAPAS

In Andalucía, tapas are more than just a way of eating – they're a way of life. *Tapeando* (going out for tapas) is a favourite Andalucian pastime and while it may serve as the prelude to lunch, it's often also the main event in the evening when Andalucians drag out their evening meal through a combination of tapas and drink. It's an ideal way to sample a range of tastes.

Tapas can draw on the culinary peculiarities of the region. In Huelva, it would be a culinary crime to order anything but the local *jamón ibérico,* while in Granada, North African tagine tapas reflect the city's days as the historical capital of Islamic Al-Andalus. In Cádiz province, the real luxury is seafood tapas, whether marinated, fried or fresh.

Here are a few more *tapa*-bar tips:

➡ Tapas bars are often situated in clusters enabling you to go bar-hopping between drinks.

➡ Ordering tapas is a physical contact sport; be prepared to elbow your way to the bar.

➡ That massive crowd at the bar usually means something. Good tapas places aren't always fancy, but they're invariably crowded.

➡ Don't worry about all those discarded serviettes on the floor – it's the Andalucian way to brush them off the table.

➡ The best *tapa* times are from 1pm to 3pm and 7pm to 9pm (slightly later in summer).

➡ Granada, Almería and Jaén all offer a free *tapa* with every drink you order. Almería goes one better and allows you to choose which free *tapa* you would like.

Where to Eat

Like elsewhere in Spain, bars are places to eat and socialise as much as they are for drinking, but they do come in many guises. These include bodegas (traditional wine bars), *cervecerías* (beer bars), *tascas* (tapas bars), *tabernas* (taverns) and even pubs (especially where there's an English influence). In many of them you'll be able to eat tapas at the bar but there will usually be a *comedor* (dining room) too, for a sit-down meal. You'll often save 10% to 20% by eating at the bar rather than a table.

Restaurantes are usually more formal places where you sit down to eat. A *mesón* is a simple restaurant attached to a bar with homestyle cooking. A *venta* is a roadside inn – the food can be delicious and inexpensive. A *marisquería* is a seafood restaurant, while a *chiringuito* is a small open-air bar or kiosk, usually fronting onto the beach.

Menu Tips

➡ Always ask for the house-special *tapa*.

➡ *Medias raciones* are a step up from tapas. They are small plates of food that are ideal for sharing between a couple or group, and are usually enjoyed in a more leisurely fashion sitting down.

➡ *Raciones* are a step up from *medias raciones* – full plates that are great for sharing if you're particularly hungry.

➡ Andalucian paella is often made with almonds, sherry, chicken and sausages, as well as seafood.

➡ Olives and a bread basket accompany most meals. Olives are nearly always served green as opposed to black.

➡ Gazpacho is usually only available in spring and summer and usually comes in a glass.

➡ Sangria isn't ubiquitous, but *tinto de verano* is a good substitute during spring and summer.

➡ Andalucians rarely drink sweet sherry; they prefer *fino* or *manzanilla,* especially with tapas.

Top: Paella with olives, bread and sangria

Bottom: *Gazpacho andaluz* (Andalucian gazpacho; p354)

Plan Your Trip

Outdoor Activities

One of the most epiphanic Andalucian experiences is discovering that the bulk of the region remains traditional, untouristed and bursting with outdoor adventure opportunities. Ancient walking trails lead to time-worn villages, cycling paths wind past ruined castles. Try diving, kitesurfing, horse riding, snowboarding, even paragliding, or go searching for emblematic wildlife.

Best Walking

Mountain Hikes
Sierra Nevada; Parque Natural Sierra de Grazalema

Hike up Peaks
Mulhacén (Sierra Nevada); El Torreón (Parque Natural Sierra de Grazalema

For Thrill-Seekers
Málaga province's newly reopened Caminito del Rey

For Wildlife Spotting
Parque Natural Sierras de Cazorla, Segura y Las Villas

For Birdwatching
Parques Nacional and Natural de Doñana; Parque Natural Sierras de Cazorla, Segura y Las Villas; Parque Natural Sierra de Grazalema

Pastoral Hikes
Sierra de Aracena; Parque Natural Sierra Norte de Sevilla

Coastal Hikes
Parque Natural de Cabo de Gata-Níjar; Parque Natural de la Breña y Marismas del Barbate

Long-Distance Hikes
GR7 trail in Las Alpujarras; GR247 trail around Parque Natural Sierras de Cazorla, Segura y Las Villas

Walking

Walking in Andalucía gets you to where 95% of visitors never go. If you're after some alone time while exercising your way through unblemished rural bliss, hit the *senderos* (footpaths).

All of Andalucía's *parques naturales* (natural parks) and *parques nacionales* (national parks) are criss-crossed by numerous well-marked day-walk trails, ranging from half-hour strolls to full-day mountain ascents. The scenery is rarely less than lovely and often majestic. You can sometimes string together day walks into a several-day trek, sleeping along the way in a variety of hotels, *hostales* (budget hotels) and campgrounds, or the occasional mountain refuge.

Maps and signage are steadily improving, but are often still iffy. The best markers are in the *parques naturales* and *nacionales,* and on major routes such as the GR7, identified by red-and-white paint splashes.

The two main categories of marked walking routes in Spain are *senderos de gran recorrido* (GRs; long-distance footpaths) and *senderos de pequeño recorrido* (PRs; shorter routes of a few hours or one or two days).

GREENWAYS, HERE WE COME

Spain's greatest environmental idea in the last 20 years might just be its *vías verdes* (greenways): disused railway lines that have been transformed into designated paths for cyclists, walkers and other nonmotorised transport, including wheelchairs. Spain has 7500km of abandoned railway tracks, and since 1993, 2100km of them have been converted into *vías verdes*. Andalucía currently has 23 (a total of 500km).

Aside from their natural attractions (bird reserves, olive groves), the *vías* guard uncommon chapters of human history. The Vía Verde del Aceite (Jaén province) once carried olive oil to the coast for export; the Vía Verde de Riotinto (Huelva province) ferried miners to the famous opencast Río Tinto mines. Many of the original engineering features have been preserved, including bridges, viaducts, tunnels and stations, some of which have been converted into cafes or rural hotels that hire bikes.

Andalucía's finest greenway is often considered to be the Vía Verde de la Sierra (p138; Cádiz). Three more leading lights are the Vía Verde de la Sierra Norte (p105; Sevilla), the Vía Verde del Aceite (p223; Jaén) and the Vía Verde de la Subbética (p213; Córdoba); these last two join at the spectacular Guadajoz viaduct to form an unbroken 160km path.

As ex-railway lines, the *vías verdes* have relatively slight gradients. They're well-marked with kilometre posts and equipped with maps, lookouts and picnic spots. More information at www.viasverdes.com.

When to Go

The best months for walking are generally May, June, September and October. July and August are ideal for the high Sierra Nevada, but unbearably hot elsewhere; some trails close due to fire risk.

Information

The *parques naturales* and *nacionales* offer detailed walking information (sometimes in Spanish only) at their official visitors centres, and online at www.ventanadelvisitante.es. Local tourist offices can be helpful.

Numerous English-language guides to localised regions are available. Among the best maps are those of Editorial Alpina (www.editorialalpina.com) to the Grazalema, Cabo de Gata, Sierra Nevada and Cazorla parks, available in English and Spanish.

Cycling

Andalucía has increasingly widespread bike-hire opportunities, increasingly well-maintained and signposted touring and off-road trails, and a growing number of urban bike-sharing schemes and cycle paths – most notably in Seville (p66).

Beware of hot weather, particularly in July and August.

Where to Go

The safest, flattest and most family-friendly paths for cyclists are the *vías verdes* (greenways).

Mountain-biking hot spots include the El Chorro and Ronda/Grazalema areas, the Parque Natural Sierras de Cazorla, Segura y Las Villas, and Las Alpujarras. The Parque Natural Sierra Nevada maintains 12 mountain-bike trails, of which the king is the 450km Ruta Cicloturística Trans-nevada, which circles the entire mountain range between 1500m and 2000m.

Diving & Snorkelling

Andalucía has some worthwhile spots for underwater exploration.

Where to Go

The Atlantic coast, with its strong currents, is best avoided (aside from some interesting wrecks around Gibraltar), and the western part of Andalucía's Mediterranean coast is of similarly limited interest to divers and snorkellers. This leaves the coast of eastern Andalucía:

➡ **Cabo de Gata, Almería** (p300) Andalucía's top diving and snorkelling spot, with clear protected waters and a varied seabed of seagrass, sand and rock dotted with caves, crevices, canyons and a wreck.

➡ **Costa Tropical, Granada** (p282)
Multicoloured fish, octopuses, corals and crustaceans, plus (relatively) warm waters make for excellent year-round diving and snorkelling; the gentle, shallow sea off La Herradura (p284) is ideal for beginners.

Information

Most establishments offer PADI or NAUI courses, plus dives for qualified divers and introductory 'baptisms'. A single dive with full equipment costs around €50; three-hour 'baptisms' are about €70.

Horse Riding

Beautiful horses define Andalucía as much as feisty flamenco, and an ever-growing number of *picaderos* (stables) offer guided rides or classes across the region. Many of the horses are Andalucian or Andalucian-Arab crosses – medium-sized, intelligent, good in traffic and usually easy to handle.

Where to Go

The hub of Andalucía's horse culture is Jerez de la Frontera (Cádiz), home of the famous Real Escuela Andaluza del Arte Ecuestre (p121) and Feria del Caballo (p122). The nearby Yeguada de la Cartuja – Hierro del Bocado (p122) breeding centre offers a fascinating insight into Andalucía's equestrian world.

Horse-riding highlights include:

➡ Beach and dune rides outside Tarifa (p143) on Cádiz' Costa de la Luz.

➡ Mountain trails around Lanjarón (p275) in Las Alpujarras.

WILDLIFE SPOTTING

Bounding deer, majestic sea mammals, flocks of migrating birds, the elusive Iberian lynx – Andalucía plays host to a fantastic array of wildlife (p334). A number of local companies run wildlife-spotting and birdwatching trips in the most popular areas.

Andalucía's famously endangered lynx population is split between the Parques Nacional and Natural de Doñana (about 100) and the Sierra Morena (around 200 to 220 in and around the Sierra de Cardeña y Montoro, Sierra de Andújar and Despeñaperros natural parks). Local operators run 4WD trips into the Parque Natural Sierra de Andújar (Jaén province) and the Parques Nacional and Natural de Doñana, which are your best bet for spotting lynxes (though chances remain low).

PLACE	ANIMAL	TOUR OPERATOR
Parques Nacional y Natural de Doñana (p87)	Wild boar, Spanish imperial eagles, red and fallow deer, greater flamingos, waterbirds	Cooperativa Marismas del Rocío (p89), Doñana Reservas (p89), Doñana Nature (p89)
Parque Natural Sierras de Cazorla, Segura y Las Villas (p239)	Ibexes, red and fallow deer, wild boar, mouflons, red squirrels, bearded vultures, black vultures, golden eagles, peregrine falcons	Turisnat (p238)
Sierra Nevada (p273)	Andalucía's largest ibex population, wild boar, golden eagles, Bonelli's eagles, griffon vultures, kestrels	Nevadensis (p277), Alpujarras Birdwatching & Nature (p275)
Parque Natural Sierra de Andújar (p226)	Ibexes, red and fallow deer, wild boar, mouflons, black vultures, black storks, Spanish imperial eagles	Turismo Verde (p226), IberianLynxLand (p226)
Parque Natural Sierra de Grazalema (p137)	Ibexes, griffon vultures	Independent visits recommended
Strait of Gibraltar (p154)	Marine mammals (April to October), over 300 species of migrating birds	FIRMM (p145), Aviantours (www.aviantours.net)
Laguna de Fuente de Piedra (p189)	Birds, especially greater flamingos (February to August)	Alpujarras Birdwatching & Nature (p275)
Peñón de Zaframagón (p138)	Griffon vultures	Independent visits recommended

BEN WELSH / GETTY IMAGES ©

Kitesurfer, Tarifa (p144)

➡ Woodland rides around Doñana (p89).

➡ Estepona's renowned Escuela de Arte Ecuestre Costa del Sol (p176).

Information

Typical ride or lesson prices are €25 per hour, €40 for two hours, and €60 for a half-day. Most stables cater to all levels, offering beginner lessons alongside challenging trail rides.

Kitesurfing, Windsurfing & Surfing

Thanks to the stiff winds that batter the Strait of Gibraltar, Cádiz' Costa de la Luz plays host to Europe's liveliest windsurfing and kitesurfing scene. Windsurfing, the original favourite, kicked off in the early 1980s. Kitesurfing, the newer, cooler, more extreme younger sibling, is equally popular.

Be warned: the choppy seas off the Costa de la Luz aren't always beginner's territory. May, June and September are usually the best months (calmer water, fewer crowds).

Where to Go

➡ **Tarifa** (p144) Europe's windsurfing and kitesurfing capital.

➡ **Los Caños de Meca** (p141) Another surfing/kitesurfing hot spot, northwest of Tarifa.

➡ **El Palmar** (p141) Andalucía's best board-riding waves.

Information

There are over 30 schools in and around Tarifa.

Kitesurfing Full-day equipment hire €60; six-hour beginner course €120.

Windsurfing Half-day equipment hire €90; six-hour beginner course €70.

Surfing Half-day equipment hire €30; two-hour class €30.

Paragliding & Hang-Gliding

Parapente (paragliding) and, to a lesser extent, *ala delta* (hang-gliding) are popular in Andalucía. You can take to the skies year-round from a growing number of launch points.

Where to Go

Little-known Algodonales, on the edge of Cádiz' Parque Natural Sierra de Grazalema, is among Andalucía's top free-flying centres, with an abundance of take-off points and strong enough winds to have attracted the World Hang-Gliding Championships in 2001. Locally based Zero Gravity (p138) offers one-week learn-to-fly paragliding courses (€900).

El Yelmo, in Jaén's Parque Natural de Cazorla, Segura y Las Villas, is another major paragliding spot, attracting thousands of people with its June free-flying fair, the Festival Internacional del Aire (p242).

The Sierra Nevada has some of Andalucía's highest launch sites.

Information

A good online resource is www.andalucia.org/en/sports.

Rock Climbing

Mention Andalucía to rock-climbing enthusiasts and they'll reply 'El Chorro'. This sheer limestone gorge above the Río Guadalhorce, 50km northwest of Málaga, contains hundreds of climbing routes, from easy to ultra-difficult. Many of them start from the infamous Caminito del Rey (p187), a notoriously narrow (and recently reopened) path that clings to the rock face.

Other climbable limestone crags are El Torcal de Antequera (Málaga) and Los Cahorros gorge (Sierra Nevada).

Information

For El Chorro, you can organise rock-climbing trips and classes through Finca La Campana (www.fincalacampana.com) or Andalucía Aventura (p185). The season is October to April.

A good climbing guidebook is *Andalucía* by David Munilla (2007).

Skiing & Snowboarding

The Sierra Nevada (p273) is Europe's most southerly ski area. Although its slopes lack the mega-steep, off-piste action of France or Switzerland, their skiing potential is fantastic. These are the highest mountains in Europe outside the Alps and the Caucasus, with cross-country routes, over 100km of runs and a top skiing elevation of 3300m. Snow can fall as early as November and linger until early May; the slopes are well-suited to beginners and families, along with advanced skiers.

Information

One-day adult ski passes cost between €34 and €45. Add on €23 for equipment rental. Six hours of group classes with a ski school cost around €60. Peak season is between Christmas and New Year, and from early February to early March.

The small settlement of Pradollano at the base (2100m) is an ugly, purpose-built ski resort for the Sierra Nevada; it's linked to the mightier attractions of Granada, about 30km away, by three daily buses (four on the weekend).

Plan Your Trip

Travel with Children

Andalucía is a family-friendly destination. The culture revolves around the (extended) family, and children are made welcome at all but the most formal restaurants, as well as at bars, and the majority of hotels. Stripped back to basics, the facilities, climate and attractions are ideal for families. To get the most of what is on offer, plan ahead.

Andalucía for Kids

The Andalucian basics – beaches and fabulous climate – are pretty good raw ingredients for starters. Add to this water sports, museums, parks, boat rides and loads of ice cream and it becomes serious spoil-them-rotten time. Note that the majority of theme parks and entertainment for children are in Málaga province, especially along the Costa del Sol.

Away from the coast, you may not find so many dedicated kiddie attractions, but every town will have at least one good-sized children's playground. Public spaces, such as town and village plazas, also morph into informal play spaces with children kicking a ball, riding bikes and playing, while parents enjoy a drink and tapa in one of the surrounding terrace bars. Many Andalucian towns also have municipal swimming pools, ideal in summer.

Eating & Drinking

Whole families, often including several generations, sitting around a restaurant or bar table eating and chatting is a fundamental element of the lifestyle here, and it is rare to find a restaurant where children are not welcome. Even if restaurants do

Best Regions for Kids

Málaga Province
Parents may balk, but the theme parks around Torremolinos and Benalmádena on the Costa del Sol have undeniable appeal for children, while beaches with shallow waters and boat rides should have the whole family smiling.

Almería Province
And now for something completely different... the Wild West shoot-'em-up shows in *tabernas* (taverns) are bound to blow their little socks off (not literally, you understand...).

Seville
Seville has a great leafy park, horse-drawn-carriage rides, boat trips and an amusement park on the former Expo site.

Cádiz Province & Gibraltar
Older kids will love the kite- and windsurfing in Tarifa – one of the major destinations for the sport in Europe. You can also hop on a ferry to Morocco for the day – something different for their show-and-tell back home.

not advertise children's menus (and few do), they will normally be willing to prepare a small portion for your child or suggest a suitable tapa or two.

High chairs in restaurants are increasingly common but by no means universal, and nappy-changing facilities are rare.

Favourite Foods

Perhaps not the healthiest of snacks, but you can't go wrong with ordering your child a churro (or two). These thick tubular doughnuts are irresistible to children – and to children at heart.

Discerning young diners may like to ease themselves into Andalucian cuisine by tasting various tapas; this will allow them to sample new flavours gradually and on a small scale. *Tortilla de patatas* (potato omelette), *albondigas* (meatballs) and, of course, chips (or French fries) are a good bet. You can also find kebabs or *shwarmas* in places with a large North African population – they are essentially a hot chicken wrap, and tasty (and messy) enough to be a big hit with most youngsters.

Aside from the normal selection of soft drinks on offer, you can generally find freshly squeezed orange juice in most bars. Another popular choice for children is *Cola Cao* (chocolate drink) served hot or cold with milk.

Discounts

Children pay two-thirds on the high-speed AVE train, but full price on most buses and ferries. There are generally discounts for admissions to sights, and those under four generally go free.

Children's Highlights

Theme Parks

➡ **Tivoli World** (p171) As well as various rides and slides, there are daily dance, musical and children's events.

➡ **Isla Mágica** (p68) Plenty of rides, including a roller coaster, plus pirate shows, bird-of-prey displays and more.

➡ **Oasys Mini Hollywood** (p294) Wild West shows, stagecoaches, can-can dancers and a zoo at this former film set for Westerns.

➡ **Aventura Amazonia** (p174) Adventure theme park with zip wires.

Museums

➡ **Museo Lara** (p179) Vast private museum; includes an exhibition on witchcraft and torture instruments which little boys (in particular) will doubtless enjoy!

➡ **Centro de Interpretación Cuevas de Guadix** (p271) Cave museum re-creating typical cave life for a family.

➡ **Casa Museo de Mijas** (p177) Folk-themed museum with models, artefacts and a donkey made from esparto grass.

➡ **Museo del Bandolero** (p179) Dedicated to the local bandits with lots of photos, exhibits and weapons, plus a gift shop.

➡ **Museo del Baile Flamenco** (p64) Includes daily flamenco performances at the family-friendly time of 7pm.

Caves, Caverns & Castles

➡ **Cueva de Nerja** (p192) Full of spooky stalactites and stalagmites.

➡ **St Michael's Cave** (p153) A huge natural grotto with a lake and atmospheric auditorium.

➡ **Gruta de las Maravillas** (p93) Explore 12 caverns here including stunning underground pools.

➡ **Cueva de la Pileta** (p184) Fascinating uncommercial caves with narrow low walkways, lakes and cave paintings.

➡ **Castles** Jaén, Segura de la Sierra, Alcalá La Real, Almodóvar del Rio and Málaga have castles with displays designed to amuse children, as well as adults.

Wildlife

➡ **Biopark** (p172) Refreshingly animal-friendly and enclosure-free zoo in the centre of the town.

➡ **Selwo Aventura** (p176) Wild-animal park with an African theme and animals including rhinos, giraffes, hippos and cheetahs.

➡ **Dolphin-Watching** (p154) The strait of Gibraltar is home to several different species of dolphin. Whales can be occasionally spotted, too.

➡ **Parque Ornitológico Loro-Sexi** (p283) Vast aviary with thousands of birds, plus parrot and birds-of-prey shows.

➡ **Mariposario de Benalmádena** (p171) A butterfly park with several reptiles, including iguanas and a giant tortoise.

➡ **Centro de Fauna Silvestre Collado del Almendral** (p240) Kids can take a minitrain on a 5km ride around a 1-sq-km enclosure and see wild boar, mouflon, ibex and deer, as well as rescued birds recovering in cages.

Other Sights & Activities

➡ **Fairs & fiestas** Annual fairs are held in every Andalucian town and village and always include a funfair with rides for kids.

➡ **Rowing boats** Rent a rowing boat to paddle along the moat at Seville's Plaza de España or a four-wheel bike to explore the park further.

➡ **Windsurfing & kiteboarding** Older children can take courses in both sports at Tarifa on the Cádiz coast.

➡ **Trip to Morocco** Take the speedy ferry from Tarifa to Tangier, Morocco for the day.

Planning

This is an easygoing, child-friendly destination with precious little advance planning necessary.

When to Go

July and August can be very busy with Spanish families, as well as foreign tourists, in the main tourist resorts, and some

BEFORE YOU GO
••••••••••••••••••••••••••••••••••••

➡ You can hire car seats for infants and children from most car-rental firms, but you should always book them in advance.

➡ No particular health precautions are necessary. Sun protection is essential but can be purchased here.

➡ Avoid tears and tantrums by planning which activities, theme parks, museums and leisure pursuits you want to opt for and, more importantly, can afford early on in the holiday.

➡ English books can be hard to find, so if your child enjoys reading or you have a bedtime-story routine, be sure to pack a couple.

hotels are block-booked by tour companies. May to June and September to October are good times to travel with young children; the weather is still warm enough for paddling in the sea but the weather has not yet reached serious sizzle factor. The theme parks and attractions are also not too crowded – aside from the Easter holidays, that is.

Accommodation

Most hotels and even *hostales* (budget hotels) will be able to provide an extra bed or cot for a child or baby. However, always check and reserve in advance as there will be a limited number available. You will be charged a supplement for this. When selecting a hotel, check whether it has a kids club, activities geared for youngsters and/ or babysitting facilities.

What's Available

You can buy baby formula in powder or liquid form, as well as sterilising solutions such as Milton, at *farmacias* (pharmacies). Disposable nappies are widely available at supermarkets and *farmacias*.

Regions at a Glance

Seville

Festivals
Architecture
Music

Spring Events

No other city changes its personality so radically in the space of just one week as Seville, when the constrained mourning of Semana Santa erupts into the carefree celebrations of the Feria de Abril.

Catedral & Alcázar

You can walk from bright geometric Mudéjar to dark atmospheric Gothic in less than 200 paces in central Seville, where the Alcázar and the Catedral sit ambiguously side by side. Indeed the cathedral itself is something of a Moorish-Christian hybrid with its three-quarter Moorish Giralda bell tower.

Flamenco

Seville has the largest and most varied stash of flamenco venues in Andalucía. Triana is the best haunt for intimate *peñas* (clubs), Barrio de Santa Cruz hosts authentic *tablaos* (choreographed flamenco shows), while during the raucous Feria de Abril, folksy *sevillanas* (folk dances) are de rigueur.

p48

Huelva & Sevilla Provinces

Wildlife
Walking
History

Delta Birds

Parque Nacional de Doñana is surely one of Spain's – and Europe's – finest protected areas. Located in Huelva and Sevilla provinces in the Río Guadalquivir delta, the park treats visitors to sightings of rare birds and mammals.

Pastoral Trails

Guided and unguided walks are an obvious draw in Parque Nacional de Doñana, but Huelva province's north harbours the contrasting topography of the Parque Natural Sierra de Aracena y Picos de Aroche, an ancient pastoral region criss-crossed with easy walking trails.

Columbus et al

Huelva and Sevilla provinces are often bracketed as being 'on the way to Portugal', but they hide some surprising historical heirlooms, including Christopher Columbus paraphernalia, baroque Osuna, the old Almohad walled town of Niebla and Moorish Almonaster la Real.

p79

Cádiz Province & Gibraltar

Food
White Towns
Music

Fish & Sherry

Where the Atlantic meets the Mediterranean you're bound to find good fish, traditionally deep-fried in olive oil to create *pescaito frito*. Then there's the sherry made from grapes that grow near the coast – a perfect complement.

Hilltop Settlements

They're all here, the famous white towns with their ruined hilltop castles, geranium-filled flower boxes and small somnolent churches. Arcos, Jimena, Castellar, Vejer...the ancient sentinels on a once-volatile frontier that divided two cultures.

Font de Flamenco

With a little help from Seville, the towns of Cádiz province pretty much created modern flamenco. Look no further than the flamenco songs – *bulerías* of Jerez or the *alegrías* of Cádiz – all still performed in local *tablaos* and *peñas*.

p108

Málaga Province

Beaches
Art
Food

Coastal Resorts

Málaga's beaches are an industry, bagging more tourist euros than the rest of the region put together. Choose according to your budget and hipster-rating between Estepona, Marbella, Fuengirola, Torremolinos, Málaga and Nerja.

Picasso & Beyond

So what if Picasso left town when he was only 10 years old? The birthplace of the great master has branched out of late, launching a slew of exciting new art museums and proving that it may have just pipped Seville and Granada as Andalucía's 'art capital'.

Regional Dishes

On the coast, simple beachside *chiringuitos* (beach bars) stand next to Michelin-star restaurants that specialise in fish. Inland, Antequera has fine soups and desserts, while Ronda is the home of mountain stews and meat dishes.

p156

Córdoba Province

Moorish Architecture
Castles
Natural Areas

Córdoba Caliphate

Córdoba, the 10th-century caliphate, pretty much defined Islamic architecture 1000 years ago. You can see it in all its glory – intact – in the famous Mezquita (Grand Mosque) or – elegantly ruined – at the Madinat al-Zahra just outside the city limits.

Border Fortifications

In Córdoba province's north, bordering the Castilla region, numerous castles stand sentinel over the craggy landscape crowned by the sinister but dramatic Almodóvar del Río, a kind of Andalucian version of Harry Potter's Hogwarts.

Off the Beaten Track

Córdoba province has three little-visited natural parks, including the wooded Sierra de Hornachuelos and the mountainous Sierras Subbéticas. North of the provincial capital lies the Sierra Morena, one of Andalucía's most remote regions.

p195

Jaén Province

Natural Areas
Wildlife
Architecture

Andalucian Wilderness

Jaén province safeguards one of Europe's largest protected areas, the Parque Natural Sierras de Cazorla, Segura y Las Villas, as well as some lesser-known, but no less beautiful, wild tracts such as the unsullied Parque Natural Sierra de Andújar.

Rare Fauna

Lynx, wild boar and mouflon are hardly ubiquitous in Andalucía. Your best chance of seeing these rare animals is probably in the quieter corners of Jaén province, where protected parks and mountains break the monotony of the olive groves.

Renaissance Towns

Renaissance architecture makes a cameo appearance in Andalucía courtesy of Jaén province's two Unesco-listed pearls – Úbeda and Baeza – plus its less-heralded provincial capital Jaén (the city), whose grandiose cathedral is befitting of Granada or Seville.

p219

Granada Province

Architecture
White Towns
Culture

Historical Eras

A celebrated Nasrid palace-fortress, a hilltop Moorish quarter, the charming Jewish 'Realejo' (a district of the city adjacent to the Alhambra that was the old Jewish quarter) and a baroque-Renaissance cathedral: Granada is a magnificent 'mess' of just about every architectural style known to European building.

Alpujarras Villages

Matching Cádiz province's white towns for spectacular beauty, Granada's *pueblos* (villages) are certainly higher, perched above the steep valleys of Las Alpujarras. They're notable for their artisan crafts, hearty mountain food and large communities of British expats.

Entertainment Scene

A university town with an arty bent and a strong literary tradition, Granada directs what happens next in Andalucía's social life. Seville might have the best festivals, but this city ultimately has the most varied entertainment scene.

p246

Almería Province

Coastal Scenery
Film Sets
History

Resort-Free Coast

Forgotten, lucky or perhaps just too arid to develop, Cabo de Gata has escaped the Costa del Sol bulldozer treatment and lived to fight another day. Now protected as a natural park, it guards the most precious flora and marine life in the southern Mediterranean.

Mini Hollywood

Hmm…doesn't that dusty desert backdrop look familiar? Hang on. Isn't that where Sergio Leone shot Clint Eastwood in the spaghetti westerns and where 'the Doctor' faced a cyborg gunslinger in *Dr Who*? Come to Oasys Mini Hollywood and relive the Wild West.

Moorish Heritage

Often overlooked by Alhambra pilgrims, the city of Almería has plenty of stories to tell, many of them hailing from the pre-Christian era. Check out the old town and Alcazaba before heading east for more Moorish mystery in Mojácar.

p285

On the Road

Huelva & Sevilla Provinces (p79)

⊙ **Seville** (p48)

Córdoba Province (p195)

Jaén Province (p219)

Cádiz Province & Gibraltar (p108)

Málaga Province (p156)

Granada Province (p246)

Almería Province (p285)

Seville

POP 703,000 / ELEV 30M

Includes ➡

Sights & Activities . . . 50
Courses 69
Tours. 69
Festivals & Events 69
Sleeping. 70
Eating 72
Drinking & Nightlife. . .75
Entertainment. 76
Shopping 77
Getting
There & Away 78
Getting Around. 78

Best Places to See Flamenco

➡ Museo del Baile Flamenco (p64)

➡ Casa de la Memoria (p76)

➡ Casa de la Guitarra (p76)

➡ El Palacio Andaluz (p76)

Best Places to Eat

➡ La Brunilda (p73)

➡ La Pepona (p74)

➡ Bar-Restaurante Eslava (p75)

➡ La Azotea (p73)

Why Go?

Some cities have looks, other cities have personality. The *sevillanos* – lucky devils – get both, courtesy of their flamboyant, charismatic, ever-evolving Andalucian metropolis founded, according to myth, 3000 years ago by the Greek god Hercules. Drenched for most of the year in spirit-enriching sunlight, this is a city of feelings as much as sights, with different seasons prompting vastly contrasting moods: solemn for Semana Santa, flirtatious for the spring fiesta and soporific for the gasping heat of summer.

Like all great cities, Seville has historical layers. Roman ruins testify the settlement's earliest face, memories of the Moorish era flicker like medieval engravings in the Santa Cruz quarter, while the riverside Arenal reeks of lost colonial glory. Yet, one of the most remarkable things about modern Seville is its ability to adapt and etch fresh new brushstrokes onto an ancient canvas.

When to Go

Mar–May The best time to visit Seville is when its two major festivals – Semana Santa and the Feria de Abril – run back to back. This is when the city wears its personality on its sleeve and is alive with colour, warm weather, orange blossom and that famous *pasión* (passion).

Jul & Aug Megahot and busy; the city is primed for tourism with all sights open and operating.

Sep & Oct The extreme heat of summer has diminished and most of the crowds have gone home.

Seville Highlights

1 Picking up expensive interior design and gardening tips at the exquisite **Alcázar** (p56)

2 Savouring an early-evening glass of something alcoholic in the **Alameda de Hércules** (p68)

3 Re-evaluating Seville's glorious Golden Age art in the **Hospital de los Venerables Sacerdotes** (p61)

4 Attending an aficionado's concert at the **Museo del Baile Flamenco** (p64)

5 Enjoying some of Andalucía's best modern tapas in **La Brunilda** (p73)

6 Strolling the panoramic walkway of the **Metropol Parasol** (p65)

7 Looking down on the Gothic Seville cathedral from the top of the **Giralda** (p50)

8 Inhaling orange blossom while cycling a Sevici bike around **Parque de María Luisa** (p66)

History

Founded by the Romans, the city of Seville didn't really flower until the Moorish Almoravid period, which began in 1085. They were replaced by the Almohads in the 12th century; Caliph Yacub Yusuf made Seville capital of the Almohad realm and built a great mosque where Seville's cathedral now stands. But Almohad power dwindled after the disastrous defeat of Las Navas de Tolosa in 1212, and Castilla's Fernando III (El Santo; the Saint) went on to capture Seville in 1248.

Fernando brought 24,000 settlers to Seville and by the 14th century it was the most important Castilian city. Seville's biggest break was Columbus' discovery of the Americas in 1492. In 1503 the city was awarded an official monopoly on Spanish trade with the new-found continent. It rapidly became one of the biggest, richest and most cosmopolitan cities on earth.

But it was not to last. A plague in 1649 caused the death of half the city's population, and as the 17th century wore on, the Río Guadalquivir became more silted and less navigable. In 1717 the Casa de la Contratación (Contracting House; the government office controlling commerce with the Americas) was transferred to Cádiz.

The beginnings of industry in the mid-19th century saw the first bridge across the Guadalquivir, the Puente de Triana (or Puente de Isabel II), built in 1852, and the old Almohad walls were knocked down in 1869 to let the city expand. In 1936 Seville fell very quickly to the Nationalists at the start of the Spanish Civil War, despite resistance in working-class areas (which brought savage reprisals).

Things have been looking up since the 1980s when Seville was named capital of the newly autonomous Andalucía (over the last quarter-century a number of provinces in Spain have been given a certain amount of autonomy from Madrid). Seville's economy was steadily improving with a mix of tourism, commerce, technology and industry in the early 2000s. Then, in 2008, the financial crisis hit the city with a sharp jolt, as it did in the rest of Andalucía. Although big metropolitan projects such as the Metropol Parasol continued, the economic situation hit rock bottom in 2012 with sky-high unemployment and serious recession. The last three years have been more optimistic with growth returning to the Spanish economy, although unemployment in Seville province still hovers stubbornly above 30%.

◉ Sights & Activities

◉ Cathedral Area

Catedral & Giralda CHURCH
(Map p54; www.catedraldesevilla.es; adult/child €9/free; ⊙11am-3.30pm Mon, 11am-5pm Tue-Sat, 2.30-6pm Sun) Seville's immense cathedral, one of the largest Christian churches in the world, is awe-inspiring in its scale and sheer majesty. It stands on the site of the great 12th-century Almohad mosque, with the mosque's minaret (the Giralda) still towering beside it.

After Seville fell to the Christians in 1248, the mosque was used as a church until 1401. Then, in view of its decaying state, the church authorities decided to knock it down and start again. 'Let's construct a church so large future generations will think we were mad,' they quipped (or so legend has it). When it was completed in 1502 after one hundred years of hard labour, the Catedral de Santa María de la Sede, as it is officially known, was (and remains) the largest church in the world by volume and pretty much defines the word 'Gothic'. It is also a veritable art gallery replete with notable works by Zurbarán, Murillo, Goya and others.

➡ Exterior

From close up, the bulky exterior of the cathedral with its Gothic embellishments gives hints of the treasures within. Pause to look at the **Puerta del Perdón** on Calle Alemanes, a legacy of the Islamic mosque.

➡ Sala del Pabellón

Selected treasures from the cathedral's art collection are exhibited in this room, the first after the ticket office. Much of what's displayed here, as elsewhere in the cathedral, is the work of masters from Seville's 17th-century artistic Golden Age.

➡ Southern & Northern Chapels

The chapels along the southern and northern sides of the cathedral hold more riches of sculpture and painting. Near the western end of the northern side is the **Capilla de San Antonio**, housing Murillo's humungous 1656 canvas depicting the vision of St Anthony of Padua. The painting was victim of a daring art heist in 1874.

➡ Tomb of Christopher Columbus

Inside the **Puerta del Príncipe** (Door of the Prince) stands the monumental tomb of Christopher Columbus (Cristóbal Colón in

SEVILLE IN FIVE WORKS OF ART

A leading player in the Golden Age of Spanish art, Seville reveals a lot through its paintings. Here are five not-to-be-missed masterpieces and the stories behind them.

Visión de San Antonio (*Vision of St Anthony*, 1656) This giant Murillo inside Seville cathedral was the victim of a notorious art theft in 1874 when an opportunistic thief cut the figure of the kneeling St Anthony from the canvas and absconded with it to America. Miraculously, the painting turned up several months later in New York where it was spotted by a savvy art dealer who bought it for $250 and sent it back to Seville to be skillfully reinserted into the canvas.

Misericordia (*Mercy*, 1666–70) In the 1660s, Murillo was commissioned to complete a series of six paintings on the theme of mercy for Seville's newly inaugurated Hospital de la Caridad, a task he completed with customary aplomb. In 1810 four of the series were stolen when Napoleon's army occupied Seville. The thief was a French general named Jean de Dieu Soult who amassed a huge personal art collection from stolen Spanish classics. The paintings were never given back (they remain scattered around museums in Paris, London and Canada) meaning four of the 'Murillos' in the hospital today are 21st-century copies.

Santa Rufina (*St Rufina*, 1629–32) One of only a handful of canvases by Diego Velázquez on display in his native city, this rendering of Santa Rufina (a 3rd-century Christian martyr) was bought by the local Focus-Abengoa Foundation in 2007 with the aim of bringing the artist 'home'. The painting cost a hefty €12.4 million and is now on display alongside two other Velázquez works in the Hospital de los Venerables Sacerdotes.

Inmaculada concepción (*Immaculate Conception*, 1650) Debate over Mary's Immaculate Conception obsessed Spanish artists in the 16th and 17th centuries and you'll see iconography celebrating it displayed everywhere. Murillo alone painted more than a dozen versions of the holy scene. One of his most notable lights up a restored convent chapel in Seville's Museo de Bellas Artes. A more sober rendering by Zurbarán can be seen in the Hospital de los Venerables Sacerdotes.

Virgen de los mareantes (*Virgin of the Navigators*, 1531–36) Hung in the Sala de Audiencias in the Alcázar, a chapel where sailors went to pray before sailing for the Indies, Alejo Fernández' masterpiece was painted sometime between 1531 and 1536 and is generally accepted as being the oldest known depiction of the discovery of the New World in art form. It depicts Columbus, Amerigo Vespucci, Charles V and a cluster of American natives sheltering beneath the Virgin Mary's outstretched cape.

Spanish) – the subject of a continuous riddle – containing what were long believed to be the great explorer's bones, brought here from Cuba in 1898.

Columbus died in 1506 in Valladolid, in northern Spain. His remains lay at La Cartuja monastery in Seville before being moved to Hispaniola in 1536. Even though there were suggestions that the bones kept in Seville's cathedral were possibly those of his son Diego (who was buried with his father in Santo Domingo, Hispaniola), recent DNA tests seemed to finally prove that it really is Christopher Columbus lying in that box. Yet, unfortunately, to confuse matters further, the researchers also say that the bones in Santo Domingo could also be real, since Columbus' body was moved several times after his death. It seems that even death couldn't dampen the great explorer's urge to travel.

➡ **Capilla Mayor**

East of the choir is the Capilla Mayor (Main Chapel). Its Gothic retable is the jewel of the cathedral and reckoned to be the biggest altarpiece in the world. Begun by Flemish sculptor Pieter Dancart in 1482 and finished by others in 1564, this sea of gilt and polychromed wood holds more than 1000 carved biblical figures. At the centre of the lowest level is the tiny 13th-century silver-plated cedar image of the Virgen de la Sede (Virgin of the See), patron of the cathedral.

➡ **Sacristía de los Cálices**

South of the Capilla Mayor are rooms containing some of the cathedral's main art

Seville Cathedral

'We're going to construct a church so large future generations will think we were mad,' declared the inspired architects of Seville in 1401 at the beginning of one of the most grandiose building projects in medieval history. Just over a century later their madness was triumphantly confirmed.

WHAT TO LOOK FOR

To avoid getting lost, orient yourself by the main highlights. Directly inside the southern (main) entrance is the grand **Tomb of Columbus** ❶. Turn right here and head into the south-eastern corner to uncover some major art treasures: a Goya in the Sacristía de los Cálices, a Zurbarán in the **Sacristía Mayor** ❷, and Murillo's shining *Immaculada* in the Sala Capitular. Skirt the cathedral's eastern wall taking a look inside the **Capilla Real** ❸ with its important royal tombs. By now it's impossible to avoid the lure of **Capilla Mayor** ❹ with its fantastical altarpiece. Hidden over in the northwest corner is the **Capilla de San Antonio** ❺ with a legendary Murillo. That huge doorway almost in front of you is the rarely opened **Puerta de la Asunción** ❻. Make for the **Giralda** ❼ next, stealing admiring looks at the high, vaulted ceiling on the way. After looking down on the cathedral's immense footprint, descend and depart via the **Patio de los Naranjos** ❽.

Capilla Mayor
Behold! The cathedral's main focal point contains its greatest treasure, a magnificent gold-plated altarpiece depicting various scenes in the life of Christ. It constitutes the life's work of one man, Flemish artist Pieter Dancart.

Patio de los Naranjos
Inhale the perfume of 60 Sevillan orange trees in a cool patio bordered by fortress-like walls – a surviving remnant of the original 12th-century mosque. Exit is gained via the horseshoe-shaped Puerta del Perdón.

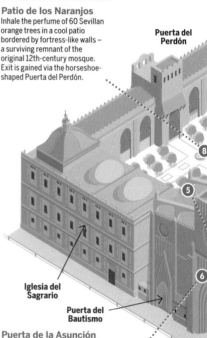

Puerta del Perdón

Iglesia del Sagrario

Puerta del Bautismo

Puerta de la Asunción
Located on the western side of the cathedral and also known as the Puerta Mayor, these huge, rarely opened doors are pushed back during Semana Santa to allow solemn processions of Catholic *hermandades* (brotherhoods) to pass through.

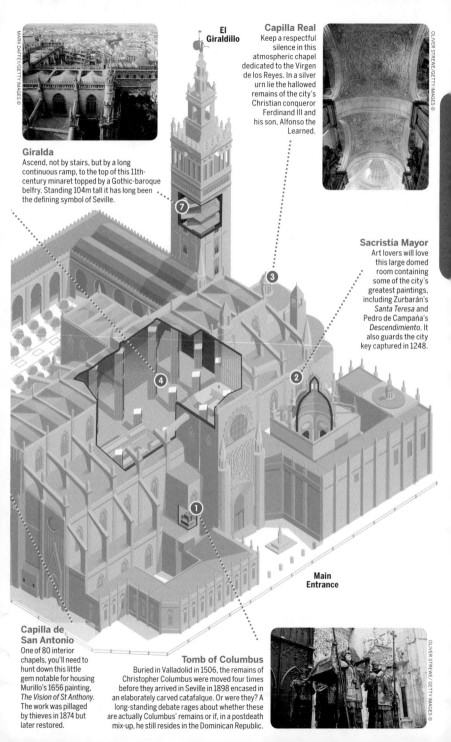

El Giraldillo

Capilla Real
Keep a respectful silence in this atmospheric chapel dedicated to the Virgen de los Reyes. In a silver urn lie the hallowed remains of the city's Christian conqueror Ferdinand III and his son, Alfonso the Learned.

Giralda
Ascend, not by stairs, but by a long continuous ramp, to the top of this 11th-century minaret topped by a Gothic-baroque belfry. Standing 104m tall it has long been the defining symbol of Seville.

Sacristía Mayor
Art lovers will love this large domed room containing some of the city's greatest paintings, including Zurbarán's *Santa Teresa* and Pedro de Campaña's *Descendimiento*. It also guards the city key captured in 1248.

Main Entrance

Capilla de San Antonio
One of 80 interior chapels, you'll need to hunt down this little gem notable for housing Murillo's 1656 painting, *The Vision of St Anthony*. The work was pillaged by thieves in 1874 but later restored.

Tomb of Columbus
Buried in Valladolid in 1506, the remains of Christopher Columbus were moved four times before they arrived in Seville in 1898 encased in an elaborately carved catafalque. Or were they? A long-standing debate rages about whether these are actually Columbus' remains or if, in a postdeath mix-up, he still resides in the Dominican Republic.

Barrio de Santa Cruz, El Arenal & Triana

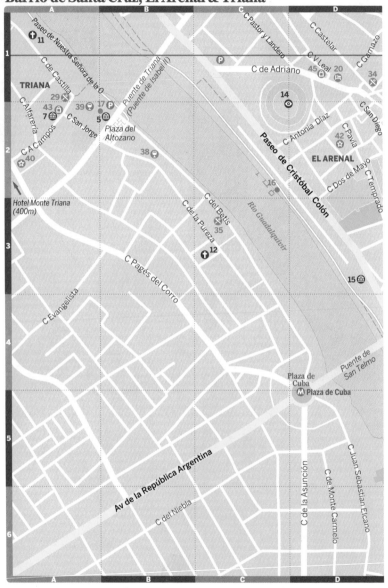

treasures. The westernmost of these is the Sacristy of the Chalices, where Francisco de Goya's painting of the Seville martyrs, *Santas Justa y Rufina* (1817), hangs above the altar.

➡ **Sacristía Mayor**

This large room with a finely carved stone dome was created between 1528 and 1547: the arch over its portal has carvings of 16th-century foods. Pedro de Campaña's 1547 *Descendimiento* (Descent from the

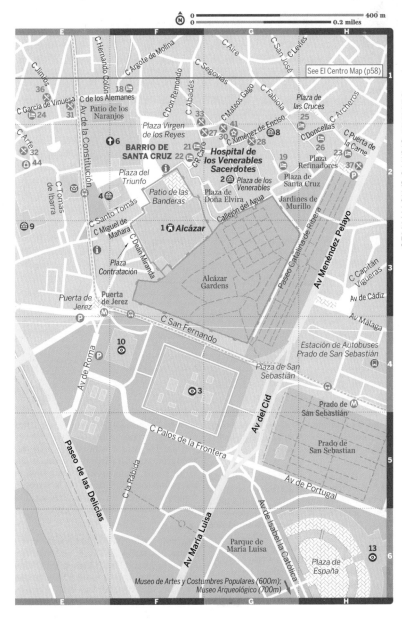

See El Centro Map (p58)

SEVILLE SIGHTS & ACTIVITIES

Cross), above the central altar at the southern end, and Francisco de Zurbarán's *Santa Teresa,* to its right, are two of the cathedral's most precious paintings. The room's centrepiece is the **Custodia de Juan de Arfe**, a huge 475kg silver monstrance made in the 1580s by Renaissance metalsmith Juan de Arfe.

➡ **Sala Capitular**

The beautifully domed chapter house, also called the Cabildo, in the southeastern corner, was originally built between 1558 and

Barrio de Santa Cruz, El Arenal & Triana

◉ Top Sights
1 Alcázar F3
2 Hospital de los Venerables
  Sacerdotes G2

◉ Sights
3 Antigua Fábrica de Tabacos..................F4
4 Archivo de Indias E2
5 Castillo de San Jorge............................ B2
6 Catedral & Giralda................................F2
7 Centro Cerámica Triana A2
8 Centro de Interpretación Judería
  de Sevilla G2
9 Hospital de la Caridad..........................E3
10 Hotel Alfonso XIII F4
11 Parroquia de Nuestra Señora de
   la O A1
12 Parroquia de Santa Ana C3
13 Plaza de España...................................H6
14 Plaza de Toros de la Real
   Maestranza....................................... C2
15 Torre del Oro D3

◉ Activities, Courses & Tours
16 Cruceros Turísticos Torre del
   Oro C2
17 Taller Andaluz de Cocina B2

◉ Sleeping
18 EME Catedral Hotel F1
19 Hostal Plaza Santa Cruz G2
20 Hotel Adriano.......................................D1
21 Hotel Casa 1800....................................F2

22 Hotel Palacio Alcázar............................ F2
23 Hotel Puerta de Sevilla H2
24 Hotel Simón E1
25 Pensión San Pancracio.........................H2
26 Un Patio en Santa Cruz H2

◉ Eating
27 Bodega Santa Cruz G2
28 Café Bar Las Teresas...........................G2
29 Casa Cuesta A1
30 Casa Tomate..G2
31 Horno de San Buenaventura E1
32 Infanta E2
33 L'Oca Giuliva F1
34 Mesón Cinco Jotas............................... D1
35 T de Triana C3
36 Taberna Los Coloniales E1
37 Vinería San Telmo H2

◉ Drinking & Nightlife
38 Café de la Prensa................................. B2
39 Cervezas Taifa A2

◉ Entertainment
40 Casa Anselma A2
41 Casa de la Guitarra..............................G2
42 Tablao El Arenal...................................D2

◉ Shopping
43 Cerámica Santa Ana A2
44 El Postigo..E2
45 Padilla Crespo......................................D1

1592 as a venue for meetings of the cathedral hierarchy. Hanging high above the archbishop's throne at the southern end is a Murillo masterpiece, *La inmaculada*.

➡ **Giralda**

In the northeastern corner of the cathedral you'll find the passage for the climb up to the belfry of the Giralda. The ascent is quite easy, as a series of ramps goes all the way to the top, built so that the guards could ride up on horseback. The decorative brick tower stands 104m tall and was the minaret of the mosque, constructed between 1184 and 1198 at the height of Almohad power. Its proportions, delicate brick-pattern decoration and colour, which changes with the light, make it perhaps Spain's most perfect Islamic building. The top-most parts of the Giralda – from the bell level up – were added in the 16th century, when Spanish Christians were busy 'improving on' surviving Islamic buildings. At the very top is El Giraldillo, a 16th-century bronze weathervane representing 'faith' that has become a symbol of Seville.

➡ **Patio de los Naranjos**

Outside the cathedral's northern side, this patio was originally the courtyard of the mosque. It's planted with 66 *naranjos* (orange trees), and a Visigothic fountain sits in the centre. Hanging from the ceiling in the patio's southeastern corner is a replica stuffed crocodile – the original was a gift to Alfonso X from the Sultan of Egypt.

★ **Alcázar**   CASTLE
(Map p54; ☑ tours 954 50 23 24; www.alcazarsevilla.org; adult/child €9.50/free; ☺ 9.30am-7pm Apr-Sep, to 5pm Oct-Mar) If heaven really *does* exist, then let's hope it looks a little bit like the inside of Seville's Alcázar. Built primarily in the 1300s during the so-called 'dark ages' in Europe, the castle's intricate architecture is anything but dark. Indeed, compared to our modern-day shopping malls, the Alcázar marks one of history's architectural high points. Unesco agreed, making it a World Heritage site in 1987.

Originally founded as a fort for the Cordoban governors of Seville in 913, the Alcázar has been expanded or reconstructed many times in its 11 centuries of existence. In the 11th century Seville's prosperous Muslim *taifa* (small kingdom) rulers developed the original fort by building a palace called Al-Muwarak (the Blessed) in what's now the western part of the Alcázar. The 12th-century Almohad rulers added another palace east of this, around what's now the Patio del Crucero. Christian Fernando III moved into the Alcázar when he captured Seville in 1248, and several later Christian monarchs used it as their main residence. Fernando's son Alfonso X replaced much of the Almohad palace with a Gothic one. Between 1364 and 1366 Pedro I created the Alcázar's crown jewel, the sumptuous Mudéjar Palacio de Don Pedro.

➡ **Patio del León**

From the ticket office inside the **Puerta del León** (Lion Gate) you emerge into the Patio del León (Lion Patio), which was the garrison yard of the original Al-Muwarak palace. Just off here is the **Sala de la Justicia** (Hall of Justice), with beautiful Mudéjar plasterwork and an *artesonado* (ceiling of interlaced beams with decorative insertions). This room was built in the 1340s by Christian king Alfonso XI, who disported here with one of his mistresses, Leonor de Guzmán, reputedly the most beautiful woman in Spain. It leads to the pretty **Patio del Yeso**, part of the 12th-century Almohad palace reconstructed in the 19th century.

➡ **Patio de la Montería**

The rooms on the western side of this patio were part of the **Casa de la Contratación** (Contracting House), founded by the Catholic Monarchs in 1503 to control trade with Spain's American colonies. The **Salón del Almirante** (Admiral's Hall) houses 19th- and 20th-century paintings showing historical events and personages associated with Seville. The room off its northern end has an international collection of beautiful, elaborate fans. The **Sala de Audiencias** (Audience Hall) is hung with tapestry representations of the shields of Spanish admirals and Alejo Fernández' landmark 1530s painting *Virgen de los mareantes* (Virgin of the Navigators; see boxed text on p51).

➡ **Cuarto Real Alto**

The Alcázar is still a royal palace. In 1995 it staged the wedding feast of Infanta Elena, daughter of King Juan Carlos I, after her marriage in Seville's cathedral. The **Cuarto Real Alto** (Upper Royal Quarters), the rooms used by the Spanish royal family on their visits to Seville, are open for (heavily subscribed) tours (€4.50) several times a day; some in Spanish, some in English. It's essential to book ahead. Highlights of the tour include the 14th-century **Salón de Audiencias**, still the monarch's reception room, and Pedro I's bedroom, with marvellous Mudéjar tiles and plasterwork.

➡ **Palacio de Don Pedro**

Posterity owes Pedro I a big thank you for creating this palace (also called the Palacio Mudéjar), the single most stunning architectural feature in Seville.

Though at odds with many of his fellow Christians, Pedro had a long-standing alliance with the Muslim emir of Granada, Mohammed V, the man responsible for much of the Alhambra's finest decoration. So in 1364, when Pedro decided to build a new palace within the Alcázar, Mohammed sent along many of his best artisans. These were joined by others from Seville and Toledo. Their work, drawing on the Islamic traditions of the Almohads and caliphal Córdoba, is a unique synthesis of Iberian Islamic art.

Inscriptions on the palace's facade, facing the Patio de la Montería, encapsulate the collaborative nature of the enterprise. While one announces in Spanish that the building's creator was 'the very high, noble and conquering Don Pedro, by the grace of God king of Castila and León', another proclaims repeatedly in Arabic that 'there is no conqueror but Allah'.

At the heart of the palace is the wonderful **Patio de las Doncellas** (Patio of the Maidens), surrounded by beautiful arches, plasterwork and tiling. The sunken garden in the centre was uncovered by archaeologists in 2004 from beneath a 16th-century marble covering.

The **Alcoba Real** (Royal Quarters), on the northern side of the patio, has stunningly beautiful ceilings and wonderful plaster- and tilework. Its rear room was probably the monarch's summer bedroom.

From here you can move west into the little **Patio de las Muñecas** (Patio of the Dolls), the heart of the palace's private quarters, featuring delicate Granada-style decoration; indeed, plasterwork was actually brought here from the Alhambra in the 19th century when the mezzanine and top gallery were added for Queen Isabel II. The **Cuarto del Príncipe** (Prince's Room), to its north, has a superb wooden cupola ceiling trying to re-create a starlit night sky.

El Centro

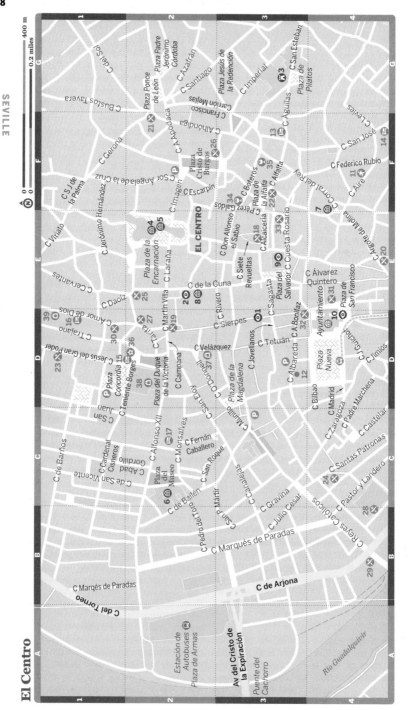

400 m

0.2 miles

Estación de
Autobuses
Plaza de Armas

Puente del
Cachorro

Av del Cristo de
la Expiración

Río Guadalquivir

C del Torneo

C Marqués de Paradas

C de Arjona

C Marqués de Paradas

C de Barros

C de San Vicente

C Cardenal Cisneros

C Abad Gordillo

C Alfonso XII

C San Juan

Plaza del Museo

C de Bailén

C Pedro del Toro

C San d Mártir

C Canalejas

C San Roque

C Monsalves

C Fernán Caballero

C Gravina

C Julio César

C Reyes Católicos

C Pastor y Landero

C Santas Patronas

C Zaragoza

C Madrid

C Bilbao

C Padre Marchena

C Castelar

EL CENTRO

Plaza de la
Encarnación

C Laraña

C de la Cuna

C Martín Villa

C Rivero

C Sierpes

C Velázquez

C Tetuán

C Jovellanos

C Albareda

C Gamazo

C Barcelona

Plaza
Nueva

Ayuntamiento

Plaza de
San Francisco

Plaza del
Salvador

C Cuesta Rosario

C Álvarez
Quintero

C Alcaicería

C Siete
Revueltas

C Sagasta

C A Bonifaz

C Don Alonso el Sabio

C Pérez Galdós

C Boteros

C Alfalfa

C de la Alfalfa

Plaza
Cristo de
Burgos

Plaza de la Cruz

Sor Ángela de la Cruz

C Imagen

C Escarpín

C Amor de Dios

C Daoíz

C Jerónimo Hernández

C Viriato

C S J de
la Palma

C Cervantes

C Jesús del Gran Poder

C Teniente Borges

Plaza
Concordia

Plaza del Duque
de la Victoria

C Campana

C Trajano

C San Eloy

C Tarifa

C O'Donnell

Plaza de la
Magdalena

C Canalejas

C de la Cuna

C Aguilas

C Santiago

C Azafrán

Plaza Ponce
de León

Plaza Padre
Jerónimo
Córdoba

C del Sol

C Bustos Tavera

C Gerona

C Apodaca

C A Apodaca

C Francisco
Carrión Mejías

Plaza Jesús de
la Redención

C Imperial

C San Esteban

Plaza de
Pilatos

C Levíes

C San José

C Federico Rubio

C Aire

C Corral del Rey

C Argote de Molina

C Álvarez
Quintero

C GIimíos

C Alhóndiga

1 **2** **3** **4** **5** **6** **7** **8** **9** **10** **11** **12** **13** **14** **15** **16** **17** **18** **19** **20** **21** **22** **23** **24** **25** **26** **27** **28** **29** **30** **31** **32** **33** **34** **35** **36** **37** **38** **39**

A B C D E F G

1 2 3 4

El Centro

⊙ Sights
1 Calle Sierpes...............................D3
2 Casa de la Memoria.....................E2
3 Casa de Pilatos...........................G3
4 Metropol Parasol.........................E2
5 Museo Antiquarium......................E2
6 Museo de Bellas Artes.................C2
7 Museo del Baile Flamenco...........F4
8 Palacio de la Condesa de Lebrija..........E2
9 Parroquia del Divino Salvador.................E3
10 Plaza de San Francisco.........................D4

⊙ Activities, Courses & Tours
11 Aire Baños Árabes.....................F4
12 CLIC..D3
Pancho Tours................................(see 17)
Past View..(see 4)

⊙ Sleeping
13 Hotel Abanico.............................F3
14 Hotel Amadeus............................F4
15 Hotel América.............................D2
16 Hotel Boutique Doña Lola...................D1
17 Oasis Backpackers' Hostel...................C2

⊙ Eating
18 Bar Europa...................................E3
19 Confitería La Campana..........................D2
20 Egaña Santo Restaurante.....................E4

21 El Rinconcillo............................F2
22 Horno de San Buenaventura................F3
23 La Azotea.....................................D1
24 La Brunilda.................................C4
25 La Pepona...................................E2
26 Los Coloniales............................F2
27 Luso Tapas..................................D2
Mercado de la Encarnación..........(see 4)
28 Mercado del Arenal.....................B4
29 Mercado Lonja del Barranco.................B4
30 Redhouse Art & Food...........................D1
31 Restaurante Albarama..........................E4
32 Robles Laredo............................D3
33 The Room....................................E3

⊙ Drinking & Nightlife
34 Cabo Loco...................................F3
35 El Garlochi..................................F3

⊙ Entertainment
Casa de la Memoria.......................(see 2)
Sevilla de Ópera............................(see 28)
36 Teatro Duque La Imperdible.................D2

⊙ Shopping
37 Casa del Libro.............................D2
38 El Corte Inglés.............................D2
39 Record Sevilla.............................D1

The spectacular **Salón de Embajadores** (Hall of Ambassadors), at the western end of the Patio de las Doncellas, was the throne room of Pedro I's palace. The room's fabulous wooden dome of multiple star patterns, symbolising the universe, was added in 1427. The dome's shape gives the room its alternative name, **Sala de la Media Naranja** (Hall of the Half Orange).

On the western side of the Salón de Embajadores, the beautiful Arco de Pavones, named after its peacock motifs, leads into the **Salón del Techo de Felipe II**, with a Renaissance ceiling (1589–91).

➡ **Salones de Carlos V**

Reached via a staircase at the southeastern corner of the Patio de las Doncellas, these are the much remodelled rooms of Alfonso X's 13th-century Gothic palace. The rooms are now named after the 16th-century Spanish king Carlos I, using his title as Holy Roman Emperor, Charles V.

➡ **Patio del Crucero**

This patio outside the Salones de Carlos V was originally the upper storey of the patio of the 12th-century Almohad palace. Initially it consisted only of raised walkways along the four sides and two cross-walkways that met in the middle. Below grew orange trees, whose fruit could be plucked at hand height by the lucky folk strolling along the walkways. The patio's lower level was built over in the 18th century after earthquake damage.

➡ **Gardens & Exit**

From the Salones de Carlos V you can go out into the Alcázar's large somnolent gardens. Formal gardens with pools and fountains sit closest to the palace. From one, the **Jardín de la Danza** (Garden of the Dance), a passage runs beneath the Salones de Carlos V to the **Baños de Doña María de Padilla** (María de Padilla Baths). These are the vaults beneath the Patio del Crucero – originally that patio's lower level – with a grotto that replaced the patio's original pool.

The gardens' most arresting feature is the **Galería de Grutesco**, a raised gallery with porticoes fashioned in the 16th century out of an old Muslim-era wall. There is also a fun hedge maze, which will delight children. The gardens to the east, beyond a long wall, are 20th-century creations, but don't hold that against them – they are heavenly indeed.

SEVILLE

Alameda de Hércules, Macarena & Isla de la Cartuja

Complejo Hospitalario Virgen Macarena

C San Juan de Ribera

Parlamento de Andalucía

C Don Fadrique

Buses C2 & C4

Buses C1 & C3

C Andueza

C Muñoz León

Old City Wall

El Palacio Andaluz (400m)

C San Luis

MACARENA

C Arrayán

C Parras

C Bustos Tavera

C Castellar

C de Resolana

C Bécquer

C Peral

C Alvarez

C de la Feria

C Relator

C de la Feria

Plaza San Martín

C Viriato

Alameda de Hércules

C Calatrava

C Crédito

C Lumbreras

C Santa Clara

C Amor de Dios

C Jesús del Gran Poder

C Trajano

C José Gálvez

Av de Ribera

Puente de la Bárqueta

C de San Vicente

C del Torneo

C Santa Ana

C Eslava

Plaza de San Lorenzo

Plaza San Antonio de Padua

C Juan Rabadán

C Curtidurías

C Miguel Cid

C Teodosio

C Pascual de Gayangos

C de Barros

Isla Mágica

Río Guadalquivir

Auditorio de la Cartuja

Camino de los Descubrimientos

Puente de la Cartuja

Bus C2

Bus C1

See El Centro Map (p58)

C Marie Curie

C Marie Curie

ISLA DE LA CARTUJA

C Albert Einstein

C Albert Einstein

C Charles Darwin

C Leonardo da Vinci

C Américo Vespucio

Bus C1

Bus C2

El Pabellón de la Navegación (150m)

0   500 m
0   0.25 miles

Alameda de Hércules, Macarena & Isla de la Cartuja

◎ **Sights**
1 Basílica de La Macarena F2
  Centro Andaluz de Arte
  Contemporáneo ....(see 3)
2 Centro de la Interpretación
  Mudéjar F3
3 Conjunto Monumental de la
  Cartuja B3
4 Isla Mágica C1
  Palacio de los Marqueses
  de la Algaba ....(see 2)

◎ **Activities, Courses & Tours**
5 Taller Flamenco E2

◎ **Sleeping**
6 Hotel Sacristía de Santa Ana E4
7 Hotel San Gil F2

◎ **Eating**
8 Bar-Restaurante Eslava D4
9 Duo Tapas E3

◎ **Drinking & Nightlife**
10 Bulebar Café E4

◎ **Entertainment**
11 Naima Café Jazz E4

SEVILLE SIGHTS & ACTIVITIES

Archivo de Indias
MUSEUM

(Map p54; Calle Santo Tomás; ⊙9.30am-4.45pm Mon-Sat, 10am-2pm Sun) FREE Housed in the former Casa de la Contratación (Contracting House) on the western side of Plaza del Triunfo, the Archivo de Indias has, since 1785, been the main archive of Spain's American empire, with 80 million pages of documents dating from 1492 to the end of the empire in the 19th century – a most effective statement of Spain's power and influence during its Golden Age.

A short film inside tells the full story of the building along with some fascinating original colonial maps and documents. The Renaissance building was extensively refurbished in 2005.

◎ Barrio de Santa Cruz

Seville's medieval *judería* (Jewish quarter), east of the cathedral and Alcázar, is today a tangle of atmospheric, winding streets and lovely plant-decked plazas perfumed with orange blossom. Among its most characteristic plazas is Plaza de Santa Cruz, which gives the *barrio* (district) its name. Nearby, Plaza de Doña Elvira is perhaps the most romantic small square in Andalucía, especially in the evening.

★Hospital de los
Venerables Sacerdotes
ART GALLERY

(Map p54; 954 56 26 96; www.focus.abengoa.es; Plaza de los Venerables 8; adult/child €5.50/2.75, Sun afternoon free; ⊙10am-2pm & 4-8pm) Inside this 17th-century baroque mansion once used as a hospice for ageing priests, you'll find one of Seville's greatest and most admirable art collections. The on-site Centro Velázquez was founded in 2007 by the local Focus-Abengoa Foundation with the intention of reviving Seville's erstwhile artistic glory. Its collection of masterpieces anchored by Diego Veláquez' *Santa Rufina* (see boxed text, p51) is one of the best and most concise art lessons the city has to offer. The excellent audio commentary explains how medieval darkness morphed into Velázquezian realism.

The 'Hospital' also guards what is perhaps the city's most typical Sevillano patio – intimate, plant-embellished and spirit-reviving – plus a chapel adorned with more golden-age paintings.

Centro de Interpretación
Judería de Sevilla
MUSEUM

(Map p54; 954 04 70 89; www.juderiadesevilla.es; Calle Ximenez de Enciso; admission €6.50; ⊙10.30am-3.30pm & 5-8pm Mon-Sat, 10.30am-7pm Sun) A reinterpretation of Seville's weighty Jewish history has been long overdue and what better place to start than in the city's former Jewish quarter. This newish museum is in an old Sephardic Jewish house in the higgledy-piggledy Santa Cruz quarter, the one-time Jewish neighbourhood that never recovered from a brutal pogrom and massacre in 1391. The events of the pogrom and other historical happenings are catalogued inside, along with a few surviving mementos including documents, costumes and books. It's small but poignant.

Guided walks of the Jewish sites of Seville are offered for €22. They run when there are enough people. Call ahead.

Aire Baños Árabes
HAMMAM

(Map p58; 955 01 00 25; www.airedesevilla.com; Calle Aire 15; bath/bath with massage €26/41; ⊙every 2hr 10am-midnight) Jumping on the

Seeing Flamenco

The intensity and spontaneity of flamenco has never translated well onto CDs or studio recordings. Instead, to ignite the goosebumps and inspire the powerful emotional spirit known to aficionados as *'duende'*, you have to be there at a performance, stamping your feet and passionately yelling *'¡óle!'*.

Peñas

Peñas are private local clubs run by enthusiasts determined to preserve flamenco in its traditional form. To find an appropriate *peña* ask around in flamenco bars, check posters on noticeboards (or lamp posts) and use your ears to follow any interesting sounds you might hear in the street. Not surprisingly, *peñas* present some of the most authentic and passionate shows in Spain. They also incorporate flamenco's oft-overlooked fourth component, the *jaleo* (audience participation).

Tablaos

Tablaos are grand and well-rehearsed flamenco extravaganzas that showcase the art in a highly professional and choreographed way. Unlike *peñas, tablao* shows are held in specific theatres or clubs where drinks and sometimes dinner is included in the price of the ticket. While the artistic talent at these events is of a high standard, *tablaos* are sometimes derided by flamenco experts for lacking the spit and sawdust that makes the music so unique.

Cultural Centres

A growing stash of cultural centres in Andalucía's bigger cities offer a more authentic and intimate alternative to *tablaos*. Cultural centres are sometimes attached to museums and attract small, savvy audiences who shout encouraging *'olés'* from the sidelines, willing the show to a soulful climax. Food and drink are rarely available.

1. *Peña*, Jerez de la Frontera (p124) **2 & 3.** Flamenco dancers, Seville (p76) **4.** Sign outside Peña La Platería (p268), Granada

hammam bandwagon, Seville's Arabic-style baths win prizes for tranquil atmosphere, historic setting (in the Barrio de Santa Cruz) and Moroccan riad-style decor – living proof that those Moors knew a thing or two about how to relax. It's best to book baths and massages one day in advance.

◉ El Arenal

Colonising caballeros made rich on New World gold once stalked the streets of El Arenal on the banks of the Río Guadalquivir, watched over by Spanish galleons offloading their American booty. There's no port here today, but the compact quarter retains plenty of rambunctious bars and a seafaring spirit.

Torre del Oro   MUSEUM

(Map p54; Paseo de Cristóbal Colón; admission €3, Mon free; ⊙ 9.30am-6.45pm Mon-Fri, 10.30am-6.45pm Sat & Sun) This 13th-century Almohad watchtower by the river supposedly had a dome covered in golden tiles, hence its name, 'Tower of Gold'. Today, it hosts a small maritime museum spread over two floors and a rooftop viewing platform.

The tower was also once used to store the booty siphoned off the colonial coffers by the returning conquistadors from Mexico and Peru. Since then it has become one of the most recognisable architectural symbols of Seville.

Hospital de la Caridad   ART GALLERY

(Map p54; Calle Temprado 3; admission €5; ⊙ 9am-1pm & 3.30-7pm Mon-Sat, 9am-12.30pm Sun) The Hospital de la Caridad, a large sturdy building one block east of the river, was once a hospice for the elderly. It was founded by Miguel de Mañara, by legend a notorious libertine who changed his ways after seeing a vision of his own funeral procession. Its main set piece is its gilded chapel decorated profusely by several Golden Age painters and sculptors, most notably Murillo and Roldán.

The hospital was famously pillaged by Napoleon's troops in 1810 when a kleptomaniac French officer named General Soult stole several of the Murillo paintings that adorned the chapel's walls. The paintings were never returned, though copies were made and hung up in place of the originals in 2008. See if you can spot the fakes.

Plaza de Toros de la Real Maestranza   BULLRING, MUSEUM

(Map p54; ☎ 954 22 45 77; www.realmaestranza. com; Paseo de Cristóbal Colón 12; tours adult/child €7/4; ⊙ half-hourly 9.30am-8pm, to 3pm bullfight days) In the world of bullfighting Seville's bullring is the Old Trafford and Camp Nou. In other words, if you're selected to fight here then you've made it. In addition to being regarded as a building of almost religious significance to fans, it's also the oldest ring in Spain (building began in 1758) and it was here, along with the bullring in Ronda, that bullfighting on foot began in the 18th century.

Slightly rushed guided visits, in English and Spanish, take you into the ring and its museum.

◉ El Centro

As the name suggests, this is Seville's centre, and the densely packed zone of narrow streets and squares north of the cathedral is the heart of the Seville shopping world as well as the home of some excellent bars and restaurants.

Museo del Baile Flamenco   MUSEUM

(Map p58; www.museoflamenco.com; Calle Manuel Rojas Marcos 3; adult/seniors & students €10/8; ⊙ 10am-7pm) The brainchild of *sevillano* flamenco dancer Cristina Hoyos, this museum spread over three floors of an 18th-century palace makes a noble effort to showcase the mysterious art with sketches, paintings and photos of erstwhile (and contemporary) flamenco greats, plus a collection of dresses and shawls. Even better than that are the fantastic nightly concerts (7pm; €20) in the on-site courtyard.

Classes and workshops can also be organised, and there's an interesting shop with unique books and garments.

Museo de Bellas Artes   ART GALLERY

(Fine Arts Museum; Map p58; Plaza del Museo 9; admission €1.50, EU citizens free; ⊙ 10am-8.30pm Tue-Sat, to 5pm Sun) Housed in the beautiful former Convento de la Merced, Seville's Museo de Bellas Artes does full justice to Seville's leading role in Spain's 17th-century artistic Siglo de Oro (Golden Age). Much of the work here is of the dark, brooding religious type.

The museum's flow is chronological, with the Golden Age masterpieces clustered in *salas* VII to X. The most visually startling room is the former convent's church, hung with paintings by masters of Sevillan baroque, above all Murillo. His *Inmaculada concepción grande* (1650) at the head of the church displays all the curving, twisting movement so central to baroque art (see p51). Other well-represented artists include Pacheco (the teacher and father-in-law of Velázquez), Zurbarán (look for his deeply sombre *Cristo crucificado,* c 1630–35) and sculptor Juan Martínez Montañes. Search and you'll find El Greco's portrait of his son Jorge Manuel, and – perhaps disappointingly – only one Velázquez: *Cabeza de apóstol* (1620).

Casa de Pilatos   PALACE, MUSEUM

(Map p58; ☑ 954 22 52 98; www.fundacionmedinaceli.org; Plaza de Pilatos; admission ground fl €6, whole house €8; ◎ 9am-7pm Apr-Oct, to 6pm Nov-Mar) The haunting Casa de Pilatos, which is still occupied by the ducal Medinaceli family, is one of the city's most glorious mansions. It's a mixture of Mudéjar, Gothic and Renaissance styles, with some beautiful tilework and *artesonados* (ceilings of interlaced beams with decorative insertions). The overall effect is like a poor man's Alcázar.

The staircase to the upper floor has the most magnificent tiles in the building, and a great golden *artesonado* dome above. Visits to the upper floor, still partly inhabited by the Medinacelis, are guided. Of interest are several centuries' worth of Medinaceli portraits and a small Goya bullfighting painting.

Palacio de la
Condesa de Lebrija   MUSEUM, PALACE

(Map p58; Calle Cuna 8; admission ground fl €5, whole bldg €8, ground fl 9am-noon Wed free; ◎ 10.30am-7.30pm Mon-Fri, 10am-2pm & 4-6pm Sat, 10am-2pm Sun) This 16th-century mansion, a block east of Calle Sierpes, has a rich collection of art and artisanry and a beautiful Renaissance-Mudéjar courtyard. The late Countess of Lebrija was an archaeologist, and she remodelled the house in 1914, filling many of the rooms with treasures from her travels.

Ancient Rome was the countess's speciality, so the library is full of books on antiquity and there are plenty of remains from Roman Itálica, including some marvellous mosaics. If you want to see the top floor, with its Arabic, baroque and Spanish rooms, you must wait for the guided tour, but it's worth it.

Plaza de San Francisco   SQUARE

(Map p58) Plaza de San Francisco has been Seville's main public square since the 16th century. The southern end of the **Ayuntamiento** (Town Hall; Map p58) here is encrusted with lovely Renaissance carving from the 1520–30s.

Calle Sierpes   STREET

(Map p58) Pedestrianised Calle Sierpes, heading north from the Plaza de San Francisco, and the parallel Calle Tetuán/Velázquez are the hub of Seville's fanciest shopping zone. This being Andalucía, it's busiest in the evenings between about 6pm and 9pm.

Parroquia del Divino Salvador   ARCHITECTURE

(Map p58; Plaza Salvador; admission €4; ◎ 11am-6pm Mon-Sat, 3-7pm Sun) A big baroque church in Plaza Salvador built between 1674 and 1712 on the site of Muslim Ishbiliya's main mosque. The facade is actually Mannerist (a more imaginative extension of the Renaissance influenced by Michelangelo). The interior reveals a fantastic richness of carving and gilding. At sunset, colour from stained-glass windows plays on the carvings to enhance their surreal beauty.

Metropol Parasol   MUSEUM, LANDMARK

(Map p58; www.metropolsevilla.com; Plaza de la Encarnación; admission €3; ◎ 10.30am-midnight Sun-Thu, to 1am Fri & Sat) Smarting with the audacity of a modern-day Eiffel Tower, the opinion-dividing Metropol Parasol, which opened in March 2011 in the Plaza de la Encarnación, claims to be the largest wooden building in the world. Its undulating honeycombed roof is held up by five giant mushroom-like pillars, earning it the local nickname *Las Setas de la Encarnación* (the mushrooms of Plaza de la Encarnación).

Six years in the making, the construction covers a former dead zone in Seville's central district once filled with an ugly car park. Roman ruins discovered during the building's conception have been cleverly incorporated into the foundations of the **Museo Antiquarium** (Map p58; Plaza de la Encarnación; admission €2.10; ◎ 10am-8.30pm Tue-Sat, to 2.30pm Sun), while upstairs on level 2 you can (for €2.10) stroll along a surreal panoramic walkway with killer city views. The Metropol also houses the plaza's former market, a restaurant and a concert space. Though costly and controversial, Jürgen Mayer-Hermann's daring creation has slotted into Seville's ancient core with a weird kind of harmony, turning (and tilting) the heads of all who pass.

Casa de la Memoria   CULTURAL CENTRE

(Map p58; ☑ 954 56 06 70; www.casadelamemoria.es; Calle Cuna 6; admission €3; ⊙ 10.30am-6.30pm) Lucid memories will be hard to shake off after visiting the Casa de la Memoria, especially if you stay for an evening flamenco show (p76). This flamenco cultural centre inhabits the former stables of the adjacent Palacio de la Condesa de Lebrija. A suite of exposition rooms display revolving flamenco exhibits. An exposé of Seville's Cafe Cantantes was showing at last visit. It is the only centre of its kind in Seville.

⊙ Triana

The legendary *barrio* of Triana sits on the west bank of the Río Guadalquivir. This atmospheric quarter was once home to many of Seville's most quintessential characters and it still hosts some of its most poignant sights.

Castillo de San Jorge   MUSEUM

(Map p54; ☑ 954 33 22 40; Plaza del Altozano; ⊙ 9am-1.30pm & 3.30-8pm Mon-Fri, 10am-2pm Sat & Sun) **FREE** 'Nobody expects the Spanish Inquisition!' Monty Python once quipped, but in Seville it's not so easy to escape the trauma. After all, this is where the Inquisition Court held its first ever council, in the infamous Castillo de San Jorge in 1481, an act that ignited 325 years of fear and terror. When the Inquisition fires were finally doused in the early 1800s, the castle was destroyed and a market built over the top; but its foundations were rediscovered in 1990.

A modern museum overlays the castle's foundations and takes viewers on a journey around the ruins juxtaposing details of each room's function with macabre stories of the cruelty dished out inside them. It's sometimes gruesome reading.

The Castillo is adjacent to the Isabel II bridge.

Centro Cerámica Triana   MUSEUM

(Map p54; Antillano Campos 14; admission €2.10; ⊙ 10am-2pm & 5-8pm Mon-Sat, 10am-3pm Sun) Triana's – and Seville's – newest museum is an attempt to rekindle the flames that once lit the kilns of the neighbourhood's erstwhile ceramic industry. It cleverly mixes the methodology and history of ceramic production with the wider history of Triana and its people.

⊙ South of the Centre

South of Santa Cruz and El Centro, the city opens out into expansive parks and broad streets which in recent years have been reclaimed by trams, bikes and strollers.

Parque de María Luisa   PARK

(⊙ 8am-10pm Sep-Jun, to midnight Jul & Aug; 🚻🎢) The lungs of central Seville are the dreamy Parque de María Luisa, which is a delightful place to escape from the noise of the city, with duck ponds, snoozing *sevillanos* and paths snaking under the trees.

If you'd rather continue your cultural education than commune with the flowers, the park contains a couple of sites that'll keep you smiling. Curving round the

---

CYCLING SEVILLE

Since the inauguration of the **Sevici** (☑ 902 011032; www.sevici.es; ⊙ 7am-9pm) bike-sharing scheme in April 2007, Seville has logged a phenomenal 1300% increase in daily cycling usage and become a blueprint for urban cycling planning everywhere. Sevici was the second bike-sharing initiative in Spain (there are now dozens), opening a couple of weeks after Barcelona's Bicing program. Despite newer competition, it remains one of the largest schemes of its kind in Europe with 2500 bikes. Grab a two-wheeled machine from any one of 250 docking stations and you'll quickly discover that cycling rather suits this flat, balmy metropolis that was seemingly designed with visceral experiences in mind.

Most of Sevici's 25,000-plus daily users are locals, but visitors can take advantage of the sharing system by purchasing a seven-day pass online for €13.33 (plus a €150 returnable deposit). Proceed to the nearest docking station, punch in the number from your coded receipt and, hey presto. Seville has 130km of city bike lanes (all painted green and equipped with their own traffic signals) and the first 30 minutes of usage are free. Beyond that, it's €1.03 for the first hour and €2.05 an hour thereafter.

Another way of taking advantage of the new cycling infrastructure is a bike tour of the city's main sights. **Pancho Tours** (p69) organises 2½-hour rides for €25, including bike hire.

TRIANA – THE OUTSIDER NEIGHBOURHOOD INSIDE SEVILLE

To fully understand the modern montage that makes up Seville there are several essential pilgrimages. Arguably, the most important is to Triana, the neighbourhood situated on the west bank of the Río Guadalquivir, a place whose past is littered with stories of sailors, ceramicists, bullfighters, flamenco artists, religious zealotry and a strong working-class identity.

Triana's 'outsider' reputation was first cemented in the Middle Ages when it was labelled *extramuros* (outside the walls) by Seville's authorities, a place where 'undesirables' were sent to live. In 1481 infamy was established when the seat of the Inquisition Court was set up in the Castillo de San Jorge on the banks of the Guadalquivir from where it began trying suspected religious deviants for heresy. The outsider myth burgeoned in the 15th century as itinerant Roma people drifted in from the east and started to put down roots, an influx that gave Triana much of its musical personality.

By the 19th century, Triana's interlinked Roma families were producing the finest bullfighters and flamenco singers of the age. The neighbourhood also began to supplement its long-established fishing industry with pottery and tile-making using thick clay dug out of the banks of the Guadalquivir.

Most of Seville's Roma were resettled in Seville's new suburbs in the 1960s, a move that altered the demographics of Triana, but not its essence. Unlike the more sanitised Santa Cruz quarter, Triana has kept much of its authenticity. Its outdoor living room in summer is the bar-filled **Calle Betis** overlooking the river, while its kitchen is the fish-biased **Mercado de Triana**. The quarter's religious devotion can be glimpsed in numerous churches, most notably the Gothic-Mudéjar **Parroquia de Santa Ana** (Map p54; Calle de la Pureza 80; donation €1.50; ⊗ 10.30am-1.30pm Mon-Fri, 4.40-6.30pm Tue & Wed), Triana's so-called 'cathedral', and the baroque **Parroquia de Nuestra Señora de la O** (Map p54; Calle Castilla 30).

Plaza de España (Map p54), with its fountains and mini-canals, is the most grandiose of the buildings built for the 1929 Exposición Iberoamericana, a brick-and-tile confection featuring Seville tilework at its gaudiest, with a map and historical scene for each Spanish province. You can hire row boats to ply the canals from only €5.

The **Museo Arqueológico** (admission €1.50, EU citizens free; ⊗10am-8.30pm Tue-Sat, to 5pm Sun), at the southern end of the park, is an unexpected depository of Roman sculptures, mosaics and statues – much of it gathered from Itálica. There is also a room of gold jewellery from the mysterious Tartessos culture.

Opposite is the **Museo de Artes y Costumbres Populares** (✆954 23 25 76; admission €1.50, EU citizens free; ⊗10am-8.30pm Tue-Sat, to 5pm Sun), with a spotlight on the ceramic tiles produced in a factory founded by Englishman Charles Pickman, in the former monastery of Cartuja (p68) in 1840.

The park is a great place for children to run off some steam; they'll enjoy feeding the doves in the plaza by the museum at the southern end of the park. Four-person quad bikes are available to rent for €12 per half-hour.

Antigua Fábrica de Tabacos   UNIVERSITY
(Map p54; Calle San Fernando; ⊗8am-9.30pm Mon-Fri, to 2pm Sat, free tours 11am Mon-Thu) **FREE** Seville's massive former tobacco factory – workplace of Bizet's passionate fictional heroine, Carmen – was built in the 18th century and has the second-largest building footprint in Spain after El Escorial. It's now the buzzing campus to the University of Seville. You can wander in at will or partake in a free tour at 11am Monday to Thursday. Meet in the main lobby.

Hotel Alfonso XIII   LANDMARK
(Map p54; Calle San Fernando 2) As much a monument as it is an accommodation option, and certainly more affordable if you come for a cup of coffee as opposed to a room, this striking only-in-Seville hotel – conceived as the most luxurious in Europe when it was built in 1928 – was constructed in tandem with the Plaza de España for the 1929 world fair. The style is classic neo-Mudéjar with glazed tiles and terracotta bricks.

There's a small museum inside relating its history. Turn left in the lobby.

Isla de la Cartuja

This former island on the Río Guadalquivir takes its name from the on-site Cartuja monastery. It was connected to Seville's west river bank in 1992 to incorporate the city's Expo '92 site. Monastery apart, most of the buildings here are modern, including the impossible-to-miss Cajasol tower completed in 2015.

El Pabellon de la Navegación MUSEUM
(www.pabellondelanavegacion.es; Camino de los Descubrimientos 2; adult/child €4.90/3.50; ⊙11am-8.30pm Tue-Sat, to 3pm Sun; 🚍) This boxy modern pavilion on the banks of the Río Guadalquivir opened in 2012 and revived a previous navigation museum that lasted from the 1992 Expo until 1999. Its permanent collection is split into four parts – navigation, mariners, shipboard life and historical views of Seville – and although its exhibits are interactive and kid-friendly, for an adult they might be a little underwhelming. The ticket includes a ride up the adjacent **Torre Schindler** (⊙9am-7pm Apr-Oct, to 6pm Nov-Mar).

Conjunto Monumental de la Cartuja MONASTERY, ART GALLERY
(Cartuja Monastery; Map p60; ☑955 03 70 70; www.caac.es; complete visit €3, monument or temporary exhibitions €1.80, free 7-9pm Tue-Fri & all day Sat; ⊙11am-9pm Tue-Sat, to 3pm Sun) This historic but offbeat art gallery was once a monastery, then a ceramics factory, but today is home to the **Centro Andaluz de Arte Contemporáneo** (Map p60).

Founded in 1399, the Conjunto Monumental de la Cartuja became the favourite *sevillano* lodging place for Christopher Columbus, who prayed in its chapel before his trip to the Americas and whose remains lay here for more than two decades in 1530–40.

In 1839 the complex was bought by an enterprising Englishman, Charles Pickman, who turned it into a porcelain factory, building the tall bottle-shaped kilns that stand rather incongruously beside the monastery. The factory ceased production in the 1980s and in 1992 the building served as the Royal Pavilion during the Expo. It has since become Seville's shrine to modern art with temporary expos revolving around some truly bizarre permanent pieces. You can't miss

Alicia, by Cristina Lucas, a massive head and arm poking through two old monastery windows that was supposedly inspired by *Alice in Wonderland*; though you could be forgiven for walking obliviously past Pedro Mora's *Bus Stop* which looks exactly like...a bus stop.

Isla Mágica THEME PARK
(Map p60; ☑902 161 716; www.islamagica.es; adult/child €29/20; ⊙high season around 11am-10pm, closed Dec-Mar; 🚍) This Disney-goes-Spanish-colonial amusement park provides a great, if expensive, day out for kids and all lovers of white-knuckle rides. Hours vary by season – see the website. Buses C1 and C2 run to Isla Mágica.

Alameda de Hércules & Around

While the Barrio de Santa Cruz and cathedral area are where things once happened in Seville, it's the Alameda de Hércules area where the young are making things happen today.

Alameda de Hércules was once a no-go area reserved only for the city's 'painted ladies', pimps and a wide range of shady characters, but the parklike strip underwent a 'Soho makeover' and these days is crammed with trendy bars, chic shops and hipsters. It's also Seville's main gay quarter.

The two distinct columns at the south end of the square are 2000-year-old Roman originals.

Basílica de La Macarena CHURCH, MUSEUM
(Map p60; ☑954 90 18 00; Calle Bécquer 1; museum €5; ⊙9am-2pm & 5-9pm) This basilica is the home of Seville's most revered Virgin and will give you a whiff of the fervour inspired by Semana Santa. The *Virgen de la Esperanza Macarena* (Macarena Virgin of Hope), a magnificent statue adorned with a golden crown, lavish vestments and five diamond-and-emerald brooches donated by famous 20th-century matador Joselito El Gallo, stands in splendour behind the main altarpiece.

The church also has a recently refurbished museum containing some of the iconography. Across the street is the longest surviving stretch of Seville's 12th-century Almohad walls.

Centro de la
Interpretación Mudéjar   MUSEUM
(Map p60; Plaza Calderón de la Barca; ☺10am-2pm & 5-8pm Mon-Fri, 10am-2pm Sat) **FREE**
The Mudéjar architectural style, which long defined Seville, has a shrine to its importance encased within one of Seville's textbook-Mudéjar buildings, the **Palacio de Los Marqueses de la Algaba** (Map p60). The small on-site museum with collected Mudéjar relics from the 12th to 20th centuries gets a little lost in the wonderfully restored mansion with its dreamy courtyard, but the captions (in Spanish and English) do a good job of explaining the nuances of the complex Mudéjar style.

📝 Courses

Seville is a great city in which to hang around for a while and learn a new skill. Many visitors from overseas join a Spanish language course and there are dozens of schools offering courses.

If learning a language is just too scholarly, then how about learning how to shimmy with the best of them? Seville has many dance and flamenco schools open to visitors staying a while.

CLIC   LANGUAGE COURSE
(Map p58; ☑954 50 21 31; www.clic.es; Calle Albareda 19) A well-established language centre headquartered in a pleasant house with a good social scene and adjacent library. Courses for children, adults and seniors. Prices are approximately €125 for 10 lessons.

Fundación Cristina Heeren de Arte Flamenco   FLAMENCO COURSE
(☑954 21 70 58; www.flamencoheeren.com; Avenida de Jerez 2) This is by far the best-known flamenco school and offers long-term courses in all flamenco arts; also offers one-month intensive summer courses.

Taller Flamenco   FLAMENCO COURSE, LANGUAGE COURSE
(Map p60; ☑954 56 42 34; www.tallerflamenco.com; Calle Peral 49) Offers one-week packages with the possibility of being taught in groups or on a one-to-one basis. It also offers Spanish language classes.

Taller Andaluz de Cocina   COOKING COURSE
(Map p54; ☑672 162621; www.tallerandaluzdecocina.com; Mercado de Triana; 3hr course €45) This recently established company in Triana market offers Spanish-Andaluz cooking courses three to four times a week at 11am. The three-hour courses use local market ingredients and include tasting afterwards. It also runs free market tours on selective days at 10.30am. Check the calendar on the website.

👣 Tours

★**Pancho Tours**   CULTURAL TOUR
(Map p58; ☑664 642 904; www.panchotours.com) **FREE** The best walking tours in the city? Join in and see – they're free, although you're welcome to tip the hard-working guide who'll furnish you with an encyclopedia's worth of anecdotes, stories, myths and theories about Seville's fascinating past. Tours kick off daily, normally at 11am – check the website for exact details. Pancho also offers bike tours (€25) and nightlife tours (€10 to €15).

Past View   TOUR
(Map p58; ☑954 32 66 46; www.pastview.es; Plaza de la Encarnación; tours €15; ☺10.30am & 1pm; 🖳) This ingenious augmented-reality video tour takes you on a guided walk using 3D video glasses that re-create scenes from the past in the actual locations they happened. The ticket office and starting point is in the Metropol Parasol (p65) and the two-hour walk (with a guide) proceeds through Seville's main sights to the Torre del Oro.

Cruceros Turísticos Torre del Oro BOAT TOUR
(Map p54; ☑954 56 16 92; www.crucerostorredeloro.com; adult/child under 14yr €16/free) One-hour sightseeing river cruises run every half-hour from 11am, departing from the river bank by the Torre del Oro. Last departure can range from 6pm in winter to 10pm in summer.

🎉 Festivals & Events

Semana Santa   HOLY WEEK
(www.semana-santa.org; ☺Mar/Apr) Every day from Palm Sunday to Easter Sunday, large, life-sized *pasos* (sculptural representations of events from Christ's Passion) are carried from Seville's churches through the streets to the cathedral, accompanied by processions that may take more than an hour to pass. The processions are organised by more than 50 different *hermandades* or *cofradías* (brotherhoods, some of which include women).

The climax of the week is the *madrugada* (early hours) of Good Friday, when some of the most respected brotherhoods file through the city. The costume worn by the marching penitents consists of a full robe and a conical hat with slits cut for the eyes. The regalia was incongruously copied by America's Ku Klux Klan.

Procession schedules are widely available during Semana Santa, or see the Semana Santa website. Arrive near the cathedral in the early evening for a better view.

Feria de Abril SPRING FAIR

(☺ Apr) The April fair, held in the second half of the month (sometimes edging into May), is the jolly counterpart to the sombre Semana Santa. The biggest and most colourful of all Andalucía's ferias (fairs) is less invasive (and also less inclusive) than the Easter celebration. It takes place on El Real de la Feria, in the Los Remedios area west of the Río Guadalquivir.

The ceremonial lighting-up of the fairgrounds on the opening Monday night is the starting gun for six nights of *sevillanos'* favourite activities: eating, drinking, dressing up and dancing till dawn.

Bienal de Flamenco FLAMENCO

(www.labienal.com; ☺ Sep) Most of the big names of the flamenco world participate in this major flamenco festival. Held in September in even-numbered years.

🛏 Sleeping

🏨 Barrio de Santa Cruz

Pensión San Pancracio PENSIÓN €

(Map p54; ☎ 954 41 31 04; Plaza de las Cruces 9; d €50, s/d/tr with shared bathroom €33/36/52) A rare budget option in Santa Cruz, this old, rambling family house has plenty of different room options (all cheap) and a pleasant flower-bedizened patio-lobby. Friendly staff make up for the lack of luxury. The compromise: shared bathrooms.

★Hotel Amadeus HOTEL €€

(Map p58; ☎ 954 50 14 43; www.hotelamadeussevilla.com; Calle Farnesio 6; s/d €100/114; 🅿 ❄ 🛜) Just when you thought you couldn't find hotels with pianos in the rooms anymore, along came Hotel Amadeus. It's run by an engaging musical family in the old *judería* (Jewish quarter) – several of the astutely decorated rooms come complete with soundproof walls and upright pianos, ensuring you don't miss out on your daily practice.

Other perks include in-room classical CDs, wall-mounted instruments and a roof-

top terrace with a jacuzzi. Composers and Mozart lovers will be suitably impressed.

Hotel Palacio Alcázar BOUTIQUE HOTEL €€

(Map p54; ☎ 954 50 21 90; www.hotelpalacioalcazar.com; Plaza de Alianza 12; s €65, d €76-108; ❄ @ 🛜) Fresh, white minimalism in the lush *barrio* of Santa Cruz, Palacio Alcázar is a recent addition to Seville's oldest quarter. It sports 12 lovely rooms and an equally lovely roof-terrace tapas bar where you call the waiter by ringing a bell on your table.

Hotel Puerta de Sevilla HOTEL €€

(Map p54; ☎ 954 98 72 70; www.hotelpuertadesevilla.com; Calle Puerta de la Carne 2; s/d €50/70; 🅿 ❄ @ 🛜) This superfriendly – and super-positioned – hotel is a great mix of the chintz and the stylish. In the lobby there's an indoor water feature lined with superb Seville tilework. The rooms are all flower-patterned textiles, wrought-iron beds and pastel wallpaper. It also features an unbeatable people-watching roof terrace.

Hostal Plaza Santa Cruz HOTEL €€

(Map p54; ☎ 954 22 88 08; www.hostalplazasantacruz.com; Calle Santa Teresa 15; d/ste €67/95; ❄ 🛜) This place in the old quarter has two options: a small hotel with unflashy creamy-white rooms just off Plaza Santa Cruz, or some more upmarket suites enhanced with deluxe touches such as tiles, art and heavy wooden furniture a block away.

Un Patio en Santa Cruz HOTEL €€

(Map p54; ☎ 954 53 94 13; www.patiosantacruz.com; Calle Doncellas 15; s €65-85, d €65-120; ❄ 🛜) Feeling more like an art gallery than a hotel, this place has starched white walls coated in loud works of art, strange sculptures and preserved plants. The rooms are immensely comfortable, staff are friendly, and there's a cool rooftop terrace with mosaic Moroccan tables. It's easily one of the hippest and best-value hotels in town.

★Hotel Casa 1800 LUXURY HOTEL €€€

(Map p54; ☎ 954 56 18 00; www.hotelcasa1800sevilla.com; Calle Rodrigo Caro 6; r from €195; ❄ @ 🛜) Reigning as number one in Seville's 'favourite hotel' charts is this positively regal Santa Cruz pile where the word *casa* (house) is taken seriously. This really is your home away from home (albeit a posh one), with charming staff catering for your every need. Historic highlights include a complimentary afternoon-tea buffet, plus a quartet of penthouse garden suites with Giralda views.

SEVILLE FOR CHILDREN

Many of Seville's adult attractions will appeal to kids on a different level, including the **cathedral** (p50) and the **Alcázar** (p56) (both free to those under 16 years old). The latter has a dedicated booklet for kids, available in most newsagents. The city abounds in open spaces and parks often have special kids' sections; head for the banks of the Río Guadalquivir, **Parque de María Luisa** (p66) and the Jardines de Murrillo. Ice cream and churros (long, deep-fried doughnuts) cafes are also ubiquitous. If the tapas get too sophisticated, try a good Italian restaurant. There are many around the Plaza de la Alfalfa. **Isla Mágica** (p68) is specifically targeted at kids, particularly those aged 10 or above, and the nearby **Pabellon de la Navegación** (p68) has lots of interactive exhibits. Tours by boat, open-top double-decker bus or horse-drawn carriage also prove popular with children.

It's also one of the only places in the city that doesn't hike its Semana Santa rates up to ridiculous levels.

EME Catedral Hotel LUXURY HOTEL €€€
(Map p54; ☑ 954 56 00 00; www.emecatedral-hotel.com; Calle de los Alemanes 27; d/ste from €250/446; ✳@🖥🌊) Take 14 fine old *sevillano* houses and knock them into one. Bring in a top designer and one of Seville's most respected chefs. Carve out a *hammam,* a rooftop pool, four restaurants, including Santo Restaurante, and slick, striking rooms with red accents. Then stick it all nose-to-nose with the largest Gothic cathedral in the world.

The result: EME Catedral Hotel, the city's most talked about accommodation where ancient Seville has been fused with something a bit more cutting edge. Does it work? Cough up the €200-plus a night and find out.

El Arenal

⭐**Hotel Adriano** HOTEL €€
(Map p54; ☑ 954 29 38 00; www.adrianohotel.com; Calle Adriano 12; s/d €65/75; 🅿✳🖥) A solid Arenal option with great staff, rooms with attractive *sevillano* features and one of the best coffee shops in Seville out front.

Hotel Simón HOTEL €€
(Map p54; ☑ 954 22 66 60; www.hotelsimonsevilla.com; Calle García de Vinuesa 19; s/d €88/125; ✳@) This well-used but grand 18th-century Sevillan house in El Arenal has an ornate patio and quiet, old-fashioned rooms, some of them embellished with rich *azulejo* tilework. Character and location are its two hallmarks (it's 100m from the cathedral). You won't find better at this price.

El Centro

Oasis Backpackers' Hostel HOSTEL €
(Map p58; ☑ 955 26 26 96; www.oasissevilla.com; Calle Almirante Ulloa 1; dm/d incl breakfast €15/50; ✳@🖥🌊) It's not often you get to backpack in a palace. A veritable oasis in the busy city-centre district, this place is a friendly welcoming hostel set in a palatial 19th-century mansion with some private room options, a cafe-bar and a rooftop deck with a small pool.

You can organise tonnes of activities here and meet plenty of multilingual fellow travellers in an atmosphere that's sociable but never over-the-top noisy.

Hotel Boutique Doña Lola BOUTIQUE HOTEL €€
(Map p58; ☑ 954 91 52 75; www.donalolasevilla.com; Calle Amor de Dios 19; s/d €79/87; ✳🖥) Hidden improbably in a rather ordinary tenement in El Centro, Doña Lola is a little haven of modernity and well-positioned for sorties pretty much everywhere. The reception area resembles a psychedelic chess board. Rooms are smallish and surgically clean, making good use of the limited space.

Hotel Abanico HOTEL €€
(Map p58; ☑ 954 21 32 07; www.hotelabanico.com; Calle Águilas 17; s/d €86/90; ✳🖥) If you want to wake up and know instantly that you're in Seville, book into this underdog hotel where the distinctive tilework, wrought-iron balconies and radiant religious art have Seville written all over them.

Hotel América HOTEL €€
(Map p58; ☑ 954 22 09 51; www.hotelamericasevilla.com; Plaza del Duque de la Victoria 9; s/d €75/90; ✳@🖥) If you like reliability and minimal fuss, then head for the Hotel América, a well-located, professionally run hotel with a

business-like sheen. It might not offer you fancy tilework or carnations on your pillow, but it *will* give you all you need to set up a decent sightseeing base.

Triana

Hotel Monte Triana HOTEL €€
(☑ 954 34 31 11; www.hotelesmonte.com; Clara de Jesús Montero 24; d from €79; P ✱ ☜) Staying in Triana has its advantages, aside from the fact that you're within fish-throwing distance of Seville's most soulful quarter. The businesslike Monte Triana has spacious rooms, a 42-car garage (a luxury in Seville), a fitness room (ditto), and its own bar and cafe. You can even choose your own pillow stuffing – latex, feather or viscoelastic.

Alameda de Hércules & Around

**Hotel Sacristía
de Santa Ana** BOUTIQUE HOTEL €€
(Map p60; ☑ 954 91 57 22; www.hotelsacristia.com; Alameda de Hércules 22; d from €95; ✱ ☜) Possibly the best deal in Seville, this delightful hotel is located on the Alameda. It's great for visiting neighbouring bars and restaurants, and the hotel itself is a heavenly place with a small fountain surrounded by bonsai trees greeting you in the central courtyard. Away from the courtyard are old-fashioned rooms with big arty bedheads, circular baths and cascading showers.

Service is equally excellent.

Hotel San Gil HOTEL €€
(Map p60; ☑ 954 90 68 11; www.hotelsangil.com; Calle Parras 28; s/d €96/119; ✱ ☜ ☜) Shoehorned at the northern end of the Macarena neighbourhood, San Gil's slightly out-of-the-way location is balanced by its proximity to the nightlife of the Alameda de Hércules. The nearby web of bike lanes provides a good excuse to get acquainted with the Sevici bike-sharing scheme. An ostentatiously tiled lobby fronts plain but modern rooms with large beds and ample space.

✗ Eating

Seville produces Andalucía's most inventive tapas – end of story – and, if you're not enamoured with the new culinary alchemists, there are plenty of decent salt-of-the-earth tapas bars too.

Mercado del Arenal (Map p58; Calle Pastor y Landero) and **Mercado de la Encarnación**

(Map p58; Plaza de la Encarnación) are central Seville's two food markets. The Encarnación, which mainly sells fruit, veggies and fish, is located under the giant mushroom pillars of the Metropol Parasol (p65).

Barrio de Santa Cruz, Alcázar & Cathedral

Bodega Santa Cruz TAPAS €
(Map p54; Calle Mateos Gago; tapas €2; ☉ 11.30am-midnight) This forever crowded bodega is where eating tapas becomes a physical contact sport. Watch out for flying elbows and admire those dexterous waiters who bob and weave like prizefighters amid the chaos. The fiercely traditional tapas are best enjoyed alfresco with a cold beer as you watch marching armies of Santa Cruz tourists go squeezing past.

Café Bar Las Teresas TAPAS €
(Map p54; Calle Santa Teresa 2; tapas €3; ☉ 10am-midnight) The hanging hams look as ancient as the bar itself, a sinuous wraparound affair with just enough room for two stout waiters to pass carrying precariously balanced tapas plates. The atmosphere is dark but not dingy, the food highly traditional, and the crowd an integrated mix of tourists and Santa Cruz locals.

L'Oca Giuliva ITALIAN €
(Map p54; ☑ 954 21 40 30; www.ocagiuliva.es; Mateos Gago 9; mains €9-12; ☉ 1.30-4pm & 8.30pm-midnight) For a night off tapas, keep the Med in sight and head over – metaphorically – to Italy. L'Oca is arguably Seville's finest purveyor of the cuisine of 'La Dolce Vita' representing all Italian regions with Puglian orecchiette, Genovese pesto, Boloñesa lasagne and Piedmontese ravioli. The pizzas are – as you'd expect – gloriously authentic.

Chandeliers and photos of professional Italians heighten the atmosphere.

Horno de San Buenaventura CAFE €
(Map p54; www.hornosanbuenaventura.com; Avenida de la Constitución; pastries from €1; ☉ 7.30am-10pm Mon-Fri, 8am-10pm Sat & Sun) There are actually two of these gilded pastry/coffee/snack bars in Seville, one here on Avenida de la Constitución opposite the cathedral and the other (inferior one) at the **Plaza de la Alfalfa** (Map p58; ☉ 9am-9pm). All kinds of fare are on show though it's probably best for its lazy continental breakfasts (yes, the service can be slow) or a spontaneous late-night cake fix.

La Azotea
FUSION, ANDALUCIAN €€

(Map p58; ☑ 955 11 67 48; Jesús del Gran Poder 31; raciones €10; ⊘ 1.30-4.30pm & 8.30pm-midnight Thu-Mon) The latest word in *nueva cocina* comes from Azotea whose proliferating empire – there are now four branches – testifies to a growing legend. The decor is Ikea-friendly, staff wear black, and the *raciones* (full servings of tapas items), which are sweetened and spiced with panache, arrive like pieces of art in a variety of plates, dishes and boxes.

Vinería San Telmo
TAPAS, FUSION €€

(Map p54; ☑ 954 41 06 00; www.vineriasantelmo. com; Paseo Catalina de Ribera 4; tapas €3.50, medias raciones €10; ⊘ 1-4.30pm & 8pm-midnight) San Telmo invented the *rascocielo* (skyscraper) *tapa*, an 'Empire State' of tomatoes, aubergine, goat's cheese and smoked salmon. If this and other creative nuggets such as foie gras with quail's eggs and lychees, or exquisitely cooked bricks of tuna, don't make you drool with expectation then you're probably dead.

Casa Tomate
TAPAS, ANDALUCIAN €€

(Map p54; ☑ 954 22 04 21; Calle Mateos Gago 24; tapas €3-4, raciones €12; ⊘ 9am-midnight) Hams swing from ceiling hooks, old feria posters are etched with art-nouveau and art-deco designs, and outdoor blackboards relay what's cooking in the kitchen of Casa Tomate on Santa Cruz' most intense tourist strip. The staff recommend dishes like garlic prawns and pork sirloin in a white-wine-and-pine-nut sauce, and who are you to argue?

✗ El Arenal

★La Brunilda
TAPAS, FUSION €€

(Map p58; ☑ 954 22 04 81; Calle Galera 5; tapas €3.50-6.50; ⊘ 1-4pm & 8.30-11.30pm Tue-Sat, 1-4pm Sun) Seville's crown as Andalucía's tapas capital is regularly attacked by well-armed rivals from the provinces, meaning it constantly has to reinvent itself and offer up fresh competition. Enter La Brunilda, a newish font of fusion tapas sandwiched into an inconspicuous backstreet in the Arenal quarter where everything – including the food, staff and clientele – is pretty.

If you have an unlimited appetite, try the whole menu. For those with smaller bellies, the creamy mushroom risotto is unmissable.

Mesón Cinco Jotas
TAPAS €€

(Map p54; www.mesoncincojotas.com; Calle Castelar 1; medias raciones €10; ⊘ 8am-midnight Mon-Fri, from noon Sat & Sun) In the world of *jamón* (ham) making, if you are awarded Cinco Jotas (Five Js) for your *jamón*, it's like getting an Oscar. The owner of this place, Sánchez Romero Carvajal, is the biggest producer of Jabugo ham, and has a great selection on offer.

It's best to try a range of different things, but note that the top-pig *jamones* can cost just under €40!

Infanta
ANDALUCIAN €€€

(Map p54; ☑ 954 56 15 54; www.infantasevilla.es; Calle Arfe 34-36; mains €16-24; ⊘ 12.30-5pm & 8pm-midnight Mon-Sat, 12.30-5pm Sun) A onetime spit and sawdust Arenal tapas bar that has moved around the corner and reinvented itself as something a little slicker and 'nouveau'. Nonetheless, the bright interior includes some beautiful throwback architectural features and the food never strays far from local ingredients. For a break from tapas, try the on-site sit-down restaurant with a full à la carte menu.

✗ El Centro

Plaza de la Alfalfa is the hub of the tapas scene and has some excellent bars.

★Redhouse Art & Food
INTERNATIONAL €

(Map p58; ☑ 661 615 646; www.redhousespace. com; Calle Amor de Dios 7; snacks from €4; ⊘ 11.30am-12.30am Tue-Sun; ☎) It's hard to classify Redhouse. With its mismatched chairs and abstract wall art, it's flirting with hipster territory, yet inside you'll find families, seniors, college geeks and the obviously not-so-hip enjoying a whole variety of food from casual coffee to romantic meals. Whatever you opt for, save room for the best homemade cakes in Andalucía.

Fashion shows, art expos, poetry readings and music all happen here.

Mercado Lonja del Barranco
INTERNATIONAL €

(Map p58; www.mercadodelbarranco.com; Calle Arjona; snacks €5-12; ⊘ 10am-midnight Sun-Thu, to 2am Fri & Sat) ✗ Fabulous new food court in an Eiffel-esque structure near the Isabel II bridge, with posh stalls stashed with the full cornucopia of *sevillano* food products. Float through the stalls and load up on cakes, fried fish, beer, miniburgers and tapas. There are plenty of nooks and crannies filled with shared tables. It's a mouth-watering and highly sociable experience.

Bar Europa
TAPAS €

(Map p58; ☑ 954 22 13 54; www.bareuropa.info; Calle Siete Revueltas 35; tapas €3, medias raciones €6-8; ☺8am-1am) An old-school bar with no pretensions that's been knocking out tapas since 1925. Notwithstanding, Europa isn't afraid to experiment. Its signature *tapa* is the *quesadilla los balanchares gratinada sobre manzana* which turns a boring old Granny Smith apple into a taste sensation by covering it in goat's cheese and laying it on a bed of strawberries.

Confitería La Campana
CAFE, BAKERY €

(Map p58; www.confiterialacampana.com; cnr Calles Sierpes & Martín Villa; large cakes from €7; ☺8am-10pm) A bakery and cafe with the words 'institution' written all over it, La Campana has been heaving with sugar addicts since 1885. Workers and the elite alike storm Seville's most popular bakery for a *yema* (soft, crumbly biscuit cake wrapped like a toffee), or a delicious *nata* (custard cake) that quivers under the glass.

Arrive early for a standing pew at the bar where waistcoated staff will slam down a coffee and *pan con tomate* (toasted roll with crushed tomato).

★ La Pepona
TAPAS, MODERN €€

(Map p58; ☑ 954 21 50 26; Javier Lasso de la Vega 1; tapas €3.50-6.50; ☺1.30-4.30pm & 8pm-midnight Mon-Sat) One of the best newcomer restaurants of 2014, La Pepona gets all the basics right, from the bread (doorstop-sized rustic slices), to the service (fast but discreet), to the decor (clean Ikea lines and lots of wood). Oscar status is achieved with the food, which falls firmly into the nouveau tapas camp.

Try the goat with yoghurt, couscous and mint – an epic amalgamation of Iberia and Morocco.

Restaurante Albarama
TAPAS €€

(Map p58; ☑ 954 22 97 84; www.restaurantealbarama.com; Plaza de San Francisco 5; tapas €5.50; ☺1-4.15pm & 8.15-11.45pm) A long, slim restaurant usually inhabited with plenty of long, slim people who tuck into tapas that are more about quality than quantity. Come here to enjoy the true beauty of tapas – the opportunity to taste a small sample of fancy food without breaking the bank.

Los Coloniales
CONTEMPORARY ANDALUCIAN €€

(Map p58; www.tabernacoloniales.es; cnr Calle Dormitorio & Plaza Cristo de Burgos; mains €10-12; ☺12.30pm-midnight) The quiet ones are always the best. It might not look like much from the outside, but Los Coloniales is something very special. The quality plates line up like models on a catwalk: *chorizo a la Asturiana,* a divine spicy sausage in an onion sauce served on a bed of lightly fried potato; eggplants in honey; and pork tenderloin *al whisky* (a whisky-flavoured sauce).

There is another inferior, more touristy branch, **Taberna Los Coloniales** (Map p54; Calle Jimios), near the cathedral.

Luso Tapas
TAPAS, PORTUGUESE €€

(Map p58; ☑ 955 09 75 53; Calle Javier Lasso de la Vega 9; tapas €4-6.50; ☺noon-5pm & 8-11.30pm Tue-Sun) Save on a day trip to Lisbon and decamp to Luso for a Portuguese take on tapas. The people from across the border treat their Iberian cousins to some impressive bites of Portuguese flavour – the fish is a highlight – and they're *muito bom* (very good) as they say on the other side of the frontier. On Thursday nights there's live *fado* at 9.30pm.

The Room
INTERNATIONAL €€

(Map p58; ☑ 619 200 946; www.theroomartcuisine.com; Calle Cuesta del Rosario 15; tapas €2.75-5; ☺noon-4.30pm & 8pm-1am; ☏) Another new 'art-cuisine' place, The Room sticks its succinct menu on a blackboard and circumnavigates the globe with everything from British-style fish and chips to pad thai noodles, Peruvian ceviche and Italian risotto. The interior is megacasual with Chaplin movies often projected onto a wall.

El Rinconcillo
TAPAS, ANDALUCIAN €€

(Map p58; ☑ 954 22 31 83; www.elrinconcillo.es; Calle Gerona 40; tapas €3, raciones €12; ☺1pm-1.30am) Some say the Rinconcillo is resting on its laurels. Maybe so; but, with more than 345 years of history, there are a lot to rest on. Seville's oldest bar first opened in 1670, when the Inquisition was raging and tapas were still just tops you screwed on bottles.

Come here for the sense of history rather than for the food, but stay for the *ortiguillas fritas* (fried sea anemones) and a saucerful of the biggest olives you've ever seen.

Robles Laredo
CONTEMPORARY SPANISH €€

(Map p58; www.casa-robles.com; Plaza de San Francisco; raciones €9-12; ☺11am-1am Sun-Wed, to 2am Thu-Sat) This small Italianate cafe-restaurant is fairly dwarfed by its two huge chandeliers and a vast collection of delicate desserts displayed in glass cases. The tapas are equally refined. Try the foie gras, beef burgers with truffle sauce, or oysters and whitebait.

Egaña Santo Restaurante   BASQUE, FUSION €€€
(Map p58; ☑ 954 21 28 73; www.eganagastrogroup.com; Calle Argote de Molina 29; mains €24-38; ⊙12.30-4pm & 8pm-late Wed-Sat & Mon, 12.30-4pm Sun) The former stomping ground of Michelin-starred Basque chef Martin Berasategui has changed hands and is now ruled over by another Basque, Josemari Egaña, a man with a long history on the Seville culinary scene. It's affiliated with the posh EME Catedral Hotel (p71) next to the cathedral, and the food remains headily experimental with a passing nod to Andalucian tradition.

Foie gras escalopes and roast octopus headline a menu doused in the elegance of Basque cuisine.

🍴 Triana

Casa Cuesta   CONTEMPORARY SPANISH €
(Map p54; ☑ 954 33 33 37; www.casacuesta.net; Calle de Castilla 3-5; mains €10; ⊙12.30-4.30pm & 8pm-12.30am) Massive glass windows look out onto a crowded plaza, mirrors artfully reflect framed bullfighting posters and flamenco iconography, and gleaming gold beer pumps furnish a wooden bar shielding bottles that look older than most of the clientele. Casa Cuesta has that wonderful sensation of *sevillano* authenticity.

T de Triana   ANDALUCIAN €€
(Map p54; ☑ 954 33 12 03; Calle Betis 20; ⊙8pm-2am) The T is Triana being itself: simple fish-biased tapas, walls full of history, *fútbol* on the big screen whenever local boys Sevilla or Real Betis are playing, and live, gutsy flamenco shows every Friday night at 10pm.

🍴 Alameda de Hércules

★ Bar-Restaurante
Eslava   FUSION, ANDALUCIAN €€
(Map p60; www.espacioeslava.com; Calle Eslava 3; medias raciones €9-13; ⊙12.30pm-midnight Tue-Sat, 12.30-4.30pm Sun) A legend in its own dinnertime, Eslava shirks the traditional tilework and bullfighting posters of tapas-bar lore and delivers where it matters: fine food backed up with equally fine service.

There's a 'nouvelle' tinge to the memorable *costillas a la miel* (pork ribs in a honey and rosemary glaze) and vegetable strudel in a cheese sauce, but there's nothing snobby about the atmosphere which is local and pretty fanatical after 9pm. An equally good restaurant (with shared kitchen) sits next door.

Duo Tapas   TAPAS, FUSION €€
(Map p60; Calle Calatrava 10; tapas €3-4.50, medias raciones €9-12; ⊙12.30-4.30pm & 8.30pm-midnight) Missed by the masses who rarely wander north from the Alameda de Hércules, Duo Tapas is 'new school' to the old school of El Rinconcillo (p74). But, what it lacks in *azulejo* (tiles) and illustrious past patrons, it makes up for in inventive tapas with an Asian twist. Alameda trendies swear by its green chicken with rice and spicy noodles.

🍷 Drinking & Nightlife

Bars usually open from 6pm to 2am on weekdays and 8pm to 4am on weekends. Drinking and partying get going as late as midnight on Friday and Saturday (daily when it's hot), upping the tempo as the night goes on.

In summer dozens of *terrazas de verano* (summer terraces; temporary, open-air, late-night bars), many of them with live music and plenty of room to dance, spring up along both banks of the river. They change names and ambience from year to year.

Drinking neighbourhoods are legion. Classic spots include drinks on the banks of the Río Guadalquivir in Triana (the wall along Calle del Betis forms a fantastic makeshift bar), Plaza de la Alfalfa (cocktail and dive bars), the Barrio de Santa Cruz and the Alameda de Hércules. The latter is the hub for young *sevillanos* and the city's gay nightlife.

Cervezas Taifa   MICROBREWERY
(Map p54; ☑ 954 04 27 31; www.cervezastaifa.es; Mercado de Triana 36; ⊙7.30am-3pm Mon-Fri, 12.30pm-5pm Sat & Sun) A tiny nano-brewery in Triana market, Taifa is at the forefront of Andalucía's newborn craft-beer movement that is slowly challenging the monopoly of Cruzcampo et al (Cruzcampo is Spain's bestselling beer). Its diminutive market stall (equivalent to that of a small fruit stall) also serves as a factory, shop and bar.

Drop by for a bottle of pilsen, pale ale or IPA, and you'll probably end up chatting about how to start brewing your own with the friendly bilingual owners.

Café de la Prensa
BAR

(Map p54; ☑954 00 29 69; Calle del Betis 8; ◑3pm-2.30am Mon-Thu, 2pm-3.30am Fri-Sun) Calle del Betis is second only to the Alameda de Hércules as a communal Seville watering hole and Café de la Prensa is a fine place to kick off a riverside bar crawl. You can sit inside and stare at walls covered in old newspapers or squeeze outside for better views of the river with the Giralda beckoning in the background.

El Garlochi
BAR

(Map p58; Calle Boteros 4; ◑10pm-6am) Dedicated entirely to the iconography, smells and sounds of Semana Santa, the ultracamp El Garlochi is a true marvel. Taste the rather revolting sounding cocktail, Sangre de Cristo (Blood of Christ) and Agua de Sevilla, both heavily laced with vodka, whisky and grenadine, and pray they open more bars like this.

Bulebar Café
BAR

(Map p60; ☑954 90 19 54; Alameda de Hércules 83; ◑9am-2am) This place gets pretty *caliente* (hot) at night but is pleasantly chilled in the early evening, with friendly staff. Don't write off its spirit-reviving alfresco breakfasts that pitch earlybirds with up-all-nighters. It's in the uber-cool Alameda de Hércules.

Cabo Loco
BAR

(Map p58; Calle Pérez Galdós 26; ◑5pm-1am Tue-Wed, to 3am Thu-Sat, to midnight Sun) Two really is a crowd in this Alfalfa-district dive bar, hole-in-the-wall, cheap-shot heaven...call it what you like. It's a good stop on any elongated bar crawl, if you don't mind standing – alfresco.

☆ Entertainment

★ Casa de la Memoria
FLAMENCO

(Map p58; ☑954 56 06 70; www.casadelamemoria.es; Calle Cuna 6; €18; ◑shows 7.30pm & 9pm) Neither a *tablao* (choreographed flamenco show) nor a private *peña* (club, usually of flamenco aficionados), this cultural centre (see p66) offers what are, without doubt, the most intimate and authentic nightly flamenco shows in Seville. It's accommodated in the old stables of the Palacio de la Condesa de Lebrija.

It's perennially popular and space is limited to 100, so reserve tickets a day or so in advance by calling or visiting the venue.

★ Sevilla de Ópera
THEATRE

(Map p58; ☑955 29 46 61; www.sevilladeopera.com; Mercado del Arenal, Calle Pastor y Landero; ◑shows 9pm Fri & Sat) Seville has served as the fictional setting for countless operas, so it made sense when in 2012 a group of opera singers and enthusiasts decided to initiate the Sevilla de Ópera club. The setting in the Arenal market is like a kind of 'Opera *tablao*' with shows designed to make the music more accessible.

You can come for drinks and/or dinner and enjoy renditions of pieces from the likes of *Carmen, The Marriage of Figaro* and *The Barber of Seville*. Prebook online.

Casa de la Guitarra
FLAMENCO

(Map p54; ☑954 22 40 93; Calle Mesón del Moro 12; tickets adult/child €17/10; ◑shows 7.30pm & 9pm) Tiny newish flamenco-only venue in Santa Cruz (no food or drinks served) where a miscued step from the performing dancers would land them in the front row of the audience. Glass display cases filled with guitars of erstwhile flamenco greats adorn the walls.

El Palacio Andaluz
FLAMENCO

(☑954 53 47 20; www.elpalacioandaluz.com; Calle de María Auxiliadora; admission with drink/dinner €38/76; ◑shows 7pm & 9.30pm) The purists will, no doubt, tell you that these highly choreographed performances in a 400-seat theatre are for tourists, but go along anyway and decide for yourself. You may be surprised – the Palacio's performers are absolute masters of their art with talent to write home about. What a show!

Tablao El Arenal
FLAMENCO

(Map p54; www.tablaoelarenal.com; Calle Rodo 7; admission with drink/dinner €38/72; ◑restaurant from 7pm, shows 8pm & 10pm) Of all the places in Seville that offer flamenco 'dinner shows', this is one of the best. With a seating capacity of 100 in an old-school tavern, it lacks the grit and – invariably – *duende* (flamenco spirit) of the *peñas* (small flamenco clubs), although you can't fault the skill of the performers. Tickets include one drink. Skip the food.

Casa Anselma
FLAMENCO

(Map p54; Calle Pagés del Corro 49; ◑midnight-late Mon-Sat) True, the music is often more folkloric than flamenco, but Casa Anselma is the antithesis of a touristy flamenco *tablao*, with cheek-to-jowl crowds, zero amplification and spontaneous outbreaks of dexterous dancing. Beware: there's no sign, just a doorway embellished with *azulejos* (tiles).

Anselma is in Triana about 200m from the western side of the Puente de Isabel II.

Teatro Duque La Imperdible THEATRE
(Map p58; ☑954 38 82 19; www.imperdible.org; Plaza del Duque de la Victoria; adult/child €12/5) This epicentre of experimental arts stages lots of contemporary dance, theatre and flamenco, usually around 9pm. The bar here also hosts varied music events from around 11pm Thursday to Saturday.

Naima Café Jazz JAZZ
(Map p60; ☑954 38 24 85; Calle Trajano 47; ⊙live performances from 11pm Sat & Sun) Very mellow bar with live jazz most nights, Naima is so small you'll probably find yourself squeezed in next to the drummer with a hi-hat crashing inches from your nose.

Shopping

Shopping in Seville is a major pastime, and shopping for clothes is at the top of the list for any *sevillano*. Shoes fetishists beware: Seville possibly has the densest quota of shoe shops on the planet.

Calles Sierpes, Velázquez/Tetuán and Cuna have retained their charm with a host of small shops selling everything from polka-dot *trajes de flamenca* (flamenco dresses) to antique fans. Most shops open between 9am and 9pm, but expect it to be ghostly quiet between 2pm and 5pm when they close for siesta.

For a more alternative choice of shops, head for Calles Amor de Dios and Doctor Letamendi, close to Alameda de Hércules.

Triana is famous for its pottery and tile-making. A dozen shops and workshops still sell charming and artistic ceramics on the corner of Calles Alfarería and Antillano Campos.

Cerámica Santa Ana CERAMICS
(Map p54; ☑954 33 39 90; www.ceramicasantaana.com; Calle San Jorge 31; ⊙10am-8.30pm Mon-Fri, to 3pm Sat) Seville specialises in distinctive *azulejos* (ceramic tiles) and they are best seen in Triana. Cerámica Santa Ana has been around for more than 50 years and the shop itself almost qualifies as a tourist attraction.

El Postigo MARKET
(Map p54; cnr Calles Arfe & Dos de Mayo; ⊙11am-2pm & 4-8pm) This covered arts and crafts market in the Arenal houses a few shops selling everything from pottery and textiles to silverware.

SEVILLE SHOPPING

Casa del Libro BOOKS
(Map p58; www.casadellibro.com; Calle Velázquez 8; ⊙9.30am-9.30pm Mon-Sat) Part of Spain's oldest bookshop chain, this branch is spread over four floors and stocks plenty of multilingual fiction and guidebooks (including this one).

Record Sevilla MUSIC
(Map p58; Calle Amor de Dios 27; ⊙10am-2pm & 5-9pm Sun-Fri, 5-9pm Sat) Fancy mixing flamenco with house? Then grab your vinyl here. Staff are knowledgeable about the local music scene too.

Padilla Crespo ACCESSORIES, CLOTHING
(Map p54; ☑954 21 29 88; Calle Adriano 18B; ⊙10am-8.30pm Mon-Sat) If you're really immersing yourself in the culture, you can pick up your wide-brimmed hat and riding outfit for the Feria de Abril right here.

El Corte Inglés DEPARTMENT STORE
(Map p58; Plaza del Duque de la Victoria 8; ⊙10am-10pm Mon-Sat) The mega Spanish department store occupies four separate buildings in and around Plaza de la Magdalena and Plaza del Duque de la Victoria.

ⓘ Information

EMERGENCIES
Ambulance (☑061)
Fire (☑085)
Policía Local (☑092)
Policía Nacional (☑091)

POST
Post Office (Map p54; Avenida de la Constitución 32; ⊙8.30am-9.30pm Mon-Fri, to 2pm Sat)

TOURIST INFORMATION
Infhor (☑954 54 19 52; Estación Santa Justa; ⊙8am-10pm, closes for lunch Sat & Sun) Independent tourist office at the train station.

Turismo Sevilla (Map p54; www.turismosevilla.org; Plaza del Triunfo 1; ⊙10.30am-7pm Mon-Fri) Information on all of Sevilla province.

Regional Tourist Office (Map p54; Avenida de la Constitución 21; ⊙9am-7pm Mon-Fri, 10am-2pm & 3-7pm Sat, 10am-2pm Sun, closed holidays) The Constitución office is well informed but often very busy. There is also a branch at the airport (☑954 44 91 28; Aeropuerto San Pablo; ⊙9am-8.30pm Mon-Fri, 10am-6pm Sat, 10am-2pm Sun, closed holidays).

❶ Getting There & Away

AIR

Seville's **airport** (SVQ; ☑954 44 90 00; www.aena.es) has a fair range of international and domestic flights.

Numerous international carriers fly in and out of Seville; carrier and schedule information changes frequently, so it's best to check with specific airlines or major online booking agents.

BUS

Seville has two main bus stations serving different destinations and bus companies. Plaza de Armas is the larger of the two.

Estación de Autobuses Plaza de Armas (Map p58; www.autobusesplazadearmas.es; Avenida del Cristo de la Expiración) The main HQ for Spain's intercity bus company, Alsa, linking to other major cities in Andalucía including Málaga (€19, three hours, eight daily), Granada (€23, three hours, nine daily), Córdoba (€12, two hours, seven daily) and Almería (€37, 5½ hours, three daily). Damas runs buses to Huelva province and Eurolines has international services to Germany, Belgium, France and beyond.

Estación de Autobuses Prado de San Sebastián (Map p54; Plaza San Sebastián) Primarily home to smaller companies running buses to lesser towns in western Andalucía. Of note are Amarillos serving the provinces of Sevilla, Cádiz and parts of Málaga, and Comes who run to some of the harder-to-reach 'white towns'.

TRAIN

Seville's **Estación Santa Justa** (☑902 43 23 43; Avenida Kansas City) is 1.5km northeast of the centre.

High-speed AVE trains go to/from Madrid (from €79, 2½ hours, 20 daily) and Córdoba (from €30, 40 minutes, 30 daily). Slower trains head to Cádiz (€16, 1¾ hours, 15 daily), Huelva (€12, 1½ hours, three daily), Granada (€30, three hours, four daily) and Málaga (€44, two hours, 11 daily).

❶ Getting Around

TO/FROM THE AIRPORT
Bus

The EA bus (€4) makes the trip between the airport and the city centre roughly every 20 to 30 minutes throughout the day. The service is reduced slightly on Sundays, as well as very early in the morning and late in the evening. The first bus from the airport to the city is at 5.45am and the last at 12.15am. From the city to the airport the first bus is at 5.15am and the last at 12.45am. It runs to/from the Plaza de Armas bus station via Santa Justa train station, the Prado de San Sebastián bus station and the Torre del Oro.

Taxi

A taxi costs a set €22 with a charge of €1 per bag from the airport to the centre, but going the other way you'll be lucky to pay less than €25. There's a €3 to €4 surcharge late at night, and on weekends and holidays.

BUS

Buses C1, C2, C3 and C4 do useful circular routes linking the main transport terminals and the city centre. The standard ticket is €1.40 but a range of passes are available (from stations and kiosks next to stops) if you're likely to use it a lot.

CAR & MOTORCYCLE

For car hire there's **Avis** (☑902 48 03 21; www.avis.com; Avenida de Italia 107) or **National Atesa** (☑959 28 17 12; www.atesa.es) at the Santa Justa train station concourse, and all the normal brands at the airport.

METRO

Seville's **metro system** (www.sevilla21.com/metro) connects Ciudad Expo with Olivar de Quinto (this line isn't that useful for visitors). Three more lines are due for completion by 2017. The standard ticket is €1.35. A one-day travel card costs €4.50.

TAXI

Taxis are common and a journey across the city centre during daylight hours will cost around €5 to €7.

TRAM

Tranvia (www.tussam.es) is the city's sleek tram service, first introduced in 2007. Two parallel lines run in pollution-free bliss between Plaza Nueva, Avenida de la Constitucíon, Puerta de Jerez, San Sebastián and San Bernardo. The standard ticket is €1.40 but a range of passes are available if you're likely to use it a lot.

Huelva & Sevilla Provinces

Includes ➡

Huelva 82
Moguer 85
Isla Cristina 86
Parque Nacional
de Doñana 87
El Rocío 90
Minas de Riotinto 92
Aracena 93
Sierra de Aracena 95
Carmona 99
Osuna 102
Écija 103
Parque Natural Sierra
Norte de Sevilla 105

Why Go?

Glittering white cities of spires and palaces, endless stretches of untainted coastline, fishing ports serving up the day's catch in unpretentious restaurants, sleepy mountain villages and Spain's most beloved national park: the western chunk of Andalucía, comprising the provinces of Sevilla and Huelva, packs in an unexpected combination of historical intrigue, culinary wizardry, natural beauty and sun worship. Capital Seville gets all the attention, but to its east stands a much less touristed trio of towns – Carmona, Osuna and Écija – with seductive historic cores and top tapas stops. Southwest of Seville lies the vast Parque Nacional de Doñana, with its protected marshes, dunes and forest. West to Portugal runs the Costa de la Luz, an exquisite yet relatively undiscovered coastline, quite unlike the packaged chaos further east. North, towards Extremadura, rises the rarely visited Sierra Morena, dotted with cobblestoned villages and criss-crossed by some of Andalucía's finest walking trails.

Best Places to Eat

➡ Casa Curro (p103)
➡ Jesús Carrión (p95)
➡ Restaurante Toruño (p91)
➡ Agustina (p107)

Best Places to Stay

➡ Posada de San Marcos (p96)
➡ Las Navezuelas (p105)
➡ Finca La Fronda (p97)
➡ Hotel Palacio Marqués de la Gomera (p103)

Driving Distances

	Aracena	Ayamonte	El Rocío	Huelva
Ayamonte	142			
El Rocío	118	107		
Huelva	101	52	60	
Niebla	87	75	35	29

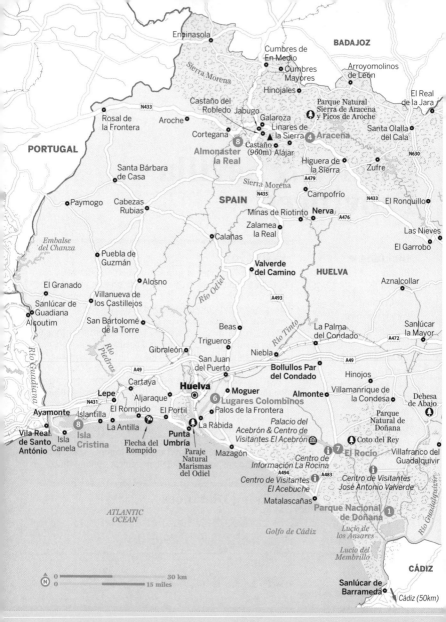

Huelva & Sevilla Provinces Highlights

1 Exploring the untrammelled wilderness of the **Parque Nacional de Doñana** (p87)

2 Delving into the past at the wonderfully preserved Roman settlement of **Itálica** (p98)

3 Digging up riches in **Osuna** (p102), a palace-studded showcase of ducal wealth and the bullring that starred in *Game of Thrones*

4 Hiking from one enchanted village to the next and tasting creative mountain cooking around **Aracena** (p93)

5 Hitting the tapas trail in **Carmona** (p99), a gorgeous hilltop enclave of towers and churches

6 Retracing the historic steps of Christopher

Columbus in the **Lugares Colombinos** (p84)

7 Feeling the festive fervour of Spain's largest religious pilgrimage in **El Rocío** (p90)

8 Checking out Islamic architecture in remote, labyrinthine **Almonaster la Real** (p98)

> **DON'T MISS**
>
> ## BEST OUTDOOR ADVENTURES
>
> ➡ Venturing into the wild at the **Parque Nacional de Doñana** (p87)
>
> ➡ Rambling off the beaten path(s) between picture-perfect villages in Huelva's **Sierra de Aracena** (p95)
>
> ➡ Cycling or hiking the disused mining railway of the **Vía Verde de la Sierra Norte** (p105)
>
> ➡ Birdwatching in and around **El Rocío** (p90)

HUELVA

POP 147,000

The capital of Huelva province is a modern, unpretentious industrial port set between the Odiel and Tinto estuaries. Despite its unpromising approaches and slightly grimy feel, central Huelva is a lively enough place, and the city's people – called *choqueros* because of their supposed preference for the locally abundant *chocos* (cuttlefish) – are noted for their warmth.

Huelva's history dates back 3000 years to the Phoenician town of Onuba. Onuba's river-mouth location made it a natural base for exporting inland minerals to the Mediterranean. The town was devastated by the 1755 Lisbon earthquake, but later grew when British company Rio Tinto developed mines in the province's interior in the 1870s. Today Huelva has a sizeable fishing fleet and a heavy dose of petrochemical industry (introduced in the 1950s by Franco).

👁 Sights

More a scene than a collection of dazzling sights, Huelva nevertheless offers a few worthwhile stops.

> ### ℹ RESOURCES
>
> **Turismo de Huelva** (www.turismo huelva.org) Huelva province information.
>
> **Sierra de Aracena** (www.sierrade aracena.com) Downloadable hiking directions for the mountainous north.
>
> **Turismo Sevilla** (www.turismosevilla. org) Tourist information for Sevilla province.

Museo de Huelva   MUSEUM
(☑959 65 04 24; www.museosdeandalucia.es; Alameda Sundheim 13; ☺9am-3.30pm Tue-Sat, 10am-5pm Sun Jun–mid-Sep, 9am-7.30pm Tue-Sat, 9am-3.30pm Sun mid-Sep–May) **FREE** This excellent town museum is stuffed with history and art. The permanent ground-floor exhibition concentrates on the province's impressive archaeological pedigree, with interesting items culled from its Roman and mining history; don't miss the blue-toned 16th-century *azulejos* (tiles) from nearby walled-town Niebla.

**Muelle-Embarcadero
de Mineral de Río Tinto**   HISTORIC SITE
An odd legacy of the area's mining history, this impressive iron pier curves out into the Odiel estuary 500m south of the port. It was designed for the Rio Tinto company in the 1870s by British engineer George Barclay Bruce. Equipped with boardwalks on upper and lower levels, it makes for a delightful stroll or jog to admire the harbour and ships. It's 1km southwest of Plaza de las Monjas.

**Santuario de Nuestra
Señora de la Cinta**   CHAPEL
(Avenida de la Cinta; ☺9am-1pm & 4-7pm; **P**) Of Gothic-Mudéjar origins but reconstructed in the 18th and 19th centuries, this pretty, plain white sanctuary looks out across the Odiel estuary from its peaceful hillside spot 3km north of the centre. Columbus allegedly promised to pray here upon returning to Spain across the turbulent Atlantic in 1493; the story is depicted in tiles by artist Daniel Zuloaga. Take city bus 6 from outside the bus station.

✦ Festivals & Events

Fiestas Colombinas   HISTORICAL
(☺1st week Aug) Huelva celebrates Columbus' departure for the Americas (3 August 1492) with this six-day festival of music, dance, cultural events and bullfighting.

🛏 Sleeping

Hotel Familia Conde   BUSINESS HOTEL €
(☑959 28 24 00; www.hotelfamiliaconde.com; Alameda Sundheim 14; s/d €52/60; ❋@❂) True, it's housed in a soulless block, but this central business-class operation is efficiently run with friendly service, and the airy, fresh-smelling rooms have gleaming bold-coloured bathrooms. It's a few steps east of the cafe-lined Gran Vía (Avenida Martín Alonso Pinzón).

Huelva

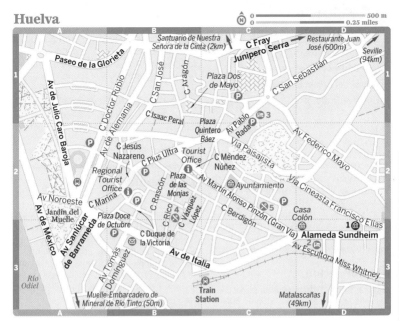

Hotel Monte Conquero   BUSINESS HOTEL €€
(☑959 28 55 00; www.hotelesmonte.com; Avenida Pablo Rada 10; r from €65; ❄ ☎) Catering to the business set, this impeccably maintained hotel is probably your best bet in Huelva. Bright-red banisters draped in greenery liven up the lobby and staff are charmingly efficient. 'Executive' women's rooms feature complimentary haircare and beauty kits, and all 162 rooms are smartly outfitted with dark-wood desks, crisp white sheets and those all-important back-up internet cables.

✖ Eating

In a salty city such as Huelva it's no surprise that the fruits of the sea star on the menu. Busy tapas bars line Avenida Pablo Rada, just north of the centre.

Restaurante Juan José   ANDALUCIAN €
(☑959 26 38 57; Calle Villamundaka 1; tapas €2-3, raciones €8-14; ☉6.30am-6pm & 8pm-midnight Mon-Sat) It's 1.5km northeast of Plaza de las Monjas, but Huelva's crowds regularly pack into this humble establishment for its fabulously gooey *tortilla de patatas* (potato and onion omelette). The tuna (fresh from Isla Cristina) and *carne mechada* (meat stuffed with pepper and ham) are tasty too. Arrive before 2pm to snag a table.

Huelva

⊙ **Sights**
  1 Museo de Huelva D3

🛏 **Sleeping**
  2 Hotel Familia Conde D3
  3 Hotel Monte Conquero C1

✖ **Eating**
  4 Azabache B2
  5 La Mirta C2

Catch bus 6 from the city bus station to Plaza Huerto Paco; walk one block south down Avenida de las Adoratrices and turn left on Calle Villamundaka.

Azabache   TAPAS, ANDALUCIAN €€
(☑959 25 75 28; www.restauranteazabache.com; Calle Vázquez López 22; raciones €6-16; ☉8am-11pm Mon-Fri, to 4pm Sat) After a taste of traditional Huelva? Squeeze into this narrow tiled tapas bar where busy, helpful waiters are quick to deliver cheese and *jamón* (ham) platters, plus scrambled *gurumelos* (local wild mushrooms), fried *chocos* (cuttlefish) and fresh fish specials.

DON'T MISS

HUELVA'S BEST BEACHES

Matalascañas (p87)

Isla Cristina (p86)

Flecha del Rompido (p86)

Isla Canela (p87)

La Mirta TAPAS, ANDALUCIAN €€

(📞959 28 36 57; www.lamirta.com; Avenida Martín Alonso Pinzón 13; tapas €3.50-5.50, raciones €6.50-15; ⊗noon-4pm & 8pm-midnight) This popular modern-rustic restaurant/wine bar on the bubbly Gran Vía specialises in local flavours thrown together with contemporary flair. *Chocos* come as linguine (with prawns), mushrooms are stuffed with goat's cheese and *pisto* (Spanish ratatouille), and it's all accompanied by hot crispy bread.

❶ Information

Regional Tourist Office (www.turismohuelva. org; Calle Jesús Nazareno 21; ⊗9am-7.30pm Mon-Fri, 9.30am-3pm Sat & Sun) Helpful on the whole province.

Tourist Office (📞959 54 18 17; Plaza de las Monjas; ⊗10am-2pm & 5-8.30pm Mon-Fri, to 2pm Sat)

❶ Getting There & Around

BUS

Most buses from the **bus station** (Calle Doctor Rubio) are operated by **Damas** (📞959 25 69 00; www.damas-sa.es). Destinations include Almonte (for El Rocío), Aracena, Isla Cristina, La Rábida, Moguer, Matalascañas, Palos de la Frontera, Seville and Faro (Portugal). Frequency is reduced on Saturday, Sunday and public holidays.

CAR & MOTORCYCLE

There's metered street parking around town (Monday to Saturday), indicated by blue and orange lines, and a useful parking lot off Calle Duque de la Victoria.

TRAIN

Renfe (📞902 43 23 43; www.renfe.com) runs three services to Seville (€12, 1½ hours) and one high-speed ALVIA train to Córdoba (€38, 1¾ hours) and Madrid (€72, 3¾ hours) daily.

LUGARES COLOMBINOS

The 'Columbian Sites' are the three townships of La Rábida, Palos de la Frontera and Moguer, along the eastern bank of the Tinto estuary. All three played a key role in Columbus' preparation for his journey of discovery and can be visited in a fun day trip from Huelva, Doñana or Huelva's eastern coast. As the countless greenhouses suggest, this is Spain's main strawberry-growing region (Huelva province produces 90% of Spain's crop).

❶ Getting There & Away

At least 11 daily buses leave Huelva for La Rábida (€1.55, 25 minutes) and Palos de la Frontera (€1.55, 30 minutes); half continue to Moguer (€1.55, 45 minutes).

La Rábida

POP 500

Monasterio de la Rábida MONASTERY

(📞959 35 04 11; www.monasteriodelarabida.com; Paraje de la Rábida; admission €3; ⊗10am-1pm & 4-7pm Tue-Sun; 🅿) In the pretty, peaceful village of La Rábida, don't miss this 14th- and 15th-century Franciscan monastery, visited several times by Columbus before his great voyage of discovery.

Here Columbus met Abbot Juan Pérez, who took up his cause and drummed up support for his far-fetched plans to discover new lands and in the process make Spain very rich. Within the monastery is a chapel with a 13th-century alabaster Virgin before which Columbus prayed, and a fresco-lined Mudéjar cloister, one of the few parts of the original structure to survive the 1755 earthquake. Fine early 20th-century frescoes by Huelvan cubist painter Daniel Vázquez Díaz detail Columbus' adventures.

Muelle de las Carabelas HISTORIC SITE

(Wharf of the Caravels; admission €3.55; ⊗10am-9pm Tue-Sun mid-Jun–mid-Sep, 9.30am-7.30pm Tue-Sun mid-Sep–mid-Jun; 🅿) On the waterfront below the Monasterio de la Rábida is this pseudo 15th-century quayside, where you can board replicas of Columbus' tiny three-ship fleet. The ships are moored behind an interesting museum covering the history of the great explorer's journeys.

Palos de la Frontera

POP 5300

It was from the port of Palos de la Frontera that Columbus and his merry band set sail into the unknown. The town provided the explorer with two of his ships, two captains (Martín Alonso Pinzón and Vicente Yáñez Pinzón) and more than half his crew.

THE FOUR VOYAGES OF CHRISTOPHER COLUMBUS

In April 1492 Christopher Columbus (Cristóbal Colón to Spaniards) finally won the Spanish royal support of the Reyes Católicos (Catholic Monarchs; Fernando and Isabel) for his proposed westward voyage of exploration to the spice-rich Orient. This proposal was to result in four great voyages and a fabulous golden age for Spain, though some historians now argue that Columbus' captains, the Pinzón brothers, really deserve the credit for finding the New World.

On 3 August 1492 Columbus embarked from Palos de la Frontera with 100 men and three ships. After a near mutiny as the crew despaired of finding land, they finally made landfall on the Bahamian island of Guanahaní on 12 October, naming it San Salvador. The expedition went on to discover Cuba and Hispaniola, where the *Santa María* sank. The *Niña* and the *Pinta* made it back to Palos on 15 March 1493.

Columbus – with animals, plants, gold ornaments and six Caribbean Indians – received a hero's welcome on his return, as all were convinced that he had reached the fabled East Indies (in fact, his calculations were some 16,000km out). Martín Alonso Pinzón died on arrival in Spain, supposedly having failed to beat Columbus back with the big news.

Columbus made further voyages in 1493 and 1498, discovering Jamaica, Puerto Rico, Trinidad and the mouth of the Orinoco River. But he proved a disastrous colonial administrator, enslaving the indigenous peoples and alienating Spanish settlers. Eventually he was arrested by a Spanish royal emissary and sent home in chains. In an attempt to redeem himself, Columbus embarked on his fourth and final voyage in May 1502. This time he reached Honduras and Panama, but then became stranded for a year in Jamaica, having lost his ships to sea worms.

Columbus died in 1506 in Valladolid, northern Spain – impoverished and apparently still believing he had reached Asia. His remains were eventually returned to the Caribbean, as he had wished, before being brought back to Seville (p50). Or were they? The story of Columbus' posthumous voyages has become quite the saga itself.

◉ Sights

Casa Museo Martín Alonso Pinzón MUSEUM
(☑ 959 10 00 41; Calle Colón 24; admission €1; ⊙ 10am-2pm Mon-Fri) The former home of the *Pinta*'s captain now houses a permanent exhibition on Palos' crucial contribution to Columbus' famous first expedition.

Museo Naval MUSEUM
(☑ 959 10 55 69; Calle Colón 52; ⊙ 10am-2pm Mon-Fri) FREE In an old sailors' hospital, Palos' naval museum hosts an impressive collection of ship models, from prehistoric canoes to Columbus' *Niña*.

Iglesia de San Jorge CHURCH
(Calle Fray Juan Pérez) Towards the northern end of Calle Colón is this 15th-century Gothic-Mudéjar church where Columbus and his sailors took communion before embarking on their great expedition. Water for their ships came from La Fontanilla well nearby.

✖ Eating

El Bodegón GRILL, ANDALUCIAN €€
(☑ 959 53 11 05; Calle Rábida 46; mains €12-25; ⊙ noon-4pm & 8.30-11.30pm Wed-Mon) Stop to take on supplies at this noisy, atmospheric grotto of a restaurant, which cooks up fish and meat on wood-fired grills.

Moguer

POP 14,300

The sleepy whitewashed town of Moguer, 8km northeast of Palos de la Frontera on the A494, is where Columbus' ship, the *Niña*, was built. The main Columbus site in town is the 14th-century **Monasterio de Santa Clara** (☑ 959 37 01 07; www.monasteriode santaclara.com; Plaza de las Monjas; guided tours €3.50; ⊙ tours 10.30am, 11.30am & 12.30pm Tue-Sun & 4.30pm, 5.30pm & 6.30pm Tue-Sat), with a lovely Mudéjar cloister and an impressive collection of Renaissance religious art; Columbus spent a night of vigil and prayer here after returning from his first voyage in March 1493. Visits are by guided tour.

Hotel Plaza Escribano (☑ 959 37 30 63; www.hotelplazaescribano.com; Plaza Escribano 5; s/d €39/56; P ✱ 🛜) is a friendly, modern hotel in Moguer's historic core. Large, stylish rooms are splashed in pastels that complement bright bedspreads; there's a small

DON'T MISS

MOGUER & JUAN RAMÓN JIMÉNEZ

Moguer has its own charming flavour of Andalucian baroque, and its sunny beauty was fulsomely expressed by local poet laureate Juan Ramón Jiménez (1881–1958), who won the Nobel Prize for literature in 1956. The **Casa Museo Zenobia y Juan Ramón Jiménez** (☑959 37 21 48; Calle Juan Ramón Jiménez 10; admission €3.50; ☉10.15am-1pm Tue-Sun & 5.15-7pm Tue-Sat), the old home of the poet and his writer wife, is open for visits.

As you wander around town, keep an eye out for tiled quotes marking key locations from Jiménez' most famous poem *Platero y yo* (Platero and I), which was inspired by his beloved donkey Platero and celebrated its centenary in 2014, and for sculptures of Jiménez' well-known characters.

library for guests plus a cute courtyard and lots of lively tiling.

About 300m southwest of the central Plaza del Cabildo, **Mesón El Lobito** (☑959 37 06 60; Calle Rábida 31; mains €7-19; ☉10.30am-5pm & 8.30pm-midnight) dishes up huge, great-value platters of traditional country fare in a cavernous bodega (wine cellar); grilled fish and meats come fresh from the open log fire.

There's an excellent **tourist office** (☑959 37 18 98; Calle Andalucía 17; ☉10am-2pm & 5-7pm Tue-Sat) inside the Teatro.

HUELVA'S COSTA DE LA LUZ

Huelva province's modestly developed Costa de la Luz consists of beautiful broad white sands backed by dunes and pine trees. West of Huelva, the main beach hot spots are Punta Umbría, Flecha del Rompido, Isla Cristina and Ayamonte. All are friendly, unpretentious places, more popular with Spanish holidaymakers than with foreign visitors.

The Costa de la Luz continues southeast from Huelva, along almost the entire coastline of neighbouring Cádiz province (p139).

Flecha del Rompido

Possibly the most spectacular beach on Huelva's Costa de la Luz, this 8km-long sand bar along the mouth of the Río Pie-

dras can be reached only by ferry, which keeps the crowds away, even in midsummer. The waters on the inland side remain calm, while the south side faces the open sea. Part of the Río Piedras wetlands reserve, it's a place of great ornithological and botanical interest.

From spring to autumn, hourly **Flechamar** (☑959 39 99 42; www.flechamar.com; one-way/return €2.50/4; ☉Apr-Oct) boats go to the Flecha from the port at the western end of El Rompido (23km west of Huelva). At least two daily buses go from Huelva to El Rompido (€2.35, 50 minutes).

Isla Cristina

POP 18,500

Founded after the 1775 earthquake, Isla Cristina is first and foremost a bustling fishing port with a 250-strong fleet. Besides the tuna and sardines, it's famous for its lively **February Carnaval**.

◉ Sights & Activities

If you can't make February's Carnaval, pop into the **Museo del Carnaval** (☑959 33 26 94; Tourist Office, Calle San Francisco 12; ☉10am-2pm) **FREE**, which hosts a permanent display of prize-winning costumes.

At the southern end of Avenida Federico Silva Muñoz (the continuation of the central Gran Vía), a bridge crosses a lagoon to reach the sprawling **Playa de la Gaviota**. Along the rear of the beach, a boardwalk trail heads east to **Playa Central**, the main tourism zone with a few hotels and restaurants. Further east a nature trail winds through forested marshlands, with good birdwatching opportunities.

🛏 Sleeping & Eating

Hotel Sol y Mar   HOTEL €€

(☑959 33 20 50; www.hotelsolymar.org; Playa Central; s/d €70/114; ☉mid-Feb–Oct; P ❋ 🛜) Possibly the best-value hotel on this coast, with perfect balconies overlooking a broad swathe of beach and little else. It has plenty of style, and welcome extras like rain showers and friendly service. The on-site **restaurant** (☑959 33 20 50; Playa Central; mains €10-14; ☉mid-Feb–Oct) serves mostly seafood on a lovely beachfront terrace.

Hermanos Moreno   SEAFOOD €€

(☑959 34 35 71; Avenida Padre Mirabent 39; raciones €6-10; ☉noon-4pm & 8pm-midnight

Apr-Sep, noon-4pm Oct-Mar) A popular choice among several busy seafood spots on a square on the northwest tip of the peninsula, opposite the seafood auction market (you can watch restaurant buyers from across Spain bid for the day's catch). *Chocos* (cuttlefish), *castañuelas* (small cuttlefish), *chipirones* (squid), stuffed tuna – it just doesn't get any fresher.

ⓘ Getting There & Away

Damas (www.damas-sa.es) runs at least five daily buses between Isla Cristina's **bus station** (Calle Manuel Siurot) and Huelva (€4, one hour).

Ayamonte

POP 15,800

Staring across the Río Guadiana to Portugal, Ayamonte has a cheerful border-town buzz.

⊙ Sights & Activities

The old town, between Paseo de la Ribera and the ferry dock (400m west), is dotted with attractive plazas, old churches, cafes, boutiques and restaurants.

Portugal-bound romantics can skip the fast, modern A49 motorway and enjoy a slower 15-minute ferry trip across the Guadiana to Portugal's Vila Real de Santo António with **Transporte Fluvial del Guadiana** (☑959 47 06 17; www.rioguadiana.net; Muelle de Portugal; passenger/bicycle/car €1.80/1.15/5.50; ☺half-hourly departures 9.30am-9pm Jul–mid-Sep, hourly departures 10am-7pm mid-Sep–Jun). The same operator runs cruises up the Guadiana, one of Spain's longest rivers, to Sanlúcar de Guadiana (nine hours). Check timings and buy tickets at the kiosk facing the ferry dock.

South of town are the broad beaches of **Isla Canela** and **Punta del Moral**, both quite developed.

✗ Eating

Casa Luciano   SEAFOOD €€
(www.casaluciano.com; Calle de la Palma 1; mains €10-20; ☺1-4.30pm & 8.30pm-midnight Tue-Sat, 1-4.30pm Sun) Of Ayamonte's many seafood restaurants, Casa Luciano is a worthy favourite. Everything on your plate is freshly cooked, minutes out of the water. Its version of tuna, particularly prized along this stretch of coast, is excellent; the *tortilla de patatas* and paella tapas are equally popular.

ⓘ Information

Tourist Office (☑959 32 07 37; Plaza de España; ☺9am-8pm Mon-Fri, to 2pm Sat)

ⓘ Getting There & Away

There are no customs or immigration checks when crossing the Spain–Portugal border here, by road or ferry.

From the **bus station** (Avenida de Andalucía), four daily buses go to Isla Cristina (€1.55, 25 minutes), six to Huelva (€5.30, 1¼ hours) and one to Faro (Portugal; €15, 40 minutes).

EAST OF HUELVA

Matalascañas

Abutting the Parques Nacional and Natural de Doñana, 50km southeast of Huelva, Matalascañas is a slap-it-up-quick tourist resort (much like Mazagón to its west). Thanks to national park regulations, development is confined to a 4km by 1km space, and the beach here is simply gorgeous.

Follow the main road east to a boardwalk trail leading down along the edge of the national park to the best part of beach. From a control post on the beach below the Gran Hotel del Coto, a 1.5km boardwalk trail snakes through the dunes, here dotted with umbrella pine and maritime juniper.

On the western edge of Matalascañas, the **Parque Dunar** (Avenida de las Adelfas; ☺8am-9pm) is a 1.3-sq-km expanse of high, pine-covered dunes laced with a maze of sandy pathways and boardwalk trails. Facing the beach at this end of town are half a dozen *chiringuitos* (beach bars) dishing up fresh seafood.

For accommodation, try the flower-filled compound of **Hotel Doñana Blues** (☑959 44 98 17; www.donanablues.com; Sector I, Parcela 129; s/d from €88/99; ☺mid-Mar–Oct; ❋@☂☀): decor is standard rural kitsch, but lovingly done, and you get your own terrace/balcony amid the jasmine, roses, bougainvillea and ivy. There's also a cool blue pool out back.

Parque Nacional de Doñana

The World Heritage–listed Parque Nacional de Doñana is a place of haunting natural beauty and exotic horizons, where flocks of flamingos tinge the evening skies pink above one of Europe's most extensive wetlands (the Guadalquivir delta), huge herds of deer and boar flit through *coto* (woodlands), and the elusive Iberian lynx battles for survival. Here, in the largest roadless region in Western Europe, and Spain's most celebrated national park, you can literally taste the scent of nature at her most raw and powerful.

The 542-sq-km national park extends 30km along or close to the Atlantic coast and up to 25km inland. Much of the perimeter is bordered by the separate **Parque Natural de Doñana**, under less strict protection, which forms a 538-sq-km buffer for the national park. The two *parques* together provide a refuge for 360 bird species and 37 types of mammal, including endangered species such as the Iberian lynx and Spanish imperial eagle (nine breeding pairs). They're also a crucial habitat for half a million migrating birds.

Since its inception in 1969, the national park has been under pressure from tourism operators, farmers, hunters, developers and builders who oppose the restrictions on land use. Ecologists, for their part, argue that Doñana is increasingly hemmed in by tourism and agricultural schemes, roads and other infrastructure that threaten to deplete its water supplies and cut it off from other undeveloped areas.

Some resident lynxes have been run over attempting to cross roads around Doñana (Spain lost 20 lynxes in road accidents in 2014). On the bright side, lynx numbers in the Doñana area now stand at around 80 to 100 individuals, despite a disastrous slump in numbers of its main prey, the rabbit, which led to park authorities introducing 10,000 new rabbits into the area in 2015. There's also an increasingly successful captive breeding program – up to 27 breeding pairs in 2015 (check out www.lynxexsitu.es). The Centro de Visitantes El Acebuche (p89) streams a live video of lynxes in its nearby breeding centre, but you can't visit them.

Access to the interior of the national park is restricted, although anyone can walk or cycle along the 28km Atlantic beach between Matalascañas and the mouth of the Río Guadalquivir (which can be crossed by boat from Sanlúcar de Barrameda in Cádiz province), as long as they do not stray inland.

The only way to visit the national park is by guided jeep tour with one of three licensed companies: Cooperativa Marismas del Rocío (p89), from the Centro de Visitantes El Acebuche; Doñana Reservas (p89), from El Rocío; and Visitas Doñana (p130), from Sanlúcar de Barrameda, in Cádiz province.

🏃 Activities

Four-hour, land-based trips in 20- to 30-person all-terrain vehicles are the only way to get inside the national park from the western side. The experience can feel a bit theme-park-like, but guides have plenty of in-depth information to share. You can pretty much count on seeing deer and wild boar, though ornithologists may be disappointed by the limited birdwatching opportunities, and you'd be very lucky to spot a lynx.

DOÑANA: LIFE CYCLES

The many interwoven ecosystems that make up the Parque Nacional de Doñana give rise to fantastic diversity. About 380 sq km of the park consists of *marismas* (marshes). These are almost dry from July to October, but in autumn they fill with water, eventually leaving only a few islets of dry land. Hundreds of thousands of waterbirds arrive from the north to winter here, including an estimated 80% of Western Europe's wild ducks. As the waters sink in spring, greater flamingos, herons, storks, spoonbills, avocets, hoopoes, bee-eaters and albatrosses arrive for the summer, many of them to nest. Fledglings flock around the *lucios* (ponds) and, as these dry up in July, herons, storks and kites move in to feast on trapped perch.

Between the marshlands and the park's 28km-long beach is a band of sand dunes, pushed inland by the wind by 2m to 5m per year. When dune sand eventually reaches the marshlands, rivers carry it back down to the sea, which washes it up on the beach – and the cycle begins again.

Elsewhere in the park, stable sands support 144 sq km of *coto* (woodland and scrub). *Coto* is the favoured habitat of many nesting birds and the park's abundant mammal population – 37 species including red and fallow deer, wild boar, wildcats and genets.

DOÑANA WALKS

The walking trails near the park's visitors centres are easy enough to be undertaken by most. The March–May and September–November migration seasons are the most exciting for birdwatchers.

Sendero Lagunas del Acebuche From the **Centro de Visitantes El Acebuche** (p89), the two Senderos del Acebuche (1.5km and 3.5km round trip) lead to birdwatching hides overlooking nearby lagoons (though these can get quite dry).

Sendero Charco de la Boca At the **Centro de Visitantes La Rocina** (p90), the Sendero Charco de la Boca is a 3.5km return walk along a stream, then through a range of habitats, passing four birdwatching hides.

Centro de Visitantes José Antonio Valverde (☑671 564145; ⊙10am-8pm Apr-Sep, to 6pm Oct-Mar) The remote Centro de Visitantes José Antonio Valverde, on the eastern edge of the park, is generally an excellent birdwatching spot as it overlooks a year-round *lucio* (pond). The easiest way to reach the centre is by authorised tour from El Rocío; the alternative is to drive yourself on rough roads from Villamanrique de la Condesa or La Puebla del Río to the northeast.

Raya Real The Raya Real, one of the most important routes used by Romería pilgrims on their journeys to and from El Rocío (p90), can be accessed from the northeastern edge of that village by crossing the Puente del Ajolí and following the track into the woodland. It crosses the Coto del Rey, a large woodland zone where you may spot deer or boar in the early morning or late evening.

During spring, summer and holidays, book at least a month ahead, but otherwise a week is usually sufficient notice. Bring binoculars (if you like), drinking water and mosquito repellent (except in winter). English-, German- and French-speaking guides are normally available if you ask in advance.

Cooperativa Marismas del Rocío WILDLIFE TOUR
(☑959 43 04 32; www.donanavisitas.es; Centro de Visitantes El Acebuche; tours €29.50) Runs four-hour tours of the national park in 20- to 30-person all-terrain vehicles, departing from the Centro de Visitantes El Acebuche (p89). Tours traverse 75km of the southern part of the park and cover all the major ecosystems – coast, dunes, marshes and Mediterranean forest. Trips start with a long beach drive, then head inland.

Doñana Reservas WILDLIFE TOUR
(☑959 44 24 74; www.donanareservas.com; Avenida de la Canaliega, El Rocío; tours per person €28) Runs four-hour tours in 20- to 30-person all-terrain vehicles, focusing on the marshes and woods in the northern section of the park, and including a stop at the Centro de Visitantes José Antonio Valverde (usually an excellent birdwatching spot). Recent reports of lynx sightings.

Doñana Nature WILDLIFE TOUR
(☑959 44 21 60; www.donana-nature.com; Calle Las Carretas 10, El Rocío; tours per person €28) Runs half-day, general interest tours of the Parque Natural de Doñana at 8am and 3pm daily (binoculars provided). Specialised ornithological and photographic trips are also offered. English-speaking guides available on request.

Doñana a Caballo HORSE RIDING
(☑674 219568; www.donanaacaballo.com; Avenida de la Canaliega, El Rocío; per 1hr/2hr/half-day €20/30/60) Guided horse rides for all levels through the Coto del Rey woodlands east of El Rocío.

ⓘ Information
The park has seven information points.
Centro de Visitantes El Acebuche (☑959 43 96 29; ⊙8am-9pm Apr–mid-Sep, to 7pm mid-Sep–Mar) Twelve kilometres south of El Rocío on the A483, then 1.6km west, El Acebuche is the national park's main visitor centre. It has paths to birdwatching hides and a live film of Iberian lynxes at its breeding centre.
Centro de Visitantes El Acebrón (☑671 593138; ⊙9am-3pm & 4-7pm) Located 6km along a minor paved road west from the Centro de Visitantes La Rocina (p90), this centre offers a Doñana information counter and an

ethnographic exhibition on the park inside a palatial 1960s residence, plus walking paths.

Centro de Visitantes La Rocina ([☑] 959 43 95 69; ⊙ 9am-3pm & 4-7pm) Beside the A483, 1km south of El Rocío. Has a national park information desk and walking paths.

⊙ Getting There & Away

You cannot enter the park in your own vehicle. **Damas** (www.damas-sa.es) runs eight to 10 buses daily between El Rocío and Matalascañas, which stop at the El Acebuche turn-off on the A483 on request. Some tour companies will pick you up from Matalascañas with advance notice.

El Rocío

POP 1340

El Rocío, the most significant town in the vicinity of the Parque Nacional de Doñana, surprises first-timers. Its streets, unpaved and covered in sand, are lined with colourfully decked-out single-storey houses with sweeping verandahs, left empty half the time. But this is no ghost town: these are the well-tended properties of 115 *hermandades* (brotherhoods), whose pilgrims converge on the town every Pentecost (Whitsunday) weekend for the Romería del Rocío, Spain's largest religious festival. And at most weekends, the *hermandades* arrive in a flurry of festive fun for other ceremonies.

Beyond its uniquely exotic ambience, El Rocío impresses with its striking setting in front of luminous Doñana *marismas* (wetlands), where herds of deer drink at dawn and, at certain times of year, pink flocks of flamingos gather in massive numbers.

Whether it's the play of light on the marshes, an old woman praying to the Virgin at the Ermita, or a girl passing by in a sultry flamenco dress, there's always something to catch the eye on El Rocío's dusky, sand-blown streets.

⊙ Sights & Activities

The marshlands in front of El Rocío, which have water most of the year, offer some of the best bird- and beast-watching in the entire Doñana region. Deer and horses graze in the shallows and you may be lucky enough to spot a big pink cloud of flamingos wheeling through the sky. Pack a pair of binoculars and stroll the waterfront promenade.

Ermita del Rocío CHURCH
(⊙ 8am-9pm Apr-Sep, to 7pm Oct-Mar) A striking splash of white at the heart of the town, the Ermita del Rocío was built in its present form in 1964. This is the permanent home of the celebrated Nuestra Señora del Rocío (Our Lady of El Rocío), a small wooden image of the Virgin dressed in long, jewelled robes, which normally stands above the main altar.

People arrive to see the Virgin every day of the year, and especially on weekends, when El Rocío's brotherhoods often gather for colourful celebrations.

DON'T MISS

SPAIN'S GREATEST RELIGIOUS PILGRIMAGE: ROMERÍA DEL ROCÍO

Every Pentecost (Whitsunday) weekend, seven weeks after Easter, El Rocío transforms from a quiet backwater into an explosive mess of noise, colour and passion. This is the culmination of Spain's biggest religious pilgrimage, the **Romería del Rocío**, which draws up to a million joyous pilgrims.

The focus of all this revelry is the tiny image of Nuestra Señora del Rocío (Our Lady of El Rocío), which was found in a marshland tree by a hunter from Almonte village back in the 13th century. When he stopped for a rest on the way home, the Virgin magically returned to the tree. Before long, a chapel was built on the site of the tree (El Rocío) and pilgrims started arriving.

Solemn is the last word you'd apply to this quintessentially Andalucian event. Participants dress in their finest Andalucian costume and sing, drink, dance, laugh and romance their way to El Rocío. Most belong to the 115 *hermandades* (brotherhoods) who arrive from towns all across southern Spain on foot, horseback and in colourfully decorated covered wagons.

The weekend reaches an ecstatic climax in the very early hours of Monday. Members of the Almonte *hermandad*, which claims the Virgin as its own, barge into the church and bear her out on a float. Violent struggles ensue as others battle for the honour of carrying La Blanca Paloma (the White Dove). The crush and chaos are immense, but somehow the Virgin is carried round to each of the *hermandad* buildings before finally being returned to the church in the afternoon. Upcoming dates: 15 May 2016, 4 June 2017 and 20 May 2018.

NIEBLA

Thirty kilometres east of Huelva on the A472 to Seville (4km north of the A49), the brilliantly preserved medieval town of Niebla makes a fascinating stop. Encircled by 2km of dusty-orange Moorish-era walls and with five original gates plus 46 towers, Niebla's old town and its narrow streets simmer with history.

Castillo de los Guzmán (☑959 36 22 70; Calle Campo del Castillo; admission €4.50; ☺10am-2pm & 4-7pm) Niebla's main attraction is the majestic 15th-century Castillo de los Guzmán, probably of Roman origins but built up into a palace fortress under Moorish rule. It's set around two open patios; in the dungeon below there's a spine-chilling torture museum. Also here is Niebla's **tourist office** (☑959 36 22 70; www.turismoniebla.com; ☺10am-2pm & 4-7pm).

Iglesia de San Martín (Plaza de San Martín; ☺mass 9am Fri) Just inside the Puerta del Socorro, the main gate into the old town, stands this Gothic-Mudéjar church split in two by a plaza.

Iglesia de Santa María de Granada (Plaza de Santa María; ☺mass 7pm Mon-Sat, noon Sun) On the central Plaza de Santa María, the beautiful Iglesia de Santa María de Granada was originally a Visigothic cathedral before becoming a 9th-century mosque then a Gothic-Mudéjar church in the 15th century.

Francisco Bernis Birdwatching Centre BIRDWATCHING
(☑959 44 23 72; www.seo.org; ☺9am-2pm & 4-6pm Tue-Sun) **FREE** About 700m east of the Ermita along the waterfront, this birdwatching facility backs on to the marshes. Flamingos, glossy ibis, spoonbills and more can be observed through the rear windows or from the observation deck with high-power binoculars (free). Experts here can help you identify species and inform you about visiting migratory birds and where to see them.

🛏 Sleeping

Hotels get booked up to a year ahead for the Romería del Rocío (p90).

Pensión Cristina PENSIÓN €
(☑959 44 24 13; pensioncristina@hotmail.com; Calle El Real 58; s/d incl breakfast €40/55; ❄🖧🛜) Just east of the Ermita, the friendly Cristina provides perfectly comfy, colourful rooms around a tile-lined patio with lots of plants (sadly, no marsh views). Downstairs, there's a popular **restaurant** (mains €9-14; ☺2-5pm & 8-11pm) serving paella, seafood and venison (the house special).

Hotel Toruño HOTEL €€
(☑959 44 23 23; www.toruno.es; Plaza Acebuchal 22; s/d incl breakfast €48/67; 🅿❄🛜) About 350m east of the Ermita, this brilliantly white villa stands right by the *marismas* (wetlands), where you can spot flamingos going through their morning beauty routine.

Inside, tile murals continue the ornithological theme – even in the shower! Rooms are bright and cosy, but only a few actually overlook the marshes. Breakfast is in the wonderful restaurant (p91), opposite.

Hotel La Malvasía HOTEL €€
(☑959 44 38 70; www.lamalvasiahotel.com; Calle Sanlúcar 38; s/d €66/94; ❄🖧🛜) This idyllic hotel occupies a grand *casa señorial* (manor house) overlooking the marshes at the eastern end of town. Rooms are crushed with character including rustic tiled floors, vintage El Rocío photos and floral-patterned iron bedsteads. Top-level units make great bird-viewing perches.

🍴 Eating

★ **Restaurante Toruño** ANDALUCIAN €€
(☑959 44 24 22; www.toruno.es; Plaza Acebuchal 22; mains €12-20; ☺8am-midnight) With its traditional Andalucian atmosphere, authentically good food and huge portions, this is El Rocío's one must-try restaurant. A highlight on the menu is the free-range *mostrenca* calf, unique to Doñana; for noncarnivores, the huge grilled veg *parrillada* is fantastic. On warm evenings dine in front of the restaurant by the 1000-year-old *acebuche* tree.

La Ermita ANDALUCIAN €€
(Calle El Real 5; mains €8.50-15; ☺8.30am-11.30pm daily Jun–mid-Sep, to 7.30pm Sun-Thu mid-Sep–May) Behind the Ermita, this tourist-oriented place relishes serving outsiders. Orders are

shouted back and forth, tables spill out onto the sand, and the food is classic homemade: *salmorejo* (a thick, garlicky, tomato-based version of gazpacho, with bits of ham), grilled fish or local *mostrenca* calf.

ℹ️ Information

Tourist Office (☑ 959 44 23 50; www.turismoalmonte.com; Calle Muñoz Pavón; ⊙9.30am-2pm) Inside the town hall.

ℹ️ Getting There & Away

Damas (www.damas-sa.es) buses run from Seville's Plaza de Armas to El Rocío (€6.36, 1½ hours, two daily), continuing to Matalascañas. From Huelva, take a Damas bus to Almonte, then another to El Rocío (eight daily).

NORTH OF HUELVA

North of Huelva, straight highways are replaced by winding byways and you enter a more temperate zone, up to 960m higher than the coast. The rolling hills of Huelva's portion of the Sierra Morena are covered with a thick pelt of cork oak and pine, punctuated by winding river valleys, enchanting stone-and-tile villages, and the bustling 'capital' of the area, Aracena.

Word is slowly getting out about this still little-discovered rural world, threaded with walking trails and blessed with a rich, and increasingly renowned, hill-country cuisine. Game, local cheeses and fresh vegetables abound, though the region's best-known product is its prized *jamón serrano* (mountain-cured ham). Most of the area lies within the 1870-sq-km Parque Natural Sierra de Aracena y Picos de Aroche, Andalucía's second-largest protected zone.

Minas de Riotinto

POP 3260 / ELEV 420M

Tucked away on the southern fringe of Huelva's Sierra Morena is one of the world's oldest mining districts; even King Solomon of faraway Jerusalem is said to have mined gold here for his famous temple. The Romans were digging up silver by the 4th century BC, but the mines were then left largely untouched until the British Rio Tinto company transformed the area into one of the world's key copper-mining centres in the 1870s (leading, incidentally, to the foundation of Spain's first football club here). The mines were sold back to Spain in 1954. Though the

miners clocked off for the last time in 2001, it's still a fascinating place to explore, with a superb museum, and the opportunity to visit the old mines and ride the mine railway.

The Río Tinto itself rises a few kilometres northeast of town, its name ('red river') stemming from the deep red-brown hue produced by the reaction of its acidic waters to the abundant iron and copper ores.

◉ Sights & Activities

Museo Minero MUSEUM
(☑ 959 59 00 25; www.parquemineroderiotinto.es; Plaza Ernest Lluch; adult/child €4/3; ⊙10.30am-3pm & 4-7pm; ℗) Riotinto's mining museum is a figurative goldmine for devotees of industrial archaeology, taking you through the area's unique history from the megalithic tombs of the 3rd millennium BC to the Roman and British colonial eras, the 1888 *año de los tiros* (year of the gunshots) upheaval and finally the closure of the mines in 2001. The tour includes an elaborate 200m-long re-creation of a Roman mine.

Within the display on the railways that served the mines, pride of place goes to the Vagón del Maharajah, a luxurious carriage built in 1892 for a tour of India by Britain's Queen Victoria, though she never actually used it.

Peña de Hierro MINE
(☑ 959 59 00 25; www.parquemineroderiotinto.es; adult/child €8/7; ⊙10.30am-3pm & 4-7pm) These are old copper and sulphur mines 3km north of Nerva (6km east of Minas de Riotinto). Here you see the source of the Río Tinto and a 65m-deep opencast mine, and are taken into a 200m-long underground mine gallery. There are three guaranteed daily visits but schedules vary, so it's essential to book ahead through the Museo Minero (by phone or online).

Ferrocarril Turístico-Minero TRAIN TOUR
(☑ 959 59 00 25; www.parquemineroderiotinto.es; adult/child €10/9; ⊙1.30pm & 5.30pm mid-Jul–mid-Sep, 1.30pm mid-Sep–mid-Jul, closed Mon-Fri Nov-Jan) A fun way to see the area (especially with children) is to ride the old mining train, running 22km (round trip) through the surreal landscape in restored early 20th-century carriages. The train parallels the river for the entire journey, so you can appreciate its constantly shifting hues. It's mandatory to book ahead. Tickets may be purchased either at the town's museum or the railway station.

Trips start at the old railway repair workshops 4km east of Minas de Riotinto off the road to Nerva. Commentary is in Spanish (with English-language handouts).

❶ Getting There & Away

Damas (www.damas-sa.es) runs five daily buses between Minas de Riotinto and Huelva (€6.88, 1¾ hours) Monday to Friday, three on weekends.

Aracena

POP 6700 / ELEV 730M

Sparkling white in its mountain bowl, the thriving old market town of Aracena is an appealingly lively place that's wrapped like a ribbon around a medieval church and ruined castle. With a stash of good places to eat and sleep, it makes an ideal Sierra de Aracena base.

⊙ Sights

Gruta de las Maravillas CAVE

(Cave of Marvels; ☑ 663 937876; Calle Pozo de la Nieve; tours adult/child €8.50/6; ☉ 10am-1.30pm & 3-6pm) Beneath the town's castle hill is a web of caves and tunnels carved from the karstic topography. An extraordinary 1km route takes you through 12 chambers and past six underground lakes, all beautifully illuminated and filled with weird and wonderful rock formations, which provided a backdrop for the film *Journey to the Center of the Earth*.

Tours are in Spanish (audio guides available) and depart according to demand. Tickets can sell out in the afternoons and on weekends when busloads of visitors arrive.

Museo del Jamón MUSEUM

(Gran Vía; adult/child €3.50/2.50; ☉ 10.45am-2.15pm & 3.30-7pm) The *jamón* for which the sierra is famed gets due recognition in this modern museum. You'll learn why the acorn-fed Iberian pig gives such succulent meat, about the importance of the native pastures in which they are reared, and about traditional and contemporary methods of slaughter and curing. One room is devoted to local wild mushrooms.

A discount is available when combined with a ticket for the Gruta de las Maravillas.

⊙ The Old Town

The handsome, cobbled Plaza Alta was originally the centre of the town. Here stands the elegant 15th-century Cabildo Viejo, the former town hall, with a grand Renaissance doorway (and a natural park information centre). From Plaza Alta, Calle Francisco Rincón descends the hill back towards town, passing a series of narrow streets attractively lined with humbler whitewashed houses, before finally entering the main Plaza del Marqués de Aracena, a lively square fronted by a few cafe-restaurants.

Castillo de Aracena CASTLE

Dramatically dominating the town are the tumbling, hilltop ruins of the *castillo*, an atmospheric fortification built by the kingdoms of Portugal and Castilla in the 12th century. Right beside is the Iglesia Prioral de Nuestra Señora del Mayor Dolor (☉ 10am-5pm, to 7.30pm Jul & Aug), a Gothic-Mudéjar hybrid built about a century later with attractive brick tracery on the tower, noted for its distinctive Islamic influence. Both are reached via a steep lane from Plaza Alta.

🏃 Activities

The hills and mountains around Aracena offer some of the most beautiful, and least known, walking country in Andalucía. Any time of year is a good time to hike here but spring, when the meadows are awash with wildflowers and carnival-coloured butterflies, is the best time to hit the trails. The Centro de Visitantes Cabildo Viejo (p95) can recommend walks of varying difficulty and give you basic maps; the tourist office (p95) sells a good map with dozens of suggested hikes.

Linares de la Sierra Walk HIKING

This sublime and fairly gentle 5km, two-hour ramble takes you down a verdant valley to beautifully sleepy Linares de la Sierra (p95). The signposted path (PRA48) is easy to find off the HU8105 on the southwestern edge of Aracena, 500m beyond the municipal swimming pool.

You can extend the walk to Alájar (4km, 1½ hours), with the option of returning to Aracena on the 4pm or 4.30pm bus (except Sunday).

Escuela de Equitación Barquera Alta HORSE RIDING

(☑ 627 594929; Finca Valbono, Ctra Aracena-Carboneras Km 1; 2hr rides per person €30) A friendly establishment organising horse rides through the countryside east of Aracena, plus classes. It's 1km northeast of town.

HUELVA & SEVILLA PROVINCES ARACENA

Aracena

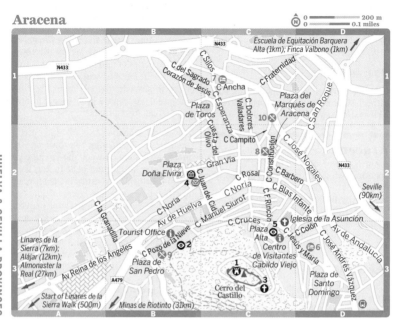

Aracena

◉ Sights
1 Castillo	C3
2 Gruta de las Maravillas	B3
3 Iglesia Prioral de Nuestra Señora del Mayor Dolor	C3
4 Museo del Jamón	B2
5 Plaza Alta	C3

🛏 Sleeping
6 Hotel Convento Aracena	D3
7 Molino del Bombo	C1

✗ Eating
8 Café-Bar Manzano	C2
9 Jesús Carrión	B3
10 Rincón de Juan	C1

🛏 Sleeping

Molino del Bombo BOUTIQUE HOTEL €
(☑959 12 84 78; www.molinodelbombo.com; Calle Ancha 4; s/d €36/60; ❈ 🛜) Though of recent vintage, the top-of-town Bombo has a rustic style that blends in with Aracena's time-worn architecture. Bright rooms have wonderfully comfy, pillow-laden beds, plus frescoes and exposed stone and brick designs; some bathrooms are done up as picturesque grottoes. The cosy salon and courtyard with trickling fountain are perfect for lounging.

Finca Valbono RURAL HOTEL €€
(☑959 12 77 11; www.fincavalbono.com; Ctra Aracena-Carboneras Km 1; s €64-80, d €80-100; 🅿❈🛜♨👪) Just 1km northeast of Aracena, this lovingly run farmhouse surrounded by greenery has 20 *casitas* (cottages) set up with log fires, kitchenettes and extra sofa-beds (perfect for groups or families), plus six rustic rooms. Most beds are twins. Other standout features include all-day breakfast (€8), a lovely pool and an on-site riding school (p93).

Hotel Convento Aracena HISTORIC HOTEL €€
(☑959 12 68 99; www.hotelconventoaracena. es; Calle Jesús y María 19; s €84-130, d €94-145; 🅿❈🛜♨) Glossy, straight-lined, modern rooms contrast with flourishes of original Andalucian baroque architecture at this recently converted 17th-century convent, your finest option in Aracena town. Room 9 is fabulously set in the church dome. Enjoy the on-site spa, good sierra cuisine, and year-round saltwater pool, with gorgeous village views and summer bar.

✗ Eating

The hills around Aracena have given rise to some superb, and increasingly innovative, cuisine. Delights include the region's mushrooms; dozens of different varieties pop up out of the ground every autumn. And then there's the ham: the *jamón ibérico* of nearby Jabugo is considered the finest in the entire country and as you explore these hills you won't fail to notice the providers of this bounty – contented-looking black pigs foraging in the forests for acorns.

★ Rincón de Juan TAPAS €

(Calle José Nogales; tapas €1.80-3, raciones €7-10; ⊙ 7.30am-4pm & 6.30pm-midnight Mon-Sat, 7.30am-4pm Sun) It's standing room only at this wedge-shaped, stone-walled corner bar, indisputably the top tapas spot in town. Iberian ham is the star attraction and forms the basis for a variety of *montaditos* (small stuffed rolls) and *rebanadas* (sliced loaves for several people). The local goat's cheese is always a good bet.

★ Jesús Carrión TAPAS, ANDALUCIAN €€

(☑ 959 46 31 88; www.jesuscarrionrestaurante.com; Calle Pozo de la Nieve 35; tapas €5-9, mains €10-17; ⊙ 1-4.30pm & 8-11pm Thu-Sat, 1-4.30pm Wed & Sun; ☎☑) Devoted chef Jesús heads up the creative kitchen at this wonderful family-run restaurant, which is causing quite the stir with its lovingly prepared, contemporary twists on traditional Aracena dishes. Try the Iberian ham carpaccio or the local boletus mushroom risotto. Homemade breads come straight from the oven and salads are deliciously fresh – not a tinned vegetable in sight!

Café-Bar Manzano TAPAS €€

(☑ 959 12 81 23; Plaza del Marqués de Aracena 22; raciones €6-14; ⊙ 8.30am-midnight Wed-Mon) This classy terrace cafe on the main plaza makes a great spot to watch Aracena go by as you enjoy tapas and *raciones* (full-plate servings) celebrating wild mushrooms and other local goodies. Such tempting toadstools as *tentullos, gurumelos* and *tanas* are served up sautéed or in enticing scrambles.

ℹ Information

Centro de Visitantes Cabildo Viejo (☑ 959 12 95 53; Plaza Alta; ⊙ 9.30am-2pm Thu-Sun) Gives out hiking information and maps, and has an exhibit on the Parque Natural Sierra de Aracena y Picos de Aroche.

Tourist Office (☑ 663 937877; www.aracena. es; Calle Pozo de la Nieve; ⊙ 10am-2pm & 4-6pm) Opposite the Gruta de las Maravillas; sells a good walking map.

ℹ Getting There & Around

The **bus station** (Avenida de Sevilla) is 700m southeast of Plaza del Marqués de Aracena.

Damas (www.damas-sa.es) runs one morning and two afternoon buses (one on Sunday) from Seville (€7.46, 1¼ hours), continuing to Cortegana via Alájar or Jabugo. From Huelva, there are two afternoon departures Monday to Friday, one at weekends (€11, three hours). There's also local service between Aracena and Cortegana via Linares, Alájar and Almonaster la Real.

Sierra de Aracena

Stretching west of Aracena is one of Andalucía's most unexpectedly picturesque landscapes, a flower-sprinkled hillcountry dotted with old stone villages and imposing castles. Woodlands alternate with expanses of *dehesa* (evergreen oak pastures where the region's famed black pigs forage for acorns). The area is threaded by an extensive network of well-maintained walking trails, with ever-changing vistas and mostly gentle ascents and descents, making for some of the most delightful rambling in Andalucía.

Great hiking routes are particularly thick in the area between Aracena and Cortegana, making attractive villages such as Alájar, Castaño del Robledo, Galaroza and Almonaster la Real perfect bases from which to set forth.

You can download Spanish- and English-language hiking information and maps from www.sierradearacena.com and www.ventanadelvisitante.es, but ideally you need a reliable map and walking guide. The best are Discovery Walking Guides' *Sierra de Aracena* and its partner *Sierra de Aracena Tour & Trail Map*.

ℹ Getting There & Around

BUS

All buses are operated by **Damas** (www.damas-sa.es). Monday to Saturday, morning and afternoon buses travel the HU8105 from Cortegana to Aracena, via Almonaster la Real, Alájar and Linares de la Sierra. Both return in the afternoon.

TRAIN

There's at least one daily train each way between Huelva and the stations of Almonaster-Cortegana (€9.50, 1¾ hours) and Jabugo-Galaroza (€11, two hours). Almonaster-Cortegana station is 1km off the Almonaster-Cortegana road, halfway between the two villages.

Linares de la Sierra

POP 230 / ELEV 505M

Just 7km west of Aracena along the HU8105, you'll bump into one of the area's cutest

Sierra de Aracena

villages, Linares de la Sierra. Surrounded by a verdant river valley, its cobbled streets are renowned for their 300-odd *llanos* (front-patio mosaics) and are lined with oddly angled, tiled-roof houses. In the centre, beside the 18th-century Iglesia de San Juan Bautista, a minute bullring plaza is paved with concentric rings around a shield of flowers. There's a little **visitors centre** (www.elvalleescondido.com; ☺9am-6pm Tue-Sun) with (limited) information on walks around Linares here.

Nearby, sample delicious, creative versions of local pork products and wild mushrooms, including mushroom-and-apple-stuffed *solomillo* (pork sirloin), at **Restaurante Arrieros** (☑959 46 37 17; www.arrieros.net; Calle Arrieros 2; mains €9-15; ☺1.30-4pm Tue-Sun, closed mid-Jun–mid-Jul), one of the sierra's top restaurants.

Alájar

POP 800 / ELEV 570M

Five kilometres west of Linares de la Sierra is possibly the region's most picturesque village, Alájar, which retains its narrow cobbled streets and cubist stone houses along with a fine baroque church. Several good walking routes leave from or pass through here.

◉ Sights & Activities

Peña de Arias Montano HISTORIC SITE

(P) High above Alájar, this rocky spur provides magical views over the village. The site takes its name from remarkable 16th-century polymath and humanist Benito Arias Montano, who repeatedly visited this spot for retreat and meditation. The *peña*'s

16th-century chapel, the **Ermita de Nuestra Señora Reina de los Ángeles** (☺11am-sunset), contains a small carving of the Virgin that is considered the patron of the whole Sierra de Aracena. Outside the chapel are stalls selling local honey and cheeses, and a **hiking information stall** (☑625 512442; ☺Fri-Sun, hours vary).

Castaño del Robledo Walk HIKING

Starting beside the bus stop on the western edge of Alájar, across the HU8105, this moderately difficult 5km uphill route leads you past the once deserted hamlet of El Calabacino, now an international artist/hippy colony, then on to the beautiful little village of Castaño del Robledo, passing through cork-oak and chestnut forest. Allow two hours.

🛏 Sleeping

★ **Posada de San Marcos** CASA RURAL €€

(☑959 12 57 12; www.posadasalajar.com; Calle Colón 12; s/d incl breakfast €60/95; P ✳ @ 🛜 🌊) 🌿 Hot on sustainability, this brilliantly restored 200-year-old village house bordering a stream on the southeastern edge of town runs on geothermal energy, rain harvesting and natural-cork insulation. The six comfortably rustic, airy rooms have big terraces, breakfast is homemade, and welcoming Spanish-English hosts Ángel and Lucy are experts on local hiking. The pool looks across the village to the *peña*.

They also run the cosy, more budget-friendly **Posada de Alájar** (Calle Médico Emilio González 2; s/d €40/55; ✳ 🛜 🌊) 🌿, where room 6 has gorgeous *peña* views.

★ Finca La Fronda RURAL HOTEL **€€**
(☑959 50 12 47; www.fincalafronda.com; Ctra
Cortegana-Aracena Km 22; r incl breakfast €115-
145; P✳🔊🛏📶) Pocketed away amid cork/
chestnut forest, La Fronda makes the perfect
hillside hideaway. Its modern-rustic beauty
comes out in the bright lounge, Mudéjar-in-
spired patio, and huge, flowery rooms with
splashes of British character (warm pastels,
smart armchairs). You can gaze out over Alájar's *peña* from the rose-fringed pool.

The efficient owners arrange *jamón* tastings, horse riding, live piano concerts and
hiking. It's signposted off the HU8105 2km
northeast of Alájar.

✗ Eating

Casa El Padrino ANDALUCIAN **€€**
(☑959 12 56 01; Plaza Miguel Moya 2; mains
€10-15; ⊙1.30-4pm & 9pm-midnight Fri & Sat,
1.30-4pm Sun) With atmospheric dining by
a brick-ring fireplace or on a sunny terrace,
El Padrino serves scrumptious country fare
loosely based on old village recipes. The
pencas de acelgas (Swiss chard stuffed
with Iberian pork) is memorable, as is the
lomo ibérico (Iberian pork loin) in chestnut
sauce, broiled to perfection.

Castaño del Robledo

POP 188 / ELEV 740M

North of Alájar on the minor HU8114 road
between Fuenteheridos and Jabugo, little
Castaño del Robledo is a truly idyllic spot,
surrounded by hazy green olive and cork
forests. Its jigsaw of tiled terracotta roofs
is overlooked by two large churches (one
unfinished), either of which could easily
accommodate the entire village population.

✦ Activities

**Castaño del Robledo–
Galaroza Loop Walk** HIKING
A nice 10km loop can be hiked by taking the
PRA38 trail from Castaño del Robledo to
Galaroza village and returning via the alternate SLA129 riverside route. The walk traverses varied woodlands interspersed with
long-distance panoramas. Wildflowers pop
up in spring and you're likely to spot some
of the *pata negra* pigs (black pigs) of Jabugo
fame rooting about for acorns. Allow about
three hours, excluding stops.

Leave via the unsigned path beside the
shrine in the Área Recreativa Capilla del
Cristo, on the HU8114 road passing along

the north of the village. To the left you'll
soon see Cortegana and Jabugo, before you
fork right, 15 minutes along the track. Your
path winds downhill until you cross the
Jabugo–Fuenteheridos trail after 10 minutes. About 50m beyond, go right at a fork.
In 10 minutes Galaroza comes into view as
you pass between its outlying *fincas* (rural
properties). Cross a small river on a footbridge and emerge on the N433 road three
minutes later. Walk left towards Galaroza,
skirting the town along the N433 for around
800m. Just before you reach a palm-studded
plaza, leave by a track on the left marked by
a 'Sendero Ribera del Jabugo' sign.

Fork right at a green-and-white-striped
post one minute from the sign, then turn left
at a 'Camino Galaroza-Castaño Bajo' sign five
minutes later down to a footbridge over a
stream. The path soon starts winding up the
Río Jabugo valley, a particularly lovely stretch
lined with poplars, willows and alders. Half an
hour from the footbridge you'll reach a vehicle track marked 'Camino de Jabugo a Fuenteheridos'. Head right, passing some *cortijos*
(farmhouses), to cross the river on a low
bridge. Turn left 50m past the bridge, then left
at a fork 30m further on. You recross the river
by stepping stone. Fifteen minutes from the
river, turn left at a red-tile-roofed house and
arrowed stump; in 15 minutes (mostly uphill)
you're re-entering Castaño del Robledo.

🛏 Sleeping

Posada del Castaño CASA RURAL **€**
(☑959 46 55 02; www.posadadelcastano.com; Calle
José Sánchez Calvo 33; s/d incl breakfast €40/50;
📶) This chilled-out converted village house,
with its bendy roof beams, big book collection and colourful throws, has walkers foremost in mind. The young British owners
(experienced travellers and hikers) are full
of information and offer self-guided walking tours and horse-riding holidays. Weather
permitting, homemade breakfast is served
on the back terrace overlooking the lush
garden.

✗ Eating

Restaurante Maricastaña ANDALUCIAN **€€**
(☑654 248583; Plaza del Álamo 7; mains €14-
19; ⊙1-4.30pm Thu-Sun, 8.30pm-midnight Fri &
Sat) Popular with weekending *sevillanos,*
Maricastaña puts an upscale urban spin on
sierra classics such as wild mushrooms and
jamón de bellota (served with eggplant, chestnut and sugar-cane syrup). Dining is by the

HUELVA & SEVILLA PROVINCES SIERRA DE ARACENA

open fire in the old house or on a brilliant terrace overlooking the village. You'll definitely need reservations on Sunday afternoon.

Almonaster la Real

POP 650 / ELEV 613M

Almonaster la Real is a peaceful village that harbours a fabulous gem of Islamic architecture.

◎ Sights & Activities

★ **Mezquita** MOSQUE
(Mosque; ⊗9am–dusk) FREE This little *mezquita* stands above the town about five minutes' walk from the main square. The almost perfectly preserved mosque, a rare find in this region, is like a miniature version of Córdoba's great mosque. Despite being Christianised in the 13th century, it retains nearly all its original Islamic features: the horseshoe arches, the semicircular mihrab, an ablutions fountain and various Arabic inscriptions. Even older are the capitals of the columns nearest the mihrab, which are Roman. The original square minaret adjoins the building. Just below is Almonaster's 19th-century bullring.

Iglesia de San Martín CHURCH
(Placeta de San Cristóbal) The Mudéjar Iglesia de San Martín has a 16th-century portal in the Portuguese Manueline style, unique in the region.

Cerro de San Cristóbal Walk HIKING
From the western end of town, this circular hiking route (5.5km, about 2½ hours) leads up to the Cerro de San Cristóbal (912m) for fantastic views across the sierra.

🛏 Sleeping & Eating

Posada El Camino HOTEL €
(⌨959 50 32 40; www.posadaelcamino.es; Ctra Cortegana-Aracena Km 6.8; s/d/tr €36/50/65; P✲🅢🅦) Popular with Spanish families, this salmon-pink motel-like lodging stands at the bottom of a hill of cork trees, with trails heading off nearby. Good regional cooking (wild mushrooms, ham-stuffed chard) is served in the country-style **restaurant** (mains €10-16; ⊗9am-midnight Tue-Sat, to 6pm Sun) with fireplace. It's half a kilometre east of Almonaster, just off the HU8105 to Alájar.

Restaurante Casa García ANDALUCIAN €€
(⌨959 14 31 09; Avenida San Martín 2; mains €11-17; ⊗1-4pm & 8.30-11.30pm) Serves gourmet versions of local fare in a cosy setting with a fireplace and brick arches.

SEVILLA PROVINCE

Just northwest of Seville you'll find the Roman ruins of Itálica, at Santiponce. To the east, the flat and fertile farmlands of La Campiña stretch into the fiery distance, a land of huge agricultural estates belonging to a few landowners, dotted with romantic old towns like Carmona, Osuna and Écija. Heading north, you'll hit the tranquil, largely untouristed hills of the Sierra Norte de Sevilla.

Santiponce

The plain town of Santiponce, 6km northwest of Seville (off the A66), is the location of Itálica, the most formidable Roman site in Andalucía, as well as the grand Gothic-Mudéjar former Monasterio de San Isidoro del Campo. It makes a fantastic day trip from Seville.

◎ Sights

★ **Itálica** ARCHAEOLOGICAL SITE
(⌨955 12 38 47; www.museosdeandalucia.es; Avenida de Extremadura 2; admission €1.50, EU citizens free; ⊗9am-3.30pm Tue-Sun mid-Jun–mid-Sep, 9am-5.30pm Tue-Sat & 9am-3.30pm Sun mid-Sep–mid-Jun; P) Itálica was the first Roman town in Spain, founded in 206 BC. It was the birthplace of the 2nd-century AD Roman emperor Trajan, and probably of his adopted son and successor Hadrian (he of the wall across northern England). Although emperors are fairly rare here today, what remains of those times are broad paved streets and ruins of houses built around patios of beautiful mosaics. Itálica also contains one of the biggest of all Roman **amphitheatres** (20,000 spectators).

The most notable houses are the **Casa de los Pájaros** (House of the Birds) and the **Casa del Planetario** (House of the Planetarium), with a mosaic depicting the gods of the seven days of the week.

Monasterio de San Isidoro del Campo MONASTERY
(⌨955 62 44 00; Avenida de San Isidoro del Campo 18; ⊗10am-2pm Wed-Sat year-round, 4-7pm Fri & Sat Oct-Mar, 5.30-8.30pm Fri & Sat Apr-Sep; P) FREE At the southern end of Santiponce, this exquisite, two-church former monastery was founded in 1301 by Guzmán El Bueno (p143) (hero of the 1294 battle at Tarifa). Over the centuries it hosted a succession of different religious orders, including the hermetic Hieronymite

monks who embellished the Patio de Evange-listas with particularly striking 15th-century murals of saints and Mudéjar-style floral and geometric patterns. It was here that the Bible was first translated into Castilian (1569).

Among the monastery's impressive Spanish art collection is a wonderful altarpiece by 17th-century Sevillan sculptor Juan Martínez Montañés.

❶ Getting There & Away

From Seville's Plaza de Armas, the M172 bus goes half-hourly to Santiponce (€1.17, 25 minutes), making its final stop at the entrance to the archaeological site.

Carmona

POP 23,200

Perched on a low hill 35km east of Seville, over-looking a hazy *vega* (valley) that sizzles in the summer heat, and dotted with ancient palaces and majestic monuments, Carmona comes as a surprise highlight of western Andalucía.

This strategic site was important as long ago as Carthaginian times. The Romans laid out a street plan that survives to this day: the Via Augusta, running from Rome to Cádiz, entered Carmona by the eastern Puerta de Córdoba and left by the western Puerta de Sevilla (both of which are still standing strong). The Muslims built a strong defensive wall around Carmona, but the town fell in 1247 to Fernando III. Later on Mudéjar and Christian artisans constructed grand churches, convents and mansions.

⊙ Sights

From the Puerta de Sevilla, it's an easy stroll through the best of old-town Carmona. Inside the **town hall** (☎954 14 00 11; Calle El Salvador; admission free; ⊙8am-3pm Mon-Fri) is a large, very fine Roman mosaic of the gorgon Medusa.

Alcázar de la Puerta de Sevilla　　　GATE
(adult/child €2/1, free Mon; ⊙10am-6pm Mon-Sat, to 3pm Sun) The impressive main gate of Carmona's old town is one element of a fortification that had already been standing for five centuries when the Romans reinforced it and built a temple on top. The Muslim Almohads added an *aljibe* (cistern) to the upper patio, which remains a hawklike perch from which to admire the typically Andalucian tableau of white cubes and soaring spires.

**Iglesia Prioral de
Santa María de la Asunción**　　　CHURCH
(☎954 19 14 82; Plaza Marqués de las Torres; admission €3; ⊙9.30am-2pm & 5.30-6.30pm Tue-Fri, to 2pm Sat) This splendid church was built mainly in the 15th and 16th centuries on the site of the former main mosque. The Patio de los Naranjos by which you enter has a Visigothic calendar carved into one of its pillars. Inside, the plateresque altar is detailed to an almost perverse degree, with 20 panels of biblical scenes framed by gilt-scrolled columns.

Museo de la Ciudad　　　MUSEUM
(☎954 14 01 28; www.museociudad.carmona.org; Calle San Ildefonso 1; adult/child €3/1, free Tue; ⊙10am-2pm Mon-Sun & 6.30-8.30pm Mon-Fri mid-Jun–Aug, 11am-7pm Tue-Sun & 11am-2pm Mon Sep–mid-Jun) Explore the town's fascinating history at the city museum, housed in a centuries-old palace, with pieces dating back to Paleolithic times. The sections on the Tartessians and their Roman successors are highlights: the former includes a unique collection of large earthenware vessels with Middle Eastern decorative motifs, the latter several excellent mosaics.

Convento de Santa Clara　　　CONVENT
(☎954 14 21 02; www.clarisasdecarmona.word-press.com; Calle Torno de Santa Clara; adult/child €2/1; ⊙11am-2pm & 4-6pm Thu-Mon) With its Gothic ribbed vaulting, carved Mudéjar-style ceiling and dazzling altarpiece – a shining example of Sevillan baroque – the Santa Clara convent appeals to both art and architecture buffs. Visits start with a spiral ascent of the tower, an 18th-century addition. Don't miss the pretty arch-lined cloister out the back.

★Necrópolis Romana　　　HISTORICAL SITE
(Roman cemetery; ☎600 143632; www.museos deandalucia.es; Avenida de Jorge Bonsor 9; ⊙9am-7pm Tue-Sat & 9am-3.30pm Sun Apr-May, 9am-3.30pm Tue-Sun Jun–mid-Sep, 9am-5.30pm Tue-Sat & 9am-3.30pm Sun mid-Sep–Mar) **FREE** On the southwestern edge of Carmona lie the remains of a Roman city of the dead. A dozen or more family tombs, some elaborate and many-chambered, were hewn into the rock here in the 1st and 2nd centuries AD. Most of the inhabitants were cremated, and in the tombs are wall niches for the boxlike stone urns. You can enter the huge Tumba de Servilia, the tomb of a family of Hispano-Roman VIPs, and climb down into several others.

Carmona

0 ――――――― 0.25 miles
N 500 m

Seville (35km)
Carmona Bike Tours (40m)
Constantina (59km)
Écija (53km)

Carretera de Brenes
C Cristo de la Sedia
C Juan de Ortega
Plaza de Lasso
Mirador
Plaza de las Descalzas
C de las Descalzas
C S M de Gracia
Plazuela de Santiago
C de Dolores Quintanilla
Iglesia de Santiago
C Calatrava
C Torno de Santa Clara
C María Auxiliadora
C Fermín Molpeceres
C San José
C San Ildefonso
C Ramón y Cajal
C General Freire
C Sor Ángela de la Cruz
C Hermanas de la Cruz
C Puerta de Marchena
Mirador
C Pedro I
C San Felipe
Iglesia de San Felipe
C Extramuros de San Felipe
Antigua Nacional IV
Osuna (62km)
C Arco de la Carne
C San Bartolomé
C San Felipe
Iglesia de San Bartolomé
C Domínguez
C Prim
C Madre de Dios
C Sancho Ibáñez
C Torno
Plaza Marqués de las Torres
Plaza de San Fernando
C El Salvador
la Plaza
C Torre del Oro
C Barbacana Alta
Buses to Córdoba & Écija
Buses to Seville
C González Parejo
C González Girón
C Santa Ana
C Beato Juan Grande
C B E Cerezo
C Antequera
C San Pedro
Iglesia de San Pedro
C La Fuente
Alameda de Alfonso XIII
C Real
Paseo del Estatuto
C San Francisco
C Enmedio
C Sevilla
Ronda León de San Francisco
Anfiteatro Romano (300m)
Necrópolis Romana (500m)

Carmona

⊙ **Sights**
1 Alcázar de la Puerta de Sevilla............C3
2 Ayuntamiento...E3
3 Convento de Santa Clara.....................E2
4 Iglesia Prioral de Santa María
  de la Asunción E2
5 Museo de la Ciudad E2

🛏 **Sleeping**
6 El Rincón de las Descalzas E2
7 Hostal Comercio C3
8 Parador de Carmona...........................G3
9 Posada San Fernando D3

🍴 **Eating**
10 Bar Goya D3
11 Mingalario E3
12 Molino de la Romera...........................F3

The site also features an interesting museum displaying objects found in the tombs. Across the street is the 1st-century BC **Anfiteatro Romano**, though you can't go in.

🚴 Activities

Carmona Bike Tours　　BICYCLE TOUR
(✆617 265798; www.carmonabiketours.com; Calle Mimosa 15; tours per person €18, bicycle hire per day €10) This energetic operation is run by two keen local cyclists. Tours (English or Spanish) take historical routes through town or venture out into the beautiful, little-explored surrounding Campiña. Book ahead.

🛏 Sleeping

Hostal Comercio　　HOSTAL €
(✆954 14 00 18; hostalcomercio@hotmail.com; Calle Torre del Oro 56; s/d €35/50; ※ 🛜) Just inside the Puerta de Sevilla, the long-standing, old-fashioned Comercio provides 14 spiffy, simple rooms around a plant-filled patio with Mudéjar-style arches. Unpretentious decor is matched by friendly service, cultivated over generations.

Posada San Fernando　　BOUTIQUE HOTEL €€
(✆954 14 14 08; www.posadasanfernando.es; Plaza de San Fernando 6; s/d €55/68; ※ 🛜) This excellent-value hotel stands on Carmona's liveliest square. Each room in the 16th-century building oozes individual character thanks to hand-painted bathroom tiles, antique furnishings and the odd claw-foot bathtub; some have balconies overlooking the palm-lined plaza. Downstairs, there's a breakfast cafe.

El Rincón de las Descalzas　　BOUTIQUE HOTEL €€
(✆954 19 11 72; www.elrincondelasdescalzas.com; Calle de las Descalzas 1; incl breakfast s €52, d €66-82; ※ 🛜) Tucked into a quiet old-town corner, this stylishly revamped 18th-century home offers 13 elegant rooms in all different colours, rambling up around orange-toned patios with fountains. All have their own quirk (exposed stone walls, 100-year-old wood-carved beds); some are noticeably nicer, and 'Antífona', with its raised bath and brick arches, is a great choice.

Parador de Carmona　　HISTORIC HOTEL €€€
(✆954 14 10 10; www.parador.es; Calle Alcázar; r €188; P ※ @ 🛜 ☲) With jaw-dropping, unexpected views of the surrounding valley roasting under the Sevillan sun, Carmona's luxuriously equipped *parador* (top-end state-owned hotel) feels even more sumptuous for the ruined Alcázar in its grounds. Most of the smart, shiny-terracotta-floored rooms overlook the plains. The beautiful dining room serves a three-course €33 *menú*, or just pop in for coffee: the terrace is divine. Best rates online.

🍴 Eating

Mingalario　　TAPAS, ANDALUCIAN €
(✆954 14 38 93; Calle El Salvador; montaditos €2.50, tapas €2-4; ⊙1-4pm & 7.30pm-midnight Wed-Mon) This small, old eatery with hams hanging from the rafters is big on *montaditos* – small toasted sandwiches stuffed with goodies like roast pork or garlic prawns. You'll find all kinds of homemade local favourites like *presa ibérica* (Iberian pork), spinach with chickpeas (a Carmona special) and *bacalao* (cod) gratin.

Bar Goya　　TAPAS, RACIONES €€
(Calle Prim 2; raciones €5-12; ⊙8am-11pm Sat-Mon & Thu, 8am-3pm Tue, noon-11pm Fri; 🌱) From the kitchens of this ever-crammed bar on Plaza de San Fernando comes forth a fabulous array of tasty tapas. Apart from such carnivores' faves as *carrillada* (pigs' cheeks) and *menudo* (tripe), chef Isabel offers pure vegetarian treats such as *alboronía* (a delicious veg stew) and an excellent Carmona spinach (blended with chickpeas).

Molino de la Romera　　TAPAS, ANDALUCIAN €€
(✆954 14 20 00; www.molinodelaromera.com; Calle Sor Ángela de la Cruz 8; mains €17-20; ⊙1-4pm & 8-11pm Tue-Sat, 1-4pm Sun) Housed in a cosy 15th-century olive-oil mill with wonderful views across the *vega* (valley), this

HUELVA & SEVILLA PROVINCES CARMONA

popular restaurant serves hearty, well-prepped meals with a splash of contemporary flair. Traditional Andalucian flavours rule (try the Carmona spinach), but tasty novel variations include fish flambéed in vodka, and *secreto ibérico* (a succulent section of Iberian pork loin) with candied pumpkin.

ℹ Information

Tourist Office (☑ 954 19 09 55; www.turismo. carmona.org; Alcázar de la Puerta de Sevilla; ☺10am-6pm Mon-Sat, to 3pm Sun)

ℹ Getting There & Away

BUS

Monday to Friday, **Casal** (www.autocarescasal. com) runs hourly buses to Seville (€2.80, one hour) from the **stop** on Paseo del Estatuto, less often on weekends. **Alsa** (www.alsa.es) has three daily buses to Córdoba (€9.72, 1½ hours) via Écija (€4.71, 35 minutes) from the car park next to the Puerta de Sevilla.

CAR & MOTORCYCLE

There's 24-hour underground parking on Paseo del Estatuto (€1.20 per hour).

Osuna

POP 17,300

The legacy of a fabulously wealthy line of dukes who loaned the town its name, Osuna dazzles unsuspecting visitors with its beautifully preserved baroque mansions and impressive Spanish Renaissance monastery filled with art treasures. This startling tableau unfolds like a mirage amid an otherwise empty landscape, as if its cache of architectural and artistic gems were no big deal.

It's 91km southeast of Seville, along the Granada–Seville A92.

◉ Sights

★**Colegiata de Santa María de la Asunción** CHURCH
(☑954 81 04 44; Plaza de la Encarnación; guided tours €3; ☺10am-1.30pm & 4-6.30pm Tue-Sun) This imposing Renaissance structure – two churches above a crypt – overlooks Osuna from the site of the ancient parish church. Its halls contain a wealth of fine art and treasure collected by the House of Osuna, including paintings by José de Ribera (El Españoleto) and sculpted works by Juan de Mesa.

Visits are by Spanish-language guided tour, which includes the grand underground sepulchre, created in 1548 as the family vault of the Osunas, who are entombed in wall niches.

Museo de Osuna MUSEUM
(☑954 81 57 32; Calle Sevilla 37; admission €2; ☺10am-2pm & 5-8pm Tue-Sat, to 2pm Sun) Housed in the 18th-century Palacio de los Hermanos Arjona y Cubas, Osuna's museum displays an eclectic mix of local relics, including an excellent presentation on the area's scholarly prowess.

Monasterio de la Encarnación MUSEUM
(Plaza de la Encarnación; admission €2.50; ☺10am-1.30pm & 3.30-6.30pm) This former monastery is now Osuna's museum of religious art. Its church boasts baroque sculpture and art, while the cloister features tiled tableaux depicting various biblical, hunting, bullfighting, monastic and seasonal scenes that are among the most beautiful of Sevillan tilework. Entry is by guided tour only (in Spanish), led by one of the resident nuns.

OSUNA'S BAROQUE MANSIONS

The triangle west of Plaza Mayor is sprinkled with mansions and churches and cut up by lovely little streets and passages. Calle Sevilla, which leads west off the main square, and Calle San Pedro, a few blocks north, are particularly packed with stately buildings. You can't go inside most, but their facades are still mesmerising.

One of the most impressive is the late 18th-century **Palacio de los Cepeda** (Calle de la Huerta 10), with rows of churrigueresque columns topped by stone halberdiers holding the Cepeda family coat of arms; now Osuna's courthouse, it's just behind the town hall. The portal of the 18th-century **Palacio de Govantes y Herdara** (Calle Sevilla 44), 350m west of Plaza Mayor, has twisted pillars encrusted with grapes and vine leaves. The facade of the 1773 **Cilla del Cabildo Colegial** (Calle San Pedro 16) bears a sculpted representation of Seville's Giralda.

The **Palacio Marqués de la Gomera** (Calle San Pedro 20), now a **hotel** (p103), features elaborate pillars on its facade, with the family shield at the top.

🛏 Sleeping

Five Gates Hostal　　　　　　HOSTAL €
(☑626 620717; www.fivegates.es; Calle Carrera
79; s/d €30/50; ❄🛜) A simple, modern establishment with plenty of colour and flair.
The 14 compact rooms are stylishly decorated with cheery bedspreads, colourful walls
and massage showers, and the facilities are
great: a big lounge with games and DVDs,
a terrific guest kitchen and complimentary
coffee and pastries. It's 350m north of Osuna's main square.

**★Hotel Palacio Marqués
de la Gomera**　　　　　HISTORIC HOTEL €€
(☑954 81 22 23; www.hotelpalaciodelmarques.
es; Calle San Pedro 20; incl breakfast s €68-79, d
€78-98; P❄@🛜) Occupying one of Osuna's
finest baroque mansions, this is an exceptionally beautiful place to stay, with individually styled rooms of princely proportions
and quiet luxury. It even has its own ornate
private chapel beside a sumptuous arched
courtyard, plus a smart restaurant and
peaceful back patio.

From Plaza Mayor, head 300m up Calle
Carrera and turn left on Calle San Pedro; it's
one block west, facing Plaza del Marqués.

🍴 Eating

★Casa Curro　　　　　　　TAPAS €
(☑955 82 07 58; www.facebook.com/restauran-
tecasacurro; Plazuela Salitre 5; tapas €2, mains
€6-12; ⊙noon-4pm & 8pm-midnight Tue-Sun; 🖊)
Welcome to the tapas bar of your dreams, a
fabulous blend of tradition and nouvelle cuisine. Plate after plate issues from the corner
kitchen at this popular hall: crunchy grilled
wild mushrooms, cheese-and-ham-stuffed
courgette, Iberian 'secret' in a quince sauce.
And yes, that's a dedicated *Game of Thrones*
menu – the avocado, spinach and pomegranate Khaleesi salad is delicious.

It's 500m west of Plaza Mayor.

Confitería Santo Domingo　　　BAKERY €
(Calle Carrera 63; pastries €1; ⊙10am-2pm &
4-9.30pm Wed-Mon) This little bakery on Osuna's main street is famous for its *aldeanas*:
elongated, sugar-dusted pastries filled with
vanilla-y cream.

Restaurante Doña Guadalupe ANDALUCIAN €€
(☑954 81 05 58; Plaza Guadalupe 6; mains €11-
21; ⊙noon-5pm & 8pm-midnight Tue-Sat) To the
happy murmurings of its many patrons,
the smart Doña Guadalupe serves up quality Andalucian cooking from partridge with

OSUNA'S GAME OF THRONES MOMENT

In late 2014 Osuna sprang into the spotlight as an unlikely filming location for
the fifth season of hit TV show *Game of
Thrones*. Osuna's 100-year-old **Plaza
de Toros** (adult/child €2/1; ⊙10am-2pm
& 4-6pm Sat, 10am-2pm Sun) starred as
the Great Pit of Daznak, the fighting pit
of Meereen, and around 600 *osunense*
extras jumped in as battling slaves and
spectating nobles. The town has embraced its newfound fame with a flurry
of excitement. Just mention *Juego de
Tronos* to someone at **Hotel Palacio
Marqués de la Gomera** (p103), which
hosted the actors, or dig into *Game of
Thrones*–themed tapas at cast favourite
Casa Curro.

rice to wild asparagus casserole and all
kinds of tasty tortillas, along with a good
Spanish wine list. It opens out on a semi-
private courtyard between Calles Quijada
and Gordillo.

ℹ Information

Oficina Municipal de Turismo (☑954 81 57
32; www.turismosuna.org; Calle Sevilla 37;
⊙10am-2pm & 5-8pm Tue-Sat, 10am-2pm Sun)
Inside the Museo de Osuna.

ℹ Getting There & Away

The **bus station** (Avenida de la Constitución)
is 1km southeast of Plaza Mayor. **Autocares
Valenzuela** (☑954 98 82 20; www.grupovalen-
zuela.com) runs at least seven daily buses (four
on Sunday) to Seville (€8.05, 1¼ hours).

Ten trains daily go to Seville (€11, one hour)
and five to Málaga (€14, 1½ hours), from the
train station 1km west of Plaza Mayor.

Écija

POP 38,700

Easily the least visited of the Campiña
towns, Écija for that very reason offers a
genuine insight into Andalucian urban life.
Crammed with Gothic-Mudéjar palaces and
churches, the towers of which glitter in the
sun, this is *la ciudad de las torres* (the city
of towers). To the Romans, it was Colonia
Augusta Firma Astigi, one of the main cities
of their Iberian realm, which struck it rich
supplying far-flung markets with olive oil.

ÉCIJA'S CHURCHES & BELL TOWERS

Écija's spire-studded townscape is a constant reminder of its prosperous past, though some structures toppled as a result of Lisbon's great earthquake in 1755. One of the finest towers belongs to the Giralda-like **Iglesia de Santa María** (Plaza de Santa María; ⊘ 9.30am-1.30pm & 5-8.30pm Mon-Sat, 9.30am-1.30pm Sun), just off Plaza de España, while that of the **Iglesia de San Juan** (Plaza de San Juan; admission €2; ⊘ 10.30am-1.30pm & 4-7pm Tue-Sat, 10.30am-1.30pm Sun) rises like a frosted wedding cake a few blocks northeast (this is the only bell tower you can climb). The Gothic-Mudéjar **Iglesia de San Pablo-Santo Domingo** (Plaza de Santo Domingo; ⊘ 6.30-7.30pm Tue-Fri, 7-8pm Sat, 11.30am-12.30pm & 7-8pm Sun), north of the square, is startlingly strung with a gigantic set of rosary beads.

The **Parroquia Mayor de Santa Cruz** (Plazuela de Nuestra Señora del Valle; ⊘ 10am-1pm & 4-8pm Tue-Sat, 10am-1pm & 6-9pm Sun), four blocks north of Plaza de España, was once the town's principal mosque and still has traces of Islamic features and some Arabic inscriptions. Beyond a roofless atrium is an interior crammed with sacred paraphernalia and baroque silverwork. A sarcophagus in front of the altar dates from the early Christian period, with a chiselled likeness of Daniel flanked by a pair of lions.

Roman remains lie strewn across town, including under the main plaza.

Écija is 53km east of Carmona on the A4 between Córdoba and Seville. Try to avoid July and August, when temperatures soar to a suffocating 45°C and Écija sizzles as *la sartén de Andalucía* (the frying pan of Andalucía).

◉ Sights

The centre of life is the cafe-lined Plaza de España, otherwise known as El Salón (the parlour), around which sprawls the old quarter.

Museo Histórico Municipal　　MUSEUM
(⊘ 954 83 04 31; http://museo.ecija.es; Plaza de la Constitución 1; ⊘ 10am-2pm Tue-Sun Jun-Sep, 10am-1.30pm & 4.30-6.30pm Tue-Sat, 10am-3pm Sun Oct-May) **FREE** The 18th-century Palacio de Benamejí houses the city's impressive history museum. Pride of place goes to the best Roman finds from the area, including a marble sculpture of an Amazon (legendary female warrior). The upper level features a hall devoted to six fantastically preserved Roman mosaics, some unearthed beneath Écija's central square, with one tableau depicting the 'birth' of wine. If you ask, someone will lead you up to the *mirador* (lookout), which has wonderful panoramic city views.

Palacio de Peñaflor　　PALACE
(Calle Emilio Castelar 26) The huge 18th-century 'Palace of the Long Balconies', 300m east of Plaza de España, is Écija's most iconic image. Though the interior is closed indefinitely for potential renovations, the curved, fresco-lined facade is bewitching enough, morning or evening.

🛏 Sleeping

Hotel Palacio de los Granados　　HISTORIC HOTEL €€
(⊘ 955 90 53 44; www.palaciogranados.com; Calle de Emilio Castelar 42; d/ste incl breakfast €88/110; P ❄ 🛜 🏊) This small palace, some sections of which date back to the 16th century, has been carefully restored by its architect owner. Lavishly furnished chambers surround a quiet patio. From central Plaza de España, go south on Avenida Miguel de Cervantes, then 450m east on Calle de Emilio Castelar.

Hidden away out the back is a romantic little courtyard full of jasmine and orange trees overlooking a turquoise swimming pool.

🍴 Eating

Hispania　　TAPAS €€
(⊘ 954 83 26 05; www.hispaniacafe.com; Pasaje Virgen de Soterraño; tapas €2-5, mains €10-16; ⊘ noon-4pm & 8.30pm-1am Tue-Sun) Stylish, friendly and packed with *ecijanos*, this sidestreet operation has a bold colour scheme that matches its experimental kitchen. The innovative chefs just keep coming up with new creations that give classic Spanish cooking a contemporary zing, whether they're doing tapas, *bocatas* (sandwiches), desserts or *revueltos* (scrambled egg dishes). Book ahead Thursday to Saturday.

ℹ Information

Tourist Office (⊘ 955 90 29 33; www.turismo ecija.com; Calle Elvira 1; ⊘ 9am-3pm & 5-7pm)

ℹ Getting There & Away

Alsa (www.alsa.es) buses depart from the **bus station** (Avenida del Gil) for Carmona (€4.71, 35 minutes, two daily), Córdoba (€5.01, one hour, five daily) and Seville (€7.32, 1¼ hours, three daily).

Parque Natural Sierra Norte de Sevilla

This 1775-sq-km protected zone, stretching across the far north of Sevilla province, presents an ever-changing landscape of deep green valleys and gentle hills, woodlands, rivers and atmospheric old towns and villages with Islamic-era forts or castles and tight white streets. Combined with Huelva province's Parque Natural Sierra de Aracena y Picos de Aroche (p95), it makes up the most westerly section of Andalucía's great Sierra Morena. You could spend days drifting around these lazy back roads enjoying the sierra's numerous walking and cycling trails with little to no competition from other foreign travellers.

Eighteen walks, mostly of a few hours' duration, are signposted in various areas. The tourist offices in Cazalla de la Sierra (p107) and Constantina (p107) can suggest local hikes and give you a basic map; there are further resources online at www.ventanadel visitante.es. The Centro de Visitantes El Robledo (p107), 1km west of Constantina, also hands out hiking information.

ℹ Getting There & Away

Autocares Valenzuela (www.grupovalenzuela. com) runs buses between Cazalla de la Sierra and Seville (€6.79, 1¾ hours) via El Pedroso four times daily Monday to Friday, twice on weekends.

Cazalla de la Sierra

POP 4800 / ELEV 600M

This attractive little white town spread around a hilltop, 85km northeast of Seville, sits in the heart of the Parque Natural Sierra Norte, making it the ideal base for exploring. Cazalla has a great selection of places to stay and eat, and lovely walks through the surrounding woods.

✦ Activities

Las Laderas–
Camino Viejo Loop Walk   HIKING
These two hiking tracks lead down from Cazalla to the Huéznar Valley, passing through typical Sierra Norte evergreen oak woodlands, olive groves and small cultivated plots, plus the odd chestnut wood and vineyard. By combining them you can enjoy a 9km round trip (about three hours).

The first is the **Sendero de las Laderas**, which starts at El Chorrillo fountain on the eastern edge of Cazalla at the foot of Calle Azahín. A 'Sendero de las Laderas 900m' sign on Paseo El Moro, just down from the Posada del Moro, directs you to this starting point. The path leads down to the Puente de los Tres Ojos bridge on the Río Huéznar, from where you go up the western bank of the river a short way, then head west under the Puente del Castillejo railway bridge and return to Cazalla by the **Camino Viejo de la Estación** (Old Station Track).

Vía Verde de la Sierra Norte   CYCLING
(www.viasverdes.com) One of the most popular among Andalucía's 23 *vías verdes* (greenways), this 18km cycling (and walking) route leads north through the Huéznar Valley below Cazalla to the village of San Nicolás del Puerto and on south to the old Cerro del Hierro mines, running along a disused mining railway. Bicycle hire is available from Paraíso del Huéznar (p105) at the beginning of the *vía*, 8km east of Cazalla on the A455.

☰ Sleeping

La Plazuela   CASA RURAL €
(☐ 954 42 14 96; www.casarural-laplazuela.es; Calle Caridad 4; s €42, d €60-75; ✳ 🛜) This tastefully converted old townhouse overlooks the main pedestrian lane in Cazalla's core. Aimed at weekending *sevillanos,* all nine rooms have been uniquely renovated in neo-rustic style with brightly coloured walls, lively tiling and smart white bedspreads.

Paraíso del Huéznar   RURAL HOTEL €
(☐ 955 95 42 03; www.paraisodelhueznar.com; Ctra A455 Km 8; per person incl breakfast €30; 🅿 🛜 🏊) At the start of the Vía Verde (p105), 8km east of Cazalla on the A455 to Constantina, the efficiently managed Paraíso has five straightforward, welcoming *casitas* (cottages; some doubles, others for up to eight) with fully equipped kitchens, log fires and hydromassage showers. There's handy on-site **bicycle hire** (per day guest/nonguest €5/10; ⏰ 9am-dusk).

★ Las Navezuelas   COUNTRY HOUSE €€
(☐ 954 88 47 64; www.lasnavezuelas.com; Ctra A432 Km 43.5; s/d/ste incl breakfast €50/62/88, 4-person apt €130; ⏰ Mar-Dec; 🅿 🏊 🐾) ⭑ From the dusty, olive-tree-lined track to the vines clambering up the balcony of your rustic

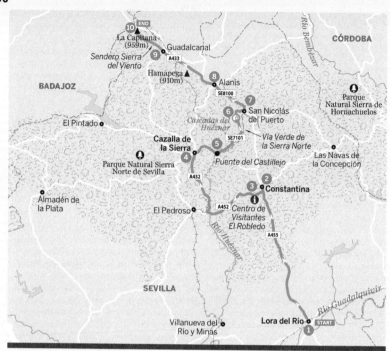

Driving Tour
Sierra Norte de Sevilla

START LORA DEL RÍO
END LA CAPITANA
LENGTH 105KM; 10 HOURS

Venturing up into the Parque Natural Sierra Norte de Sevilla from the south makes for a startling transition and an exhilarating drive. From Seville, follow the A4 and the A457 to ❶ **Lora del Río**, then take the A455 north. The orange groves recede and you start climbing, at each bend enjoying varied vistas of green hills. Soon you enter the park proper; continue climbing to ❷ **Constantina** (p107) and pop into one of its wonderfully traditional cafes. Then head west along the A452 to the ❸ **Centro de Visitantes El Robledo** (p107), where you can pick up walking maps and wander the botanical garden. Wind west on the A452 through hilly countryside, mists clinging to the mountains as they recede into the distance. As you cross the Río Huéznar an old aqueduct appears. Turn right on the A432 and drive 12km north to ❹ **Cazalla de la Sierra** (p105), the

shining 'capital' of the sierra. Lunch on the exquisitely traditional and inventive mountain tapas here, then wander the town and stay overnight. Head north out of Cazalla and pick up the A455 back towards Constantina. This road crosses the Río Huéznar just east of the Cazalla-Constantina train station. A bumpy 1km drivable track leads downstream from here to the ❺ **Puente del Castillejo** railway bridge. Upstream, the river is paralleled by the SE7101 road which runs 13km to San Nicolás del Puerto. Two kilometres before the village are the ❻ **Cascadas del Huéznar**, a series of powerful waterfalls. From ❼ **San Nicolás del Puerto**, take the SE8100 northwest. The landscape gets more dramatic as you approach ❽ **Alanís**, topped by a medieval castle. Continue northwest on the A433, along the edge of the park, to remote, windswept ❾ **Guadalcanal**. North of town, get out of the car and hit the hiking trail: the 5km (two-hour) Sendero Sierra del Viento follows a ridge to ❿ **La Capitana**, the park's highest peak (959m) and the perfect lookout point for wrapping up your tour.

room, this 16th-century, eco-conscious *cortijo* (farmhouse) is the ideal rural retreat. You could stay for weeks lounging by the pool and exploring the sunburnt hills. It's signposted 3km south of Cazalla on the A432 to Seville.

Italian owner Luca and family prepare wonderful meals (hotel guests only) using organic ingredients from their garden. Their heating system is powered by solar and geothermal energy.

✗ Eating

★ Agustina
TAPAS, ANDALUCIAN €€

(☑954 88 32 55; Plaza del Concejo; tapas €3.50-7, mains €8-12; ☺noon-5pm & 7pm-midnight Wed-Mon) The youthful owners of this sophisticated, city-feel bar/restaurant create traditional sierra dishes with a creative, wider-world flourish – a lovely surprise in little Cazalla. The speciality *queso de cabra con miel* (goat's cheese with honey) is fabulous, as is the *revuelto* of local wild mushrooms. It's 300m south of the main Calle La Plazuela, along Calle Cervantes.

Cortijo Vistalegre
ANDALUCIAN, ITALIAN €€

(☑954 88 35 13; www.cortijovistalegre.es; Ctra Real de la Jara Km 0.5; mains €8-15; ☺noon-4pm & 8pm-midnight Wed-Sun) Fancy sierra wines and platters of local *jamón ibérico* or goat's cheese, followed by...delicious homemade pizza or mushroom-stuffed pasta? Then you'll love this smartly rustic *cortijo,* just off the A450 on the southwestern edge of town. Colourful wall hangings, candle-lit tables and an open log fire set the indoors scene, or you can dine on the huge terrace outside.

ℹ Information

Tourist Office (☑954 88 35 62; www.cazalladelasierra.es; Plaza Mayor; ☺10am-2pm Tue-Thu, 10am-2pm & 4-7pm Fri & Sat, 11am-1pm Sun)

Constantina

POP 6300 / ELEV 555M

Constantina is the Sierra Norte's biggest town, but it still has plenty of charm. Cars and trucks rumble down the central Calle del Peso and everyone retreats into utterly traditional cafes where the purest olive oil is poured from silver ewers.

◉ Sights & Activities

Castillo Árabe
CASTLE

(☺9am-9pm) FREE Topping the western side of town, Constantina's ruined Almoravid-era Islamic fort is worth the climb for the views alone. Below are the medieval streets and 18th-century mansions of the Barrio de la Morería.

Los Castañares Walk
HIKING

The 5.5km Sendero Los Castañares trail takes you up through thick, peaceful chestnut woods to a hilltop viewpoint, then loops back down into Constantina to the driveway of the ruined fort (about two hours total). It's signposted from Paseo de la Alameda at the north of town.

✗ Eating

Asador Los Navarro
GRILL €

(☑954 49 63 61; www.asadorlosnavarro.com; Paseo de la Alameda 39; tapas €2.50, raciones €7-12; ☺9am-11pm Thu-Tue) Often filled with families and friends, this rustic barn at the north end of town dishes up succulent grilled meats as big combo plates or tapas, plus local wines.

ℹ Information

Centro de Visitantes El Robledo (☑610 663214; Ctra Constantina-El Pedroso Km 1; ☺10am-2pm Wed-Sun Feb-May, 10am-2pm Thu-Sun Oct-Dec & Jun, 10am-2pm Fri-Sun Jul-Sep & Jan) The park's main visitors centre, 1km west of Constantina along the A452, offers limited hiking information and maps. There's also a clearly labelled botanical garden of Andalucian plants divided into regional environments.

Oficina Municipal de Turismo (☑955 88 12 97; Avenida de Andalucía; ☺10am-2pm Tue-Sun)

El Pedroso

A pleasant village of broad cobbled streets, El Pedroso lies 16km south of Cazalla de la Sierra on the A432 from Seville. The **Sendero del Arroyo de las Cañas**, a 10km marked walking loop route around the flattish country west of El Pedroso, beginning opposite Bar Triana on the western side of town, is one of the prettiest hikes in the park. It traverses a landscape strewn with boulders and, in spring, gorgeous wildflowers. Allow 3½ hours.

Cádiz Province & Gibraltar

Includes ➜

Cádiz...............109
Jerez de la Frontera...119
El Puerto
de Santa María......125
Arcos de la Frontera...131
Grazalema..........135
Parque Natural
Sierra de Grazalema...137
Olvera.............138
Vejer de la Frontera...139
Tarifa..............142
Parque Natural Los
Alcornocales........148
Gibraltar...........150

Why Go?

If you had to choose just one province to explain Andalucía in its full, complex beauty, it'd probably be Cádiz province. Thrillingly sited white towns, craggy mountains, endless olive trees, a stunning white-sand coastline dotted with surfer-cool villages, flamenco in its purest incarnation, the font of Andalucian horse culture, fortified sherry, festivals galore, and – just when you'd half-sussed it out – that idiosyncratic British anomaly, Gibraltar. Packed in among all this condensed culture are two expansive natural parks covering an unbroken tract of land that runs from Olvera in the north to Algeciras in the south. The same line once marked the blurred frontier between Christian Spain and Moorish Granada, and that ancient border remains dotted with castle-topped white towns, many with a 'de la Frontera' suffix that testifies to their fascinating, volatile history.

Best Places to Stay

➜ V... (p140)

➜ La Casa Grande (p133)

➜ La Casa del Califa (p140)

➜ Hostal África (p145)

➜ Parador de Cádiz (p113)

Best Beaches

➜ Punta Paloma (p143)

➜ El Palmar (p141)

➜ Bolonia (p148)

➜ Zahara de los Atunes (p142)

➜ Playa de la Victoria (p113)

Driving Distances

	Cádiz	Jerez de la Frontera	Tarifa	Gibraltar
Jerez de la Frontera	32			
Tarifa	103	113		
Gibraltar	144	113	43	
Arcos de la Frontera	63	32	113	115

CÁDIZ

POP 121,700

You could write several weighty tomes about Cádiz and still fall miles short of nailing its essence. Old age accounts for much of the complexity. Cádiz is generally considered to be the oldest continuously inhabited settlement in Europe, founded as Gadir by the Phoenicians in about 1100 BC. Now well into its fourth millennium, the ancient centre, surrounded almost entirely by water, is a romantic jumble of sinuous streets where Atlantic waves crash against eroded sea walls, salty beaches teem with sun-worshippers, and cheerful taverns echo with the sounds of cawing gulls and frying fish.

Spain's first liberal constitution (La Pepa) was signed here in 1812, while the city's distinctive urban model provided an identikit for fortified Spanish colonial cities in the Americas. Indeed, the port – with its crenellated sea walls and chunky forts – is heavily reminiscent of Cuba's Havana or Puerto Rico's San Juan.

Enamoured return visitors talk fondly of Cádiz' seafood, sands and stash of intriguing monuments and museums. More importantly, they gush happily about the *gaditanos* (people from Cádiz), an upfront, sociable bunch whose crazy Carnaval (p112) is an exercise in ironic humour and whose upbeat *alegrías* (flamenco songs) will bring warmth to your heart.

Sights

To understand Cádiz, first you need to befriend its *barrios* (districts). The old city is split into classic quarters: the Barrio del Pópulo, home of the cathedral, and nexus of the once prosperous medieval settlement; Barrio de Santa María, the old Roma and flamenco quarter; Barrio de la Viña, a former vineyard that became the city's main fishing quarter and Carnaval epicentre; and Barrio del Mentidero (said to take its name from the many rumours spread on its streets) in the northwest.

Plaza de San Juan de Dios   SQUARE

Glammed up for the 200th anniversary of the 1812 constitution, cafe-lined Plaza San Juan de Dios is dominated by the grand neoclassical **ayuntamiento** (Town Hall) built around 1800.

★ Catedral de Cádiz   CATHEDRAL

(956 28 61 54; Plaza de la Catedral; adult/child €5/3; 10am-6pm Mon-Sat, 1.30-6pm Sun)

Cádiz' beautiful yellow-domed cathedral is an impressively proportioned baroque-neoclassical construction, best appreciated from seafront Campo del Sur in the evening sun. Though commissioned in 1716, the project wasn't finished until 1838, by which time neoclassical elements (the dome, towers and main facade) had diluted architect Vicente Acero's original baroque plan.

With the same ticket you can check out religious treasures at the **Museo Catedralicio** (Cathedral Museum; 956 25 98 12; Plaza de Fray Félix; adult/child €5/3; 10am-6pm Mon-Sat, 1-6pm Sun), just east. You may be able to climb the cathedral's **Torre de Poniente** (Western Tower), although it was closed indefinitely at the time of research.

Casa del Obispo   MUSEUM

(www.lacasadelobispo.com; Plaza de Fray Félix; adult/child €5/4; 10am-8pm, to 6pm mid-Sep–mid-Jun) Outside the cathedral's eastern exterior wall, this expansive museum of glass walkways over 1500 sq metres of excavated ruins takes you through Cádiz' eventful history, from the 8th century BC to the 18th century. It served as a Phoenician funerary complex, Roman temple and mosque, before becoming the city's Episcopal Palace in the 16th century. It was closed temporarily at research time: enquire at the tourist office (p118).

Teatro Romano   ARCHAEOLOGICAL SITE

(Campo del Sur) On the seaward edge of the Barrio del Pópulo is Cádiz' Roman theatre. Though the theatre itself is closed for renovation works, you can see parts of it at the adjacent, recently reopened **Centro de Interpretación del Teatro Romano** (Calle Mesón 12; 11am-5pm Mon-Sat & 10am-2pm Sun Apr-Sep, 10am-4.30pm Mon-Fri & 10am-2pm Sun Oct-Mar, closed 1st Mon of month Apr-Sep) FREE.

Plaza de Topete   SQUARE

About 250m northwest of the cathedral, this triangular plaza is one of Cádiz' most intimate. Bright with flowers, it's usually talked about as Plaza de las Flores (Square of the Flowers). Right beside is the revamped **Mercado Central de Abastos** (Plaza de la Libertad; 9am-3pm), built in 1837 and the oldest covered market in Spain.

Torre Tavira   TOWER

(www.torretavira.com; Calle Marqués del Real Tesoro 10; admission €6; 10am-8pm, to 6pm Oct-Apr) Northwest of Plaza de Topete, the Torre Tavira opens up dramatic panoramas of Cádiz and has a camera obscura that projects live,

Cádiz Province & Gibraltar Highlights

1. Soaking up the chilled-out kitesurfing, windsurfing and beach scene in **Tarifa** (p142)

2. Exploring the fashionable world of flamenco, sherry and horses in **Jerez de la Frontera** (p119)

3. Absorbing 3000 years of history as you wander the sea-encircled old city of **Cádiz** (p109)

4. Getting lost in the white-town magic of **Vejer de la Frontera** (p139)

5. Hiking the sheer-sided **Garganta Verde** (p137) in the Sierra de Grazalema

6. Going back in time at ruined Roman town **Baelo Claudia** (p148)

7. Tucking into fresh-from-the-ocean fish in Sanlúcar de Barrameda's **Bajo de Guía** (p131)

8. Gazing out to Africa from Jimena de la Frontera's **Castillo** (p148)

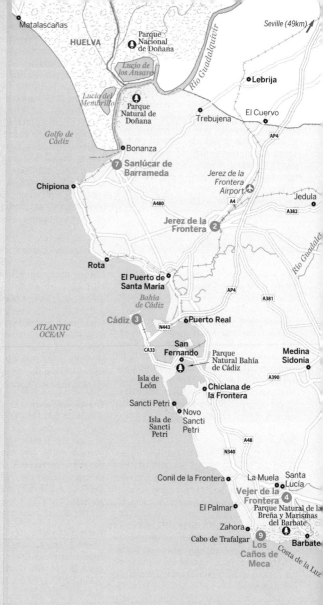

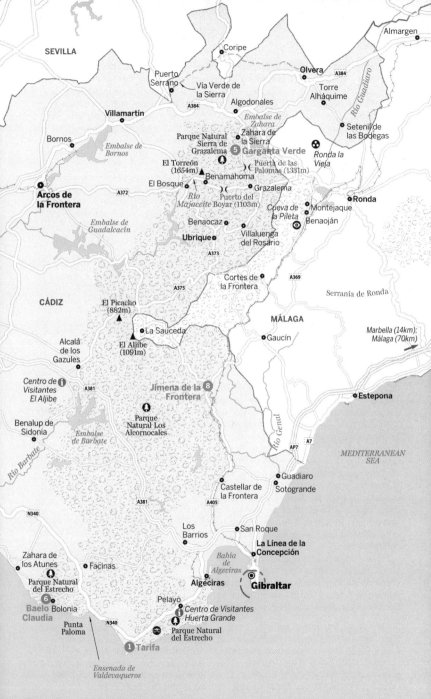

SEVILLA

Almargen

Coripe

Puerto Serrano

Olvera A384

Vía Verde de la Sierra

Torre Alháquime

Villamartín

A384

Algodonales

Embalse de Zahara

Setenil de las Bodegas

Bornos

Embalse de Bornos

Parque Natural Sierra de Grazalema

Zahara de la Sierra

5 Garganta Verde

Río Guadiaro

Ronda la Vieja

El Torreón (1654m)

Benamahoma

Puerta de las Palomas (1331m)

Arcos de la Frontera

A372

El Bosque

Río Majaceite

Puerto del Boyar (1103m)

Grazalema

Cueva de la Pileta

Montejaque

Ronda

Benaoján

Embalse de Guadalcacín

Benaocaz

Villaluenga del Rosario

Ubrique

A373

Cortes de la Frontera

A369

Serranía de Ronda

CÁDIZ

A375

El Picacho (882m)

La Sauceda

MÁLAGA

Marbella (14km); Málaga (70km)

Gaucín

Alcalá de los Gazules

El Aljibe (1091m)

Centro de Visitantes El Aljibe

A381

Jimena de la Frontera **8**

Estepona

Benalup de Sidonia

Embalse de Barbate

Parque Natural Los Alcornocales

Río Genal

AP7

A7

MEDITERRANEAN SEA

Río Barbate

N340

Guadiaro

Sotogrande

Castellar de la Frontera

A405

A381

Los Barrios

San Roque

La Línea de la Concepción

Zahara de los Atunes

Facinas

Bahía de Algeciras

Gibraltar

Parque Natural del Estrecho

6 Baelo Claudia

Bolonia

Punta Paloma

N340

Pelayo

Algeciras

Centro de Visitantes Huerta Grande

Parque Natural del Estrecho

1 Tarifa

Ensenada de Valdevaqueros

Strait of Gibraltar

LOCAL KNOWLEDGE

CÁDIZ CARNAVAL

No other Spanish city celebrates **Carnaval** (⊙Feb) with as much spirit, dedication and humour as Cádiz. Here it becomes a 10-day singing, dancing and drinking fancy-dress street party spanning two February weekends. The fun, fuelled by huge amounts of alcohol, is irresistible. Check www.turismo.cadiz.es for updates on the next festival.

Costumed groups of up to 45 people, called *murgas*, tour the city on foot or on floats and tractors, dancing, drinking, singing satirical ditties or performing sketches. The biggest hits are the 12-person *chirigotas* with their scathing humour, irony and double meanings, often directed at politicians. Most of their famed verbal wit will be lost on all but fluent Spanish speakers.

This being carefree Cádiz, in addition to the 300 or so officially recognised *murgas* (who are judged by a panel in the Gran Teatro Falla), there are also plenty of *ilegales* – any singing group that fancies taking to the streets.

The heart of Carnaval, where you'll stumble across some of the liveliest and most drunken scenes, is the working-class Barrio de la Viña, between the Mercado Central de Abastos and Playa de la Caleta, and along Calle Ancha and around Plaza de Topete, where *ilegales* tend to congregate.

Typically, the first weekend sees the mass arrival of nonlocal partygoers, while the second weekend is when the *gaditanos* (people from Cádiz) really come out to play. Surprisingly, things can be quiet midweek.

If you plan to sleep in Cádiz during Carnaval, book accommodation months ahead.

moving images of the city on to a screen (sessions every 30 minutes).

★**Museo de Cádiz**   MUSEUM
(www.museosdeandalucia.es; Plaza de Mina; admission €1.50, EU citizens free; ⊙9am-3.30pm Tue-Sun mid-Jun–mid-Sep, 9am-7.30pm Tue-Sat & 9am-3.30pm Sun mid-Sep––mid-Jun) Yes, it's a bit dusty, but the Museo de Cádiz is the province's top museum. Stars of the ground-floor archaeology section are two Phoenician marble sarcophagi carved in human likeness, along with lots of headless Roman statues and a giant marble Emperor Trajan (with head) from the Baelo Claudia (p148) ruins. Upstairs, the excellent fine arts collection displays 18 superb 17th-century canvases of saints, angels and monks by Francisco de Zurbarán.

Equally important is the beautifully composed altarpiece from the chapel of Cádiz' Convento de Capuchinas, which cost artist Bartolomé Esteban Murillo his life when he fell from its scaffolding in 1682.

Museo de las Cortes de Cádiz   MUSEUM
(Calle Santa Inés 9; ⊙9am-6pm Tue-Fri, to 2pm Sat & Sun) **FREE** The remodelled Museo de las Cortes de Cádiz is full of memorabilia of the revolutionary 1812 Cádiz parliament. One exhibit jumps out at you: the huge, marvel-lously detailed model of 18th-century Cádiz, made in mahogany and ivory by Alfonso Ximénez between 1777 and 1779.

Puerta de Tierra   GATE
(Land Gate; ⊙10am-6pm Tue-Sun) **FREE** The imposing 18th-century Puerta de Tierra guards the southeastern (and only land) entry to Cádiz' old town. You can wander the upper fortifications and defence tower, where Spanish- and English-language panels detail visible sights and the evolution of Cádiz' complex fortification system.

🏃 Activities

Playa de la Caleta   BEACH
Hugging the western side of the Barrio de la Viña, this small, popular city beach catches the eye with its mock-Moorish *balneario* (bathhouse). It's flanked by two forts: the **Castillo de San Sebastián** (Paseo Fernando Quiñones; adult/child €2/free; ⊙9.30am-5pm), for centuries a military installation, and the star-shaped **Castillo de Santa Catalina** (📞956 22 63 33; Calle Antonio Burgos ; ⊙11am-7pm, to 8.30pm Mar-Oct) **FREE**, built after the 1596 Anglo-Dutch sacking of the city.

Mimicking Ursula Andress in *Dr. No*, Halle Berry famously strode out of the sea here in an orange bikini in the 2002 James Bond film *Die Another Day*.

Playa de la Victoria   BEACH

Often overshadowed by the city's historical riches, Cádiz' beaches are Copacabana-like in their size, vibe and beauty. This fine, wide strip of Atlantic sand starts 1km south of the Puerta de Tierra and stretches 4km back along the peninsula.

Take bus 1 (Plaza España-Cortadura; €1.10) from Plaza de España, or walk or jog along the promenade from the Barrio de Santa María.

🎓 Courses

Cádiz is an inspiring place to study Spanish language and culture. About 300m southeast of the Puerta de Tierra, Gadir Escuela Internacional de Español (📞956 26 05 57; www.gadir.net; Calle Pérgolas 5) is a long-established school with a wide range of classes in small, specialised groups. Other good language schools include K2 Internacional (📞956 21 26 46; www.k2internacional. com; Plaza Mentidero 19) and Melkart Centro Internacional de Idiomas (📞956 22 22 13; www.centromelkart.com; Calle General Menacho 7), both based in the Barrio del Mentidero and offering special courses for people over 50 years old. The schools also organise flamenco, cooking and even surf courses, as well as accommodation.

🛏 Sleeping

★Casa Caracol   HOSTEL €

(📞956 26 11 66; www.hostel-casacaracol.com; Calle Suárez de Salazar 4; hammock/dm/d incl breakfast €10/18/40; @🛜) 🏄 Casa Caracol is Cádiz' original old-town backpacker hostel. Friendly as only Cádiz can be, it has colourful bunk dorms for four, six or seven, a sociable communal kitchen, and a roof terrace with hammocks. Other perks include home-cooked dinners, yoga, and bike and surfboard rental. No lift.

Hotel Argantonio   HOTEL €€

(📞956 21 16 40; www.hotelargantonio.com; Calle Argantonio 3; incl breakfast s €75-95, d €100-125; ❄@🛜) This characterful, small-is-beautiful hotel in Cádiz' old quarter sparkles with its hand-painted and wood-carved doors, colourfully tiled floors adorning bedrooms, bathrooms and corridors, and intricate Moorish arch and fountain in the lobby. The 1st floor is Mudéjar, the 2nd 'colonial romantic', the 3rd a mix. Tucked away on the roof is a lounge terrace.

Hotel Patagonia Sur   HOTEL €€

(📞856 17 46 47; www.hotelpatagoniasur.es; Calle Cobos 11; s €105, d €110-135; ❄@🛜) A relative newcomer, this glossy Argentine-run gem offers clean-lined modernity just steps from the cathedral. Rooms, all with tea and coffee sets, are smart, fresh and snug. Bonuses include a glass-fronted cafe and sun-filled 5th-floor attic rooms with cathedral views and sun-loungers on private terraces.

★Parador de Cádiz   HOTEL €€€

(📞956 22 69 05; www.parador.es; Avenida Duque de Nájera 9; incl breakfast s €192-272, d €210-290; ❄🛜🏊) Bold, beautiful and right beside Playa de la Caleta, the so-called Parador Atlántico contrasts with Andalucía's other *paradores* (luxurious state-owned hotels) in that it's super-modern and built from scratch. Bright reds and blues throw character into the sleek, contemporary rooms with balcony and floor-to-ceiling windows. Choose from four sea-view swimming pools.

🍴 Eating

Just as the air in Jerez de la Frontera is thick with sherry, Cádiz smells unforgettably of fresh fish. Calle Virgen de la Palma, in the Barrio de la Viña, is the city's go-to seafood street, where fantastic fish restaurants plate up the day's catch at alfresco tables. Calles Plocia and Sopranis, off Plaza de San Juan de Dios, are the gourmet eat-streets.

★Casa Manteca   TAPAS €

(📞956 21 36 03; Calle Corralón de los Carros 66; tapas €2.50; ⏰noon-4pm & 8.30pm-12.30am, closed Sun & Mon evenings approx Nov-Mar) The hub of La Viña's Carnaval fun, with every inch of its walls covered in flamenco, bullfighting and Carnaval memorabilia, Casa Manteca is a *barrio* classic full of old tapas faves. Ask the chatty waiters for a *tapa* of mussels or *chicharrones* (pressed pork dressed with a squeeze of lemon), and it'll fly across the bar on wax paper.

La Candela   SPANISH, TAPAS €

(📞956 22 18 22; www.lacandelatapasbar.com; Calle Feduchy 3; tapas €3.50-7; ⏰1.30-4pm & 8.30-11pm; 🛜) Like a quirky London or Melbourne cafe turned cool, colourful tapas bar, La Candela surprises with its floral-stamped windows and rustic-industrial decor. From the busy little open kitchen at the back come tasty innovative creations with local inspiration – tuna brochette with wasabi mayonnaise, *rabo de toro* (bull's tail) lasagne, and honey-goat's-cheese salad.

Cádiz

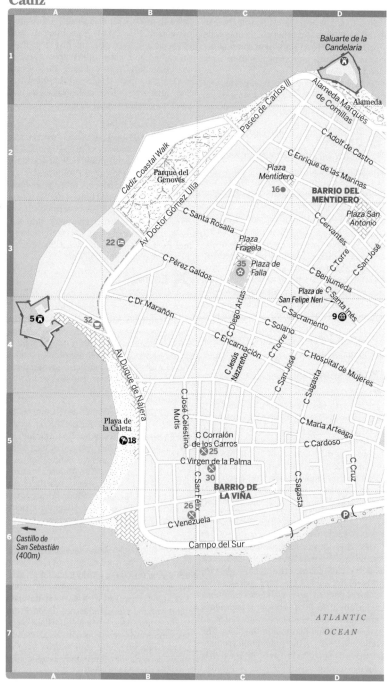

Baluarte de la Candelaria

Alameda Marqués de Comillas

Alameda

Paseo de Carlos III

Cádiz Coastal Walk

Parque del Genovés

C Adolf de Castro

C Enrique de las Marinas

Plaza Mentidero

16

BARRIO DEL MENTIDERO

Plaza San Antonio

C Cervantes

Av Doctor Gómez Ulla

C Santa Rosalía

22

Plaza Fragela

C Pérez Galdos

35 Plaza de Falla

C Torre

C San José

C Benjumeda

Plaza de San Felipe Neri

C Santa Inés

C Sacramento

9

C Dr Marañón

5

32

C Diego Arias

C Solano

C Encarnación

C Torre

C San José

C Sagasta

C Hospital de Mujeres

Av Dique de Nájera

C Jesús Nazareño

C José Celestino Mutis

Playa de la Caleta

18

C Corralón de los Carros

25

C Virgen de la Palma

30

C San Félix

26

C Venezuela

BARRIO DE LA VIÑA

C María Arteaga

C Cardoso

C Sagasta

C Cruz

P

Castillo de San Sebastián (400m)

Campo del Sur

ATLANTIC OCEAN

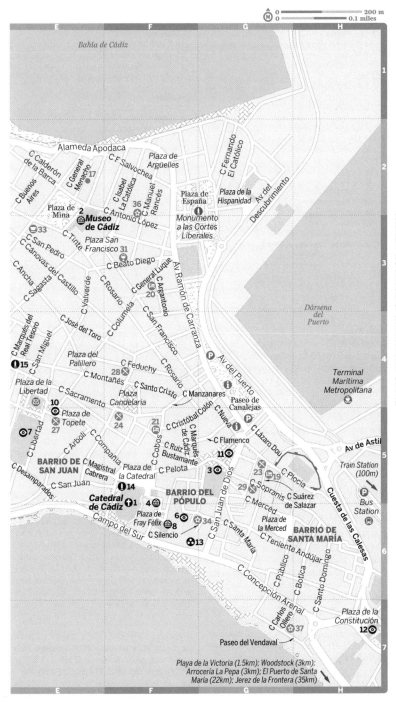

Bahía de Cádiz

Alameda Apodaca

C Calderón de la Barca
C General Menacho 17
C F Salvochea
Plaza de Argüelles
C Fernando El Católico

C Buenos Aires
C Isabel La Católica
C Manuel Rancés
Plaza de España
Plaza de la Hispanidad
Av del Descubrimiento

Plaza de Mina 2
Museo de Cádiz
C Antonio López
36
Monumento a las Cortes Liberales

33
C San Pedro
C Tinte
Plaza San Francisco 31

C Cánovas del Castillo
C Beato Diego
C General Luque
C Argantonio
20

C Ancha
C Sagasta
C Valverde
C Rosario
C Columela
C San Francisco
Av Ramón de Carranza

Dársena del Puerto

C Marqués del Real Tesoro
C José del Toro

15
C San Miguel

Plaza del Palillero
C Feduchy
C Rosario
Av del Puerto

Terminal Marítima Metropolitana

Plaza de la Libertad
28
C Montañés
C Santo Cristo
C Manzanares
Paseo de Canalejas

10
C Sacramento
Plaza Candelaria
C Cristóbal Colón
C Nueva
C Lázaro Dou

Plaza de Topete
27
24
21
C Marqués de Cádiz
C Flamenco

7
C Libertad
C Arbolí
C Compañía
C Cobos
C Ruiz Bustamante
11
Av de Astil

BARRIO DE SAN JUAN
C Magistral Cabrera
Plaza de la Catedral
C Pelota
3
23
19
C Plocia
Train Station (100km)

14
C San Juan
BARRIO DEL PÓPULO
29
C Sopranis
C Suárez de Salazar
Bus Station

C Desamparados
Catedral de Cádiz 1
6
4
C San Juan de Dios
C Merced
Cuesta de las Calesas

Plaza de Fray Félix
8
34
Plaza de la Merced
BARRIO DE SANTA MARÍA

C Silencio
13
C Santa María
C Teniente Andújar

Campo del Sur
C Concepción Arenal
C Público
C Botica
C Santo Domingo

C Carlos Ollero
37
Plaza de la Constitución
12

Paseo del Vendaval

Playa de la Victoria (1.5km); Woodstock (3km); Arrocería La Pepa (3km); El Puerto de Santa María (22km); Jerez de la Frontera (35km)

Cádiz

◎ Top Sights
1 Catedral de Cádiz F5
2 Museo de Cádiz..E3

◎ Sights
3 Ayuntamiento...G5
4 Casa del Obispo F5
5 Castillo de Santa Catalina.................... A4
6 Centro de Interpretación del
   Teatro Romano F6
7 Mercado Central de Abastos E5
8 Museo Catedralicio................................F6
9 Museo de las Cortes de Cádiz.............. D4
10 Plaza de San Juan de Dios.................... G5
11 Plaza de Topete E5
12 Puerta de Tierra H7
13 Teatro Romano F6
14 Torre de Poniente F5
15 Torre Tavira...E4

◎ Activities, Courses & Tours
16 K2 Internacional......................................C2
17 Melkart Centro Internacional de
   Idiomas...E2
18 Playa de la Caleta...................................B5

◎ Sleeping
19 Casa Caracol..G5
20 Hotel Argantonio F3
21 Hotel Patagonia Sur F5
22 Parador de Cádiz B3

◎ Eating
23 Atxuri...G5
24 Café Royalty F5
25 Casa Manteca..C5
26 El Faro B6
27 Freiduría Las Flores E5
28 La Candela..F4
29 La Esquina de Sopranis G5
30 Mesón Criollo C5

◎ Drinking & Nightlife
31 Nahu... F3
32 Quilla A4
33 Tetería El Oasis E3

◎ Entertainment
34 El Pay Pay F6
35 Gran Teatro Falla....................................C3
36 La Cava F2
37 Peña Flamenca La Perla G7

Café Royalty
CAFE €

(☏956 07 80 65; www.caferoyalty.com; Plaza Candelaria; snacks €3.50-12; ☺9am-midnight Jun-Sep, 11am-11pm Oct-May) Originally opened in 1912 on the centenary of the 1812 constitution, the Royalty was once a discussion corner for the intellectuals of the day, including beloved *gaditano* composer Manuel de Falla. The cafe closed in the 1930s, but thanks to an inspired renovation project overseen by a local *gaditano* it reopened in 2012, 100 years after its initial inauguration.

The frescoed, mirrored, intricately carved interior is – no exaggeration – breathtaking. Fantastic for brunch or *merienda* (afternoon snack).

Freiduría Las Flores
SEAFOOD €

(☏956 22 61 12; Plaza de Topete 4; tapas €1.50, raciones €6-8; ☺noon-4.30pm & 8.30pm-midnight) Cádiz' addiction to fried fish reaches new heights here. If it comes from the sea, chances are it's been fried and dished up at Las Flores as *tapa, media racion* (larger tapas serving) or *racion* (full-plate serving), or in an improvised paper cup, fish-and-chips style. If you can't choose, try a *surtido* (mixed fry-up). Don't count on a table.

★ La Esquina de Sopranis
TAPAS €€

(☏956 26 58 42; www.sopranis.es; Calle Sopranis 5; tapas €1.50-5.50; ☺1-4pm & 8.30-11.30pm Tue-Sat, 1-4pm Sun) One of those bubbly, contemporary tapas places you'll never want to leave, packed-out Sopranis blends casual and sophisticated to perfection. The food is equally exquisite. Local seasonal ingredients are thrown together in beautifully presented creative combos, like mini-*solomillo* (pork sirloin) with chorizo sauce or market-fresh *timbal de verduras* (vegetable stack). Our top pick: the melt-in-the-mouth cheeses.

Atxuri
BASQUE, ANDALUCIAN €€

(☏956 25 36 13; www.atxuri.es; Calle Plocia 7; raciones €12-18; ☺1.15-5pm & 9-11.30pm Thu-Sat, 1.15-5pm Sun-Wed) One of Cádiz' most long-standing restaurants, Atxuri fuses Basque and Andalucian influences into a refined range of flavours. As you'd expect in a place with Basque roots, *bacalao* (cod; perhaps scrambled or *al pil pil*) and high-quality steaks are recurring themes; Andalucian fish and meat staples blur the boundary.

Arrocería La Pepa
SPANISH, SEAFOOD €€

(☏956 26 38 21; www.restaurantelapepa.es; Paseo Marítimo 14; paella per person €12-15; ☺1.30-4pm & 8.30-11pm Thu-Sat, 1.30-4pm Sun-Wed) For a decent paella, leave the old town behind and head 3km southeast along Playa de la Victoria – take an appetite-inducing oceanside stroll or jog, or a quick ride on bus 1 to Estadio (Plaza España-Cortadura; €1.10). The fish in La Pepa's seafood paella tastes like it's just jumped 100m from the Atlantic on to your plate.

Mesón Criollo   SEAFOOD €€
(www.mesoncriollo.com; cnr Calles Virgen de la Palma & Lubet; mains €7-14; ⊘noon-4pm & 8-11.30pm, closed Sun-Tue & Wed night Oct-Feb) Amid La Viña's countless fish restaurants, this one stands out for its prawns, fish brochettes and – if you happen to arrive at the right time – individual paella. Sit out on the palm-studded street at tapas time and you'll feel like there's a permanent carnival going on in what is Cadiz' primary Carnaval quarter.

El Faro   SEAFOOD €€€
(☑956 21 10 68; www.elfarodecadiz.com; Calle San Félix 15; mains €16-25; ⊘1-4pm & 8.30-11.30pm) Ask any *gaditano* for their favourite Cádiz restaurant and there's a high chance they'll choose El Faro, at once jam-packed tapas bar and upmarket restaurant decorated with pretty ceramics. Seafood is why people come here, although the *rabo de toro* has its devotees.

If any place in this relaxed city has a dress code, it's El Faro, but even here it only extends to banning swimsuits...

🍷 Drinking & Nightlife

With limitations on outdoor drinking spaces and enforced closing times, Cádiz nightlife isn't quite what it used to be, but there are still plenty of places for after-dark fun.

In the old city, the Plaza de Mina–Plaza San Francisco–Plaza de España triangle is the centre of the late-night bar scene, especially Calle Beato Diego; things get going around midnight, but can be quiet early in the week. More bars are scattered around the Barrio del Pópulo, east of the cathedral. Punta San Felipe (La Punta), on the northern side of the harbour, has a string of drinks/dance bars packed with a youngish crowd from about 3am to 6am Thursday to Saturday.

Cádiz' other nocturnal haunt, particularly in summer, is down along Playa de la Victoria and the Paseo Marítimo, on and around Calle Muñoz Arenillas near the Hotel Playa Victoria (about 2.5km south of the Puerta de Tierra).

Quilla   CAFE, WINE BAR
(www.quilla.es; Playa de la Caleta; ⊘10am-11pm; 🛜) A bookish cafe-bar encased in what appears to be the rusty hulk of an old ship overlooking Playa de la Caleta, with coffee, pastries, tapas, wine, art expos and gratis sunsets. Opening hours spill over in summer.

Nahu   BAR
(www.nahucadiz.es; Calle Beato Diego 8; ⊘4pm-3am Mon-Sat; 🛜) Stylish student-oriented cocktail bar with mood lighting, Moroccan lamps and chill-out sofas. At its best when you're perched at the bar, G&T in hand, but good for coffee and wi-fi too. DJ sessions Friday or Saturday.

Tetería El Oasis   TEAHOUSE
(Calle San José 6; ⊘5pm-midnight Mon-Fri, 4pm-2am Sat) Find dark nooks under the red and orange lace curtains and sip discreetly on a Darjeeling in a state of contemplative meditation – until the belly dancers arrive (Friday, 11pm)!

Woodstock   BAR
(Paseo Marítimo 11; ⊘2pm-3am) Popular beer bar overlooking Playa de la Victoria, with 80-plus international beers, pool table and occasional live jazz, rock and blues.

☆ Entertainment

★ Peña Flamenca La Perla   FLAMENCO
(☑956 25 91 01; www.laperladecadiz.es; Calle Carlos Ollero; admission €3) Paint-peeled La Perla, set romantically next to the crashing Atlantic surf off Calle Concepción Arenal in the Barrio de Santa María, hosts flamenco at 10pm most Fridays, more often in spring and summer, for an audience full of aficionados. It's an unforgettable experience.

Gran Teatro Falla   THEATRE
(☑956 22 08 34; www.facebook.com/TeatroFalla; Plaza de Falla) Named for Andalucía's finest classical composer and native *gaditano* Manuel de Falla, this red-bricked neo-Mudéjar theatre hosts Cádiz' annual Carnaval competitions (p112). The rest of the year it's busy with theatre, dance and music.

La Cava   FLAMENCO
(☑956 21 18 66; www.flamencolacava.com; Calle Antonio López 16; admission €22, with dinner €37; ⊘Mar-Dec) Cádiz' main *tablao* (choreographed flamenco show) happens in a rustically bedecked tavern with drinks and dinner on Tuesdays (April to November), Thursdays and Saturdays at 9.30pm.

> **ℹ️ RESOURCES**
>
> **Cádiz Turismo** (www.cadizturismo.
> com) Official government tourist infor-
> mation.

El Pay Pay   MUSIC, THEATRE
(www.cafeteatropaypay.com; Calle Silencio 1;
⊙10am-3am Wed-Sat) In the Barrio del Pópulo, this 'cafe-theatre' runs a hugely varied arts
program including drama, storytelling, stand-
up comedy and live jazz, blues and flamenco,
plus regular Thursday jams (10.30pm).

ℹ️ Information

Centro de Recepción de Turistas (☑956 24
10 01; www.turismo.cadiz.es; Paseo de Canale-
jas; ⊙9am-6.30pm Mon-Fri, to 5pm Sat & Sun)
Near the bus and train stations.
Hospital Puerta del Mar (☑956 00 21 00;
Avenida Ana de Viya 21) Main general hospital,
2.5km southeast of the Puerta de Tierra.
Policía Nacional (☑091, 956 29 75 00;
Avenida de Andalucía 28) National police;
500m southeast of the Puerta de Tierra.
Regional Tourist Office (☑956 20 31 91;
Avenida Ramón de Carranza; ⊙9am-7.30pm
Mon-Fri, 9.30am-3pm Sat & Sun)

ℹ️ Getting There & Around

BICYCLE

Urban Bike (www.urbanbikecadiz.es; Calle
Marques de Valdeíñigo 4; bicycle hire per
1/3/24hr €5/10/16; ⊙10am-5pm Mon-Fri)
rents bicycles.

BOAT

From the **Terminal Marítima Metropolitana**, 17
daily catamarans (www.cmtbc.es) leave Monday
to Friday for El Puerto de Santa María (€2.65, 30
minutes); there are six on Saturday, five on Sunday.

BUS

All out-of-town buses currently leave from the
provisional **bus station** (☑956 80 70 59; Plaza
Sevilla), next to the train station. Cádiz' new bus
station, on Avenida Astilleros on the east side of
the train station, is due to be completed in late
2015; all services are likely to switch to the new
station once it opens.

Most buses are operated by **Comes** (☑956
29 11 68; www.tgcomes.es) or **Los Amarillos**
(☑902 210317; www.samar.es). The **Consorcio
de Transportes Bahía de Cádiz** (☑856 10 04
95; www.cmtbc.es) runs buses between Jerez de
la Frontera airport and Cádiz, via Jerez city.

CAR & MOTORCYCLE

The AP4 motorway from Seville to Puerto Real
on the eastern side of the Bahía de Cádiz carries
a €7.25 toll.

There's lots of underground parking, including
on Paseo de Canalejas near the port (€20 per
24 hours).

TRAIN

From the train station, on the southeastern edge
of the old town, trains go to/from El Puerto de
Santa María (€3.40, 35 minutes, 23 daily), Jerez
de la Frontera (€4.05 to €6.05, 45 minutes, 33
daily) and Seville (€16 to €24, 1¾ hours, 15 daily). Three or four daily high-speed ALVIA trains
go to Madrid (€74, 4½ hours).

THE SHERRY TRIANGLE

North of Cádiz, Jerez de la Frontera, Sanlúcar
de Barrameda and El Puerto de Santa María
mark the three corners of the famous 'sherry
triangle'. Even if Andalucía's unique, smooth

BUSES FROM CÁDIZ

TO	COST (€)	DURATION (HR)	FREQUENCY
Arcos de la Frontera	7.25	1½	1-4 daily
El Bosque	8.80	2½	2-4
El Puerto de Santa María	2.65	45min	hourly
Granada	36	5¼	4 daily
Jerez de la Frontera	3.75	50min	3-7 daily
Málaga	28	4½	4 daily
Ronda	16	3½	1-2 daily
Sanlúcar de Barrameda	5	1	5-10 daily
Seville	13	1¾	9 daily
Tarifa	9.91	1¾	7 daily
Vejer de la Frontera	5.67	1½	5-7 daily

wine isn't your cup of tea, don't forget the history, the beaches, the horses, the food, the flamenco and the environmental marvel that is the Parque Nacional de Doñana.

Jerez de la Frontera

POP 190,600

Stand down all other claimants. Jerez, as most savvy Hispanophiles know, *is* Andalucía. It just doesn't broadcast it in the way that Seville and Granada do. Jerez is the capital of Andalucian horse culture, stop one on the famed sherry triangle and – cue the protestations from Cádiz and Seville – the cradle of Spanish flamenco. The *bulería*, Jerez' jokey, tongue-in-cheek antidote to Seville's tragic *soleá*, was first concocted in the legendary Roma *barrios* of Santiago and San Miguel. But Jerez is also a vibrant, chic modern Andalucian city, where fashion brands live in old palaces and stylishly outfitted businesspeople sit down to distinctly contemporary cuisine. If you really want to unveil the eternal riddle that is Andalucía, start here.

◉ Sights

Scattered across town, often tucked behind other buildings, Jerez' understated sights creep up on you. It can take a day or two to bond with the city. But once you're bitten, it's like *duende* (flamenco spirit) – there's no turning back.

Jerez (the word even *means* 'sherry') has around 20 sherry bodegas. Most require bookings for visits, but a few offer tours where you can just turn up. The tourist office (p125) has details.

★ Alcázar   FORTRESS
(⎆956 14 99 55; Alameda Vieja; admission excl/incl camera obscura €5/7; ⊙9.30am-7.30pm Mon-Fri Jul–mid-Sep, 9.30am-5.30pm Mon-Fri mid-Sep–Oct & Mar-Jun, 9.30am-2.30pm Nov-Feb & Sat & Sun year-round) Jerez' muscular yet elegant 11th- or 12th-century fortress is one of Andalucía's best-preserved Almohad-era (1140–1212) relics. It's noted for its octagonal tower, a classic example of Almohad defensive forts and a fabulous spot for city views.

You enter the Alcázar via the **Patio de Armas**. On the left is the beautiful *mezquita* (mosque), transformed into a chapel by Alfonso X in 1264. On the right, the 18th-century **Palacio Villavicencio**, built over the ruins of the old Almohad palace, displays artwork but is best known for its bird's-eye views of Jerez; the camera obscura inside its tower provides a picturesque panorama of the city.

Beyond the Patio de Armas, the peaceful gardens re-create the ambience of Islamic times with geometric flower beds and tinkling fountains. The well-preserved, domed Baños Árabes (Arabic Baths), with their shafts of light, are particularly worth a look.

★ Catedral de San Salvador   CATHEDRAL
(Plaza de la Encarnación; admission €5; ⊙10am-6.30pm Mon-Sat) Echoes of Seville colour Jerez' dramatic cathedral, a surprisingly harmonious mix of baroque, neoclassical and Gothic styles. Standout features are its broad flying buttresses and intricately decorated stone ceilings. Behind the main altar, a series of rooms and chapels shows off the cathedral's collection of art (including works by Zurbarán and Pacheco), religious garments and silverware.

You can also enjoy an orange-tree-lined patio (the church was built by Alfonso X on the site of an old mosque) and a 'secret staircase' to nowhere. Though erected between 1695 and 1778, the building only officially became a cathedral in 1980.

Centro Andaluz de Flamenco   ARTS CENTRE
(Andalucian Flamenco Centre; ⎆956 90 21 34; www.centroandaluzdeflamenco.es; Plaza de San Juan 1; ⊙9am-2pm Mon-Fri) **FREE** At once architecturally intriguing – note the entrance's original 15th-century Mudéjar *artesonado* (ceiling of interlaced beams with decorative inserts) and the intricate Andalucian baroque courtyard – and a fantastic flamenco resource, this unique centre holds thousands of print and musical works. Flamenco videos are screened at 10am, 11am, noon and 1pm. Staff can provide a list of 17 local *peñas* (small private clubs), plus information on classes in flamenco dance and singing, and upcoming performances.

Museo Arqueológico   MUSEUM
(⎆956 14 95 60; Plaza del Mercado; admission €5; ⊙10am-2pm Tue-Sun year-round, 4-7pm Tue-Fri mid-Sep–mid Jun) In the Santiago quarter, Jerez' revamped archaeology museum houses fascinating local relics ranging from Paleolithic to 16th-century times. Look especially for the 7th-century BC Greek helmet found in the Río Guadalete and a fragment of a rare 15th-century Gothic-Mudéjar painting.

Jerez de la Frontera

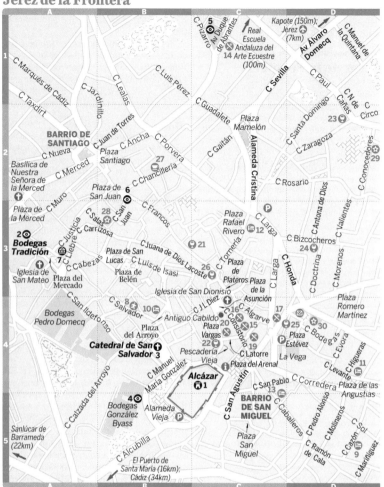

★**Bodegas Tradición** SHERRY BODEGA
(📞956 16 86 28; www.bodegastradicion.com; Plaza Cordobeses 3; tours €20; ⏰8am-3pm Mon-Fri Jul-Aug, 10am-6pm Mon-Fri & 10am-2pm Sat Sep-Jun, closed Sat Dec-Feb) An intriguing bodega, not only for its extra-aged sherries (at least 20 years old), but also because it houses the Colección Joaquín Rivera, a private Spanish art collection that includes important works by Goya, Velázquez and Zurbarán. Tours (in English, Spanish and German) require prior booking.

Bodegas González Byass SHERRY BODEGA
(Bodegas Tío Pepe; 📞956 35 70 16; www.bodegastiopepe.com; Calle Manuel María González 12; tours €13; ⏰tours hourly noon-5pm Mon-Sat, noon-2pm Sun) Home to the famous Tío Pepe brand, González Byass is one of Jerez' biggest sherry houses, handily located just west of the Alcázar. Five or six daily tours run in English and Spanish, and a couple in German. You can book online, but it isn't essential.

Bodegas Sandeman SHERRY BODEGA
(📞675 647177; www.sandeman.com; Calle Pizarro 10; tours €7.50; ⏰tours 11am-2.30pm Mon, Wed &

Jerez de la Frontera

◉ Top Sights
1	Alcázar	C4
2	Bodegas Tradición	A3
3	Catedral de San Salvador	B4

◉ Sights
4	Bodegas González Byass	B5
5	Bodegas Sandeman	C1
6	Centro Andaluz de Flamenco	B2
7	Museo Arqueológico	A3

⊕ Activities, Courses & Tours
8	Hammam Andalusí	B4

🛏 Sleeping
9	Hostal Fenix	D5
10	Hotel Bellas Artes	B4
11	Hotel Casa Grande	D4
12	Hotel Palacio Garvey	C3
13	Nuevo Hotel	C4

✖ Eating
14	Albalá	C1
15	Albores	C4
16	Cruz Blanca	C4
17	El Gallo Azul	C4
18	La Carboná	E4
19	Mesón del Asador	C4
20	Reino de León	C4

🍸 Drinking & Nightlife
21	Damajuana	C3
22	Dos Deditos	C4
23	Plaza de Canterbury	D2
24	Tabanco El Guitarrón de San Pedro	D3
25	Tabanco El Pasaje	C4
26	Tabanco Plateros	C3
27	Tetería La Jaima	B2

⊕ Entertainment
28	Centro Cultural Flamenco Don Antonio Chacón	B3
29	Puro Arte	D2
30	Teatro Villamarta	D4

CÁDIZ PROVINCE & GIBRALTAR JEREZ DE LA FRONTERA

Fri, 10.15am-2pm Tue & Thu) Three or four daily tours (no bookings needed) each in English, Spanish and German, and one in French, all including tastings; the website has up-to-date schedules. In honour of their Scottish creator, Sandeman sherries carry the black-caped 'Don' logo.

🏃 Activities

★ Real Escuela
Andaluza del Arte Ecuestre EQUESTRIAN SHOW
(📞 956 31 80 08; www.realescuela.org; Avenida Duque de Abrantes; training sessions adult/child €11/6.50, exhibicións adult/child €21/13; ⊙ training sessions 10am-1pm Mon, Wed & Fri, exhibicións noon Tue & Thu) The famous Royal Andalucian School of Equestrian Art trains horses and riders. You can watch them going through their paces in training sessions and visit the **Museo del Enganche** (Horse Carriage Museum; adult/child €4.50/2.50; ⊙ 10am-2pm Mon-Fri), which includes an 18th-century Binder hunting break (carriage). The big highlight is the official *exhibición* (show), in which the handsome horses show off their tricks to classical music. Book tickets online.

Hammam Andalusí   HAMMAM

(☑956 34 90 66; www.hammamandalusi.com; Calle Salvador 6; baths €24, with 15/30min massage €34/53; ⊙10am-10pm) Jerez is full of echoes of its Moorish past, but there's none more magical than the Hammam Andalusí. Incense, essential oils and the soothing sound of tinkling water welcome you through the door, then you pass through three turquoise pools (tepid, hot and cold). You can even throw in a massage. Numbers are limited, so book ahead.

Yeguada de la Cartuja –
Hierro del Bocado   EQUESTRIAN SHOW

(☑956 16 28 09; www.yeguadacartuja.com; Finca Suerte del Suero; adult/child €16/10; ⊙11am-1.30pm Sat) This stud farm is dedicated to improving the fine Cartujano stock. The guided visit is followed by a spectacular show consisting of free-running colts, demonstrations by a string of mares, and dressage. Book ahead. To get here, turn off the A381 11km southeast of central Jerez at the 'Yeguada de la Cartuja' sign.

✦ Festivals & Events

Festival de Jerez   FLAMENCO

(www.facebook.com/FestivalDeJerez; ⊙late Feb–early Mar) Jerez' biggest flamenco celebration.

Motorcycle Grand Prix   MOTORCYCLES

(⊙May) The Circuito de Jerez (Racing Circuit; ☑956 15 11 00; www.circuitodejerez.com), on the A382 10km east of town, usually hosts motorcycle- and car-racing events in March, April or May, including one of the Grand Prix races of the World Motorcycle Championship.

Feria del Caballo   HORSES

(⊙late Apr–early May) Jerez' week-long horse fair is one of Andalucía's grandest festivals, with music and dance, and equestrian competitions and parades.

🛌 Sleeping

Hostal Fenix   HOSTAL €

(☑956 34 52 91; www.hostalfenix.com; Calle Cazón 7; incl breakfast s €30-35, d €35-40; ❄🔲) There's nothing flash about the Fenix, which is part of its charm. The 14 simple, characterful rooms are well-maintained by ultra-friendly owners, who'll bring breakfast to your room. Cute Arabic-inspired patios are dotted around. The impressive art adorning the walls is painted by the *dueña* (owner) and her cousin.

Hotel Bellas Artes   HOTEL €

(☑956 34 84 30; www.hotelbellasartes.net; Plaza del Arroyo 45; s/d €48/55; ❄@🔲) This converted neoclassical palace overlooks Jerez' Catedral de San Salvador from its rooftop terrace and suites. An exquisite carved stone corner pillar graces its sand-toned exterior. Strong interior colours contrast with white marble floors, rooms come with Nespresso machines and free-standing bathtubs (though some feel slightly too dated), and there's a summer rooftop jacuzzi.

Nuevo Hotel   HOTEL €

(☑956 33 16 00; www.nuevohotel.com; Calle Caballeros 23; s/d/tr €30/42/57; ❄🔲📶) One of the sweetest family-run hotels in Andalucía, the Nuevo's comfortable rooms are complemented by spectacular room 208, replete with Islamic-style stucco work and *azulejos* (tiles). You'll wake up thinking you've taken up residence in the Alhambra. Breakfast (€5) is available.

Hotel Casa Grande   HOTEL €€

(☑956 34 50 70; www.hotelcasagrande.eu; Plaza de las Angustias 3; r/ste €100/165; 🅿❄🔲) This brilliant hotel occupies a beautifully restored 1920s mansion. Rooms are set over three floors around a light-flooded patio, or beside the fantastic roof terrace with views across Jerez' rooftops. All is overseen by the congenial Monika Schroeder, a mine of information about Jerez.

Hotel Palacio Garvey   HOTEL €€

(☑956 32 67 00; www.sferahoteles.com; Calle Tornería 24; r/ste incl breakfast €70/100; 🅿❄🔲) Jerez' nominal posh hotel is a sensational 19th-century neoclassical palace conversion, with part of the ancient city wall visible from the lift. The public areas sport leopard prints, African-themed paintings and low-slung tables, while subtle colours, luxurious leather furniture, tiled bathrooms and mirrored Moroccan-inspired bowls feature in the 16 individually decorated rooms.

🍴 Eating

Jerez gastronomy combines Moorish heritage and maritime influences with international touches. Sherry, of course, flavours many traditional dishes such as *riñones al jerez* (sherry-braised kidneys) and *rabo de toro* (bull's tail), and there's been a notable turn towards creative contemporary cuisine.

Cruz Blanca   TAPAS, ANDALUCIAN €

(www.restaurantelacruzblanca.com; Calle Consistorio 16; tapas €2.50-4; ⊙8am-midnight Mon-Fri,

THE GREAT TABANCO REVIVAL

Sprinkled across the city centre, Jerez' famous old *tabancos* are basic, bubbly taverns serving sherry from the barrel. Most date from the early 20th century and, although *tabanco* comes from the fusion of *tabaco* (tobacco) and *estanco* (tobacco shop), the focus is indisputably the local plonk (ie sherry). In danger of dying out just a few years ago, Jerez' *tabancos* have suddenly sprung back to life as fashionable modern-day hang-outs, frequented by crowds of stylish young *jerezanos* as much as old-timers. Several stage regular flamenco, but you're just as likely to catch an impromptu performance. All are fantastic, cheap, down-to-earth places to capture that old Jerez atmosphere – sherry in hand.

The **tourist office** (p125) has information on the official **Ruta de los Tabancos de Jerez** (www.facebook.com/rutadelostabancosdejerez).

Tabanco El Pasaje (956 33 33 59; www.tabancoelpasaje.com; Calle Santa María 8; 11am-3pm & 7-11pm, shows 8.30pm Thu-Sun & 2.30pm Fri & Sat) Born back in 1925, Jerez' oldest *tabanco* serves up its sherry with suitably raw flamenco.

Tabanco El Guitarrón de San Pedro (www.facebook.com/guitarrondesanpedro; Calle Bizcocheros 16; noon-midnight, shows 10pm Thu & Fri, 3pm Sat, 8pm Sun) Regular flamenco and occasional jazz. Sunday flamenco sessions are spontaneous – and open to all!

Tabanco Plateros (www.tabancoplateros.com; Calle Francos 1; noon-3.30pm & 7.30pm-1am) Join the crowd spilling out from this lively drinking house for sherry, beer, wine, and simple meat and cheese tapas.

9am-midnight Sat, 1pm-midnight Sun) The Cruz whips up good seafood, *revueltos* (scrambled egg dishes), meat and salads, served at outdoor tables on a quiet little plaza or inside surrounded by smart, modern design. The marinated *salsa verde* (pesto and parsley) fish and wild tuna with soy sauce are specialities.

★**Albores** CONTEMPORARY ANDALUCIAN €€
(956 32 02 66; Calle Consistorio 12; tapas €2.40-5, mains €10-16; 9am-midnight Mon-Sat, 11am-midnight Sun) Pitching itself among age-old city-centre favourites, Albores brings a sophisticated, contemporary edge to local flavours with its original tapas and mains combos. If there's one overall highlight it's probably the fish, particularly the monkfish, asparagus and bacon puff pastry, though the beautifully presented goats' cheese *tosta* (open sandwich on toasted bread) is just as fantastic. One of Jerez' top breakfast spots.

Reino de León CONTEMPORARY ANDALUCIAN €€
(956 32 29 15; www.reinodeleongastrobar.com; Calle Latorre 8; mains €10-17; 8am-midnight Mon-Fri, noon-midnight Sat & Sun) More 'nouveau' than most Jerez institutions, this self-styled gastrobar takes the region's staple ingredients – sherry, tuna, cured ham – and douses them with creative embellishments. Think nut-and-mascarpone-stuffed salmon or mini tandoori chicken brochettes, thrown

in with tasty salads and a fantastic wine list featuring sherry and other Cádiz wines. It's created quite the local buzz.

Mesón del Asador SPANISH, GRILL €€
(956 32 26 58; www.mesondelasador.com; Calle Remedios 2; tapas €2.80-3.25, mains €8-16; noon-4pm & 8.30-11.30pm) This big-and-busy place is a carnivore's dream that dishes up generous grilled meat tapas and full meaty spreads ranging from sizzling pork/beef/chicken brochettes to a two-person *chuletón de buey* (big beef chop). The *solomillo de cerdo* (pork tenderloin) in Cabrales or Roquefort comes highly recommended.

Albalá CONTEMPORARY ANDALUCIAN €€
(956 34 64 88; www.restaurantealbala.com; cnr Calle Divina Pastora & Avenida Duque de Abrantes; tapas €2-4, mains €8-15; noon-4pm & 8.30pm-midnight) Slide into light-wood booths amid minimalist oriental decor for chef Israel Ramos' beautifully creative modern meat, fish and veg dishes infused with typical Andalucian ingredients. House specials include *rabo de toro* croquettes and king prawn burgers with ginger noodles, plus deliciously crispy chunky asparagus tempura. It's 1km north of Plaza del Arenal.

La Carboná ANDALUCIAN €€
(956 34 74 75; www.lacarbona.com; Calle San Francisco de Paula 2; mains €13-20; 1-4pm &

8pm-midnight Wed-Mon) This popular, cavernous restaurant with an imaginative menu occupies an old bodega with a hanging fireplace that's oh-so-cosy in winter. Delicately presented specialities include grilled meats, fresh fish and the quirky mini wild boar burger with mango and yoghurt sauce, plus a good local wines list. If you can't decide, try the sherry pairing menu (€32).

El Gallo Azul
SPANISH, TAPAS €€

(Calle Larga 2; tapas €2.50-4, mains €9-15; ⏰12.30-4.30pm & 8.30-11.30pm Mon-Sat, 12.30-4.30pm Sun) Housed in what has become Jerez' signature building, a circular facade emblazoned with a sherry logo, El Gallo Azul has a smartish upstairs restaurant with a three-course *menú* (€13.50) and a tiny tapas bar at street level. It's more about the location, perfect for coffee and cake as the city springs back to life post-siesta.

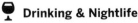

Drinking & Nightlife

Tucked away on the narrow streets north of Plaza del Arenal are a few bars catering mostly to the under-30s. Northeast of the centre, **Plaza de Canterbury** (cnr Calles Zaragoza & N de Cañas; ⏰8.15am-2.30am Mon-Wed, 8.15am-4am Thu-Sat, 4pm-4am Sun)has a couple of pubs popular with a 20s crowd, while the late-night *bares de copas* (drinks bars) northeast along Avenida de Méjico attract a younger clientele. Jerez' tabancos (p123) are busy drinking spots.

Kapote
BAR

(www.kapote.es; Avenida Álvaro Domecq 45; ⏰3.30pm-3am Sun-Thu, to 5am Fri & Sat) One of three popular side-by-side *bares de copas* next to the Hotel Sherry Park, north of the centre, Kapote keeps lively until late with chart favourites and a mixed crowd.

Dos Deditos
BAR

(Plaza Vargas 1; ⏰7pm-midnight Sun-Thu, 6pm-3am Fri, 4pm-3am Sat) A friendly, central beer bar with a never-ending list of Spanish and international brews.

JEREZ' FERTILE FLAMENCO SCENE

Jerez' moniker as the 'cradle of flamenco' is regularly challenged by aficionados in Cádiz and Seville, but the claim has merit. This surprisingly untouristed city harbours not just one but *two* Roma quarters, Santiago and San Miguel, which have produced a glut of renowned artists including Roma singers Manuel Torre and Antonio Chacón. Like its rival cities, Jerez has also concocted its own flamenco *palo* (musical form), the intensely popular *bulería*, a fast rhythmic musical style with the same *compás* (accented beat) as the *soleá*.

Begin your explorations at the Centro Andaluz de Flamenco (p119), Spain's only bona fide flamenco library, where you can pick up information on clubs, performances, and singing, dance and guitar lessons. From here, stroll down Calle Francos past a couple of legendary flamenco bars where singers and dancers still congregate. North of the Centro Andaluz de Flamenco, in the Santiago quarter, you'll find dozens of *peñas* (small private clubs) known for their accessibility and intimacy; entry is normally free if you buy a drink. The *peña* scene is particularly lively during the February flamenco festival (p122). Jerez' newly revitalised tabancos (p123), taverns that serve sherry from the barrel, are great for spur-of-the-moment flamenco.

Centro Cultural Flamenco Don Antonio Chacón (☎956 34 74 72; www.facebook.com/pages/D-Antonio-Chacón-Centro-Cultural-Flamenco; Calle Salas 2) One of the best *peñas* in town (and hence Andalucía), the Chacón, named for the great Jerez-born flamenco singer, is run by the jovial Tota twins, who often host top-notch flamenco performers. Happenings are usually impromptu, especially during the February flamenco festival. Call to find out about upcoming events, or contact the Centro Andaluz de Flamenco (p119).

Puro Arte (☎647 743832; www.puroarteflamencojerez.com; Calle Conocedores 28; €25, with dinner €42) Jerez' brand-new *tablao* (choreographed flamenco show) stages popular local-artist performances at 10pm daily. Advance bookings essential.

Damajuana (www.facebook.com/damajuanajerez; Calle Francos 18; ⏰8pm-3.30am Tue-Thu, 4pm-4am Fri-Sun) One of two historic bars on Calle Francos where flamenco singers and dancers have long met and drunk, with varied live music and a fun *movida flamenca* (flamenco scene).

Tetería La Jaima TEAHOUSE
(Calle Chancillería 10; dishes €9-14; ☉4-11.30pm Tue-Thu, to 2am Fri & Sat, to 9pm Mon & Sun; 🛜) You'll feel like a Moorish sultan reclining with a fruity, aromatic brew in this atmospherically dark tearoom, decked out with the best in Moroccan trinkets. If you're hungry, try some couscous or a tagine.

☆ Entertainment

Jerez is home to one of Andalucía's liveliest and most authentic flamenco (p124) scenes.

Teatro Villamarta THEATRE
(☑956 14 96 85; www.teatrovillamarta.es; Plaza Romero Martínez) Runs a busy program where you can pick up Bizet, Verdi, Mozart, Shakespeare and – of course – flamenco.

❶ Information

Oficina de Turismo (☑956 33 88 74; www.turismojerez.com; Plaza del Arenal; ☉9am-3pm & 5-6.30pm Mon-Fri, 9.30am-2.30pm Sat & Sun)

❶ Getting There & Away

AIR

Jerez airport (☑956 15 00 00; www.aena.es), the only one serving Cádiz province, is 7km northeast of town on the A4. Taxis to/from the airport cost €15. Eight to 10 daily trains run between the airport and Jerez (€1.80, 10 minutes), El Puerto de Santa María (€2, 15 minutes) and Cádiz (€4.05, 45 minutes). Local airport buses run twice/once on weekdays/weekends, continuing from Jerez (€1.30, 30 minutes) to El Puerto de Santa María (€1.60, 50 minutes) and Cádiz (€3.75, 1½ hours).

Ryanair (www.ryanair.com) To/from Barcelona, London Stansted and Frankfurt (seasonal).

Air Berlin (www.airberlin.com) To/from Mallorca, Frankfurt, Berlin and Düsseldorf (via Madrid).

Vueling (www.vueling.com) To/from Barcelona.

Iberia (www.iberia.com) Daily to/from Madrid.

BUS

The **bus station** (☑956 14 99 90; Plaza de la Estación) is 1.3km southeast of the centre.

TO	COST (€)	DURATION	FREQUENCY
Arcos de la Frontera	1.90	30min	1-4 daily
Cádiz	3.75	1hr	3-9 daily
El Puerto de Santa María	1.60	20min	3-10 daily
Ronda	13	2¼hr	1-2 daily
Sanlúcar de Barrameda	1.90	35min	7-13 daily
Seville	8.90	1¼hr	5-7 daily

CAR & MOTORCYCLE

There's 24-hour parking (€5) under the Alameda Vieja (beside the Alcázar); press the red button.

TRAIN

Jerez' train station is beside the bus station.

TO	COST (€)	DURATION	FREQUENCY
Cádiz	4.05	45min	16 daily
Córdoba	24	2½hr	13 daily
El Puerto de Santa María	2	10min	half hourly
Seville	11	1¼hr	15 daily

El Puerto de Santa María

POP 88,700

When you're surrounded by such cultural luminaries as Cádiz, Jerez de la Frontera and Seville, it's easy to get lost in the small print; such is the fate of El Puerto de Santa María, despite its collection of well-known icons. Osborne sherry, with its famous bull logo (which has become the national symbol of Spain), was founded and retains its HQ here, as do half a dozen other sherry bodegas. With its abundance of good beaches, sherry bodegas, elaborate cuisine, weighty bullfighting legacy and smattering of architectural heirlooms, El Puerto can seem like southern Andalucía in microcosm. It's an easy day trip from Cádiz or Jerez.

◉ Sights

Castillo de San Marcos CASTLE
(☑627 569335; servicios.turisticos@caballero.es; Plaza Alfonso X El Sabio; adult/child €6/3, free Tue; ☉tours hourly 11.30am-1.30pm Tue, 10.30am-1.30pm Thu & Sat) Heavily restored in the 20th century, El Puerto's fine castle was constructed over an Islamic mosque by Alfonso X of Castilla after he took the town in 1260. The old mosque inside, now converted into a church, is the highlight. Tuesday tours require bookings; Thursday and Saturday tours end with a sherry tasting (the castle

CÁDIZ PROVINCE & GIBRALTAR EL PUERTO DE SANTA MARÍA

El Puerto de Santa María

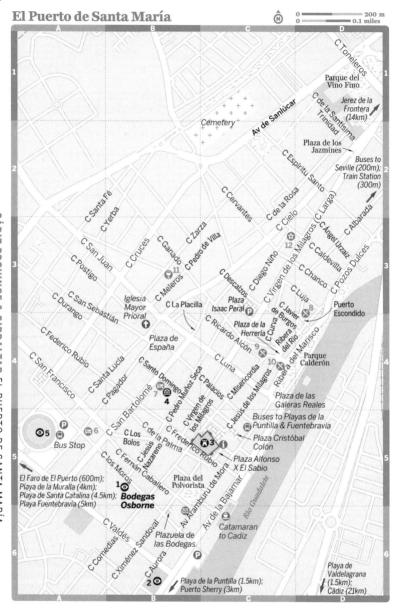

is owned by Bodegas Caballero); all 11.30am sessions are in English.

Fundación Rafael Alberti   MUSEUM
(☎956 85 07 11; www.rafaelalberti.es; Calle Santo Domingo 25; adult/child €4/2; ☺10am-2pm Tue-Sun) Two blocks inland from Plaza Alfonso X El Sabio, this foundation has interesting, well-displayed exhibits on Rafael Alberti (1902–99), one of Spain's great Generation of '27 poets, who grew up here. Free English, French or Spanish audio guides.

El Puerto de Santa María

◎ **Top Sights**
  1 Bodegas Osborne B5

◎ **Sights**
  2 Bodegas Gutiérrez Colosía.................B6
  3 Castillo de San Marcos C5
  4 Fundación Rafael Alberti B4
  5 Plaza de Toros.......................................A5

🛏 **Sleeping**
  6 El Baobab Hostel.................................A5
  7 Palacio San Bartolomé........................B4

🍴 **Eating**
  8 Aponiente...D3
  9 Mesón del Asador C4
  10 Romerijo... C4

◎ **Drinking & Nightlife**
  11 Bodega Obregón.................................B3

◎ **Entertainment**
  12 Peña Flamenca Tomás El Nitri...........C3

★**Bodegas Osborne**   SHERRY BODEGA
(☎956 86 91 00; www.osborne.es; Calle los Moros 7; tours €8; ◎tours noon & 12.30pm, in English 10.30am) Creator of the legendary black bull logo still exhibited on life-sized billboards all over Spain (now without the name), Osborne, the best known of El Puerto's sherry wineries, was set up – with no intentional irony – by an Englishman, Thomas Osborne Mann, in 1772. It remains one of Spain's oldest companies run continuously by the same family.

The gorgeous whitewashed bodega, hidden in flower-fringed gardens, adds extra tours from June to mid-September. Book ahead.

Bodegas Gutiérrez Colosía   SHERRY BODEGA
(☎956 85 28 52; www.gutierrezcolosia.com; Avenida de la Bajamar 40; tours €6; ◎tours 12.15pm Mon-Fri, 1pm Sat) No bookings needed for English-, Spanish- or German-language tours of this intimate, family-run sherry bodega, right beside the catamaran dock. Visits end with a five-wine tasting, which can include tapas and flamenco on request. Timings vary.

Plaza de Toros   BULLRING
(www.plazadetorospuertosantamaria.es; Plaza Elías Ahuja; admission €4; ◎10am-2pm & 5-7pm Tue-Fri, 10am-2pm Sat; 🅿) Four blocks southwest of Plaza de España is El Puerto's grand Plaza de Toros, built in 1880 with room for 15,000 spectators and still one of Andalucía's most important bullrings. Entry is from Calle Valdés.

🎉 Festivals & Events

Feria de Primavera y Fiestas del Vino Fino   WINE
(Spring Fair; ◎Apr-May) Around 200,000 half-bottles of *fino* (sherry) are drunk during this six-day fiesta.

Festividad Virgen del Carmen   RELIGIOUS
(◎16 Jul) Fisherfolk Andalucía-wide pay homage to their patron; El Puerto parades the Virgin's image along the Río Guadalete.

🛏 Sleeping

El Baobab Hostel   HOSTEL €
(☎956 54 21 23; www.casabaobab.es; Calle Pagador 37; dm €18-20, s €22-30, d €45-55; ❄🌐) Facing the Plaza de Toros in a converted 19th-century building, this small, six-room hostel is El Puerto's best budget choice with a homey, friendly feel, tastefully done interiors and communal kitchen and bathrooms.

★**Palacio San Bartolomé**   LUXURY HOTEL €€€
(☎956 85 09 46; www.palaciosanbartolome.com; Calle San Bartolomé 21; s €54-98, d €78-195; ❄@🌐) Every now and again along comes a hotel that blows away even the most jaded hotel reviewer. Fancy a room with its own mini swimming pool, sauna, jacuzzi, bathrobes and deckchairs? It's all yours for €198 at the deftly designed, welcoming San Bart, set in a former palace.

If you don't bag the pool room, the others are equally luxurious: four-poster beds, giant showers and cool, contemporary elegance.

🍴 Eating

El Puerto is famous for its outstanding seafood and tapas bars. Look along the central Calles Luna and Misericordia, Calle Ribera del Marisco to the north, and Avenidas de la Bajamar and Aramburu de Mora to the south.

Romerijo   SEAFOOD €
(☎956 54 12 54; www.romerijo.com; Ribera del Marisco 1; seafood per 250g from €4.50, raciones €8-12; ◎11am-11.30pm) A huge, always-busy El Puerto institution, Romerijo has three sections: one boiling seafood, another (opposite) frying it, and the third a *cervecería* (beer bar). Buy by the quarter-kilo in paper cones. The *freiduría* (fried-fish shop) closes 4pm to 7pm.

★**Mesón del Asador**   SPANISH, GRILL €€
(www.mesondelasador.com; Calle Misericordia 2; tapas €2-3, mains €10-20; ◎12.30-4pm &

EL PUERTO'S BEACHES

Drawing a predominantly Spanish crowd, El Puerto's white-sand beaches are among southern Spain's more popular coastal escapes. Closest to town is pine-flanked **Playa de la Puntilla**, a 1.5km walk southwest – or take bus 1 or 2 (€1.05) from Avenida Aramburu de Mora. A couple of kilometres further west is the swish Puerto Sherry marina, beyond which are little **Playa de la Muralla** and 3km-long **Playa de Santa Catalina**, with beach bars. Bus 3 from the centre runs out to **Playa Fuentebravía** (Playa Fuenterrabía), at the far end of Playa de Santa Catalina. By car, take the Rota road west from the roundabout at the northwest end of Calle Valdés.

On the eastern side of the Río Guadalete is popular **Playa de Valdelagrana**, backed by high-rise hotels, apartments, bars and restaurants. Bus 3 also goes here.

8pm-midnight) It's a measure of El Puerto's gastronomic nous that, in such a seafood-orientated town, there's a meat restaurant that could compete with any Buenos Aires steakhouse. The power of the Mesón's delivery is in the smell that hits you the moment you open the door – chargrilled beef and pork sizzling away on mini-barbecues brought to your table. Try the chorizo or the chicken brochette.

El Faro del Puerto   ANDALUCIAN, SEAFOOD €€
(☑956 87 09 52; www.elfarodelpuerto.com; Ctra de Fuentebravía Km 0.5; tapas €6-10, mains €17-22; ⊙1-4.30pm & 9-11pm Mon-Sat, 1-4.30pm Sun; 🖪) El Faro is worth hunting down for its traditional-with-a-hint-of-innovation take on local seafood, excellent wine list, and classically smart, multiroom setting inside an old *casa señorial* (manor house). The tuna tartare is a highlight. The (cheaper) bar/tapas menu has good vegetarian and gluten-free choices. It's on the roundabout at the northwest end of Calle Valdés.

Aponiente   SEAFOOD, FUSION €€€
(☑956 85 18 70; www.aponiente.com; Puerto Escondido 6; 12-course tasting menu €136; ⊙1.45-2.45pm & 8.45-9.45pm Tue-Sat Apr-Nov) Audacious is the word for the bold experimentation of leading Spanish chef Angel León, whose seafood-biased *nueva cocina* menu has won a cavalcade of awards including two Michelin stars and a 2011 plug from the *New York Times* as one of 10 restaurants in the world 'worth a plane ride'.

The restaurant splits local opinion in traditional El Puerto. Some snort at its prices and pretension, others salivate at the thought of fish 'chorizo', yeast-fermented mackerel and creamy rice with microseaweeds. It's set to relocate to a restored 18th-century mill near the train station in summer 2015.

🍷 Drinking & Nightlife

Bodega Obregón   BAR
(Calle Zarza 51; ⊙9am-3pm & 6-9pm Mon-Fri, 9am-4pm Sat, 10am-3pm Sun) Think sherry's just a drink for grandmas? Come and have your illusions blown to pieces at this spit-and-sawdust-style bar where the sweet stuff is siphoned from woody barrels. The home-cooked Saturday-lunch *guisos* (stews) are a local favourite.

☆ Entertainment

Peña Flamenca Tomás El Nitri   FLAMENCO
(☑956 54 32 37; Calle Diego Niño 1) This good honest *peña* (small private club), with the air of a foot-stomping, 19th-century flamenco bar, showcases some truly amazing guitarists, singers and dancers in a club full of regulars. Shows are usually on Saturday nights.

ℹ Information

Tourist Office (☑956 48 37 15; www.turismoelpuerto.com; Plaza de Alfonso X El Sabio 9; ⊙10am-2pm & 6-8pm Mon-Sat, 10am-2pm Sun)

ℹ Getting There & Away

BOAT

The **catamaran** (www.cmtbc.es) leaves from in front of the Hotel Santa María for Cádiz (€2.65, 30 minutes) 16 times daily Monday to Friday, five on weekends.

BUS

El Puerto has two bus stops. Buses to Cádiz (€2.65, 45 minutes, hourly), Jerez de la Frontera (€1.60, 20 minutes, two to seven daily) and Sanlúcar de Barrameda (€1.90, 25 minutes, 13 daily) go from the **bus stop** outside the Plaza de Toros. Buses to Seville (€10, 1¾ hours, two daily) go from outside the train station.

A VERY BRITISH DRINK

The names give it away: Harvey, Sandeman (p120), Terry, Humbert, Osborne (p127). Andalucía's sherry industry might be Spanish in character but it is firmly Anglo-Irish in origin. Francis Drake sacked Cádiz in 1587 and greedily made off with over 3000 barrels of local *vino* – a whole new industry was inauspiciously born.

Thomas Osborne Mann, from Exeter, was among the first to jump on board. Befriending local wine-growers in El Puerto de Santa María in 1772, he set up what is today one of Spain's oldest family firms, Osborne, famous for its imposing black bull logo. George Sandeman, a Scotsman from Perth, founded his fledgling sherry empire in Tom's Coffee House in the City of London in 1790. John Harvey from Bristol began importing sherry from Spain in 1796 and concocted the world's first cream sherry, Harvey's Bristol Cream, in the 1860s. The Terry family, from southern Ireland, founded their famous bodegas in El Puerto de Santa María in 1865. Even Spain's most illustrious sherry dynasty González-Byass – producers of the trademark Tío Pepe brand – was formed from an 1835 Anglo-Spanish alliance between Andalucian Manuel María González and his English agent Robert Byass.

CAR & MOTORCYCLE

There's supervised parking at the Plaza de Toros and the catamaran dock. Plaza Isaac Peral has an underground car park (€3.95 per 24 hours).

TRAIN

From the train station at the northeast end of town, frequent trains go to/from Jerez de la Frontera (€2, 10 minutes), Cádiz (€3.40, 35 minutes) and Seville (€14, 1¼ hours).

Sanlúcar de Barrameda

POP 67,300

Sanlúcar is one of those lesser-known Andalucian towns that will pleasantly surprise you. Firstly, there's the gastronomy: Sanlúcar cooks up some of the region's best seafood on a hallowed waterside strip called Bajo de Guía. Secondly, Sanlúcar's unique location at the northern tip of the esteemed sherry triangle enables its earthy bodegas, nestled in the somnolent, monument-strewn old town, to produce the much-admired one-of-a-kind *manzanilla* (sherry). Thirdly, plonked at the mouth of the Río Guadalquivir estuary, Sanlúcar provides a quieter, less trammelled entry point into the ethereal Parque Nacional de Doñana than the popular western access points in Huelva province.

As if that wasn't enough, the town harbours a proud nautical history. Both Christopher Columbus, on this third sojourn (p85), and Portuguese mariner Ferdinand Magellan struck out from here on their voyages of discovery. Don't miss out.

◉ Sights

Palacio de Orleans y Borbón   PALACE

(cnr Calles Cuesta de Belén & Caballeros; ⊙10am-1.30pm Mon-Fri) FREE From central Plaza del Cabildo, cross Calle Ancha and head up Calle Bretones, which becomes Calle Cuesta de Belén. At the top you'll come to this beautiful neo-Mudéjar old-town palace, built as a 19th-century summer home for the aristocratic Montpensier family. It's now Sanlúcar's town hall; you can only visit the gardens.

Palacio de los Duques de Medina Sidonia   PALACE, MUSEUM

(✆956 36 01 61; www.fcmedinasidonia.com; Plaza Condes de Niebla 1; admission €5; ⊙tours noon Tue-Fri, 11.30am & noon Sun) Just off Calle Caballeros, this was the rambling home of the aristocratic family (p323) that once owned more of Spain than anyone else. The mostly 17th-century house bursts with antiques, and paintings by Goya, Zurbarán and other Spanish greats. Stop for coffee and cake in its old-world cafe (cakes €2-3.50; ⊙9am-9pm Tue-Sun, 9am-1pm & 4-8.30pm Mon).

Iglesia de Nuestra Señora de la O   CHURCH

(Plaza de la Paz; ⊙mass 7pm Mon & Wed-Fri, 9am, noon & 7pm Sun) Fronting the old town's Calle Caballeros, this medieval church stands out among Sanlúcar's many others for its fine 1360s Gothic-Mudéjar portal and its rich interior decoration, particularly the Mudéjar *artesonado* (ceiling of interlaced beams with decorative insertions).

THE SHERRY SECRET

Once sherry grapes have been harvested, they're pressed and the resulting must is left to ferment. When a frothy veil of *flor* (yeast) appears on the surface, the wine is transferred to bodegas in big American-oak barrels.

Wine enters the *solera* (from *suelo*, 'floor') process when it's a year old. The barrels, five-sixths full, are lined up in rows at least three barrels high. Those on the bottom contain the oldest wine. From these, about three times a year, 10% of the wine is drawn out. This is replaced with the same amount from the barrels directly above, which is then replaced from the next layer. The wines age for three to seven years. A little brandy is added before bottling, bringing alcohol content to 16% to 18%, which stops fermentation.

Castillo de Santiago   CASTLE
(☑956 92 35 00; www.castillodesantiago.com; Plaza del Castillo de Santiago; adult/child €6/4; ☺10am-2.30pm Tue-Sat, 11am-2.30pm Sun) Surrounded by Barbadillo's bodegas, Sanlúcar's restored 15th-century castle has great views from its hexagonal Torre del Homenaje (keep). The story goes that Isabel la Católica first saw the sea from here. Entry to the Patio de Armas and its restaurant is free.

★ **Bodegas Barbadillo**   WINERY
(☑956 38 55 00; www.barbadillo.com; Calle Sevilla; tours €6; ☺tours noon & 1pm Tue-Sat, noon Sun, in English 11am Tue-Sat) Barbadillo was the first family to bottle Sanlúcar's famous *manzanilla* and also produces one of Spain's most popular *vinos*. Bodega tours end with a tasting. Also in this 19th-century building is the informative **Museo de la Manzanilla** (☺10am-3pm Tue & Thu-Sat, 10am-6pm Wed, 11am-2pm Sun) **FREE**, which traces the 200-year history of *manzanilla*.

☞ Tours

Sanlúcar is a potential base for exploring the Parque Nacional de Doñana (p87), which glistens just across the Río Guadalquivir.

Trips here are run by the licensed **Visitas Doñana,** (☑956 36 38 13; www.visitasdonana.com; Bajo de Guía; tours €35; ☺9am-7pm) whose boat, the *Real Fernando,* chugs up the river for

wildlife viewing. Your first option is a three-hour boat/jeep combination, which goes 30km through the park's dunes, marshlands and pine forests in 20-person 4WD vehicles. There's usually one trip in the morning and another in the afternoon. The second (less interesting) option is a hop-on-hop-off ferry tour with a little walking. You can book and find out more about Doñana at the **Centro de Visitantes Fábrica de Hielo** (☑956 38 65 77; Bajo de Guía; ☺9am-7pm). Trips depart from Bajo de Guía. It's best to reserve a week ahead.

Viajes Doñana (☑956 36 25 40; viajesdonana@hotmail.com; Calle San Juan 20; tours €35; ☺9am-2pm & 5-8.30pm Mon-Fri, 10.30am-2pm Sat) agency books the same trips.

★ Festivals & Events

Feria de la Manzanilla   WINE FESTIVAL
(☺late May/early Jun) A big *manzanilla*-fuelled fair kicks off Sanlúcar's summer.

Romería del Rocío   RELIGIOUS
(☺7th weekend after Easter) Many pilgrims and covered wagons set out for El Rocío (p90) from Sanlúcar.

Carreras de Caballos   HORSES
(www.carrerassanlucar.es; ☺Aug) Two horse-race meetings held almost every year since 1845, on the beaches beside the Guadalquivir estuary.

🛏 Sleeping

★ **Hostal Alcoba**   HOTEL €€
(☑956 38 31 09; www.hostalalcoba.es; Calle Alcoba 26; s €70-80, d €80-90; ⓟ❄🅿🌐▣) The beautifully quirky but stylish 11-room Alcoba, with a slick, modernist courtyard complete with loungers, pool and hammocks, looks like something that architect Frank Lloyd-Wright might have conceived. Skilfully put together (and run), it's a genius design creation that's somehow wonderfully homey, functional and central (just off the northeastern end of Calle Ancha), all at the same time.

Hotel Barrameda   HOTEL €€
(☑956 38 58 78; www.hotelbarrameda.com; Calle Ancha 10; s €70-85, d €68-90; ❄🌐) This gleaming, 40-room hotel overlooks the tapas bar fun on Plaza del Cabildo, and makes an excellent, central choice for the sparkling modern rooms in its new wing (some with little terraces), ground-floor patio, marble floors and super-efficient service. Rates drop outside July and August.

Hotel Posada de Palacio   HISTORIC HOTEL €€
(☑ 956 36 50 60; www.posadadepalacio.com; Calle Caballeros 11; d incl breakfast €88-174; ☺ Mar-Oct; ✳🖭) Plant-filled patios, high ceilings, gracious historical charm and 18th-century luxury add up to one of the most elegantly characterful places to stay in this region. Each room is different – tiled floors, brick arches, loft-like set-ups – but the superior doubles are standouts. There's antique furniture, but it's never too overdone.

From central Plaza del Cabildo, cross Calle Ancha and head up Calle Bretones, which becomes Calle Cuesta de Belén.

✕ Eating

Strung out along **Bajo de Guía**, 750m northeast of the centre, is one of Andalucía's most famous eating strips, once a fishing village and now a haven of high-quality seafood restaurants that revel in their simplicity. The undisputed speciality is *arroz caldoso a la marinera* (seafood rice); the local *langostinos* (king prawns) are another favourite.

★Casa Balbino   TAPAS, SEAFOOD €
(www.casabalbino.com; Plaza del Cabildo 11; tapas €2-3; ☺ noon-5pm & 6-11.30pm) It doesn't matter when you arrive, Casa Balbino is always overflowing with people, drawn in by its fantastic seafood tapas. Whether you're perched at the bar, tucked into a corner or lucky enough to score one of the outdoor plaza tables, you'll have to elbow your way to the front and shout your order to a waiter, who'll shout back and hand over your dish.

The options are endless, but the *tortillas de camarones* (crisp shrimp fritters), fried-egg-topped *tagarninas* (thistles) and *langostinos a la plancha* (grilled king prawns) are exquisite.

Helados Artesanos Toni   ICE CREAM €
(www.heladostoni.com; Plaza del Cabildo 2; ice creams €1.30-4; ☺ 9am-midnight mid-Mar–mid-Oct) For some of the best ice cream in Andalucía, don't miss Helados Artesanos Toni, family run since 1986. Now they even do frozen yoghurt.

★Poma   SEAFOOD €€
(☑ 956 36 51 53; www.restaurantepoma.com; Bajo de Guía 6; mains €10-16; ☺ 1-4.30pm & 7.30pm-midnight) You could kick a football on Bajo de Guía and guarantee it'd land on a decent plate of fish, but you should probably aim for Poma, where the *frito variado* (€14) comes with

five different varieties of lightly fried species plucked out of the nearby sea and river.

Casa Bigote   SEAFOOD €€€
(☑ 956 36 26 96; www.restaurantecasabigote.com; Bajo de Guía 10; mains €12-20; ☺ 12.30-4pm & 8pm-midnight Mon-Sat) Classier than most places, Casa Bigote is the most renowned of Bajo de Guía's seafood-only restaurants. Waiters flit back and forth across a small lane to its permanently packed tapas bar on the corner opposite.

❶ Information

Oficina de Información Turística (☑ 956 36 61 10; www.sanlucarturismo.com; Avenida Calzada Duquesa Isabel; ☺ 10am-2pm & 4-6pm)

❶ Getting There & Away

BUS

From the **bus station** (Avenida de la Estación), **Los Amarillos** (☑ 902 21 03 17; www.losamarillos.es) goes hourly to/from El Puerto de Santa María (€2.17, 30 minutes), Cádiz (€2.65, one hour) and Seville (€8.84, two hours), less on weekends.

Autocares Valenzuela (☑ 956 18 10 96; www.grupovalenzuela.com) has hourly buses to/from Jerez de la Frontera (€1.90, 40 minutes), less on weekends.

CAR & MOTORCYCLE
There's underground parking on Avenida Calzada Duquesa Isabel.

THE WHITE TOWNS

Arcos de la Frontera
POP 22,450

Everything you've ever dreamed a *pueblo blanco* (white town) to be miraculously materialises in Arcos de la Frontera (33km east of Jerez): a thrilling strategic clifftop location, a soporific old town full of winding streets and mystery, a swanky *parador*, and a volatile frontier history. The odd tour bus and foreign-owned guesthouse do little to dampen the drama.

For a brief period during the 11th century, Arcos was an independent Berber-ruled *taifa* (small kingdom). In 1255 it was claimed by Christian King Alfonso X El Sabio for Seville and it remained 'de la Frontera' (on the frontier) until the fall of Granada in 1492.

Arcos de la Frontera

Arcos de la Frontera

⊙ Top Sights
1 Basílica Menor de Santa María
   de la Asunción B2
2 Plaza del Cabildo B3

⊙ Sights
3 Castillo de los Duques B2
4 Iglesia de San Pedro D4
5 Mirador B3

🛏 Sleeping
6 Casa Campana D3
7 La Casa Grande C3
8 Parador de Arcos de la Frontera C3

🍴 Eating
9 Babel A1
10 Bar La Cárcel B2
   Parador de Arcos de la
   Frontera ....(see 8)
11 Taberna Jóvenes Flamencos B2

⊙ Sights

★ Plaza del Cabildo   SQUARE

Lined with fine ancient buildings, Plaza del Cabildo is the centre of the old town, its vertiginous **mirador** (Lookout) affording exquisite vistas over the Río Guadalete. The 11th-century, Moorish-built **Castillo de los Duques** is closed to the public, but its outer walls frame classic Arcos views. On the square's eastern side, the Parador de Arcos de la Frontera (p133) is a reconstruction of a 16th-century magistrate's house.

★ Basílica Menor
de Santa María de la Asunción   CHURCH

(Plaza del Cabildo; admission €2; ⊙10am-1pm & 4-6.30pm Mon-Fri, 10am-2pm Sat Mar-Dec) This Gothic-cum-baroque creation is one of Andalucía's more beautiful and intriguing small churches, built over several centuries on the site of a mosque. Check out the ornate gold-leaf altarpiece (a miniature of the one in

Seville cathedral) carved between 1580 and 1608, a striking painting of San Cristóbal (St Christopher), a 14th-century mural uncovered in the 1970s, an ornate wood-carved choir and the lovely Isabelline ceiling tracery.

Iglesia de San Pedro CHURCH
(Calle San Pedro 4; admission €1; ⊙ 9.30am-1.30pm & 3.30-6.30pm Mon-Fri, 9.30am-1.30pm Sat) A Gothic-baroque confection, sporting what is perhaps one of Andalucía's most magnificent small-church interiors.

☞ Tours

Old-Town Tour WALKING TOUR
(per person €5) The tourist office (p133) organises daily guided old-town walking tours (1½ hours) at 11am and 5pm (6pm June to September); book ahead.

✵ Festivals & Events

Semana Santa HOLY WEEK
(⊙ Mar/Apr) Dramatic Semana Santa processions see hooded penitents inching through Arcos' narrow streets. On Easter Sunday, a hair-raising running of the bulls takes over.

Feria de San Miguel FAIR
(⊙ late Sep) Arcos celebrates its patron saint with a colourful four- or five-day fair.

⌂ Sleeping

Casa Campana GUESTHOUSE €
(⊘ 600 284928; www.casacampana.com; Calle Núñez de Prado 4; r/apt €50/80; ✴ @ 🛜 📶) One of several charming guesthouses in old Arcos, Casa Campana has two simple doubles and a massive five-person apartment with kitchenette that's filled with character. The flowery patio with sun loungers is a lovely private spot and the rooftop terrace is flooded with views. It's run by very knowledgeable owners, who hand out an excellent old-town walking tour brochure.

★ La Casa Grande HISTORIC HOTEL €€
(⊘ 956 70 39 30; www.lacasagrande.net; Calle Maldonado 10; r €79-105, ste €94-105; ✴ @ 🛜) This gorgeous, rambling, cliffside mansion dating back to 1729 once belonged to the great flamenco dancer Antonio Ruiz Soler. With each of the seven rooms done in different but wonderfully tasteful design (all with divine views), it feels more like a home-cum-artists-retreat than a hotel. Great breakfasts, a well-stocked library, a fabulous rooftop terrace, and massage and yoga top off the perfect package.

It closes for two weeks in mid- or late January.

Parador de Arcos de la Frontera HISTORIC HOTEL €€€
(⊘ 956 70 05 00; www.parador.es; Plaza del Cabildo; r €100-170; ✴ @ 🛜) A rebuilt 16th-century magistrate's residence that combines typical *parador's* luxury with a magnificent cliffside setting and the best views in town. Eight of the 24 rooms have balconies opening out to sweeping clifftop panoramas; most others look out on pretty Plaza del Cabildo. The classically smart *restaurant* (mains €10-21; ⊙ 8-11am, noon-4pm & 8.30-11pm) offers a short but select local menu. Good discounts online.

✗ Eating

Taberna Jóvenes Flamencos ANDALUCIAN, TAPAS €
(⊘ 657 133552; www.tabernajovenesflamencos. blogspot.com; Calle Deán Espinosa 11; tapas €2-3, raciones €6-10; ⊙ noon-midnight Thu-Tue; ⊘) You've got to hand it to this popular place, which successfully opened up midrecession in 2012. Along with wonderful flamenco/bullfighting decor and brilliantly red tables, it has an easy-to-navigate menu of meat, fish, vegetarian and scramble dishes – including a delicious chunky courgette and Parmesan omelette. Service is impeccable and music and dance break out regularly.

Bar La Cárcel TAPAS €€
(⊘ 956 70 04 10; Calle Deán Espinosa 18; tapas €2.50, raciones €8-13; ⊙ noon-1am Tue-Sun) A *cárcel* (prison) in name only, this low-key bar-restaurant offers no-nonsense tapas – honeyed eggplant with goat's cheese, spinach-cheese crêpes – with ice-cold *cañas* (small draught beer) and *tinto de verano* (red wine with lemonade and ice). It's friendly and authentic.

Babel MOROCCAN, FUSION €€
(www.restaurantebabel.es; Calle Corredera 11; dishes €7-12; ⊙ 1-4pm & 7.30-11.30pm Mon-Sat) Arcos' Moorish fusion spot has some tasteful decor (the ornate stools were shipped in from Casablanca) and some equally tasty dishes: choose from tagines, couscous and hummus, or the full Arabic tea treatment with silver pots and sweet pastries.

❶ Information

Tourist Office (⊘ 956 70 22 64; www. turismoarcos.es; Calle Cuesta de Belén 5;

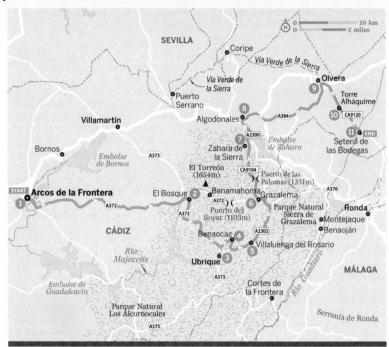

Driving Tour
White Towns

START ARCOS DE LA FRONTERA
END SETENIL DE LAS BODEGAS
LENGTH 130KM; TWO DAYS

Rev up in dramatic **1 Arcos de la Frontera** (p131), a Roman-turned-Moorish-turned-Christian citadel perched atop a sheer-sided sandstone ridge. Head 32km east along the A372 to **2 El Bosque**, the western gateway to Cádiz province's Parque Natural Sierra de Grazalema and location of the park's main information centre (p137). The A373 takes you 13km round to leather-making **3 Ubrique**, close to the borders of the Grazalema and Alcornocales natural parks. Mountains rise quickly as you drive 7km up the A2302 to tiny **4 Benaocaz**, where several Grazalema park hikes start/finish, and another 7km on to equally diminutive **5 Villaluenga del Rosario** with its artisan cheese museum. Plying the craggy eastern face of the sierra then taking the A372 west brings you to **6 Grazalema** (p135), a red-roofed park-activity nexus also famous for its blanket-making and homemade honey; it's

the perfect overnight stop. Count the switch-backs on the steep CA9104 as you climb up to the view-splayed Puerto de las Palomas and, beyond, quintessential white town **7 Zahara de la Sierra** (p136), with its huddle of houses spread around the skirts of a rocky crag above a glassy reservoir at the foot of the Grazalema mountains. The A2300 threads north to **8 Algodonales**, a white town on the edge of the natural park known for its guitar-making workshop and hang-gliding/paragliding (p138) obsession. Take the A384 east from here past the Peñón de Zaframagón (an important refuge for griffon vultures) to reach **9 Olvera**, visible for miles around thanks to its Arabic castle but also known for its high-quality olive oil and Vía Verde (p138) cycling/hiking path. Following the CA9106 you'll pass the little-known white town of **10 Torre Alháquime**. From here, the CA9120 winds south towards the border with Málaga province and **11 Setenil de las Bodegas**, a village instantly recognisable for its cave houses. Once used for storing wine, today they offer a shady antidote to the summer heat plus some good tapas bars.

⏱ 9.30am-2pm & 3-7.30pm Mon-Sat, 10am-2pm Sun) Doubles up as a Centro de Inter-pretación with history exhibits and a model of present-day Arcos.

ⓘ Getting There & Around

BUS

Buses from Arcos' **bus station** (Calle Los Alcaldes) in the new town down to the west of the old town, off Avenida Miguel Mancheño, are operated by **Los Amarillos** (☏ 902 21 03 17; www.losamarillos.es), **Comes** (www.tgcomes.es) and/or the **Consorcio de Transportes Bahía de Cádiz** (www.cmtbc.es). Frequency is reduced at weekends.

TO	COST (€)	DURATION	FREQUENCY
Cádiz	7.25	1hr	12 daily
Jerez de la Frontera	1.90	40min	23 daily
Málaga	19	3¾hr	2 daily
Olvera	7.83	1½hr	1 daily
Ronda	9.56	2hr	2 daily
Seville	8.97	2hr	2 daily

CAR & MOTORCYCLE

There's underground parking below Paseo de Andalucía, west of the old town. A half-hourly 'microbus' (€0.90) runs up to the old town from adjacent Plaza de España.

Grazalema

POP 1650 / ELEV 825M

Few white towns are as generically per-fect as Grazalema, with its spotless white-washed houses sporting rust-tiled roofs and wrought-iron window bars, sprinkled on the steep rocky slopes of its eponymous moun-tain range. With hikes fanning out in all directions, Grazalema is the most popular base for adventures into the Parque Natu-ral Sierra de Grazalema (p137). It's also an age-old producer of blankets, honey, cheese, meat-filled stews and an adrenalin-filled bullrunning festival, and has its own special mountain charm.

◉ Sights

Plaza de España SQUARE
The centre of the village is Plaza de Es-paña, overlooked by the 18th-century **Iglesia de la Aurora** (⏱ 11am-1pm) and refreshed by a four-spouted Visigothic **fountain**.

Museo de Artesanía Textil MUSEUM
(www.mantasdegrazalema.com; Ctra de Ronda; ⏱ 8am-2pm & 3-6.30pm Mon-Thu, 8am-2pm Fri; Ⓟ) Grazalema's delicate wool shawls and blankets rose to fame in the 18th and 19th centuries. At this artisan textile factory, 350m northwest of Plaza de España, you can still witness the traditional weaving methods.

🏃 Activities

Horizon ADVENTURE SPORTS
(☏ 956 13 23 63; www.horizonaventura.com; Calle Las Piedras 1; ⏱ 10am-2pm & 5-8pm Mon-Sat) Just off Plaza de España, highly experienced Hori-zon offers all the most exciting activities in the Parque Natural Sierra de Grazalema, includ-ing hiking, kayaking, climbing, canyoning, caving and paragliding, with English-, French or German-speaking guides. Prices per person range from €13 for a half-day walk to €90 for tandem paragliding (but may rise for less than six people).

El Calvario-Corazón de Jesús WALKING
A signposted 500m route that splits in two leads up to El Calvario, a chapel ruined during the civil war, and to a larger-than-life statue of Jesus (Corazón de Jésus), both with fine mountain and village views. The path starts on the left side of the A372, about 500m uphill from the swimming pool at the east end of Grazalema.

🛏 Sleeping

Casa de las Piedras HOTEL €
(☏ 956 13 20 14; www.casadelaspiedras.net; Calle Las Piedras 32; s/d €35/48, with shared bathroom €15/25; ✳ 🛜) Mountain air and a homey feel go together like Isabel and Fernando at this rustic-design hotel with a snug down-stairs lounge and masses of park activities information. The simple cosy rooms, in var-ious shapes and sizes, are decorated with Grazalema-made blankets. It's 100m west of Plaza de España.

La Mejorana CASA RURAL €
(☏ 956 13 23 27, 649 613272; www.lamejorana.net; Calle Santa Clara 6; s/d incl breakfast €45/58; ✳ @ 🛜 ▦) A beautiful, welcoming house towards the upper end of Grazalema, La Mejorana has smartened up its six colour-ful, comfy rooms. Some have private loung-es and bright blue Moroccan-style arches; others balconies, huge mirrors or wrought-iron bedsteads. There's a big country-style sitting room plus a terrace with gorgeous

village views – and a leafy garden that even includes in a pool.

Eating

Cafetería Rotacapa
CAFE €

(www.facebook.com/cafeteria.rotacapa; Calle Las Piedras 9; dishes €1-2.50; ⊙8am-1.30pm & 5-9pm Mon-Thu, 8am-9pm Fri-Sun) Join the local chatter at this bubbly, flowery-walled haven of homemade cakes, croissants, coffee and cooked breakfasts.

Restaurante El Torreón
ANDALUCIAN €€

(📋956 13 23 13; www.restauranteeltorreongrazalema.com; Calle Agua 44; mains €7-15; ⊙1-3.30pm & 7.30-11.30pm Thu-Tue) This cosy, friendly restaurant with a log fire specialises in traditional mountain cuisine, from local chorizo and cheese platters to *tagarnina* (thistle) scrambles (a Cádiz delicacy), sirloin in green-pepper sauce, and a tasty spinach blended with pine nuts. Tables spill out on to the street when it's sunny.

ℹ Information

Tourist Office (www.grazalema.es; Plaza de Asomaderos; ⊙10am-2pm & 4-7pm Mon-Sat) Parque Natural Sierra de Grazalema walking information.

ℹ Getting There & Away

Los Amarillos (www.losamarillos.es) runs two daily buses to/from Ronda (€2.87, one hour); three daily to/from Ubrique (€2.34, 30 minutes) via Benaocaz (€1.62, 20 minutes); and one daily Monday to Friday to El Bosque (€1.45, 30 minutes), where you can change for Arcos de la Frontera.

Zahara de la Sierra

POP 1320 / ELEV 550M

Rugged Zahara, strung around a vertiginous crag at the foot of the Grazalema mountains, overlooking the turquoise Embalse de Zahara, hums with Moorish mystery. For over 150 years in the 14th and 15th centuries, it stood on the old medieval frontier facing off against Christian Olvera, clearly visible in the distance. These days Zahara ticks all the classic white-town boxes and is a great base for hiking the Garganta Verde (p137), so it's popular. Come during the afternoon siesta, however, and you can still hear a pin drop.

The precipitous CA9104 road over the ultra-steep 1331m Puerto de las Palomas (Doves' Pass) links Zahara with Grazalema (17km) and is a spectacular drive full of white-knuckle switchbacks.

◉ Sights & Activities

With vistas framed by tall palms and hot-pink bougainvillea, Zahara's streets invite exploration. The village centres on Calle San Juan; towards its eastern end stands the 18th-century baroque **Iglesia de Santa María de Mesa** (⊙hours vary). To climb to the 12th-century **castle keep** (admission free; ⊙24hr), a hike of about 10 to 15 minutes, take the path almost opposite the Hotel Arco de la Villa. The castle's recapture from the Christians by Abu al-Hasan of Granada, in a 1481 night raid, provoked the Reyes Católicos (Catholic Monarchs) to launch the last phase of the Reconquista, which ended with the fall of Granada.

Zahara Catur
ADVENTURE SPORTS

(📋657 926394; www.zaharacatur.com; Plaza del Rey 3) This Zahara-based adventure outfit rents two-person canoes (€18 per hour) and runs guided walks and canyoning. Minimum six people, but you can join other groups.

🛏 Sleeping

Los Tadeos
RURAL HOTEL €€

(📋956 12 30 86; www.alojamientoruralcadiz.com; Paseo de la Fuente; s/d/ste €45/63/100; 🅿✳🛜🚭) On the western edge of Zahara, Los Tadeos has been glammed up from a family-run *pensión* (small budget hotel) to a comfy, well-equipped *rural hotel* and restaurant. The 17 rooms are tastefully done in modern-rustic style, many with big balconies and three with private jacuzzis. The highlight is the beautiful infinity pool for drinking in the countryside and village views.

ℹ Information

Punto de Información Zahara de la Sierra (📋956 12 31 14; Plaza del Rey 3; ⊙9am-2.30pm & 4-6pm Tue-Fri, 11am-3pm & 4-6pm Sat & Sun) Official Parque Natural Sierra de Grazalema information.

ℹ Getting There & Away

Comes (📋956 29 11 68; www.tgcomes.es) runs two daily buses to/from Ronda (€4.47, one hour).

Parque Natural Sierra de Grazalema

The rugged pillar-like peaks of the Parque Natural Sierra de Grazalema rise abruptly from the plains northeast of Cádiz, revealing sheer gorges, rare firs, wild orchids and the province's highest summits against a beautifully green backdrop. This is the wettest part of Spain – stand aside Galicia and Cantabria, Grazalema village logs an average 2000mm annually. It's gorgeous walking country (best months: May, June, September and October). For the more intrepid, adventure activities abound.

The 534-sq-km park, named Spain's first Unesco Biosphere Reserve in 1977, extends into northwestern Málaga province, where it includes the Cueva de la Pileta (p184).

🏃 Activities

Hiking, caving, canyoning, kayaking, rock climbing, cycling, birdwatching, paragliding – this gorgeous protected area crams it all in. For the more technical stuff, go with a guide; Zahara Catur (p136) and Grazalema-based Horizon (p135) are respected adventure-activity outfits.

The Sierra de Grazalema is criss-crossed by beautiful marked trails. Four of the best – the Garganta Verde (p137), El Pinsapar (p137), Llanos del Rabel and El Torreón (p138) paths – enter restricted areas and require free permits from the Centro de Visitantes El Bosque (📞956 70 97 33; cv_el-bosque@agenciamedioambienteyagua.es; Calle Federico García Lorca 1; ⏰9.30am-2pm Sun-Tue, 9.30am-2pm & 4-6pm Wed-Sat). Ideally, book a month or two ahead. The Centro will email permits on request, usually in Spanish only. Additional (leftover) permits are sometimes available on the day; you can ask ahead by phone or email, but you'll have to collect them at the Centro on the day. Some trails are off-limits June to October due to fire risk.

The Centro de Visitantes El Bosque, the Punto de Información Zahara de la Sierra (p136) and the Grazalema tourist office (p136) have decent maps outlining the main walking possibilities. There's downloadable Spanish- and English-language hiking information with maps online at www.ventanadelvisitante.es.

DON'T MISS

GARGANTA VERDE WALK

The 2.5km path that winds down into the precipitous Garganta Verde (Green Throat), a lushly vegetated gorge over 100m deep, is one of the Sierra de Grazalema's most spectacular walks. A large colony of enormous griffon vultures, whose feathers ruffle in the wind as they whoosh by close-up, makes the one-hour descent even more dramatic. The best viewpoint is 30 minutes in.

At the bottom of the ravine, you follow the riverbed to an eerie cavern known as the Cueva de la Ermita. Then it's a 1½-hour climb back up!

The trail starts 3.5km south of Zahara de la Sierra, at Km 10 on the CA9104 to Grazalema. You'll need a free prebooked permit from the Centro de Visitantes El Bosque (p137). The route is partially closed June to mid-October.

El Pinsapar Walk   HIKING

The 12km Sendero del Pinsapar to Benamahoma starts from a car park 1km along the CA9104 to Zahara de la Sierra, 2km uphill from Grazalema. Keep an eye out for the rare dark-green *pinsapo*, a relic of the great Mediterranean fir forests of the Tertiary period, which survives only in southwest Andalucía and northern Morocco. Allow six hours one-way.

This hike requires a permit from the Centro de Visitantes El Bosque (p137).

Salto del Cabrero Walk   HIKING

Of the park's free-access paths, the most dramatic is the 7.2km Sendero Salto del Cabrero between the Puerto del Boyar and Benaocaz, traversing the western flanks of the Sierra del Endrinal. The Camino de los Charcones leads from the top of Grazalema to the Puerto del Boyar (1.8km). From here, the well-signposted Sendero Salto del Cabrero proceeds mainly downhill through a broad vista-laden valley.

Allow three to four hours from Grazalema to Benaocaz. A daily bus returns from Benaocaz to Grazalema at 3.40pm. The Sendero Salto del Cabrero was closed at the Grazalema end at research time, but may well reopen. You can still reach the Salto del Cabrero (Goatherd's Leap) itself, a gaping fissure in the earth's surface, from Benaocaz (about one hour).

VÍA VERDE DE LA SIERRA

Regularly touted as the finest of Spain's *vías verdes* (greenways which have transformed old railway lines into traffic-free thoroughfares for bikers, hikers and horse-riders), the Vía Verde de la Sierra (www.fundacionviaverdedelasierra.com) between Olvera and Puerto Serrano is one of 23 such schemes in Andalucía. Aside from the wild, rugged scenery, the 36km-route is notable for four spectacular viaducts, 30 tunnels (with sensor-activated lighting) and three old stations-turned-hotel/restaurants. Ironically, the train line itself was never actually completed. It was constructed in the 1920s as part of the abortive Jerez to Almargen railway, but the Spanish Civil War put a stop to construction works. The line was restored in the early 2000s.

The Hotel/Restaurante Estación Verde (661 463207; Calle Pasadera 4; s/d/tr €25/40/60) just outside Olvera is the official starting point. Here you can hire bikes, including tandems, kids' bikes and chariots, from €12 per day, and check out the Centro de Interpretación Vía Verde de la Sierra (adult/child €2/1; 9.30am-5.30pm Thu-Mon). Bike hire is also available at Coripe and Puerto Serrano stations. Other services include the Patrulla Verde (638 280184; 9am-5pm Sat & Sun), a staff of bike experts who help with info and mechanical issues.

A highlight of the Vía Verde is the Peñón de Zaframagón, a distinctive crag that's a prime breeding ground for griffon vultures. The Centro de Interpretación y Observatorio Ornitológico (956 13 63 72; adult/child €2/1; 11am-4pm Sat & Sun), in the former Zaframagón station building 16km west of Olvera, allows close-up observations activated directly from a high-definition camera placed up on the crag.

El Torreón Walk
HIKING

(Nov-May) El Torreón (1654m) is Cádiz province's highest peak and from the summit on clear days you can see Gibraltar, the Sierra Nevada and Morocco's Rif Mountains. The route starts 100m east of Km 40 on the Grazalema–Benamahoma A372, 8km west of Grazalema. It takes about 2½ hours to the summit. You'll need a permit from the Centro de Visitantes El Bosque (p137).

Zero Gravity
ADVENTURE SPORTS

(615 372554; www.paraglidingspain.es; Calle Zahara de la Sierra 11-13, Algodonales; 1-week courses €900) Little-known Algodonales, 6km north of Zahara de la Sierra, surprises as a major paragliding and hang-gliding centre of Andalucía. Long-standing Zero Gravity offers an extensive range of beginner and 're-fresher' paragliding programs, plus tandem flights with instructors (€100).

Olvera

POP 8180 / ELEV 643M

Dramatically topped by an Arabic castle, Olvera (27km northeast of Zahara de la Sierra) beckons from miles away across olive-covered country. A bandit refuge until the mid-19th century, the town now supports more family-run farming cooperatives than anywhere else in Spain. Most come to Olvera for the Vía Verde de la Sierra, but as a white town par excellence, it's renowned for its olive oil, striking neoclassical church and roller-coaster history, which probably started with the Romans.

☉ Sights & Activities

Castillo Árabe
CASTLE

(Plaza de la Iglesia; adult/child €2/1; 10.30am-2pm & 4-7pm Tue-Sun) Perched on a crag high atop town is Olvera's late-12th-century Arabic castle, which later formed part of Nasrid Granada's defensive systems.

La Cilla
MUSEUM

(Plaza de la Iglesia; adult/child €2/1; 10.30am-2pm & 4-7pm Tue-Sun) The old grain store of the Dukes of Osuna, beside the castle, houses the tourist office, the Museo La Frontera y los Castillos, and an exposition on Olvera's Vía Verde de la Sierra (p138) cycling/hiking path.

Iglesia Parroquial
Nuestra Señora de la Encarnación
CHURCH

(Plaza de la Iglesia; admission €2; 11am-1pm Tue-Sun) Built over a Gothic-Mudéjar predecessor, Olvera's neoclassical top-of-town church was commissioned by the Dukes of Osuna and completed in 1843.

🛏 Sleeping & Eating

Hotel Sierra y Cal   HOTEL €
(☏ 956 13 03 03; www.tugasa.com; Calle Nuestra
Señora de los Remedios 2; s/d incl breakfast
€36/56; ❄ 🛜 🏊) This simple but efficiently
managed hotel towards the eastern end of
untouristed Olvera delivers a few surprises including small-town friendly rooms, a
pool, a reading room and a decent **cafe-
restaurant** (mains €8-12) that pulls in locals,
especially on football nights.

Taberna Juanito Gómez   TAPAS €
(Calle Bellavista; tapas €2-3; ⊙ 1.30-4.30pm &
8.30-11.30pm Mon-Sat) A simple little place
that does tasty, decent-value tapas and
montaditos (bite-sized filled rolls) taking in
all your usual faves: garlic prawns, grilled
mushrooms, Manchego cheese and Iberian
ham.

ℹ Information

Tourist Office (☏ 956 12 08 16; www.turism
olvera.es; Plaza de la Iglesia; ⊙ 10.30am-2pm &
4-7pm Tue-Sun)

ℹ Getting There & Away

Los Amarillos (☏ 902 21 03 17; www.losamaril-
los.es) runs one or two daily buses to/from Jerez
de la Frontera (€9.18, two hours) and Málaga
(€12, three hours), and one daily Monday to
Friday to/from Ronda (€5.44, 1½ hours). **Comes**
(☏ 956 29 11 68; www.tgcomes.es) has one daily
bus Monday to Friday to/from Cádiz (€15, three
hours).

COSTA DE LA LUZ & THE SOUTHEAST

Arriving on the Costa de la Luz from the
Costa del Sol is like flinging open the window and breathing in the fresh air. Bereft of
tacky resorts and unplanned development,
this is a world of flat-capped farmers, grazing bulls and Sunday mass followed by a furtive slug of dry sherry and lunchtime tapas.
Throw in beautiful, broad, blonde beaches
bubbling with a fun-loving surf scene and a
string of spectacularly located white towns,
and you're unequivocally back in Spain.
Spaniards, well aware of this, flock here in
July and August. It's by no means a secret,
but the stunning Costa de la Luz somehow
remains the same old, chilled-out beach
hang-out it's always been.

The Costa de la Luz continues west into
neighbouring Huelva province (p86), up to
the Portugal border.

Vejer de la Frontera

POP 9280

Vejer – the jaw drops, the eyes blink, the eloquent adjectives dry up. Looming moodily
atop a rocky hill above the busy N340, 50km
south of Cádiz, this serene, compact white
town is something very special. Yes, there's
a labyrinth of twisting old-town streets plus
some serendipitous viewpoints, a ruined
castle, a surprisingly elaborate culinary
scene and a tangible Moorish influence. But
Vejer has something else – an air of magic and mystery, an imperceptible touch of
duende (spirit).

⊙ Sights

Plaza de España   SQUARE
With its elaborate 20th-century, Seville-tiled
fountain and perfectly white town hall,
Vejer's palm-studded Plaza de España is a
favourite hang-out. There's a small lookout
above its western side (accessible from Calle
de Sancho IV El Bravo).

Casa del Mayorazgo   HOUSE
(Callejón de la Villa; admission by donation; ⊙ hours
vary) If the door's open, pop into this private
18th-century house to find two stunning
flower-filled patios and one of just three
original towers that kept watch over the city,
with panoramic views down to Plaza de España and across town.

Iglesia del Divino Salvador   CHURCH
(Plaza Padre Ángel; ⊙ mass 6.30pm Mon, Wed &
Fri, 7pm Sat, 10am Sun) Built atop an earlier
mosque, this unusual church is 14th-century
Mudéjar at the altar end and 16th-century
Gothic at the other. In the late afternoon the
sun shines surreally through the stained-
glass windows, projecting multicoloured
light above the altar.

Castillo   CASTLE
(Calle del Castillo; tours per person €4-6; ⊙ 10am-
2pm & 4pm-8pm) Vejer's much-reworked castle, once home of the Duques de Medina
Sidonia, dates from the 10th or 11th century. Its small, erratically open **museum**
preserves one of the black cloaks that Vejer
women wore until just a couple of decades
ago (covering everything but the eyes).

Currently, the only way to visit the castle is by private guided tour; check with the tourist office (p141).

Old-Town Walls
WALLS

Enclosing the 40,000-sq-metre old town, Vejer's imposing 15th-century walls are particularly visible between the Arco de la Puerta Cerrada and the Arco de la Segur, two of the four original gateways to survive. The Arco de la Segur area was, in the 15th century, the *judería* (the Jewish quarter).

🍃 Courses

⭐ Annie B's
Spanish Kitchen
COOKING COURSE

(☑ 620 560649; www.anniebspain.com; Calle Viñas 11; 1-day course €135) This is your chance to master the fine art of Andalucian cooking with top-notch local expertise. Annie's popular day classes (Andalucian-, Moroccan- or seafood-focused) end with lunch by the pool or on the fabulous roof terrace at her gorgeous old-town house. She also does a great selection of full-board six-day courses, including 'Low-Carb Deliciousness' and 'Spanish Culinary Classics'.

La Janda
LANGUAGE COURSE

(☑ 956 44 70 60; www.lajanda.org; Calle José Castrillón 22; per 20hr week €180) Who wouldn't want to study Spanish in Vejer, with its winding streets, authentic bars and mysterious feel? La Janda's courses emphasise cultural immersion, integrating everything from flamenco, yoga and cooking classes to Almodóvar movie nights in a lovely 18th-century village mansion.

🎊 Festivals & Events

Velada de Nuestra Señora
de la Oliva
MUSIC, RELIGIOUS

(⊙10-24 Aug) Nightly themed music and dancing in Plaza de España (flamenco, jazz etc).

🛏 Sleeping

⭐ La Casa del Califa
BOUTIQUE HOTEL €€

(☑ 956 44 77 30; www.lacasadelcalifa.com; Plaza de España 16; incl breakfast s €88-123, d €99-148, ste €169-220; ⊙mid-Feb–mid-Dec; P❋🐾🛈) Rambling over several floors of maze-like corridors, this gorgeous old hotel oozes character. All rooms are peaceful, chic and wonderfully comfortable, with Moroccan-style decor. The top-floor 'Africa' suite is particularly beautiful. Special 'emir' service (€45) bags

you fresh flowers, chocolates and champagne. Breakfast is a wonderful spread and, downstairs, there's a fabulous Moroccan/Middle Eastern restaurant (p140).

⭐ V...
BOUTIQUE HOTEL €€€

(☑ 956 45 17 57; www.hotelv-vejer.com; Calle Rosario 11-13; d €218-328; ❋@🐾) V... (that's V for Vejer, and, yes, the three dots are part of the name) is one of Andalucía's most exquisite creations. It's a brilliantly run, 12-room, old-world boutique hotel where trendy, modern design features (luxurious open-plan bathrooms with huge tubs and giant mirrors) mix with antique artefacts (pre-Columbus doors).

Communal areas include a massage room in the ancient *aljibe* (cistern) and a waterfall – wait for it – on a vista-laden roof terrace next to a bubbling jacuzzi.

🍴 Eating

Vejer has quietly morphed into a gastronomic highlight of Andalucía, where you can just as happily tuck into traditional, age-old recipes as Moroccan fusion dishes.

Mercado
de Abastos
ANDALUCIAN, INTERNATIONAL €

(Calle San Francisco; dishes €2-8; ⊙11am-4.30pm & 7pm-1am) Freshly glammed up with cool, modern gastrobar design, Vejer's Mercado de San Francisco has been transformed into a foodie hot spot. Grab a *vino* and choose between classic favourites and contemporary creations at the wonderfully varied tapas stalls: ham *raciones, tortilla de patatas* (potato-and-onion omelette), fried fish in paper cups, even sushi.

⭐ El Jardín del Califa
MOROCCAN, FUSION €€

(☑ 956 44 77 30; www.jardin.lacasadelcalifa.com; Plaza de España 16; mains €12-18; ⊙1-4pm & 8-11.30pm mid-Feb–mid-Dec; 🐾) The sizzling atmosphere matches the food at this exotically beautiful restaurant – also a hotel (p140) and *tetería* (teahouse). It's buried away in a cavernous house where even finding the toilets is a full-on adventure. The menu is Moroccan/Middle Eastern – tagines, couscous, hummus, falafel – and, while the presentation is fantastic, it's the Maghreb flavours (saffron, figs, almonds) that linger the longest. Book ahead.

Valvatida
ANDALUCIAN, FUSION €€

(☑ 622 468594; Calle Juan Relinque 3; dishes €7-12; ⊙noon-4pm & 8-11.30pm; 🐾) Creative cookery meets market-fresh Andalucian ingredients at this cute modern-rustic spot with fold-out chairs, dangling fishing nets and posters in the window. The short seasonal menu plays with contemporary twists on local fish and meats (fancy pigs' cheeks fajitas?), but also features delicious veggie-friendly pastas, salads and stir-fries. Your *café* is served on a tiny wooden tray.

Mesón Pepe Julián ANDALUCIAN €€
(☑956 45 10 98; Calle Juan Relinque 7; dishes €7-12; ⊙12.30-5pm & 7.30-11.30pm Thu-Tue) Opposite the market, family-run Pepe Julián shines for its wholesome traditional home-cooking. It's a hit with local Spaniards, who pack in for the carefully prepped meats, fish, *platos combinados* (meat-and-three-veg dishes) and tortillas (try the cheese one), as well as for perfectly simple *jamón* and *ensaladilla* (Russian salad) tapas in the tile-walled bar.

☆ Entertainment

**Peña Cultural Flamenca
'Aguilar de Vejer'** FLAMENCO
(Calle Rosario 29) Part of Vejer's magic is its genuine small-town flamenco scene, best observed in this atmospheric old-town bar/performance space. Free shows usually happen on Saturdays at 9.30pm; ask at the tourist office.

❶ Information

Oficina Municipal de Turismo (☑956 45 17 36; www.turismovejer.es; Avenida Los Remedios 2; ⊙8am-3pm Mon-Fri) About 500m below the town centre, beside a big free car park.

❶ Getting There & Around

From Avenida Los Remedios, **Comes** (☑956 29 11 68; www.tgcomes.es) runs bus services to Cádiz, Barbate, Jerez de la Frontera and Seville. More buses stop at La Barca de Vejer, on the N340 at the bottom of the hill. From here, it's a steep 20-minute walk or €6 taxi ride up to town.

TO	COST (€)	DURATION	FREQUENCY
Algeciras	7.17	1¼hr	8 daily
Barbate	1.35	15min	6 daily
Cádiz	5.68	1½hr	5 daily
Jerez de la Frontera	7.79	1½hr	1 daily Mon-Fri
La Línea (for Gibraltar)	9.05	1¾hr	5 daily
Málaga	22	3¼hr	2 daily
Seville	15	2hr	4 daily
Seville (from Avenida Los Remedios)	16	2hr	1 daily Mon-Fri
Tarifa	4.52	45min	8 daily

Los Caños de Meca

POP 170

Little laid-back Los Caños de Meca, 15km southwest of Vejer, straggles along a series of spectacular open white-sand beaches that will leave you wondering why Marbella even exists. Once a hippie haven, Caños still attracts beach lovers of all kinds and nations – especially in summer – with its alternative, hedonistic scene and nudist beaches, as well as kitesurfing, windsurfing and boardsurfing opportunities.

◉ Sights & Activities

Caños' main beach is straight in front of Avenida de Trafalgar's junction with the A2233 to Barbate. Nudists head to its eastern end where there are more-isolated coves, including Playa de las Cortinas, and to Playa del Faro beside Cabo de Trafalgar.

Sleepy El Palmar, 5km northwest of Caños, has Andalucía's best board-surfing waves from October to May.

Cabo de Trafalgar CAPE
At the western end of Los Caños de Meca, a side road (often half-covered in sand) leads out to a lighthouse (set to become a hotel) on a low spit of land. This is the famous Cabo de Trafalgar, off which Spanish naval power was swiftly terminated by a British fleet under Admiral Nelson in 1805.

**★Parque Natural de la
Breña y Marismas del Barbate** HIKING
This 50-sq-km coastal park protects important marshes and pine forest from Costa del Sol–type development. Its main entry point is the 7.2km Sendero del Acantilado between Los Caños de Meca and Barbate, along clifftops that rival Cabo de Gata in their beauty.

The hike's high point is the 16th-century Torre del Tajo with its tranquil mirador (lookout) perched above the Atlantic. The path starts just behind Hotel La Breña at

CÁDIZ PROVINCE & GIBRALTAR LOS CAÑOS DE MECA

the eastern end of Los Caños de Meca and emerges by Barbate's fishing port.

Escuela de Surf 9 Pies
SURFING

(📞 620 104241; www.escueladesurf9pies.com; Avenida de la Playa, El Palmar; board & wetsuit rental per 2/4hr €13/20, classes €28) Recommended surf school offering board hire and year-round, all-level classes, towards the north end of El Palmar beach.

🛏 Sleeping

Casas Karen
HOTEL €€

(📞 956 43 70 67, 649 780834; www.casaskaren. com; Camino del Monte 6; d €85-125, q €155-190; 🅿 🕿 🐾) This eccentric, laid-back Dutch-owned hideaway has characterful rustic rooms and apartments across a flower-covered plot. Options range from a converted farmhouse to thatched *chozas* (traditional huts) and two recently remodelled split-level 'studios'. Decor is casual Andalucian-Moroccan, full of throws, hammocks and colour. It's 1km east of the Cabo de Trafalgar turn-off.

🍴 Eating

Las Dunas
CAFE, BAR

(www.barlasdunas.es; Ctra del Faro de Trafalgar; dishes €6-11; ⏱ 10.30am-11.30pm Sep-Jun, to 3am Jul & Aug; 🕿) Say *hola* to the ultimate relaxation spot, where kitesurfers kick back between white-knuckle sorties launched from the beach outside. Bob Marley tunes, great *bocadillos* (filled rolls), a warming winter fire, and a laid-back, beach-shack feel.

ⓘ Getting There & Away

Comes (📞 956 29 11 68; www.tgcomes.es) has two daily weekday buses from Los Caños de Meca (€1.25, 15 minutes) to Cádiz (€6.25, 1½ hours) via El Palmar (€2.02, 30 minutes). Additional summer services may run to Cádiz and Seville.

Zahara de los Atunes
POP 1115

About 20km southeast of Los Caños de Meca, Zahara de los Atunes fronts a fantastic broad, 12km-long, west-facing sweep of white sand. For years a traditional fishing village famous for its Atlantic bluefin tuna caught using the ancient *almadraba* method, today Zahara is an increasingly popular summer beach hang-out that's paving its way into the local culinary scene. Its tiny

old core of narrow streets and lively bars centres on the ruined 15th-century **Castillo de las Almadrabas**, where the tuna catch was once processed. In summer *chiringuitos* (beach bars) spill out on to the sand, though things can be quiet the rest of the year. South of Zahara is the more developed resort of Atlanterra.

🛏 Sleeping

Hotel Avenida Playa
HOTEL €€

(📞 956 43 93 38; www.avenidaplayahotel.com; Avenida Hermanos Doctores Sánchez Rodríguez 12; incl breakfast s €90-118, d €100-128; ⏱ late Jan-Dec; ✴ 🕿) It's all tasteful rustic design, flowery paintings and warm yellow walls at this friendly eight-room hotel in the heart of Zahara. Best are the two airy top-floor 'suites' with big terraces, sun loungers and castle/sea views. The owners rent out three nearby apartments, too.

🍴 Eating

Restaurante Antonio
SEAFOOD €€

(📞 956 43 95 42; www.restauranteantoniozahara.com; Bahía de la Plata Km 1, Atlanterra; mains €12-25; ⏱ Feb-Nov) Prize-winning sea-view Antonio's, 1km south of Zahara, is widely recommended for its high-quality seafood, brought to you by attentive waiters in crisp white shirts. Tuna, of course, is the star, dished up in a million different incarnations from *atún encebollado* (tuna stew) to sashimi. The tartare of locally caught tuna is a speciality.

ⓘ Getting There & Away

Comes (📞 956 29 11 68; www.tgcomes.es) runs daily buses to Vejer de la Frontera (€2.50, 25 minutes), Los Caños de Meca (€2.12, 30 minutes) and Cádiz (€8.21, two hours, weekdays only). Additional buses run in summer.

Tarifa
POP 13,500

Tarifa's tip-of-Spain location, where the Mediterranean and the Atlantic meet, gives it a different climate and character to the rest of Andalucía. Stiff Atlantic winds draw in surfers, windsurfers and kitesurfers who, in turn, lend this ancient yet deceptively small settlement a refreshingly small international vibe. Tarifa is the last stop in Spain before Morocco, and it's also a taste of things to come. With its winding whitewashed streets and tangible North African feel, the

TARIFA: BEACH BLISS

Jazzed up by the colourful kites and sails of kitesurfers and windsurfers whizzing across turquoise waves, the exquisite bleach-blonde beaches that stretch northwest from Tarifa along the N340 are some of Andalucía's most beautiful. In summer they fill up with sun-kissed beach lovers and chill-out bars, though the relentless winds can be a hassle. If you tire of lazing on the sand, kitesurfing, windsurfing and horse riding await.

Playa Chica On the isthmus leading out to Isla de las Palomas at the southernmost tip of Tarifa town, tiny Playa Chica is more sheltered than other local beaches.

Playa de los Lances This spectacular, broad sweep of sand stretches for 7km northwest from Tarifa. The low dunes behind it are a *paraje natural* (protected natural area); you can hike across them on the 1.5km **Sendero de los Lances**, signposted towards the northwest end of Calle Batalla del Salado.

Playa de Valdevaqueros Sprawling between 7km and 10km northwest of Tarifa, to the great white dune at Punta Paloma, Valdevaqueros is one of Tarifa's most popular kitesurfing spots.

Punta Paloma Punta Paloma, 10km northwest of Tarifa, is famous for its huge sand dune. At its far western end, you can lather yourself up in a natural mud bath.

walled windswept old town could easily pass for Chefchaouen or Essaouira. It's no secret, however, and, in August especially, the town is packed – that's half the fun.

Tarifa may be as old as Phoenician Cádiz and was definitely a Roman settlement. It takes its name from Tarif ibn Malik, who led a Muslim raid in AD 710, the year before the main Islamic invasion of the peninsula.

◎ Sights

Tarifa's narrow old-town streets, mostly of Islamic origin, hint at Morocco. Pass through the Mudéjar **Puerta de Jerez**, built after the Reconquista, then pop into the action-packed **Mercado de Abastos** (Calle Colón; ⊙ 8.30am-2pm Tue-Sat) before winding your way to the mainly 16th-century **Iglesia de San Mateo** (Calle Sancho IV El Bravo; ⊙ 8.45am-1pm Mon, 8.45am-1pm & 6-8pm Tue-Sat, 10am-1pm & 7-8.30pm Sun). Head south of the church along Calle Coronel Moscardó then up Calle Aljaranda; the **Miramar** (atop part of the castle walls) has spectacular views across to Africa.

★**Castillo de Guzmán**　　　CASTLE
(Calle Guzmán El Bueno; adult/child €2/0.60; ⊙ 11am-2.30pm & 4-6.30pm May–mid-Sep, to 6.30pm mid-Sep–Apr) Though built in 960 on the orders of Cordoban caliph Abd ar-Rahman III, this restored fortress is named after Reconquista hero Guzmán El Bueno. In 1294, when threatened with the death of his captured son unless he surrendered the castle to Merenid attackers from Morocco, El Bue-

no threw down his own dagger for his son to be killed. Guzmán's descendants later became the Duques de Medina Sidonia, one of Spain's most powerful families (p323).

A new castle museum should be open by the time you read this; timings may change.

🏃 Activities

Diving

Aventura Marina　　　DIVING
(☑ 956 68 19 32; www.aventuramarina.org; Recinto Portuario) Diving in Tarifa is usually done from boats around Isla de las Palomas, where shipwrecks, corals, dolphins and octopuses await. Port-based Aventura Marina offers three-hour 'baptisms' (€75) and equipment rental (€50).

Horse Riding

Aventura Ecuestre　　　HORSE RIDING
(☑ 956 23 66 32; www.aventuraecuestre.com; Hotel Dos Mares, Ctra N340 Km 79.5) Well-organised, English-speaking equestrian outfit running one-hour rides along Playa de los Lances (€30) and four-hour forays into the Parque Natural Los Alcornocales (€60), plus private lessons (€30 per hour) and kids' pony rides (€25 per hour). It's 5km northwest of Tarifa.

Molino El Mastral　　　HORSE RIDING
(☑ 679 193503; www.mastral.com; Ctra Santuario Virgen de la Luz; per hr €30) This excellent horse-riding establishment, 5km north of Tarifa, offers fun excursions into the hilly countryside. It's signposted off the CA9210 (off the N340).

Tarifa

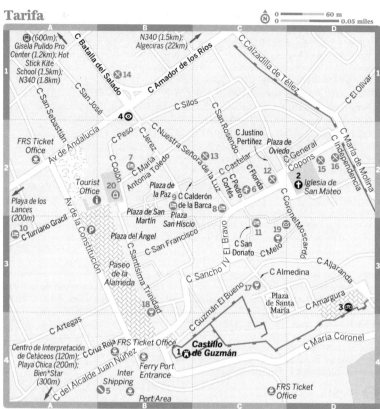

CÁDIZ PROVINCE & GIBRALTAR TARIFA

Tarifa

◎ Top Sights
1 Castillo de Guzmán B4

◎ Sights
2 Iglesia de San Mateo D2
3 Miramar D3
4 Puerta de Jerez B1

✚ Activities, Courses & Tours
5 Aventura Marina B4
6 FIRMM C2

🛏 Sleeping
7 Hostal África B2
8 Hotel Misiana C2
9 La Casa de la Favorita B2
10 Melting Pot A3
11 Posada La Sacristía C3

✖ Eating
12 Bar-Restaurante Morilla C2
13 Café 10 .... C2
14 Café Azul B1
15 La Oca da Sergio D2
16 Mandrágora D2

🍷 Drinking & Nightlife
17 Almedina C3
18 La Ruina B3
19 Moby Dick C3

🛍 Shopping
20 Mercado de Abastos B2

Kitesurfing & Windsurfing

Tarifa's legendary winds have turned the town into one of Europe's premier windsurf-ing and kitesurfing destinations. The most popular strip is along the coast between Tar-ifa and Punta Paloma, 10km northwest. Over

30 places offer equipment hire and classes, from beginner to expert. The best months are May, June and September, but bear in mind that the choppy seas aren't always beginner's territory.

Gisela Pulido Pro Center   KITESURFING
(☏608 577711; www.giselapulidoprocenter.com; Calle Mar Adriático 22; 3hr group courses per person €70) World champion Gisela Pulido's highly rated kitesurfing school offers year-round group/private courses, including six-hour 'baptisms' (€140) and nine-hour 'complete' courses (€210), in Spanish, French, English and German.

Hot Stick Kite School   KITESURFING, SURFING
(☏647 155516; www.hotsticktarifa.com; Calle Batalla del Salado 41; 1-day courses €70-80, kit rental per day €60; ☉Mar–mid-Nov) Daily three- to four-hour kitesurfing classes, plus two- to five-day courses (Spanish, English, French and German). Also two-hour surfing and paddle-boarding sessions (€50).

Club Mistral   WINDSURFING, KITESURFING
(☏619 340913; www.club-mistral.com; Hurricane Hotel, Ctra N340 Km 78; equipment rental per day €90; ☉Mar-Dec) Recommended group/private windsurfing and kitesurfing classes (beginner, intermediate or advanced level), and paddle-boarding (€25 per hour), 7km northwest of Tarifa. Three-hour group windsurfing classes are €80 per person, kitesurfing €110. Spanish, English, French and German spoken. Also at Valdevaqueros, 9km northwest of town.

Whale-Watching
The waters off Tarifa are one of the best places in Europe to see whales and dolphins as they swim between the Atlantic and the Mediterranean from April to October; sightings of some kind are almost guaranteed during these months. In addition to striped and bottlenose dolphins, long-finned pilot whales, orcas (killer whales) and sperm whales, you may also spot endangered fin whales and common dolphins. Sperm whales swim the Strait of Gibraltar from April to August; the best months for orcas are July and August. Find out more at Tarifa's brand-new Centro de Interpretación de Cetáceos (Avenida Fuerzas Armadas 17; ☉11am-3pm Tue-Sun Mar-Oct) FREE.

FIRMM   WHALE-WATCHING
(☏956 62 70 08; www.firmm.org; Calle Pedro Cortés 4; adult/child €30/20; ☉Apr-Oct) Of Tarifa's dozens of whale-watching outfits, not-for-profit FIRMM is a good choice. Its primary purpose is to study the whales, record data and encourage environmentally sensitive tours.

⚜ Festivals & Events
Feria de la Virgen de la Luz   FAIR
(☉1st week Sep) Tarifa's town fair, honouring its patron, mixes religious processions, beautiful horses and your typical Spanish fiesta.

🛏 Sleeping
★Hostal África   HOSTAL €
(☏956 68 02 20; www.hostalafrica.com; Calle María Antonia Toledo 12; s/d €50/65, with shared bathroom €35/50; ☉Mar-Nov; 🛜) This revamped 19th-century house just southwest of the Puerta de Jerez is one of the Costa de la Luz' best *hostales* (budget hotels). Full of plant pots and sky-blue-and-white arches, it's run by hospitable owners, and the 13 all-different rooms sparkle with bright colours. Enjoy the lovely, big roof terrace, with exotic cabana and views of Africa.

La Casa de la Favorita   HOTEL, APARTMENT €€
(☏690 180253; www.lacasadelafavorita.com; Plaza de San Hiscio 4; r €80-115; ❄🛜🅿) La Favorita has become a lot of people's favourite, and fills up fast. It must be something to do with the creamy contemporary furnishings, surgical cleanliness, kitchenettes and coffee-makers in every room, small library, roof terrace, and dynamic colourful art.

Hotel Misiana   BOUTIQUE HOTEL €€
(☏956 62 70 83; www.misiana.com; Calle Sancho IV El Bravo 16; d/ste €95/200; ❄🛜) Thanks to its exquisite penthouse suite with private roof terrace and Morocco views, super-central Misiana is the best place to stay in Tarifa if you've got the money. But the doubles are pretty lovely too, with their stylish whiteness, pale greys and driftwood decor. This is real Tarifa chic and it's predictably popular; book well ahead.

Posada La Sacristía   BOUTIQUE HOTEL €€
(☏956 68 17 59; www.lasacristia.net; Calle San Donato 8; r €135; ❄🛜) Tucked inside a beautifully renovated 17th-century townhouse is Tarifa's most elegant boutique accommodation. Attention to detail is impeccable with 10 smart doubles that ooze style, tasteful colour schemes, big comfy beds, a sumptuous lounge, and rooms spread over two floors around a central courtyard. Buffet breakfast

costs €6; a good Mediterranean fusion restaurant (mains €10-18) opens in summer.

Hotel Dos Mares
HOTEL €€€

(☎956 68 40 35; www.dosmareshotel.com; Ctra N340 Km 79.5; r incl breakfast €195-225; ❄☎☲⌨) Tarifa is all about the beach, and inviting accommodation options line the coast to its northwest. Opening on to the sand, 5km northwest of town, Moroccan-flavoured Dos Mares has comfy, bright, tile-floored rooms and bungalows in yellows, blues and burnt oranges, some with sea-facing balconies. Other perks: a sleepy cafe, a gym, a pool, and an on-site horse-riding school (p143).

✖ Eating

Tarifa is full of good food with a strong international flavour, Italian in particular. It's also one of Andalucía's top breakfast spots – time to break out of the *tostada* and coffee monotony! Other treats to look for are smoothies, ethnic fusion food, organic ingredients and wonderful vegetarian meals.

★ Café Azul
BREAKFAST €

(www.facebook.com/cafeazultarifa; Calle Batalla del Salado 8; breakfasts €3.50-7.50; ⊙9am-3pm) This eccentric Italian-run place with eye-catching blue-and-white Moroccan-inspired decor whips up the best breakfasts in town, if not Andalucía. You'll want to eat everything. It does a wonderfully fresh fruit salad topped with muesli and yoghurt, plus good coffee, smoothies, juices, *bocadillos* (filled rolls) and cooked breakfasts. The fruit-and-yoghurt-stuffed crêpe is a work of art.

Café 10
CAFE €

(Calle Nuestra Señora de la Luz 10; dishes €2-6; ⊙9.30am-2am Mar-Sep, 9.30am-2.30pm & 5.30-11pm Oct–mid-Dec & Feb; ☎) This old-town cafe delivers the breakfast/snack goods in a cosy, neo-rustic lounge with pink-cushioned chairs spilling out on to the sloping street. Homemade cakes, great coffee, fresh juices, sweet and salty crêpes, and *revueltos* and *bocadillos* in exciting international-themed combinations (avocado, mozzarella). Yes, there's even latte art. Later on, the G&Ts and cocktails come out.

Mandrágora
MOROCCAN, ANDALUCIAN €€

(☎956 68 12 91; www.mandragoratarifa.com; Calle Independencia 3; mains €12-18; ⊙6.30pm-midnight Mon-Sat Mar-Jan) On a quiet street behind the Iglesia de San Mateo, this intimate palm-dotted spot serves Andalucian-Arabic food and does so terrifically well. It's hard to know where to start, but tempting choices include lamb with plums and almonds, Moroccan vegetable couscous, chicken tagine, and monkfish in a wild-mushroom-and-sea-urchin sauce.

GR7: SPAIN'S OTHER CAMINO

After the Camino de Santiago, the Sendero de Gran Recorrido 7 (GR7) is probably Spain's most iconic footpath, crossing the nation from Tarifa to Andorra and comprising a crucial segment of the E4 footpath that travels over 10,000km across Europe to Greece and then Cyprus.

The Andalucian section, based on old hunting and trading paths, takes in seven natural parks and the Parque Nacional Sierra Nevada (p272), crossing copious mountain ranges and vast expanses of cultivated and wild land.

The GR7 tracks 268.5km northeast from Tarifa across Cádiz and Málaga provinces, before splitting southeast of Antequera at Villanueva de Cauche. The more popular southern route (451km) heads south of the Sierra Nevada through Las Alpujarras. The isolated northern route (443km) traverses Córdoba and Jaén provinces including the crinkled Cazorla highlands. The two paths rejoin at Puebla de Don Fadrique, the final town on Andalucía's portion of the GR7.

The whole thing, via either route, takes 35 to 40 days, though most walkers focus on smaller segments, particularly in Las Alpujarras and the Grazalema/Ronda area. There's generally plenty of accommodation available en route in local *hostales* (budget hotels) and hotels, though some sections require tents for camping. Waymarking (red-and-white markers plus signposts with distance and/or time to next destination) is sporadic in places. Fortunately Cicerone produces a comprehensive guidebook detailing every section called *Walking the GR7 in Andalucía* (2013; Kirstie Shirra and Michelle Lowe).

La Oca da Sergio
ITALIAN €€

(☑615 686571; Calle General Copons 6; mains €10-20; ⊙1-4pm & 8pm-midnight daily Jun-Oct, 8pm-midnight Mon & Wed-Fri, 1-4pm & 8pm-midnight Sat & Sun Dec-May) Italians rule the Tarifa food scene. Amiable Sergio roams the tables Italian-style, armed with loaded plates and amusing stories, and resides over genuine home-country cooking at this popular restaurant tucked away behind the Iglesia de San Mateo. Look forward to homemade pasta, wood-oven thin-crust pizzas, cappuccinos and postdinner *limoncello*.

Bar-Restaurante Morilla
TAPAS, ANDALUCIAN €€

(☑956 68 17 57; Calle Sancho IV El Bravo 2; mains €10-15; ⊙8.30am-11.30pm) One of numerous eateries lying in wait along Calle Sancho IV El Bravo in the heart of the old town, busy no-frills Morilla attracts more *tarifeños* than others. They pop in for the quality tapas, seafood *raciones* and lamb dishes, and for the excellent *cazuela de pescado y marisco* (fish-and-seafood stew).

🍸 Drinking & Nightlife

With all the surfers, kitesurfers and beach-goers breezing through, Tarifa has a busy bar scene (especially in summer), plus a few lively late-night clubs thrown into the mix. Lots of the after-dark fun centres on narrow Calles Cervantes, San Francisco and Santísima Trinidad, just east of the Alameda. Don't even bother going out before 11pm. A few *chiringuitos* get going with music and *copas* (drinks) on Playa de los Lances and the beaches northwest of town.

★Bien*Star
BEACH BAR

(www.bienstartarifa.com; Playa de los Lances; ⊙12.30pm-1am Sat-Thu, to 3am Fri Jul & Aug, 12.30-9pm Sun-Thu, to 3am Fri Oct-Jun) Perched on perfectly white sands, this shabby-chic wind-battered beach bar is what Tarifa is all about – cool drinks, a kitesurfing crowd and a contagiously laid-back vibe. Live music happens on Fridays around 10pm. It's one of the few *chiringuitos* to stay open virtually year-round.

Almedina
BAR

(☑956 68 04 74; www.almedinacafe.net; Calle Almedina 3; ⊙8.30pm-midnight; 🛜) Built into the old city walls, cavernous Almedina squeezes a flamenco ensemble into its clamorous confines on Thursdays at 10.30pm.

La Ruina
CLUB

(www.facebook.com/pages/La-Ruina-Tarifa; Calle Santísima Trinidad 2; ⊙midnight-3am Sun-Thu, to 4am Fri & Sat) This old town ruin turned club amps things up with a steady early-hours diet of electro and house.

Moby Dick
BAR

(www.facebook.com/TabernaMobyDyck; Calle Melo 2; ⊙7.30pm-1am Wed-Sun) A warm, traditional-feel beer bar serving up international and local brews and tapas to a regular live-music soundtrack. Gets packed on gig nights.

❶ Information

Tourist Office (☑956 68 09 93; Paseo de la Alameda; ⊙10am-1.30pm & 4-6pm Mon-Fri, 10am-1.30pm Sat & Sun)

❶ Getting There & Away

BOAT
FRS (☑956 68 18 30; www.frs.es; Avenida de Andalucía 16) runs 35-minute ferries up to eight times daily between Tarifa and Tangier (Morocco; adult/child/car/motorcycle one-way €37/20/102/30). All passengers need a passport. **Inter Shipping** (☑956 68 47 29; www.inter shipping.es; Recinto Portuario, Local 4) offers similar schedules to Tangier (€37/19/100/60).

BUS
Comes (☑956 29 11 68; www.tgcomes.es) operates from the **bus station** beside the petrol station at the northwestern end of Calle Batalla del Salado. In July and August, **Horizonte Sur** (www.horizontesur.es) has several daily buses from here to Punta Paloma via Tarifa's beaches.

TO	COST (€)	DURATION	FREQUENCY
Cádiz	9.91	1½hr	5 daily
Jerez de la Frontera	11	2½hr	1 daily
La Barca de Vejer (for Vejer de la Frontera)	4.52	40min	6 daily
La Línea (for Gibraltar)	4.49	1hr	6 daily
Málaga	17	2¾hr	3 daily
Seville	20	3hr	4 daily

CAR & MOTORCYCLE
There's metered parking on Avenida de la Constitución beside the Alameda (€2 per two hours; free 8pm to 10am).

Bolonia

POP 111

Tiny Bolonia village, signposted off the N340 15km northwest of Tarifa, fronts a gloriously white beach framed by a big dune, rolling green hills, and the impressive Roman remains of Baelo Claudia.

In July and August, three daily buses run between Tarifa and Bolonia. Otherwise it's your own wheels.

◉ Sights

★ Baelo Claudia
ARCHAEOLOGICAL SITE

(✆956 10 67 96; www.museosdeandalucia.es; admission €1.50, EU citizens free; ⊙9am-5.30pm Tue-Sat Jan-Mar & mid-Sep–Dec, to 7.30pm Apr–mid-Jun, to 3.30pm mid-Jun–mid-Sep & Sun year-round) The ruined town of Baelo Claudia is one of Andalucía's most important Roman archaeological sites. These majestic beach-side ruins – with fine views across to Africa – include the substantial remains of a theatre, a paved forum, thermal baths, the market, the marble statue and columns of the basilica, and the workshops that turned out the products that made Baelo Claudia famous in the Roman world: salted fish and *garum* (spicy seasoning made from leftover fish parts). There's a good museum.

Baelo Claudia particularly flourished during the reign of Emperor Claudius (AD 41–54), but declined after an earthquake in the 2nd century. Live musical performances sometimes happen on July and August evenings.

Parque Natural Los Alcornocales

The beautiful, 1677-sq-km Parque Natural Los Alcornocales is rich in archaeological, historical and natural interest, but it's still off the beaten track. Stretching 75km north almost from the Strait of Gibraltar to the border of the Parque Natural Sierra de Grazalema (p137) and into Málaga province, it's a spectacular jumble of sometimes rolling, sometimes rugged medium-height hills, much of it covered in Spain's most extensive *alcornocales* (cork-oak woodlands). There are plenty of walks and outdoor-activity options, but you'll need a car to explore properly.

Five walking routes, including the 3.3km **Sendero Subida al Picacho** up the park's second-highest peak (El Picacho; 882m), require free permits, which you must request at least three days in advance from the **Oficina del Parque Natural Los Alcornocales** (✆856 58 75 08; pn.alcornocales.cmaot@juntadeandalucia.es; Ctra Alcalá-Benalup Km 1 , Alcalá de los Gazules; ⊙9am-2pm Mon-Fri); they'll email your permit. Downloadable hiking information is available online at www.ventanadelvisitante.es.

ℹ Information

Ayuntamiento de Jimena de la Frontera (Town Hall; ✆956 64 02 54; Calle Sevilla 61, Jimena de la Frontera; ⊙9am-2pm Mon-Fri)

Centro de Visitantes El Aljibe (Ctra Alcalá-Benalup Km 1, Alcalá de los Gazules; ⊙9am-3pm Tue-Sun mid-May–mid-Sep, 10am-2pm & 3-5pm Tue-Sun mid-Sep–mid-May) Off the Jerez–Los Barrios A381, 4km southwest of Alcalá de los Gazules.

Centro de Visitantes Huerta Grande (✆671 590887; Km 96 N340; ⊙9.30am-2pm Tue-Sun) Off the Tarifa–Algeciras N340, at the western end of Pelayo. Walking information and maps, plus a butterfly/bird observation garden.

Jimena de la Frontera

POP 3090

Tucked away in crinkled hills on the eastern edge of the Parque Natural Los Alcornocales, Jimena sits in prime cork-oak country. Its blanched whiteness and crumbled Nasrid-era castle look out towards Gibraltar and Africa (both magnificently visible). Property-seeking Brits have discovered the town, but so far it's kept its Andalucian feel and makes a great base for exploring the park. The trails here are lovely, including treks along the cross-continental E4 (GR7) path, and forays out to Bronze Age cave paintings at Laja Alta.

◉ Sights & Activities

Castillo de Jimena
CASTLE

(⊙24hr) FREE Jimena's romantically ruined 13th-century Nasrid castle, probably built on Roman ruins, once formed part of a defence line stretching from Olvera down through Setenil, Zahara de la Sierra, Castellar and Algeciras to Tarifa. Note the Islamic cisterns and the remains of an ancient rock-carved Mozarabic church known as El Baño de la Reina Mora (the Moorish Queen's Bath).

Sendero Río Hozgarganta
HIKING

This 3km walk, the most accessible of several good hikes around Jimena, starts towards the northwest end of town where a track to the Río Hozgarganta heads west off the road

ALGECIRAS: GATEWAY TO MOROCCO

The major port linking Spain with Africa is an ugly industrial fishing town notable for producing the greatest flamenco guitarist of the modern era, Paco de Lucía, who was born here in 1947 and died in 2014 in Playa del Carmen, Mexico. The **tourist office** (☑670 949047; Paseo Río de la Miel ; ⊙9am-7.30pm Mon-Fri, 9.30am-3pm Sat & Sun) has info on a self-guided **Paco de Lucía tour** that uncovers local landmarks connected with the great musician. New arrivals usually leave quickly, by ferry to Morocco or bus to Tarifa.

To get from Algeciras bus or train station to the port, walk 600m east along Calle San Bernardo.

Buses from Algeciras

Bus station (Calle San Bernardo)

TO	COST (€)	DURATION	FREQUENCY
Cádiz	13	2½hr	7 daily
Jerez de la Frontera	11	1½hr	6 daily
La Línea (for Gibraltar)	2.45	30min	every 30min
Málaga	15	2½hr	15 daily
Seville	22	3hr	12 daily
Tarifa	2.25	30min	12 daily

Trains from Algeciras

Train station (☑956 63 10 05; Avenida Gesto por la Paz)

TO	COST (€)	DURATION	FREQUENCY
Granada	30	4¼hr	3 daily
Madrid	7	5½hr	3 daily
Ronda	20	1½hr	3 daily

Ferries from Algeciras

Ferries from Algeciras to Tangier drop you in Tangier Med, 40km east of Tangier itself. Remember your passport when headed to Tangier; no passport is required for trips to the Spanish Moroccan enclave of Ceuta, although you will need to show identification (such as a passport or national ID card) to board the ferry.

FRS (☑956 68 18 30; www.frs.es)

Inter Shipping (☑956 65 73 69; www.intershipping.es)

Trasmediterránea (☑902 45 46 45; www.trasmediterranea.es)

TO	FERRY COMPANY	COST (€; ONE-WAY), ADULT/CHILD/CAR	DURATION	FREQUENCY
Ceuta	FRS	38/15/117	1hr	5 daily
Ceuta	Trasmediterránea	35/20/115	1¼hr	4 daily
Tangier Med	FRS	21/15/115	1½hr	7 daily
Tangier Med	Inter Shipping	20/10/105	1½hr	3 daily
Tangier Med	Trasmediterránea	21/15/120	1½hr	5 daily

soon after passing the last houses. You can also pick it up west off Plaza del Puerto Mora (northwest side of Jimena). Allow an hour or two.

Turn left at the river and follow a stonier path past old mills, rustling cork oaks and the remnants of the Real Fábrica de Artillería, a 1780s artillery factory where they made the cannonballs fired at Gibraltar during the Great Siege (1779–83). The route deposits you at the southwest corner of town.

Sleeping & Eating

Posada La Casa Grande INN, APARTMENT €
(☏956 64 11 20; www.posadalacasagrande.es; Calle Fuente Nueva 42; r €50, apt €60-70; ✳@ ☎ 🖶) Spread around plant-dotted patios, La Casa Grande has everything you need for a delightful central Jimena stay, including colourfully rustic rooms and two-to four-person apartments, friendly staff, a library/painting studio with wraparound views, and an excellent hiking information centre.

Restaurante El Anón INTERNATIONAL, FUSION €€
(☏956 64 01 13; www.hostalanon.com; Calle Consuelo 34; mains €12-15; ⊙1-3.30pm & 8-11.30pm Thu-Tue; ☎🖶) Picture a rambling townhouse full of hidden nooks, tiled tables, and big terraces bursting with flowers, plus a rooftop pool with exquisite Africa views. El Anón's menu is incredibly varied, with tasty hummus and falafel accompanied by tagines, Greek salads, lamb moussaka and wild honeyed mushrooms. It also rents 12 rustic rooms (s/d €38/60; ☎🖂).

Getting There & Away

Three daily trains go to Algeciras (€5.05, 40 minutes), Granada (€26, four hours) and Ronda (€7.35, one hour) from the station in Los Ángeles, 1km southeast of Jimena. Jimena's bus stop, at the bottom of town, has weekday services to Ronda (€6.48, two hours) and Algeciras (€4.59, 50 minutes).

GIBRALTAR

POP 32,700

Red pillar boxes, fish-and-chip shops and creaky 1970s seaside hotels; Gibraltar – as British writer Laurie Lee once commented – is a piece of Portsmouth sliced off and towed 500 miles south. As with many colonial outposts, 'the Rock' overstates its Britishness, a bonus for pub-grub and afternoon-tea lovers, but a confusing double-take for modern Brits who thought their country had moved on since the days of Lord Nelson memorabilia. Poised strategically at the jaws of Europe and Africa, Gibraltar, with its Palladian architecture and camera-hogging Barbary macaques, makes for an interesting break from Cádiz province's white towns and tapas. Playing an admirable supporting role is the swashbuckling local history; lest we forget, the Rock has been British longer than the United States has been American.

ℹ GIBRALTAR: PRACTICALITIES

Border Crossings
The border is open 24 hours. Customs bag searches are *usually* perfunctory.

Electricity
Electric current is the same as in Britain: 220V or 240V, with plugs of three flat pins. You'll need an adaptor to use your Spanish plug lead (available from electronics shops on Main St).

Money
Currencies are the interchangeable Gibraltar pound (£) and pound sterling. You can spend euros, but conversion rates are poor. Change unspent Gibraltar currency before leaving. Banks (mostly on Main St) are generally open weekdays from 8.30am to 4pm.

Telephone
To phone Gibraltar from Spain, precede the eight-digit local number with ☏00350; from other countries dial the international access code, then ☏350 (Gibraltar's country code) and the local number. To call Spain from Gibraltar, dial ☏0034 then the nine-digit number.

Visas & Documents
To enter Gibraltar, you need a passport or EU national identity card. American, Canadian, Australian, New Zealand and EU passport holders are among those who do not need visas for Gibraltar. For further information, contact Gibraltar's **Civil Status and Registration Office** (Map p152; ☏20070071; www.gibraltar.gov.gi; 6 Convent Pl).

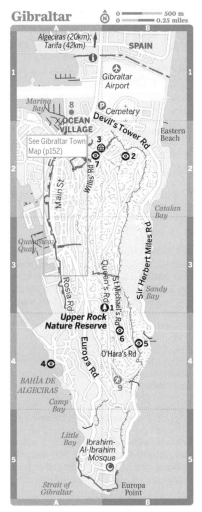

Gibraltar

◎ **Top Sights**
1 Upper Rock Nature Reserve...............B3

◎ **Sights**
2 Great Siege Tunnels B2
3 Military Heritage Centre A2
4 Nelson's Anchorage A4
5 O'Hara's Battery B4
6 St Michael's Cave...............................B4
7 WWII Tunnels A2

🔶 **Activities, Courses & Tours**
8 Dolphin Adventure...............................A1
   Dolphin Safari...............................(see 8)
9 Mediterranean Steps B4

sula, landing with an army of 10,000 men. The name Gibraltar derives from Jebel Tariq (Tariq's Mountain).

The Almohad Muslims founded a town here in 1159 and were usurped by the Castilians in 1462. In 1704 an Anglo-Dutch fleet captured Gibraltar during the War of the Spanish Succession. Spain ceded the Rock to Britain by the 1713 Treaty of Utrecht, but didn't give up military attempts to regain it until the failure of the Great Siege of 1779–83; Spain has wanted it back ever since.

In 1969 Francisco Franco (infuriated by a referendum in which Gibraltarians voted by 12,138 to 44 to remain under British sovereignty) closed the Spain–Gibraltar border. The same year a new constitution committed Britain to respecting Gibraltarians' wishes over sovereignty, and gave Gibraltar domestic self-government and its own parliament, the House of Assembly. In 1985, just before Spain joined the European Community (now the EU), the border was reopened after 16 long years.

In a 2002 vote, Gibraltarians resoundingly rejected the idea of joint British-Spanish sovereignty. Today, the thorny issue of Gibraltar's long-term future still raises its head from time to time, with recent debates sparked by conflict over who controls the waters off the Rock. Gibraltarians believe in their right to self-determination, and the big-picture problems remain unresolved.

◎ Sights

Gibraltar Town

Most Gibraltar sojourns start in Grand Casemates Sq, accessible through Landport

This towering 5km-long limestone ridge rises to 426m, with dramatic cliffs on its northern and eastern sides. Gibraltarians speak English, Spanish, and a curiously accented, sing-song mix of the two, swapping back and forth midsentence. Signs are in English.

History

Both the Phoenicians and the ancient Greeks left traces here, but Gibraltar really entered the history books in AD 711 when Tariq ibn Ziyad, the Muslim governor of Tangier, made it the initial bridgehead for the Islamic invasion of the Iberian Penin-

Gibraltar Town

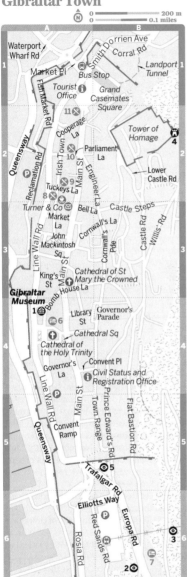

N

0 ———————— 200 m
0 ———————— 0.1 miles

Gibraltar Town

◎ Top Sights
1 Gibraltar Museum A4

◎ Sights
2 Alameda Botanic Gardens B6
3 Apes' Den B6
4 Moorish Castle B2
5 Trafalgar Cemetery B5

🛏 Sleeping
6 Hotel Bristol A4
7 Rock Hotel B6

⊗ Eating
8 Clipper A2
9 House of Sacarello A2
10 Star Bar A2
11 Verdi Verdi A2

★ **Gibraltar Museum**   MUSEUM

(Map p152; www.gibmuseum.gi; 18-20 Bomb House Lane; adult/child £2/1; ⊙10am-6pm Mon-Fri, to 2pm Sat) Gibraltar's swashbuckling history quickly unfolds in this fine museum, which comprises a labyrinth of rooms ranging from prehistoric and Phoenician Gibraltar to the infamous Great Siege (1779–83). Don't miss the well-preserved 14th-century Islamic baths, and an intricately painted 7th-century BC Egyptian mummy found in the bay in the 1800s.

Trafalgar Cemetery   CEMETERY

(Map p152; Prince Edward's Rd; ⊙8.30am-sunset) Gibraltar's cemetery gives a poignant history lesson, with its graves of British sailors who perished here after the 1805 Battle of Trafalgar, and of 19th-century yellow-fever victims.

Alameda Botanic Gardens   GARDENS

(Map p152; Grand Pde; ⊙8am-sunset) **FREE** Take a break from Gibraltar's inexplicably manic traffic amid these lush gardens, scene of Molly Bloom's famous sexual exploits in James Joyce's *Ulysses*.

Nelson's Anchorage   LANDMARK

(Map p151; Rosia Rd; admission £1; ⊙9am-6.15pm) At the southwest end of town, Nelson's Anchorage pinpoints the site where Nelson's body was brought ashore from the HMS *Victory* – preserved in a rum barrel, so legend says. A 100-tonne British-made Victorian supergun (1870) commemorates the spot.

Tunnel (at one time the only land entry through Gibraltar's walls), then continue along Main St, a slice of the British high street under the Mediterranean sun.

Upper Rock

★**Upper Rock**
Nature Reserve NATURE RESERVE
(Map p151; adult/child incl attractions £10/5, vehicle £2, pedestrian excl attractions £0.50; ⊙9am-6.15pm, last entry 5.45pm) The Rock is one of the most dramatic landforms in southern Europe. Most of its upper sections (but not the main lookouts) fall within the Upper Rock Nature Reserve. Entry tickets include admission to St Michael's Cave, the Apes' Den, the Great Siege Tunnels, the Moorish Castle, the Military Heritage Centre and the 100-tonne gun. The upper Rock is home to 600 plant species and is the perfect vantage point for watching bird migration (p154) between Europe and Africa.

The Rock's most famous inhabitants are the tailless Barbary macaques. Many of the 200 apes hang around the top cable-car station, the **Apes' Den** (Map p152) (near the middle cable-car station) and the Great Siege Tunnels. Legend has it that when the apes (possibly introduced from North Africa in the 18th century) disappear from Gibraltar, so will the British. Summer is best for seeing newborn apes, but keep a safe distance to avoid run-ins with protective parents. Several visitors have been attacked by apes in recent years, which led to some apes being 'exported' in 2014.

About 1km (15 minutes' walk) south down St Michael's Rd from the top cable-car station, O'Hara's Rd leads left up to **O'Hara's Battery** (Map p151; adult/child £3/2; ⊙10am-5pm Mon-Fri), an emplacement of big guns on the Rock's summit (not included in your nature-reserve ticket). Slightly further down is the extraordinary **St Michael's Cave** (Map p151; St Michael's Rd; ⊙9am-5.45pm, to 6.15pm Apr-Oct), a spectacular natural grotto full of stalagmites and stalactites. People once thought the cave was a possible subterranean link with Africa. Today, apart from attracting tourists in droves, it's used for concerts, plays and even fashion shows. For a more extensive look, the **Lower St Michael's Cave Tour** (tours per person £10) is a three-hour guided adventure into the lower cave system. The tourist office (p155) can recommend guides. Children must be over 10; wear appropriate footwear.

A 1.5km (30-minute) walk north (downhill) from the top cable-car station is Princess Caroline's Battery, housing the **Military Heritage Centre** (Map p151; ⊙9-5.45pm, to

6.15pm Apr-Oct). From here one road leads down to Princess Royal Battery – more gun emplacements – while another heads 300m up to the **Great Siege Tunnels** (Map p151; ⊙9.30am-6.15pm), a complex defence system hewn out of the Rock by the British during the siege of 1779–83 to provide gun emplacements. The **WWII tunnels** (Map p151; adult/child £8/4; ⊙10am-4pm Mon-Sat), where the Allied invasion of North Africa was planned, can also be visited; these aren't included in your nature-reserve ticket, but you must have a nature-reserve ticket to visit them. Even combined, these tunnels constitute only a tiny proportion of the Rock's more than 50km of tunnels and galleries, most off-limits to the public.

On Willis' Rd, the way down to town from Princess Caroline's Battery, you'll find Gibraltar's **Moorish Castle** (Tower of Homage; Map p152; ⊙9.30am-6.45pm Apr-Sep, 9am-5.45pm Oct-Mar), rebuilt in 1333 after being won back from the Spanish.

🏃 Activities

Hiking

★**Mediterranean Steps** HIKING
(Map p151) Not the most well-known attraction in Gibraltar, but surely the most spectacular, this narrow, ancient path with steep steps – many hewn into the limestone – starts at the nature reserve's entrance at Jews' Gate and traverses the south end of Gibraltar before steeply climbing the crag on the eastern escarpment. It comes out on the ridge; it's best to take the road down.

---

❶ CABLE CAR–NATURE RESERVE COMBO

The best way to explore the Rock is to whizz up on the **cable car** (Lower Cable-Car Station; Red Sands Rd; adult one-way/return £8.50/11, child one-way/return £4.50/5; ⊙9.30am-7.45pm Apr-Oct, to 5.15pm Nov-Mar), weather permitting, then stop off at all the nature reserve sights on your way down. You can get special cable car–nature reserve one-way combo tickets for this (adult/child £20/12). Note that the lower cable-car station stops selling these about two hours before the reserve closes. For the Apes' Den, hop out at the middle station.

The views along the way are stupendous; ornithologists won't know where to look with birds soaring above, below and around you. The 1.5km trail is mildly exposed. Allow 45 minutes to an hour.

Birdwatching

One of Gibraltar's best views is right above your head. The Strait of Gibraltar is a key point of passage for migrating birds between Africa and Europe; over 300 species have been recorded in the Gibraltar area. Soaring birds such as raptors, black and white storks and vultures rely on thermals and updraughts for their crossings, and there are just two places where the seas are narrow enough for storks to get into Europe by this method. One is the Bosphorus, between the Black Sea and the Sea of Marmara; the other is the Strait of Gibraltar. White storks sometimes congregate in flocks of up to 5000 to cross the strait. Northward migrations generally occur between mid-February and early June, and southbound flights between late July and early November. When a westerly wind is blowing, Gibraltar is normally a good spot for seeing the birds. When the wind is calm or easterly, the Tarifa area is usually better.

Dolphin-Watching

The Bahía de Algeciras has a sizeable year-round population of dolphins and a Gibraltar highlight is spotting them. Dolphin Adventure (Map p151; ☑20050650; www.dolphin.gi; 9 The Square, Marina Bay; adult/child £25/13) and Dolphin Safari (Map p151; ☑20 071914; www.dolphinsafari.gi; 6 The Square, Marina Bay; adult/child £25/15; ☺Feb-Nov) run excellent dolphin-watching trips of one to 1½ hours. Most of the year they usually make three daily excursions; from about April to September there may be extra trips. Dolphin Adventure also does occasional whale-watching trips (adult/child £40/25). Advance bookings essential.

🛏 Sleeping

Hotel Bristol
HOTEL **€€**

(Map p152; ☑20076800; www.bristolhotel.gi; 10 Cathedral Sq; s/d/tr £69/86/99; P❋🛜🏊) Where else can you stay in a retro 1970s hotel that isn't even trying to be retro? The dated but decent Bristol has creaking floorboards, red patterned carpets, an attractive walled garden and a small swimming pool, though staff aren't particularly helpful. It's in a prime location just off Main St.

Rock Hotel
HOTEL **€€€**

(Map p152; ☑20073000; www.rockhotelgibraltar. com; 3 Europa Rd; incl breakfast s £150-174, d £160-184; P❋🛜🏊) As famous as the local monkeys, Gibraltar's grand old dame is looking fab and fresh after a massive makeover. The 86 smart but cosy, creamy, wood-floored rooms with fresh flowers and sea views still smelt of paint when we visited. Tick off gym, pool, welcome drink, writing desks, bathrobes, a sparkling cafe-bar and Sunday roasts (£25).

Eating

Goodbye tapas, hello fish and chips. Gibraltar's food is unashamedly British – and pretty pricey by Andalucian standards. The staples are pub grub, beer, sandwiches, chips and stodgy desserts, though a few international flavours can be found at Queensway Quay, Marina Bay and Ocean Village.

Verdi Verdi
INTERNATIONAL **€**

(Map p152; www.verdiverdi.com; International Commercial Centre, Main St 2A; dishes £2-5; ☺7.30am-5pm Mon-Fri) This energetic kosher cafe serves up good home-made quiches, salads, soups, hummus, falafel wraps and cakes. Eat in or takeaway.

House of Sacarello
INTERNATIONAL **€€**

(Map p152; www.sacarellosgibraltar.com; 57 Irish Town; mains £8-11; ☺8.30am-7.30pm Mon-Fri, 9am-3pm Sat; 🛜🌱) A jack of all trades and master of...well...some, Sacarello's offers a great range of vegetarian options (pastas, quiches) alongside pub-style dishes in an old multilevel coffee warehouse. There's a good long coffee list, plus lots of cakes, a salad bar and daily specials. From 3.30pm to 7.30pm, you can linger over afternoon tea (£5.90).

Clipper
BRITISH, PUB **€€**

(Map p152; 78B Irish Town; mains £5-9; ☺9am-10pm Mon-Fri, 10am-4pm Sat, 10am-10pm Sun; 🛜) Ask five...10...20 people in Gibraltar for their favourite pub and, chances are, they'll choose the Clipper. Looking sparklingly modern after a refurb that cleared out some of the dated naval decor, the Clipper does real pub grub in traditionally large portions. British faves include jacket potatoes, chicken tikka masala, Sunday roasts and that essential all-day breakfast (£5.95).

Star Bar
PUB, INTERNATIONAL **€€**

(Map p152; www.starbargibraltar.com; 12 Parliament Lane; mains £7-11; ☺8am-11pm Mon-Sat, 10am-9pm Sun) The Rock's oldest bar (if house advertising is to be believed) has been revamped with contemporary flair and a Mediterranean-influenced pub menu that even features tapas. Squeeze inside for wraps, burgers, salads, ribeye steak, spinach-and-goat's-cheese pasta and, of course, fish and chips.

Shopping

Main St is full of British high-street shops, including Topshop, Next, Monsoon and Marks & Spencer. Shops usually open from 10am to 7pm weekdays (without siesta breaks), and until 2pm Saturdays.

Information

Emergency (☑199) Police, ambulance.
Police Headquarters (☑20072500; New Mole House, Rosia Rd)
St Bernard's Hospital (☑20079700; Harbour Views Rd) With 24-hour emergency facilities.
Tourist Office (Map p152; www.visitgibraltar.gi; Grand Casemates Sq; ☺9am-5.30pm Mon-Fri, 10am-3pm Sat, 10am-1pm Sun)

Getting There & Away

AIR

EasyJet (www.easyjet.com) Flies daily to/from London Gatwick and three times weekly to/from Bristol.

British Airways (www.britishairways.com) Flies daily to/from London Heathrow.

Monarch (www.monarch.co.uk) Flies five times weekly to/from London Luton, four to/from Manchester and three to/from Birmingham.

BOAT

One weekly **FRS** (www.frs.es) ferry sails from Gibraltar to Tangier Med (Morocco; adult/child one-way £38/25, one hour) on Friday at 7pm. Book tickets at **Turner & Co** (Map p152; ☑20 078305; 67 Irish Town; ☺9am-1pm & 2-5pm Mon-Fri).

BUS

No buses go directly to Gibraltar, but the **bus station** in La Línea de la Concepción (Spain) is only 400m from the border. From here, there are regular buses to/from Algeciras, Cádiz, Málaga, Seville and Tarifa.

CAR & MOTORCYCLE

Long vehicle queues at the border and congested streets in Gibraltar make it far less time-consuming to park in La Línea and walk across the frontier (1.5km to Casemates Sq). To take a car into Gibraltar (free) you need an insurance certificate, registration document, nationality plate and driving licence. Gibraltar drives on the right.

In Gibraltar, there are car parks on Line Wall Rd, Reclamation Rd and Devil's Tower Rd. Street parking in La Línea costs €1.25 per hour, but it's easier/safer to use the underground car parks just north of Avenida Príncipe de Asturias.

Getting Around

Bus 5 runs between town and the border every 10 to 20 minutes. Bus 2 serves Europa Point, bus 3 the southern town; bus 4 and bus 8 go to Catalan Bay. All these buses stops at Market Pl, immediately northwest of Grand Casemates Sq. Tickets cost £1.50, or £2.25 for a day pass.

Málaga Province

POP 1.64 MILLION

Includes ➜

Málaga 157
Marbella 173
Estepona 175
Mijas 177
Ronda 178
Ardales
& El Chorro 185
Antequera 185
Paraje Natural Torcal
de Antequera 188
La Axarquía 189
Nerja 191

Best Places to Eat

➜ La Consula (p172)

➜ Óleo (p165)

➜ El Mesón de Cervantes (p165)

➜ Casanis (p174)

➜ Arte de Cozina (p188)

Best Places to Stay

➜ El Molino de los Abuelos (p190)

➜ El Molino del Santo (p181)

➜ Hotel Linda Marbella (p174)

➜ La Fructuosa (p185)

Why Go?

Málaga is the hip revitalised Andalucian city everyone is talking about after decades of being pointedly ignored, particularly by tourists to the coastal resorts. The city's 30-odd museums and edgy urban art scene are well matched by the contemporary chic dining choices, spanking new metro line and a shopping street voted as one of the most stylish (and expensive) in Spain. And besides Málaga, each region of the province has equally fascinating diversity, ranging from the breathtaking mountains of La Axarquía to the tourist-driven razzle dazzle of the Costa del Sol.

Inland are the *pueblos blancos* (white towns) crowned by spectacularly situated Ronda. Or the underappreciated, elegant old town of Antequera with its nearby archaeological site and fabulous *porra antequera* (garlic-laden soup).

Málaga is at its most vibrant during the annual feria, when the party atmosphere is infused with flamenco, *fino* (dry straw-coloured sherry) and carafe-loads of fiesta spirit.

Driving Distances

	Málaga	Antequera	Ronda	Mijas
Antequera	40			
Ronda	64	87		
Mijas	25	70	70	
Nerja	53	89	117	88

MÁLAGA

POP 568,479

Málaga is a world apart from the adjoining Costa del Sol; a historic and culturally rich provincial capital which has long lived in the shadow of the iconic Andalucian cities of Granada, Córdoba and Seville. Yet, it has rapidly emerged as the province's city of culture with its so-called 'mile of art' being compared to Madrid, and its dynamism and fine dining to Barcelona.

The tastefully restored historic centre is a delight: its Gothic cathedral is surrounded by narrow pedestrian streets flanked by traditional and modern bars, and shops that range from idiosyncratic and family owned, to urban-chic and contemporary. Cast your eyes up to enjoy a skyline that reflects the city's eclectic character; church spires jostle for space with russet-red tiled roofs and lofty apartment buildings while, like a grand old dame, the 11th-century Gibralfaro castle sits grandly aloft and provides the best view of all.

The former rundown port has also been grandly rebuilt and cruise-line passengers are now boosting the city's coffers and contributing to the overall increase in tourism to the city.

History

Málaga comes from *malaka,* meaning 'to salt', the name given to the city by the Phoenicians in the 8th century BC after their culinary custom of salting fish. The city grew to become a major port in Roman times, exporting olive oil and *garum* (fish paste), as well as copper, lead and iron from the mines in the mountains around Ronda. Málaga continued to flourish under Moorish rule from the 8th century AD, especially as the chief port of the Emirate of Granada. The city held out against the invading Christian armies until 1487 and displayed equal tenacity against Franco's fascists during the Spanish Civil War. More recently the city has happily managed to stave off the mass development that typifies the adjacent Costa del Sol.

⊙ Sights

Málaga's major sights are clustered in or near the charming old town, which is situated beneath the Alcazaba and the Castillo de Gibralfaro. A good place to start your exploring is the landmark cathedral, which towers above the surrounding streets and is thus reassuringly easy to find. The port area is home to a further three museums.

⊙ Historic Centre

★ Catedral de Málaga   CATHEDRAL

(Map p166; ☑952 21 59 17; Calle Molina Lario; cathedral & museum €5, tower €6; ⊙10am-6pm Mon-Sat) Málaga's cathedral was started in the 16th century on the site of the former mosque. Of this, only the Patio de los Naranjos survives, a small courtyard of fragrant orange trees.

Inside, the fabulous domed ceiling soars 40m into the air, while the vast colonnaded nave houses an enormous cedar-wood choir. Aisles give access to 15 chapels with gorgeous 18th-century retables and religious art. Climb the tower (200 steps) to enjoy stunning panoramic views of the city skyline and coast.

Building the cathedral was an epic project that took some 200 years. Such was the project's cost that by 1782 it was decided that work would stop. One of the two bell towers was left incomplete, hence the cathedral's well-worn nickname, *La Manquita* (the one-armed lady). The cathedral's museum displays a collection of religious items covering a period of 500 years.

★ Museo Picasso Málaga   MUSEUM

(Map p166; ☑902 44 33 77; www.museopicassomalaga.org; Calle San Agustín 8; admission €7, incl temporary exhibition €10; ⊙10am-8pm Tue-Thu & Sun, to 9pm Fri & Sat) The Museo Picasso has an enviable collection of 204 works, 155 donated and 49 loaned to the museum by Christine Ruiz-Picasso (wife of Paul, Picasso's eldest son) and Bernard Ruiz-Picasso (his grandson), and includes some wonderful paintings of the family, including the heartfelt *Paulo con gorro blanco* (Paulo with a white cap), a portrait of Picasso's eldest son painted in the 1920s.

Don't miss the Phoenician, Roman, Islamic and Renaissance archaeological remains in the museum's basement, discovered during construction works.

There are also excellent year-round temporary exhibitions.

★ Alcazaba   CASTLE

(Map p166; Calle Alcazabilla; admission €2.20, incl Castillo de Gibralfaro €3.40; ⊙9.30am-8pm Tue-Sun) No time to visit Granada's Alhambra? Then Málaga's Alcazaba can provide a taster. The entrance is next to the Roman amphitheatre, from where a meandering path climbs amid lush greenery: crimson bougainvillea, lofty palms, fragrant jasmine bushes and rows of orange trees. Extensively

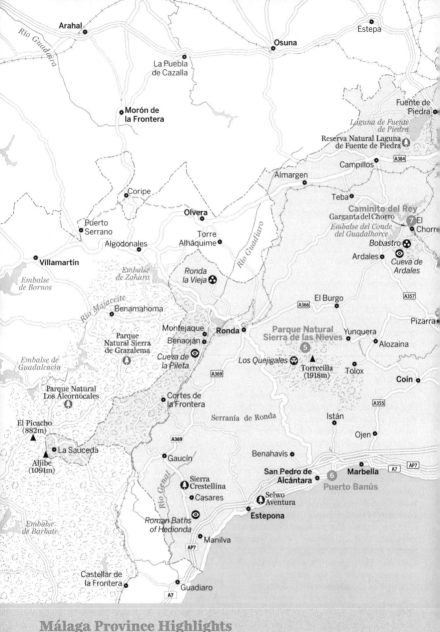

Málaga Province Highlights

1 Embarking on an art trail visiting world-class museums in **Málaga** (p157)

2 Following the polka dots to the **Feria de Málaga** (p163), the province's top annual fiesta

3 Marvelling at the architectural gems in the old centre of **Antequera** (p185)

4 Admiring breathtaking mountaintop views in **Comares** (p190)

MEDITERRANEAN SEA

Melilla
(180km)

0   20 km
0   10 miles

5 Exploring the fascinating backcountry around the **Parque Natural Sierra de las Nieves** (p183) near Ronda

6 Checking out all the glitz and glamour at a Puerto Banús nightclub, such as **Tibu** (p175)

7 Taking the walk of a lifetime along El Chorro's **Caminito del Rey** (p187)

ℹ FREE ENTRY TO MUSEUMS

The **Museo Picasso** (p157) and the **Centre Pompidou Málaga** (p160) offer free admission on Sunday afternoons from 6pm and 4pm, respectively, until closure time.

restored, this palace-fortress dates from the 11th-century Moorish period; the caliphal horseshoe arches, courtyards and bubbling fountains are evocative of this influential period in Málaga's history.

Don't miss the small **archaeological museum** located within the former servants' quarters of the Nazari palace, with its exhibits of Moorish ceramics and pottery.

Museo Carmen Thyssen   MUSEUM
(Map p166; www.carmenthyssenmalaga.org; Calle Compañía 10; admission €4.50, incl temporary exhibition €9; ⊙10am-7.30pm Tue-Sun) Located in an aesthetically renovated 16th-century palace in the heart of the city's former Moorish quarter, the extensive collection concentrates on 19th-century Spanish and Andalucian art and includes paintings by some of the country's most exceptional painters, including Joaquín Sorolla y Bastida, Ignacio Zuloaga and Francisco de Zurbarán. Temporary exhibitions similarly focus on 19th-century art.

Castillo de Gibralfaro   CASTLE
(Map p162; admission €2.20, incl Alcazaba €3.40; ⊙9am-9pm Apr-Sep) One remnant of Málaga's Islamic past is the craggy ramparts of the Castillo de Gibralfaro, spectacularly located high on the hill overlooking the city. Built by Abd ar-Rahman I, the 8th-century Cordoban emir, and later rebuilt in the 14th century when Málaga was the main port for the emirate of Granada, the castle originally acted as a lighthouse and military barracks.

Nothing much is original in the castle's interior, but the airy walkway around the ramparts affords the best views over Málaga.

There is also a military museum, which includes a small scale model of the entire castle complex and the lower residence, the Alcazaba.

The best way to reach the castle on foot is via the scenic Paseo Don Juan de Temboury, to the south of the Alcazaba. From here a path winds pleasantly (and steeply) through lushly gardened terraces with viewpoints over the city. Alternatively, you can drive up the Camino de Gibralfaro or take bus 35 from Avenida de Cervantes.

Museo de Málaga   MUSEUM
(Palacio de la Aduana; Map p166; ☏951 29 40 51; Plaza de la Aduana; ⊙10am-7pm Tue-Sun) **FREE**
The Museum of Málaga opened in 2015. It includes an archaeological-history section with reproductions of wall paintings found in Nerja caves and a magnificent 1.7m sculpture of a Roman soldier dating to the 2nd century AD. A further gallery concentrates on the Moorish period with a large model of Málaga's one-time medina-like market and several Nasrid ceramics. The museum also contains a fine-arts section of 19th- and 20th-century Spanish paintings.

Museo de Arte Flamenco   MUSEUM
(Map p166; ☏952 22 13 80; www.museoflamencojuanbreva.com; Calle Franquelo 4; suggested donation €1; ⊙10am-2pm Tue-Sun) Fabulously laid-out over two floors in the HQ of Málaga's oldest and most prestigious *peña* (private flamenco club), this collection of fans, costumes, posters and other flamenco paraphernalia is testimony to the city's illustrious flamenco scene.

Museo del Vidrio y Cristal   MUSEUM
(Museum of Glass & Crystal; Map p162; ☏952 22 02 71; www.museovidrioycristalmalaga.com; Plazuela Santísimo Cristo de la Sangre 2; admission €5; ⊙11am-7pm Tue-Sun) This enthralling museum is housed in an 18th-century palatial house, complete with three central patios, in a charmingly dilapidated part of town. Aesthetically restored by aristocratic owner and historian Gonzalo Fernández-Prieto, this private collection concentrates on glass and crystal but includes antique furniture, priceless carpets, pre-Raphaelite stained-glass windows and huge 16th-century ancestral portraits.

◉ Alameda Principal & Around

The Alameda Principal, now a busy thoroughfare, was created in the late 18th century as a boulevard on what were then the sands of the Guadalmedina estuary. Adorned with mature trees from the Americas, the wide road is lined with 18th- and 19th-century buildings while the central reservation is home to a row of colourful flower stalls.

★ Centre Pompidou Málaga   MUSEUM
(Map p162; ☏951 92 62 00; www.centrepompidou.es; Pasaje Doctor Carrillo Casaux, Muelle Uno; admission €7, incl temporary exhibition €9; ⊙9.30am-8pm Wed-Mon) Opened in 2015 in the port, this offshoot of the Paris Pompidou Centre is housed in a low-slung modern building

crowned by a playful multicoloured cube. The permanent exhibition includes the extraordinary *Ghost* by Kader Attia depicting rows of Muslim women bowed in prayer created from domestic aluminum foil, plus works by such contemporary masters as Frida Kahlo, Francis Bacon and Antoni Tàpies. There are also audiovisual installations, talking 'heads' and temporary exhibitions.

The museum is contracted to be here for five years at an annual cost of a cool €1 million.

Centro de Arte Contemporáneo MUSEUM
(Contemporary Art Museum; Map p162; www.cacmalaga.org; Calle Alemania; ⊙10am-8pm Tue-Sun) FREE The contemporary art museum is housed in a skilfully converted 1930s wholesale market on the river estuary. The bizarre triangular floor plan of the building has been retained, with its cubist lines and shapes brilliantly displaying the modern art. Painted entirely white, windows and all, the museum exhibits works from well-known contemporary artists such as Tracey Emin and Damien Hirst.

Paseo de España PARK
(Map p166; Paseo del Parque; P) A palm-lined extension of the Alameda, this park was created in the 1890s on land reclaimed from the sea. The garden along its southern side is full of exotic tropical plants and trees, making a pleasant refuge from the bustle of the city. Elderly and young *malagueños* (people from Málaga) stroll around and take shelter in the deep shade of the tall palms, and on Sundays buskers and entertainers play to the crowds.

Mercado Atarazanas MARKET
(Map p166; Calle Atarazanas; P) North of the city's main artery, the Alameda Principal, you'll find this striking 19th-century iron-clad building incorporating the original Moorish gate that once connected the city with the port. The magnificent stained-glass window depicts historical highlights of the city.

The daily market here is pleasantly noisy and animated. Choose from swaying legs of ham and rolls of sausages or cheese, fish and endless varieties of olives. The fruit and veg stalls are the most colourful, selling everything that is in season, ranging from big misshapen tomatoes, sliced and served with olive oil, chopped garlic and rough salt, to large purple onions, mild-flavoured and sweet.

DON'T MISS

URBAN REGENERATION IN SOHO

The antithesis of Málaga's prestigious world-class art museums is the refreshingly down-to-earth **MUES** (Málaga Arte Urbano en el Soho; Map p162), a grassroots movement originally born from an influx of street artists to the area. The result is a total transformation of the formerly rundown district between the city centre and the port (now called Soho), with edgy contemporary murals several stories high, as well as jazzy cafes, ethnic restaurants, craft shops and street markets.

Muelle Uno PORT
(Map p162; P) The city's long beleaguered port area underwent a radical rethink in 2013 and was redesigned to cater to the increase in cruise passengers to the city. Wide quayside walkways now embellish Muelle 1 and Muelle 2, which are lined by palm trees and backed by shops, restaurants, bars and a small aquarium, the **Museo Alborania** (Map p166; ☑ 951 60 01 08; www.museoalborania.com; Palmeral de las Sopresas, Muelle 2; adult/child €7/5; ⊙11am-2pm & 5pm-midnight Jul–15 Sep, 10.30am-2.30pm & 4.30-6:30pm 15 Sep–Jun; ♦).

◉ West of the Centre

Museo Ruso de Málaga MUSEUM
(☑951 92 61 50; www.coleccionmuseoruso.es; Avenida de Sor Teresa Plat 15; adult/child €8/free; ⊙11am-10pm Tue-Sun; P) This offshoot of the Russian State Museum in St Petersburg opened in 2015 in a former 1920s tobacco factory. It is dedicated to Russian art from the 16th to 20th centuries, featuring works by Ilya Repin, Wassily Kandinsky and Vladimir Tatlin, among others. From Málaga Centre Alameda Principal, take bus 3, 15 or 16 and get off at Avenida La Paloma (€1.35, 10 minutes).

This museum is essentially a 'pop-up' with a 10-year contract to remain in Málaga.

Museo Automovilístico Málaga MUSEUM
(☑951 13 70 01; www.museoautomovilmalaga.com; Avenida Sor Teresa Prat 15; adult/child €7.50/free; ⊙10am-7pm Tue-Sun) Housed in a former tobacco factory, petrol heads and fashionistas will love this museum which combines the history of the automobile with 20th-century

Málaga

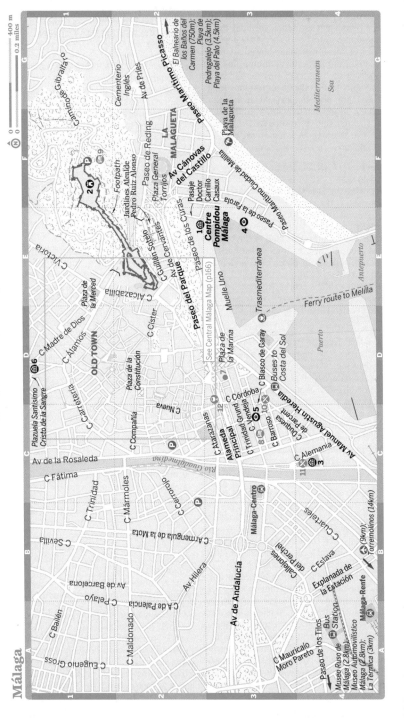

0 0

N

0.2 miles

400 m

Mediterranean Sea

El Balneario de los Baños del Carmen (750m); Playa de Pedregalejo (3.5km); Playa de Palo (4.5km)

Playa de la Malagueta

LA MALAGUETA

Paseo Marítimo Picasso

Cementerio Inglés

Av de Pries

Camino de Gibralfaro

Paseo General Torrijos

Plaza General Torrijos

Paseo de Reding

Jardines Alcaide Pedro Ruiz Alonso

Footpath

Av Cánovas del Castillo

Paseo Marítimo Ciudad de Melilla

Pasaje Doctor Carrillo Casaux

Centre Pompidou Málaga

Paseo de la Farola

Paseo de los Curas

C Guillén Sotelo

Av de Cervantes

C Victoria

C Alcazabilla

Paseo del Parque

See Central Málaga Map (p166)

Muelle Uno

Trasmediterránea

Antepuerto

Ferry route to Melilla

Puerto

C Cister

Plaza de la Merced

C Madre de Dios

C Álamos

OLD TOWN

Plaza de la Constitución

C Nueva

Plaza de la Marina

C Blasco de Garay

Costa del Sol

Buses to Costa del Sol

C Córdoba

C Duquesa de Parcent

Av Manuel Agustín Heredia

C Carretería

Plazuela Santísimo Cristo de la Sangre

C Compañía

C Atarazanas

Alameda Principal

C Trinidad Grund

C Vendeja

C Barroso

C Alemania

Av de la Rosaleda

C Fátima

Río Guadalmedina

Málaga-Centro

C Trinidad

C Mármoles

C Cerrojo

Armengula de la Mota

Av Hilera

Av de Andalucía

Callejones del Perchel

C Eslava

Explanada de la Estación

Málaga-Renfe

C Sevilla

C Barcelona

Av de Barcelona

C Pelayo

C A de Palencia

C Bailén

C Maldonado

C Eugenio Gross

Bus Station

C Cuarteles

(9km); Torremolinos (14km)

Museo Ruso de Málaga (2.8km); Museo Automovilístico Málaga (2.8km); La Térmica (3km)

Museo Ruso de Málaga (2.8km); Museo Automovilístico Málaga (2.8km)

C Mauricalo Moro Pareto

Paseo de los Tilos

A1 A2 A3 A4 B1 B2 B3 B4 C1 C2 C3 C4 D1 D2 D3 D4 E1 E2 E3 E4 F1 F2 F3 F4 G1 G2 G3 G4

Málaga

⊙ Top Sights
1 Centre Pompidou Málaga...................E2

◎ Sights
2 Castillo de Gibralfaro...........................F1
3 Centro de Arte Contemporáneo........C4
4 Muelle Uno...E3
5 MUES..C3
6 Museo del Vidrio y Cristal...................D1

☉ Activities, Courses & Tours
7 Málaga Bike Tours D3

⊜ Sleeping
8 Feel Málaga Hostel C3
9 Parador Málaga Gibralfaro F1

⊗ Eating
10 Al Yamal D3
11 Óleo.. C4

⊝ Drinking & Nightlife
12 Antigua Casa de Guardia D3

fashion from style gurus such as Chanel, Yves Saint Laurent and Dior. Around 85 cars have been immaculately restored, including a Bugatti, a Bentley and a fabulous flower-power-painted Rolls. From Málaga Centre Alameda Principal, take bus 3, 15 or 16 and get off at Avenida La Paloma (€1.35, 10 minutes).

La Térmica   CULTURAL CENTRE
(www.latermicamalaga.com; Avenida de Los Guindos 48; ⊙hours vary; P) FREE Come here for the architecture alone; this fabulous Modernista building has dazzling tilework, courtyards and fountains and has been a military hospital, orphanage and civic centre in its time. It is now home to a lively program of concerts, courses and exhibitions (the graffiti artist Banksy was the subject of a recent show), plus an antique market held the first Sunday of every month.

⊙ La Malagueta & the Beaches

At the end of the Paseo del Parque lies the exclusive residential district of La Malagueta. Situated on a spit of land protruding into the sea, apartments here have frontline sea views, and some of Málaga's best restaurants are found near the **Playa de la Malagueta** (the beach closest to the city centre). Head 2km east to the fabulous setting of the seafood restaurant, El Balneario de los Baños de Carmen (p165).

East of Playa de la Malagueta, sandy beaches continue to line most of the waterfront for several kilometres. Next along are **Playa de Pedregalejo** and **Playa el Palo**, El Palo being the city's original, salt-of-the-earth fishing neighbourhood. This is a great place to bring children and an even better place to while away an afternoon with a cold beer and a plate of sizzling seafood. To reach either beach, take bus 11 from Paseo del Parque.

🏃 Activities

Hammam Al-Andalus   HAMMAM
(Map p166; ☑952 21 50 18; www.hammamal andalus.com; Plaza de los Mártires 5; €30; ⊙10am-midnight) These Moorish-style baths provide *malagueños* with a luxury marble-clad setting to enjoy the same relaxation benefits as those offered by similar facilities in Granada and Córdoba. Massages are also available.

Málaga Bike Tours   CYCLING
(Map p162; ☑606 978513; www.malagabiketours. eu; Calle Trinidad Grund 1; tours €25) Bike tours are an excellent way to see the sights and you can't do better than Málaga Bike Tours, which runs daily tours leaving from outside the municipal tourist office in Plaza de la Marina at 10am. Reservations are required. Book at least 24 hours ahead.

Alternatively, you can rent your own bike for €10 a day.

🎉 Festivals & Events

There's a whole host of festivals throughout the year in Málaga province, listed in the booklet *¿Qué Hacer?*, available each month from the municipal tourist office.

Fiesta Mayor de Verdiales   FOLK MUSIC
(⊙28 Dec) Thousands congregate for a grand gathering of *verdiales* folk groups at Puerto de la Torre. The groups perform an exhilarating brand of music and dance unique to the Málaga area. Buses 20 and 21 from the Alameda Principal go to Puerto de la Torre.

Semana Santa   HOLY WEEK
Each night from Palm Sunday to Good Friday, six or seven *cofradías* (brotherhoods) bear holy images for several hours through the city, watched by large crowds.

Feria de Málaga   FAIR
(⊙mid-Aug) Málaga's nine-day feria (fair), launched by a huge fireworks display, is the most ebullient of Andalucía's summer ferias. It resembles an exuberant Rio-style street

LOCAL KNOWLEDGE

DINNER IN THE CITY

The Renfe rail company has a latish last train on the Málaga–Fuengirola route at 11.30pm, so if you are staying in one of the Costa resorts you can dine (and drink) in the big city before hightailing it to the station and heading home.

party with plenty of flamenco and *fino*; head for the city centre to be in the thick of it.

At night, festivities switch to large fairgrounds and nightly rock and flamenco shows at Cortijo de Torres, 3km southwest of the city centre; special buses run from all over the city.

🛏 Sleeping

★ **Dulces Dreams** HOSTEL €

(Map p166; ☑ 951 35 78 69; www.dulcesdreamshostel.com; Plaza de los Mártires 6; r incl breakfast €45-60; ✴ 🛜) Run by an enthusiastic young team, the rooms at Dulces (sweet) Dreams are appropriately named after desserts; 'Cupcake' is a good choice with its terrace overlooking the imposing red-brick church across the way. This is an older building so there's no lift and the rooms vary in size, but they are bright and whimsically decorated using recycled materials as far as possible. Breakfast is healthy and cosmopolitan with choices including avocado, cheese, fruit and muesli, plus organic coffee that guests claim to be the best in town.

Feel Málaga Hostel HOSTEL €

(Map p162; ☑ 952 22 28 32; www.feelmalagahostel.com; Calle Vendeja 25; d €45, without bathroom €35, shared rooms per person from €16; @ 🛜) Located within a suitcase trundle of the city-centre train station, the accommodation here is clean and well-equipped with a choice of doubles and shared rooms. The downstairs communal area has a colourful seaside look with stripey deckchairs and minifootball, bathrooms sport classy mosaic tiles and the top-floor kitchen has all the essentials necessary to whip up a decent meal.

★ **Molina Lario** HOTEL €€

(Map p166; ☑ 952 06 20 02; www.hotelmolinalario.com; Calle Molina Lario 20-22; r €116-130; ✴ 🛜 ⬚) Perfect for romancing couples, this hotel has a sophisticated contemporary feel with spacious rooms decorated in a cool

palette of earthy colours. There are crisp white linens, marshmallow-soft pillows and tasteful paintings, plus a fabulous rooftop terrace and pool with views to the sea. Situated within confessional distance of the cathedral.

El Hotel del Pintor BOUTIQUE HOTEL €€

(Map p166; ☑ 952 06 09 81; www.hoteldelpintor.com; Calle Álamos 27; s/d €59/70; ✴ @ 🛜) The red, black and white colour scheme of this friendly, small hotel echoes the abstract artwork of *malagueño* artist Pepe Bornov, whose paintings are on permanent display throughout the public areas and rooms. Although convenient for most of the city's main sights, pack your earplugs, as the rooms in the front can be noisy, especially on a Saturday night.

El Riad Andaluz GUESTHOUSE €€

(Map p166; ☑ 952 21 36 40; www.elriadandaluz.com; Calle Hinestrosa 24; s/d/tr €62/89/119; ✴ @ 🛜) This French-run guesthouse, in the historic part of town, has eight rooms set around the kind of atmospheric patio that's known as a *riad* in Morocco. The decoration is Moroccan but each room is different, including colourful tiled bathrooms. Breakfast is available.

Parador Málaga Gibralfaro HISTORIC HOTEL €€€

(Map p162; ☑ 952 22 19 02; www.parador.es; Castillo de Gibralfaro; r incl breakfast €130-155; P ✴ 🛜 ⬚) With an unbeatable location perched on the pine-forested Gibralfaro, Málaga's stone-built *parador* (luxurious state-owned hotel) is a popular choice, although the rooms are fairly standard. Most have spectacular views from their terraces, however, and you can dine at the excellent terrace restaurant, even if you are not a guest at the hotel.

🍴 Eating

Málaga has a staggering number of tapas bars and restaurants, particularly around the historic centre (over 400 at last count), so finding a place to eat poses no problem. A gourmet food market, Mercado de La Merced is also slated to open in the historic centre, just off Plaza de la Merced, offering an eclectic choice of international and local cuisine to sample or take away.

El Calafate VEGETARIAN €

(Map p166; Calle Andrés Pérez 6; mains €7-10; ⊙ 1.30-4pm & 8.30-11pm Mon-Sat; 🍴) Squeezed into a corner in a tangle of narrow pedestrian streets, this vegetarian restaurant has a menu that encompasses veggie favourites such as breaded seitan and tofu cutlets, plus international imports ranging from Thai rice to Greek moussaka.

Casa Aranda
CAFE €

(Map p166; www.casa-aranda.net; Calle Herrería del Rey; churro €0.45; ⊙8am-3pm Mon-Sat; ⊕) Casa Aranda is in a narrow alleyway next to the market and, since 1932, has been *the* place in town to enjoy chocolate and churros (tubular-shaped doughnuts). The cafe has taken over the whole street with several outlets all overseen by a team of mainly elderly white-shirted waiters who welcome everyone like an old friend (and most are).

★Óleo
FUSION €€

(Map p162; ☑952 21 90 62; www.oleorestaurante.es; Edificio CAC, Calle Alemania; mains €12-16; ⊙10am-midnight Mon-Sat; ☜) Located at the city's contemporary art museum with white-on-white minimalist decor, Óleo provides diners with the unusual choice of Mediterranean or Asian food with some subtle combinations such as duck breast with a side of seaweed with hoisin, as well as more purist Asian and gourmet palate-ticklers such as candied, roasted piglet.

Vegetarians are well catered to and the service is attentive and swift.

★El Mesón de Cervantes
TAPAS, ARGENTINIAN €€

(Map p166; ☑952 21 62 74; www.elmesonde cervantes.com; Calle Álamos 11; mains €13-16; ⊙7pm-midnight Wed-Mon) Cervantes started as a humble tapas bar run by expat Argentinian Gabriel Spatz (the original bar is still operating around the corner), but has expanded into plush spacious digs with an open kitchen, fantastic family-style service and incredible meat dishes.

Al Yamal
MOROCCAN €€

(Map p162; Calle Blasco de Garay 7; mains €9-12; ⊙noon-3pm & 7-11pm Mon-Sat) In the heart of the buzzing Soho *barrio* (district), this family-run restaurant serves delicious authentic Moroccan cuisine, including tagines, couscous, hummus and *kefta* (meatballs). The dining room has just six tables and is decorated with warm Moroccan colours and fabrics; finish off your meal with a mint tea delicately spiced with the essence of orange blossom.

GASTROARTE

In 2012, a group of around 30 culinary experts, including chefs and food producers, mainly based around Málaga, formed **Gastroarte** (www.gastroarte.es) to rediscover and celebrate the cuisine of Andalucía. This was, in part, a reaction to the bland international cuisine that typifies many restaurants on the Costa. Both **Arte de Cozina** (p188) in Antequera and **Óleo** (p165) in Málaga are members of Gastroarte, and numbers are increasing as more and more restaurants celebrate the bounty and quality of fresh produce available in Andalucía, and such delights as superb olive oil, local wine and an abundance of fresh fish and seafood.

Batik
MODERN SPANISH €€

(Map p166; ☑952 22 10 45; www.batikmalaga.com; Calle Alcazabilla 12; mains €12-20; ⊙10am-midnight; ☜) Located on the top floor of a hostel, views don't get much better than this: an outdoor terrace overlooking the Alcazaba across the way. The cuisine combines art-on-a-plate good looks with innovative culinary flair in the style of grilled beef with juniper-scented chocolate jus. Reservations recommended.

Vino Mio
INTERNATIONAL €€

(Map p166; www.restaurantevinomio.com/en; Plaza Jeronimo Cuervo 2; mains €10-15; ⊙1pm-2am; ☜) This Dutch-owned restaurant has a diverse menu that includes dishes such as kangaroo steaks, vegetable stir-fries and duck breast with sweet chilli, that hit the mark, most of the time. International tapas, like hummus and Roquefort croquettes, are also available, making it a good place for lighter bites, too.

El Balneario de los Baños del Carmen
SEAFOOD €€

(www.elbalneariomalaga.com; Calle Bolivia 40, La Malagueta; mains €8-15; ⊙11am-9pm Sun-Wed, to 2am Thu-Sat; ℗) A wonderful place to sit outside on a warm balmy evening and share a plate of prawns or grilled sardines, along with some long, cold beverages. It was built in 1918 to cater to Málaga's bourgeoisie and is rekindling its past as one of the city's most celebrated venues for socialising.

The dining room still has a tangible feel of its former ballroom days; there is live music

MÁLAGA PROVINCE MÁLAGA

Central Málaga

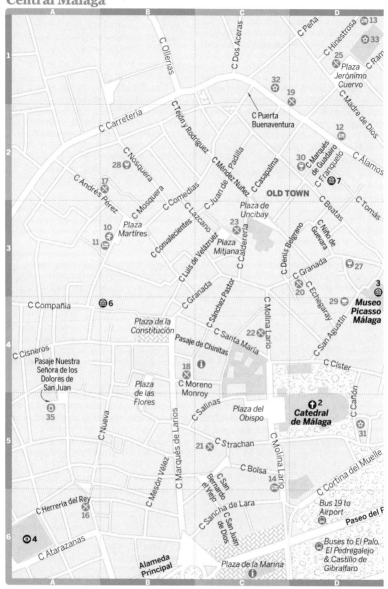

on Saturdays in case you feel like breaking into a waltz. There is also an **Organic Produce & Craft Market** held in the car park every Sunday (9am to 3pm)

El Chinitas ANDALUCIAN €€€

(Map p166; ☎ 952 21 09 72; Calle Moreno Monroy; mains €16-25; ☺noon-midnight) This longstanding popular restaurant offers a menu of solidly traditional Andalucian cuisine

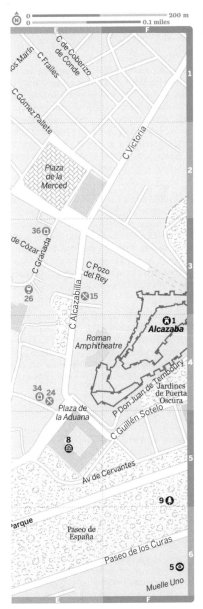

Central Málaga

◎ Top Sights
1 Alcazaba...F4
2 Catedral de Málaga.........................D5
3 Museo Picasso Málaga.....................D3

◎ Sights
4 Mercado Atarazanas..........................A6
5 Museo Alborania................................F6
6 Museo Carmen Thyssen....................B4
7 Museo de Arte Flamenco..................D2
8 Museo de Málaga...............................E5
9 Paseo de España................................F5

⊕ Activities, Courses & Tours
10 Hammam Al-Andalus........................B3

⊟ Sleeping
11 Dulces Dreams...................................B3
12 El Hotel del Pintor............................D2
13 El Riad Andaluz D1
14 Molina Lario.......................................C5

⊗ Eating
15 Batik..E3
16 Casa Aranda.......................................A6
17 El Calafate..B2
18 El Chinitas..B4
19 El Mesón de Cervantes D1
20 El Piyayo...D3
21 Gorki...C5
22 La Rebaná C4
23 Pepa y Pepe..C3
24 Uvedoble Taberna E4
25 Vino Mío D1

⊜ Drinking & Nightlife
26 Bodegas El Pimpi...............................E3
27 Casa Lola...D3
28 La Casa Invisible B2
29 La Tetería D4
30 Los Patios de Beatas.........................D2

⊕ Entertainment
31 Clarence Jazz Club D5
32 Kelipe..C1
33 Teatro Cervantes...............................D1

⊜ Shopping
34 Alfajar...E4
35 La Recova A5
36 Ultramarinos Zoilo............................E3

🍷 Drinking & Nightlife

The best bar hop areas are from Plaza de la Merced in the northeast to Calle Carretería in the northwest, plus Plaza Mitjana and Plaza de Uncibay.

with an emphasis on meat and fish dishes; the oxtail is a speciality. The atmosphere is elegant old world with sumptuous tile-work, twinkling chandeliers, and superb service and attention to detail.

Los Patios de Beatas WINE BAR

(Map p166; Calle Beatas 43; ⏰1-5pm & 8pm-midnight Mon-Sat, 1-6pm Sun; 🛜) Two 18th-century mansions have metaphorphised into this sumptuous space where you can sample fine wines from a selection reputed to be the most extensive in town. Stained-glass windows and beautiful resin tables inset with mosaics and shells add to the overall art-infused atmosphere. Innovative tapas and *raciones* are also served.

Bodegas El Pimpi BAR

(Map p166; www.bodegabarelpimpi.com; Calle Granada 62; ⏰11am-2am; 🛜) This rambling bar is an institution in this town. The interior encompasses a warren of rooms with a courtyard and open terrace overlooking the Roman amphitheatre. Walls are decorated with historic feria posters and photos of visitors, while the enormous barrels are signed by more well-known folk, including Tony Blair and Antonio Banderas. Tapas and meals are also available.

Antigua Casa de Guardia BAR

(Map p162; www.antiguacasadeguardia.net; Alameda Principal 18; ⏰11am-midnight) This atmospheric old tavern dates to 1840 and is the oldest bar in Málaga. The peeling custard-coloured paintwork, black-and-white photographs of local boy Picasso and elderly bar staff look fittingly antique. Try the dark brown, sherry-like *seco* (dry) Málaga wine or the romantically named *lagrima tranañejo* (very old tear).

La Casa Invisible BAR

(Map p166; www.lainvisible.net; Calle Nosquera 11; ⏰11am-late Mon-Sat; 🛜) This place is indeed hard to find, but persevere and you will be rewarded with a wonderful courtyard setting, albeit mildly dilapidated, with shady palms, a goldfish pond and colourful murals. As well as the bar, there are regular concerts ranging from African percussion to flamenco, plus classes like yoga and tango.

La Tetería TEAHOUSE

(Map p166; www.la-teteria.com; Calle San Agustín 9; speciality teas €2.50; ⏰9am-midnight Mon-Sat) Serves heaps of aromatic and classic teas, herbal infusions, coffees and juices, with teas ranging from peppermint to '*antidepresivo*'. Sit outside and marvel at the beautiful church opposite or stay inside to enjoy the wafting incense and background music.

Casa Lola BAR

(Map p166; Calle Granada 46; ⏰11am-4pm & 7pm-midnight) Fronted by traditional blue-and-white tiles, this sophisticated spot specialises in vermouth on tap, served ice cold and costing just a couple of euros. Grab a pew on one of the tall stools and peruse the arty decor and clientele.

TAPAS TRAIL

The pleasures of Málaga are essentially undemanding, easy to arrange and cheap. One of the best is a slow crawl around the city's numerous tapas bars and old bodegas (cellars).

El Piyayo (Map p166; ☎952 22 90 57; www.entreplatos.es; Calle Granada 36; raciones €6-10; ⏰12.30pm-midnight) A popular, traditionally tiled bar and restaurant, famed for its *pescaitos fritos* (fried fish) and typical local tapas, including wedges of crumbly Manchego cheese, the ideal accompaniment to a glass of hearty Rioja wine.

Uvedoble Taberna (Map p166; www.uvedobletaberna.com; Calle Císter 15 ; tapas €2.70; ⏰12.30-4pm & 8pm-midnight Mon-Sat; 🛜) If you are seeking something a little more contemporary, head to this popular spot with its innovative take on traditional tapas.

La Rebaná (Map p166; www.larebana.com; Calle Molina Lario 5; raciones €7-12; ⏰12.30-5pm & 7.30pm-midnight Mon-Fri, 12.30pm-1am Sat & Sun) A great, noisy and central tapas bar. The dark wood-clad interior (with its wrought-iron gallery) creates an inviting ambience. Goats' cheese with cherries, foie gras and cured meats are among the offerings.

Pepa y Pepe (Map p166; ☎615 656984; www.barpepaypepe.com; Calle Calderería 9; tapas €1.50-2, raciones €3.60-5.50; ⏰12.30-4.30pm & 7.30pm-12.30am) A snug tapas bar that brims with young diners enjoying tapas such as *calamares fritos* (battered squid) and fried green peppers.

Gorki (Map p166; www.grupogorki.com; Calle Strachan 6; mains €9-12; ⏰12.30pm-midnight) A tastefully decorated tapas bar for enjoying sophisticated small bites such as miniburgers and sweetbreads encased in light flaky pastry.

☆ Entertainment

Teatro Cervantes THEATRE
(Map p166; www.teatrocervantes.com; Calle Ramos Marín; ⊙Sep–mid-Jul) The handsome art-deco Cervantes has a fine program of music, theatre and dance, including some well-known names on the concert circuit.

Kelipe FLAMENCO
(Map p166; ☑692 829885; www.kelipe.net; Calle Pena 11; €24-35; ⊙9pm show Thu-Sat) Málaga's substantial flamenco heritage has its nexus to the northwest of Plaza de la Merced. This flamenco centre puts on authentic performances Thursday to Saturday at 9.30pm; €24 entry includes two drinks – reserve ahead.

Clarence Jazz Club LIVE MUSIC
(Map p166; ☑951 91 80 87; www.clarencejazzclub.com; Calle Cañón 5; admission €5; ⊙8pm-2am Wed & Thu, 4pm-4am Fri & Sat) Enjoy quality jazz gigs at this intimate club across from the cathedral. It's advisable to reserve a table at weekends.

🔒 Shopping

The chic marble-clad Calle Marqués de Larios is increasingly home to designer stores and boutiques. In the surrounding streets are family-owned small shops in handsomely restored old buildings, selling everything from flamenco dresses to local sweet Málaga wine. Don't miss the fabulous daily market Mercado Atarazanas (p161).

La Recova CRAFTS
(Map p166; www.larecova.es; Pasaje Nuestra Señora de los Dolores de San Juan; ⊙9.30am-1.30pm & 5-8pm Mon-Thu, 9.30am-8pm Fri, 10am-2pm Sat) Seek out this intriguing Aladdin's cave of an art, crafts and antique shop selling traditional *sevillana* tiles, handmade jewellery, antique irons, textiles and much more. It also has a small local bar tucked in the corner, handy for enjoying a beer between browsing.

Ultramarinos Zoilo FOOD
(Map p166; Calle Granada 65; ⊙10am-2pm & 5-7pm Mon-Fr, to 2pm Sat) This lovely deli has been a family-run business since the early 1950s. Choose from great wheels of crumbly Manchego cheese, several grades of local chorizo and the speciality, *jamón serrano*, which hangs over the main counter, gently curing and intensifying in flavour.

TINTO DE VERANO

If you are visiting during summer, consider ordering a *tinto de verano* at any local bar. This long cold drink is made with red wine, local lemonade (not too sweet), lashings of ice and a slice of lemon. Refreshing, and it shouldn't make your head reel too much on a hot day.

Alfajar ARTS & CRAFTS
(Map p166; www.alfajar.es; Calle Císter 3; ⊙10am-2pm & 5-8pm Mon-Fri, to 2pm Sat) Perfect for handcrafted Andalucian ceramics produced by local artisans. You can find traditional designs and glazes, as well as more modern, arty and individualistic pieces.

ℹ️ Information

Municipal Tourist Office (Map p166; Plaza de la Marina; ⊙9am-8pm Mar-Sep, to 6pm Oct-Feb) Offers a range of city maps and booklets. It also operates information kiosks at the Alcazaba entrance (Calle Alcazabilla), at the main train station (Explanada de la Estación), on Plaza de la Merced and on the eastern beaches (El Palo and La Malagueta).

Regional Tourist Office (Map p166; www.andalucia.org; Plaza de la Constitución 7; ⊙9.30am-7.30pm Mon-Fri, 10am-7pm Sat, 10am-2pm Sun) Located in a stunning 18th-century former Jesuit college with year-round art exhibitions, this small tourist office carries a range of information, including maps of the regional cities.

ℹ️ Getting There & Away

TO/FROM THE AIRPORT
Málaga's **airport** (AGP; ☑952 04 88 38; www.aena.es), the main international gateway to Andalucía, is 9km southwest of the city centre. It is a major hub in southern Spain, serving top global carriers as well as budget airlines.

Bus
Bus 75 to the city centre (€1.50, 20 minutes) leaves from outside the arrivals hall every 20 minutes, from 7am to midnight. The bus to the airport leaves from the western end of Paseo del Parque, and from outside the bus and train stations, about every half-hour from 6.30am to 11.30pm.

Car
Numerous local and international agencies have desks at the airport.

Taxi

A taxi from the airport to the city centre costs around €20.

Train

Trains run every 20 minutes from 6.50am to 11.54pm to the **María Zambrano station** (www.renfe.es; Explanada de la Estación) and the Málaga-Centro station beside the Río Guadalmedina. Departures from the city to the airport are every 20 minutes from 5.30am to 11.30pm.

BUS

The **bus station** (Map p162; ☎ 952 35 00 61; www.estabus.emtsam.es; Paseo de los Tilos) is 1km southwest of the city centre, with links to all major cities in Spain.

Destinations include the following, note that the prices listed are the minimum quoted for the route.

TO	COST	DURATION (HR)	FREQUENCY (DAILY)
Almería	€19	4¾	8
Cádiz	€27	4	3
Córdoba	€12	3-4	4
Granada	€12	2	18
Jaén	€20	3¼	4
Madrid airport	€45	10	5
Seville	€19	2¾	6

TRAIN

The **Maria Zambrano (Málaga-Renfe) train station** (www.renfe.es) is near the bus station. Destinations include Córdoba (€26, 2½ hours, 18 daily), Seville (€24, 2¾ hours, 11 daily) and Madrid (€80, 2½ hours, 10 daily). Note that for Córdoba and Seville the daily schedule includes faster trains at roughly double the cost.

ⓘ Getting Around

BUS

Useful buses around town (€1.35 for all trips around the centre) include bus 11 to El Palo, bus 34 to El Pedregalejo and El Palo, and bus 35 to Castillo de Gibralfaro, all departing from Avenida de Cervantes. Destinations further afield include Antequera (€7.45, one hour, nine daily) and Ronda (€12.75, 2½ hours, nine daily).

CAR

There are several well-signposted underground car parks in town. The most convenient are on Avenida de Andalucía, Plaza de la Marina and Plaza de la Merced.

TAXI

Taxi fares typically cost around €6 per 2km to 3km. Fares within the city centre, including to the train and bus stations and Castillo de Gibralfaro, are around €8.

TRAIN

There is a train from Málaga (centre) to Fuengirola running every 20 minutes from 5.30am to 11.30pm and from Fuengirola to Málaga from 6.20am to 12.40pm.

METRO

Metro Málaga (www.metrodemalaga.info) opened in 2015 with two lines linking the suburbs to the east with Málaga University (single, €1.35), which formerly suffered from serious traffic congestion. More lines are being added including one that will run to the city centre; check the website for updates.

COSTA DEL SOL

While the Costa del Sol has long attracted both foreign residents and tourists to its shores, it has also attracted a fair amount of negative press over the years, mainly related to mass development and the spiralling cost of a pint. The truth is that, while there has been unsightly overbuilding here, there are still places that are genuinely picturesque and traditional, and a world away from the soulless urbanisations and Sid-and-Dot-style pubs.

In the resorts of the Costa del Sol, you'll find an abundance of hotels with an international flavour and bilingual staff. These will include some of the more well-known chains. Torremolinos alone sports more than 75 accommodation options.

Torremolinos & Benalmádena

POP 128,340

Torremolinos was developed in the 1950s and, while many of the not-so-modern blocks are Stalin-era in their grimness, there remain attractive quarters, such as the La Carihuela. Torremolinos has been known as the Costa del Sol's gay capital since its first gay bar opened in 1962. The highest concentration of gay bars and clubs lies just west of Plaza La Nogalera in the centre.

The adjacent resort of Benalmádena comprises a fairly bland built-up coastal stretch with the highlights being the **Puerto Deportivo** (leisure port), and the relatively unspoiled **Benalmádena Pueblo** (village) inland. Another resort, Arroya de la Miel, also falls under the Benalmádena banner and is best known as being home to the Tivoli theme park.

◉ Sights & Activities

The centre of Torremolinos revolves around the pedestrian shopping street of San Miguel from where several flights of steps lead down to the beach at Playamar (there is also a lift). Together with Mijas, Benalmádena Pueblo has maintained its traditional charm with cobbled streets, orange trees and simple, flower-festooned houses. There is a magnificent view of the coast from the tiny church at the top of the village.

La Carihuela   BEACH
La Carihuela, flanking the beach, was formerly the fishing district of Torremolinos and is one of the few parts of town that has not suffered from rampant overdevelopment. The beachside promenade is lined with lowrise shops, bars and restaurants, and is one of the most popular destinations for *malagueños* to enjoy fresh seafood at weekends.

Puerto Deportivo de Benalmádena   PORT
(Benalmádena; P) This port on the coast in Benalmádena is striking for its GaudÍ-cum-Asian-cum-Mr-Whippy-style architecture, and large choice of bars, restaurants and shops overlooking the boats.

Playamar   BEACH
This long stretch of beach in Torremolinos is lined with reliably good *chiringuitos* (beach bars) and is also extremely family friendly with pedalos, playgrounds, sunbeds and parasols for hire. The wide promenade is popular with strollers and joggers, and in midsummer films are often screened on the beach.

Mariposario de Benalmádena   BUTTERFLY PARK
(www.mariposariodebenalmadena.com; Benalmádena Pueblo; adult/child €9/5; ⊙10am-6pm; P ⊕) Situated next to the Buddhist stupa, in a quasi Thai temple, this butterfly park is a delight with some 1500 fluttery creatures, including exotic subtropical species, moths and cocoons (in action). There are some impressive plants and water features, plus two resident iguanas, a wallaby and a giant tortoise.

Buddhist Stupa   MUSEUM, MONUMENT
(Benalmádena Pueblo; ⊙10am-2pm & 3.30-6.30pm Tue-Sat, 10am-7.30pm Sun; P) FREE The largest Buddhist stupa in Europe is in Benalmádena Pueblo. It rises up, majestically out of place,

---

> **BEST COSTA DEL SOL FAMILY ATTRACTIONS**
>
> The Costa del Sol is a particularly welcoming area for those travelling with children and there's plenty going on to keep them occupied.
>
> **Biopark** (p172)
>
> **Tivoli World** (p171)
>
> **Selwo Aventura** (p176)
>
> **Mariposario de Benalmádena** (p171)
>
> **Aventura Amazonia** (p174)

---

on the outskirts of the village, surrounded by new housing and with sweeping coastal views. The lofty interior is lined with exquisitely executed devotional paintings.

Tivoli World   AMUSEMENT PARK
(www.tivolicostadelsol.com; Arroya de la Miel; admission €8, Supertivolino ticket €15; ⊙4pm-midnight Apr-Sep) The oldest and largest amusement park in Málaga province, with various rides and slides, as well as daily dance, flamenco and childrens' events. Consider the good-value 'Supertivolino', which covers admission and unlimited access to some 35 rides.

🛏 Sleeping

Hotel Zen   HOTEL €
(☎952 37 38 82; www.hotelzen.es; Urbanizacion El Pinar, Torremolinos; r incl breakfast €50; P ❄ 🛜 🏊) Located between the airport and Torremolinos, this hotel is ideal for travellers as a free airport shuttle (also to the beach and town centre) is included in the price. The name is a bit of a mystery as there is nothing particularly oriental about the decor, which is beige-on-beige bland, but the situation, in a quiet residential area, is very tranquil.

Most rooms have balconies and there is a pool, heated in the winter.

Hostal Guadalupe   HOSTAL €€
(☎952 38 19 37; www.hostalguadalupe.com; Calle del Peligro, Torremolinos; s €35-70, d €45-80, apt €55-90; 🛜) A superb choice across from the beach; rooms are plain but comfortable and several have terraces overlooking the sea. The apartment has kitchen facilities that are great for longer stays. The staff are extremely attentive; they will park your car for you if you can't find a spot and advise on what's going on in town. There is no lift.

✖ Eating & Drinking

For the best seafood restaurants, head to the fishing district of La Carihuela on the coast, just west of the centre. The best source of information on the town's gay scene can be found at www.gaytorremolinos.eu.

Rincon de la Paquita SEAFOOD €
(Calle del Cauce, Arroyo de la Miel, Benalmádena; mains €8-9, raciones €5-6; ⊙noon-11pm) This place looks like it belongs in a fishing village on the beach rather than a tourist-driven resort. Squeezed into a narrow pedestrian street, with plastic tables, football on the telly and a blackboard of specials, locals rate this place as having the best seafood in town; order a selection of *raciones* to share.

La Zoca SEAFOOD €€
(☑95 238 5925; www.restaurantelazoca.com; Calle Bulto 61, La Carihuela, Torremolinos; mains €15-20; ⊙9.30am-11.30pm; 🚲) Firstly, families take note. This seaside restaurant has a playground across the way. The emphasis is on seafood such as *gambas pil-pil* (prawns in a spicy oil-based sauce) and rice-based dishes (with five to choose from). Gets packed with boisterous Spanish families on Sundays, so not the time for an intimate *tête a deux*.

Vinoteca Las Tablas ANDALUCIAN €€
(☑95 237 3740; Calle de las Mercedes 12, Torremolinos; mains €10; ⊙1-4.30pm & 8-11.30pm) Glide up in the lift and step out onto the terrace for a sweeping panoramic view of the coast. Superb wines are available by the glass and the menu includes light bites such as cheese plates and salads, as well as heartier fare including barbecued meats.

★La Consula MODERN SPANISH €€€
(☑952 436 026; www.laconsula.com; Finca Consula Churriana; set menu €27.50; ⊙1-4pm Mon-Fri Jul-Sep) This is one of the coast's top professional culinary schools. Located around 6km northwest of Torremolinos in Churriana, the daily menu reflects an innovative twist on traditional Spanish dishes with beautifully crafted plates and faultless delicious flavours.

The service is the best you will find anywhere – these students don't want to mess up – and the atmosphere is elegant and formal. Don't turn up in flip-flops.

The history of the main building has an interesting twist for literary buffs. It was owned by Americans who were apparently good pals with Ernest Hemingway. Hemingway wrote *The Dangerous Summer* while staying here in 1959, just two years before his death.

Monet BAR
(www.monetbar.com; Puerto Deportivo, Benalmádena; ⊙11am-late) Located front line in the port, this place is a cool low-lit coffee bar by day but morphs into a disco and nightclub post sunset, with regular salsa and theme nights.

❶ Information

Tourist Office (www.pmdt.es; Plaza de la Independencia, Torremolinos; ⊙9.30am-1.30pm Mon-Fri) There are additional tourist kiosks at Playamar and La Carihuela.

❶ Getting There & Away

BUS

Avanza (www.avanzabus.com) runs services from Málaga (€2.50, 25 minutes, 14 daily) and from Marbella (€5.50, 1¼ hours, 24 daily).

TRAINS

Trains (www.renfe.es) run to Torremolinos and Arroyo de la Miel-Benalmádena every 20 minutes from Málaga (€2.35, 20 minutes) from 5.30am to 10.30pm, continuing on to the final stop, Fuengirola.

Fuengirola

POP 78,000

Fuengirola is a genuine Spanish working town, as well as being firmly on the tourist circuit. It attracts mainly northern European visitors and also has a large foreign-resident population, many of whom arrived here in the '60s – and stayed (yes, there are a few grey ponytails around). The beach stretches for a mighty 7km, encompassing the former fishing quarter of Los Boliches.

◉ Sights

Biopark ZOO
(☑952 66 63 01; www.bioparcfuengirola.es; Avenida Camilo José Cela; adult/child €18/13; ⊙10am-sunset; 🅿) This is a zoo that treats its animals very well with spacious enclosures, conservation and breeding programs, plus educational activities. There is also a bat cave, reptile enclosure, cafes for refreshments and a large gift shop.

✖ Eating

La Cepa SEAFOOD €
(Plaza Yate 21; tapas €3, mains €7-10; ⊙noon-4pm & 7-11pm Mon-Sat, to 3.30pm Sun) Hidden away on an attractive bar-and-restaurant-lined

FUENGIROLA'S FERIA

Fuengirola has arguably the best and biggest annual feria on the Costa. Held from 6 to 12 October, festivities include a *romería* (religious pilgrimage) when locals head to the *campo* (countryside) for flamenco, paella and pitchers of *cerveza* (beer). A flamenco mass is held in the main church on 6 October, and is followed by drinking and dancing in the street with most women dressed in their traditional flamenco frills.

square, the menu concentrates on seafood, including such tentacle ticklers as fried squid, and prawns wrapped in bacon.

Cafe Fresco   INTERNATIONAL €
(Las Rampas; wraps €4.80, salads €7.50; ⊗10am-4pm Mon-Sat) This breezy restaurant is popular with the waistline-watchers for its menu of homemade soups, salads, and wraps (including curried chicken and Greek salad), best accompanied with an energising smoothie. There is a second branch in Los Boliches.

 Drinking

Plenty of tacky disco-pubs line the Paseo Marítimo (promenade), and a cluster of music bars and discos can be found opposite the port.

Colón   BAR
(www.casacolon.es; Plaza de los Chinorros; ⊗6pm-late; 🛜) Take note of the accent here...this place is one of a clutch of similar traditional Spanish bars with sprawling terraces behind the main post office. The wines are good, and the weekend ambience has a big-city feel and seems reassuringly Spanish despite being just a couple of blocks from the banks of sunbeds on the sand.

Pogs   LIVE MUSIC
(www.pogsfuengirola.com; Calle de Lamo de Espinosa; ⊗6pm-late Wed-Sat, 1.30-8pm Sun) This spirited Irish pub is one of the most popular places for live music in town and has a reputable line-up of local musicians, playing everything from blues to jazz, together with Guinness, the perfect draught accompaniment. It has an afternoon live session on Sundays for the more mature, early-to-bed folk.

ℹ **Information**

Tourist office (www.visitfuengirola.com; Paseo Jesús Santos Rein; ⊗9.30am-1.30pm Mon-Fri; 🛜) Has a wealth of information on the town.

ℹ **Getting There & Away**

BUS

Avanza (www.avanzabus.com) runs bus services including to Fuengirola from Málaga (€4.20, 40 minutes, 15 daily) and from Estepona (€8.75, 1¾ hours, 11 daily).

CAR

A toll road (AP-7) connects Fuengirola with Estepona (€14), providing a (costly) alternative to the hazardous N340 coast road.

TRAIN

Trains (www.renfe.es) run every 20 minutes to Málaga from 6.20am to 12.40am with stops including the airport and Torremolinos.

Marbella

POP 136,322

Marbella is the Costa del Sol's classiest (and most expensive) resort. This wealth glitters most brightly along the Golden Mile, a tiara of star-studded clubs, restaurants and hotels stretching from Marbella to Puerto Banús, the flashiest marina on the Costa del Sol, where black-tinted Mercs slide along a quayside of luxury yachts. Marbella has a magnificent natural setting, sheltered by the beautiful Sierra Blanca mountains, as well as a surprisingly attractive *casco antiguo* (old town) replete with narrow lanes and well-tended flower boxes.

Marbella has a long history and has been home to Phoenicians, Visigoths and Romans, as well as being the most important town on the coast during Moorish times. Arab kings still own homes here, as do plenty of rich and famous people, such as native *malagueño* Antonio Banderas.

◎ **Sights & Activities**

Marbella's picturesque old town is chocolate-box perfect with pristine white houses, narrow, mostly traffic-free streets and geranium-filled balconies. You can easily spend an enjoyable morning or evening exploring the cafes, restaurants, bars, designer boutiques and antique and craft shops.

Plaza de los Naranjos   PLAZA
At the heart of Marbella's *casco antiguo* is pretty Plaza de los Naranjos, dating back to 1485, with its tropical plants, palms, orange trees and, inevitably, overpriced bars.

Museo Ralli   MUSEUM
(www.therallimuseums.com; Urbanización Coral Beach; ⊗10am-2pm Tue-Sat) **FREE** This superb

private art museum exhibits paintings by primarily Latin American and European artists in bright well-lit galleries. Part of a nonprofit foundation, its exhibits include sculptures by Henry Moore and Salvador Dalí, vibrant contemporary paintings by Argentinian surrealist Alicia Carletti and Cuban Wilfredo Lam, plus works by Joan Miró, Chagall and Chirico.

Museo del Grabado Español
MUSEUM
(Calle Hospital Bazán; admission €3; ☺10am-2pm & 5.30-8.30pm) This small art museum in the old town includes works by some of the great masters, including Picasso, Joan Miró and Salvador Dalí, among other, primarily Spanish painters.

Aventura Amazonia
ADVENTURE SPORTS
(📞952 83 55 05; www.aventura-amazonia.com; Avenida Valeriano Rodriguez 1; adult/child €24/20; ☺10am-6pm Tue-Fri, to 7pm Sat & Sun) Twenty zip lines are located over six adventure circuits, which includes the longest in the province, at 240m. Tots are catered to with an adventure playground and there is even a crèche for parents who want a quick escape-whiz through the trees.

🛌 Sleeping

★Hotel Linda Marbella
HOTEL €€
(📞952 85 71 71; www.lindamarbella.com; Calle Ancha 21; s €25-38, d €40-82; 🖀) Look for the bright-blue shutters and crimson bougainvillea; this perfectly placed small hotel is in the centre of old town and offers very comfortable rooms (albeit with very little storage space), set around a small central patio festooned with ivy. Bag one with a terrace overlooking the picturesque pedestrian street.

Hotel San Cristóbal
HOTEL €€
(📞952 86 20 44; www.hotelsancristobal.com; Avenida Ramñon y Cajal 3; s/d incl breakfast €60/85; 🖀) Dating back to the '60s, this solid midrange hotel has recently revamped rooms sporting tasteful pale-grey and cream decor contrasting with smart navy fabrics. Most rooms have balconies and a pool is being planned.

Claude
BOUTIQUE HOTEL €€€
(📞952 90 08 40; www.hotelclaudemarbella.com; Calle San Francisco 5; d/ste €280/330; 🌐🖀) Situated in the quieter upper part of town, this sumptuous hotel is housed in a 17th-century mansion of some historical significance – it was the former summer home of Napoleon's third wife. The decor successfully marries contemporary flourishes with

the original architecture, while claw-foot tubs and crystal chandeliers add to the classic historical feel.

🍴 Eating

In general, the restaurants in the historic centre tend to be priced for tourists; an exception is the picturesque Calle San Lázaro near the Plaza de los Naranjos, which is home to several excellent tapas bars mainly frequented by locals.

El Estrecho
TAPAS €
(Calle San Lázaro; tapas €2.50-3.50; ☺noon-midnight) It's always crammed, so elbow your way to a space in the small back dining room and order from a massive menu that includes tapas such as *salmorejo* (Córdoba-style thick gazpacho) and seafood salad.

Mirto
ITALIAN €€
(Travesia Carlos Mackintosh 15; mains €10-14; ☺noon-4pm & 7-11pm Tue-Sun) Tucked down a pedestrian alley and utterly unpretentious, the handful of tables here get filled up fast, as the word is out that this is the best Italian in town. The owners are from Naples and star of the show is the pasta, homemade daily. Generous portions, great coffee and attentive service add to the agreeable eating experience.

Garum
INTERNATIONAL €€
(📞952 858 858; www.garummarbella.com; Paseo Marítimo; mains €12-15; ☺11am-11.30pm; 🖀) Finnish-owned and set in a dreamy location right on the promenade across from the beach, Garum's menu will especially please those seeking a little gourmet variety. Expect dishes that range from smoked-cheese soup to Moroccan chicken samosas and red lentil falafal.

★Casanis
BISTRO €€€
(📞952 90 04 50; www.casanis-restaurante-marbella.es; Calle Ancha 8; mains €20-25; ☺10.30am-4pm & 7.30-11pm Mon-Sat) Situated on one of the prettiest streets in town, step into the dining room and be transported to a Tintin fantasy world, with walls covered in cartoon-style murals, and interspersed with (real) leafy ferns and plants. The cuisine spans the seas with dishes such as Bourgogne snails, beef Wellington and bluefin tuna from Barbate on the Cadíz coast; all prepared with culinary flair.

🍷 Drinking

For the most spirited bars and nightlife, head to Puerto Banús, 6km west of Marbella. In town, the best area is around the small Puerto Deportivo. There are also some beach clubs open only in summer.

Buddha CLUB
(www.buddhamarbella.net; Avenida del Mar; ⊘7pm-late; 🐾) As Buddhist statues overlook the heathens on the dance floor, the DJ spins almost everything from funk and acid jazz to hip hop and rock. The interior is all plush fabrics and suitably posh with moody lighting and comfortable sofas. There are regular theme nights.

Nikki Beach CLUB
(www.nikkibeach.com; Don Carlos Hotel; ⊘noon-late Apr-Sep; 🐾) Sprawl out on white sofas overlooking the surf as you nibble on haute tapas and enjoy the live music or DJ playing a riveting mix. A fixture on the glam clubbing scene; don your best party garb, shine those shoes and assume some attitude – it's that kind of place.

Tibu CLUB
(www.tibubanus.com; Plaza Antonio Banderas, Puerto Banús; ⊘11pm-7am) A spirited sexy nightclub with dancers, acrobats, guest DJs and predictably costly cocktails.

🛍 Shopping

Déjà Vu VINTAGE
(📷952 82 55 21; Calle Pedraza 8; ⊘11.30am-3pm & 5-8.30pm Mon-Fri, noon-3pm Sat) This is the place for your designer vintage fashion from 1960s Chanel suits to classic Yves Saint Laurent three-piece suits. Also sells accessories, jewellery and some truly fabulous hats.

ℹ Information

Tourist Office (www.marbellaexclusive.com; Plaza de los Naranjos; ⊘9am-8pm Mon-Fri, 10am-2pm Sat) Has plenty of leaflets and a good town map.

ℹ Getting There & Away

BUS
Buses to Fuengirola (€3.75, one hour), Puerto Banús (€2.10, 20 minutes) and Estepona (€3.30, one hour) leave about every 30 minutes from Avenida Ricardo Soriano.

PARKING
Marbella's streets are clogged with traffic and street parking is notoriously difficult to find. The most central underground car park is on Avenida del Mar (per hour €2.20).

Estepona
POP 67,100

Estepona was one of the first resorts to attract foreign residents and tourists some 45 years ago and, despite the surrounding development, the centre of the town still has a cosy old-fashioned feel – for good reason: the town's roots date back to the 4th century. Centuries later during the Moorish era, Estepona was an important and prosperous town due to its strategic proximity to the Straits of Gibraltar.

Estepona is steadily extending its promenade to Marbella; at its heart is the pleasant Playa de la Rada beach. The Puerto Deportivo is the centre of the nightlife, especially at weekends, and is also excellent for water sports, as well as bars and restaurants.

◉ Sights

Orchidarium GARDENS
(www.orchidariumestepona.es; Calle Terraza 86; ⊘11am-2pm & 5-9pm Tue-Thu & Sun, to 11pm Fri & Sat) **FREE** The orchidarium is housed in a glass-domed contemporary building and surrounded by lush landscaping. There are 1500 species of orchids here, the largest collection in Europe, as well as 5000 subtropical plants, flowers and trees. A meandering path takes you through the exhibition space and past a dramatic 17m-high waterfall; the sound of water acts as a soothing backdrop to your visit. Note that an entry charge may be introduced in due course.

Colección Arte Garó ART GALLERY
(Plaza de las Flores; ⊘9am-3.30pm Mon-Fri, 10am-2pm Sat) **FREE** Shares digs with the tourist office and spreads six centuries of art over three well laid-out floors.

Museo Arqueológico MUSEUM
(Plaza Blas Infante 1; ⊘8am-3pm Mon, 8am-8pm Tue-Fri, 10am-2pm & 4-8.30pm Sat) **FREE** Testifies to Estepona's 4th-century AD roots with many of the displayed pieces dug out of offshore shipwrecks, often by local divers and fishermen.

Ruta de los Murales PUBLIC ART
(Calle Terraza) Look out for the giant murals covering the whole sides of buildings on Calle Terraza and the surrounding streets (the tourist office can provide you a map). The murals are the work of local artist José

ROMAN SULPHUR BATHS OF HEDIONDA

These natural sulphur springs date back to Roman times; it is reputed that Julius Caesar even took a dip here to cure some nasty skin ailment or other. Although covered with a crude, albeit protective, concrete structure, the stone-vaulted ceiling over the first pool is still intact; a small arch leads to a second larger pool. Nearby, a pretty waterside glade is backed by a bank of alluvial mud, with telltale scoop marks from its removal for face packs and poultices.

The baths lie unexploited and neglected, located within two municipalities neither of which want to, perhaps thankfully, foot the bill to commercialise the site. It's popular at weekends with Spanish picnicking families; be prepared for the telltale smell of rotten eggs and the waters' milky-like appearance. But don't forget to appreciate the fact that these restorative baths can be enjoyed completely free of charge.

To get here, take the A-377 off the AP-7 toll road signposted Casares and Gaucín, follow the signs to the Roman Oasis restaurant and take the rough road located just before the restaurant entrance for around 1km. Look for a picnic area on your right; the baths are just beyond it.

Fernández Ríos; there are 26 to date and the number is growing. The murals range from exquisitely lifelike botanical themes to whimsical portraits of children.

🏃 Activities

Selwo Aventura
WILDLIFE RESERVE
(www.selwo.es; Carretera A7 Km 162.5; adult/child €25/17; ⊙10am-6pm) This popular safari park has more than 200 exotic animal species. You can tour the park by 4WD or on foot and enjoy various adventure activities. It is home to the only Asian elephant born in Spain, and there is even a lodge if you fancy an overnight stay in – erm – Africa.

Buceo Estepona
DIVING
(☑645 610374; www.buceoestepona.com; Puerto Deportivo; dive €25; ⊙10am-3pm & 4.30-8pm) A reputable diving outfit offering a wide range of diving options and courses, including diving trips to Tarifa, Gibraltar and Algeciras.

Escuela de Arte Ecuestre Costa del Sol
HORSE RIDING
(☑952 80 80 77; www.escuela-ecuestre.com; El Padrón; 45min class €67; ⊙10am-2pm & 5-7pm) This British Horse Society–approved riding school offers a range of classes and treks for all ages and levels of ability.

🛏 Sleeping

Hostal El Pilar
HOSTAL €
(☑952 80 00 18; www.hostalelpilar.es; Plaza de las Flores 10, Estepona; s/d €35/50; ❀) This is a charming old-fashioned *hostal* with original tile-work and a central courtyard. Wedding photos, plants and antiques contribute to the homey feel. The position is ideal, right on the town's most historic square.

🍴 Eating

Estepona has no shortage of good restaurants, particularly in the old town and port.

La Escollera
SEAFOOD €
(Puerto Pesquero, Puerto Deportivo; mains €7-10; ⊙1-4.30pm & 8-11.30pm Tue-Sat, 1-4.30pm Sun) Locals in the know arrive in shoals to dine on arguably the freshest and best seafood in town. Located in the port, the atmosphere is no-frills basic with plastic tables and paper cloths. When the fish tastes this good and the beer is this cold – who cares?

Thai Thapa
THAI €
(13 Edificio Poniente, Puerto Deportivo; mains €6.50-8, menú €11; ⊙12.30-4.30pm & 6.30pm-midnight) Somehow you expect to pay more for this front-line position overlooking the harbour, but the dishes are reasonably priced and authentic, including fragrantly spiced curries and soups with just enough chilli to break a sweat. The *menú del día* (daily set lunch menu) covers two courses, plus rice, with plenty of choice for fussy families.

La Esquina del Arte
TAPAS €
(Calle Villa; tapas €2-3; ⊙noon-midnight Mon-Sat; 🛜) This place may be in the centre of the historic centre but there is nothing old fashioned about the creative tapas and *pintxos* (Basque tapas) here. Expect tasty bites such as prawns wrapped in flaky pastry, pâté with fig jam and peppers stuffed with salt cod. It has excellent wines by the glass.

Venta Garcia
MODERN EUROPEAN €€
(☑952 89 41 91; Carretera de Casares Km 7; mains €12-18; ℗) Venta Garcia specialises in superbly presented and conceived dishes

using local produce. There is an emphasis on game and venison; rabbit and quail are cooked to perfection and served with simple sides like wild asparagus with fresh lemon. The countryside views are similarly sublime, but the word is out, so be sure to reserve – especially on weekends.

It's on the road to Casares, around 7km from the centre of town.

Drinking

The Puerto Deportivo is the best place to head for late-night bars. Beach clubs also swing into action in the summer. Check flyers around town to see where the action is.

Puro Beach BAR
(www.purobeach.com; Laguna Village; ⊘ noon-late Apr-Oct) This bar enjoys prime position in Laguna Village and is the place to luxuriate with its private 'nomad' tents, pool, DJs and overall summer-in-the-sun party setting.

Laguna Village is an Asian-inspired beachside complex of bars, restaurants and shops set around lush landscaping, tinkling fountains and snaking waterways.

Siopa CAFE
(80 Calle Real; ⊘ 9am-late) This stylish stamp-sized place on a pedestrian street specialises in craft beers, including several from local Estepona brewery Babel. It reputedly serves the best coffee in town and is also good for breakfast.

ⓘ Information

Tourist Office (www.estepona.es; Plaza de las Flores; ⊘ 9am-8pm Mon-Fri) Located on an historical square, it has brochures and a decent map of town.

ⓘ Getting There & Away

BUS

There are regular buses to Marbella (€3.30, one hour), and Málaga (€8, two hours).

PARKING

Estepona has several well-signposted car parks on Avenida España (per hour €1.50).

Mijas

POP 82,124 / ELEV 428M

The story of Mijas encapsulates the story of the Costa del Sol. Originally a humble village, it is now the richest town in the province. Since finding favour with discerning bohemian artists and writers in the 1950s

and '60s, Mijas has sprawled across the surrounding hills and down to the coast, yet managed to retain the picturesque charm of the original *pueblo* (village).

Mijas has a foreign population of at least 40% and the municipality includes Mijas Costa and La Cala de Mijas, both located on the coast southwest of Fuengirola.

◉ Sights & Activities

Virgen de la Peña HISTORIC SITE
(Avenida Virgen de la Peña) If you walk past the *ayuntamiento* (town hall), you will reach this grotto where the Virgin is said to have appeared to two children who were led here by a dove in 1586. During the annual village procession on 8 September, the effigy of the Virgin is carried 2km up to the **Ermita del Calvario**, a tiny chapel built by Carmelite brothers. Black-iron crosses mark a short walking trail that leads up to the hermitage.

Centro de Arte Contemporáneo de Mijas MUSEUM
(CAC; www.cacmijas.info; Calle Málaga 28; admission €3; ⊘ 10am-7pm Tue-Sun) This art museum houses an extraordinary exhibition of Picasso ceramics (the second-largest collection in the world), plus some exquisite Dalí bronze figurines, glassware and bas-relief. There are also temporary exhibitions. Note that, despite the name, this museum is not affiliated with Málaga's CAC museum.

Casa Museo de Mijas MUSEUM
(Plaza Libertad 2; adult/child €1/free; ⊘ 10am-2pm & 5-8pm) This quaint folk museum was created and is run by Carmen Escalona, who specialises in crafting folk-themed models which, together with other artefacts, show perfectly the style and mode of living some 50 years ago.

Plaza de Toros BULLRING
(museum €3; ⊘ 10am-8pm) This unusual square-shaped bullring is located at the top of the village, and is surrounded by lush ornamental gardens with wonderful views of the coast. There is a modest museum dedicated to local bullfighting history.

Coastal Footpath WALKING
(Playa La Luna, La Cala de Mijas, Mijas Costa; ♿ 🐕) Enjoy a gentle coastal stroll along a wooden promenade constructed in 2014 and currently stretching 6km from La Cala de Mijas to Calahonda, with plans to eventually extend it to Estepona. The meandering walkway passes several beachside *chiringuitos* (beach bars), quiet coves and rocky headlands.

🛏 Sleeping

Casa Tejón APARTMENT €

(☑ 661 669469; www.casatejon.com; Calle Málaga 15; 2-person apt €45) The small apartments are homily furnished with a happy mishmash of furniture and textiles. Set around a small central courtyard decorated with pots of scarlet geraniums, the location is bang in the centre of the village and the owners run a handy bar and restaurant next door.

TRH Mijas HOTEL €€

(☑ 952 48 58 00; www.trhhoteles.com; Plaza de la Constitución; s/d €65/85; P ❄ ☎) This tastefully furnished Andalucian-style hotel has excellent facilities, and activities including horse riding, tennis and hydromassage. The exquisitely landscaped gardens have views stretching down to the coast. On the downside – you're a long way from the beach. Check online for excellent deals.

🍴 Eating & Drinking

It's not the most exciting of places to eat, but Mijas has a couple of decent restaurants.

Aroma INTERNATIONAL €€

(www.aromacafeandsecretgarden.com; Calle San Sebastián 8; mains €7-15; ☺ noon-late; 🚗) The house dates to 1872, but the real charmer (aside from the Canadian owner) is the so-called 'secret garden' out back, which is a divine dining space under mature orange, fig and olive trees with a well that dates from Moorish times. An Argentinian barbecue is served nightly, while other dishes include traditional tapas, crêpes, pasta and pizza.

Lew Hoad SPANISH €€

(☑ 952 46 76 73; www.lew-hoad.com; Carretera de Mijas, Km 3.5; mains €11-18; ☺ 1-5pm & 7.30-11pm; P 🛜) Founded in 1964 by the late Wimbledon tennis champion, Australian Lew Hoad, this elegant restaurant is surrounded by mature gardens, plus tennis and padel courts (available for hourly rent). The cuisine befits the setting with classic dishes such as *zarzuela* (seafood stew) and oxtail, plus lighter snacks for those hoping to play a few sets rather than sink into a siesta.

Museo de Vino WINE BAR

(www.museovinomalaga.org; Calle San Sebastián 14; ☺ 11am-4pm & 7pm-late) Located on the prettiest street in the village, this is a more of a wine bar than a museum although there is some literature and photographs on local viticulture. More striking is the sheer number of bottles here, lining the walls. You can taste three wines for €6 and also enjoy platters of cheese and ham to share.

ℹ Information

Mijas Tourist Office (☑ 958 58 90 34; www.mijas.es; Plaza Virgen de la Peña; ☺ 9am-8pm Mon-Fri, 10am-3pm Sat) Helpful tourist office with plenty of information about the village and area.

ℹ Getting There & Away

Frequent buses run from Fuengirola (€2.10, 25 minutes).

THE INTERIOR

The mountainous interior of Málaga province is an area of raw beauty and romantic white villages sprinkled across craggy landscapes. Beyond the mountains, the verdant countryside opens out into a wide chequerboard of floodplains. It's a far cry from the tourist-clogged coast.

Ronda

POP 37,000 / ELEV 744M

Perched on an inland plateau riven by the 100m fissure of El Tajo gorge, Ronda is Málaga province's most spectacular town. It has a superbly dramatic location, and owes its name ('surrounded' by mountains), to the encircling Serranía de Ronda.

Established in the 9th century BC, Ronda is also one of Spain's oldest towns. Its existing old town, La Ciudad (the City), largely dates to Islamic times, when it was an important cultural centre filled with mosques and palaces. Its wealth as a trading depot made it an attractive prospect for bandits and profiteers, and the town has a colourful and romantic past in Spanish folklore.

Ronda was a favourite with the Romantics of the late 19th century, and has attracted an array of international artists and writers, such as David Wilkie, Alexandre Dumas, Rainer Maria Rilke, Ernest Hemingway and Orson Welles.

⦿ Sights

La Ciudad, the historic old town on the southern side of El Tajo gorge, is an atmospheric area for a stroll with its evocative, still-tangible history, Renaissance mansions and wealth of museums. But don't forget the newer town, which has its distinctive charms and is home to the emblematic bullring, plenty of good tapas bars and restaurants, and the leafy Alameda del Tajo gardens. Three bridges crossing the gorge connect the old town with the new.

Plaza de Toros   BULLRING

(Calle Virgen de la Paz; admission €7, €8.50 incl audioguide; ⊙ 10am-8pm) Ronda's Plaza de Toros is a mecca for bullfighting aficionados. In existence for more than 200 years, it is one of the oldest and most revered bullrings in Spain and has been the site of some of the most important events in bullfighting history.

The on-site Museo Taurino is crammed with memorabilia such as blood-spattered costumes worn by 1990s star Jesulín de Ubrique. It also includes artwork by Picasso and photos of famous fans such as Orson Welles and Ernest Hemingway.

Built by Martín Aldehuela, the bullring is universally admired for its soft sandstone hues and galleried arches. At 66m in diameter, it is also the largest and, therefore, most dangerous bullring, yet it only seats 5000 spectators – a tiny number compared with the huge 50,000-seat bullring in Mexico City.

Behind the Plaza de Toros, spectacular clifftop views open out from Paseo de Blas Infante and the nearby Alameda del Tajo park.

Museo Lara   MUSEUM

(www.museolara.org; Calle de Armiñán 29; adult/child €4/2; ⊙ 11am-8pm; ⊞) The museum is the private collection of Juan Antonio Lara Jurado who has been a collector since the age of 10. Now in his 70s, he still lives above the museum, but his living space is set to shrink as he wants to expand still further. You name it, it is here: priceless, historic collections of clocks, weapons, radios, gramophones, sewing machines, telephones, opera glasses, Spanish fans, scales, cameras and far, far more.

There is an impressive archaeological section, plus a grisly exhibit on the Inquisition with various torture apparatus, including head crushers and stocks. Then there is the witchcraft room, which kids, in particular, will love. Think pickled toads and the like.

Casa del Rey Moro   GARDENS

(House of the Moorish King; Calle Santo Domingo 17; admission €4; ⊙ 10am-7pm) The terraces give access to La Mina, an Islamic stairway of more than 300 steps cut into the rock all the way down to the river at the bottom of the gorge. These steps enabled Ronda to maintain water supplies when it was under

---

RONDA WINE ROUTE

The Ronda region was a major wine-producing area in Roman times; Ronda la Vieja (p184) is the archaeological site of the great Roman city of Acinipo, which means 'among the vineyards'. Coins have been found here embellished with bunches of grapes. Other viticultural relics include remains of ceramic kilns and even a bronze head of Bacchus at a Roman villa in nearby Los Villares. Since 1990 there has been a renaissance of the wine industry in these parts and today you can visit up to 21 wineries in the region (by prior appointment). Check the www.ruta-vinos-ronda.com website for more details.

---

attack. It was also the point where Christian troops forced entry in 1485. The steps are not well lit and are steep and wet in places. Take care.

Museo de Ronda   MUSEUM

(Palacio Mondragón, Plaza Mondragón; admission €3; ⊙ 10am-7pm Mon-Fri, to 3pm Sat & Sun) The city museum has artefacts and information especially related to both Roman and Islamic funerary systems. Of even more interest to some will be the palatial setting. Built for Abomelic, ruler of Ronda in 1314, the palace retains its fountains and internal Patio Mudéjar courtyard, from where a horseshoe arch leads to a clifftop garden with splendid views.

Iglesia de Santa María La Mayor   CHURCH

(Calle José M Holgado; adult/child €4/1.50; ⊙ 10am-8pm) The city's original mosque metamorphosed into this elegant church. Just inside the entrance is an arch covered with Arabic inscriptions, which was part of the mosque's *mihrab* (prayer niche indicating the direction of Mecca). The church has been declared a national monument, and its interior is an orgy of decorative styles and ornamentation. A huge central, cedar choir stall divides the church into two sections: aristocrats to the front, everyone else at the back.

Museo del Bandolero   MUSEUM

(www.museobandolero.com; Calle de Armiñán 65; adult/child €3.75/free; ⊙ 10.30am-8pm) This small museum is dedicated to the banditry for which central Andalucía was once renowned. Old prints reflect that when the youthful *bandoleros* (bandits) were not

MÁLAGA PROVINCE RONDA

Ronda

0   200 m
0   0.1 miles

A   **B**   **C**   **D**

Train Station

C Jerez
C de Sevilla
C Jerez
Paseo de las Inglesas
C Molino
C José María Castelló Madrid
Av de Andalucía
Av de Córdoba
Av Martínez Astein

Bus Station
Plaza Concepción García Redondo
C de San José
C de Monterejas
C Lauria
C de Infantes
Plaza del Ahorro

21
C Pozo
22
C de Sevilla
C Mariano Soubirón
C Doctor Ramón y Cajal
C Naranja
C Calvo Asensio
Carrera del Espinel
C Setenil
Iglesia de los Descalzos
Plaza de los Descalzos

Iglesia de la Merced

Alameda del Tajo

24
C Borrego Gómez
Iglesia de Nuestra Señora del Socorro
Plaza del Socorro
19
C Pedro Romero
Plaza Carmen Abela
C María Cabrera
Capitán Cortés
C San Vicente de Paul

Plaza de Toros
7
Plaza Teniente Arce
Paseo de Blas Infante
20
23
C Nueva
17
C Villanueva
C Santa Cecilia
15
EL MERCADILLO

C Virgen de la Paz

12
Plaza de España
C Los Remedios
El Tajo Gorge
C Madre Petra
8
9
Iglesia de Nuestro Padre Jesús

Centro de Interpretación Puente Nuevo
Río Guadalevín

18
16
C Tenorio
C Santo Domingo
2
10
LA CIUDAD
6
La Mina
Puente Viejo
C Real

Plaza María Auxiliadora
11
C José M Holgado
C de Armiñán
C Marqués de Salvatierra
Puente Árabe
1

Plaza del Campillo
4
3
5
C Espíritu Santo
Hoyo San Miguel
Arroyo

Plaza Mondragón
Plaza Duquesa de Parcent

C Imágenes
Puerta de Almocábar
Iglesia del Espíritu Santo
Puerta de Carlos V
Plaza Arquitecto Pons Sorolla
13
14
BARRIO DE SAN FRANCISCO

1   **2**   **3**   **4**   **5**   **6**   **7**

Ronda

◎ Sights
1 Baños Arabes C5
2 Casa del Rey Moro C5
3 Iglesia de Santa María La Mayor B6
4 Museo de Ronda B6
5 Museo del Bandolero C6
6 Museo Lara B5
7 Plaza de Toros B3

⊟ Sleeping
8 Aire de Ronda D4
9 Enfrente Arte D4
10 Hotel Ronda C5
11 Hotel San Gabriel B5
12 Parador de Ronda B4

⊗ Eating
13 Almocábar C7

14 Casa María B7
15 Faustino C3
16 La Casa del Dulce B5
17 Nonno Peppe B4
18 Restaurante Albacara B5
19 Restaurante Pedro Romero B3
20 Restaurante Tragabuches B4

◉ Drinking & Nightlife
21 Entre Vinos B2
22 Malastrana B2
23 Tragatapas B4

◉ Entertainment
24 Círculo de Artistas B3

being shot, hanged or garrotted by the authorities, they were stabbing each other in the back, literally as much as figuratively. You can pick up your fake pistol or catapult at the gift shop.

Baños Arabes   HISTORIC SITE
(Arab Baths; Hoyo San Miguel; admission €3, free Mon; ☺10am-7pm Mon-Fri, to 3pm Sat & Sun) Enjoy the pleasant walk here from the centre of town. Backing on to Ronda's river, these 13th- and 14th-century Arab baths are in good condition, with horseshoe arches, columns and clearly designated divisions between the hot and cold thermal baths. They're some of the best-preserved Arab baths in Andalucía.

★☆ Festivals & Events

Corpus Cristi   RELIGIOUS
(☺May-Jun) On the Thursday after Trinity (usually falling somewhere between May and June) there are bullfights and festivities after the 900kg Station of the Cross is carried 6km through the town.

Feria de Pedro Romero   BULLFIGHTS
(☺1-14 Sep) An orgy of partying including the important flamenco event, Festival de Cante Grande, culminates in the Corridas Goyesca (bullfights in honour of legendary bullfighter Pedro Romero).

⊨ Sleeping

Ronda has some of the most atmospheric and well-priced accommodation in Málaga province. In the first half of May and from July to September, you definitely need to book ahead.

★ Hotel San Gabriel   HOTEL €€
(☑952 19 03 92; www.hotelsangabriel.com; Calle José M Holgado 19; s/d incl breakfast €72/100; ❄⊙) This charming hotel is filled with antiques and photographs that offer an insight into Ronda's history – bullfighting, celebrities and all. Ferns hang down the huge mahogany staircase and there is a billiard room, a cosy living room stacked with books, as well as a DVD-screening room with 10 velvet-covered seats rescued from Ronda's theatre.

Check the website for packages that include a private wine tasting, chocolates and cava (sparkling wine) in the room, and dinner for two at the renowned Restaurante Pedro Romero (p183).

★ El Molino del Santo   HOTEL €€
(☑952 16 71 51; www.molinodelsanto.com; Estación de Benaoján, Benaoján; s/d incl breakfast €89/127; ☺Feb-Nov; P❄⊡) Located near the well-signposted Benaoján train station, this British-owned hotel has a stunning setting next to a rushing stream; the main building was a former olive mill. The rooms are set amid the pretty gardens and have private terraces or balconies. The restaurant is popular with local residents and serves contemporary international cuisine.

Management can provide maps of local walks and the village of Benaoján is nearby (around 15km southwest of Ronda). There are no TVs.

Aire de Ronda   BOUTIQUE HOTEL €€
(☑952 16 12 74; www.airederonda.com; Calle Real 25; r from €85; P⊙) Located near the Arab Baths in a particularly tranquil part

MÁLAGA PROVINCE RONDA

of town, this hotel has smart minimalist rooms in punchy black and white, plus fabulous bathrooms with shimmering silver- or gold-coloured mosaic tiles, walk-in showers and, in one romantic couples' room, a glass partition separating the shower from the bedroom.

Enfrente Arte HOTEL €€
(☑ 952 87 90 88; www.enfrentearte.com; Calle Real 40; r incl breakfast €80-90; ✻@✉) On an old cobblestone street, Belgian-owned Enfrente offers a huge range of facilities and funky modern-cum-oriental decor. It has a bar, pool, sauna, recreation room, flowery patio with black bamboo, film room and fantastic views out to the Sierra de las Nieves. What's more, the room price includes all drinks, to which you help yourself, and a sumptuous buffet breakfast.

Hotel Ronda BOUTIQUE HOTEL €€
(☑ 952 87 22 32; www.hotelronda.net; Ruedo Doña Elvira; s/d €53/70; ✻☎) With its geranium filled window boxes and whitewashed *pueblo* exterior, this cute-as-a-button small hotel has surprisingly contemporary rooms painted in vivid colours and accentuated by punchy original abstracts. Several overlook the beautiful Mina gardens across the way.

✗ Eating

Typical Ronda food is hearty mountain fare, with an emphasis on stews (called *cocido*, *estofado* or *cazuela*), *trucha* (trout), *rabo de toro* (bull's-tail stew) and game such as *conejo* (rabbit), *perdiz* (partridge) and *codorniz* (quail).

La Casa del Dulce BAKERY €
(Calle Tenorio 11; cakes €0.80; ✦) Stop by La Casa del Dulce and ogle the trays of freshly baked *mantecada* biscuits; a delicious crumbly speciality based on almonds and topped with icing sugar. Don't worry, they can't be that sinful – they're made by nuns.

Casa María ANDALUCIAN €
(☑ 951 083 663; Plaza Ruedo Alameda 27; menú €20; ⊙ noon-3.30pm & 7.30-10.30pm Thu-Tue; ✦) This no-frills restaurant has a kitchen run by a passionate cook who prepares dishes strictly according to what is fresh in the market. There is no menu. The selection is not huge but most diners opt for the five-course *poco de todo* tasting *menú* reflecting Maria's delicious homestyle cooking.

Nonno Peppe ITALIAN €
(Calle Nueva 18; pasta dishes from €7; ⊙ 11am-midnight; ✦) If you're on a long haul and need a break from tapas, you can't go wrong with the genuine Italian fare served up in this economical place run by a couple from Salerno, near Naples. There's great *spaghetti alla vongole* (with clams), pesto and pizzas, along with homey Italian-style service.

Faustino ANDALUCIAN €
(Calle Santa Cecilía; tapas €1.50, raciones €6-8; ⊙ 11.30am-midnight Tue-Sun) This is the real deal, a lively atmospheric tapas bar with plenty of seating in the open traditional atrium decorated with plants, feria posters, and bullfighting and religious pictures. Tapas and *raciones* are generous. Go with the recommendations like *champingnones a la plancha* (grilled mushrooms with lashings of

RONDA'S FIGHTING ROMEROS

Ronda can bullishly claim to be the home of bullfighting – and it does. It proudly boasts the Real Maestranza de Ronda equestrian school, founded in 1572 for the Spanish aristocracy to learn to ride and fight. They did this by challenging bulls in an arena, and thus was born the first bullfight.

Legend has it that one of these fights went awry when a nobleman fell from his horse and risked being gored to death. Without hesitation local hero Francisco Romero (b 1698) leapt into the ring and distracted the bull by waving his hat. By the next generation, Francisco's son, Juan, had added the *cuadrilla* (the matador's supporting team), consisting of two to three *banderilleros* (who work on foot) and two to three picadors (men on horseback with pike poles).

Juan's son Pedro Romero (1754–1839) invented the rules and graceful ballet-like movements of the modern bullfight, introducing the *muleta* (a variation on his grandfather's hat), a red cape used to attract the bull's attention.

In 1932 Ronda also gave birth to one of Spain's greatest 20th-century bullfighters, the charismatic Antonio Ordóñez, who was immortalised by Hemingway in *The Dangerous Summer*.

PARQUE NATURAL SIERRA DE LAS NIEVES

Southeast of Ronda lies the 180-sq-km Parque Natural Sierra de las Nieves, noted for its rare Spanish fir, the *pinsapo,* and fauna including some 1000 ibex and various species of eagle. The *nieve* (snow) after which the mountains are named usually falls between January and March. **El Burgo**, a remote but attractive village 10km north of Yunquera on the A366, makes a good base for visiting the east and northeast of the park. Information is available from Yunquera's **tourist office** (Calle del Pozo 17; ⊘ 8am-3pm Tue-Fri).

The most rewarding walk in the Sierra de las Nieves is an ascent of the highest peak in western Andalucía, **Torrecilla** (1918m). Start at the Área Recreativa Los Quejigales, which is 10km east by unpaved road from the A376 Ronda–San Pedro de Alcántara road. The turn-off, 12km from Ronda, is marked by signs. From Los Quejigales you have a steepish 470m ascent by the **Cañada de los Cuernos gully**, with its tranquil Spanish-fir woods, to the high pass of **Puerto de los Pilones**. After a fairly level section, the final steep 230m to the summit rewards you with marvellous views. The walk is a five- to six-hour round trip, and is easy to moderate in difficulty.

garlic). The only downside is the uncomfortable, if pretty, rustic-style painted chairs. Ouch!

Almocábar
ANDALUCIAN €€

(Calle Ruedo Alameda 5; tapas €2, mains €10; ⊘ noon-5pm & 8-11pm Wed-Mon) Tasty tapas here include *montaditos* (small pieces of bread) topped with a variety of delicacies like duck breast and chorizo. Mains are available in the elegant dining room and concentrate on Ronda-style specialities such as hearty stews and oxtail. There's a bodega upstairs, and wine tastings and dinner can be arranged for a minimum of eight people (approximately €50 per person).

Restaurante Pedro Romero
ANDALUCIAN €€

(⊋ 952 87 11 10; www.rpedroromero.com; Calle Virgen de la Paz 18; menú €16, mains €15-18; ⊘ noon-4.30pm & 7.30-11pm; ⊕) Opposite the bullring, this celebrated eatery dedicated to bullfighting turns out classic *rondeño* dishes (dishes from Ronda), such as partridge stew with dried fruits and a celebrated *rabo de toro* (braised oxtail). A recent addition to the menu – chicken curry with chips – seems woefully out of place. Let's hope it stays that way.

The walls are covered with bullfighting memorabilia, including a cape that once belonged to the famous bullfighter from Córdoba, Manolete.

Restaurante Albacara
INTERNATIONAL €€€

(⊋ 952 16 11 84; www.hotelmontelirio.com; Calle Tenorio 8; mains €15-22) One of Ronda's best restaurants, the Albacara is in the old stables of the Montelirio palace and teeters on the edge of the gorge. It serves up delicious meals – try the beef stroganoff or classic magret of duck. Be sure to check out the

extensive wine list. Reserve your table in advance.

Restaurante Tragabuches
MODERN SPANISH €€€

(⊋ 952 19 02 91; Calle José Aparício 1; set menus €59-87; ⊘ 1.30-3.30pm & 8-10.30pm Tue-Sat) Ronda's most famous restaurant is a 180-degree-turn away from the ubiquitous 'rustic' look and cuisine. Tragabuches is modern and sleek with an innovative menu to match. Choose from three set menus. People flock here from miles away to taste the food prepared by its creative chef.

🍷 Drinking & Nightlife

Tragatapas
BAR

(www.tragatapas.com; Calle Nueva 4; ⊘ noon-4.30pm & 8-11.30pm; ⊛) Although a tad too brightly lit (like most bars in Ronda), this place has a contemporary vibe with its background jazz, black beamed ceiling and arty bites such as curried-chicken *pinchos* (snacks).

Malastrana
BAR

(Calle Pozo 13; ⊘ noon-4pm & 8pm-late Tue-Sun) If you have grown weary of all that *vino,* this bar specialises in craft beers with imports from Norway, Germany, England and the US as well as local Spanish brews, Asturian cider and locally produced vermouth.

Entre Vinos
WINE BAR

(Calle Pozo; ⊘ noon-4pm & 7-11pm Mon-Sat; ⊛) A stylish small wine bar with exposed brick and wood panelling, frequented mainly by locals. This is a good place to taste local Ronda wines, as they feature heavily on the wine list. Creative tapas are also served.

☆ Entertainment

Círculo de Artistas FLAMENCO
(Plaza del Socorro; admission €15; ⊙ Wed-Mon May-Sep) Stages flamenco shows in a sumptuous historical building on the square from 10pm, as well as other song and dance performances.

❶ Information

Tourist Office (www.turismoderonda.es; Paseo de Blas Infante; ⊙10am-7pm Mon-Fri, to 5pm Sat, to 2pm Sun) Helpful staff with a wealth of information on the town and region.

❶ Getting There & Around

BUS

The bus station is at Plaza Concepción García Redondo 2. **Comes** (www.tgcomes.es) has buses to Arcos de la Frontera (€9.56, two hours, one to two daily), Jerez de la Frontera (€13, three hours, one to three daily) and Cádiz (€18, two hours, one to three daily). **Los Amarillos** (www. losamarillos.es) goes to Seville via Algodonales and Grazalema, and to Málaga via Ardales.

CAR

There are a number of underground car parks and some hotels have parking deals for guests. Parking charges are about €1.50 per hour, or €18 to €25 for 14 to 24 hours.

TRAIN

Ronda's **train station** (☑ 952 87 16 73; www. renfe.es; Avenida de Andalucía) is on the line between Bobadilla and Algeciras. Trains run to Algeciras via Gaucín and Jimena de la Frontera. This train ride is incredibly scenic and worth taking just for the views. Other trains depart for Málaga, Córdoba, Madrid, and Granada via Antequera. For Seville change at Bobadilla or Antequera. It's less than 1km from the train station to most accommodation. A taxi will cost around €7.

Serranía de Ronda

Curving around the south and southeast of the town, the Serranía de Ronda may not be the highest or most dramatic mountain range in Andalucía, but it's certainly among the prettiest. Any of the roads through it between Ronda and southern Cádiz province, Gibraltar or the Costa del Sol make a picturesque route. Cortés de la Frontera, overlooking the Guadiaro Valley, and Gaucín, looking across the Genal Valley to the Sierra Crestellina, are among the most beautiful spots to stop.

To the west and southwest of Ronda stretch the wilder Sierra de Grazalema and Los Alcornocales natural parks. There are plenty of walking and cycling possibilities and Ronda's tourist office can provide details of these as well as maps.

◉ Sights

Ronda la Vieja ARCHAEOLOGICAL SITE
(⊙9am-3pm Tue-Sat, 8am-2pm Sun) FREE To the north of Ronda, off the A374, is the relatively undisturbed Roman site of Acinipo at Ronda la Vieja, with its partially reconstructed theatre. Although completely ruinous, with the exception of the theatre, it is a wonderfully wild site with fantastic views

OFF THE BEATEN TRACK

THE PILETA CAVES

Twenty kilometres southwest of Ronda la Vieja are some of Andalucía's most ancient and fascinating caves: the **Cueva de la Pileta** (☑952 16 73 43; www.cuevadelapileta. org; Benaoján; adult/child €8/5; ⊙hourly tours 10am-1pm & 4-6pm; ⊕). The guided tour, by torchlight, into the dark belly of the cave reveals Stone Age paintings of horses, goats and fish from 20,000 to 25,000 years ago. Beautiful stalactites and stalagmites add to the effect. The guided tours are given by members of the Bullón family, who discovered the paintings in 1905 and who speak some English.

The fact that the caves are so uncommercial is a real plus. Although the family is finding the upkeep a battle, they are loathe to give in to pressure from the local authority who would obviously like to exploit the caves for maximum tourist euros.

Benaoján village is the nearest you can get to the Cueva de la Pileta by public transport. The caves are 4km south of the village, about 250m off the Benaoján–Cortés de la Frontera road; there is no transport to the caves, so you will need your own car to get here. The turn-off is signposted. Benaoján is served by two Los Amarillos buses (from Monday to Friday) and up to four daily trains to/from Ronda. Walking trails link Benaoján with Ronda and villages in the Guadiaro Valley.

GAUCÍN

Gaucín is a picturesque whitewashed village located on the edge of the Serranía de Ronda mountain range with views to Gibraltar and Morocco. The village was impoverished until the late 1970s when it gradually became discovered by a group of footloose bohemians and artists mainly from chilly northern European climes. Since then Gaucín has continued to grow as an artist's colony. Every May **Art Gaucín** (www.artgaucin.com) takes place, with around 25 local painters, sculptors and photographers opening their studios to the public.

The village is also home to a boutique hotel, **La Fructuosa** (☑ 617 692784; www.lafructuosa.com; Calle Luís de Armiñán 67; s/d incl breakfast €80/90; ❋ ⊗) and several restaurants, ranging from the superchic **La Granada Divino** (☑ 951 70 90 75; www.lagranadadivino.com; Calle de las Piedras; mains €13-23; ⊗ noon-3pm & 7-11pm Wed-Sun, 7-11pm Mon & Tue), famously overhauled by Gordon Ramsey (try his signature King prawns' dish), to the earthy local **Casa Antonia** (Plaza del Santo Niño 10; mains €7-9; ⊗ 9am-11pm Tue-Sun), with its terrace seating on the main square watched over by a quaint 17th-century six-spout fountain. Gaucín is also an excellent spot for birdwatchers and there are handy identification plaques throughout the meandering narrow lanes; look skywards and you may spy vultures and booted eagles circling above.

To get here take the signposted A377 from the A-7 (or AP-7 toll road) at Manilva, signposted Casares and Gaucín; the village is approximately 25km from the turn-off.

of the surrounding countryside. You can happily while away a few hours wandering through the fallen stones, trying to guess the location of various baths and forums.

Ardales & El Chorro

Fifty kilometres northwest of Málaga, the Río Guadalhorce carves its way through the awesome **Garganta del Chorro** (El Chorro gorge). Also called the Desfiladero de los Gaitanes, the gorge is about 4km long, as much as 400m deep and sometimes just 10m wide. Its sheer walls, and other rock faces nearby, are a major magnet for rock climbers, with hundreds of bolted climbs snaking their way up the limestone cliffs.

The pleasant, quiet town of Ardales (population 2700) is the main centre and a good base for exploring further afield. The picturesque **Embalse del Conde del Guadalhorce** is 6km from here – a huge reservoir that dominates the landscape and is noted for its carp fishing. However, most people aim for the hiking and climbing mecca of El Chorro, a small village in the midst of a spectacular and surreal landscape of soaring limestone crags. There are also a couple of easy circular hikes that start from the reservoir, including the 5km **Sendero del Guaitenejo**.

 Activities

Andalucía Aventura ROCK CLIMBING
(www.andalucia-aventura.com) Andalucía Aventura organises rock climbing and abseiling for various levels of skill, as well as hiking excursions. See the website for full details.

Antequera

POP 42,000 / ELEV 577M

Antequera is a fascinating town, both architecturally and historically, yet it has somehow avoided being on the coach-tour circuit – which only adds to its charms. The three major influences in the region, Roman, Moorish and Spanish, have left the town with a rich tapestry of architectural gems. The highlight is the opulent Spanish-baroque style that gives the town its character and which the civic authorities have worked hard to restore and maintain. There is also an astonishing number of churches here – more than 30, many with wonderfully ornate interiors. Little wonder that the town is often referred to as the 'Florence of Andalucíá.

And there's more! Some of Europe's largest and oldest dolmens (burial chambers built with huge slabs of rock), from around 2500 BC to 1800 BC, can be found just outside the town's centre.

The flip side to all this antiquity is a vibrant city centre with some of the best tapas bars this side of Granada.

⊙ Sights

The substantial remains of the Alcazaba, a Muslim-built hilltop castle, dominate Antequera's historic quarter and are within easy (if uphill) distance of the town centre.

★ Alcazaba FORTRESS

(adult/child incl Colegiata de Santa María la Mayor €6/3; ⊙ 10am-7pm Mon-Sat, 10.30am-3pm Sun) Favoured by the Granada emirs of Islamic times, Antequera's hilltop Moorish fortress has a fascinating history and covers a massive 62,000 sq metres. The main approach to the hilltop is from Plaza de San Sebastián, up the stepped Cuesta de San Judas and then through an impressive archway, the **Arco de los Gigantes**, built in 1585 and formerly bearing huge sculptures of Hercules. All that is left today are the Roman inscriptions on the stones.

The admission price includes a multilingual audioguide, which sets the historical scene as you meander along tidy pathways, flanked by shrubs and some archaeological remains of a Gothic church and Roman dwellings from the 6th century AD.

Climb the 50 steps of the **Torre del Homenaje** for great views, especially towards the northeast and of the **Peña de los Enamorados** (Rock of the Lovers), about which there are many legends.

Admission to the Colegiata de Santa María la Mayor is included in the price. Don't miss the ruins of **Roman Baths** dating from the 3rd century AD, which can be viewed from Plaza Santa María, outside the church entrance. Although a tad overgrown, you can clearly see the layout, aided by an explanatory plaque.

Colegiata de Santa María la Mayor CHURCH

(Plaza Santa María; adult/child incl Alcazaba €6/3; ⊙ 10am-7pm Mon-Fri, 10.30am-3pm Sun) Just below the Alcazaba is the large 16th-century Colegiata de Santa María la Mayor. This church-cum-college played an important part in Andalucía's 16th-century humanist movement, and boasts a beautiful Renaissance facade, lovely fluted stone columns inside and a Mudéjar *artesonado* (a ceiling of interlaced beams with decorative insertions). It also plays host to some excellent musical events and exhibitions.

Museo de la Ciudad de Antequera MUSEUM

(www.antequera.es; Plaza del Coso Viejo; compulsory guided tour €3; ⊙ 9.30am-2pm & 4.30-6.30pm Tue-Fri, 9.30am-2pm Sat, 10am-2pm Sun) Located in the town centre, the pride of the Museo

Municipal is the elegant and athletic 1.4m bronze statue of a boy, *Efebo*. Discovered on a local farm in the 1950s, it is possibly the finest example of Roman sculpture found in Spain.

The museum also displays some pieces from a Roman villa in Antequera, where a superb group of mosaics was discovered in 1998. The collection includes a treasure trove of religious items, containing so much silver that you can only visit by guided tour on the half-hour.

Dolmens ARCHAEOLOGICAL SITE

(Cerro Romeral; ⊙ 9am-7.30pm Tue-Sat, to 3.30pm Sun) FREE The **Dolmen de Menga** and **Dolmen de Viera**, both dating from around 2500 BC, are 1km from the town centre in a small, wooded park beside the road that leads northeast to the A45. Head down Calle Encarnación from the central Plaza de San Sebastián and follow the signs.

A third chamber, the **Dolmen del Romeral** (Cerro Romeral; ⊙ 9am-6pm Tue-Sat, 9.30am-2.30pm Sun) FREE, is 5km further out of town. It is of later construction (around 1800 BC) and features the use of small stones for its walls.

Prehistoric people of the Copper Age transported dozens of huge slabs from the nearby hills to construct these burial chambers. The stone frames were covered with mounds of earth. The engineering implications for the time are astonishing. Menga, the larger, is 25m long, 4m high and composed of 32 slabs, the largest of which weighs 180 tonnes. In midsummer the sun rising behind the Peña de los Enamorados hill to the northeast shines directly into the chamber mouth.

To get here, continue 2.5km past Menga and Viera through an industrial estate, then turn left following 'Córdoba, Seville' signs. After 500m, turn left at a roundabout and follow 'Dolmen del Romeral' signs for 200m.

Museo Conventual de las Descalzas MUSEUM

(Plaza de las Descalzas; compulsory guided tour €3.30; ⊙ 10.30am-2pm & 5-8pm Tue-Sat, 10am-1.30pm Sun) This museum, in the 17th-century convent of the Carmelitas Descalzas (barefoot Carmelites), approximately 150m east of town's Museo Municipal, displays highlights of Antequera's rich religious-art heritage. Outstanding works include a painting by Lucas Giordano of St Teresa of Ávila (the 16th-century founder of the Carmelitas Descalzas), a bust of the Dolorosa by Pedro de Mena and a *Virgen de Belén* sculpture by La Roldana.

CAMINITO DEL REY

El Chorro gorge is particularly famous for the **Caminito del Rey** (www.caminitodelrey.info; €6; ☉10am-6pm), or 'King's Path', so named because Alfonso XIII walked along it when he opened the Guadalhorce hydroelectric dam in 1921. The path had fallen into severe disrepair by the late 1990s and became famously known as the most dangerous pathway in the world; if you need proof, you can search for the videos on YouTube. After several people fell to their death the *caminito* was closed in 2001 and, after extensive restoration and a €5.5 million tab, reopened in March 2015. It is now reputedly entirely safe and open to anyone with a reasonable head for heights.

The path hangs 100m above the Río Guadalhorce and snakes around the cliffs, affording truly breathtaking views at every turn. The boardwalk is 2.9km long and constructed with wooden slats and a 1.2m-high three-wire guard rail; in some sections the old crumbling path can be spied just below. There is a lot of information on the website, including reservation details. The cost per person is a nominal €6 and you should allow around four hours for the walk, which includes walking to your access point and from the *caminito* end (whether Alora or Ardales). Note that the walk is linear, however there are regular buses that can take you back to your start point (€1.55, 20 minutes).

The most convenient public transport to the area is the train from Málaga which leaves eight times daily to Alora (40 minutes, €3.60). Check www.renfe.com for the timetable.

Iglesia del Carmen CHURCH
(Plaza del Carmen; admission €2; ☉11am-1.30pm & 4.30-5.45pm Tue-Fri, 11am-2pm Sat & Sun) Only the most jaded would fail to be impressed by the Iglesia del Carmen and its marvellous 18th-century Churrigueresque retable. Magnificently carved in red pine by Antequera's own Antonio Primo, it's spangled with statues of angels by Diego Márquez y Vega, and saints, popes and bishops by José de Medina. While the main altar is unpainted, the rest of the interior is a dazzle of colour and design, painted to resemble traditional tilework.

★ Festivals & Events

Semana Santa HOLY WEEK
(☉Mar) One of the most traditional celebrations in Andalucía; items from the town's treasure trove are actually used in the religious processions.

Real Feria de Agosto FAIR
(☉mid-Aug) This festival celebrates the harvest with bullfights, dancing and street parades.

🛏 Sleeping

Antequera hotel prices are refreshingly moderate.

Hotel San Sebastían HOTEL €
(☑952 84 42 39; www.hotelplazasansebastian.com; Plaza de San Sebastián 4; s/d €25/40; P❉🛜) You can't get much more central

than this smartly refurbished hotel situated on a pretty square across from the magnificent Iglesia de San Sebastián. Its terrace is the best perch on the plaza to watch the evening *paseo*. The rooms are plain with dated decor but have welcome perks, such as fridges and small balconies. Breakfast is not included but there are plenty of bars nearby. Parking costs an extra €7 per day.

Hotel Coso Viejo HOTEL €
(☑952 70 50 45; www.hotelcosoviejo.es; Calle Encarnación 9; s/d incl breakfast €44/54; P❉🛜) This converted 17th-century neoclassical palace is right in the heart of Antequera, opposite Plaza Coso Viejo and the town museum. The simply furnished rooms are set around a handsome patio with a fountain, and there's an excellent tapas bar and restaurant. No TVs.

Parador de Antequera HISTORIC HOTEL €€€
(☑952 84 02 61; www.parador.es; Paseo García del Olmo; s/d incl breakfast €125/150; P❉🛜🏊) This *parador* is in a quiet area of parkland north of the bullring and near the bus station. It's comfortably furnished and set in pleasant gardens with wonderful views, especially at sunset.

🍴 Eating & Drinking

Local specialities you'll encounter on almost every Antequera menu include *porra antequerana* (a thick and delicious garlicky soup, similar to gazpacho); *bienmesabe* (literally 'tastes good to me'; a sponge dessert); and *angelorum* (a dessert incorporating meringue, sponge and egg yolk). Antequera also does a fine breakfast *mollete* (soft bread roll), served with a choice of fillings.

Rincon de Lola
TAPAS €

(www.rincondelola.net; Calle Encarnación 7; tapas €2, raciones €7; ⊙ noon-11.30pm Tue-Sun) A great place for inexpensive, varied tapas that can give you a taster of local dishes such as *cochinillo* (suckling pig), or *porra antequerana*. There are also piled high *tostas* (open sandwiches on toasted bread) and *raciones* such as tomatoes filled with cheese, salmon, wild mushrooms and prawns.

Capella Cafe y Tapas
ANDALUCIAN, CAFE €

(☑ 951 23 58 06; Calle Infanta Don Fernando 20; tapas, pastries €1; ⊙ 8am-11pm Mon-Thu, to midnight Fri & Sat; 🛜) A thoroughly pleasant place to come for any number of options: coffee, wine, tapas, *meriendas* (afternoon snacks) and wifi. It's made doubly interesting by the on-site **Maqueta de Antequera** (www.maquetade antequera.es; admission €1; ⊙ 8am-11pm, to midnight Fri & Sat), a huge scale model of the city in the 18th century, unveiled in 2013. It is said to be the largest model of its kind in Spain.

★ Arte de Cozina
ANDALUCIAN €€

(www.artedecozina.com; Calle Calzada 27-29; mains €12-15, tapas €2; ⊙ 1-11pm) The *simpática* (friendly) owner of this hotel-restaurant has her own garden that provides fresh ingredients for her dishes. Traditional dishes are reinterpreted, like gazpacho made with green asparagus or *porra* with oranges, plus meat, fish, and Antequeran specialities. On Thursday and Friday evenings classical musicians provide entertainment.

The adjacent tapas bar serves unusual light bites such as snails in a spicy almond sauce or river crab with chilli and peppers. There are plenty of dessert choices, which is unusual in these parts.

Reina Restaurante
CONTEMPORARY ANDALUCIAN €€

(☑ 952 70 30 31; Calle San Agustín 1; mains €14-18, menú €14; ⊙ 1-4pm & 8-11pm Tue-Sun) Located in a pretty restaurant-flanked cul-de-sac off Calle Infante Don Fernando, this restaurant also runs a cooking school, La Espuela, so they know what they're doing. The menu includes a fine selection of Antequeran specialities, such as chicken in almond sauce and partridge pâté, along with more daring dishes like strawberry gazpacho with goats' cheese.

The elegant dining room is painted a dark mulberry-pink, contrasting with crisp white table linens. The bow-tied waiters complete the dress-for-dinner feel.

El Angelote
BAR

(Plaza del Carmen 10; ⊙ 12.30pm-late Tue-Sat; 🛜) A lively bar with terrace seating on the picturesque square; it offers occasional live music.

ℹ Information

Municipal Tourist Office (☑ 952 70 25 05; www.antequera.es; Plaza de San Sebastián 7; ⊙ 11am-2pm & 5-8pm Mon-Sat, to 2pm Sun) A helpful tourist office with information about the town and region.

ℹ Getting There & Around

BUS

The **bus station** (Paseo Garcí de Olmo) is 1km north of the centre. **Alsa** (www.alsa.es) runs buses to Seville (€14, 2½ hours, five daily), Granada (€9, 1½ hours, five daily), Córdoba (€11, two hours 40 minutes, one daily), Almería (€23, six hours, one daily) and Málaga (€6, 1½ hours, two daily).

Buses run between Antequera and Fuente de Piedra village (€2.45, 25 minutes, three daily).

CAR

A toll road, (AP-46) running from Torremolinos to Las Padrizas (€5), is located around 21km southeast of Antequera.

PARKING

There is underground parking on Calle Diego Ponce north of Plaza de San Sebastián (per hour €1.50, 12 to 24 hours €18).

TAXIS

Taxis (€6 to €7 per 2km to 3km) wait halfway along Calle Infante Don Fernando, or you can call ☑ 952 84 55 30.

TRAIN

The **train station** (www.renfe.es; Avenida de la Estación) is 1.5km north of the centre. Six trains a day run to/from Granada (€11, 1½ hours), and there are four daily to Seville (€18, 1½ hours). Another three run to Málaga or Córdoba, but you'll need to change at Bobadilla.

Paraje Natural Torcal de Antequera

South of Antequera are the weird and wonderful rock formations of the Paraje Natural Torcal de Antequera. A 12-sq-km area of gnarled, serrated and pillared limestone, it formed as a sea bed 150 million years ago and now rises to 1336m (El Torcal). It's otherworldly out here and the air is pure and fresh. There is an **information centre** (✒ 952 24 33 24; www.visitasfuentepiedra.es; ⊙ 10am-9pm) that provides details on walks, and flora and fauna.

Two marked walking trails, the 1.5km Ruta Verde (green route) and the 3km Ruta Amarilla (yellow route) start and end near the information centre. More dramatic views are along the restricted Ruta Rojo (red route), for which guided tours are organised; contact the Antequera tourist office (p188) for details. Wear shoes with good tread as the trails are rocky.

To get to El Torcal you will need your own car or a taxi. By car, leave central Antequera along Calle Picadero, which soon joins the Zalea road. After 1km or so you'll see signs on the left to Villanueva de la Concepción. Take this road and, after about 11km, a turn uphill to the right leads to the information centre after 4km.

Laguna de Fuente de Piedra

About 20km northwest of Antequera, just off the A92 *autovía* (toll-free dual carriageway), is the Laguna de Fuente de Piedra. When it's not dried up by drought, this is Andalucía's biggest natural lake and one of Europe's two main breeding grounds for the greater flamingo (the other is in the Camargue region of southwest France). After a wet winter as many as 20,000 pairs of flamingos will breed at the lake.

The birds arrive in January or February, with the chicks hatching in April and May. The flamingos stay until about August, when the lake, which is rarely more than 1m deep, no longer contains enough water to support them. They share the lake with thousands of other birds of some 170 species.

You can watch an informative audiovisual film about the flamingos at the lakeside **Centro de Información Fuente de Piedra** (✒ 952 71 25 54; www.visitasfuentepiedra.es; Laguna de Fuente de Piedra; ⊙ 10am-2pm & 5-7pm). Staff can also advise on the best spots for birdwatching. You can buy maps here and rent binoculars (an essential).

Near the lake is the the well-regarded **Caserío de San Benito** (✒ 952 11 11 03; Km 108 Carretera Córdoba-Málaga; menú €14; ⊙ noon-5pm & 8pm-midnight Tue-Sun), which is a good place to stop for a quality lunch. A beautifully converted farmhouse, San Benito is stuffed with antiques and serves up exquisitely prepared traditional dishes.

EAST OF MÁLAGA

The coast east of Málaga, sometimes described as the Costa del Sol Oriental, is less developed than the coast to the west. The suburban sprawl of Málaga extends east into a series of unmemorable and unremarkable seaside towns – Rincón de la Victoria, Torre del Mar, Torrox Costa – which pass in a concrete high-rise blur, before culminating in more attractive Nerja, which has a large population of Brits and Scandinavians.

The area's main redeeming feature is the rugged region of La Axarquía, which is just as stunning as Granada's Las Alpujarras yet, as well as being even more difficult to pronounce (think of taking a chopper to one of those infuriating Scandinavian flatpack stores: 'axe-ikea'), is hardly known. The area is full of great walks, which are less well-known than those in the northwest of the province around Ronda. A 406-sq-km area of these mountains was declared the Parque Natural Sierras de Tejeda, Almijara y Alhama in 1999.

La Axarquía

POP 211,447

The Axarquía region is riven by deep valleys lined with terraces and irrigation channels that date to Islamic times – nearly all the villages dotted around the olive-, almond- and vine-planted hillsides date from this era. The wild inaccessible landscapes, especially around the Sierra de Tejeda, made it a stronghold of *bandoleros* who roamed the mountains without fear or favour. Nowadays, its chief attractions include fantastic scenery; pretty white villages; strong, sweet, local wine made from sun-dried grapes; and good walking in spring and autumn.

The 'capital' of La Axarquía, **Vélez Málaga**, 4km north of Torre del Mar, is a busy but unspectacular town, although its restored hilltop castle is worth a look. From Vélez the A335 heads north past the turquoise Embalse de la Viñuela reservoir and up through the **Boquete de Zafarraya** (a dramatic cleft in the mountains) towards Granada. One bus a day makes its way over this road between Torre del Mar and Granada.

Some of the most dramatic La Axarquía scenery is up around the highest villages of **Alfarnate** (925m) and **Alfarnatejo** (858m), with towering, rugged crags such as Tajo de Gomer and Tajo de Doña Ana rising to their south.

You can pick up information on La Axarquía at the tourist offices in Málaga, Nerja, Torre del Mar or Cómpeta. Prospective walkers should ask for the leaflet on walks in the Parque Natural Sierras de Tejeda, Almijara y Alhama. Good maps for walkers are *Mapa Topográfico de Sierra Tejeda* and *Mapa Topográfico de Sierra Almijara* by Miguel Ángel Torres Delgado, both at 1:25,000. You can also follow the links at www.axarquia.es for walks in the region.

Comares

POP 1435

Comares sits like a snowdrift atop its lofty hill. The adventure really is in getting there. You see it for kilometre after kilometre before a final twist in an endlessly winding road lands you below the hanging garden of its cliff. From a little car park you can climb steep, winding steps to the village. Look for ceramic footprints underfoot and simply follow them through a web of narrow, twisting lanes past the **Iglesia de la Encarnación** and eventually to the ruins of Comares' **castle** and a remarkable summit **cemetery**.

The village has a history of rebellion, having been a stronghold of Omar ibn Hafsun, but today there is a tangible sense of contented isolation, enjoyed by locals and many newcomers. The views across the Axarquía are stunning.

Have lunch at **El Molino de los Abuelos** (☑ 952 50 93 09; Plaza de la Axarquía; mains €8-16, menú €9), a converted olive mill on the main plaza, which serves Spanish cuisine, including several rice dishes (the owner is from Valencia), and doubles as a charming small **hotel** (☑ 952 50 93 09; www.hotelmolinodelosabuelos. com; Plaza de la Axarquia 2; d with/without bathroom from €75/55, ste €120; P 🛜). There are a couple of friendly bars at the heart of the village.

On weekdays only, a bus leaves Málaga for Comares at 6pm and starts back at 7am the next morning (€3.20, 1½ hours).

Cómpeta

POP 3459

This picturesque village with its panoramic views, steep winding streets and central bar-lined plaza, overlooking the 16th-century church, has long attracted a large mixed foreign population. Not only has this contributed to an active cultural scene, but Cómpeta is also home to one or two above-*pueblo*-average restaurants serving contemporary cuisine. It also has a couple of charity shops (rare in Spain) and a foreign-language bookshop. The village is a good base for hiking and other similar adrenalin-fuelled activities.

🏌 Activities

Salamandra   OUTDOORS

(☑ 952 55 34 93; www.malaga-aventura.com; Calle El Barrio 47; potholing/kayaking/canyoning per person from €25/25/45; ☉ 10am-2pm & 5-7pm; 🚶) This is a one-stop centre that organises a wide range of activities, including guided hikes, potholing, canyoning and kayaking, plus themed tours, such as orchid trips in spring, mushroom picking and historical routes. The latter includes the former merchants' pathway linking Cómpeta with Játar and covering some 20km (on foot).

Los Caballos del Mosquin   HORSE RIDING

(☑ 608 658108; www.horseriding-andalucia.com; Canillas del Albaida; half-day trek incl picnic €65) Offers guided horse-riding treks ranging from one hour to three days (including full board and accommodation) in the surrounding countryside.

🎉 Festivals & Events

Noche del Vino   WINE

(Night of the Wine; ☉ 15 Aug) Cómpeta has some of the area's best local wine, and the popular Noche del Vino features a program of flamenco and *sevillano* music and dance in the central and pretty Plaza Almijara, plus limitless free wine.

🛏 Sleeping

Hotel Balcón de Cómpeta   HOTEL €€

(☑ 952 55 36 62; www.hotel-competa.com; Calle San Antonio 75; s/d incl breakfast €54/77; ❄ 🛜 ⊠) A long-established modern hotel located at the top of the village with sweeping panoramic views. The rooms have benefited from a colour-coordinated update with charcoal greys and raspberry pinks contrasting with cool pastels and whites. There's a tennis court, as well as a pool.

🍴 Eating & Drinking

Taberna de Oscar   MODERN ANDALUCIAN €

(☑ 952 51 66 31; www.tabernadeoscar.es; Plaza Pantaleón Romero 1; medias raciónes €3.50-5.50;

⊗ restaurant 11am-11pm Wed-Mon; bar 6pm-late Wed-Mon; ☑) Tucked in an elbow behind the church, the olive oil and the produce used in dishes here is organic (as far as possible), while the robust house wine comes from the family bodega. There's a vegetarian menu with ingredients such as roast beetroot and marinated tofu as well as Andalucian staples, including gazpacho and *zarzuela* (fish and seafood stew).

Dishes are served in *medias raciones* (half rations, about double a *tapa* size). Upstairs on the terrace there is a cocktail bar with great rooftop views and even better strawberry daiquiris.

El Pilón INTERNATIONAL €€
(☑ 952 55 35 12; www.restauranteelpilon.com; Calle Laberinto; mains €13-18; ⊗ 7-11pm Mon, Wed-Sat, 1-3.30pm Sun; ☑) This former carpenter's workshop is one of the village's most popular restaurants. Dishes are created using locally sourced ingredients, whenever possible, and reflect an eclectic range including tandoori chicken, Burgo's black pudding and plenty of vegetarian options. There's a cocktail lounge with sweeping views and regular events, including wine tastings and live music.

Museo del Vino ANDALUCIAN €€
(Avenida Constitución; mains €9.50-17; ⊗ 1-4pm & 7.30-10.30pm) Exuding rustic warmth with exposed bricks and beams, this long-time tourist favourite serves excellent ham, cheese and sausage *raciónes* and wine from the barrel. It's also something of an Aladdin's cave of regional crafts and produce, plus Moroccan bits and pieces.

ⓘ Information

Tourist Office (☑ 952 55 36 85; Avenida de la Constitución; ⊗ 10am-3pm Mon-Sat, to 2pm Sun) The tourist office is located beside the bus stop at the foot of the village, and has plenty of information about the town and region.

ⓘ Getting There & Away

BUS

Three buses travel daily from Málaga to Cómpeta (€4.60, 1½ hours), stopping via Torre del Mar.

PARKING

There's a free car park up the hill from the tourist office.

Frigiliana

POP 3093

Considered by many to be the prettiest village in La Axarquía, Frigiliana is 7km north of Nerja and linked to it by several buses daily (except Sunday). The narrow streets are lined with simple whitewashed houses adorned with pots of blood-red geraniums. The tourist office (www.frigiliana.es; Plaza del Ingenio; ⊗ 9am-8pm Mon-Fri, 10am-1.30pm & 4-8pm Sat & Sun) is helpful.

El Fuerte, the hill that climbs above the village, was the scene of the final bloody defeat of the *moriscos* (converted Muslims) of La Axarquía in their 1569 rebellion, and where they reputedly plunged to their death rather than be killed or captured by the Spanish. You can walk up here if you follow the streets to the top of the town and then continue along the dusty track.

Frigiliana prides itself on its sweet local wine, local artists, local honey and by simply being just so sugar-cube perfect and picturesque.

Nerja

POP 20,700

Nerja, 56km east of Málaga with the Sierra Almijara rising behind it, has succeeded in rebuffing developers, allowing its centre to retain a low-rise village charm, despite the proliferation of souvenir shops and day-trippers. At its heart is the perennially beautiful Balcón de Europa, a palm-lined promontory built on the foundations of an old fort with panoramic views of the cobalt-blue sea flanked by honey-coloured coves.

The town is increasingly popular with package holidaymakers and 'residential tourists', which has pushed it far beyond its old confines. There is significant urbanisation, especially to the east. The holiday atmosphere, and seawater contamination, can be overwhelming from July to September, but the place is more *tranquilo* and the water cleaner the rest of the year.

◎ Sights & Activities

The town centres on the delightful Balcón de Europa, which juts out over the deep blue water and is *the* place for the local *paseo* (promenade) on a languid summer's evening; there are a couple of handy

Nerja

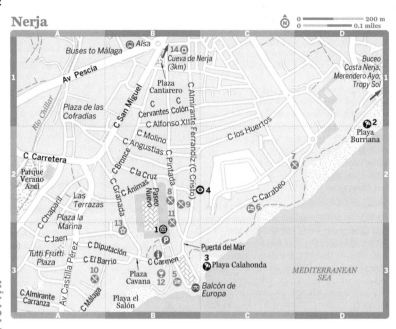

Nerja

◉ Sights
1	Museo de Nerja	B3
2	Playa Burriana	D1
3	Playa Calahonda	C3
4	Tuesday Market	C2

🛏 Sleeping
5	Hotel Balcón de Europa	B3
6	Hotel Carabeo	C2

🍴 Eating
7	Bakus	D2
8	Gusto	B2
9	La Piqueta	B2
10	Lan Sang	A3
11	Oliva	B3
	Restaurante 34	(see 6)

🍷 Drinking & Nightlife
12	Cochran's Irish Bar	B3

🎭 Entertainment
13	Centro Cultural Villa de Nerja	B3

🛍 Shopping
14	Rastro	B1

terrace bars here, as well as the predictable horses and carriages; best avoided from an animal-welfare point of view.

★**Cueva de Nerja** CAVE
(www.cuevadenerja.es; adult/child €9/5; ☉ unguided visit 10am-1pm & 4-5.30pm Sep-Jun, 10am-6pm Jul & Aug; guided visit 1-2pm & 5.30-6.30pm Sep-Jun, 11am-noon & 6.30-7.30pm Jul & Aug) The Cueva de Nerja is the big tourist attraction in Nerja, just off the N340, 3km east of town on the slopes of the Sierra Almijara. The enormous 4km-long cave complex, hollowed out by water around five million years ago and once inhabited by Stone Age hunters, is a theatrical wonderland of extraordinary rock formations, subtle shifting colours, and stalactites and stalagmites. Large-scale performances including ballet and flamenco are staged here throughout summer.

About 14 buses run daily from Málaga and Nerja, except Sunday. The whole site is very well organised for tourism, and has a huge restaurant and car park. A full tour of the caves takes about 45 minutes. Note that there is no extra charge for guided tours.

Museo de Nerja MUSEUM
(☎ 952 52 72 24; Plaza de España; adult/child €4/2; ☉ 10am-2pm & 4-6.30pm Tue-Sun, to 10pm Jul & Aug) Nerja's museum traces the history of the town from the cave dwellers of Paleolithic times to the tourist boom years of the '60s, and is well worth an hour or so of your time.

The museum's highlights centre on artefacts found in the Cueva de Nerja and range from the thought-provoking skeleton of an adult cave dweller to a fascinatingly mundane prehistoric cheese dish.

Playa Calahonda
BEACH

This small, picturesque cove is located to the east of the Balcón de Europa. You can rent sunbeds and parasols, though it does get busy at the height of summer, especially with guests from the nearby **Hotel Balcón de Europa** (☑ 952 52 08 00; www.hotelbalconeuropa. com; Paseo Balcón de Europa 1; s/d €82/115; ☒).

Playa Burriana
BEACH

(🅿) This is Nerja's longest and best beach with plenty of towel space on the sand. You can walk here via picturesque Calle Carabeo, continuing down the steps to the beach and along to Burriana.

Playa del Cañuelo
BEACH

East of Nerja the coast becomes more rugged and with your own wheels you can head to some great beaches reached by tracks down from the A7. Playa del Cañuelo, immediately before the border of Granada province, is one of the best, with a couple of summer-only restaurants.

Buceo Costa Nerja
DIVING

(☑ 952 52 86 10; www.nerjadiving.com; Playa Burriana; snorkelling from €30; ☺ 9am-7pm) Diving can be especially rewarding here due to the Atlantic stream, which results in highly varied marine life. This reputable outfit organises courses for most levels.

⚞ Festivals & Events

Noche de San Juan
SUMMER SOLSTICE

(☺ 23 Jun) Nerja's inhabitants celebrate St John's Day by dusting off their barbecue kits and heading for the beach. They eat sizzling sardines, fish and seafood, drink wine and beer, and stay up until the next morning swimming, dancing, partying and, ultimately, flaking out on the sand.

Virgen del Carmen
RELIGIOUS

(☺ 16 Jul) The fishermens' feast day is marked with a procession that carries the Virgin in fishing boats.

🛏 Sleeping

Nerja has a huge range of accommodation, but in summer rooms in the better hotels tend to be booked at least two months in advance.

★ Hotel Carabeo
HOTEL €€

(☑ 952 52 54 44; www.hotelcarabeo.com; Calle Carabeo 34, Nerja; d/ste incl breakfast from €85/180; ☺ Apr-Oct; ✱ @ 🛜 ☒) Full of stylish antiques and wonderful paintings, this small, family-run seafront hotel is set above manicured terraced gardens. There's also a good restaurant and the pool is on a terrace overlooking the sea. The building is an old school house and is located on one of the prettiest pedestrian streets in town, festooned with colourful bougainvillea.

✖ Eating

Nerja has an abundance of restaurants and bars, most geared towards undiscerning tourists. In general, avoid any advertising all-day English breakfasts or with sun-bleached posters of the dishes. Playa Burriana, Nerja's best beach, is backed by an animated strip of restaurants and bars.

La Piqueta
TAPAS €

(Calle Pintada 8; tapas €2, raciónes €4.50-6; ☺ 10am-midnight Mon-Sat) There are two very good reasons why this is the most popular tapas bar in town: first, the house wine is excellent, second, you get a free *tapa* with every drink (generally a miniburger; vegetarians can request cheese). On the menu are sturdy classics such as tripe and *huevos estrellados* (literally, broken eggs) prepared with ham, garlic, potatoes and peppers.

Gusto
INTERNATIONAL €

(Calle Pintada 23; snacks €5-7; ☺ 11am-11pm; ☝) Homemade burgers, including vegetarian with cheese, plus Med-style sandwiches such as roasted pepper and goats' cheese, salad, grilled halloumi and quiche, make this a popular snack spot. Breakfasts include classy smoked salmon, US-style waffles, healthy Swiss-style muesli and the (OK, not so healthy) full English breakfast. The children's menu is more varied than most.

Lan Sang
THAI €€

(www.lansang.com; Calle Málaga 12; mains €7-14; ☺ 1.30-3pm & 7.30-11pm Tue-Sat, 7-10.30pm Sun) The owner and chef are from Laos so dishes are a subtle combination of the two cuisines: Thai and Lao. As well as curries, stir-fries and soups, there is an emphasis on fresh local fish and seafood, prepared with spices such as tamarind, ginger, kaffir-lime leaves and chilli. Soups and salads are similarly based on delicate fragrant flavours.

Bakus
BISTRO €€

(Calle Carabeo 2; mains €12-17; ⊙12.30-3.30pm & 7-10.30pm Tue-Sun) The interior combines raspberry pink with charcoal grey, but most folk head to the sprawling terrace overlooking pristine Playa Carabello. The menu should suit most discerning diners, ranging from light bites like baked gorgonzola tart and pumpkin soup, to meat dishes with sauces that sound decidedly moreish, including tarragon, leek and bacon, truffle cream and port wine with wild mushrooms.

Merendero Ayo
SEAFOOD €€

(www.ayonerja.com; Playa Burriana; mains €9-13; ⊙9am-midnight; P ♿) At this open-air place you can enjoy paella cooked in sizzling pans over an open fire – and even go back for a free second helping. It's run by Ayo, a delightful local character famed for the discovery of the Cueva de Nerja complex. He throws the rice on the *paellera* (paella dish) in a spectacular fashion, amusing all his guests.

Restaurante 34
MODERN EUROPEAN €€

(☑952 52 54 44; www.hotelcarabeo.com; Hotel Carabeo, Calle Carabeo 34; mains €15-25; ⊙1-3.30pm & 7-11pm Tue-Sun; ☎) A truly gorgeous setting both indoors and outside in the garden, which is gently stepped to its furthest section overlooking the sea. Delicious and exotic food combinations are served, and there is an adjacent tapas bar for smaller appetites. Live music Wednesday and Sunday evening.

Oliva
MODERN EUROPEAN €€€

(☑952 52 29 88; www.restauranteoliva.com; Calle Pintada 7; mains €19-23; ⊙1-4pm & 7-11pm) Impeccable service, single orchids, a drum-and-bass soundtrack and a charcoal-grey-and-green colour scheme; in short, this place has class. The menu is reassuringly brief and changes regularly according to what's in season. The inventive dishes combine unlikely ingredients like pistachio falafel and mango panna cotta with black-olive caramel. Reservations recommended.

Drinking

Cochran's Irish Bar
IRISH PUB

(www.cochransirishpub.com; Paseo Balcón de Europa 6; ⊙8pm-3am Tue-Sat, 5pm-midnight Sun) A longstanding Irish bar with a superb atmosphere plus a foot-hopping program of live twanging at weekends. There is a beautifully sited outdoor bar with sweeping sea views and a romantic tropical-island feel, which makes it especially perfect at locked-eyes-over-cocktails time.

Tropy Sol
CAFE

(Playa Burriana; ⊙10am-10pm) Playa Burriana's top place for coffee and ice cream.

☆ Entertainment

Centro Cultural Villa de Nerja
CULTURAL CENTRE

(☑952 52 38 63; Calle Granada 45) This well-run centre organises an ambitious annual program of classical music, theatre, jazz and flamenco, featuring international and Spanish musicians and performers.

🔒 Shopping

There is a lively **market** (Calle Almirante Ferrandíz; ⊙9am-3pm Tue) on Tuesday and a **rastro** (Urbanización Flamingo, Calle Almirante Ferrandiz; ⊙9am-2pm Sun) (flea market) on Sunday morning north of town.

ℹ Information

Tourist office (www.nerja.org; Calle Carmen; ⊙10am-2pm & 6-10pm) Has plenty of useful leaflets.

ℹ Getting There & Around

BUS

Alsa (☑952 52 15 04; www.alsa.es; Avenida Pescía) runs regular buses to/from Málaga (€5.75, 1¾ hours, 23 daily), Marbella (€9.50, 1¼ hours, one daily) and Antequera (€9, 2¼ hours, two daily). There are also buses to Almería and Granada.

PARKING

Follow the signs to the central **underground car park** (1/24hr €1.20/18) in Plaza de España.

Córdoba Province

POP 798,000

Includes ➡

Córdoba 198
Baena 211
Parque Natural
Sierras Subbéticas. . . 211
Almodóvar del Río . . . 216
Parque Natural Sierra
de Hornachuelos 216

Best Places to Eat

➡ Restaurante La Fuente (p215)

➡ La Boca (p208)

➡ Garum 2.1 (p208)

➡ Bodegas Campos (p208)

➡ El Astronauta (p209)

Best Places to Stay

➡ Casa Olea (p215)

➡ Balcón de Córdoba (p208)

➡ Bed and Be (p207)

➡ Casa Baños de la Villa (p215)

➡ Hotel Zuhayra (p213)

Why Go?

Once the dazzling beacon of Al-Andalus, the historic city of Córdoba is itself the main magnet of its namesake province. Remnants of the illustrious Caliphate of Córdoba, especially the great Mezquita (Mosque), hold immense historical and architectural interest, and the city around them is full of good food and wine and captivating gardens. But there's plenty of less-trampled territory to explore outside the provincial capital. To the north looms the Sierra Morena, a rolling expanse of protected forests, remote villages and ruined castles. To the south, olive trees and grapevines carpet rippling terrain, yielding some of Spain's best oils and the unique sweet Montilla-Moriles wines. Further south, caves and canyons are carved out of the limestone massif of the Sierras Subbéticas, with bustling Priego de Córdoba and crag-perched Zuheros making perfect bases for mountain hiking and dining on homestyle local dishes.

Driving Distances

	Córdoba	Priego de Córdoba	Almodóvar del Río	Baena
Priego de Córdoba	103			
Almodóvar del Río	30	133		
Baena	60	34	90	
Montilla	46	58	76	37

Córdoba Province Highlights

❶ Discovering the marvellous Mezquita and other reminders of Al-Andalus' three-cultures golden age in colourful **Córdoba** (p195)

❷ Exploring the mountains, valleys and caves of the **Parque Natural Sierras Subbéticas** (p211)

❸ Imbibing sweet Montilla wines, especially on a winery tour in **Montilla** (p212) itself

❹ Admiring the baroque fantasies of **Priego de Córdoba** (p214)

❺ Walking through the Mediterranean woodlands of the **Parque Natural Sierra de Hornachuelos** (p216)

❻ Touring the castles, oak pastures and isolated villages of Andalucía's mysterious 'deep north', **Los Pedroches** (p217)

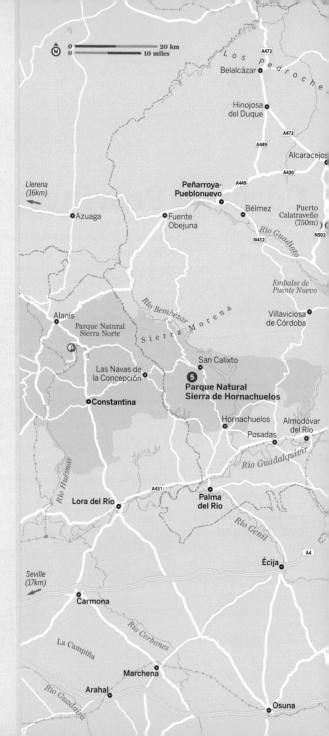

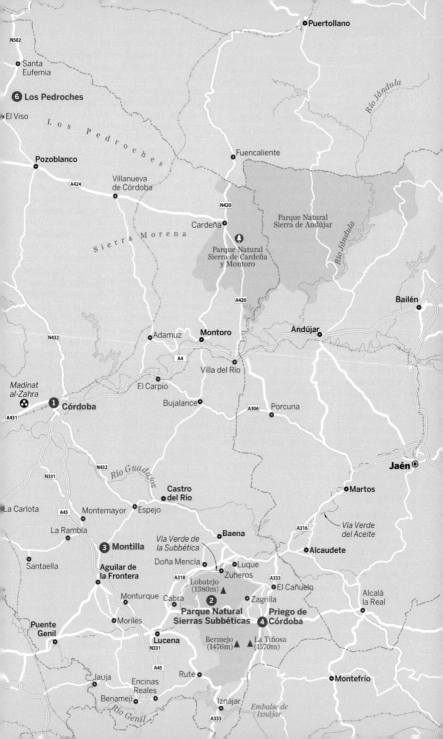

CÓRDOBA

POP 296,000 / ELEV 110M

One building alone is enough to put Córdoba high on any traveller's itinerary: the mesmerising multiarched Mezquita. One of the world's greatest Islamic buildings, it's a symbol of the worldly and sophisticated Islamic culture that flourished here more than a millennium ago when Córdoba was the capital of Islamic Spain, and Western Europe's biggest and most cultured city. Once here, you'll find there's much more to this city: Córdoba is a great place for exploring on foot or by bicycle, staying and eating well in old buildings centred on verdant patios, diving into old wine bars, and feeling millennia of history at every turn. The narrow streets of the old Judería (Jewish quarter) and Muslim quarter stretch out from the great mosque like capillaries (to the northwest and northeast respectively), some clogged with tourist bric-a-brac, others delightfully peaceful. The life of the modern city focuses a little further north, around Plaza de las Tendillas, where you'll find a more boisterous vibe with some excellent bars and restaurants. Andalucía's major river, the Guadalquivir, flows just below the Mezquita, and the riverfront streets are home to a growing band of lively restaurants and bars making the most of the view.

Córdoba bursts into life from mid-April to mid-June, when it stages most of its major fiestas. At this time of year the skies are blue, the temperatures are perfect and the city's many trees, gardens and courtyards drip with foliage and blooms. September and October are also excellent weatherwise, but July and August can sizzle.

History

The Roman colony of Corduba was established in 152 BC as a strategic provisioning point for Roman troops. In the 1st century AD, Emperor Augustus made the city capital of Baetica, one of the three Roman provinces on the Iberian Peninsula, ushering in an era of prosperity and cultural ascendancy that brought the writers Seneca and Lucan to the world. The Roman bridge over the Guadalquivir and the temple on Calle Claudio Marcelo are just the most visible remains of this important Roman city, whose traces now lie a metre or two beneath the modern city. By the 3rd century, when Christianity reached Córdoba, the Roman city was already in decline. Córdoba fell to Islamic invaders in AD 711.

The city took centre stage in 756 when Abd ar-Rahman I set himself up here as the emir of Al-Andalus (the Muslim-controlled parts of the Iberian Peninsula), founding the Omayyad dynasty, which more or less unified Al-Andalus for two and a half centuries. Abd ar-Rahman I founded the great Mezquita in 785. The city's, and Al-Andalus', heyday came under Abd ar-Rahman III (912–61). He named himself caliph (the title of the Muslim successors of Mohammed) in 929, ushering in the era of the Córdoba caliphate.

Córdoba was by now the biggest city in Western Europe, with a flourishing economy based on agriculture and skilled artisan products, and a population somewhere around 250,000. The city shone with hundreds of dazzling mosques, public baths, patios, gardens and fountains. This was the famed 'city of the three cultures', where Muslims, Jews and Christians coexisted peaceably and Abd ar-Rahman III's court was frequented by scholars from all three communities. Córdoba's university, library and observatories made it a centre of learning whose influence was still being felt in Christian Europe many centuries later.

Towards the end of the 10th century, Al-Mansur (Almanzor), a ruthless general whose northward raids terrified Christian Spain, took the reins of power from the caliphs. But after the death of Al-Mansur's son Abd al-Malik in 1008, the caliphate descended into anarchy. Berber troops terrorised and looted the city and, in 1031, Omayyad rule ended. Córdoba became a minor part of the Seville *taifa* (small kingdom) in 1069, and has been overshadowed by Seville ever since.

Twelfth-century Córdoba did nevertheless produce the two most celebrated scholars of Al-Andalus – the Muslim Averroës (1126–98) and the Jewish Maimonides (1135–1204), men of multifarious talents most remembered for their efforts to reconcile religious faith with Aristotelian reason. After Córdoba was taken by Castilla's Fernando III in 1236, it declined into a provincial city and its fortunes only looked up with the arrival of industry in the late 19th century. Christian Córdoba did, however, give birth to one of the greatest Spanish poets, Luis de Góngora (1561–1627), still much remembered in the city.

⊙ Sights

★ Mezquita   MOSQUE, CATHEDRAL
(Mosque; ☑ 957 47 05 12; www.catedraldecordoba.es; Calle Cardenal Herrero; adult/child €8/4, 8.30-

9.30am Mon-Sat free; ◔8.30-9.30am & 10am-7pm Mon-Sat, 8.30-11.30am & 3-7pm Sun Mar-Oct, to 6pm daily Nov-Feb) It's impossible to over-emphasise the beauty of Córdoba's great mosque, with its remarkably serene (despite tourist crowds) and spacious interior. One of the world's greatest works of Islamic architecture, the Mezquita hints, with all its lustrous decoration, at a refined age when Muslims, Jews and Christians lived side by side and enriched their city with a heady interaction of diverse, vibrant cultures.

Arab chronicles recount how Abd ar-Rahman I purchased half of the Hispano-Roman church of San Vicente for the Muslim community's Friday prayers, and then, in AD 784, bought the other half on which to erect a new mosque. Three later extensions nearly quintupled the size of Abd ar-Rahman I's mosque and brought it to the form you see today – with one major alteration: a 16th-century cathedral plonked right in the middle (hence the often-used description 'Mezquita-Catedral').

Mass is celebrated in the central cathedral at 9.30am Monday to Saturday, and at noon and 1.30pm Sundays.

➡ **Patio de los Naranjos**

This lovely courtyard, with its orange, palm and cypress trees and fountains, forms the entrance to the Mezquita. It was formerly the site of ritual ablutions before prayer in the mosque. Its most impressive entrance is the Puerta del Perdón, a 14th-century Mudéjar archway in the base of the bell tower. The ticket office is just inside here.

➡ **Bell Tower**

The 54m-high bell tower reopened to visitors in 2014 after 24 years of intermittent restoration work, and you can climb up to its bells for fine panoramas. Originally built by Abd ar-Rahman III in 951–52 as the Mezquita's minaret, it was encased in a strengthened outer shell, and heightened, by the Christians in the 16th and 17th centuries. You can still see caliphal vaults and arches inside.

The original minaret would have looked something like the Giralda in Seville, which was practically a copy. Córdoba's minaret influenced all minarets built thereafter throughout the western Islamic world.

➡ **The Mezquita's Interior**

The Mezquita's architectural uniqueness and importance lies in the fact that, structurally speaking, it was a revolutionary building for its time. Earlier major Islamic buildings such as the Dome of the Rock in Jerusalem and the Great Mosque in Damascus placed an emphasis on verticality, but the Mezquita was intended as a democratically horizontal and simple space, where the spirit could be free to roam and communicate easily with God – a kind of glorious refinement of the original simple Islamic prayer space (usually the open yard of a desert home).

Men prayed side by side on the *argamasa,* a floor made of compact, reddish slaked lime and sand. A flat roof, decorated with gold and multicoloured motifs, was supported by striped arches suggestive of a forest of date palms. The arches rested on, eventually, 1293 columns (of which 856 remain today). The Patio de los Naranjos, where the ablution fountains gurgled with water, was the oasis.

Abd ar-Rahman I's initial mosque was a square split into two rectangular halves: a covered prayer hall and an open ablutions courtyard. His prayer hall – the area immediately inside the door by which visitors enter today – was divided into 11 'naves' by lines of arches striped in red brick and white stone. The columns of these arches were a mishmash of material collected from the earlier church on the site, Córdoba's Roman buildings and places as far away as Constantinople. To raise the ceiling high enough to create a sense of openness, inventive builders came up with the idea of a two-tier construction, using taller columns as a base and planting shorter ones on top.

Later enlargements of the mosque, southward by Abd ar-Rahman II in the 9th century and Al-Hakim II in the 960s, and eastward by Al-Mansur in the 970s, extended it to an area of nearly 14,400 sq metres, making it one of the biggest mosques in the world. The arcades' simplicity and number give a sense of endlessness to the Mezquita.

The final Mezquita had 19 doors along its north side, filling it with light and yielding a sense of openness. Nowadays, only one door sheds light into the dim interior, dampening the vibrant effect of the red-and-white double arches. Christian additions to the building, such as the solid mass of the cathedral in the centre and the 50 or so chapels around the fringes, further enclose and impose on the airy space.

➡ **Mihrab & Maksura**

Like Abd ar-Rahman II a century earlier, Al-Hakim II in the 960s lengthened the naves of the prayer hall, creating a new

Mezquita

TIMELINE

600 Foundation of a Christian church, the Basilica of San Vicente, on the site of the present Mezquita.

785 Salvaging Visigothic and Roman ruins, Emir Abd ar-Rahman I replaces the church with a *mezquita* (mosque).

833–56 Mosque enlarged by Abd ar-Rahman II.

951–2 A new minaret is built by Abd ar-Rahman III.

962–71 Mosque enlarged, and superb new **mihrab ❶** added, by Al-Hakim II.

978–9 Mosque enlarged for the last time by Al-Mansur, who also enlarged the courtyard (now the **Patio de los Naranjos ❷**), bringing the whole complex to its current dimensions.

1236 Mosque converted into a Christian church after Córdoba is recaptured by Fernando III of Castilla.

1271 Instead of destroying the mosque, the Christians modify it, creating the **Capilla de Villaviciosa ❸** and **Capilla Real ❹**.

1523 Work on a Gothic/Renaissance-style cathedral inside the Mezquita begins, with permission of Carlos I. 'You have destroyed something unique in the world,' the king laments on seeing the finished work.

1593–1664 The 10th-century minaret is reinforced and rebuilt as a Renaissance-baroque **belltower ❺**.

2004 Spanish Muslims petition to be able to worship in the Mezquita again. The Vatican doesn't consent.

TOP TIPS

» **Among the oranges** The Patio de los Naranjos can be enjoyed free of charge at any time.

» **Early birds** Entry to the rest of the Mezquita is offered free every morning, except Sunday, between 8.30am and 9.30am.

» **Quiet time** Group visits are prohibited before 10am, meaning the building is quieter and more atmospheric in the early morning.

The mihrab
Everything leads to the mosque's greatest treasure – the beautiful prayer niche, in the wall facing Mecca, that was added in the 10th century. Cast your eyes over the gold mosaic cubes crafted by imported Byzantium sculptors.

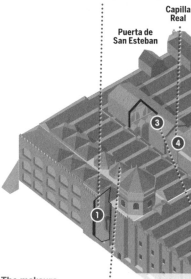

Capilla Real

Puerta de San Esteban

The maksura
Guiding you towards the mihrab, the maksura is a former royal enclosure where the caliphs and their retinues prayed. Its lavish, elaborate arches were designed to draw the eye of worshippers towards the mihrab and Mecca.

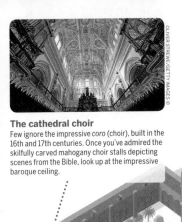

The cathedral choir

Few ignore the impressive *coro* (choir), built in the 16th and 17th centuries. Once you've admired the skilfully carved mahogany choir stalls depicting scenes from the Bible, look up at the impressive baroque ceiling.

Puerta del Perdón

❺

Belltower

Reopened to visitors in 2014 after a 24-year restoration, the 54m-tall belltower has the best views in the city. It was built in the 17th century around and above the remains of the Mezquita's 10th-century minaret.

The Mezquita arches

No, you're not hallucinating. The Mezquita's most defining characteristic is its unique terracotta-and-white striped arches that are supported by 856 pillars salvaged from Roman and other ruins. Glimpsed through the dull light they're at once spooky and striking.

❷

Patio de los Naranjos

Abandon architectural preconceptions all ye who enter here. The ablutions area of the former mosque is a shady courtyard embellished with orange trees that acts as the Mezquita's main entry point.

Capilla Mayor

A Christian monument inside an Islamic mosque sounds beautifully ironic, yet here it is: a Gothic high chapel sanctioned by Carlos I in the 16th century and planted in the middle of the world's third-largest mosque.

Capilla de Villaviciosa

Sift through the building's numerous chapels till you find this gem, an early Christian modification which fused existing Moorish features with Gothic arches and pillars. It served as the Capilla Mayor until the 1520s.

kiblah wall (indicating the direction of Mecca) and mihrab (prayer niche) at the south end. The bay immediately in front of the mihrab and the bays to each side form the *maksura,* the area where the caliphs and courtiers would have prayed. The mihrab and *maksura* are the most beautifully and intricately decorated parts of the whole mosque.

The greatest glory of Al-Hakim II's extension was the portal of the mihrab – a crescent arch with a rectangular surround known as an *alfíz.* For the portal's decoration, Al-Hakim asked the emperor of Byzantium, Nicephoras II Phocas, to send him a mosaicist capable of imitating the superb mosaics of the Great Mosque of Damascus, one of the great 8th-century Syrian Omayyad buildings. The Christian emperor sent the Muslim caliph not only a mosaicist but also a gift of 1600kg of gold mosaic cubes. Shaped into flower motifs and inscriptions from the Quran, this gold is what gives the mihrab portal its magical glitter. Inside the mihrab, a single block of white marble sculpted into the shape of a scallop shell, a symbol of the Quran, forms the dome that amplified the voice of the imam (the person who leads Islamic worship services) throughout the mosque.

The arches of the *maksura* are the mosque's most intricate and sophisticated, forming a forest of interwoven, lavishly decorated horseshoe shapes. Equally attractive are the *maksura*'s skylit domes, decorated with star-patterned stone vaulting. Each dome was held up by four interlocking pairs of parallel ribs, a highly advanced technique in 10th-century Europe.

➡ **Cathedral**

Following the Christian conquest of Córdoba in 1236, the Mezquita was used as a cathedral but remained largely unaltered for nearly three centuries. But in the 16th-century King Carlos I gave the cathedral authorities permission to rip out the centre of the Mezquita in order to construct the Capilla Mayor (the main altar area) and *coro* (choir).

Legend has it that when the king saw the result he was horrified, exclaiming: 'You have destroyed something unique in the world.' The cathedral took nearly 250 years to complete (1523–1766) and thus exhibits a range of architectural fashions, from plateresque and late Renaissance to extravagant Spanish baroque. Among the later features are the Capilla Mayor's rich 17th-century jasper and red-marble retable (altar screen), and the fine mahogany stalls in the choir, carved in the 18th century by Pedro Duque Cornejo.

◉ **Around the Mezquita**

★ **Alcázar de los Reyes Cristianos**   FORTRESS, GARDENS
(Fortress of the Christian Monarchs; www.alcazardelosreyescristianos.cordoba.es; Campo Santo de

---

CÓRDOBA'S PATIOS

Studded with pots of geraniums, with bougainvillea cascading down the walls and a trickling fountain in the middle, the famed patios of Córdoba have provided shade and cool during the searing heat of summer for centuries. The origin of these much-loved courtyards probably lies in the Roman atrium (open spaces inside buildings). The tradition was continued by the Arabs, for whom the internal courtyard was an area where women went about their family life and household jobs. The addition of a central fountain and multitudes of plants heightened the sensation of coolness.

Beautiful patios can be glimpsed – often tantalisingly, through closed wrought-iron gates – in Córdoba's Judería and many other parts of town. They are at their prettiest in spring, and happily dozens of them open up for free public viewing during the popular Fiesta de los Patios de Córdoba (p206).

Asociación de Amigos de los Patios Cordobeses (Calle San Basilio 44; ⊙ 11am-2pm & 5.30-8pm, closed Tue Nov-Feb & Sun evening year-round) This particularly lovely patio, dripping with bougainvillea and other blooms, can be visited free year-round.

Ruta de Patios del Alcázar Viejo (www.patiosdelalcazarviejo.com; Calle San Basilio 14; admission €6; ⊙ 11am-2pm & 5-8pm Wed-Mon Mar-Apr & Oct, 11am-2pm & 6-9pm Wed-Mon May, Jun & 2nd half Sep, 11am-2pm & 5-8pm Fri-Mon Nov–mid-Dec, closed Jul–mid-Sep, mid-Dec–Feb & Sun evenings year-round) Offers the chance to enter six patios in the Alcázar Viejo district outside of the patio festival season.

Los Mártires; admission 8.30am-2.30pm €4.50, other times incl water, light & sound show adult/child €7/free; ☺ 8.30am-8.45pm Tue-Fri, to 4.30pm Sat, to 2.30pm Sun Sep-Jun, to 3pm Tue-Sun Jul-Aug; ♿) Built under Castilian rule in the 13th and 14th centuries on the remains of a Moorish predecessor, this fort-cum-palace hosted both Fernando and Isabel, who made their first acquaintance with Columbus here in 1486. One hall displays some remarkable Roman mosaics, dug up from the Plaza de la Corredera in the 1950s. The Alcázar's terraced gardens – full of fish ponds, fountains, orange trees and flowers – are a delight to stroll around.

While you're here it's also interesting to visit the nearby **Baños del Alcázar Califal** (Campo Santo de los Mártires; admission €2.50; ☺ 8.30am-8.45pm Tue-Fri, to 4.30pm Sat, to 2.30pm Sun mid-Sep–mid-Jun, to 3pm Tue-Sat, to 2.30pm Sun mid-Jun–mid-Sep), the impressive 10th-century bathhouse of the Moorish Alcázar.

Puente Romano   BRIDGE

Spanning the Río Guadalquivir just below the Mezquita, the handsome, 16-arched Roman bridge formed part of the ancient Via Augusta, which ran from Girona in Catalonia to Cádiz. Rebuilt several times down the centuries, it's now traffic free and makes for a lovely stroll.

Torre de la Calahorra   MUSEUM

(📞957 29 39 29; www.torrecalahorra.com; Puente Romano; adult/child incl audioguide €4.50/3; ☺ 10am-7pm Oct-Apr, to 8.30pm May-Sep) At the south end of the Puente Romano stands this squat tower, erected under Islamic rule. It now houses the Museo Vivo de Al-Andalus, a museum highlighting the cultural achievements of Al-Andalus. You need the audioguide to make the most of it.

◎ Judería

The old Jewish quarter west and north of the Mezquita is a labyrinth of narrow streets and small squares, whitewashed buildings and wrought-iron gates allowing glimpses of plant-filled patios. Some streets are now choked with gaudy souvenir shops and tourist-oriented restaurants, but others remain quiet and unblemished. The importance of the medieval Jewish community is illustrated by the Judería's proximity to the Mezquita and the city's centres of power. Spain had one of Europe's biggest Jewish communities, recorded from as early as the

2nd century AD. Persecuted by the Visigoths, they allied themselves with the Muslims following the Arab conquests. By the 10th century they were established among the most dynamic members of society, holding posts as administrators, doctors, jurists, philosophers and poets. One of the greatest Jewish theologians, Maimonides, was born in Córdoba in 1135, though he left with his family at an early age to escape Almohad persecution, eventually settling in Egypt. His magnum opus, the *Mishne Torah,* summarised the teachings of Judaism and systematised all Jewish law.

Sinagoga   SYNAGOGUE

(Calle de los Judíos 20; EU citizen/other free/€0.30; ☺ 9am-3.30pm Tue-Sun mid-Jun–mid-Sep, to 7.30pm Tue-Sat mid-Sep–mid-Jun) Constructed in 1315, this small, probably private or family synagogue is one of the few testaments to the Jewish presence in medieval Andalucía, though it hasn't been used as a place of worship since the expulsion of Jews in 1492. Decorated with extravagant stuccowork that includes Hebrew inscriptions and intricate Mudéjar star and plant patterns, it has an upper gallery reserved for women.

Casa de Sefarad   MUSEUM

(www.casadesefarad.es; Cnr Calles de los Judíos & Averroes; admission €4; ☺ 10am-6pm Mon-Sat, 11am-6pm Sun) In the heart of the Judería, and once connected by tunnel to the Sinagoga, the Casa de Sefarad is an interesting museum is devoted to the Sephardic (Iberian Peninsula Jewish) tradition. Different rooms cover food, domestic crafts, ritual, music, prominent Jews of Córdoba and the Inquisition. There's also a section on women intellectuals (poets, artists and thinkers) of Al-Andalus.

Casa Ramón García Romero   HANDICRAFTS

(Plaza Agrupación de Cofradías; admission free; ☺ 11am-2pm & 4.30-8pm Mon-Sat) A display of beautiful embossed-leather work (one of Córdoba's traditional crafts), reviving techniques used by 10th-century Omayyad artisans.

◎ Other Areas

★ Centro Flamenco Fosforito   MUSEUM

(📞957 47 68 29; www.centroflamencofosforito.cordoba.es; Plaza del Potro; admission €2; ☺ 8.30am-7.30pm Tue-Fri, 8.30am-2.30pm Sat, 9.30am-2.30pm Sun) Possibly the best flamenco museum in Andalucía, the Fosforito centre has exhibits, film and information panels

Córdoba

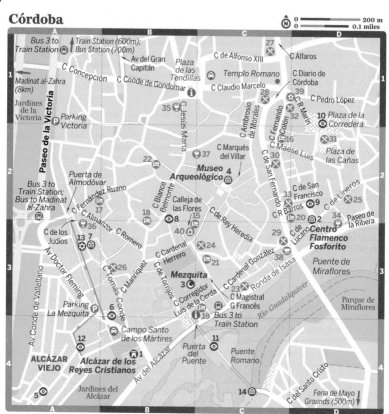

in English and Spanish telling you the history of the guitar and all the flamenco greats. Touch-screen videos demonstrate the important techniques of flamenco song, guitar, dance and percussion – you can test your skill at beating out the *compás* (rhythm) of different *palos* (song forms). Regular live flamenco performances are held here too.

The museum benefits from a fantastic location inside the Posada del Potro, a legendary inn that played a part in *Don Quijote,* where Cervantes described it as a 'den of thieves'. The famous square it stands on, once a horse market, features a lovely 16th-century stone fountain topped by a rearing *potro* (colt).

Museo Julio Romero de Torres
ART

(Plaza del Potro 1; admission €4.50; 8.30am-8.45pm Tue-Fri, to 4.30pm Sat, to 2.30pm Sun) A former hospital houses what is, surprisingly enough, Córdoba's most visited museum, devoted to much-loved local painter Julio

Romero de Torres (1874–1930), who is famed for his paintings expressing his sense of Andalucian female beauty. He was also much inspired by flamenco and bullfighting.

★ Museo Arqueológico
MUSEUM

(Plaza de Jerónimo Páez 7; EU citizen/other free/€1.50; 9am-7.30pm Tue-Sat, to 3.30pm Sun mid-Sep–mid-Jun, 9am-3.30pm Tue-Sun mid-Jun–mid-Sep) The excellent Archaeological Museum traces Córdoba's many changes in size, appearance and lifestyle from pre-Roman to early Reconquista times, with some fine sculpture, an impressive coin collection, and interesting exhibits on domestic life and religion. In the basement you can walk through the excavated remains of the city's Roman theatre.

Templo Romano
TEMPLE

(Calle Claudio Marcelo) Though generally not open to visitors, this 1st-century AD Roman temple can be viewed perfectly well from the street. Its 11 tall white columns make a strik-

Córdoba

⊙ Top Sights
1 Alcázar de los Reyes
   Cristianos.. B4
2 Centro Flamenco Fosforito D2
3 Mezquita B3
4 Museo Arqueológico C2

⊙ Sights
5 Asociación de Amigos de los
   Patios Cordobeses A4
6 Baños del Alcázar Califal B3
7 Casa de Sefarad................................. A3
8 Casa Ramón García Romero............... B2
9 Museo Julio Romero de
   Torres.. D2
10 Plaza de la Corredera.......................... D1
11 Puente Romano................................... C4
12 Ruta de Patios del Alcázar
   Viejo... A4
13 Sinagoga... A3
14 Torre de la Calahorra C4

⊜ Sleeping
15 Balcón de Córdoba.............................. B3
16 Casa de los Azulejos........................... C2
17 Hospedería Alma Andalusí.................. A2
18 Hospedería del Atalia B2
19 Hotel Hacienda Posada de
   Vallina.. C3

20 Hotel Maestre D2
21 Hotel Mezquita C3
22 Option Be Hostel B2

⊗ Eating
23 Amaltea C3
24 Bar Santos.. C3
25 Bodegas Campos D2
26 Casa Mazal.. B3
27 Delorean Bar de Tapas C1
28 El Astronauta C1
29 Garum 2.1 .... C3
30 La Boca... C2
31 Mercado de la Corredera D2
32 Taberna Salinas.................................. C1
33 Taberna Sociedad de Plateros C2

⊖ Drinking & Nightlife
34 Amapola D3
35 Bar Correo.. B1
36 Bodega Guzmán.................................. A3
37 Califa.. C2
38 La Bicicleta... C3

⊙ Entertainment
39 Jazz Café C1

⊜ Shopping
40 Meryan B3

ing sight, especially when floodlit. The band of cats that hangs out here must be the most photographed cats in Spain.

Plaza de la Corredera   PLAZA
This grand 17th-century square has an elaborate history as a site of public spectacles. It was the site of Córdoba's Roman circus (for horse races and other spectacles) and later of bullfights and Inquisition burnings. Nowadays it's ringed by balconied apartments and is home to an assortment of popular, though culinarily run-of-the-mill, cafes and restaurants. The **Mercado de la Corredera** (⊙ 8am-2.30pm Mon-Sat) is a busy morning food market selling all kinds of fresh produce.

Palacio de Viana   MUSEUM
(www.palaciodeviana.com; Plaza de Don Gome 2; admission whole house/patios €8/5; ⊙ 10am-7pm Tue-Sat, to 3pm Sun Sep-Jun, 9am-3pm Tue-Sun Jul & Aug) A stunning Renaissance palace set around 12 beautiful patios, the Viana Palace is a particular delight to visit in spring. Occupied by the aristocratic Marqueses de Viana until 1980, the large building is packed with art and antiques. The whole-house charge covers a one-hour guided tour of the

rooms and access to the patios and garden. It's an 800m walk northeast from Plaza de las Tendillas.

★ Madinat al-Zahra   ARCHAEOLOGICAL SITE
(Medina Azahara; ☑ 957 10 49 33; www.museos-deandalucia.es; Carretera Palma del Río Km 5.5; EU citizen/other free/€1.50; ⊙ 9am-7.30pm Tue-Sat Apr–mid-Jun, to 3.30pm mid-Jun–mid-Sep, to 5.30pm mid-Sep–Mar, 9am-3.30pm Sun year-round; ℗) Eight kilometres west of Córdoba stands what's left of Madinat al-Zahra, the sumptuous palace-city built by Caliph Abd al-Rahman III in the 10th century. The complex spills down a hillside with the caliph's palace (the area you visit today) on the highest levels overlooking what were gardens and open fields. The residential areas (still unexcavated) were set away to each side. A fascinating modern museum has been installed below the site.

Legend has it that Abd al-Rahman III built Madinat al-Zahra for his favourite wife, Az-Zahra. Dismayed by her homesickness and yearnings for the snowy mountains of Syria, he surrounded his new city with almond and cherry trees, replacing snowflakes with fluffy white blossoms. More realistically, it was probably Abd al-Rahman's rivalry with the Fatimid dynasty in North Africa that drove him to declare his caliphate in 929 and construct, as caliphs were wont to do, a new capital. Building started in 940 and chroniclers record some staggering construction statistics: 10,000 labourers set 6000 stone blocks a day, with outer walls stretching 1518m east to west and 745m north to south.

It is almost inconceivable to think that such a city, built over 35 years, was to last only a few more before the usurper Al-Mansur transferred government to a new palace complex of his own in 981. Then, between 1010 and 1013, Madinat al-Zahra was wrecked by Berber soldiers. During succeeding centuries its ruins were plundered repeatedly for building materials.

The visitors' route takes you down through the city's original northern gate. Highlights of the visitable area are the grand arched Edificio Basilical Superior, which housed the main state admin offices, and the Casa de Yafar, believed to have been residence of the caliph's prime minister. The crown jewel of the site, the royal reception hall known as the Salón de Abd al-Rahman III, was closed for restoration at the time of writing. This hall has exquisitely carved stuccowork and is said to have been decorated with gold and silver tiles, arches of ivory and ebony, and walls of multicoloured marble.

The museum, 2km downhill by road from the site entrance, takes you through the history of Madinat al-Zahra, with sections on its origins, planning and construction, its inhabitants and its eventual downfall. The sections are illustrated with beautifully displayed pieces from the site and some excellent interactive displays, and complemented by flawless English translations.

Drivers should leave Córdoba westward along Avenida de Medina Azahara. This feeds into the A431 road, with the turn-off to Madinat al-Zahra signposted after 6km. You must park at the museum and get tickets there for the site and the shuttle bus (*lanzadera;* €2.10 return) which takes you 2km up to the site.

A bus to Madinat al-Zahra leaves from a stop near Córdoba's Puerta de Almodóvar at 10.15am and 11am daily, 4.15pm Tuesday to Saturday and 11.45am Sunday (€8.50 return including the shuttle from museum to site and back). Tickets for the bus must be bought in advance at the Centro de Visitantes (p210)

or at the tourist offices at the train station (p210) or Plaza de las Tendillas (p210).

✦ Festivals & Events

Spring and early summer – especially May, when the weather is at its most glorious – are Córdoba's chief festival times.

Semana Santa · HOLY WEEK
(🕓 Mar/Apr) Every evening from Palm Sunday to Good Friday, up to 12 *pasos* (platforms bearing sacred statues from churches) are carried through the city, accompanied and watched by large crowds of the faithful.

All routes include a section called the *carrera oficial* (official trail), where the thickest crowds gather. Most *pasos* reach the *carrera oficial* between 7pm and 11pm. From 2016 the *carrera oficial* is expected to be the streets around the Mezquita (previously it was focused on Plaza de las Tendillas).

Cruces de Mayo · LOCAL FIESTA
(May Crosses; 🕓 early May) Crosses adorned with flowers and Manila shawls are set up in about 50 plazas and streets. The plazas too are decorated, drink and tapas stalls are set up, and the whole thing turns into a neighbourhood party with music and dancing. Wednesday to Sunday of the first week of May, peaking on the Friday night and Saturday.

Fiesta de los Patios de Córdoba · PATIOS
(www.patios.cordoba.es; 🕓 early May) This 'best patio' competition sees many of Córdoba's beautiful private courtyards open for public viewing till 10pm nightly. A concurrent cultural program stages flamenco and other concerts in some of the city's grandest patios and plazas. The festival runs for two weeks, starting in early May.

Feria de Mayo · SPRING FAIR
(May Fair; 🕓 last week May) A massive weeklong party takes over the Arenal area near the river with music, Sevillana dancing, horses, carriages, traditional dress, fireworks and loads of fun.

Festival de la Guitarra de Córdoba · MUSIC
(www.guitarracordoba.org; 🕓 1st half Jul) A two-week celebration of the guitar, with live performances of classical, flamenco, rock, blues and more by top Spanish and international names in Córdoba's theatres.

🛏 Sleeping

Córdoba's many accommodation options span the spectrum from economy to deluxe. Even some of the lower-end places offer elegantly styled and spacious rooms, while others are laden with antiques and history. Booking ahead during the main festivals is essential. We quote prices for the main tourist seasons of approximately April, May, September and October. Expect to pay more during Semana Santa and the May festivals and on some weekends, but less in July, August and the depths of winter.

⭐ Bed and Be   HOSTEL €

(☏ 661 42 07 33; www.bedandbe.com; Calle Cruz Conde 22; dm €17-20, d with shared bathroom €50-80; ❋ ⎙) 🍃 An exceptionally good hostel option a bit north of Plaza de las Tendillas. Staff are clued up about what's on and what's new in Córdoba, and they offer a social event every evening – anything from a bike tour to a sushi dinner. The assortment of double and dorm rooms are all super-clean and as gleaming white as a *pueblo blanco* (white town).

Extra value is added by the great roof terrace, bicycle rental (€6/10 per three/six hours) and communal kitchen and lounge area.

The new, contemporary-design Option Be Hostel (www.bedandbe.com; Calle Leiva Aguilar 1; dm €15-25, d €20-40; ❋ ⎙), run by the same people along similar lines but with mostly private bathrooms, should be open in the historic centre by the time you get there.

Hospedería Alma Andalusí   HOTEL €

(☏ 957 76 08 88; www.almaandalusi.com; Calle Fernández Ruano 5; r €50-60; ❋ ⎙) This guesthouse in a quiet section of the Judería (the old Jewish quarter) has been brilliantly converted from an ancient structure into a stylish, modern establishment, while rates have been kept down. There's an appealing floral theme throughout. Thoughtfully chosen furnishings, polished wood floors and blue-and-white colour schemes make for a comfortable base.

Hotel Maestre   HOTEL €

(☏ 957 47 24 10; www.hotelmaestre.com; Calle Romero Barros 4-6; d €55-65; P ❋ ⎙) Within easy reach of the Mezquita and some good restaurants, the Maestre is popular, efficiently run and well priced. Rooms are medium-sized and fairly plain, but clean and comfy. The three patios, and walls full of art, add light and colour, and there's parking (€10) right on the spot.

Hospedería del Atalia   BOUTIQUE HOTEL €€

(☏ 957 49 66 59; www.hospederiadelatalia.com; Calle Buen Pastor 19; r €70-160; ste €170-260; ❋ ⎙) Entered from a quiet patio in the Judería, the Atalia sports elegant, contemporary, owner-designed rooms in burgundies, russets and olive greens. Good breakfasts with a wide choice are €6, and there's a super sunny roof terrace with chairs, tables and a Mezquita view.

Casa de los Azulejos   HOTEL €€

(☏ 957 47 00 00; www.casadelosazulejos.com; Calle Fernando Colón 5; incl breakfast s €78, d €89-134; ❋ @ ⎙ ⎙) Mexican and Andalucian styles converge in this stylish nine-room hotel, where the patio is all banana trees, ferns and potted palms bathed in sunlight. Colonial-style rooms feature tall antique doors, big beds, walls in lilac and sky blue, and floors adorned with the beautiful old *azulejos* (tiles) that give the place its name.

Hotel Mezquita   HOTEL €€

(☏ 957 47 55 85; www.hotelmezquita.com; Plaza Santa Catalina 1; s €50-65, d €65-140; ❋ ⎙) This former mansion stands directly opposite its namesake monument and sports a broad miscellany of art and antiques in its common areas. There are some large, elegant rooms with marble floors and balconies overlooking the great mosque, and some smaller quarters in an interior wing.

Hotel Hacienda Posada de Vallina HOTEL €€

(☏ 957 49 87 50; www.hhposadadevallina.es; Calle Corregidor Luís de la Cerda 83; r €70-100; P ❋ @ ⎙) In an enviable nook on the quiet side of the Mezquita, this cleverly renovated hotel uses portraits and period furniture to enhance a plush and modern interior. There are two levels overlooking a salubrious patio, and the rooms make you feel comfortable but in-period (ie medieval Córdoba). Those upstairs are a bit airier. Columbus allegedly once stayed here.

Hotel Hesperia Córdoba   HOTEL €€

(☏ 957 42 10 42; www.hesperia.com; Avenida Fray Albino 1; s €47-139, d €55-164; P ❋ @ ⎙ ⎙) The chief advantage of this luxury franchise across the river, near the Puente Romano, is the brilliant view from some of the rooms and from the roof terrace and bar. Rooms in the hotel's new wing are larger and more modern, but lack the views.

★ **Balcón de Córdoba**   BOUTIQUE HOTEL €€€
(☏957 49 84 78; www.balcondecordoba.com; Calle Encarnación 8; r incl breakfast €120-200; ❄🌐) Offering top-end boutique luxury, the 10-room Balcón is a riveting place with a charming *cordobés* patio, slick rooms, antique doorways, and ancient stone relics dotted around as if it were a wing of the nearby archaeological museum. Service doesn't miss a beat and the rooms have tasteful, soothing, contemporary decor with a little art but no clutter.

The roof terrace affords great views across the rooftops to the Mezquita, and the classy restaurant does a carefully prepared selection of Cordoban-cum-global dishes.

✖ Eating

Córdoba's signature dish is *salmorejo,* a delicious, thick, chilled soup of blended tomatoes, garlic, bread, lemon, vinegar and olive oil, sprinkled with hard-boiled egg and strips of ham. Along with *rabo de toro* (bull's tail stew), it appears on every menu. There's traditional meaty and fishy Andalucian fare aplenty here – but also a good sprinkling of creative contemporary eateries putting successful fresh twists on Spanish and Mediterranean ingredients. Don't miss the wine from nearby Montilla and Moriles.

Taberna Salinas   ANDALUCIAN €
(www.tabernasalinas.com; Calle Tundidores 3; raciones €7-8; ☉12.30-4pm & 8-11.30pm Mon-Sat, closed Aug) A historic bar-restaurant (since 1879), with a patio and several rooms, Salinas is adorned in classic Córdoba fashion with tiles, wine barrels, art and photos of bullfighter Manolete. It's popular with tourists (and offers a five-language menu), but it retains a traditional atmosphere and the waiters are very helpful. Not least, the food is very good, from the orange-and-cod salad to the pork loin in hazelnut sauce.

Bar Santos   TAPAS €
(Calle Magistral González Francés 3; tortilla €2; ☉10am-midnight) Most restaurants close to the Mezquita are geared to an undiscriminating tourist market. But this legendary little bar serves the best *tortilla de patata* (potato omelette) in town – and don't the *cordobeses* know it. Thick wedges are deftly cut from giant wheels of the stuff and customarily served with plastic forks on paper plates to eat outside under the Mezquita's walls. Don't miss it.

Taberna Sociedad de Plateros   ANDALUCIAN €
(☏957 47 00 42; Calle de San Francisco 6; tapas €2-2.25, raciones €5-10; ☉noon-4pm & 8pm-midnight Tue-Sat, noon-4pm Sun) Run by the silversmiths' guild, this well-loved traditional bar-cum-restaurant serves a selection of generous tapas and *raciones* (full plates of tapas items) in its light, glass-roofed patio. The seafood selection is particularly good, highlighted by such items as *bacalao rebozado* (breaded cod) and *salpicón de mariscos* (shellfish salad).

Delorean Bar de Tapas   TAPAS €
(Calle de Alfonso XIII; tapas €1.20; ☉8.30am-4pm & 8pm-1am Mon-Fri, noon-4pm & 8pm-1am Sat; 🌐) Makes sense that the cheapest tapas in town are amid the alternative club zone. You get a generous tapa free with every drink, and only pay for any extra ones. Tasty offerings include mushroom quesadillas, and fried egg with chips and spicy *chistorra* sausage.

★ **La Boca**   FUSION €€
(☏957 47 61 40; www.restaurantelaboca.com; Calle San Fernando 39; mains €10-15; ☉noon-midnight Wed-Sun, to 5pm Mon) Trendy for a reason, this cutting-edge eatery whips up exciting global variations from traditional ingredients, then presents them in eye-catching ways: Iberian pork cheeks with red curry and basmati? Battered cod chunks with almonds and garlic? It's very well done, though portions are not for giant appetites. Reservations advisable at weekends.

★ **Garum 2.1**   CONTEMPORARY ANDALUCIAN €€
(Calle San Fernando 122; tapas €3-7, raciones €7-17; ☉noon-4pm & 8pm-midnight, to 2am Fri & Sat) Garum serves up traditional meaty, fishy and veggie ingredients in all sorts of creative, tasty new concoctions. We recommend the *presa ibérica con herencia del maestro* (Iberian pork with potatoes, fried eggs and ham). Service is helpful and friendly.

★ **Bodegas Campos**   ANDALUCIAN €€
(☏957 49 75 00; www.bodegascampos.com; Calle de Lineros 32; mains & raciones €11-23; ☉1.30-4.30pm daily, 8-11.30pm Mon-Sat) This atmospheric warren of rooms and patios is popular with smartly dressed *cordobeses.* The restaurant and more informal *taberna* (tavern) serve up delicious dishes, putting a slight creative twist on traditional Andalucian fare – the likes of cod-and-cuttlefish ravioli or pork sirloin in grape sauce. Campos also produces its own house Montilla.

★ **El Astronauta** MEDITERRANEAN €€
(☎957 49 11 23; www.elastronauta.es; Calle Diario de Córdoba 18; medias-raciones €5.50-8.50, raciones €9-17; ⏰1.30-5pm & 8pm-late Mon-Thu, 1.30pm-late Fri & Sat; ☝) The Astronauta produces a galaxy of Mediterranean dishes with an emphasis on fresh, healthy ingredients: zesty salads, mezes, lamb moussaka, vegetarian burgers and much more. The decor is cosmic, the vibe alternative and the local clientele loyal.

Amaltea FUSION, VEGETARIAN €€
(☎957 49 19 68; Ronda de Isasa 10; mains €12-18; ⏰1-4pm & 8pm-late Mon-Sat, 1-4pm Sun; ☝) ✈
The best of a growing number of eateries along the riverside Ronda de Isasa, Amaltea specialises in organic food and wine. There's a good mix of Spanish, Mediterranean, Middle Eastern and Asian dishes, including plenty of vegetarian and gluten-free fare.

Casa Mazal JEWISH, ANDALUCIAN €€
(☎957 94 18 88; www.casamazal.com; Calle Tomás Conde 3; mains €9-20; ⏰12.30-4pm & 7.30-11pm; ☝) A meal here makes a fine complement to the nearby Casa de Sefarad museum, as it brings the Sephardic tradition to the table, along with some *andalusí* (Moorish) dishes. Sephardic cuisine has diverse roots in Al-Andalus, Turkey, Italy and North Africa, with such varied items as Syrian lentil-and-rice salad, an array of couscous options, and *seniyeh* lamb pie on the menu.

There are regular recitals of Sephardic, *andalusí* or early Spanish music too.

🍷 Drinking & Entertainment

Córdoba has a great range of places to drink. If you're searching for authentic flamenco, the Centro Flamenco Fosforito (p203) stages regular events and is a good place to ask about what else is coming up.

★ **La Bicicleta** CAFE, BAR
(☎666 544690; Calle Cardenal González 1; ⏰10am-late Mon-Fri, noon-late Sat & Sun) ✈ This friendly, informal bar welcomes cyclists (and anyone else who's thirsty) with an array of drinks, tasty snacks (light dishes €4–€9) and – best of all – long, cool, multifruit juices. There's 20% off some drinks if you come by bike!

★ **Bodega Guzmán** WINE BAR
(Calle de los Judíos 7; ⏰noon-4pm & 8.15-11.45pm Fri-Wed) This atmospheric Judería drinking spot bedecked with bullfighting memorabilia is frequented by both locals and tourists.

Montilla wine is dispensed from three giant barrels behind the bar: don't leave without trying some *amargoso* (bitter).

Califa PUB
(www.cervezascalifa.com; Calle Juan Valera 3; ⏰noon-4pm & 7pm-midnight Mon-Thu, noon-late Fri & Sat, noon-4pm Sun) These enterprising Córdoba lads have opened one of the region's first craft beer pubs, challenging the hegemony of the Cruzcampos and San Miguels. In fact, it's more accurately described as a brewpub, as they concoct the ale on the premises. Try their Rubia, Morena, IPA or Sultana stout varieties – or select from two dozen other craft ales from around Spain.

Amapola MUSIC BAR
(www.facebook.com/amapolacordoba; Paseo de la Ribera 9; ⏰5pm-3am Mon-Thu, noon-4am Fri-Sun) The artiest bar in the riverside area, with a semigrunge feel, elaborate cocktails and a great terrace looking down to the river.

Bar Correo BAR
(Calle Jesús María 2; ⏰noon-3.30pm & 7.30-11pm Mon-Fri, noon-3.30pm Sat & Sun) Why does this tiny tiled bar just off Plaza de las Tendillas attract throngs of beer drinkers every evening? Hard to say, but it's a tradition going back to the bar's origins in 1931. The friendly staff welcome foreign visitors.

Jazz Café LIVE MUSIC
(www.facebook.com/joseluis.cabello1?fref=ts; Calle Rodríguez Marín; ⏰from 9pm; ☎) An enticing music den decked with musical paraphernalia, Jazz Café stages blues jams on Thursdays and jazz jams on Tuesdays (both from 10pm), plus other live acts as and when. It rocks on until the wee hours; on Fridays and Saturdays you may find DJs spinning soul or funk.

🛍 Shopping

Córdoba's time-honoured craft specialities are colourful embossed leather *(cuero repujado)*, silver jewellery and some attractive pottery. The embossed leather is also known as *guadamecí* (sheepskin) or *cordobán* (goatskin). Calles Cardenal González and Manríquez have some of the classier craft shops.

Meryan HANDICRAFTS
(☎957 47 59 02; Calleja de las Flores 2; ⏰9am-8pm Mon-Fri, to 2pm Sat) Has a particularly good range of embossed-leather goods: wallets, bags, boxes, notebooks, even copies of Picasso paintings.

ⓘ Information

Córdoba (www.cordobaturismo.es) Tourist information for the province.

Centro de Visitantes (Visitors Centre; ☏957 35 51 79; www.andalucia.org; Plaza del Triunfo; ☺9am-7.30pm Mon-Fri, 9.30am-3pm Sat & Sun) The main tourist-information centre, with an exhibit on Córdoba's history, and some Roman and Visigothic remains downstairs.

Municipal Tourist Information Kiosk (☏902 20 17 74; www.turismodecordoba.org; Plaza de las Tendillas; ☺9am-2pm & 5-7.30pm)

Municipal Tourist Information Office (☏902 20 17 74; www.turismodecordoba.org; train station; ☺9am-2pm & 4.30-7pm) In the station's main entry hall.

ⓘ Getting There & Away

TRAIN

Córdoba's modern **train station** (www.renfe.com; Glorieta de las Tres Culturas), 1.2km northwest of Plaza de las Tendillas, is served both by fast AVE services and by some slower regional trains.

TO	COST (€)	DURATION	FREQUENCY
Andújar	10-16	50min	5 daily
Antequera	19-33	30-40min	17 daily
Granada	38	2¾hr	6 daily
Jaén	15	1¾hr	4 daily
Madrid	38-71	1¾-2hr	30 daily
Málaga	27-41	1hr	17 daily
Seville	14-30	45-80min	35 daily

ⓘ Getting Around

BICYCLE

There are bicycle lanes throughout the city, though they're little used.

Solobici (☏957 48 57 66; www.solobici.net; Calle María Cristina 5; per 3hr/5hr/day €6/10/15; ☺10am-2pm daily, 6-9pm Mon-Fri) Rents bikes for city and out-of-town riding.

BUS

Bus 3 (€1.30, every 12 to 20 minutes), from the west end of Avenida Vía Augusta (the street between the train and bus stations), runs down Calle Diario de Córdoba and Calle de San Fer-

BUSES FROM CÓRDOBA

Bus Station (☏957 40 40 40; www.estacionautobusescordoba.es; Avenida Vía Augusta) It's located behind the train station, 1.3km northwest of Plaza de las Tendillas.

Alsa (☏902 42 22 42; www.alsa.es)

Autocares Carrera (☏957 50 16 32; www.autocarescarrera.es)

Autocares San Sebastián (☏957 42 90 30; www.autocaressansebastian.es)

Socibus (☏902 22 92 92; www.socibus.es)

Transportes Ureña (☏957 40 45 58; http://urena-sa.com)

TO	BUS COMPANY	COST (€)	DURATION	FREQUENCY
Almodóvar del Río	Autocares San Sebastián	1	30min	up to 10 daily
Baena	Autocares Carrera	5.50	1hr	8 daily
Baeza	Alsa	12	2½hr	2 daily
Granada	Alsa	15	2¾hr	8 daily
Hornachuelos	Autocares San Sebastián	2.20	1hr	2-5 daily except Sun
Jaén	Transportes Ureña	10	2hr	4-6 daily
Madrid	Socibus	17	5hr	6 daily
Málaga	Alsa	12	3hr	4 daily
Montilla	Autocares Carrera	3.80	45min	12 daily
Priego de Córdoba	Autocares Carrera	9.20	2hr	7 daily
Seville	Alsa	12	2hr	7 daily
Úbeda	Alsa	12	2¾hr	4 daily
Zuheros	Autocares Carrera	6.50	1¾hr	4 daily

nando, east of the Mezquita. For the return trip, catch it on Ronda de Isasa near the Puente Romano, or from Avenida Doctor Fleming or Paseo de la Victoria.

CAR

The one-way system is nightmarish, and cars are banned from the historic centre unless they are going to park, unload or load at hotels, most of which are reasonably well signposted as you approach. There is free, unmetered parking south of the river across the Puente de Miraflores, and a mixture of free and metered parking on Paseo de la Victoria, Avenida Doctor Fleming and streets to their west. Metered zones (with blue lines along the street) are free of charge from 2pm to 5pm and 9pm to 9am, and on Saturday afternoons and all day Sunday.

TAXI

Taxis from the bus or train stations to the Mezquita cost around €7. In the centre, taxis congregate on Campo Santo de los Mártires and just off Plaza de las Tendillas.

SOUTHERN CÓRDOBA PROVINCE

The rolling countryside south of Córdoba is almost entirely covered in olive trees and grapevines, yielding some of Spain's finest olive oils and the unique, sherrylike Montilla-Moriles wines. Back in the 13th to 15th centuries this region straddled the Islamic-Christian frontier, hence the many towns and villages that cluster around large castles. Towards the southeast, the mountainous Parque Natural Sierras Subbéticas rises up from the lowlands: 320 sq km of high summits, canyons, caves and wooded valleys surrounded by appealing villages and towns such as Zuheros and Priego de Córdoba, great bases for a scenic natural break.

Baena

POP 18,300

This small market town produces olive oil of such high quality it has gained its own Denominación de Origen (DO; a designation that indicates the product's unique geographic origins, production processes and quality). The town's periphery is dotted with huge storage tanks.

◉ Sights

Almazara Núñez de Prado   OLIVE OIL
(☑957 67 01 41; Avenida Cervantes 15; tours free; ⊙ 9am-2pm & 4-6pm Mon-Fri mid-Sep–mid-Jun, 9am-3pm Mon-Fri mid-Jun–mid-Sep; ℗) ⚑ FREE
The best reason for coming to Baena is to visit this working olive-oil mill, run by a family who own around 100,000 olive trees. Olives are hand-picked to prevent bruising, then pulped in ancient stone mills. The mill is one of the few in Spain that still use the traditional stone mills, and is famous for its *flor de aceite,* the oil that seeps naturally from the crushed olives.

Tours are given during opening hours; be there at least one hour before closing time.

You'll see a video about the production process, then tour the mill to see traditional olive-pressing techniques, the modern bottling facility and the old bodega (storage cellar).

Parque Natural Sierras Subbéticas

This 320-sq-km park in the southeast of the province encompasses a set of craggy, emerald-green limestone hills pocked with caves, springs and streams, with some charmingly appealing old villages and small towns set round its periphery. It makes for some lovely exploring among valleys, canyons and high peaks (the highest is 1570m La Tiñosa). Most visitors base themselves in or near picturesque Zuheros or Priego de Córdoba.

The park's visitors center, Centro de Visitantes Santa Rita (☑957 50 69 86; Ctra A339, Km 11.2; ⊙9am-2pm Wed-Fri, 9am-2pm & 6-8pm Sat & Sun May-Jun, 8am-2pm Fri-Sun Jul-Sep, 9am-2pm Wed-Fri, 9am-2pm & 4-6pm Sat-Sun Oct-Apr), is 15km west of Priego. An excellent walking guide is *Walking in the Subbética Natural Park Córdoba* by local resident Clive Jarman; Zuheros' Hotel Zuhayra (p213) sells the guide for €14 and individual walks sheets for €2.50. The local tourism website, www.turismodelasubbetica.es, is a useful source on the area.

Zuheros & Around

POP 700 / ELEV 625M

Rising above the olive-tree-strewn countryside on the park's northern edge, Zuheros sits in a supremely picturesque location, its tangle of white streets and crag-top castle crouching in the lee of towering hills. Approached by twisting roads up from the A318, the village has a delightfully relaxed atmosphere.

MONTILLA WINES

The rolling countryside south of Córdoba is a zone of chalky white, moisture-retaining soils, long, hot, dry summers, and sharp day/night temperature changes – disastrous conditions for most grapevines. But not for the Pedro Ximénez. The PX, as it's known (*pe equis* in Spanish), is a tough one, a Rambo of vines that thrives on extreme weather – and it's exactly these conditions that yield the unusual flavours of the wines of the Montilla-Moriles Denominación de Origen (DO), which are produced exclusively from PX grapes.

These sweet wines are endlessly compared with sherry, to the irritation of local vintners. The fundamental difference between the Jerez sherries and Montilla is the alcoholic potency – Jerez wine is fortified by the addition of extra alcohol, whereas Montilla wine achieves its own high levels of alcohol (15%-plus) and sweetness from the intense summer temperatures. The most delicate of Montilla wines is the pale, strawlike *fino*; an *amontillado* is a golden-amber wine with a nutty flavour; and the *oloroso* is a darker, full-bodied wine with 18% to 20% alcohol content. Then there's the almost black, super-sweet Pedro Ximénez wine itself – all Montilla-Moriles wines come from PX grapes but *wine* with the name Pedro Ximénez is made from grapes that are put out in the sun to dry, like raisins, before being pressed.

Montilla wines are ubiquitous in bars and restaurants throughout Córdoba province – they go very well with tapas, as predinner drinks or as dessert wines, and the lighter ones nicely accompany soups or seafood starters. If you're feeling brave, try ordering a *fiti* (fifty-fifty), a powerful mix of *fino* and PX!

To get closer to the winemaking process, head to the town of Montilla. The wineries in the area are far less visited than the sherry bodegas of Jerez, and their wines are just as alluring. Montilla's helpful **Oficina de Turismo** (☑ 957 65 23 54; www.montillaturismo.es; Centro Multifuncional, Plaza Solera, off Calle Palomar; ☺10am-2pm & 4-6pm Mon-Fri, 11am-2pm Sat & Sun) has detailed information, and the Ruta del Vino website (www.rutadelvino montillamoriles.com) is also helpful.

Bodegas Alvear (☑ 957 65 29 39; www.alvear.es; Avenida Boucau 6; 1½hr tours €6-7; ☺tours 12.30pm Mon-Sat) The most renowned of Montilla's winemakers and one of Spain's oldest, with a range of PX vintages. Located just south of Montilla's historic core. Call ahead for tours in languages other than Spanish.

Bodegas Lagar Blanco (☑ 628 319977; www.lagarblanco.es; Ctra Cuesta Blanca Km 4; ☺1½hr tours daily by arrangement; ⓟ) Owner and guide Miguel Cruz gives excellent tours in English or Spanish at this scenic spot in the Sierra de Montilla, 10km east of town (€10 by taxi). You'll see giant traditional *tinaja* storage vessels as well as modern winemaking technology. Call or email to book a visit.

Bodegas Pérez Barquero (☑ 957 65 05 00; www.perezbarquero.com; Avenida de Andalucía 27; 1hr tours in Spanish/English/French €5/10/10; ☺tours noon daily; ⓟ) The vast warehouses here are stacked high with oak barrels of highly acclaimed wines, with tastings in an atmospheric former chapel. It's in the western part of Montilla, on the way in from the N331.

Las Camachas (☑ 957 65 00 04; Avenida de Europa 3; mains €12-24; ☺1.30-5pm & 9pm-midnight) Montilla's top restaurant offers up delicious local specialities, many prepared with local wines, in six wood-beamed dining halls. It's strong on grilled and roast meats and seafood.

◉ Sights

Castillo de Zuheros CASTLE
(Plaza de la Paz; admission or tours €2; ☺10am-2pm & 5-7pm Tue-Fri, tours 11am, 12.30pm, 2pm, 5.30pm & 6.30pm Sat, Sun & holidays, all afternoon times 1hr earlier Oct-Mar) Set on a panoramic pinnacle, Zuheros' castle is of 9th-century Moorish origin, with remains of a later Renaissance palace attached. Weekend visits are guided, and it's worth booking for these; other days visits are unguided. The ticket also includes the little **Museo Arqueológico** (Archaeological Museum; ☑ 957 69 45 45; Plaza de la Paz), just across the square, which doubles as Zuheros' tourist office.

Cueva de los Murciélagos CAVE
(Cave of the Bats; ☑ 957 69 45 45; www.cuevadelos-murcielagos.es; adult/child €6/5; ⊘ guided tours 12.30pm & 5.30pm Tue-Fri, 11am, 12.30pm, 2pm, 5pm & 6.30pm Sat & Sun, afternoon tours 1hr earlier Oct-Mar; P) Carved out of the limestone massif 4km above Zuheros is this extraordinary cave. From the vast hall at the start of the tour, it's a 430m loop walk through a series of corridors filled with fantastic rock formations. Traces of Neolithic rock paintings showing abstract figures of goats can be admired along the way.

Visits are by guided tour only and should be reserved by phoning Turismo Zuheros (p214) between 10am and 1.30pm Tuesday to Friday, or by emailing them.

The drive up to the cave is exhilarating, as the road twists and turns through the looming mountains, with vertiginous views from various lookout points.

🏃 Activities

A number of wonderful walks can be done in the vicinity. Hotel Zuhayra can put you in contact with an English-speaking walking guide, **Clive Jarman** (☑ 669 700763, clivejarman@gmail.com), who lives in Zuheros. The ideal months for walking are April, May, September and October.

★**Vía Verde de la Subbética** CYCLING, HIKING
(www.viasverdes.com; 🚹) 🏁 The area's easiest and best marked path is the *vía verde* (greenway; a disused railway converted to a cycling and walking track) which you can see snaking through the countryside below Zuheros. It runs 65km across southern Córdoba province from Camporreal near Puente Genil to the Río Guadajoz on the Jaén border, skirting the western and northern fringes of the natural park.

With gentle gradients and utilising old bridges, tunnels and viaducts, the greenway makes for a fun outing for travellers of all ages. There are cafes and bike-hire outlets in old station buildings along the route, and informative map-boards – it's impossible to get lost! At the Río Guadajoz it connects with the Vía Verde del Aceite (p223), which continues a further 55km to Jaén city.

Subbética Bike's Friends (☑ 672 605088; www.subbeticabikesfriends.com; bikes per hr/half-day/day €3.50/9.50/14.50, child seats €2; ⊘ 10am-6pm Sat & Sun; 🚹) at Doña Mencía station, 4km west down the hill from Zuheros, rents a range of different bikes, including chil-dren's, and can normally provide them any day of the week if you call ahead.

Cañón de Bailón Walk WALKING
Behind Zuheros village lies a dramatic rocky gorge, the Cañón de Bailón. A pleasant circular walk of just over 4km (two to three hours) takes you into the canyon then back to Zuheros by the road from the Cueva de los Murciélagos.

To find the trail, head down Calle Barrera from the southwest corner of Zuheros to a bridge over the Río Bailón with a car park and a large 'Sendero Río Bailón' signboard. Take the track heading up past the sign and follow it as it winds uphill and then turns left along the slopes above the gorge. The valley opens out between rocky walls and the path descends and crosses the stony riverbed. It then recrosses the river twice more within 200m. Just before a fourth crossing after a further 400m, bear up to the left on what is at first a very faint path. It becomes much clearer as it zigzags past a twisted rock pinnacle up on the right. Keep climbing steadily and then, where the path levels off, keep left through trees to reach a superb viewpoint. Continue on an obvious path to the road leading up to the Cueva de los Murciélagos. Turn left for Zuheros.

🛏 Sleeping

★**Hotel Zuhayra** HOTEL €
(☑ 957 69 46 93; www.zercahoteles.com; Calle Mirador 10; s/d €48/60; ❄ 🛜 🏊) A short distance below Zuheros' castle, this hotel has breathtaking views of the countryside from every room. It makes an excellent base for exploring the area. The friendly proprietors, the Ábalos brothers (who speak English), offer masses of information about walks and other things to see and do, and can set you up with a local guide. There is also a good restaurant.

🍴 Eating

Restaurante Zuhayra ANDALUCIAN €€
(www.zercahoteles.com; Calle Mirador 10; medias-raciones €6-14; ⊘ 1-4pm & 8-10.30pm; 🍴) The restaurant of Hotel Zuhayra prepares excellent versions of local and Andalucian favourites, such as its homemade partridge pâté or lamb chops with thyme. There are good vegetarian options too; try the *ensalada Zuhayra* with baked vegetables, cress, almonds and caramelised local cheese.

Mesón Atalaya
ANDALUCIAN €€

(☑957 69 46 97; Calle Santo 58; mains €7-20; ☺1-
4pm & 9-11pm Tue-Sun) This family-run establishment at the east end of the village does
good local fare, with plenty of lamb, pork,
ham, *potajes* and *cazuelas* (types of stew),
local cheese and homemade desserts. There
are two nice, plant-filled patios inside.

Los Balanchares
CHEESE €

(☑957 69 47 14; www.losbalanchares.com; Ctra
A318, Km 68; ☺9am-2pm & 4-7pm Mon-Fri, 10am-
4pm Sat & Sun) Zuheros is renowned for its
cheeses and you can see and buy a top selection at this wonderful organic goat- and
sheep-cheese maker, on the Doña Mencía–
Baena road below Zuheros.

ℹ Information

Turismo Zuheros (☑957 69 45 45; www.
turismodezuheros.es; Plaza de la Paz 1;
☺10am-2pm Tue-Sun year-round, 5-7pm Tue-
Fri Apr-Sep, 4-6pm Tue-Fri Oct-Mar)

ℹ Getting There & Away

BUS

Buses depart from Mesón Atalaya.

Autocares Carrera (☑957 50 16 32; www.
autocarescarrera.es) Two to four daily buses
to/from Córdoba (€6.50, 1¾ hours).

Autocares Valenzuela (☑Seville 954 82 02
89; www.grupovalenzuela.com) Three or more
daily buses to/from Doña Mencía (€1.15, 20
minutes) and two or more to/from Seville (€17,
3¾ hours).

CAR

There are parking areas near Mesón Atalaya
restaurant at the east end of the village: follow
'Cueva de los Murciélagos' signs as you approach Zuheros.

Priego de Córdoba & Around

POP 13,100 / ELEV 650M

Perched on an outcrop like a big vanilla
cake, Priego de Córdoba is a surprisingly
bustling market town in a fertile pocket of
the Subbética. Founded in AD 745, it later
found itself on the Granada emirate's front
line against its Christian enemies, until its
definitive conquest by Alfonso XI in 1341.
Priego's cavalcade of extravagant baroque
churches, fine civic buildings and mansions
are the legacy of a centuries-long run of
prosperity, cresting with an 18th-century
boom in silk and velvet production.

◎ Sights

Northeast of the central Plaza de la Constitución, leafy Plaza Abad Palomino leads
to the original Moorish quarter, the **Barrio
de La Villa**. The narrow lanes of the *barrio* wind through to the clifftop Paseo del
Adarve, with its panoramic promenade
looking out over the Río Salado valley, and
the elegant Paseo de Colombia, with its
fountains, flower beds and pergola.

★ Parroquia de la Asunción
CHURCH

(Plaza Santa Ana 1; admission €3; ☺11am-1.30pm
Tue-Sat, 11-11.30am & 1-1.30pm Sun) On the edge
of the Barrio de La Villa, this church repre-
sents a high point in Andalucian baroque
chiefly thanks to its wonderful Sagrario
(Sacristy), where whirls of frothy white stuccowork surge upwards to two beautiful cupolas – all the work of local artist Francisco
Javier Pedrajas in the 1780s. Even if baroque
churches normally make you yawn, this is
something special.

For further super-lavish church ornamentation, head to the **Iglesia de la Aurora** (Carrera de Álvarez; admission €1.50; ☺10.30am-1.30pm
Tue-Sun) and **Iglesia de San Francisco** (Calle
Buen Suceso; admission free; ☺10am-1pm & 7-9pm
Mon-Fri, 10am-1pm Sat & Sun), both rebuilt in baroque style in the 18th century.

Castillo de Priego de Córdoba
CASTLE

(Plaza Abad Palomino; admission €1.50; ☺10am-
2pm & 4-7pm Tue-Thu, 11.30am-1.30pm & 5-7pm Fri
& Sat, 11.30am-1.30pm Sun) The rectilinear towers of Priego's castle stand proudly alongside
Plaza Abad Palomino. Originally an Islamic
fortress, it was thoroughly remodelled by
the new Christian overlords between the
13th and 15th centuries. Climb the towers
for aerial views of the white town.

Fuente del Rey
FOUNTAIN

(Fountain of the King; Calle del Río) Southwest of
the centre an entire plaza-cum-park is reserved for this splendid 19th-century fountain, with its three-tiered basin continually
filled with water splashing from 130 spouts.
It would be equally at home in the gardens
of Versailles.

If you take the stairs to the left of the
Fuente de la Virgen de la Salud, near the top
of the park, you can walk to the Ermita del
Calvario (Calvary Chapel), from where there
are scenic views of the town and surrounding countryside.

Museo Histórico Municipal MUSEUM
(☎957 54 09 47; Carrera de las Monjas 16; admission €2; ☺10am-1.30pm daily, 6-8.30pm Tue-Thu, 5-7pm Fri & Sat) The city's history museum features three components: an archaeology survey; two floors devoted to local painter Adolfo Lozano Sidro (1872–1935), whose realistic illustrations covered the spectrum of social life in his era; and a stylistically varied set of landscape paintings.

Jardín Micológico 'La Trufa' GARDENS
(Ctra CO8211, Km 7.25, Zagrilla Alta; ☺10am-2pm Tue-Thu, 10am-2pm & 4-6pm Fri-Sun; ｐ） FREE
In Zagrilla Alta village, 11km northwest of Priego, this botanical garden/museum complex gives perhaps the most comprehensive overview in Europe of the mysterious mushroom. Andalucía is probably the continent's most fungi-rich area. A stroll around the gardens takes you through eight ecosystems, each featuring its trademark toadstools.

🛏 Sleeping

⭐**Casa Olea** RURAL HOTEL €€
(☎696 748209; www.casaolea.com; Ctra CO7204, near El Cañuelo; s/d incl breakfast €105/118; ｐ✳☎�$⚊） ⚓ Set in its own little olive grove by a small river, this British-owned country house 12km north of Priego has a beautifully spacious and relaxed feel. It makes a great rural retreat and base for exploring the region. There are good walks in its immediate area as well as further afield in the Sierras Subbéticas, plus mountain bikes to rent (€15 per day) and a lovely pool.

Excellent dinners (two/three courses €20/25) are available five nights a week. No children under seven.

⭐**Casa Baños de la Villa** BOUTIQUE HOTEL €€
(☎957 54 72 74; www.casabanosdelavilla.com; Calle Real 63; s/d/ste incl breakfast €56/93/175; ｐ✳☎⚊） A big draw of this unique and welcoming hotel is that it has its very own *baños árabes*, a Moorish fantasy of baths and arches, and room rates include a 90-minute session in three pools of different temperatures, plus sauna. The rooms are all comfy and individually designed with homey bric-a-brac, and there's a fine roof deck.

🍴 Eating & Drinking

The Priego area produces some of Spain's finest olive oils, with their own Denominación de Origen (DO; www.dopriegodecordoba.

es): do sample some (as well as Montilla-Moriles wines!) with your meals here.

⭐**Restaurante La Fuente** ANDALUCIAN €€
(Zagrilla Alta; mains €8-15; ☺2-4pm & 8.30pm-midnight) The small village of Zagrilla Alta is 11km northwest of Priego, and more than worth the trek for the warm welcome and terrific home-style cooking you'll receive at La Fuente, set beside a spring and stream just up from the main road.

Great local specialities include *revuelto de collejas* (scrambled eggs with campion leaves, garlic, and ham or shrimps) and *remojón* (chunks of orange, fig and hard-boiled egg with strips of salted cod), or you could go for a *chuletón* or *churrasco* – big slabs of grilled beef. Leave room for the homemade cheesecake! Zagrilla is on several walking routes, and makes a very popular halt.

Restaurante Zahorí ANDALUCIAN €€
(www.hotelzahori.es; Calle Real 2; mains €10-16; ☺12.30-4.30pm & 8.30pm-midnight Thu-Tue) Overseen by Don Custodio with the same care that he brings to his adjacent small hotel, the Zahorí prepares traditional sierra fare from lamb chops to grilled *setas* (wild mushrooms), served up in various stone-walled salons or outside gazing at the Asunción church.

Balcón del Adarve ANDALUCIAN €€
(☎957 54 70 75; www.balcondeladarve.com; Paseo de Colombia 36; mains €10-16; ☺noon-4.30pm & 8pm-midnight Tue-Sun) Overlooking the valley, with a terrace that takes full advantage of this privileged setting, this excellent restaurant brings a touch of elegance to local favourites such as ox tail, pig's cheeks (done in cannelloni) and partridge pâté.

ℹ Information

Oficina de Turismo (www.turismodepriego.com; Plaza de la Constitución 3; ☺10am-2pm & 4.30-7pm Mon-Fri, 10am-2pm & 4.30-6.30pm Sat, 10am-2pm Sun)

ℹ Getting There & Around

BUS
Priego's **bus station** (☎957 70 18 75; Calle San Marcos) is about 1km west of the centre. **Autocares Carrera** (☎957 50 16 32; www.autocares-carrera.es) runs to Montilla (€5.35, two or three daily, 1¼ hours) and Córdoba (€9.20, two hours, seven times daily Monday to Friday, three times on Saturday and Sunday). **Alsa** (☎902 42 22

42; www.alsa.es) heads to Granada (€7.40, 1½ to two hours, two to four daily) via Alcalá la Real.

CAR

There's a small car park, **Aparcamiento Palenque** (Carrera de las Monjas; ⊘7.30am-9.30pm Mon-Sat), 200m along the street running west from Plaza de la Constitución. Or you can park for free in a vacant lot on Calle San Luis, 150m downhill from the Carnicerías Reales.

WESTERN CÓRDOBA PROVINCE

Towards Sevilla province unfolds a sparsely inhabited landscape cut through by the Río Guadalquivir and dotted with villages and castles, the most formidable one looming over the whitewashed jumble of Almodóvar del Río. To the north, the pleasant burg of Hornachuelos is the gateway to a remote range of forested hills interspersed with pasturelands and populated by deer, wild boar, otters and large birds of prey.

Almodóvar del Río

Castillo de Almodóvar   CASTLE
(☑957 63 40 55; www.castillodealmodovar.com; Calle del Castillo; adult/child €7/4; ⊘11am-2.30pm & 4-8pm Mon-Fri, 11am-8pm Sat & Sun Apr-Jun & Oct, 10am-3pm Mon-Sat, 10am-4pm Sun Jul-Sep, 11am-2.30pm & 4-7pm Mon-Fri, 11am-7pm Sat & Sun Nov-Mar; ℗) Almodóvar's monumental and sinister-looking castle dominates the view from far and wide, rising almost sheer above the Río Guadalquivir with just enough room for the AVE high-speed train line to squeeze in between. It was founded in the 8th century but owes most of its present appearance to post-Reconquista rebuilding. Because the castle had never been taken by force, Pedro I ('the Cruel') used it as a treasure store. Its sense of impregnability is still potent within the massive walls.

You can climb up several of the nine towers, the mightiest being the Torre del Homenaje (Tower of Homage), which also contains the dungeon, where medieval conditions are re-created by a mannequin tableau. A film on the castle's history, with English subtitles, is screened in the chapel.

There is parking below the castle, or you can also drive up the driveway and park just below the entrance, saving a 600m uphill walk.

Parque Natural Sierra de Hornachuelos

The Parque Natural Sierra de Hornachuelos is a 600-sq-km area of rolling hills in the Sierra Morena, northwest of Almodóvar del Río. The park is densely wooded with a mix of holm oak, cork oak and ash, and is pierced by a number of thickly wooded river valleys. It is renowned for its eagles and other raptors, including Andalucía's second-largest colony of black vultures.

The pleasant small town of Hornachuelos on the park's southern fringe, standing above a small reservoir on the Río Bembézar, makes the obvious base for enjoying the park's quiet charms.

◉ Sights & Activities

From Plaza de la Constitución, in the old centre of Hornachuelos, a lane called La Palmera, with a charming palm-tree pebble mosaic underfoot, leads up to the Iglesia de Santa María de las Flores. The church sits on a plaza overlooking the olive-dotted hills, with the remains of a Moorish castle just up to the left.

Walking trails start from both the village and natural park visitors centre (p218), 1.5km north.

Sendero de Los Ángeles   WALKING
This path runs 4km from the foot of Hornachuelos village up beside the Bembézar reservoir to a huge, abandoned seminary, the Seminario de los Ángeles (entry prohibited). You may well spy griffon vultures from a colony a little further up the valley.

Sendero Botánico   WALKING
Starting at the visitors centre, the Sendero Botánico climbs a hillside through mossy cork forest, levelling off momentarily, then winds down a narrow dirt trail with excellent views of the surrounding countryside, making a wonderfully varied 1.2km loop.

Sendero Guadalora   WALKING
(⊘closed Jun-Sep) This moderately demanding but rewarding walk starts 2.5km northwest of the visitors centre (you can drive that far), then wends its way 6km (about 2½ hours) through evergreen oaks and olive trees and down a thickly wooded river valley to emerge on the CO5310 road, from

LOS PEDROCHES

If you like driving empty roads across big landscapes and coming upon the occasional spectacular sight, then Córdoba's isolated far north, known as Los Pedroches, is for you. This is a plateau-like region of long, long vistas, broken up by a few ranges of hills and thinly scattered villages. It's known for its extensive *dehesas* (woodland pastures with acorn-bearing holm oaks) and for its high-quality ham, *jamón ibérico de bellota*, from the black Iberian pigs that feast on the annual acorn *(bellota)* harvest. Salted and cured for six to 12 months, the resulting dark-pink ham is usually served wafer-thin with bread and Montilla wine. You can sample it in almost every village in this area.

The gateway to Los Pedroches is the 750m **Puerto Calatraveño** pass, on the N502 about 55km north of Córdoba. From here the green landscape stretches ahead towards infinity. The first village is **Alcaracejos**, home to the district tourist office, the Oficina Comarcal de Turismo (☑957 77 40 10; www.turismolospedroches.org; Ctra Pozoblanco, Alcaracejos; ⊙9.30am-2.30pm Mon-Fri, 10am-2pm Sat & Sun). Northwest from here is **Hinojosa del Duque** with its monumental 16th-century church, the Catedral de la Sierra (Plaza de la Catedral, Hinojosa del Duque; ⊙10am-noon), the bell tower of which is claimed to have been the model for the one on Córdoba's Mezquita. The plaza cafes here are good for refreshments.

From Hinojosa it's 9km north to remote **Belalcázar** whose massive and spooky Castillo de los Sotomayor is visible from far and wide, its top-heavy main tower rising 45m above its hilltop perch. This castle was built in the 15th century by the master of the Knights of Calatrava, a Reconquista crusading order that controlled a huge swathe of territory from Córdoba to Toledo and Badajoz. Today it stands abandoned except for nesting storks, and is securely locked up, but you can walk right round the outside for a good inspection. The Albergue Camino de Santiago (☑617 715129; http://caminode-santiagobelalcazar.blogspot.com.es; Calle Pilar, Belalcázar; dm €12, platos combinados €3.50, menú €7.50; P❀❖), just below the castle, is a well-managed hostel intended primarily for walkers following the Camino Mozárabe (one of the longer and more obscure branches of the Camino de Santiago network of medieval pilgrim routes to Santiago de Compostela), but is open to all for good-value food and lodging.

The lonely CO9402 heads 27km east across empty countryside to **Santa Eufemia**, Andalucía's northernmost village. For stupendous 360-degree views over vast swathes of Andalucía and Castilla-La Mancha, head up to the Castillo de Miramontes, a tumbled ruin 2.5km above Santa Eufemia (turn west off the N502 at Bar La Paloma, and turn right at the 'Camino Servicio RTVE' sign after 1km).

Villanueva de Córdoba, a lively market town 50km southeast of Santa Eufemia, makes a good place to bed down for the night; we recommend Hotel la Casa del Médico (☑957 12 02 47; http://hotellacasadelmedico.com; Calle Contreras 4, Villanueva de Córdoba; incl breakfast s €70-80, d €95-125; ❀❖❋). Eat and drink at cheerful La Puerta Falsa (Calle Contreras 8, Villanueva de Córdoba; mains €8-16; ⊙8am-midnight), with a pretty patio and a good choice of seafood as well as hill-country meat and egg dishes.

Before returning to civilisation, nature lovers can take a wander in the Parque Natural Sierra de Cardeña y Montoro (www.ventanadelvisitante.es), 384 sq km of rolling hills and woodland that is home to a few Iberian lynx and wolves, plus otters and birds of prey. Paths branch out from Aldea del Cerezo, 6km east of Cardeña village. Head to the Centro de Visitantes Venta Nueva (☑671 593306; Junction N420 & A420; ⊙9am-2pm Wed-Fri, 9am-2pm & 6-8pm Sat & Sun May-Jun, 8am-2pm Fri-Sun Jul-Sep, 9am-2pm Wed-Fri, 9am-2pm & 4-6pm Sat-Sun Oct-Apr), 1km south of Cardeña, for information.

Autocares San Sebastián (☑957 42 90 30; www.autocaressansebastian.es) provides bus service between Córdoba and Los Pedroches.

where you must retrace your steps, if you haven't organised a taxi. Walkers must obtain a free permit for this route, quickly and easily available at the visitors centre (p218).

🛏 Sleeping & Eating

Hostal El Álamo   HOSTAL €
(☑957 64 04 76; http://complejoturisticoelalamo.com; Ctra A3151, Km 8; s/d incl breakfast €38/55;

✳ 🛜 ✉) Motel-style El Álamo, along the main road of Hornachuelos, sports a faux *cortijo* (farmhouse) style, with tiled roofs and wagon wheels strewn about. The cafe/bar/restaurant (Carretera San Calixto; mains €6-22; ⊙1-4pm & 8-11.30pm) is a popular gathering place. Ask for a room away from the road, which can be noisy.

❶ Information

Oficina de Turismo (☑ 957 64 07 86; www.hornachuelosrural.com; Recinto Ferial; ⊙9am-3pm Tue-Wed, 10am-2pm Thu-Sun) Hornachuelos' unsignposted but helpful tourist office is in the feria grounds off Carretera San Calixto (the A3151 passing through the west side of town).

Centro de Visitantes Huerta del Rey (☑957 64 11 40; Carretera Hornachuelos-San Calixto Km1.5; ⊙9am-2pm Wed-Fri, 9am-2pm & 6-8pm Sat & Sun May-Jun, 8am-2pm Fri-Sun Jul-Sep, 9am-2pm Wed-Fri, 9am-2pm & 4-6pm Sat & Sun Oct-Apr) The natural park visitors centre has interesting displays and information for visitors (including a set of six detailed walk leaflets costing €2).

❶ Getting There & Away

Autocares San Sebastián (www.autocares-sansebastian.es) runs buses to/from Córdoba (€2.20, one hour, four times daily Monday to Friday, twice on Saturday). Buses leave from Carretera San Calixto, just below the police station.

Jaén Province

POP 658,600

Includes ➜

Jaén 222

Parque Natural
Sierra de Andújar . . . 226

Baeza 227

Úbeda. 231

Cazorla 237

Parque Natural
Sierras de Cazorla,
Segura y Las Villas. . . 239

Best Places to Eat

➜ Misa de 12 (p235)

➜ Cantina de la Estación (p235)

➜ Casa Antonio (p224)

➜ Mesón Leandro (p238)

➜ Zeitúm (p235)

Best Places to Stay

➜ Afán de Rivera (p235)

➜ Parador Castillo de Santa Catalina (p224)

➜ Hostal Aznaitín (p229)

➜ Parador Condestable Dávalos (p235)

➜ Palacio de la Rambla (p235)

Why Go?

For anyone who loves culture, nature, history or good food, this relatively little-visited province turns out to be one magical combination. Endless lines of pale-green olive trees – producing one-sixth of all the world's olive oil – carpet much of the landscape. Castle-crowned hills are a reminder that this was once a frontier zone between Christians and Muslims, while the gorgeous Renaissance architecture of Unesco World Heritage sites Úbeda and Baeza displays the wealth amassed by the Reconquista nobility.

Beyond the towns and olive groves, Jaén has wonderful mountain country. The Parque Natural Sierras de Cazorla, Segura y Las Villas is a highlight of Andalucía for nature lovers, with rugged landscapes, prolific wildlife, and good hotels, roads and trails to help you make the most of it.

Products of the forests and hills such as venison, partridge and wild mushrooms feature strongly in Jaén cuisine, and in the recipes of a surprising number of wonderfully creative chefs, especially in Úbeda.

Driving Distances

	Úbeda	Jaén	Baeza	Cazorla
Jaén	60			
Baeza	16	50		
Cazorla	44	102	58	
Santa Elena	72	79	65	116

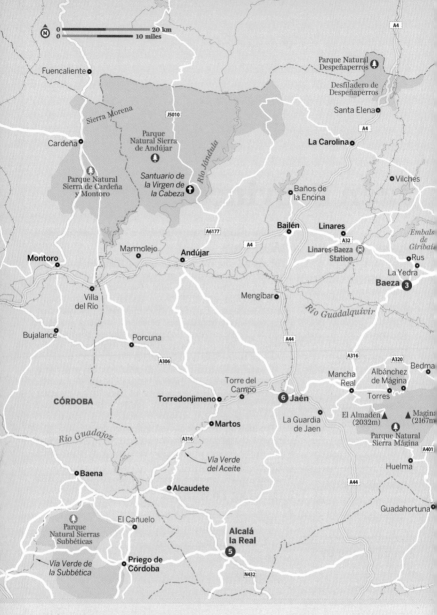

Jaén Province Highlights

❶ Indulging the senses with the inspired architecture and food of **Úbeda** (p231)

❷ Walking the green valleys and craggy mountains of the **Parque Natural Sierras de Cazorla, Segura y Las Villas** (p239)

❸ Investigating the tangle of stone lanes lined with beautiful buildings in old **Baeza** (p227)

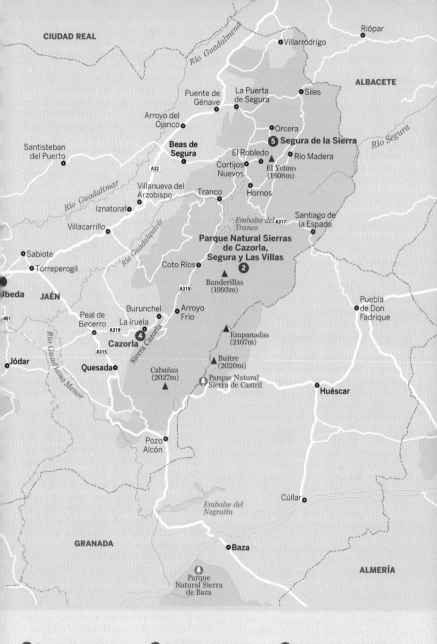

CIUDAD REAL

Río Guadalmena

Ríopar

Villarródrigo

ALBACETE

Puente de Génave

La Puerta de Segura

Siles

Arroyo del Ojanco

Orcera

Río Segura

Santisteban del Puerto

Beas de Segura

El Robledo

5 Segura de la Sierra

A32

Cortijos Nuevos

Río Madera

El Yelmo (1808m)

Villanueva del Arzobispo

Tranco

Hornos

Río Guadalimar

Iznatoraf

Embalse del Tranco

Santiago de la Espada

A317

Villacarrillo

Río Guadalquivir

Parque Natural Sierras de Cazorla, Segura y Las Villas

2

Sabiote

Coto Ríos

Puebla de Don Fadrique

Torreperogil

Banderillas (1993m)

Úbeda

JAÉN

A319

Burunchel

Arroyo Frío

401

Peal de Becerro

La Iruela

Empanadas (2107m)

Jódar

A319

4 Cazorla

A315

Sierra Cazorla

Buitre (2020m)

Río Guadiana Menor

Quesada

Cabañas (2027m)

Parque Natural Sierra de Castril

Huéscar

Pozo Alcón

Embalse del Negratín

Cúllar

GRANADA

Baza

ALMERÍA

Parque Natural Sierra de Baza

4 Enjoying the sights and atmosphere of picturesque mountain town **Cazorla** (p237)

5 Climbing up to the fascinating hilltop castles at **Alcalá la Real** (p226) and **Segura de la Sierra** (p242)

6 Exploring traditional tapas bars and the historic castle in **Jaén** (p222)

JAÉN

POP 112,000 / ELEV 575M

Set amid vast olive groves, upon which its precarious economy depends, Jaén is somewhat overshadowed by the beauty of nearby Úbeda and Baeza, and is often passed over by visitors to the province. But once you make it into town you will discover a charming, if mildly dilapidated, historic centre with hidden neighbourhoods, excellent tapas bars and a grandiose cathedral.

Muslim Yayyan was a significant city before its conquest by Castilla in 1246. Christian Jaén remained important thanks to its strategic location near the border with Nasrid Granada. After the Muslims were finally driven out of Granada in 1492, Jaén sank into a decline with many of its people emigrating to the Spanish colonies – hence the existence of other Jaéns in Peru and the Philippines.

◉ Sights & Activities

The wooded, castle-crowned hill Cerro de Santa Catalina defines Jaén's western boundary, with the streets of the old Moorish town huddling around its base.

★ Catedral de la Asunción   CATHEDRAL

(Plaza de Santa María; adult/child incl audio guide €5/1.50; ⊙10am-2pm & 4-8pm Mon-Fri, 10am-2pm & 4-7pm Sat, 10am-noon & 4-7pm Sun) The size and opulence of Jaén's cathedral still dwarf the rest of the city, especially when seen from the hilltop eyrie of Cerro de Santa Catalina. Andrés de Vandelvira, the master architect of Úbeda and Baeza, was commissioned to create this huge house of God in the 16th century, replacing a crumbling Gothic cathedral which itself had been built on the site of a mosque.

The facade on Plaza de Santa María was not completed until the 18th century, and owes more to the baroque tradition than to the Renaissance, thanks to its host of statuary by Seville's Pedro Roldán. But the cathedral's predominant aesthetic is Renaissance – particularly evident in its huge, round arches and clusters of Corinthian columns that lend it great visual strength. Inside, a great circular dome rises over the crossing before the main altar. Check out the beautiful carving on the stone ceilings of the nave and aisles, and on the wooden seats in the choir.

Palacio de Villardompardo   BATHHOUSE, MUSEUM

(Centro Cultural Baños Árabes; Plaza de Santa Luisa de Marillac; ⊙9am-10pm Tue-Sat, to 3pm Sun) **FREE** This Renaissance palace houses three excellent attractions: the beautiful 11th-century Baños Árabes (Arab Baths), one of the largest surviving Islamic-era bathhouses in Spain; the Museo de Artes y Costumbres Populares (Museum of People's Art & Customs), devoted to the rural life of preindustrial Jaén province; and the Museo Internacional de Arte Naïf (International Museum of Naïve Art) with a large collection of colourful and witty Naïve art.

The Arab baths were rediscovered in 1913 beneath the 16th-century palace, which had been built on top of them. Of their three rooms (cold, warm, hot), the warm room, with its multiple horseshoe arches, is the finest. In an adjoining room, glass flooring reveals part of a Roman street. A 10-minute explanatory film with English subtitles is part of the visit to this section.

The Museum of People's Art & Customs, spread over several floors, covers everything from wine-making to saddlery to pig-slaughtering (*matanza*). There's an antique doll's house and a recreation of an early-20th-century rural home, but perhaps most evocative are the photos of country life a century ago, showing just how tough and basic it was. The Naïve art museum is based on the work of its founder, Manuel Moral. You can spend a long time lost in the everyday detail so playfully depicted in these works.

★ Castillo de Santa Catalina   CASTLE

(Cerro de Santa Catalina; adult/child €3/1.50; ⊙10am-2pm & 3.30-7.30pm Tue-Sat, to 3pm Sun; P) High above the city, atop cliff-girt Cerro de Santa Catalina, this fortress' near-impregnable position is what made Jaén important during the Muslim and early Reconquista centuries. At the end of the ridge stands a large cross, on the spot where Fernando III had a cross planted after Jaén finally surrendered to him in 1246: the views are magnificent.

The Muslim fortress here was revamped after the Christian conquest. What exists today is only about one-third of what there used to be – the rest was demolished to make way for the adjacent *parador* hotel in the 1960s. Inside, the displays in English and Spanish give a good sense of the castle's history.

If you don't have a vehicle for the circuitous 4km drive up from the city centre, you can take a taxi (€7), or you can walk in about 40 minutes from the cathedral via Calles Maestre, Parrilla and Buenavista. At the top of Buenavista, turn right along the Carretera de

Jaén

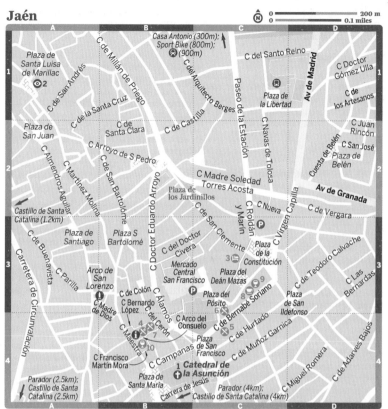

Circunvalación, and after 50m take the track up to the left and walk up through the trees.

If you aren't staying at the *parador,* drop in for a drink to see the extraordinary vaulted, decorative ceilings in the main salon and dining room.

Vía Verde del Aceite   CYCLING, WALKING
(Olive Oil Greenway; www.viasverdes.com) Fifty-five kilometres of disused railway, including two tunnels and eight viaducts, running across the southern Jaén countryside to the Río Guadajoz, west of Alcaudete, have been converted to a well-surfaced cycling and walking track, with gentle gradients that make it perfect for an extended ride.

The track starts in the Fuentezuelas area on the northwest edge of Jaén city. At the Río Guadajoz it connects with the Vía Verde de la Subbética (p213), which continues another 65km across Córdoba province. **Sport Bike** (🖉953 27 44 76; Calle San Francisco Javier

Jaén

◎ Top Sights
1 Catedral de la Asunción B4

◎ Sights
  Baños Árabes ....(see 2)
  Museo de Artes y
    Costumbres Populares ....(see 2)
  Museo Internacional de
    Arte Naïf ....(see 2)
2 Palacio de Villardompardo A1

⊜ Sleeping
3 Hotel Xauen C3

⊗ Eating
4 El Gorrión B4
5 El Pato Rojo C4
6 Panaceite C3
7 Taberna La Manchega B4

◎ Drinking & Nightlife
8 Colombia 50 Café C3
9 Deán C3
10 El Calentito B4

14; per day €15; ⊙10am-1.30pm & 5-8.30pm Mon-Fri, to 1.30pm Sat), near the train station, rents 24-speed mountain bikes.

⚔ Festivals & Events

Semana Santa   HOLY WEEK
(www.cofradiasjaen.org; ⊙Mar-Apr) The week leading up to Easter Sunday sees statue-bearing processions through the old city by 16 *cofradías* (brotherhoods).

🛏 Sleeping

Hotel Xauen   HOTEL €€
(☎953 24 07 89; www.hotelxauenjaen.com; Plaza del Deán Mazas; s/d incl breakfast €55/65; P❄🛜) The Xauen has a superb location in the centre of town. Communal areas are decorated with large photos of colourful local scenes, while the rooms are a study in brown and moderately sized, but comfy and well cared-for. The rooftop sun terrace has stunning cathedral views. Parking nearby is €12.

★ Parador Castillo
de Santa Catalina   LUXURY HOTEL €€€
(☎953 23 00 00; www.parador.es; Cerro de Santa Catalina; r €169; P❄@🛜⛲) Next to the castle on the Cerro de Santa Catalina, Jaén's *parador* has an incomparable setting and theatrically vaulted halls. Rooms are luxuriously dignified with plush furnishings, some with four-poster beds. There is also an excellent restaurant and a bar with panoramic terrace seating.

🍴 Eating

There aren't many fancy restaurants in Jaén, but some of Andalucía's quirkiest tapas bars are here, and the *jiennenses* (people of Jaén) cherish and preserve them. For the highest concentration, head for the little zone of wafer-thin streets northwest of the cathedral. Here, and throughout Jaén province, bars will give you a free tapa with every drink. You only pay for any extra tapas you order.

El Gorrión   ANDALUCIAN €
(Calle Arco del Consuelo 7; tapas from €1.50, raciones €7-15; ⊙1.30-4pm Tue-Sun & 8.30pm-12.30am Fri & Sat) Lazy jazz plays in the background, old newspaper cuttings are glued to the walls and paintings of bizarre landscapes hang lopsidedly next to oval oak barrels. It feels as though local punters have been propping up the bar for centuries (or at least since 1888, when it opened). The tapas, such as pepper sausage *(salchichón a la pimienta)* or seafood-stuffed artichokes, go very well with the local wine on offer.

El Pato Rojo   SEAFOOD €
(Calle de Bernabé Soriano 12; medias raciones €8-10; ⊙1-5pm & 8pm-midnight) No-frills but always packed to the gills, the 'Red Duck' concentrates on one thing – perfect seafood tapas. Unless you've grabbed one of the few tables out on the narrow pavement, it's a matter of squeezing up to the bar and ordering a beer or *fino* (straw-coloured sherry); a tapa will come free with each drink.

If you're hungry, order a *media ración* (larger tapas serving) of prawns, mussels or scallops.

Taberna La Manchega   ANDALUCIAN €
(www.facebook.com/tabernalamanchega.jaen; Calle Bernardo López 12; platos combinados €6, raciones €3-10; ⊙10am-5pm & 8pm-1am Wed-Mon) La Manchega has been in action since the 1880s; apart from enjoying the great, traditional tapas and *raciones* (full plates of tapas items), such as venison chorizo and goat kid in garlic *(choto al ajillo)*, you can drink wine and watch the characterful local clientele.

Panaceite   CONTEMPORARY SPANISH €
(www.panaceite.com; Calle de Bernabé Soriano 1; tapas from €2.60, raciones €6.50-15; ⊙11am-midnight) Always packed, this corner bar near the cathedral has a semicircle of outside tables. It serves some seriously good tapas and *raciones*, such as pork sirloin with a choice of four sauces, or aubergines in sugarcane syrup, as well as salads, bread-roll sandwiches and wines by the glass.

★ Casa Antonio   SPANISH €€€
(☎953 27 02 62; www.casantonio.es; Calle Fermín Palma 3; mains €19-23; ⊙1-4pm & 8.30-11.30pm Mon-Sat, 1-4pm Sun, closed Aug) This elegant little restaurant, in an unpromising street off Parque de la Victoria, prepares top-class Spanish fare rooted in local favourites, such as the partridge pâté or Segura lamb. There's also some excellent seafood. Nothing too complicated, just top ingredients expertly prepared. Service is polished and attentive.

🍷 Drinking & Nightlife

Colombia 50 Café   CAFE
(Calle de Bernabé Soriano 23; ⊙8am-9pm Mon-Thu, 9am-1am Fri, 9am-1am Sat, 9.30am-9pm Sun; 🛜) A large cafe with a sort of tropical-colonial ambience, Colombia is busy most

of the day and a fine place for breakfast. Try one of their *blankitas* (toasted bread with assorted toppings, including partridge-and-tomato), or a crêpe or croissant, along with one of the global range of coffees (including Jamaica Blue Mountain).

Deán
BAR
(www.facebook.com/dean.plazabar; Plaza del Deán Mazas; ⏰11am-late) The interior is small and cramped with punters spilling out on to the leafy square, but Deán has a pulsating late-night vibe with its industrial-steel piping and pumping music. During the day it's more of a cafe, with chairs on the square and light eats such as hummus and *tostas* (toast with toppings).

El Calentito
BAR
(Calle Arco del Consuelo; ⏰1-5.30pm & 8pm-1am Thu-Sat, to 5.30pm Sun) This bar in the *zona de tascas* (tapas zone) has a livelier atmosphere and younger clientele (20s) than most others, with everything painted in bright primary colours.

ⓘ Information

Oficina de Turismo (☑953 19 04 55; www.andalucia.org; Calle Maestra 8; ⏰9am-7.30pm Mon-Fri, 9.30am-3pm Sat & Sun) Combined city and regional tourist office with helpful multilingual staff.

ⓘ Getting There & Around

CAR
Jaén's one-way system and traffic are no fun, but the way to most hotels is well signposted. There are a couple of central underground car parks.

TRAIN
Jaén's **train station** (www.renfe.com; Paseo de la Estación) has four trains a day to Córdoba (€15, 1¾ hours), Seville (€28, three hours) and Madrid (€35, four hours).

NORTHWEST JAÉN PROVINCE

North of Jaén you pass across indifferent countryside until the Sierra Morena appears on the horizon. This range of rolling, green wooded hills stretching along Andalucía's northern border is little visited, but has a mysterious, lonely magic all its own.

Desfiladero de Despeñaperros & Santa Elena

The Desfiladero de Despeñaperros, a dramatic, deep gorge cutting through the Sierra Morena, is traditionally considered the main gateway to Andalucía from the north. The A4 highway (and a railway) zip quickly through it on viaducts and through tunnels. To get a better look at its rocky pinnacles, take the old road which has a mirador and restaurant where you can stop and take in the scenery: from the north, take exit 243 and follow 'Parque Natural Despeñaperros' signs; from the south, take exit 257 into Santa Elena town then head out past the signposted El Mesón restaurant, and from the double roundabout at the bottom of the gorge follow 'Venta de Cárdenas' signs. The hilly and beautiful country straddling the gorge is the **Parque Natural de Despeñaperros**: for

BUSES FROM JAÉN

Alsa (☑902 42 22 42; www.alsa.es) and Transportes Ureña (☑953 22 01 16; www.urena-sa.com) run buses from the bus station (☑953 23 23 00; www.epassa.es/autobus; Plaza de la Libertad).

TO	BUS COMPANY	COST (€)	DURATION	FREQUENCY
Baeza	Alsa	4.50	1hr	11 daily
Cazorla	Alsa	9.25	2½hr	3 daily
Córdoba	Transportes Ureña	10	2hr	4-7 daily
Granada	Alsa	8.90	1¼hr	12 daily
Málaga	Alsa	20	3½hr	4 daily
Seville	Transportes Ureña	23	4½hr	1 daily
Úbeda	Alsa	5.40	1¼hr	12 daily

WORTH A TRIP

ALCALÁ LA REAL

From a distance the **Fortaleza de la Mota** (www.tuhistoria.org; Alcalá la Real; adult/child €6/3; ☉10.30am-7.30pm Apr–mid-Oct, to 5.30pm mid-Oct–Mar; **P**)) looks more like a city than a mere fort, with its high church tower and doughty castle keep rising above the surrounding walls. And in a sense that's what it was, for back in the Middle Ages this fortified hill now looming over the town of Alcalá la Real *was* Alcalá la Real. It's a marvellous stop if you're heading along the Granada–Córdoba road across southwestern Jaén province, and well worth a detour even if you're not.

The modern town below only came into being in the 17th century, when fortified towns on hills had passed their use-by date. Today the fortress is as much archaeological site as monument, for what were houses, palaces, stables and streets are now lines of low ruins. The fortress was founded around AD 1000 then largely rebuilt after being conquered by Castilla's Alfonso XI in 1341. One of the most remarkable features is the inside of the church, where the floor has been removed to lay bare dozens of graves carved out of the rock beneath.

information on the park and walking routes, visit the **Centro de Visitantes Puerta de Andalucía** (☑953 66 43 07; Ctra A4 Km 257; ☉10am-2pm Thu-Fri & Sun year-round, 10am-2pm & 4-6pm Sat Sep-Jun, 8am-2pm Sat Jul-Aug) on the west side of exit 257.

◎ Sights

Museo Batalla de las Navas de Tolosa MUSEUM
(www.museobatallanavasdetolosa.es; Ctra de Miranda del Rey, Santa Elena; adult/child €3/2, audio guide €1; ☉10am-2pm & 4-7pm Tue-Sat Oct-May, to 2pm & 5-8pm Tue-Sat Jun-Sep, to 2pm & 3.30-6.30pm Sun year-round; **P**)) The course of Spanish history was changed 2km west of Santa Elena on 16 July 1212, when Christian armies defeated the Muslim Almohad army in the battle of Las Navas de Tolosa, which opened the doors of Andalucía to the Reconquista. This museum, a few hundred metres west from exit 257 on the A4, has the full fascinating story and a viewing tower from which you can see the battle site.

After the battle the Christians are believed to have tossed Muslim captives off the cliffs of the Desfiladero de Despeñaperros. It's commonly believed this is the origin of the name Despeñaperros, which means 'overthrow of the dogs'.

✖ Eating

El Mesón ANDALUCIAN €€
(Avenida Andalucía 91, Santa Elena; mains €9-18; ☉noon-midnight) A sound choice for refreshments, with local fare such as venison in mushroom sauce, and partridge salad with dried fruits.

Parque Natural Sierra de Andújar

This large (748 sq km) natural park north of Andújar town has the largest expanses of natural vegetation in the Sierra Morena as well as plenty of bull-breeding ranches. Among the many varieties of wildlife are five emblematic endangered species – Iberian lynx, wolf, black vulture, black stork and Spanish imperial eagle – which attract a good number of bird and animal watchers to the park. The Iberian lynx population here, around 120, is the largest in the world. Staff at the park visitors centre, the **Centro de Visitantes Viñas de Peñallana** (☑953 54 96 28; Ctra A6177 Km 13; ☉10am-2pm & 4-6pm Thu-Sun, hours may vary), 13km north of Andújar town, can tell you the best areas for lynx-spotting, though chances of sightings are always slim. The best months are December and January, the mating season. Local firms offering guided wildlife and birdwatching trips include **Turismo Verde** (☑629 518345; www.lasierra deandujar.com) and **IberianLynxLand** (☑636 984515; www.iberianlynxland.com).

On a hilltop in the heart of the park stands the **Santuario de la Virgen de la Cabeza** (Ctra A6177 Km 31, Cerro del Cabezo; **P**)), a chapel that is the focus of one of Spain's biggest and most emotive religious events, the **Romería de la Virgen de la Cabeza**, on the last weekend in April. Hundreds of thousands of people converge in a huge, festive tent city to witness a small statue of the Virgin Mary, known as La Morenita, being carried around the hill for several hours on the Sunday.

A great base for wildlife watchers, rural hotel La Caracola (☎ 633 515679; www.lacaracolahotelrural.com; Ctra A6177 Km 13.8; d incl breakfast €60; P🐾🖥) sits among woodlands and offers bright, contemporary rooms, comfortable common areas and good meals – they'll serve breakfast as early as you like. It's 1.4km off the A6177, less than a kilometre north of the Andújar park visitors centre.

Andújar town is served by several daily trains and buses from Jaén and Córdoba, and by buses from Baeza and Úbeda. There are buses to the sanctuary on Saturday and Sunday.

EASTERN JAÉN PROVINCE

This part of the region is where most visitors spend their time, drawn in by the allure and Renaissance architecture of the Unesco World Heritage towns Baeza and Úbeda, as well as the beautiful mountains and hiking trails of the Cazorla area.

Baeza

POP 15,500 / ELEV 90M

The twin towns of Baeza (ba-*eh*-thah) and Úbeda, 9km apart, put paid to any notion that there is little of architectural interest in Andalucía apart from Moorish buildings. Far from any of Andalucía's more famed cultural centres, these two country towns guard a treasure trove of superb Christian Renaissance buildings from a time when a few local families managed to amass huge fortunes and spent large parts of them beautifying their home towns. Baeza, the smaller of the two, can be visited in a day trip from Úbeda, though it has some good accommodation of its own. Here a handful of wealthy, fractious families, rich from grain-growing and cloth and leather production, left a marvellous catalogue of perfectly preserved Renaissance churches and civic buildings.

Baeza was one of the first Andalucian towns to fall to the Christians (in 1227), and little is left of the Muslim town of Bayyasa after so many centuries of Castilian influence.

◉ Sights

Baeza's main sights mostly cluster in the narrow streets south of the central Plaza de España and the broad Paseo de la Constitución (once Baeza's marketplace and bullring).

Plaza del Pópulo   SQUARE
(Plaza de los Leones) This handsome square is surrounded by elegant 16th-century buildings. The central Fuente de los Leones (Fountain of the Lions) is made of carvings from the Ibero-Roman village of Cástulo and is topped by a statue reputed to represent Imilce, a local princess who became one of the wives of the famous Carthaginian general Hannibal.

The Puerta de Jaén on the plaza's west side was originally a city gate of Muslim Bayyasa, though it was reconstructed in 1526. Joined to it is the Arco de Villalar, erected by Carlos I the same year to commemorate the crushing of a serious insurrection in Castilla that had threatened to overthrow him.

On the southern side of the square is the lovely 16th-century Casa del Pópulo, formerly a courthouse and now Baeza's tourist office. It was built in the plateresque style, an early phase of Renaissance architecture noted for its decorative facades. On the eastern side the Antigua Carnicería, from 1547, must rank as one of the world's most elegant butcheries. It's now used as a courthouse.

★ Catedral de Baeza   CATHEDRAL
(Plaza de Santa María; admission incl audio guide €5; ◐10.30am-2pm & 4-7pm Mon-Fri, 10am-7pm Sat, 10am-6pm Sun) As was the case in much of Andalucía, the Reconquista destroyed Baeza's mosque and in its place built a cathedral. This was the first step towards the town's transformation into a Castilian gem. The cathedral is a stylistic melange, though the predominant style is 16th-century Renaissance, visible in the facade on Plaza de Santa María and in the basic design of the three-nave interior (by Andrés de Vandelvira).

You can climb the tower for great views over the town and countryside. The tower's base dates from the 11th century and was part of the minaret of the mosque. The cathedral's next oldest feature is the 13th-century Gothic-Mudéjar Puerta de la Luna (Moon Doorway) at its western end, which is topped by a 14th-century rose window. Inside, there's a clear transition from the nave's two easternmost bays, which are Gothic, with sinuous ceiling tracery and gargoyled capitals, to the Renaissance-style bays further west with their Corinthian capitals and classical square and circle designs.

The broad Plaza de Santa María was designed to be a focus of Baeza's religious and civic life. The 17th-century Seminario de

Baeza

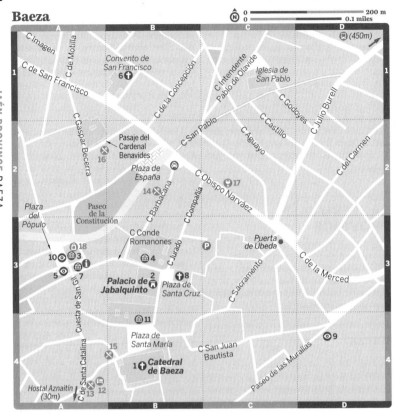

San Felipe Neri, a former seminary, now houses part of the Universidad Internacional de Andalucía, which teaches postgraduate courses.

★ **Palacio de Jabalquinto** PALACE
(Plaza de Santa Cruz; ⊙9am-2pm Mon-Fri) FREE
Baeza's most flamboyant palace was probably built in the late 15th century for a member of the noble Benavides clan. Its chief glory is the spectacular facade in decorative Isabelline Gothic style, with a strange array of naked humans climbing along the moulding over the doorway; at the top is a line of shields topped by helmets topped by mythical birds and beasts.

The interior patio has a two-tier Renaissance arcade with marble columns, an elegant fountain, and a magnificent carved baroque stairway. Across the square, the 13th-century Iglesia de la Santa Cruz (admission free; ⊙11am-1pm & 4-6pm Mon-Sat, noon-2pm Sun) was one of the first churches built in Baeza. With its round arches and semicircular apse, it is a very rare example in Andalucía of Romanesque architecture.

Antigua Universidad HISTORIC BUILDING
(Old University; Calle del Beato Juan de Ávila; admission free; ⊙10am-2pm & 4-7pm) Baeza's historic university was founded in 1538. It became a fount of progressive ideas that generally conflicted with Baeza's conservative dominant families, often causing scuffles between the highbrows and the well-heeled. Since 1875 the building has housed a secondary school. The main patio, with elegant Renaissance arches, is open to visitors, as is the early-20th-century classroom of the famed poet Antonio Machado, who taught French here from 1912 to 1919.

Paseo de las Murallas STREET
Heading southwest from Plaza del Pópulo, then looping back northeastward along the escarpment at the edge of town, this street

Baeza

⊚ **Top Sights**
1 Catedral de Baeza B4
2 Palacio de Jabalquinto B3

⊚ **Sights**
3 Antigua Carnicería A3
4 Antigua Universidad B3
5 Arco de Villalar A3
6 Capilla de los Benavides B1
7 Casa del Pópulo A3
   Fuente de los Leones ....(see 10)
8 Iglesia de Santa Cruz B3
9 Paseo de las Murallas D4
10 Plaza del Pópulo...................................A3
   Puerta de Jaén ....(see 5)
11 Seminario de San Felipe Neri B4

⊜ **Sleeping**
12 Hotel Puerta de la Luna.......................A4

⊗ **Eating**
13 Bar Paco's..A4
14 El Arcediano B2
15 El Nanchoas..B4
16 La Almazara..A2

⊙ **Drinking & Nightlife**
17 Café Teatro Central C2

⊜ **Shopping**
18 La Casa del Aceite A3

and pedestrian promenade affords superb views across the olive groves to the distant mountains of the Sierra Mágina (south) and Sierra de Cazorla (east).

Capilla de los Benavides   CHAPEL
(Calle de San Francisco) This partially restored chapel, part of the former Convento de San Francisco, was one of Andrés de Vandelvira's masterpieces, built in the 1540s as the funerary chapel of the Benavides family. Devastated by an earthquake and later sacked by Napoleonic troops, it was semirestored in the 1980s. An arrangement of curved girders traces the outline of its majestic dome, over a space where some of the fine Renaissance carvings remain, controversially left open to the elements.

🎉 Festivals & Events

Semana Santa   HOLY WEEK
(www.semanasantabaeza.es; ⊙Mar-Apr) Baeza's Easter processions are solemn, grand and rooted very deep in the town's traditions. Evenings from Palm Sunday to Good Friday.

Feria   FAIR
(⊙mid-Aug) The summer fair starts with a big Carnaval-style procession of *gigantones* (papier mâché giants) and other colourful figures, and continues with five days of fireworks, a huge funfair, concerts and bullfights.

🛏 Sleeping

★**Hostal Aznaitín**   HOSTAL €
(☑953 74 07 88; www.hostalaznaitin.com; Calle Cabreros 2; s/d incl breakfast Sun-Thu €38/46, Fri & Sat €52/59; ❊🛜☎) 🅿 Welcoming, bright and modern Aznaitín is a far cry from the dreary *hostales* of old. Rooms are stylish and well-sized, with good mattresses and large, appealing photos of Baeza sights. Reception has masses of information and ideas on things to see and do in and around Baeza.

Hotel Puerta de la Luna   HERITAGE HOTEL €€
(☑953 74 70 19; www.hotelpuertadelaluna.com; Calle Canónigo Melgares Raya 7; s €70-99, d €70-111, buffet breakfast €15; 🅿❊@🛜☎) There is no doubt where Baeza's Renaissance-era nobility would stay if they were to return today. This luxurious hotel in a 17th-century mansion sports orange trees and a pool in its elegant patio, and beautifully furnished salons with welcoming fireplaces. The spacious rooms are enhanced by classical furnishings and art, and good big bathrooms.

🍴 Eating

Paseo de la Constitución and Plaza de España are lined with bar-cafe-restaurants that are great for watching local life, but the best finds are tucked away in the narrow old-town streets.

El Arcediano   TAPAS €
(Calle Barbacana 4; montaditos €5, raciones €10-12; ⊙8.30pm-midnight Thu, 2-4pm & 8.30pm-midnight Fri-Sun) A quirky spot on a narrow lane, with chandeliers, a big vase of flowers on the bar and a grapevine painted on the ceiling. El Arcediano serves up excellent large *montaditos* (slices of toasted bread with toppings) with anything from pork to anchovies, assorted cheeses, or classic mashed tomato and olive oil.

Bar Paco's   TAPAS €
(Calle de Santa Catalina; tapas €3.50-6; ⊙1.30-4pm & 8.30pm-midnight Fri-Sun, 2-4pm & 8.30pm-midnight Mon-Thu) Permanently thronged with locals and visitors (get here early if you want to sit down), Paco's prepares a big array of tasty, well-presented, creative tapas. The

OLIVE OIL: THE FACTS

You can't fail to notice that in the province of Jaén, the *aceituna* (olive) rules. Over 60 million olive trees carpet a full 40% of the landscape, and the aroma of their oil perfumes memories of any visit. In an average year these trees yield about 500,000 tonnes of olive oil, meaning that Jaén produces 40% of Spain's and 17% of the entire world's production. Almost the whole population depends, directly or indirectly, on this one crop.

Olives are harvested from October until about February. They are taken straight to oil mills to be mashed into a pulp that is then pressed to extract the oil, which is then decanted to remove water. Oil that's good enough for consumption without being refined is sold as *aceite de oliva virgen* (virgin olive oil), and the best of that is *virgen extra*. Plain *aceite de oliva* – known in the trade as *lampante* (lamp oil) – is oil that has to be refined before it's fit for consumption. Oils are tested for chemical composition and taste in International Olive Council laboratories before they can be labelled virgin or extra virgin.

A technological revolution since the late 20th century has changed the face of the olive oil world. On the way out, except in some smaller operations, are the traditional methods of harvesting (teams of people bashing the branches with poles), pulping (great conical stone rollers), pressing (squashing layers of pulp between esparto-grass mats) and decanting (four or five repeated processes taking eight or nine hours). Today's olives are shaken off the trees by tractor-driven vibrating machines; they are pulped mechanically; and centrifuge machines separate the liquids from the solids and do most of the decanting – all in a fraction of the time it used to take.

Jaén is proud of its high-quality olive oil: many restaurants will offer you a few different types to try, soaked up with bread. Quality oil is sold in specialist shops and good groceries, and direct at some mills.

Oleícola San Francisco (☑953 76 34 15; www.oleoturismojaen.com; Calle Pedro Pérez, Begíjar; 1½hr tours €5; ☉tours 11am & 5pm) These fascinating tours of a working oil mill near Baeza will teach you all you could want to know about the process of turning olives into oil, how the best oil is made and what distinguishes extra virgin from the rest. At the end you get to taste a few varieties, and you'll probably emerge laden with a bottle or two of San Francisco's high-quality product.

Tours can be given in English or French (ring ahead to ensure availability). To get there, turn off the A316 about 4km west of Baeza at Km 14, signposted to Begíjar, and turn right immediately past the petrol station after 1.4km.

Centro de Interpretación Olivar y Aceite (www.centrodeolivaryaceitelaloma.com; Corredera de San Francisco 32, Úbeda; adult/child €3.50/free; ☉10am-1pm & 6-9pm Tue-Sat, 10am-1pm Sun Jun-Sep, 11am-2pm & 5-8pm Tue-Sat, 11am-2pm Sun Oct-May) Úbeda's olive-oil interpretation centre explains all about the area's olive-oil history, and how the oil gets from the tree to your table, with the help of models, mill equipment and videos in English and Spanish. You get the chance to taste different oils, and to buy from a broad selection.

---

crêpes (with fillings like smoked salmon, avocado and potato) are particularly good, and portions are bigger than your average tapa.

El Nanchoas
ANDALUCIAN €€

(www.elnanchoas.com; Calle Comendadores 6; mains €7-15; ☉11.30am-4.30pm & 8pm-1am Mon & Wed-Sat, to 4.30pm Sun) Relaxed and friendly Nanchoas serves up well-prepared home-style Jaén favourites in a sunny little courtyard and stone-walled dining room. Try the tasty *lomo de orza* (pork loin slow-fried with spices then conserved in a clay vessel called an *orza*) with garlicky eggs, or some sheep's cheese with honey and raisins.

La Almazara
ANDALUCIAN €€

(www.restaurantelaalmazarabaeza.com; Pasaje del Cardenal Benavides 15; mains €9-18; ☉1-4pm & 8pm-midnight Tue-Sun) Has a great terrace facing the marvellous plateresque facade of the 16th-century *ayuntamiento* (town hall) across the street, as well as a bar and indoor dining area. La Almazara serves up lots of fresh fish and classic meat dishes, plus a *parrillada de verduras* (grilled vegetables) that's great for vegetarians who have grown weary of *revueltos* (scrambled-egg dishes).

Drinking

★Café Teatro Central BAR
(www.cafeteatrocentral.com; Calle Obispo Narváez 19; ⊘4pm-4am Tue-Sun, 9pm-4am Mon) Well worth a visit, except possibly on Wednesday – karaoke night. Owner Rafael has put tons of love into creating a fascinatingly eclectic environment with his display of historic instruments, coloured lighting, and decorations ranging from giant stone Buddhas to a miniature Big Ben. There's live music at about 11.30pm every Thursday, Friday and Saturday (anything but heavy metal!).

A delightful patio, complete with bubbling fountain and languid goddess statues, adds to the fun.

🛍 Shopping

La Casa del Aceite FOOD
(www.casadelaceite.com; Paseo de la Constitución 9; ⊘10am-2pm & 5-8.30pm Mon-Sat, to 2pm Sun) Sells a big range of quality olive oil, plus other local products such as wild-boar pâté, olives, cosmetics and ceramics.

ℹ Information

Tourist Office (☑953 77 99 82; www.andalucia.org; Plaza del Pópulo; ⊘9am-7.30pm Mon-Fri, 9.30am-3pm Sat & Sun)

ℹ Getting There & Around

BUS

Alsa (☑902 42 22 42; www.alsa.es) runs services from the **bus station** (☑953 74 04 68; Avenida Alcalde Puche Pardo), 900m northeast of Plaza de España.

TO	COST (€)	DURATION	FREQUENCY
Cazorla	4.90	1¾hr	3 daily
Córdoba	12	2½hr	2 daily
Granada	13	1½-2½hr	7 daily
Jaén	4.50	1hr	8 daily
Úbeda	1.20	15min	14 daily

CAR

Street parking in the centre is fairly restricted, but there's an **underground car park** (Calle Compañía; per 1/24hr €1.10/10; ⊘7.30am-11.30pm).

TRAIN

The nearest train station is **Linares–Baeza** (www.renfe.com), 13km northwest of town. One Alsa bus runs from Baeza bus station to the train station, at 5.30pm (€2.70, one hour); two come back, at 7.10am and 3.45pm. A taxi costs €23.

TO	COST (€)	DURATION	FREQUENCY
Almería	28	3¼hr	3 daily
Córdoba	20	1½hr	1 daily
Granada	from 9	3hr	1 daily
Jaén	6	45min	3 daily
Madrid	33	3-4hr	5-6 daily
Seville	29	3hr	1 daily

Úbeda

POP 33,900 / ELEV 760M

Úbeda (*oo*-be-dah) is a slightly more sophisticated proposition than its little sister Baeza. Aside from the splendour of its architecture, the town has some top-class tapas bars and restaurants, and an age-old ceramics tradition that is still turning out some very appealing wares.

The city became a Castilian bulwark on the Christian march south. Úbeda's aristocratic lions – despite a quarrelsome tendency that led Isabel la Católica to have most of the town's fortifications knocked down in 1506 – jockeyed successfully for influence at the Habsburg court in the 16th century. Francisco de los Cobos y Molina rose to be state secretary to King Carlos I, and his nephew Juan

JAÉN PROVINCE'S RENAISSANCE MASTER BUILDER

Most of the finest architecture that you see in Úbeda, Baeza and Jaén is the work of one man: Andrés de Vandelvira (1509–75), born in Alcaraz, Castilla-La Mancha, 150km northeast of Úbeda. Thanks to the patronage of Úbeda's Cobos and Molina families, Vandelvira almost single-handedly brought the Renaissance to Jaén province. His work spanned all three main phases of Spanish Renaissance architecture – the ornamental early phase known as plateresque, as seen in Úbeda's Sacra Capilla de El Salvador (p232); the purer line and classical proportions which emerged in the later Palacio de Vázquez de Molina (p232); and the austere late-Renaissance style (called Herreresque) of his last building, the Hospital de Santiago (p234). Little is known about Vandelvira's life, but his legacy is a jewel of Spanish culture.

JAÉN TO ÚBEDA SCENIC DRIVE

If you prefer long, scenic routes to short, unexciting ones, consider driving from Jaén to Úbeda via Albánchez de Mágina. The route takes you through the mountainous and beautiful Parque Natural Sierra Mágina, and Albánchez' little castle is arguably the most daringly perched of all Jaén province's daringly perched castles.

Turn off the A316 into Mancha Real and head to the pretty village of Torres. Now comes the most dramatic stage as the narrow JA3107 winds up over the 1250m-high Puerto de Albánchez and down to Albánchez de Mágina. The leaning tower of the 14th-century **Castillo de Albánchez** (admission free; ⊘24hr) stands on top of a single rock on a sheer cliff rising directly above the village. You can, surprisingly, walk up to it in about 20 steep minutes from the central Plaza de la Constitución. The bird's-eye views over the whitewashed village and surrounding mountains are stunning.

From Albánchez, continue to Úbeda via Jimena, Bedmar (where you can investigate the remains of a 15th-century fortress) and Jódar.

Vázquez de Molina succeeded him in the job and kept it under Carlos' successor Felipe II.

High office exposed these men to the Renaissance aesthetic just then reaching Spain from Italy. Much of the wealth that the Molinas and flourishing local agriculture brought to Úbeda was invested in what are now considered to be some of the purest examples of Renaissance architecture in Spain. As a result, Úbeda (along with neighbouring Baeza) is one of the few places in Andalucía boasting stunning architecture that was *not* built by the Moors.

◉ Sights

Most of Úbeda's splendid buildings are in the maze of narrow, winding streets and expansive squares that make up the *casco antiguo* (old quarter), on the southern side of the mostly drab modern town. The old town is particularly beautiful at night with its wonderful plateresque facades floodlit gold against inky black skies.

The lovely Plaza Vázquez de Molina is the monumental heart of the old town and the perfect place to start exploring.

★**Sacra Capilla de El Salvador**   CHAPEL
(Sacred Chapel of the Saviour; www.fundacionmedinaceli.org; Plaza Vázquez de Molina; adult/child incl audio guide €5/2.50; ⊘9.30am-2pm & 5-7pm Mon-Sat, 11.30am-2pm & 5-8pm Sun, afternoon hours 30min earlier Apr-May, 1hr earlier Oct-Mar) The purity of Renaissance lines is best expressed in this famous chapel, built between 1536 and 1559. The first of many works executed in Úbeda by Andrés de Vandelvira, it was commissioned by Francisco de los Cobos y Molina as his family's funerary chapel.

Its main facade is a preeminent example of plateresque style, with an orgy of classical sculpture depicting Greek gods on the underside of the arch – a Renaissance touch that would have been inconceivable a few decades earlier.

Numerous skulls scattered among the facade's decoration are a reminder that the building is a funerary chapel.

Inside the chapel, the Capilla Mayor is suffused in golden light beneath a stately dome painted in gold, blue and red, and features a grand 1560s altarpiece sculpture of the transfiguration by Alonso de Berruguete. The chapel is still privately owned by the Seville-based ducal Medinaceli family, descendants of the Cobos.

Next to the chapel stands what was originally its chaplain's house, the **Palacio del Deán Ortega** – another Vandelvira creation. The mansion is now Úbeda's luxurious *parador* hotel (p235).

★**Palacio de Vázquez de Molina**   MANSION
(Plaza Vázquez de Molina; ⊘8am-2.30pm Mon-Fri) **FREE** Lucky Úbeda functionaries – the building where they push their pens has to be the most beautiful *ayuntamiento* (town hall) in Spain. It was built by Vandelvira in about 1562 as a mansion for Juan Vázquez de Molina, whose coat of arms surmounts the doorway.

The perfectly proportioned, deeply Italian-influenced facade is divided into three tiers by slender cornices, with the sculpted caryatids on the top level continuing the lines of the Corinthian and Ionic pilasters on the lower tiers.

Úbeda

Úbeda

◎ Top Sights
1 Casa Museo Arte Andalusí B3
2 Palacio de Vázquez de Molina............. B3
3 Sacra Capilla de El Salvador............... C3
4 Sinagoga del Agua B2

◎ Sights
5 Antiguo Ayuntamiento C3
6 Centro de Interpretación Olivar y
  Aceite.. B2
7 Iglesia de San Pablo C2
8 Iglesia de Santa María de los
  Reales Alcázares B4
9 Museo de San Juan de la Cruz C2
10 Palacio del Deán Ortega C3
11 Palacio Vela de los Cobos B3
12 Plaza 1° de Mayo C3

🛏 Sleeping
13 Afán de Rivera B4
14 Hotel El Postigo................................. A3

15 Hotel María de Molina B3
16 Palacio de la Rambla.......................... A3
  Parador Condestable
  Dávalos .... (see 10)

🍴 Eating
17 Cantina de la Estación C1
18 La Taberna B2
19 La Tintorera....................................... B2
20 Misa de 12... C2
21 Restaurante Antique.......................... B2
22 Zeitúm.. C2

🍷 Drinking & Nightlife
23 Beltraneja... B3

🛍 Shopping
24 Alfarería Tito B3
25 Artesur... A3

Iglesia de Santa María de los Reales Alcázares　　CHURCH
(www.santamariadeubeda.es; Plaza Vázquez de Molina; adult/child €4/1.50; ☺4-8pm Mon, 11am-2pm & 4-8pm Tue-Sat, 9.30am-2pm Sun) Úbeda's grand parish church, founded in the 13th century on the site of Muslim Úbeda's main mosque, is a conglomerate of Gothic, Mudéjar, Renaissance, baroque and neoclassical styles. The main portico, facing Plaza Vázquez de Molina, is a beautiful late Renaissance composition dating from 1604–12, with a relief sculpture showing the adoration of the shepherds.

Inside, the intricate Mudéjar-style *artesonado* (ceiling of interlaced beams) is the fruit of a recent restoration.

★**Casa Museo Arte Andalusí**　　MUSEUM
(✆953 75 40 14; Calle Narváez 11; admission €2; ☺11am-2pm & 5.30-8pm) This fascinating private museum comprises a 16th-century house that was inhabited by *conversos* (Jews who converted to Christianity) and a huge, diverse collection of antiques assembled by owner Paco Castro. The informal guided tours make it all come alive. The first hint that this is somewhere special is the original 16th-century heavy carved door. Ring the bell if it is closed.

Paco has lovingly restored the house without detracting from its crumbling charm. Above the central patio are balconies and a painted Mudéjar-style ceiling and eaves. It is the ideal faded-grandeur setting for Paco's collection of Renaissance doorways, 16th-century water jugs, antique bridal trunks, tapestries and artwork, collected from all over Spain. Downstairs, the barrel-vaulted bodega is lined with photos of Paco and his flamenco chums, including the late maestro Paco de Lucía, who played here. It's hoped flamenco nights here may start again.

Palacio Vela de los Cobos　　MANSION
(Calle Juan Montilla; tours €4; ☺tours noon Sat & Sun, 1.15pm Tue-Sun, 6pm Fri & Sat, 7.15pm Sat) This fascinating Vandelvira-designed 16th-century mansion, elegantly restored in the 19th century, is still a private home, fully furnished and replete with paintings, antiques and books. The owner guides tours himself: get tickets at Semer (✆953 75 79 16; Calle Juan Montilla 3; ☺9.30am-2pm Tue-Sun, 5-8pm Fri-Sat), across the street.

★**Sinagoga del Agua**　　MUSEUM
(www.sinagogadelagua.com; Calle Roque Rojas 2; 45min tours in Spanish adult/child €4/3;

☺10.30am-2pm & 4.45-7.30pm) The medieval Sinagoga del Agua was discovered in 2006 by a refreshingly ethical property developer who intended to build apartments here, only to discover that every swing of the pickaxe revealed some tantalising piece of an archaeological puzzle. The result is this sensitive re-creation of a centuries-old synagogue and rabbi's house, using original masonry whenever possible. Features include the women's gallery, a bodega with giant storage vessels, and a *mikveh* ritual bath.

There is evidence of a sizeable Jewish community in medieval Islamic Úbeda, cohabiting peacefully with the considerably larger Muslim population.

Plaza 1° de Mayo　　SQUARE
Broad Plaza 1º de Mayo was originally Úbeda's market square and bullring. It was also the grisly site of Inquisition burnings, which local worthies used to watch from the gallery of the Antiguo Ayuntamiento (Old Town Hall) in the southwestern corner. The Iglesia de San Pablo (admission free; ☺11am-1pm & 6-8pm Tue-Sat, to 1pm Sun), on the square's north side, has a particularly elaborate late-Gothic portal from 1511.

Museo de San Juan de la Cruz　　MUSEUM
(✆953 75 06 15; http://sanjuandelacruzubeda.com; Calle del Carmen 13; admission incl audio guide €3.50; ☺11am-1pm & 5-7pm Tue-Sun) This sizeable museum is devoted to the celebrated mystic and religious reformer St John of the Cross, who died here in 1591. The plethora of memorabilia includes a reconstructed monk's cell with a lifelike figure of St John writing at a table – plus a couple of fingers from his right hand in a glass case!

Hospital de Santiago　　ARCHITECTURE
(Calle Obispo Cobos; ☺10am-2pm & 5-9pm, closed Sun Jul, closed Sat & Sun Aug) **FREE** Andrés de Vandelvira's last architectural project, completed in 1575, has been dubbed the Escorial of Andalucía in reference to the famous monastery outside Madrid, built in a similarly grand, sober late-Renaissance style. The finely proportioned building, which stands outside the old town, 500m west of Plaza de Andalucía, has a broad, two-level, marble-columned patio, and a wide staircase with colourful original frescoes.

It now acts as a cultural centre, housing a library, exhibition halls, and a concert hall in the chapel.

✨ Festivals & Events

Semana Santa HOLY WEEK
(⊘Mar-Apr) Eighteen solemn brotherhoods carry sacred church statues through the town in atmospheric processions during the week leading up to Easter Sunday. Thursday and Friday see processions during the daytime as well as after dark.

Festival Internacional de Música y Danza Ciudad de Úbeda MUSIC FESTIVAL
(www.festivaldeubeda.com; ⊘May-Jun) This festival concentrates on classical music, but also includes jazz, flamenco and ethnic music, over a month from early or mid-May.

🛏 Sleeping

Hotel El Postigo HOTEL €
(☑953 75 00 00; www.hotelelpostigo.com; Calle Postigo 5; s/d Sun-Thu €46/51, Fri & Sat €70/75; ✳@🛜🏊) A small, appealing, modern hotel on a quiet street, El Postigo provides spacious, comfy rooms in red, black and white. Staff are welcoming, and there's a pleasant courtyard as well as a large sitting room with a log fire in winter.

★Afán de Rivera HERITAGE HOTEL €€
(☑953 79 19 87; www.hotelafanderivera.com; Calle Afán de Rivera 4; r €70-85; ✳🛜) This incredible small hotel lies inside one of Úbeda's oldest buildings, predating the Renaissance. Expertly run by the amiable Jorge, it has beautifully historic common areas, and comfortable rooms that offer far more than is usual at this price: shaving kits, fancy shampoos and tastefully eclectic decor combining the traditional and the contemporary.

Breakfast is a locally sourced feast worth every *céntimo* of its €10 cost.

Palacio de la Rambla HISTORIC HOTEL €€
(☑953 75 01 96; www.palaciodelarambla.com; Plaza del Marqués de la Rambla 1; incl breakfast s €70-96, d €100-130; ⊘closed Jul-Aug; ✳🛜) The lovely Palacio de la Rambla gives you the full aristocratic mansion experience. The ivy-clad patio is wonderfully romantic, there's a beautiful salon opening on to a garden-patio, and each room is clad in precious antiques, so that it feels like you're staying with aristocratic friends rather than in a hotel.

Hotel María de Molina HISTORIC HOTEL €€
(☑953 79 53 56; www.mariademolina.es; Plaza del Ayuntamiento; s/d Sun-Thu €54/80, Fri & Sat €64/91; ✳🛜🏊) The attractive María de Molina is housed in a 16th-century mansion facing a picturesque plaza. The well-appointed rooms are arranged around a central patio decorated with a few historic tapestries and leafy plants. Don't get too excited about the pool – it's minuscule.

Parador
Condestable Dávalos HISTORIC HOTEL €€€
(☑953 75 03 45; www.parador.es; Plaza Vázquez de Molina; r €188; 🅿✳🛜) One of Spain's original *paradors* (opened in 1930) and an inspiration for many that were to follow, this plush hotel occupies a historic monument, the Palacio del Deán Ortega (p232), on the wonderful Plaza Vázquez Molina. It has, of course, been comfortably modernised in period style and is appropriately luxurious.

🍴 Eating

Úbeda is the culinary hotspot of Jaén province; its talented chefs are one reason why Spaniards flock here for weekend breaks.

★Misa de 12 ANDALUCÍAN €€
(www.misade12.com; Plaza 1º de Mayo 7; raciónes €9-20; ⊘noon-midnight Wed-Sun) From the tiny cooking station in this little corner bar, a succession of truly succulent platters magically emerges – slices of *presa ibérica* (a tender cut of Iberian pork) grilled to perfection, juicy fillets of *bacalao* (cod), or *revuelto de pulpo y gambas* (eggs scrambled with octopus and shrimp).

Staff are attentive and efficient even when run off their feet, which they often are due to the place's popularity.

★Cantina de la Estación CONTEMPORARY ANDALUCIAN €€
(☑687 777230; www.cantinalaestacion.com; Cuesta Corredera 1; mains €15-19; ⊘1.30-4pm & 8.15pm-midnight Thu-Sun, to 4pm Mon-Tue) The charming originality here starts with the design – three rooms with railway themes (the main dining room being the deluxe carriage). It continues with the seasonal array of inspired fusion dishes based on locally available ingredients, such as wild boar in red-wine sauce on vegetable couscous, or millefeuille of smoked salmon, Parmesan and béchamel.

Every dish is made with a different olive oil, and food presentation is a true art form here. Service is welcoming and attentive.

Zeitúm CONTEMPORARY SPANISH €€
(www.zeitum.com; Calle San Juan de la Cruz 10; mains €12-16; ⊘1-4pm & 8.30-11.30pm Tue-Sun) Zeitúm is housed in a headily historic 14th-century building, where staff will

ÚBEDA POTTERY

Úbeda's pottery tradition dates back into the mists of time, and the town's typical emerald-green glaze has its origins in Islamic times. The traditional craft has been kept alive by a few dedicated master potters, notably Pablo Tito (1909–98) and his sons Paco Tito and Juan Tito. They have experimented with new designs, while also reviving old techniques and continuing to use some of the very few medieval Arab-type kilns left in Spain.

Today there are five workshop/showrooms along Calle Valencia in the potters' quarter, Barrio San Millán (just east of the old town), and the potters are often willing to explain some of their ancient techniques.

Alfarería Tito (Plaza del Ayuntamiento 12; ⊙9am-2pm & 4-8pm) Juan Tito's distinctive style veers away from the classic green glaze, with intricate patterns and bright colours, especially blue. His large old-town showroom/workshop displays and sells a big range of very covetable wares. You're looking at around €20 for a decorative plate; the dazzling designs and artisanship are well worth it.

happily show you the original well, and the stonework and beams bearing Jewish symbols. Olive oil tastings (a selection of oils to soak bread in) are a feature here, along with the top-class preparation of diverse dishes such as organic egg with raclette and whitebait, or pork sirloin with goats' cheese.

La Tintorera   CONTEMPORARY ANDALUCIAN €€
(www.latintorera.es; Calle Real 27; raciones €8-15; ⊙noon-4pm & 8-11.45pm Tue-Sat, to 4pm Sun; 🛜) With a warm, intimate atmosphere enjoyed by couples and small groups of friends, the Tintorera turns out inventive preparations of classic ingredients – try the timbale of aubergines, ham and cheese (a stack of the said ingredients baked juicily together), or *lomo de orza* with potatoes, fried egg and paprika oil. Everything except the silver-framed mirror is in black and white, including the staff's outfits.

Restaurante Antique   CONTEMPORARY ANDALUCÍAN €€
(📞953 75 76 18; www.restauranteantique.com; Calle Real 25; mains €12-26, raciones €9-18; ⊙1-4pm & 8-11.30pm) Antique is not at all 'antique', but puts a contemporary, high-quality twist on traditional raw materials – try its vegetable wok with partridge and rice noodles, or the mini-kebab of seafood marinated in soy, wine and mustard. Decor is fittingly simple but stylish.

La Taberna   ANDALUCIAN €€
(Calle Real 7; mains €10-20; ⊙noon-3.30pm & 7.30pm-midnight; 🐾) Simple menu, quick service, tasty food and a wide variety of clientele – La Taberna is an oasis of solid reliability in a town where food can sometimes be a little on the expensive side.

🍷 Drinking & Nightlife

Most of the drinking in Úbeda takes place in the many excellent tapas bars.

Beltraneja   MUSIC BAR
(Calle Alcolea 6; ⊙4pm-3am Sun-Thu, to 4am Fri & Sat) Hidden away in the old town's back streets, Beltraneja combines a cavernous interior of exposed stone, flocked wallpaper and graffiti-style murals with an ample open-air courtyard. Music moves from rock/soul/blues in the afternoon to indie and pop for dancing to at night; quite a party gets going on Saturdays.

🛍 Shopping

Artesur   ARTS & CRAFTS
(Plaza del Marqués de la Rambla 2; ⊙10am-9pm) A rambling shop with a big choice of ceramics, coloured-glass lights, esparto, and brass and wrought-iron decorative items – all handcrafted locally.

ℹ Information

Oficina de Turismo (📞953 77 92 04; www.andalucia.org; Calle Baja del Marqués 4; ⊙9am-3.30pm Sat-Tue, to 7.30pm Wed-Fri)

Turismo de Úbeda (www.turismodeubeda.com) The town's useful tourism website.

ℹ Getting There & Around

BUS

Alsa (📞902 42 22 42; www.alsa.es) runs services from the **bus station** (📞953 75 21 57; Calle

San José 6), which is in the new part of town, 700m west of Plaza de Andalucía.

TO	COST (€)	DURATION	FREQUENCY
Baeza	1.15	15min	12 daily
Cazorla	4.05	1hr	4 daily
Córdoba	12	2½hr	4 daily
Granada	12.80	2½hr	7 daily
Jaén	5.20	1¼hr	10 daily

CAR
Parking in the old town is free, but often difficult to find – the best bet is Redonda de Miradores. The underground **Parking Plaza** (Plaza de Andalucía; per 1/24hr €1.50/18; ☑7.30am-11.30pm) is reasonably convenient.

TRAIN
The nearest station is **Linares–Baeza** (www.renfe.com), 21km northwest, which you can reach on Linares-bound buses (€1.95, 30 minutes, four daily). Daily trains head to Madrid, Jaén, Almería, Granada, Córdoba and Seville.

Cazorla
POP 7340 / ELEV 836M

This picturesque, bustling white town sits beneath towering crags, just where the Sierra de Cazorla rises up from a rolling sea of olive trees, 45km east of Úbeda. It makes the perfect launching pad for exploring the beautiful Parque Natural Sierras de Cazorla, Segura y Las Villas, which begins dramatically among the cliffs of Peña de los Halcones (Falcon Crag) directly above the town.

◎ Sights
The heart of town is Plaza de la Corredera, with busy bars and the elegant *ayuntamiento* and clock tower looking down from the southeast corner. Canyonlike streets lead south to the Balcón de Zabaleta. This little mirador is like a sudden window in a blank wall, with stunning views up to the Castillo de la Yedra and beyond. From here another narrow street leads down to Cazorla's most picturesque square, Plaza de Santa María.

Iglesia de Santa María   CHURCH
(Plaza de Santa María; ☑10am-1pm & 4-8pm, to 7pm Oct-Mar) This picturesque shell of a grand church was designed by great Renaissance architect Andrés de Vandelvira in the 16th century, and later wrecked by Napoleonic troops in reprisal for Cazorla's tenacious resistance. It houses Cazorla's tourist office (p238), which offers interesting

half-hour tours (€2 per person) through the *bovedas* (vaults) that channel the Río Cerezuelo underneath the church.

★ Castillo de la Yedra   CASTLE, MUSEUM
(Museo del Alto Guadalquivir; EU citizen/other free/€1.50; ☑9am-7.30pm Tue-Sat, to 3.30pm Sun & daily mid-Jun–mid-Sep) Cazorla's dramatic Castle of the Ivy, a 700m walk above Plaza de Santa María, has great views and is home to the interesting Museum of the Upper Guadalquivir, whose diverse collections include traditional agricultural tools and kitchen utensils, religious art, models of an old olive mill, and a small chapel featuring a life-size Romanesque-Byzantine crucifixion sculpture.

The castle is of Muslim origin, comprehensively rebuilt in the 14th century after the Reconquista.

🏃 Activities
There are some great walks straight out of Cazorla town – all uphill to start with, but your reward is beautiful forest paths and fabulous panoramas of cliffs, crags, circling vultures and lonely monasteries. Good maps and information in anything except Spanish are hard to come by, but the main routes are signposted and waymarked. Cazorla's tourist office has maps with descriptions in Spanish. Editorial Alpina's *Sierra de Cazorla* map is useful and sold in some shops in Cazorla.

Sendero del Gilillo   WALKING
(PRA313) The best walk for the fit and energetic is this full-day 21km loop from Cazorla up to the Puerto del Gilillo pass (nearly 1100m higher than the town and with stupendous views) and back via the Loma de los Castellones ridge, Puerto del Tejo pass, Prado Redondo forest house and Ermita Virgen de la Cabeza chapel.

The route ascends from Cazorla's Iglesia de Santa María via the Ermita de San Sebastián chapel (2.2km, about two hours return) and the Riogazas picnic area (3.5km, about three hours return), either of which makes a scenic there-and-back walk if you fancy something shorter.

Sendero de Ermitas y Monasterios   WALKING
(SLA7) An 11km loop passing a few isolated chapels and monasteries in the hills, the SLA7 follows the PRA313 (Sendero del Gilillo) for 4km before diverging to the right along the La Iruela–El Chorro road, then descending back to town via the Monasterio de Montesión. The walk takes about four hours.

Turisnat DRIVING TOUR
(📞 953 72 13 51; www.turisnat.es; Avenida del Parque Natural 2; ½-day tours per person €30-39, full day €45-49) An amalgamation of seven experienced local agencies, Turisnat is a reliable option for wildlife-spotting 4WD trips along the forest tracks of the *parque natural*.

★ Festivals & Events

Bluescazorla MUSIC
(www.bluescazorla.com; 🕑 Jul) Cazorla has a surprisingly cosmopolitan vibe for a remote country town and demonstrates it with this annual three-day blues fest, which sees international musicians and several thousand fans packing into the town.

🛏 Sleeping

Hotel Guadalquivir HOTEL €
(📞 953 72 02 68; www.hguadalquivir.com; Calle Nueva 6; s/d incl breakfast €42/56; ❄️ 🖥) Welcoming, family-run Guadalquivir has well-kept, comfy, ample rooms with pine furniture, though no memorable views. It's well run, centrally located, and serves up a decent breakfast. It all equals straightforward, no-fuss, good value for money.

Casa Rural Plaza de Santa María CASA RURAL €
(📞 953 72 20 87; www.plazadesantamaria.com; Callejón Plaza Santa María 5; incl breakfast s €35, d €48-58; ❄️ 🖥) This multilevel house is set round a lovely garden-patio with a fish pond. Its terraces and a couple of the rooms enjoy superb views over Plaza de Santa María, Cazorla's castle and the mountains beyond. The attractive rooms are all different, in yellows, oranges and blues, with a variety of folksy styles.

Los Abedules APARTMENT €
(📞 953 12 43 08; www.losabedules-cazorla.com; Los Peralejos; 2-person apt €60, 4-person apt €70-80; 🅿️ 🖥 ♒) Surrounded by olive groves 6km west of Cazorla (200m off the A319 towards Úbeda), English-run Los Abedules is an ideal base if you have a car. There are fully furnished, comfortable apartments and a salt-water pool for cooling down after a long day out. Minimum two-night stay. Pets welcome.

🍴 Eating

There are good bars on Cazorla's main squares, where you can choose tapas and *raciones*.

Bar Las Vegas TAPAS €
(Plaza de la Corredera 17; tapas €1-2, raciones €10-12; 🕑 10am-midnight) It's tiny but it's the best

of Cazorla's central bars, with barrel tables outside (and packed tables inside when the weather's poor). They do great tapas including one called *gloria bendita* (blessed glory), which turns out to be scrambled eggs with prawns and capsicum, as well as *raciones* of local favourites such as cheese, ham, venison and *lomo de orza*.

★ Mesón Leandro CONTEMPORARY SPANISH €€
(www.mesonleandro.com; Calle Hoz 3; mains €9-20; 🕑 1.30-4pm & 8.30-11pm Wed-Mon) Just behind the Iglesia de Santa María, Leandro brings a touch of sophistication to Cazorla dining – professional, friendly service in a bright, attractive dining room with lazy music, and just one token set of antlers on the wall. The broad menu of nicely presented dishes encompasses the likes of *fettuccine a la marinera*, as well as partridge-and-pheasant pâté and a terrific *solomillo de ciervo* (venison sirloin).

La Cueva de Juan Pedro ANDALUCIAN €€
(Plaza de Santa María; raciones & mains €8-20, menú €10-13; 🕑 noon-10pm) An ancient, wood-beamed place with hams and drying peppers dangling from the bar ceiling, and boar and mouflon (wild sheep) heads protruding from the walls. Taste the traditional Cazorla *conejo* (rabbit), *trucha* (trout), *rin-rán* (a mix of salted cod, potato and dried red peppers), *jabalí* (wild boar) or *ciervo* (red-deer venison).

ℹ️ Information

Oficina Municipal de Turismo (📞 953 71 01 02; www.cazorla.es; Plaza de Santa María; 🕑 10am-1pm & 4-8pm, to 7pm Oct-Mar) Inside the remains of Santa María church, with useful information on the natural park as well as the town.

ℹ️ Getting There & Around

BUS

Alsa (www.alsa.es) runs three to five daily buses to Úbeda (€4, one hour), Baeza (€4.80, 1¼ hours), Jaén (€9.25, two to 2½ hours) and Granada (€18, 3¾ hours). The bus stop is on Calle Hilario Marco, 500m north of Plaza de la Corredera via Plaza de la Constitución.

CAR

Parking and driving in the old, central part of town is near impossible, but there's a reasonable amount of free parking around the periphery. **Parking Hogar Sur** (Calle Cronista Lorenzo Polaino; per 1/24hr €1.25/10; 🕑 7am-11pm), just down from Plaza de la Constitución, is convenient.

Parque Natural Sierras de Cazorla, Segura y Las Villas

One of the biggest drawcards in Jaén province – and, for nature lovers, in all of Andalucía – is the mountainous, lushly wooded Parque Natural Sierras de Cazorla, Segura y Las Villas. This is the largest protected area in Spain – 2099 sq km of craggy mountain ranges, deep, green river valleys, canyons, waterfalls, remote hilltop castles and abundant wildlife, with a snaking, 20km-long reservoir, the Embalse del Tranco, in its midst. The abrupt geography, with altitudes varying between 460m at the lowest point up to 2107m at the summit of Cerro Empanadas, makes for dramatic changes in the landscape. The Río Guadalquivir, Andalucía's longest river, begins in the south of the park, and flows northwards into the reservoir, before heading west across Andalucía to the Atlantic Ocean.

The best times to visit the park are spring and autumn, when the vegetation is at its most colourful and temperatures pleasant. The park is hugely popular with Spanish tourists and attracts several hundred thousand visitors each year. The peak periods are Semana Santa, July, August, and weekends from April to October.

Exploring the park is a lot easier if you have a vehicle, and there are plenty of places to stay within the park as well as in Cazorla town. The network of paved and unpaved roads and footpaths reaches some pretty remote areas and offers plenty of scope for panoramic day walks or drives. If you don't have a vehicle, you have the option of guided walks, 4WD excursions and wildlife-spotting trips, which will get you out into the wild areas.

🛏 Sleeping

La Mesa Segureña APARTMENT €

(📞953 48 21 01; https://es-la.facebook.com/lamesa desegura; Calle Cruz de Montoria, Segura de la

Sierra de Cazorla

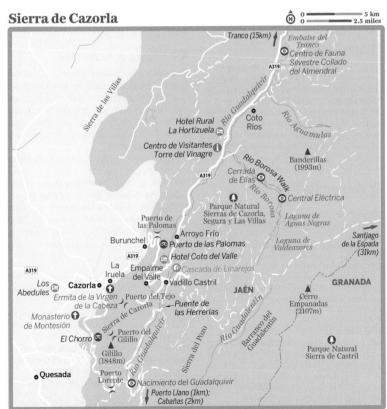

JAÉN PROVINCE PARQUE NATURAL SIERRAS DE CAZORLA, SEGURA Y LAS VILLAS

ℹ️ WALK PREPARED

The website www.sierrasdecazorla seguraylasvillas.es is a useful source of information in English, including walk descriptions and maps; www. ventanadelvisitante and (for the north of the park) www.sierradesegura.com have better walk information and maps, but in Spanish only. Tourist offices and park information offices can also help, but most handouts are again in Spanish only.

When walking, be sure to equip yourself with enough water and appropriate clothes. Temperatures up in the hills are generally several degrees lower than down in the valleys, and the wind can be cutting at any time. In winter the park is often blanketed in snow.

Sierra; 2-person apt €60-75; 🛜) Cosy apartments just below Segura castle, with great views, a touch of bright art, fireplaces and minikitchens. Good discounts are often available from the quoted rates.

ℹ️ Information

Centro de Visitantes Torre del Vinagre
(📞 953 72 13 51; Ctra A319 Km 48; ⊙10am-2pm & 4-7pm, afternoons 3-8pm Jul-Sep, 4-6pm Oct-Mar, closed Mon Sep-Jun) The park's main visitors centre is 16km north of Arroyo Frío. It can provide information on walking routes and other attractions, though staff may not speak English. There's a cafe and shop here (with some maps and guides), and a botanical garden over the road.

ℹ️ Getting There & Away

BUS

Carcesa (📞 953 72 11 42) runs buses at 7.15am and 2.30pm, Monday and Friday only, from Cazorla to Empalme del Valle, Arroyo Frío, Torre del Vinagre (€4.25, one hour) and Coto Ríos. They start back from Coto Ríos at 9am and 4.15pm. No buses link the northern part of the park with the centre or south, and there are no buses to Segura de la Sierra or Hornos.

CAR

The A319 from Cazorla heads up through the centre of the park past the Embalse del Tranco almost to Hornos, where the A317 heads southeast to Santiago de la Espada. Roads feed into the north of the park from Villanueva del Arzobispo and other towns on the A32. There are at least seven petrol stations in the park.

The South of the Park

The A319, heading northeast from Cazorla, enters the park after 7km at Burunchel, then winds 6km up to the 1200m **Puerto de las Palomas** pass. The mirador here affords wonderful views, opening out northwards down the Guadalquivir valley. Three twisting kilometres downhill from here is Empalme del Valle, a junction where the A319 turns north to follow the Guadalquivir to **Arroyo Frío** (6km). This is the most commercialised of the park's villages with a rash of restaurants, tour agencies and accommodation on and off the main road.

Past Arroyo Frío, the A319 continues 16km along the valley to the park's main visitors centre, the Centro de Visitantes Torre del Vinagre (p240) and the turn-off for the wonderful Río Borosa walk (p241). After another 10km the **Embalse del Tranco** opens out beside the road; several miradors offer panoramas over its waters as the A319 heads another 16km north, before crossing the dam that holds back the reservoir near the small village of Tranco.

🎯 Sights & Activities

Nacimiento del Guadalquivir   SPRING
(Source of the Guadalquivir) An interesting detour from Empalme del Valle will take you past Vadillo Castril village to the Puente de las Herrerías bridge (7km) and then 11km on southward by unpaved road to the Guadalquivir's source.

From here you can, if you like, continue a further 9km east then south (unpaved) to Cabañas, which, at 2027m, is one of the highest peaks in the park (it's a 3km round-trip walk of about 1½ hours from the road to the summit and back). Or you can head west then north back to Cazorla (26km) via the Puerto Lorente pass, on unpaved roads most of the way.

Centro de Fauna Silvestre Collado del Almendral   NATURE RESERVE
(📞 680 149028; Ctra A319 Km 59; adult/child €9/7; ⊙ from 10am Tue-Sun; 🅿️ 👶) On a spur of land between the Embalse del Tranco and the A319, 7km north of Coto Ríos, this is a 1 sq km enclosed animal park where you can see ibex, mouflon, deer and wild boar in semi-liberty. Visits are by minitrain along 5km of road through the park, followed by a 1.5km walk taking in three miradors.

WILD THINGS

If you're a wildlife enthusiast, you have to get yourself to the Cazorla natural park. The chances of spotting wildlife are better here than almost anywhere else in Andalucía. Creatures such as red and fallow deer, ibex, wild boar, mouflon (a wild sheep) and red squirrels are all present in good numbers, and are surprisingly visible once you get out on the trails (even along the roads in the case of deer). The autumn mating season (September and October for deer, November for mouflon and wild boar) is a particularly exciting time to observe the big mammals. The park is also home to some 180 bird species, including griffon vultures, golden eagles, peregrine falcons and even the majestic *quebrantahuesos* (lammergeier or bearded vulture), one of Europe's biggest birds, which is being reintroduced here after dying out in the 1980s. In short, get walking and keep those binoculars at the ready!

Closing times can range from 4pm in winter to as late as 10pm in July or August. Call ahead if you want to know exact times.

★ Río Borosa Walk
WALKING

The most popular walk in the Parque Natural Sierras de Cazorla, Segura y Las Villas follows the Río Borosa upstream through scenery that progresses from the pretty to the majestic, via a gorge and two tunnels to two beautiful mountain lakes – an ascent of 500m. The walk is 12km each way and takes about seven hours there and back.

To reach the start, turn east off the A319 at the 'Sendero Río Borosa' sign opposite the Centro de Visitantes Torre del Vinagre (p240), and go 1.7km. The first section of the walk criss-crosses the tumbling river on a couple of bridges. After just over 3km, where the track starts climbing to the left, take a path forking right. This leads through a beautiful 1.5km section where the valley narrows to a gorge, the Cerrada de Elías, and the path changes to a wooden walkway. You re-emerge on the dirt road and continue for 4km to the Central Eléctrica, a small hydroelectric station.

Past the power station, the path crosses a footbridge, where a 'Nacimiento de Aguas Negras, Laguna de Valdeazores' sign directs you ahead. About 1.5km from the station, the path turns left and zigzags up into a tunnel cut into the cliff for water flowing to the power station. It takes about five minutes to walk the narrow path through the tunnel, then there's a short section in the open air before a second tunnel, which takes about one minute to get through. You emerge just below the dam of the Laguna de Aguas Negras, a picturesque little reservoir surrounded by hills and trees. Cross the dam then walk about 1km south to a similar-sized natural lake, the Laguna de Valdeazores, the end-point of the walk.

Due to its popularity, it's preferable to do this walk on a weekday! Do carry a water bottle: there are good trackside springs but the last is at the Central Eléctrica. A torch is comforting, if not essential, for the tunnels.

🛏 Sleeping

Hotel Rural La Hortizuela
RURAL HOTEL €

(☑ 953 71 31 50; Ctra A319 Km 50.5; s/d €35/50; ☺ closed Dec-Feb; P 🛜 ➿) The 20 rooms here are well-kept, with splashes of colour, but nothing fancy. What's special is the beautiful natural setting in wooded four-hectare grounds, which are fenced in to protect plants such as wild orchids and wild asparagus. Wildlife, including deer, boar and red squirrels, is plentiful in the surrounding woodlands.

A bar and good-value restaurant add to the appeal. It's 1km off the A319, 3km north of Torre del Vinagre visitors centre.

Hotel Coto del Valle
HOTEL €€

(☑ 953 12 40 67; www.cotodelvalle.com; Ctra A319 Km 34.3; s/d from €68/90; ☺ closed mid-Dec–

THE GR247 CIRCUIT

One number crops up on footpath signs in every part of the Parque Natural Sierras de Cazorla, Segura y Las Villas: GR247. This 479km circuit travels right round the park, passing through or close to most of its most beautiful and interesting spots. It's designed in 21 stages, with basic overnight refuges provided where other accommodation is lacking. Nearly all of it is cyclable as well as walkable. For detailed information see www.sierrasdecazorlaseguraylas villas.es/gr247.

EL YELMO

El Yelmo (1808m) is one of the highest and most panoramic mountains in the north of the park. A 5.5km road – paved all the way, but single-track in parts – goes right to the summit, which suffers from a rash of communications towers but has magnificent 360-degree views. El Yelmo is a favourite take-off point for paragliders and is the focus of a big free-flying fiesta, the **Festival Internacional del Aire** (www.fiaelyelmo.com), which attracts thousands of people for three days every June. For tandem flights contact **Olivair** (607 301716; www.olivair.org), based in Beas de Segura.

To get to El Yelmo, take the A317A from Hornos as it winds its way east up into the pine forests, with high mountains rising on both sides. Go left (signposted to Segura and Siles) at a junction after 13km, and in 1km you'll see a road taking off to the left, between a ruined building and a smaller intact one which is the El Campillo walkers' refuge. This is the road up to El Yelmo. If you'd prefer to walk up, take the path signed 'Derivación 2 Bosques del Sur' from the El Campillo refuge. It shortens the climb to 3km (about 1½ hours).

end Jan; P❄️📶🏊🅿️) This large-ish, rustic-veneer hotel stands on a scenic spot on the Empalme del Valle–Arroyo Frío road. What really gives it an edge are the big outdoor pool in lawned gardens, and the superb, cavelike spa with its great big warm pool and panoramic Jacuzzi section.

Rooms are reasonably sized and pleasant, with wooden furniture and beams, and the restaurant decor includes two entire stuffed deer and one ibex.

Hornos

POP 410 / ELEV 867M

Like better-known Segura de la Sierra, little Hornos is fabulously located – atop a crag backed by a sweep of mountains, with marvellous views over the shimmering Embalse del Tranco and the lush, green countryside, richly patterned with olive, pine and almond trees and the occasional tossed dice of a farmhouse.

Hornos dates back to the Bronze Age when there was a settlement here; the castle on the crag was built by Christians in the mid-13th century, probably on the site of an earlier Muslim fortification. Don't expect colour-coordinated geraniums, souvenir shops or a tourist office: Hornos' charms lie in exploring the narrow, winding streets and wondering at the view from several strategically placed miradors. Seek out the early-16th-century **Iglesia de la Asunción**, which has the oldest, albeit crumbling, plateresque portal in the province, plus a vibrant 1589 *retablo* (altarpiece) with nine painted panels.

There are a couple of restaurants and basic lodgings should you want to stay. If you want to stride out, a plaque at the village entrance shows local trails including two of about 4km each to tiny outlying villages – the PRA152 south down to Hornos El Viejo and the PRA148 east up to La Capellanía.

To get to Hornos, take the A319 12km north of the Tranco dam to a T-junction; from here the A317 winds 4km up to Hornos village.

Cosmolarium INTERPRETATION CENTRE (953 00 00 29; www.cosmolarium.info; admission €3, incl planetarium €5; 11am-2pm & 4.30-7.30pm Thu-Mon) Hornos' panoramic castle now houses, curiously enough, this modern astronomy interpretation centre and planetarium. Exhibits are devoted to the universe, galaxies, the solar system and the history of astronomy (English and French audio guides are included in the ticket price). The planetarium presents projections in Spanish and English on astronomical themes.

Segura de la Sierra

POP 250 / ELEV 1145M

One of Andalucía's most picturesque villages, Segura de la Sierra perches on a 1200m-high hill crowned by a Reconquista castle, 21km north of Hornos. The village takes some of its character from its five Moorish centuries before the Knights of Santiago captured it in 1214, after which it became part of the Christian front line against the Almohads and then the Granada emirate.

As you drive up into the village, the Puerta Nueva, one of four gates of Islamic Saqura, marks the entrance to the old part of Segura. Signs two the Castillo lead you round to a junction on the northern side by the little walled bullring. Turn left here to head up to the castle itself.

◉ Sights & Activities

In the village below the magnificent castle, the sturdy 16th-century Iglesia de Nuestra Señora del Collado stands just below the main square, Plaza de la Encomienda. In addition to the Arab baths in the castle, there's a second set of **Baños Árabes** (Calle Baño Moro; admission free; ⊙ hours variable) at the foot of the village, built around 1150, with pretty red-and-white horseshoe arches. Nearby is the Puerta Catena, the best-preserved of Segura's Islamic gates; from here you can pick up the waymarked GR147 footpath to the splendidly isolated village of Río Madera (a 15km downhill hike).

★**Castillo de Segura**   CASTLE
(☑953 48 21 73; www.castillodesegura.com; adult/child incl audio guide €4/3; ⊙10.30am-2pm Wed-Sun Mar-Jun & Sep-Dec, daily Jul-Aug, 4.30-6.30pm or later Fri-Sun Mar, May-Jun & Nov-Dec, Wed-Sun Apr & Sep-Oct, daily Jul-Aug, closed Jan-Feb; 🚗) This lofty castle dates from Moorish times but was rebuilt after the Christian conquest in the 13th century. Abandoned in the 17th century, it was restored in the 1960s and has now become a 'territory of the frontier' interpretation centre. The ticket office is also Segura's tourist information office.

You can see the original Arab steam baths (with a video on the history of Segura and the castle), visit the 13th-century Mudéjar chapel, climb the tower and walk round the battlements for a bird's-eye view of El Yelmo, 5km south, and the rocky crags and olive-tree-strewn lowlands all around.

✗ Eating

Mirador de Peñalta   ANDALUCIAN €
(Calle San Vicente 29; mains €4-17; ⊙1.30-4pm & 8-10pm Tue-Sun) On the street entering Segura from below, this place caters to hungry travellers with a meaty menu that includes steaks, lamb chops and pork, as well as some sierra specialties such as *ajo atao* (a belly-filling fry-up of potatoes, garlic and eggs).

JAÉN PROVINCE PARQUE NATURAL SIERRAS DE CAZORLA, SEGURA Y LAS VILLAS

LAURA BATTIATO / GETTY IMAGES ©

Teterías & Hammams

In contrast to other parts of Spain, the Moorish residence in Andalucía had a sense of destiny and permanence. Between 711 and 1492, the region spent nearly eight centuries under North African influence, and exotic reminders still flicker in *teterías* (teahouses) and *hammams* (bathhouses) in cities such as Córdoba, Granada, Almería and Málaga.

Moorish Tearooms

Forget tall, low-fat vanilla lattes poured into cheap takeaway cups – Andalucía's caffeine lovers prefer to hang out in more exotic *teterías*: Moorish-style tearooms that display a hint of Fez, Marrakech or Cairo in their ornate interiors. Calle Calderería Nueva in Granada's Albayzín is where the best stash are buried, but they have proliferated in recent years; now even Torremolinos has one! Look out for dimly lit, cushion-filled, fit-for-a-sultan cafes, where pots of herbal tea accompanied by plates of Arabic sweets arrive at your table on silver salvers.

1. *Tetería*, Granada (p247) **2.** Moorish-style mint tea **3.** Hammam de Al Andalus (p260), Granada **4.** Arabic-style spa, Córdoba (p198)

Arabic Bathhouses

Sitting somewhere between a western spa and a Moroccan *hammam*, Andalucía's bathhouses retain enough old-fashioned elegance to satisfy a latter-day emir with a penchant for Moorish-era opulence. You can recline in candlelit subterranean bliss, sip mint tea, and experience the same kind of bathing ritual – successive immersions in cold, tepid and hot bathwater – that the Moors did. Seville, Granada, Almería, Córdoba and Málaga all have excellent Arabic-style bathhouses, with massages also available.

BEST TETERÍAS

Tetería Dar Ziryab (p267), Granada

La Tetería (p167), Málaga

Tetería Almedina (p293), Almería

Tetería Nazarí (p267), Granada

Granada Province

POP 918,000

Includes ➡

Granada 247
Guadix 271
Sierra Nevada 273
Las Alpujarras 275
Salobreña 282
Almuñécar
& La Herradura 283

Best Flamenco Venues

➡ Palacio de los Olvidados (p256)

➡ Casa del Arte Flamenco (p268)

➡ Jardines de Zoraya (p268)

➡ Le Chien Andalou (p268)

Best Places to Eat

➡ La Bicicleta (p265)

➡ Carmela Restaurante (p265)

➡ La Fábula (p266)

➡ Taberna Restaurante La Tapa (p279)

Why Go?

The last citadel of the Moors in Europe is a tempestuous place where Andalucía's complex history is laid out in ornate detail. The starting point for 99% of visitors is the Alhambra, the Nasrid emirs' enduring gift to architecture, a building whose eerie beauty is better seen than described. Below it nestles a city where brilliance and shabbiness sit side by side in bohemian bars, shadowy *teterías* (teahouses), winding lanes studded with stately *cármenes* (large houses with walled gardens), and backstreets splattered with street art.

The province's alternative muse hides in the snow-capped mountains that rise behind the Alhambra. The Sierra Nevada guard the highest peaks in mainland Spain and the country's largest ski resort. The southern side of the range shelters Las Alpujarras, which are characterised by their massive canyons where white villages replete with traditional flat-roofed Berber houses practice old-fashioned craft-making.

For more curiosities, head north to the troglodyte city of Guadix, where cave-living never went out of fashion.

When to Go

Mar–Apr The solemn build-up to Easter and the subsequent ferias and celebrations are always a good time to visit Andalucía's towns and cities. The downside – elevated accommodation prices.

May–Jun Balmy spring weather, flowers in bloom and festivals a-plenty, if you don't mind the crowds. This is also the ideal season for hiking in the Alpujarras.

Nov–Feb The South Coast has the mildest winters in Europe. Accommodation prices fall and there's skiing in the Sierra Nevada.

GRANADA

POP 258,000 / ELEV 738M

Read up on your Nasrid history, slip a copy of Federico García Lorca's *Gypsy Ballads* into your bag, and acquire a working knowledge of Andalucía's splendid Moorish architectural heritage – Granada is calling and its allure is hard to ignore.

Internationally revered for its lavish Alhambra palace, and enshrined in medieval history as the last stronghold of the Moors in Western Europe, Granada is the darker more complicated cousin of sunny, exuberant Seville. Humming with a feisty cosmopolitanism and awash with riddles, question marks, contradictions and myths, this is a place to put down your guidebook and let your intuition lead the way – through the narrow ascending streets of the Albayzín and the tumbling white-walled house gardens of the Realejo quarter. Elegant yet edgy, grandiose but gritty, monumental but marked by pockets of stirring graffiti, 21st century Granada is anything but straightforward. Instead, this sometimes stunning, sometimes ugly city set spectacularly in the crook of the Sierra Nevada is an enigmatic place where – if the mood is right – you sense you might find something that you've long been looking for. A free tapa, perhaps? An inspirational piece of street art? A flamenco performance that finally unmasks the intangible spirit of *duende*?

Endowed with relics from various epochs of history, there's lots to do and plenty to admire in Granada; the mausoleum of the Catholic monarchs, old-school bars selling generous tapas, bohemian *teterías* where Arabic youths smoke *cachimbas* (hookah pipes), and an exciting nightlife that bristles with the creative aura of counterculture. Make no mistake, you'll fall in love here, but you'll spend days and weeks trying to work out why. Best idea – don't bother. Instead, immerse yourself in the splendour, and leave the poetic stanzas to the aesthetes.

History

As lively as Granada is today, it's hardly what it was five centuries ago. The city came into its own late in Spain's Islamic era. As Córdoba and Seville fell to the Catholics in the mid 13th century, a minor potentate called Mohammed ibn Yusuf ibn Nasr established an independent state based in Granada. The town was soon flooded with Muslim refugees, and the Nasrid emirate became the last bastion of Al-Andalus.

The Alhambra was developed as royal court, palace, fortress and miniature city, and the Nasrids ruled from this increasingly lavish complex for 250 years. During this time, Granada became one of the richest cities in Europe, with a population of more than 350,000. Under emirs Yusuf I (r 1333–54) and Mohammed V (r 1354–59 and 1362–91), traders did booming business, and artisans perfected such crafts as wood inlay.

As usual, though, decadent palace life bred a violent rivalry over succession. One faction supported the emir Abu al-Hasan and his Christian concubine, Zoraya, while the other backed Boabdil (Abu Abdullah), Abu al-Hasan's son by his wife Aixa – even though Boabdil was still just a child. In 1482 Boabdil started a civil war, and following Abu al-Hasan's death in 1485, won control of the city. With the emirate weakened by infighting, the Catholics pounced in 1491. Queen Isabel in particular had been smitten by Granada – so fittingly named for the jewel-like pomegranate, she thought, its buildings clustered like seeds along the hillsides – and she wanted it for herself. After an eight-month siege, Boabdil agreed to surrender the city in return for the Alpujarras valleys, 30,000 gold coins and political and religious freedom for his subjects. Boabdil hiked out of town – letting out the proverbial 'Moor's last sigh' as he looked over his shoulder in regret – and on 2 January 1492, Isabel and Fernando entered the city ceremonially in Muslim dress, to set up court in the Alhambra.

Their promises didn't last. They soon divided the populace, relegating the Jews to the Realejo and containing the Muslims in the Albayzín. Subsequent rulers called for full-scale expulsion, first in 1570 and again in 1610. It is said that there are families in Morocco who, still today, sentimentally keep the keys to their long-lost homes.

This brutal expulsion backfired, however, and Granada – once the Catholic Monarchs' prize jewel – became a backwater. In 1828 American writer Washington Irving visited the ruined palace and decided to move in. His *Tales of the Alhambra,* published in 1832, brought tourists from all over the world to marvel at the city's Islamic heritage; they helped give the city a little push into the modern age. Now Granada thrives on a culture that mixes Spanish, Moroccan, *gitano* (Roma) and student, plus tourist, life.

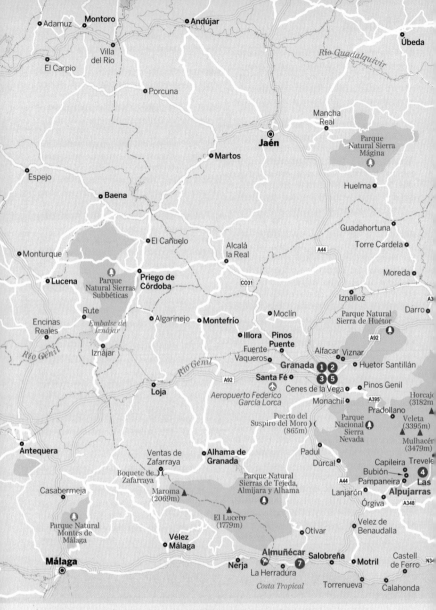

Granada Province Highlights

① Discovering that all the legends, rumours and hyperbole are true at Granada's **Alhambra** (p250)

② Admiring the golden majesty of the **Basilica San**

Juan de Dios (p259) in Granada

③ Bar-crawling for free tapas in **Granada** (p265) and calling it 'dinner'

④ Hiking from village to village amid the dramatic canyons and steep-sided valleys of **Las Alpujarras** (p275)

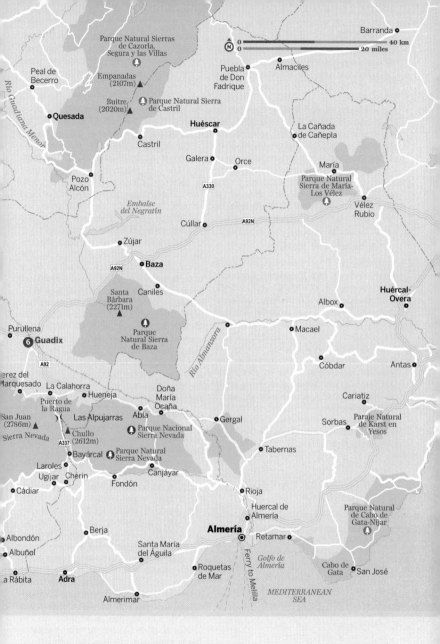

5 Reclining in a *tetería* with a pot of tea, some pastries and a *cachimba* in **Granada** (p267)

6 Detouring to unsung **Guadix** (p271) for a glimpse of Andalucía's unique cave quarter

7 Hitting the unpretentious town of **Almuñécar** (p283) for a day of unashamed beach-loafing

◉ Sights

Most major sights are an easy walk within the city centre, and there are buses for when the hills wear you out. Rectangular Plaza Nueva is Granada's main nexus. The Albayzín sits on a hill immediately to the north and is roughly demarcated by Gran Via de Colón and the Darro River. The Alhambra lies on a separate hill on the opposite side of the Darro. Granada's former Jewish quarter, the Realejo, occupies the southwestern slope of the Alhambra hill and some of the flat land beyond. Central Granada is laid out in a grid on the flat land west of the Albayzín and northwest of the Realejo. Its main square is Plaza Bib-Rambla.

◉ Alhambra & Realejo

★ Alhambra   PALACE
(Map p254; ☏ 902 44 12 21; www.alhambra-tickets. es; adult/under 12yr €14/free, Generalife only €7; ☺ 8.30am-8pm 15 Mar-14 Oct, to 6pm 15 Oct-14 Mar, night visits 10-11.30pm Tue-Sat Mar-Oct, 8-9.30pm Fri & Sat Oct-Mar) The Alhambra is Granada's – and Europe's – love letter to Moorish culture, a place where fountains trickle, leaves rustle, and ancient spirits seem to mysteriously linger. Part palace, part fort, part World Heritage site, part lesson in medieval architecture, the Alhambra has long enchanted a never-ending line of expectant visitors. As a historic monument, it is unlikely it will ever be surpassed – at least not in the lifetime of anyone reading this book.

NEW ENTRANCE GATE FOR THE ALHAMBRA

A temporary exhibition inside the Alhambra in spring 2015 outlined the competition-winning design drawn up by Portuguese architect Álvaro Siza Vieira for a new entrance gate and visitors centre for the Moorish palaces. The centre will inhabit the site of the current ticket office and car park, and incorporate an entrance facility designed to minimise queues. Also included will be a cafe, terrace, offices and visitor facilities. Fountains, courtyards and cypress trees will help create an appropriately Moorish environment. The €45 million building project is due to start in 2016 and is estimated to take five years to complete.

For most tourists, the Alhambra is an essential pilgrimage and, as a result, predictably crowded. At the height of summer, some 6000 visitors tramp through daily, making it difficult to pause to inspect a pretty detail, much less mentally transport yourself to the 14th century. Schedule a visit in quieter months, if possible; if not, then book in advance for the very earliest or latest time slots.

The Alhambra takes its name from the Arabic *al-qala'a al-hamra* (the Red Castle). The first palace on the site was built by Samuel Ha-Nagid, the Jewish grand vizier of one of Granada's 11th-century Zirid sultans. In the 13th and 14th centuries, the Nasrid emirs turned the area into a fortress-palace complex, adjoined by a village of which only ruins remain. After the Reconquista (Christian reconquest), the Alhambra's mosque was replaced with a church, and the Convento de San Francisco (now the Parador de Granada) was built. Carlos I (also known as the Habsburg emperor Charles V), grandson of the Catholic Monarchs, had a wing of the palaces destroyed to make space for his huge Renaissance work, the Palacio de Carlos V. During the Napoleonic occupation, the Alhambra was used as a barracks and nearly blown up. What you see today has been heavily but respectfully restored.

➔ **Palacios Nazaríes**

The central **palace complex** (Calle de Real de Alhama) is the pinnacle of the Alhambra's design.

Entrance is through the 14th-century **Mexuar**, perhaps an antechamber for those awaiting audiences with the emir. Two centuries later, it was converted to a chapel, with a prayer room at the far end. Look up here and elsewhere to appreciate the geometrically carved wood ceilings. From the Mexuar, you pass into the **Patio del Cuarto Dorado**. It appears to be a forecourt to the main palace, with the symmetrical doorways to the right, framed with glazed tiles and stucco, setting a cunning trap: the right-hand door leads only out, but the left passes through a dogleg hall (a common strategy in Islamic domestic architecture to keep interior rooms private) into the **Patio de los Arrayanes** (Court of the Myrtles), the centre of a palace built in the mid 14th century as Emir Yusuf I's private residence.

Rooms (likely used for lounging and sleeping) look onto the rectangular pool edged in myrtles, and traces of cobalt blue

ⓘ ALHAMBRA PRACTICALITIES

Some areas of the Alhambra can be visited at any time free of charge, but the highlight areas (the Palacios Nazaríes) can be entered only with a ticket at a pre-allocated time slot. Up to 6600 tickets are available each day. About one third of these are sold at the ticket office on the day, but they sell out early, especially in high season (March to October), when you need to start queuing by 7am to be reasonably sure of getting one.

Fortunately, it's also possible to buy tickets up to three months ahead online or by phone from Alhambra Advance Booking (☑ 902 88 80 01, for international calls +34 958 92 60 31; www.alhambra-tickets.es). Advance tickets can also be purchased (or prepaid tickets picked up) at the bookshop, Tienda Librería de la Alhambra (p269), just off Plaza Nueva, which has less manic queues than the complex itself. All advance tickets incur a 13% surcharge, meaning most visitors end up paying €15.40 for a standard entry ticket.

When full-access tickets are sold out, you can still buy a ticket to the Generalife and gardens (€7). The Palacios Nazaríes are also open for night visits (Map p254; €8; ⊗ 10-11.30pm Tue-Sat Mar-Oct, 8-9.30pm Fri & Sat Nov-Feb), good for atmosphere rather than detail.

There is no explanatory signage in the complex, but a reasonable audioguide is available for €6.50. No outside food is allowed, but there is a slightly pricey cafeteria at the Parador de Granada (Map p254; ☑ 958 22 14 40; Calle Real de la Alhambra; mains €19-22; ⊗ 1-4pm & 8.30-11pm), plus vending machines by the ticket office and the Alcazaba.

The best access on foot is to walk up the Cuesta de Gomérez from Plaza Nueva through the *bosque* (woods) to the Puerta de la Justicia (Map p254). Enter here if you already have your ticket, otherwise proceed further along to the ticket office. Buses C3 and C4 run up to the ticket office from Plaza Isabel la Católica.

---

paint cling to the *muqarnas* (honeycomb vaulting) in the side niches on the north end. Originally, all the walls were lavishly coloured; with paint on the stucco-trimmed walls in the adjacent Sala de la Barca, the effect would have resembled flocked wallpaper. Yusuf I's visitors would have passed through this annex room to meet him in the Salón de los Embajadores (Chamber of the Ambassadors), where the marvellous domed marquetry ceiling uses more than 8000 cedar pieces to create its intricate star pattern representing the seven heavens.

Adjacent is the restored Patio de los Leones (Courtyard of the Lions), built in the second half of the 14th century under Muhammad V, at the political and artistic peak of Granada's emirate. But the centrepiece, a fountain that channelled water through the mouths of 12 marble lions, dates from the 11th century. The courtyard layout, using the proportions of the golden ratio, demonstrates the complexity of Islamic geometric design – the varied columns are placed in such a way that they are symmetrical on numerous axes. The stucco work, too, hits its apex here, with almost lacelike detail.

Walking counterclockwise around the patio, you first pass the Sala de los Abencerrajes. The Abencerraje family supported the young Boabdil in a palace power struggle between him and his own father, the reigning sultan. Legend has it that the sultan had the traitors killed in this room, and the rusty stains in the fountain are the victims' indelible blood. But the multicoloured tiles on the walls and the great octagonal ceiling are far more eye-catching. In the Sala de los Reyes (Hall of the Kings) at the east end of the patio, the painted leather ceilings depict 10 Nasrid emirs.

On the patio's north side, doors once covered the entrance to the Sala de Dos Hermanas (Hall of Two Sisters) – look for the holes on either side of the frame where they would have been anchored. The walls are adorned with local flora – pine cones and acorns – and the band of calligraphy at eye level, just above the tiles, is a poem praising Muhammad V for his victory in Algeciras in 1369, a rare triumph this late in the Islamic game. The dizzying ceiling is a fantastic *muqarnas* dome with some 5000 tiny cells. The carved wood screens in the upper level enabled women (and perhaps others involved in palace intrigue) to peer down from hallways above without being seen. At the far end, the tile-trimmed Mirador de Lindaraja (Lindaraja lookout) was a lovely place for palace denizens to look onto the garden below. Traces of paint still cling to the window frames, and a few panels of coloured glass set in the wood ceiling cast a warm glow.

Alhambra

TIMELINE

900 The first reference to al-qala'at al-hamra (red castle) atop Granada's Sabika Hill.

1237 Founder of the Nasrid dynasty, Muhammad I, moves his court to Granada. Threatened by belligerent Christian armies he builds a new defensive fort, the **Alcazaba** ❶.

1302–09 Designed as a summer palace-cum-country estate for Granada's foppish rulers, the bucolic **Generalife** ❷ is begun by Muhammad III.

1333–54 Yusuf I initiates the construction of the **Palacio Nazaríes** ❸, still considered the highpoint of Islamic culture in Europe.

1350–60 Up goes the **Palacio de Comares** ❹, taking Nasrid lavishness to a whole new level.

1362–91 The second coming of Muhammad V ushers in even greater architectural brilliance, exemplified by the construction of the **Patio de los Leones** ❺.

1527 The Christians add the **Palacio de Carlos V** ❻. Inspired Renaissance palace or incongruous crime against Moorish art? You decide.

1829 The languishing, half-forgotten Alhambra is 'rediscovered' by American writer Washington Irving during a protracted sleep-over.

1954 The Generalife gardens are extended southwards to accommodate an outdoor theatre.

TOP TIPS

» **Queue-dodger** Reserve tickets in advance online at www.alhambra-tickets.es

» **Money-saver** You can visit the general areas of the palace free of charge any time by entering through the Puerta de Justica.

» **Stay over** Two fine hotels are housed on the grounds: Parador de Granada (expensive) and Hotel América (more economical).

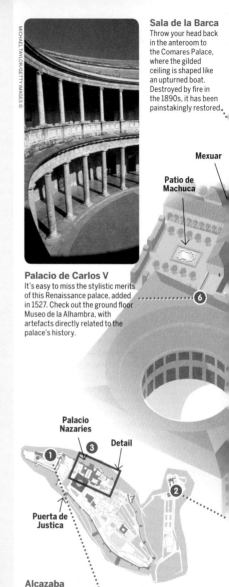

Sala de la Barca
Throw your head back in the anteroom to the Comares Palace, where the gilded ceiling is shaped like an upturned boat. Destroyed by fire in the 1890s, it has been painstakingly restored.

Mexuar

Patio de Machuca

Palacio de Carlos V
It's easy to miss the stylistic merits of this Renaissance palace, added in 1527. Check out the ground floor Museo de la Alhambra, with artefacts directly related to the palace's history.

Palacio Nazaries

Detail

Puerta de Justica

Alcazaba
Find time to explore the towers of the original citadel, the most important of which – the Torre de la Vela – takes you, via a winding staircase, to the Alhambra's best viewpoint.

Patio de los Arrayanes

If only you could linger longer beside the rows of *arrayanes* (myrtle bushes) that border this calming rectangular pool. Shaded porticos with seven harmonious arches invite further contemplation.

Palacio de Comares

The neck-ache continues in the largest room in the Comares Palace, renowned for its rich geometric ceiling. A negotiating room for the emirs, the Salón de los Embajadores is a masterpiece of Moorish design.

Sala de Dos Hermanas

Focus on the *dos hermanas* – two marble slabs either side of the fountain – before enjoying the intricate cupola embellished with 5000 tiny moulded stalactites. Poetic calligraphy decorates the walls.

Salón de los Embajadores

④

Patio de los Arrayanes

Baños Reales

Washington Irving Apartments

Patio de la Lindaraja

⑤

Sala de los Reyes

Palacio del Partal

Sala de los Abencerrajes

Jardines del Partal

Patio de los Leones

Count the 12 lions sculpted from marble, holding up a gurgling fountain. Then pan back and take in the delicate columns and arches built to signify an Islamic vision of paradise.

Generalife

A coda to most people's visits, the 'architect's garden' is no afterthought. While Nasrid in origin, the horticulture is relatively new: the pools and arcades were added in the early 20th century.

Alhambra

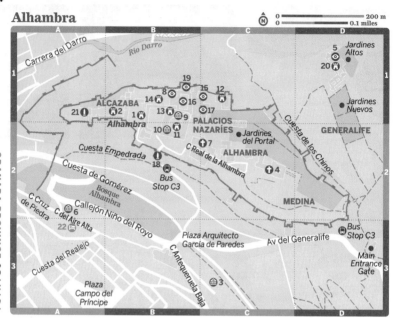

0 ————— 200 m
0 ————— 0.1 miles

From the Sala de Dos Hermanas, a passageway leads past the domed roofs of the baths on the level below and into rooms built for Carlos I in the 1520s, and later used by Washington Irving. From here you descend to the pretty Patio de la Lindaraja. In the southwest corner is the bathhouse – you can't enter, but you can peer in at the rooms lit by star-shaped skylights.

You emerge into an area of terraced gardens created in the early 20th century. The reflecting pool in front of the small Palacio del Partal with the Albayzín glimering in the background is the oldest surviving palace in the Alhambra, from the time of Mohammed III (r 1302–09). You can leave the gardens by a gate facing the Palacio de Carlos V or continue along a path to the Generalife.

➡ Alcazaba, Christian Buildings & Museums

The west end of the Alhambra grounds are the remnants of the Alcazaba, chiefly its ramparts and several towers. The Torre de la Vela (Watchtower), with a narrow staircase leading to the top terrace, is where the cross and banners of the Reconquista were raised in January 1492.

By the Palacios Nazaríes, the hulking Palacio de Carlos V clashes spectacularly with its surroundings. In a different setting its merits might be more readily appreciated – it is the only example in Spain of the Renaissance-era circle-in-a-square ground plan. Begun in 1527 by Pedro Machuca, a Toledo architect who studied under Michelangelo, it was financed, perversely, from taxes on Granada's *morisco* (converted Muslim) population but never finished because funds dried up after the *morisco* rebellion.

Inside, the Museo de la Alhambra (☉ 8.30am-8pm Wed-Sat, to 2.30pm Tue & Sun) FREE has a collection of Alhambra artefacts, including the door from the Sala de Dos Hermanas, while the Museo de Bellas Artes (Fine Arts Museum; non-EU/EU citizen €1.50/free; ☉ 2.30-8pm Tue, 9am-8pm Wed-Sat, to 2.30pm Sun) displays paintings and sculptures from Granada's Christian history.

Further along, the 16th-century Iglesia de Santa María de la Alhambra sits on the site of the palace mosque, and at the crest of the hill the Convento de San Francisco, now the Parador de Granada hotel, is where Isabel and Fernando were laid to rest while their tombs in the Capilla Real were being built.

Alhambra

◎ **Top Sights**
1 Alhambra B1

◎ **Sights**
2 Alcazaba.. B1
3 Casa-Museo Manuel de Falla C3
4 Convento de San Francisco C2
5 Escalera del Agua D1
6 Fundación Rodríguez-Acosta A2
7 Iglesia de Santa María de la
   Alhambra C2
8 Mexuar B1
   Mirador de Lindaraja ....(see 15)
9 Museo de Bellas Artes B1
10 Museo de la Alhambra B2
11 Palacio de Carlos V B2
12 Palacio del Partal C1
13 Palacios Nazaríes B1
14 Palacios Nazaríes Night Visits B1
15 Patio de la Lindaraja C1
16 Patio de los Arrayanes B1
17 Patio de los Leones............................. C1
   Patio del Cuarto Dorado .... (see 8)
18 Puerta de la Justicia B2
19 Sala de la Barca B1
   Sala de los Abencerrajes ....(see 17)
   Sala de los Reyes ....(see 17)
   Salón de los Embajadores .... (see 19)
20 Summer Palace.................................... D1
21 Torre de la Vela A1

◉ **Sleeping**
22 Carmen de la Alcubilla del
   Caracol..A3
   Parador de Granada .... (see 4)

◈ **Eating**
   Parador de Granada .... (see 4)

➜ Generalife

From the Arabic *jinan al-'arif* (the overseer's gardens), the Generalife is a soothing arrangement of pathways, patios, pools, fountains, tall trees and, in season, flowers of every imaginable hue. To reach the complex you must pass through the Alhambra walls on the east side, then head back northwest. You approach through topiary gardens on the south end, which were once grazing land for the royal herds. At the north end is the emirs' summer palace (Map p254), a whitewashed structure on the hillside facing the Alhambra. The courtyards here are particularly graceful; in the second courtyard, the trunk of a 700-year-old cypress tree suggests what delicate shade once graced the patio. Climb the steps outside the courtyard to the Escalera del Agua (Map p254), a delightful

bit of garden engineering, where water flows along a shaded staircase.

Fundación Rodríguez-Acosta   MUSEUM

(Map p254; ☏ 958 22 74 97; www.fundacionrodriguezacosta.com; Callejón Niño del Royo 8; guided tour €5 (€6 with library tour); ⓧ 10am-6:30pm) One of the largest structures on the Realejo hill, the so-called 'Carmen Blanco' hosts the Rodríquez-Acosta foundation in a building designed and built by the Granada-born modernist artist, José María Rodriquez-Acosta in 1914. It's an unusual and whimsical place (with incredible gardens) that borrows from all number of architectural genres including art deco, Nasrid, Greek and baroque. The guided tour includes a walk through the house's subterranean tunnels, and entry to a well-curated museum containing original works by Pacheco, Cano and Zurbarán.

Pay an extra €1 and the tour is extended to the library, considered to be the house's finest room, replete with rare items collected during Rodríguez-Acosta's world travels, particularly in Asia.

Museo Sefardí   MUSEUM

(Map p262; ☏ 958 22 05 78; www.museosefardidegranada.es; Placeta Berrocal 5; admission €5; ⓧ 10am-2pm, 5-9pm) Since being expelled en masse in 1492, there are very few Sephardi Jews left living in Granada today. But this didn't stop one enterprising couple from opening up a museum to their memory in 2013, the year that the Spanish government began offering Spanish citizenship to any Sephardi Jew who could prove their Iberian ancestry. The museum is tiny, but the selected artifacts make excellent props to the passionate and fascinating historical portrayal related by the owners.

Casa-Museo Manuel de Falla   MUSEUM

(Map p254; ☏ 958 22 21 88; www.museomanueldefalla.com; Paseo de los Mártires; adult/reduced €3/1; ⓧ 9am-2.30pm & 3.30-7pm Tue-Fri, to 2.30pm Sat & Sun) Arguably Spain's greatest classical composer and an artistic friend of Lorca, Manuel de Falla (1876–1946) was born in Cádiz, but spent the key years of his life in Granada until the Civil War forced him into exile. You can find out all about the man at this attractive *cármen* where he lived and composed, and which has been preserved pretty much as he left it. Tours are guided and intimate.

GRAFFITI ART

While the UK has Banksy, Granada has El Niño de las Pinturas (real name Raúl Ruíz), a street artist whose creative graffiti has become a defining symbol of a city where the grandiose and the gritty often sit side by side. Larger-than-life, lucid and thought-provoking, El Niño's giant murals, the majority of which adorn the Realejo neighbourhood, juxtapose vivid close-ups of the human countenance with short poetic stanzas written in highly stylised lettering. Over the last two decades, El Niño has become a famous underground personality in Granada and has sometimes been known to give live painting demonstrations at the university. Although he risks criticism and occasional fines for his work, most Granadinos agree that his street art brings creative splashes of colour to their ancient city, ensuring it remains forward-thinking and edgy.

Pancho Tours (p260) do a street-art tour, which takes in some of these works of public art.

Plaza Nueva & Around

Palacio de los Olvidados   MUSEUM
(Map p262; ☑ 655 55 33 40; www.palaciodelosolvidados.com; Cuesta de Santa Inés 6; admission €5; ☉10am-7pm) Lest we forget, Jews played a vital role in the glorious Nasrid Emirate of Granada that reigned from the 1200s to 1492, built on peaceful Christian, Muslim and Jewish coexistence. The aptly named 'palace of the forgotten', which opened in 2014 in the Albayzín, revisits this oft-ignored Jewish legacy. It's the second and best of Granada's new Jewish-related museums, with seven rooms filled with attractively displayed relics (scrolls, costumes and ceremonial artifacts) amassed from around Spain.

A well-versed guide takes you round the exhibits.

Iglesia de Santa Ana   CHURCH
(Map p262; Plaza Santa Ana) Extending from the northeast corner of Plaza Nueva, Plaza Santa Ana is dominated by the Iglesia de Santa Ana, a church which incorporates a mosque's minaret in its belltower.

Archivo-Museo San Juan de Dios   MUSEUM
(Map p262; ☑ 958 22 21 44; www.museosanjuandedios.es; Calle de la Convalencia 1; admission €3; ☉10am-2pm Mon-Sat) This museum of liturgical art in the ancient Casa de los Pisa is a little more esoteric than other Granada art museums, though the compulsory guided tour will fill you in on its finer details and raison d'être. It catalogues the life of Granada's resident saint, San Juan Robles (San Juan de Díos).

Baños Árabes El Bañuelo   BATHHOUSE
(Map p262; Carrera del Darro 31; ☉10am-5pm Tue-Sat) FREE Located along narrow Carrera del Darro is this simple, yet well-preserved, 11th-century Islamic bathhouse.

Albayzín

On the hill facing the Alhambra across the Darro valley, Granada's old Muslim quarter (the Albayzín) is a place for aimless wandering; you'll get lost regularly whatever map you're using. The cobblestone streets are lined with signature only-in-Granada *cármenes* (large mansions with walled gardens, from the Arabic *karm* for garden). The Albayzín survived as the Muslim quarter for several decades after the Christian conquest in 1492.

Bus C1 runs circular routes from Plaza Nueva around the Albayzín about every seven to nine minutes, from 7.30am to 11pm.

Colegiata del Salvador   CHURCH
(Map p258; Plaza del Salvador; admission €0.75; ☉10am-1pm & 4.30-6.30pm) Plaza del Salvador, near the top of the Albayzín, is dominated by the Colegiata del Salvador, a 16th-century church on the site of the Albayzín's former main mosque, the patio of which still survives at the church's western end.

Palacio de Dar-al-Horra   PALACE
(Map p258; Callejón de las Monjas) Close to the Placeta de San Miguel Bajo, off Callejón del Gallo and down a short lane, is the 15th-century Palacio de Dar-al-Horra, a romantically dishevelled mini-Alhambra that was home to the mother of Boabdil, Granada's last Muslim ruler. It's not open to the public, but viewable from the outside.

Carmen Museo Max Moreau   MUSEUM
(Map p258; ☑ 958 29 33 10; Camino Nuevo de San Nicolás 12; ☉10.30am-1.30pm & 4-6pm Tue-Sat)

FREE Most of the Albayzín's *cármenes* are true to their original concept – quiet, private houses with high walls that hide beautiful terraced gardens. But you can get a rare (and free) glimpse of one of these secret domains at the former home of Belgium-born portrait painter and composer Max Moreau. His attractive house has been made into a museum displaying his former living quarters and work space, along with a gallery that showcases his best portraits.

There are fine Alhambra views.

Mirador San Nicolás LOOKOUT
(Map p258; Callejón de San Cecilio) Callejón de San Cecilio leads to the Mirador San Nicolás, a lookout with unbeatable views of the Alhambra and Sierra Nevada. Come back here for sunset (you can't miss the trail then!). At any time of day take care: skilful, well-organised wallet-lifters and bag-snatchers operate here. Don't be put off – it is still a terrific atmosphere, with buskers and local students intermingling with camera-toting tourists.

Calle Calderería Nueva STREET
(Map p262) Linking the upper and lower parts of the Albayzín, Calle Calderería Nueva is a narrow street famous for its *teterías,* but also a good place to shop for slippers, hookahs, jewellery and North African pottery from an eclectic cache of shops redolent of a Moroccan souk.

◉ Plaza Bib-Rambla & Around

★ Capilla Real HISTORIC BUILDING
(Map p262; www.capillarealgranada.com; Calle Oficios; admission €4; ◷10.15am-1.30pm & 3.30-6.30pm Mon-Sat, 11am-1.30pm & 2.30-5.30pm Sun) Here they lie, Spain's notorious Catholic Monarchs, entombed in a chapel adjoining Granada's cathedral; far more peaceful in death than their tumultuous lives would have suggested. Isabella and Ferdinand commissioned the elaborate Isabelline-Gothic-style mausoleum that was to house them, but it was not completed until 1521, hence their temporary interment in the Alhambra's Convento de San Francisco.

The monarchs lie in simple lead coffins in the crypt beneath their marble monuments in the chancel, enclosed by a stunning gilded wrought-iron screen created in 1520 by Bartolomé de Jaén. Also here are the coffins of Isabella and Ferdinand's unfortunate daughter, Juana the Mad, and her husband, Philip of Flanders.

The sacristy contains a small but impressive museum, with Ferdinand's sword and Isabella's sceptre, silver crown and personal art collection, which is mainly Flemish but also includes Botticelli's *Prayer in the Garden of Olives*. Felipe de Vigarni's two fine early-16th-century statues of the Catholic Monarchs at prayer are also here.

Catedral de Granada CATHEDRAL
(Map p262; ☑958 22 29 59; www.catedraldegranada. com; Gran Vía de Colón 5; admission €4; ◷10:45am-7.45pm Mon-Sat, 4-7pm Sun) Too boxed in by other buildings to manifest its full glory to observers at ground level, Granada's cavernous cathedral is, nonetheless, a hulking classic that sprang from the fertile imagination of the 17th-century painter cum sculptor cum architect Alonso Cano. Although commissioned by the Catholic Monarchs in the early 1500s, construction began only after Isabella's death, and didn't finish until 1704.

The result is a mishmash of styles: baroque outside, courtesy of Cano, and Renaissance inside, where the Spanish pioneer in this style, Diego de Siloé, directed operations to construct huge piers, white as meringue, a black-and-white tile floor and the gilded and painted chapel. Even more odd, the roof vaults are distinctly Gothic.

Corral del Carbón HISTORIC SITE
(Map p262; Calle Mariana Pineda; ◷10am-8pm) Tucked away just to the east of Calle Reyes Católicos is this Nasrid-era corn exchange framed by an elaborate horseshoe arch, which began life as a 14th-century inn for merchants. It has since been used as an inn for coal dealers (hence its modern name, Coal Yard) and later a theatre. It was closed for renovations at last visit, but can still be viewed from the outside.

Centro José Guerrero ART GALLERY
(Map p262; ☑958 22 51 85; www.centroguerrero. org; Calle Oficios 8; ◷10.30am-2pm & 4.30-9pm Tue-Sat, to 2pm Sun) FREE An art gallery named for the Granada-born abstract painter (1914–91) who went to live in the US. Exhibitions are temporary and with a modernist bent, though the gallery keeps half a dozen of Guerrero's characteristically vibrant works in a permanent collection.

La Madraza de Granada HISTORIC BUILDING
(Map p262; Calle Oficios; guided tour €2; ◷10am-8pm) La Madraza was founded in 1349 by Sultan Yusuf I as a school and university. It still belongs to Granada University. Since

Granada

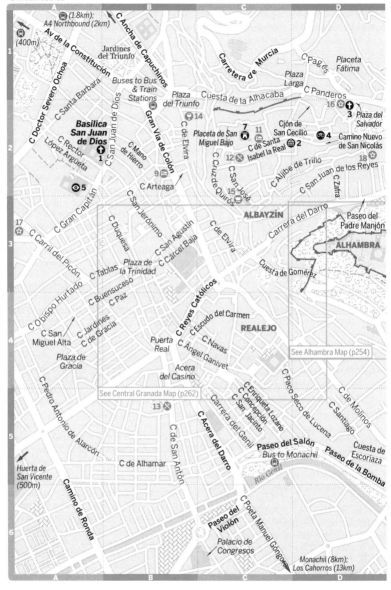

See Alhambra Map (p254)

See Central Granada Map (p262)

extensive excavations and remodeling in the early 2010s, it is now possible to view its interesting sometimes contradictory mix of Arabic, Christian, Mudéjar and baroque architecture. The oldest remains date from an 11th century country house.

Highlights include an elaborate mihrab, a baroque dome and some coloured stucco. Student guides take you through the details. The building is easily recognisable by the *trompe d'oeil* on its front facade.

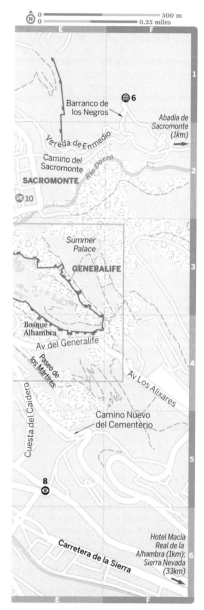

Granada

◎ **Top Sights**
  1 Basilica San Juan de Díos...................A2

◎ **Sights**
  2 Carmen Museo Max Moreau..............C2
  3 Colegiata del Salvador D2
  4 Mirador San Nicolás.............................D2
  5 Monasterio de San Jerónimo..............A2
  6 Museo Cuevas del Sacromonte..........F1
  7 Palacio de Dar-al-Horra C2
  8 Placeta Joe Strummer E5

◎ **Sleeping**
  9 AC Palacio de Santa Paula B2
  10 Casa Morisca Hotel E2
  11 Santa Isabel La Real C2

◎ **Eating**
  12 El Ají C2
  13 La Fábula Restaurante.......................B5

◎ **Drinking & Nightlife**
  14 Al Sur de Granada..............................B2
  15 Albayzín Abaco Té C3

◎ **Entertainment**
  16 Jardines de Zoraya.............................D2
  17 La Tertulia A3
  18 Peña La Platería.................................D2

want to see? Come to the Basilica of St John of God. If Seville cathedral is the world's most voluminous church, this basilica is surely one of the most opulently decorated. Barely a square inch of the interior lacks embellishment, most of it rich and glittering.

Once you've taken in the head-spinning details, climb upstairs behind the altar to where the saint's remains are set deep in a niche surrounded by gold, gold and more gold.

Monasterio de San Jerónimo   MONASTERY
(Map p258; Calle Rector López Argüeta 9; admission €4; ⊙10am-1.30pm & 4-8pm Mon-Fri, to 2.30pm & 4-7.30pm Sat & Sun) Another of Granada's stunning Catholic buildings is a little out of the centre. At the 16th-century Monasterio de San Jerónimo, where nuns still sing vespers, every surface of the church has been painted – the stained glass literally pales in comparison.

Gonzalo Fernández de Córdoba, known as El Gran Capitán and the Catholic Monarchs' military man, is entombed here, at the foot of the steps, and figures of him and his wife stand on either side of the enormous gilt retable, which rises eight levels. Almond

◎ Outside the Centre

★ **Basilica San Juan de Díos**   CHURCH
(Map p258; Calle San Juan de Díos; admission €4; ⊙10am-1pm & 4-7pm) Bored of baroque churches? Seen every gilded altarpiece you

cookies, baked by the nuns, are for sale at the front desk, to stop your head from spinning.

Placeta Joe Strummer   SQUARE
(Map p258) The premature death of Joe Strummer of The Clash awakened a new awareness about the cultural significance of the band, especially in Granada where Strummer was a regular visitor in the 1980s and 90s. In May 2013, Placeta Joe Strummer was inaugurated in the Realejo quarter by his widow and several hundred gathered fans. The small square with its trees, fountain and Sierra Nevada view is adorned with a mural of Strummer by street artist El Niño de las Pinturas.

🏃 Activities

Hammam de Al Andalus   HAMMAM
(Map p262; ☑902 33 33 34; www.granada.hammamalandalus.com; Calle Santa Ana 16; bath/bath & massage €24/36; ⊙10am-midnight) With three pools of different temperatures, plus a steam room and the option of a proper skin-scrubbing massage, this is the best of Granada's three Arab-style baths. Sessions are booked for two-hour sessions (reserve ahead) and the dim, tiled rooms are suitably sybaritic and relaxing.

⎙ Tours

Cicerone Cultura y Ocio   WALKING TOUR
(Map p262; ☑958 56 18 10; www.ciceronegranada.com; tour €15) Informative walking tours of central Granada and the Albayzín leave daily from Plaza Bib-Rambla at 10.30am and 5pm (10am & 4pm in winter) Wednesday to Sunday.

Play Granada   CULTURAL TOUR
(Map p262; www.playgranada.com; Calle Santa Ana 2; segway tour €30) 🍃 The make or break of a good tour is the tour guide, and Play Granada's are truly fantastic. Even if you don't do a tour, you'll see the congenial guides buzzing around Plaza Nueva on their Segways, stopping to chat with anyone and everyone.

Highly recommended is the Segway Tour, which lasts 1¾ hours and covers 8km. You'll cover twice the distance in the same time period if you partake in the electric bike tour instead.

Pancho Tours   CULTURAL TOUR
(☑664 64 29 04; www.panchotours.com) FREE Excellent free tours of Granada by the guys in the orange t-shirts. Choose from the daily Albayzín tour (11am), or the more esoteric 'street art tour' (Monday, Wednesday, Friday at 5pm). Guides are knowledgeable and humorous, and tours are loaded with interesting anecdotes. Book online.

🎊 Festivals & Events

Semana Santa   HOLY WEEK
The two most striking events in Granada's Easter week are Los Gitanos (Wednesday), when the *fraternidad* (brotherhood) toils to the Abadía de Sacromonte, lit by bonfires, and El Silencio (Thursday), when the streetlights are turned off for a silent candlelit march.

Feria del Corpus Cristi   RELIGIOUS
(Corpus Christi Fair) The big annual fair, which starts 60 days after Easter Sunday, is a week of bullfights, dancing and street puppets;

GRANADA'S SACRED MOUNTAIN

Sacromonte, the primarily *gitano* (Roma) neighbourhood northeast of the Albayzín, is renowned for its flamenco traditions, drawing tourists to nightclubs and aficionados to music schools. But it still feels like the fringes of the city, literally and figuratively, as the homes dug out of the hillside alternate between flashy and highly extemporaneous, despite some of the caves having been established since the 14th century.

The area is good for an idle stroll, yielding great views (especially from an ad hoc cafe on Vereda de Enmedio). For some insight into the area, the **Museo Cuevas del Sacromonte** (Map p258; www.sacromontegranada.com; Barranco de los Negros; admission €5; ⊙10am-6pm) provides an excellent display of local folk art. This wide-ranging ethnographic and environmental museum and arts centre is set in large herb gardens and hosts art exhibitions, as well as flamenco and films (10pm on Wednesday and Friday from June to September). The diligent can press on to the **Abadía de Sacromonte** (admission €4; ⊙10am-1pm & 4-6pm Tue-Sat, 11am-1pm & 4-6pm Sun), at the very top of the hill, where you can squeeze into underground cave chapels.

Note that it is not considered safe for lone women to wander around the uninhabited parts of Granada's Sacromonte area, day or night.

most of the action is at fairgrounds by the bus station.

Día de la Cruz
RELIGIOUS

On 3 May, squares, patios and balconies are adorned with floral crosses, beginning three days of revelry.

Festival Internacional de Música y Danza
MUSIC

(www.granadafestival.org) For three weeks in June and July, first-class classical and modern performance takes over the Alhambra and other historic sites.

🛏 Sleeping

Central Granada – the level ground from the Realejo across to Plaza de la Trinidad – is very compact, so hotel location doesn't matter much. The prettiest lodgings are the Albayzín courtyard houses, though these call for some hill-walking, and many aren't accessible by taxi. The handful of hotels up by the Alhambra are scenic but a hassle for sightseeing further afield. Rates are highest in spring and fall, spiking over Easter. Parking, where offered, costs €15 to €20 per day, and is usually at a municipal parking lot, not on the hotel grounds.

Hotel Posada del Toro
HOTEL €

(Map p262; ☑958 22 73 33; www.posadadeltoro. com; Calle de Elvira 25; d from €50; 🖸🛜) A lovely small hotel with rooms set around a tranquil central patio. Walls are coloured like Italian gelato in pistachio, peach and cream flavours. The rooms are similarly tasteful with parquet floors, Alhambra-style stucco, rustic-style furniture and small but perfectly equipped bathrooms with double sinks and hydromassage showers. A bargain – especially considering its central location.

★ Carmen de la Alcubilla del Caracol
HISTORIC HOTEL €€

(Map p254; ☑958 21 55 51; www.alcubilladelcaracol. com; Calle del Aire Alta 12; s/d €100/120; 🖸@🛜) This much-sought-after small hotel inhabits a traditional *cármen* on the slopes of the Alhambra. It feels more like a B&B than a hotel thanks to the attentiveness of its Granada-loving host, Manuel. The seven rooms are washed in pale pastel colours and furnished luxuriously, but not ostentatiously.

The highlight? The fabulous views from the spectacular terraced garden and the sounds of Granadian life wafting up from the streets below.

Santa Isabel La Real
BOUTIQUE HOTEL €€

(Map p258; ☑958 29 46 58; www.hotelsantais-abellareal.com; Calle de Santa Isabel La Real 19; r €105; 🖸@🛜) Ideally situated between the Plaza San Miguel Bajo and Mirador San Nicolas (Plaza de San Nicolás), this gorgeous 16th-century building has been tastefully restored into an exquisite small hotel. Many of the original architectural features endure, including the marble columns. Rooms are set around a central patio and are individually decorated with lacy bedspreads, embroidered pictures and hand-woven rugs.

Go for room 11 if you can, for its Alhambra view.

Hotel Palacio de Los Navas
HISTORIC HOTEL €€

(Map p262; ☑958 21 57 60; www.palaciodelosna-vas.com; Calle Navas 1; r from €120; 🖸🛜) This Don Quijote–era 16th-century building has individually furnished rooms with lots of cool creams and whites, original columns and doors, terracotta-tiled floors and desks. The rooms surround a traditional columned patio. The hotel's location is convenient for nightlife – Calle Navas, one of Granada's quintessential tapa-crawling streets is just outside the door.

Hotel Párraga Siete
HOTEL €€

(Map p262; ☑958 26 42 27; www.hotelparra-gasiete.com; Calle Párraga 7; s/d €65/85; 🖸🛜) Seemingly furnished out of an Ikea-inspired style guide, the Párraga Seven has small modern rooms that feel as new as a freshly starched shirt. Aside from the high standard of cleaning, bonuses include an afternoon bottle of water delivered to your room and a sleek downstairs bar/restaurant called Vitola Gastrobar – ideal for breakfast or tapas.

Hotel Zaguán del Darro
HISTORIC HOTEL €€

(Map p262; ☑958 21 57 30; www.hotelzaguan.com; Carrera del Darro 23; s/d €55/70; 🖸@🛜) This place offers excellent value for the Albayzín. The 16th-century house has been tastefully restored, with sparing use of antiques. Its 13 rooms are all different; some look out over the Río Darro. There's a good bar-restaurant below, and the main street in front means easy taxi access – but also a bit of evening noise.

Hotel Casa del Capitel Nazarí
HISTORIC HOTEL €€

(Map p262; ☑958 21 52 60; www.hotelcasaca-pitel.com; Cuesta Aceituneros 6; s/d €68/85; 🖸@🛜) Another slice of Albayzín magic in a 1503 Renaissance palace that's as much

Central Granada

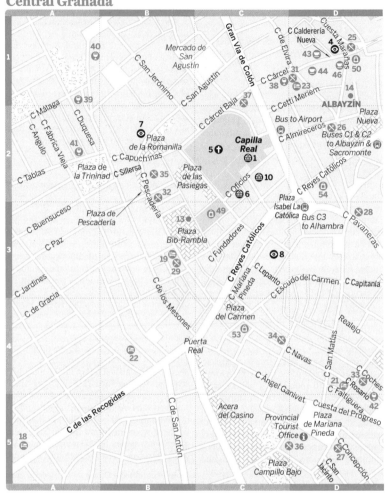

architectural history lesson as midrange hotel. Rooms have Moroccan inflections and the courtyard hosts art exhibits. It's just off Plaza Nueva, too.

Hotel Molinos
HOTEL €€

(Map p262; ☎958 22 73 67; www.hotelmolinos. es; Calle Molinos 12; s/d/tr €53/85/115; ❄ ☎) Don't let the 'narrowest hotel in the world' moniker put you off (and yes, it actually is – with a certificate from the *Guinness Book of Records* to prove it), there's plenty of breathing space in Molinos' nine recently boutique-ised rooms, and warm hospitality

in its information-stacked lobby. Situated at the foot of the Realejo, it's an economical central option.

Hotel Los Tilos
HOTEL €€

(Map p262; ☎958 26 67 12; www.hotellostilos.com; Plaza Bib-Rambla 4; s/d €45/75; ❄) The Tilos' spacious (for downtown) rooms are simple but regularly renovated and overlook Plaza Bib-Rambla. Double-glazed windows keep out the shouts of late-night bar crawlers crawling home at 5am. Bonus: there's a small but panoramic rooftop terrace if you

den, the Roman Emperor spa or the carnations they leave on your bed in the afternoon.

Expensive, but worth every penny.

Casa Morisca Hotel
HISTORIC HOTEL €€€

(Map p258; ☑958 22 11 00; www.hotelcasamorisca.com; Cuesta de la Victoria 9; d/ste €167/220; ❋@🖥) You can recline like a Nasrid emir in this late-15th-century mansion, which perfectly captures the spirit of the Albayzín and nearby Alhambra. Atmosphere and history are laid on thick without sacrificing home comforts, and beautiful architectural details abound from the silver candelabras to the tiled ornamental pool.

AC Palacio de Santa Paula
LUXURY HOTEL €€€

(Map p258; ☑902 29 22 93; www.palaciodesantapaula.com; Gran Vía de Colón 31; r from €200; P❋@🖥) There's a surfeit of five stars in Granada including this luxury operation, which occupies a former 16th-century convent, some 14th-century houses with patios and wooden balconies, and a 19th-century aristocratic house, all with a contemporary overlay. The rooms sport every top-end luxury you might desire, and the hotel also has a fitness centre, sauna and Turkish bath.

Parador de Granada
HISTORIC HOTEL €€€

(Map p254; ☑958 22 14 40; www.parador.es; Calle Real de la Alhambra; r €335; P❋@🖥) This is the most luxurious and highly priced of Spain's *paradores*. Head here if you are looking for romance and want to recline on a divan like Boabdil, the last emir, or, perhaps, Washington Irving (it's encased in a converted 15th-century convent located in the Alhambra grounds). Book ahead; it's megapopular – obviously.

🍴 Eating

Granada's a place where gastronomy remains reassuringly down to earth – and cheap. What it lacks in flashy *alta cocina* (haute cuisine) it makes up for in generous portions of Andalucian standards. The city has a wealth of places serving decent tapas and *raciones* (large tapas servings). It also excels in Moroccan cuisine.

★ Gran Café Bib-Rambla
CAFE €

(Map p262; Plaza Bib-Rambla 3; chocolate & churros €4; ⏰8am-11pm; 🚇) It's 5pm, you've just traipsed around five vaguely interesting churches and hypoglycemia is rapidly setting in. Time to hit Plaza Bib-Rambla, where Granada's best churros (fried dough strips) are served in a no-nonsense 1907-vintage

don't get your own Alhambra view from your room.

★ Hotel Hospes Palacio de Los Patos
LUXURY HOTEL €€€

(Map p262; ☑958 53 57 90; www.hospes.com; Solarillo de Gracia 1; r/ste €200/400; P❋@🖥🏊) Put simply, the best hotel in Granada – if you can afford it – offering lucky guests sharp modernity and never-miss-a-beat service in a palatial Unesco-protected building. You could write a novella about its many memorable features: the grand staircase, the post-modern chandeliers, the Arabian gar-

Central Granada

⦿ Top Sights
1 Capilla Real C2

◉ Sights
2 Archivo-Museo San Juan de Dios.......... E1
3 Baños Árabes El Bañuelo...................... F1
4 Calle Calderería Nueva.......................... D1
5 Catedral de Granada............................. C2
6 Centro José Guerrero C2
7 Centro Lorca... B2
8 Corral del Carbón.................................. C3
9 Iglesia de Santa Ana............................. E1
10 La Madraza de Granada........................ C2
11 Museo Sefardí....................................... E3
12 Palacio de los Olvidados F1

◔ Activities, Courses & Tours
13 Cicerone Cultura y Ocio........................ B3
14 Escuela Delengua D1
15 Hammams de Al Andalus E1
16 Play Granada.. E2

🛌 Sleeping
17 Hotel Casa del Capitel Nazarí E1
18 Hotel Hospes Palacio de Los
     Patos.. A5
19 Hotel Los Tilos....................................... B3
20 Hotel Molinos F4
21 Hotel Palacio de Los Navas.................. D4
22 Hotel Párraga Siete B4
23 Hotel Posada del Toro........................... D1
24 Hotel Zaguán del Darro......................... F1

⊗ Eating
25 Arrayanes D1
26 Bodegas Castañeda D2

27 Café Futbol.. D5
28 Carmela Restaurante............................. D3
29 Gran Café Bib-Rambla.......................... B3
30 Hicuri Art Restaurant............................ E4
31 La Bella y La Bestia D1
32 La Bicicleta.. B2
33 La Botillería D4
34 Los Diamantes...................................... C4
35 Oliver... B2
36 Restaurante Chikito C5
37 Siloé Café & Grill C1

◒ Drinking & Nightlife
38 Boom Boom Room................................. C1
39 Botánico A1
40 El Bar de Eric.. A1
41 Mundra... A2
42 Taberna La Tana.................................... D5
43 Tetería Dar Ziryab................................. D1
44 Tetería Kasbah...................................... D1
45 Tetería La Cueva de Ali Baba................ F1
46 Tetería Nazarí D1

◓ Entertainment
47 Casa del Arte Flamenco E2
48 Le Chien Andalou.................................. E1

🛍 Shopping
49 Alcaicería.. C3
50 Alquimía Pervane D1
51 Artesanías González E2
52 Daniel Gil de Avalle E4
53 La Carta des Vins C4
    La Oliva .... (see 33)
54 Tienda Librería de la Alhambra D2

cafe. Check their freshness by watching Mr Churro-maker lower them into the fryer behind the bar, and then enjoy them dipped in cups of ulta-thick hot chocolate.

La Bella y La Bestia   ANDALUCIAN, TAPAS €
(Map p262; ☎958 22 51 87; www.bodegaslabel-laylabestia.com; Calle Carcel Baja 14; tapas €2-3; ⊗noon-midnight) Lots of beauty, but no real beast – this place wins the prize for Granada's most generous free tapas: a huge plate of bagels, chips and pasta arrives with your first drink. There are four branches, though this one is particularly well-placed, just off Calle de Elvira.

Bodegas Castañeda   TAPAS €
(Map p262; Calle Almireceros; tapas €2-3, raciónes €6-8; ⊗11.30am-4.30pm & 7.30pm-1.30am) A much loved relic among locals and tourists alike, the buzzing Castañeda is the Granada tapas bar to trump all others. Don't ex-

pect any fancy new stuff here, but do expect lightning-fast service, booze from big casks mounted on the walls, and eating as a physical contact sport.

Café Futbol   CAFE €
(Map p262; www.cafefutbol.com; Plaza de Mariana Pineda 6; churros €2; ⊗6am-1am; 🖰) More about chocolate and ice cream than football, this three-storey cafe with its butter-coloured walls and gaudy chandeliers, dates from 1910 and is generally packed with coiffured señoras, foreign students and families. Elderly, white-shirted waiters attend to the Sunday afternoon rush, when everyone in Granada seemingly turns up for hot chocolate and churros.

Hicuri Art Restaurant   VEGAN €
(Map p262; Plaza de los Girones 3; mains €7-12; ⊗10am-10pm Mon-Sat; ☑) Granada's leading graffiti artist, El Niño de las Pinturas, has

been let loose on the inner and outer walls of Hicuri, and the results are positively psychedelic. The food used to be vegetarian with a few dishes for diehard carnivores, but it recently went full-on vegan.

Tofu and seitan are liberally used in the food, and the almond tiramisu makes a persuasive dessert.

★**La Bicicleta** BISTRO €€
(Map p262; ☑958 25 86 36; Plaza Pescadería 4; raciones €8-15; ⊙11am-11:30pm Thu-Tue) For something new and a bit different, head to this lovely bistro, which adds a touch of Parisian panache to Granada – truly the best of both worlds. It's small and intimate, and good for many things, including an excellent *huevos a la flamenca* (tomato sauce and eggs). Placed strategically by the door, the cake tray is crying out for an afternoon *merienda* (afternoon snack).

★**Carmela Restaurante** TAPAS, ANDALUCIAN €€
(Map p262; ☑958 22 57 94; www.restaurantecarmela.com; Calle Colcha 13; tapas €5-10; ⊙12.30pm-midnight) Long a bastion of traditional tapas, Granada has taken a leaf out of Seville's book and come up with something a little more out-of-the-box at this new streamlined restaurant, guarded by the statue of Jewish philosopher Yehuba ibn Tibon at the jaws of the Realejo quarter. The best of Carmela's creative offerings is the made-to-order tortilla and cured-ham croquettes the size of tennis balls.

Arrayanes MOROCCAN €€
(Map p262; ☑958 22 84 01; www.rest-arrayanes.com; Cuesta Marañas 4; mains €15; ⊙1.30-4.30pm & 7.30-11.30pm Sun-Fri, to 4:30pm Sat; ☑) The best Moroccan food in a city that is well known for its Moorish throwbacks? Recline on lavish patterned seating, try the rich, fruity tagine casseroles and make your decision. Note that Arrayanes does not serve alcohol.

La Botillería TAPAS, FUSION €€
(Map p262; ☑958 22 49 28; Calle Varela 10; mains €13-20; ⊙1pm-1am Wed-Sun, 1-8pm Mon) Establishing a good reputation for nouveau tapas, La Botillería is just around the corner from the legeandary La Tana bar, to which it has family connections. It's a more streamlined modern place than its cousin, where you can *tapear* (eat tapas) at the bar or sit down for the full monty Andalucian-style. The *solomillo* (pork tenderloin) comes in a rich, wine-laden sauce.

Siloé Café & Grill INTERNATIONAL €€
(Map p262; ☑958 22 07 52; Plaza de Diego Siloé; mains €12-17; ⊙9am-midnight) Contrasting with the old-school Café Gran Via de Colon next door, the new-in-2014 Siloé is one of those adaptable restaurants that fits many budgets and meal configurations. Its sleek cafe-booth interior is good for late breakfasts, afternoon *meriendas*, wine and tapas, or full-blown lunch or dinner. Tasty and a bit different are the tapa-sized burgers, which are satisfying without being too over-indulgent.

The restaurant overlooks a small square by the cathedral.

Los Diamantes SEAFOOD €€
(Map p262; www.barlosdiamantes.com; Calle Navas 26; racionés €8-10; ⊙noon-6pm & 8pm-2am Mon-Fri, 11am-1am Sat & Sun) Granada's great tapas institution has two central outlets. This old-school scruffy joint in tapa bar–lined Calle Navas, and a newer hipper Ikea-esque version in Plaza Nueva. What doesn't change is

---

FREE TAPAS

Granada – bless its generous heart – is one of the last bastions of that fantastic practice of free tapas with every drink. Place your drink order at the bar and, hey presto, a plate will magically appear with a generous portion of something delicious-looking on it. Order another drink and another plate will materialise. The process is repeated with every round you buy – and each time the tapa gets better. As Spanish bars serve only small glasses of beer (cañas measure just 250ml) it is perfectly easy to fill up on free tapas over an enjoyable evening without getting totally inebriated. Indeed, some people 'crawl' from bar to bar getting a drink and free tapa in each place. Packed shoulder-to-shoulder with tapas institutions, Calle de Elvira and Calle Navas are good places for bar crawls. If you're hungry you can always order an extra plate or two to soak up the cervezas.

The free tapa practice is carried on throughout most of Granada and Jaén provinces, and also extends into Almería, where bars will even allow you to choose the tapas you wish to try.

DEAD POET'S SOCIETY

Murmurs of intellectual debate have long provided a musical commentary in Granada's bars, cafes and *teterías*. It's a tradition that harks back to the early 1920s, when a nascent group of poets, writers and musicians came together in a *tertulia* (a Spanish artistic/literary gathering) known as 'El Rinconcillo' in Café Alameda. The Rinconcillo took its name from the small corner of the cafe where the group convened, a cramped space furnished with divans, tables and a piano. Regularly holding court was Federico García Lorca, who had returned to Granada from studies in Madrid in 1921, and classical composer Manuel de Falla, who had moved to the city from Cádiz the previous year. They were joined by the likes of classical guitarist Andrés Segovia, painter Ismael González de la Serna, poet Miguel Pizarro, Lorca's brother Francisco, and many others. Fascinated by flamenco and inspired by the baroque poetry of Luis de Góngora, the Rinconcillo wanted to celebrate the authenticity of Andalucian culture while, at the same time, vanquish the picturesque vision of Spain erroneously expounded by outsiders. In 1922 the group was instrumental in organising the Concurso de Cante Jondo, a flamenco singing competition staged in the Alhambra that aimed to save the art from over-commercialisation. Five years later they reappeared at an event organised by the Ateneo de Sevilla to celebrate the 300th anniversary of Góngora's death, the first unofficial gathering of what became known as the Generación de '27 (an influential group of Spanish writers and artists that included Salvador Dalí and Luis Buñuel).

Granada still emits an edgy literary air in its diverse drinking establishments, although the Café Alameda is no longer in business. Its former digs are now occupied by the Restaurante Chikito (p266), which in February 2015 placed a statue of the Rinconcillo's most famous member, Lorca, in its hallowed front bar, in the corner where he and his compatriots once met, drank and – in the process – reinvented Spanish culture.

---

the tapa specialty – fish, which you'll smell sizzling in the fryer as soon as you open the door.

El Ají
MODERN SPANISH €€

(Map p258; ☎958 29 29 30; Plaza San Miguel Bajo 9; mains €12-20; ⊙1-11pm; ☷) Up in the Albayzín, this chic but cosy neighbourhood restaurant is no bigger than a shoebox, but serves from breakfast right through to the evening. Chatty staff at the tiny marble bar can point out some of the highlights of the creative menu (such as prawns with tequila and honey). It's a good place to get out of the sun and rest up, especially if you are hiking up from Plaza Nueva.

Oliver
SEAFOOD €€

(Map p262; ☎958 26 22 00; www.restauranteoliver.com; Calle Pescadería 12; mains €12-18; ⊙1-4pm & 8pm-midnight Mon-Sat) The seafood bars on this square are a Granada institution, and Oliver is one of the best for food and unflappable service in the midst of the lunch rush. Sleek business types pack in alongside street-sweepers to devour *raciónes* of garlicky fried treats at the mobbed bar, which can be ankle deep in crumpled napkins and shrimp shells come 4pm.

The only place for any peace is the back dining room or the terrace tables, which fill up early.

★ La Fábula Restaurante
MODERN EUROPEAN €€€

(Map p258; ☎958 25 01 50; www.restaurantelafabula.com; Calle San Antón 28; mains €22-28; ⊙1.30-4.30pm, 8.30-11pm Tue-Sat) In Fábula it's hard to avoid the pun – the place is pretty fabulous. Hidden in the highly refined confines of the Hotel Villa Oniria, the setting matches the food, which is presented like art and tastes equally good. Stand-outs are the venison with chestnuts and quince, or the baby eels with basil in venere rice.

The 11-course tasting menu is €65 (€80 with wine pairing) and there's a lovely garden out back. Be sure to book ahead.

Restaurante Chikito
ANDALUCIAN €€€

(Map p262; ☎958 22 33 64; www.restaurantechikito.com; Plaza Campillo Bajo 9; mains €16-22; ⊙12.30-3.30pm & 7.30-11.30pm Thu-Tue) Occupying the site of the legendary Café Alameda, the Chikito is perennially popular with the smart local set; its walls are plastered with Andaluz celeb pics, while its front bar contains a recently imported statue of Federico García Lorca, who once convened here with other intellectuals.

The tapas bar specialty is snails. The adjacent restaurant concentrates on hearty dishes like oxtail stew and pork medallions, which it has spent many years getting right.

🍷 Drinking & Nightlife

The best street for drinking is the rather scruffy Calle de Elvira, but other chilled bars line Río Darro at the base of the Albayzín and Calle Navas. Just north of Plaza de Trinidad are a bunch of cool hipster-ish bars.

Old stalwarts on the drinking/tapas scene are Los Diamontes (two branches), Bodega La Bella y la Bestia (four branches including one in Calle de Elvira) and the eternal classic Bodegas Castañeda.

★ Taberna La Tana   BAR
(Map p262; Calle Rosario; ⊙12.30-4pm & 8.30pm-midnight) Possibly the friendliest family-run bar in Granada, La Tana specialises in Spanish wines and backs it up with some beautifully paired tapas. You can't go wrong with the 'surtido' plate of Spanish hams. Ask the bartender about the 'wines of the month' and state your preference – a *suave* (smooth) red, or a *fuerte* (strong).

The small interior is old-fashioned, packed to the rafters (usually) and is filled with the aroma of fine wine.

El Bar de Eric   BAR
(Map p262; Calle Escuelas 8; ⊙8.30am-2am Sun-Thu, to 3am Fri & Sat) Imagine Keith Moon reincarnated as a punk rocker and put in charge of a modern tapas restaurant. Eric's is the brainchild of Spanish rock'n'roll drummer Eric Jiménez, of Los Planetas – but in this new bastion of rock chic, things aren't as chaotic as you might think.

Indulge in some fusion tapas served with cocktails and admire photo art that highlights band shoots and old rock-gig posters. Punters often arrive brandishing guitars and start up some spontaneous strumming.

Botánico   BAR
(Map p262; www.botanicocafe.es; Calle Málaga 3; ⊙10am-1am Mon-Fri, noon-1am Sat & Sun) A haven for cool dudes with designer beards, students finishing off their Lorca dissertations, and anyone else with arty inclinations, Botánico is a casual snack restaurant by day, a cafe at *merienda* time (5-7pm), and a bar and club come dusk, with DJs or live music emphasising jazz and blues.

GRANADA'S BEST TETERÍAS

Granada's *teterías* (teahouses) have proliferated in recent years, but there's still something exotic and dandyish about their dark atmospheric interiors, stuffed with lace veils, stucco, low cushioned seats and an invariably bohemian clientele. Most offer a long list of aromatic teas along with sticky Arabic sweets. Some serve up music and more substantial snacks. Many still permit their customers to indulge in the *chachima* (shisha pipe). Narrow Calle Calderería Nueva is Granada's best 'tetería street'. Cafe hours are roughly noon to midnight.

Tetería Nazari (Map p262; Calle Calderería Nueva 13) Snuggle down on the misshapen pouffes with the flamenco singers, the earnest art students and the winner of last year's Che Guevara look-alike contest.

Tetería La Cueva de Ali Baba (Map p262; Puente de Epinosa 15) Slightly more refined *tetería*, where you can sip wine and pick at tapas, overlooking the Darro River.

Tetería Dar Ziryab (Map p262; ☑ 655 44 67 75; Calle Calderería Nueva 11) A warm stove and regular live music provide two reasons to duck into the *Arabian Nights* interior of Dar Ziryab, where amorous undergraduates share *chicambas* (hookah pipes with water filters). Then there's the 40+ teas, sweet milk shakes and lovely white-chocolate tarts.

Tetería Kasbah (Map p262; Calle Calderería Nueva 4; mains €8-12) Savoury food, ample student-watching potential and amazing stucco make up for the sometimes slow service in Calle Calderería Nuevo's biggest and busiest *tetería*.

✂ Albayzín Abaco Te (Map p258; ☑ 958 22 19 35; Calle Alamo de Marqués 5; 🎤) Hidden high up in the Albayzín maze, Abaco's Arabian minimalist interior allows you to enjoy Alhambra views from a comfy-ish floor mat. Health freaks hog the carrot juice; sweet tooths bag the excellent cakes.

The bright colour scheme screams 'orange', while the name comes from the peaceful botanical garden across the road.

Al Sur de Granada
BAR

(Map p258; ☑ 958 27 02 45; www.alsurdegranada. net; Calle de Elvira 150; ⊙ 10am-4pm & 6-11.30pm) This delicatessen, dedicated to the best food and wine from around Granada province, doubles as a bar. Get a sampler cheese platter and try some of the various mountain liqueurs. It's also a great place to pick up some local products to take home.

Mundra
BAR

(Map p262; Plaza de la Trinidad; platters €10; ⊙ 8.30pm-2am Mon-Thu, to 3am Fri & Sat) Overlooking the leafy square, Mundra has a global-chic feel with its black barrel tables, Buddha statues and chill-out soundracks. There are platters to share for the peckish, including fresh prawns, which come from Motril, and provolone cheese, which doesn't.

Boom Boom Room
CLUB

(Map p262; ☑ 646 81 96 00; Calle Carcel Baja 11; ⊙ 3pm-6am Sun-Thu, to 7am Fri & Sat) A glittery converted cinema is now Granada's top club for the glam crowd, who recline on the gold sofas and get hip-swivelling to cheesy Spanish pop tunes.

☆ Entertainment

Do not miss the nightly shows (8pm; €30) in the Palacio de los Olvidados (p256), which combine Lorca's plays with some magnificent self-penned flamenco. Best night out in Granada. No contest!

Peña La Platería
FLAMENCO

(Map p258; www.laplateria.org.es; Placeta de Toqueros 7) Buried in the Albayzín warren, Peña La Platería claims to be the oldest flamenco aficionados' club in Spain, founded in 1949. Unlike other more private clubs,

it regularly opens it doors to nonmembers for performances on Thursday nights (and sometimes Saturdays) at 10.30pm.

Casa del Arte Flamenco
FLAMENCO

(Map p262; ☑ 958 56 57 67; www.casadelarte flamenco.com; Cuesta de Gomérez 11; tickets €18; ⊙ shows 7.30pm & 9pm) A small newish flamenco venue that is neither *tablao* (tourist show) nor *peña* (private club), but something in between. The performers are invariably top-notch, while the atmosphere depends largely on the tourist-local make-up of the audience.

Jardines de Zoraya
FLAMENCO

(Map p258; ☑ 958 20 60 66; www.jardinesde zoraya.com; Calle Panaderos 32; tickets with drink/ dinner €20/45; ⊙ shows 8pm & 10.30pm) A little larger than some of Andalucía's new flamenco cultural centres, and hosted in a restaurant that serves food and drink, the Jardines de Zoraya appears, on first impression, to be a touristy flamenco *tablao*. But reasonable entry prices, top-notch performers and a highly atmospheric patio make the Abayzín venue a worthwhile stop for any aficionado.

La Tertulia
LIVE PERFORMANCE

(Map p258; www.tertuliagranada.com; Calle Pintor López Mezquita 3; ⊙ 9pm-3am Tue-Sat) In Spain, a *tertulia* is an artistic gathering, and that's what you generally get at this bohemian bar where the emphasis is less on the beer and more on what's taking off on stage – comic guitarists, poetry jams and the like.

Le Chien Andalou
FLAMENCO

(Map p262; www.lechienandalou.com; Carrera del Darro 7; tickets €6-10; ⊙ shows 9.30pm & 11.30pm) Small cavernous bar that was once a cistern, but now hosts two nightly flamenco shows for half the price of the bigger places. Performances can be hit or miss, but at this price, it's probably worth the gamble.

ALSA BUSES FROM GRANADA

DESTINATION	COST (€)	DURATION (HR)	FREQUENCY (DAILY)
Almuñécar	8.36	1¼	9
Jaén	8.89	1¼	16
Córdoba	15	2¾	8
Guadix	5.50	1	15
Málaga	12	1½	22
Lanjarón	4.28	1	9
Seville	23	3	9

🛍 Shopping

Granada's craft specialities include *taracea* (marquetry) – the best work has shell, silver or mother-of-pearl inlay, applied to boxes, tables, chess sets and more.

Artesanías González   ARTS & CRAFTS
(Map p262; Cuesta de Gomérez 12; ⊘11am-8pm) Specialises in exceptionally fine examples of marquetry, ranging from small easy-to-pack boxes to larger pay-the-overweight-allowance chess sets.

Daniel Gil de Avalle   MUSIC
(Map p262; www.gildeavalle.com; Plaza del Realejo 15; ⊘10am-1pm & 5-8pm) This longstanding music store specialises in exquisite hand-made guitars. Step inside and you may well see the *guitarrero* (guitar maker) at work. Sheet music is also available, with an obvious emphasis on flamenco.

Tienda Librería de la Alhambra   SOUVENIRS
(Map p262; ✆ 958 22 78 46; Calle Reyes Católicos 40; ⊘9.30am-8.30pm) This is a fabulous shop for Alhambra aficionados, with a tasteful selection of quality gifts, including excellent coffee table–style tomes, children's art books, hand-painted fans, arty stationery and stunning photographic prints, which you select from a vast digital library (from €14 for A4 size).

Alquímía Pervane   PERFUME
(Map p262; Calderería Nueva) A fragrant hole in the wall near the top of this Moroccan-themed street, with its teashops and hookah pipes, selling a wide choice of wonderful oils in pretty bottles, plus rose water and similar.

La Carta des Vins   WINE
(Map p262; Calle Navas 29; ⊘10am-3pm & 5.30-9pm Mon-Fri; to 3pm Sat) This small wineshop has an excellent selection of vintages from around Granada and Andalucía, as well as the rest of Spain and further afield, including Argentina and Chile. The owner holds wine-tasting courses and one-off tasting sessions.

Alcaicería   SOUVENIRS
(Map p262; Calle Alcaicería) Formerly a grand Moorish bazaar where silk was made and sold, the stalls are now taken up with souvenir shops. The setting is still very reminiscent of the past, however, especially in the early morning before the coach tours descend. You can still see where the gates once stood at the entrances, there to guard against looting and closed at night. Opening hours vary, depending on the individual shops.

La Oliva   FOOD
(Map p262; Calle Rosario 9; ⊘11am-2.30pm & 7-10pm Mon-Sat) For a superb range of quality deli items, with an emphasis on fine wines and olive oil.

ℹ Information

Provincial Tourist Office (Map p262; ✆ 958 24 71 28; www.turismodegranada.org; Plaza de Mariana Pineda 10; ⊘9am-8pm Mon-Fri, 10am-7pm Sat, 10am-3pm Sun) Information on all of Granada province.

Tourist Office (Map p262; ✆ 958 22 10 22; Calle Santa Ana 1; ⊘9am-7.30pm Mon-Sat, 9.30am-3pm Sun) Close to Plaza Nueva.

ℹ Getting There & Away

AIR
Aeropuerto Federico García Lorca (www.aena.es) is 17km west of the city, near the A92. **Autocares J González** (www.autocaresjose-gonzalez.com) runs buses (one way €3) to Gran Vía de Colón opposite the cathedral. Links to destinations outside Spain are limited to **British Airways** (www.ba.com), who run thrice weekly flights to London City Airport.

TRAINS FROM GRANADA

DESTINATION	COST (€)	DURATION (HR)	FREQUENCY (DAILY)
Almería	20	2½	4
Madrid	69	4	4
Barcelona	60	7-11	3
Córdoba	36	2½	6
Algeciras	30	4¼	3
Linares-Baeza	24	2¼	1
Seville	30	3	4

BUS

Granada's **bus station** (Carretera de Jaén) is 3km northwest of the city centre. Take city bus SN2 to Cruz del Sur and change onto the LAC bus for the Gran Via de Colón in the city centre. Taxis cost around €7-9. **Alsa** (www.alsa.es) handles buses in the province and across the region, plus a night bus direct to Madrid's Barajas airport (€25, six hours).

TRAIN

The **train station** (958 24 02 02; Avenida de Andaluces) is 1.5km northwest of the centre, off Avenida de la Constitución. For the centre, walk straight ahead to Avenida de la Constitución and turn right to pick up the LAC bus to Gran Vía de Colón; taxis cost about €5.

ⓘ Getting Around

BUS

Individual tickets are €1.20. Pay with notes or coins to the bus driver. The most useful lines are C1, which departs from Plaza Nueva and does a full circuit of the Albayzín; C2, which runs from Plaza Nueva up to Sacramonte; and C3, which goes from Plaza Isabel II up through the Realejo quarter to the Alhambra.

CAR

Driving in central Granada – in common with most large Andalucian cities – can be frustrating and should be avoided if possible. Park your car on the outskirts and use public transport; there are plenty of options. If you have to drive, there are several central car parks: **Alhambra Parking** (Avenida Los Alixares; per hr/day €2.50/17), **Parking San Agustín** (Calle San Agustín; per hr/day €1.75/20) and **Parking Plaza Puerta Real** (Acera del Darro; per hr/day €1.45/17).

METRO

Stalled by the economic crisis, Granada's long-awaited new metro was still not operational in early 2015, although the lines have been built. The 16km route, which will run between Albolote in the north and Amarilla in the southwest, includes 26 stations and will take 45 minutes to ride in its entirety. As only 2.5km of the route in central Granada will travel beneath the ground, the metro is better described as a light-rail link.

TAXI

Taxis congregate in Plaza Nueva and at the train and bus stations.

LORCA'S LEGACY

It is debatable whether you can truly understand modern Andalucía without at least an inkling of knowledge about Spain's greatest poet and playwright, Federico García Lorca (1898–1936). Lorca epitomised many of Andalucía's potent hallmarks – passion, ambiguity, exuberance and innovation – and brought them skilfully to life in a multitude of precocious works. Early popularity was found with *El Romancero Gitano* (Gypsy Ballads), a 1928 collection of verses on Roma themes, full of startling metaphors yet crafted with the simplicity of flamenco song. Between 1933 and 1936 he wrote the three tragic plays for which he is best known: *Bodas de Sangre* (Blood Wedding), *Yerma* (Barren) and *La Casa de Bernarda Alba* (The House of Bernarda Alba) – brooding and dark, dramatic works dealing with themes of entrapment and liberation. Lorca was murdered at the start of the Civil War in August 1936. Although the whereabouts of his remains have proved elusive, recent research reaffirms the longstanding notion that he was executed by military authorities loyal to Franco, due to his perceived left-leaning political views and homosexuality.

Lorca's summer house, **Huerta de San Vicente** (958 25 84 66; Calle Virgen Blanca; admission only by guided tour in Spanish €3, Wed free; 9.15am-1.30pm & 5-7.30pm Tue-Sun), is a museum in a tidy park, a 15-minute walk from Puerta Real (head 700m down Calle de las Recogidas). In 2015 it was joined by the much delayed **Centro Lorca** (Map p262; Plaza de la Romanilla), the new home of the Lorca foundation that will host a library, 424-seat theatre, and expo space in a super-modern building.

In Lorca's birthplace, the village of Fuente Vaqueros, 17km west of Granada, the **Museo Casa Natal Federico García Lorca** (958 51 64 53; www.patronatogarcialorca.org; Calle Poeta Federico García Lorca 4; admission €1.80; guided visits hourly 10am-2pm & 5-7pm Tue-Sat) displays photos, posters and costumes for the writer's plays. Buses (€2, 20 minutes) operated by **Ureña** (958 45 41 54) leave from Avenida de Andaluces in front of Granada train station roughly hourly between 7am and 9pm weekdays, and every two hours from 9am on weekends.

LA VEGA & EL ALTIPLANO

Surrounding Granada is a swathe of fertile land known as La Vega, planted with shimmering poplar groves, as well as food crops. Heading northeast, the A92 passes through the hilly Parque Natural Sierra de Huétor before entering an increasingly arid landscape, made all the more dramatic by the white peaks of the Sierra Nevada looming to the south. Up close, the terrain around the town of Guadix is also fascinating, with the largest concentration of cave houses in Spain, and possibly in Europe.

Guadix sits on an elevated plateau. To the southeast lies the Marquesado de Zenete district below the northern flank of the Sierra Nevada; to the northeast sits the Altiplano, Granada's 'High Plain', which breaks out into mountains here and there and affords superb long-distance views all the way to northern Almería province.

Guadix

POP 20,400

Guadix (gwah-*deeks*), 55km from Granada near the foothills of the Sierra Nevada, is famous for its cave dwellings – not prehistoric remnants, but the homes of at least 3000 present-day townspeople, carved into the hills' heavy clay. Cave hotels, which are wonderfully cool in summer and cosy in winter, let you try the lifestyle. The *accitanos* (from the town's Moorish name, Wadi Acci) also enjoy some excellent, tourist-free tapas bars. The tourist office (☑958 66 26 65; Avenida Mariana Pineda; ◐9am-1.30pm & 4-6pm Mon-Fri) is on the road leaving the town centre towards Granada.

◉ Sights

Most visitors make a beeline to the cave district, but the town's old quarter has its own distinctive architecture, much of it rendered in warm sandstone. At the centre is a fine cathedral (Calle Santa María del Buen Aire; admission with audioguide €5; ◐10.30am-2pm & 5-7.30pm Mon-Sat, 7.30-9pm Sun), built between the 16th and 18th centuries on the site of the town's former main mosque in a mix of Gothic, Renaissance and baroque styles. The entry price includes a small art museum (which has the same opening hours and uses the same audio-guide).

Near Guadix Cathedral, the Plaza de la Constitución feels almost fortified, edged with porticos and gracefully worn brick steps. Just up the hill, look for the off-kilter tile Mudéjar tower of the 16th-century Iglesia y Monasterio de Santiago (Placeta de Santiago; ◐11am & 7-8.30pm Sun, 7-8.30pm Mon-Sat) with an elaborate plateresque facade by Diego Siloé.

Just to the west of the Iglesia y Monasterio de Santiago, you'll find the 10th- and 11th-century Islamic castle, the Alcazaba (Calle Barradas 3; admission €1.20), from where there are fine views across town and into the main cave quarter. It was closed for renovations at last visit.

Barriada de las Cuevas CAVES

Up in the hills on the south side of town is Guadix's largest cave district, some 2000 whitewashed dwellings nestled among rolling hills, with spindly chimneys, satellite dishes and full connections to the town's power and water lines. You can walk or drive a route past some rather splendid homes, as well as some more ramshackle ones.

Centro de Interpretación Cuevas de Guadix MUSEUM

(Plaza de Padre Poveda; admission €2.60; ◐10am-2pm & 5-7pm Mon-Fri, to 2pm Sat) Re-creates cave life of years past, with an audiovisual presentation and displays of traditional housewares and furnishings, including ox yokes, clay water pots, woven esparto grass, and wooden furniture painted in bright primary colours.

For more insight, peruse the Iglesia Nuestra Señora de Gracia (◐11.30am-1pm & 5-8pm Tue-Fri) opposite, a relatively modern church with an older cave chapel leading off the nave.

🛏 Sleeping

Hotel Palacio de Oñate HOTEL €€

(☑958 66 05 00; www.palaciodeonate.es; Calle Mira de Amezcua, Guadix; s/d €50/70; ❊☞) Guadix's former Hotel Comercio has been rebranded and updated to make it more like something you'd find in Granada. The palacio itself dates from 1905 and has an elegant ochre-washed facade with wrought-iron balconies. General rooms are fairly boring, but the '*suite presidencial mudéjar*' is something else.

The large public spaces include a spa with Turkish bath, sauna and massage parlour. There's also a gym plus an adjacent jazz bar/cafe called Diwan. All pretty regal for Guadix.

WORTH A TRIP

CASTILLO DE LA CALAHORRA

During the Reconquista, the flatlands between Guadix and the mountains fell under the command of Marqués Rodrigo de Mendoza, whose tempestuous life included a spell in Italy unsuccessfully wooing Lucrezia Borgia. About 20km southeast of Guadix, his forbidding **Castillo de La Calahorra** (958 67 70 98; admission €3; 10am-12.30pm & 4-5.30pm Wed) looms on a hilltop, guarding the pass over the Sierra Nevada.

Built between 1509 and 1512, the domed corner towers and blank walls enclose an elegant Renaissance courtyard with a staircase of Carrara marble. Guided tours (in Spanish) take about 30 minutes, and if you arrive while one is going on, you'll have to wait for the door to be opened.

For guided tours outside of regular hours, contact the caretaker Antonio Trivaldo on the castle phone number to arrange a time. To drive up to the castle, turn onto the dirt road opposite La Hospedería del Zenete in La Calahorra and take the winding route up-hill, or park in the town plaza and walk up the stone footpath.

✖ Eating & Drinking

No need for a sit-down meal in Guadix – you can feed yourself well, and meet the locals, at the exceptional bars around town. At every place, you'll pay less than €1.50 for a beer, and *raciónes* cost about €5.

La Bodeguilla
TAPAS €

(Calle Doctor Pulido 4; drink & tapa €1.70, raciónes €6) Between Avenida Medina Olmos and the river, La Bodeguilla is one of the best traditional bars in town – and the oldest, dating from 1904. Here, old men in flat caps line the bar tucking into delicious tapas, like *habas y jamon* (broad beans and ham), accompanied by wine, vermouth, muscatel or *fino* (sherry) direct from one of the stacked-up barrels lining the far wall of the room.

Bodega Calatrava
TAPAS €

(Calle La Tribuna; drink & tapa €1.70, raciónes €6) An atmospheric traditional bar tucked down a side street in the centre of town, and specialising in simple tapa treats like juicy fried prawns and wedges of crumbly well-aged Manchego cheese, as well as more substantial *raciónes*.

Cafetería Versalles
CAFE €

(Calle Medina Olmos 1; churros €3.50; 7am-1am;) Across from the municipal park, this time-tested cafe is *the* place in town for breakfast, including, reputedly, the best *churros con chocolate* (tubular deep-fried doughnuts and thick hot chocolate) in town.

Café Jazz Diwan
BAR

(958 66 05 00; Hotel Palacio de Oñate, Calle Mira de Amezcua) Part of a tastefully reformed hotel, this elegant small bar with a mezzanine floor has an intimate sophisticated vibe. There's occasional live jazz, or – more often – a live pianist.

❶ Getting There & Away

BUS

Buses run to Granada (€5.50, one hour, 15 daily), Almería (€10, two hours, two daily), Málaga (€18, three hours, three daily) and Mojácar (€16, 3½ hours, two daily). The **bus station** (958 66 06 57; Calle Concepción Arenal) is off Avenida Medina Olmos, about 700m southeast of the centre.

TRAIN

There are four trains daily to Granada (€9.50, one hour) and six to Almería (€11, 1¼ hours). The station is off the Murcia road, about 2km northeast of the town centre – walkable, but dusty and drab; a cab costs €5 to the centre, and about €9 to the cave district.

SIERRA NEVADA & LAS ALPUJARRAS

Granada's dramatic alpine backdrop is the Sierra Nevada range, which extends about 75km from west to east and into Almería province. Its wild snow-capped peaks include the highest point in mainland Spain, while the lower reaches of the range, known as Las Alpujarras (sometimes just La Alpujarra), are dotted with tiny scenic villages. From July to early September, the higher elevations offer wonderful multiday trekking and day hikes. Outside of this period, there's risk of seriously inclement weather, but the lower Alpujarras are always welcoming, with most snow melting away by May.

The 862-sq-km Parque Nacional Sierra Nevada, Spain's largest national park, is home to 2100 of Spain's 7000 plant species, among them unique types of crocus, narcissus, thistle, clover, poppy and gentian. Andalucía's largest ibex population (about 5000) is here, too, frolicking above 2800m. Surrounding the national park at lower altitudes is the Parque Natural Sierra Nevada, with a lesser degree of protection.

Along the southern edge of the protected area, the Alpujarras is a 70km-long jumble of valleys along the southern flank of the Sierra Nevada. It is a beautiful, diverse and even slightly strange place. Its landscape of arid slopes, deep crags and egg-white villages look as if they were spilled onto the mountainside, the towns on the mountain's lower belts simmer with spiritual seekers, long-term travellers and rat-race dropouts, while the higher villages have a disorienting timelessness.

Even the most-visited Alpujarran towns are appealing, as the villages' Berber-style flat-roofed houses and the winding lanes between them look out on hillsides that have been carefully terraced and irrigated since the earliest Moorish times. With well-trod footpaths connecting each settlement, it's a delightful area to explore on foot.

Getting There & Away

BUS

Alsa (www.alsa.es) operates local buses. From Granada, it runs on two routes: one twice daily on the low road through Cádiar and Válor; the other three times daily to the higher villages and ending in Trevélez or Bérchules. Return buses start before 6am and mid-afternoon. There is a Málaga–Órgiva bus (€12, three hours, once daily except Sunday), and a bus from Almería to Válor (€7.60, three hours) on Monday, Wednesday and Friday.

Sierra Nevada

Los Cahorros

A short drive southeast of Granada, not far from the village of Monachil, the area known as Los Cahorros is good for short walks, with trails running through the dramatic gorges that guard the Río Monachil. The most pop-

ular route – the Cahorros Altos, heading upstream – passes over a suspension bridge and alongside waterfalls. Look for the start of the 5km route just east of Monachil. The gorge walls are popular with rock-climbers.

You can take a bus from Granada to Monachil (€3, 30 minutes), from Paseo del Salón in Granada; buses run nearly hourly from 8.10am to 11.10pm, except Saturday afternoon and Sunday.

Sierra Nevada Ski Station

The ski station Sierra Nevada Ski (☎902 70 80 90; www.sierranevada.es; one-day ski pass €33-45), has its base at the resort 'village' of Pradollano, 33km from Granada on the A395. It is popular with day-skiers and hence supremely busy at weekends in season. A few of the 121 marked runs start almost at the top of 3395m-high Veleta. There are cross-country routes, too, and a dedicated snowboard area (with Spain's longest half-pipe), a new family slope and kids' snow park, and night-skiing on Thursday and Saturday. In summer, the station becomes a mountain bike park keeping three of its 22 lifts open and offering 30km of trails.

In winter Tocina (☎958 46 50 22) operates three daily buses (four on the weekend) to the resort from Granada's bus station (€5/8 one way/return, one hour). Outside the ski season there's just one daily bus (9am from Granada, 5pm from the ski station). A taxi from Granada costs about €50.

Mulhacén & Veleta

The Sierra Nevada's two highest peaks are Mulhacén (3479m) and Veleta (3395m). Two of three known as Los Tresmiles, because they rise above 3000m, they're on the western end of the range, close to Granada. From the ski station on the mountains' north flank, a road climbs up and over to Capileira,

Sierra Nevada & Las Alpujarras

the highest village in the Barranco de Poqueira in the Alpujarras on the south side, but it's closed to motor vehicles on the highest stretch. From late June to the end of October (depending on snow cover), the national park operates a shuttle bus to give walkers access to the upper reaches of the range – or just a scenic guided drive.

The bus runs up from 3km above the ski station, starting at the national park information post at **Hoya de la Mora** (✏671 56 44 07; ⊘8.30am-2.30pm & 3.30-7.30pm Jun-Oct). Tickets are €5 one way or €9 return. It's best to phone ahead to check availability and reserve a space.

From the end of the bus route on the north side, it's about 4km up Veleta, an ascent of about 370m with 1½ hours' walking (plus stops); or 14km to the top of Mulhacén, with four to five hours' walking. To tackle Mulhacén from the south side, base yourself in Capileira in Las Alpujarras. From here a national park summer shuttle runs up to the Mirador de Trevélez, from where it's around three hours to the top of Mulhacén (6km, 800m ascent).

To make the trip into an overnight loop, you can bunk down at the 84-bed Refugio Poqueira (p279), which sits at 2500m below the southwestern face of Mulhacén. The loop to Mulhacén from Mirador de Trevélez incorporating the refugio takes six to seven hours. Book in advance.

The **Centro de Visitantes El Dornajo** (✏958 34 06 25; ⊘10am-5pm), about 23km from Granada, on the A395 towards the ski station, has plenty of information on the Sierra Nevada.

Las Alpujarras

Lanjarón

The closest of Las Alpujarras villages to Granada, leafy Lanjarón often bustles with tourists. Second only to Trevélez in ham production, it's also packed with shops selling the stuff. And that bottled water you've been drinking? It's from here as well. The therapeutic waters have been harnessed at the large **Balneario de Lanjarón** (✏958 77 01 37; www.balneariodelanjaron.com; Avenida de la Constitución; 1hr bath €30), a spa on the west edge of town, just opposite the tourist office. Promoting more active pursuits is the excellent **Caballo Blanco Trekking Centre** (✏627 79 48 91; www.caballoblancotrekking.com; two-/four-hour treks €40/70), offering horse-riding lessons and treks into the surrounding hills and mountains. English and German are spoken. Book in advance. Top-notch birdwatching tours, both around Lanjarón and further afield, are also available via **Alpujarras Birdwatching & Nature** (www.alpujarras birdwatching.com).

For snacks, wander down the main street to the middle of town, to **Arca de Noé**

LAS ALPUJARRAS WALKING TRAILS

For those without summit fever, the alternating ridges and valleys of Las Alpujarras are criss-crossed with a network of mule paths, irrigation ditches and hiking routes, for a near-infinite number of good walks between villages or into the wild. The best time for walking in Las Alpujarras is April to mid-June, and also mid-September to early November, when the temperatures are just right and the vegetation is at its most colourful.

The villages in the Barranco de Poqueira are the most popular starting point, but even there, you'll rarely pass another hiker on the trail. Colour-coded routes ranging from 4km to 23km (two to eight hours) run up and down the gorge, and you can also hike to Mulhacén from here. Get maps and advice at the **Nevadensis** (p277) office in Pampaneira, or you can make do with the Editorial Alpina map, which shows most of the trails in the gorge.

Of the long-distance footpaths that traverse Las Alpujarras, the **GR-7** (which runs all the way to Greece) follows the most scenic route; you can walk it from Lanjarón to Válor in around five days staying in the villages of Pampaneira, Pitres, Trevélez, and Bérchules en route. Buses serve all these villages, allowing you to split it into shorter day walks. The Bubión–Pitres section makes a good afternoon outing.

A newer path, the **GR-240** (better known as the *Sulayr*) runs in a 300km circuit around the Sierra Nevada at a higher altitude than the GR-7. Inaugurated in 2007, it is relatively well-signposted and takes 15–19 days to walk in its entirety. Most people join it for shorter segments.

(Jamones Gustavo Rubio; Avenida de la Alpujarra 38; ☉10am-9pm), one of the better ham shops, where you can stock up on supplies or order a tasting tray and have a swig of sherry out the back. On the same street **Cafetería Denebola** (☎958 77 22 78; Avenida de Andalucia 38; snacks €2-3; ☉8.30am-9pm) does fantastic coffee confections and decent breakfasts.

Órgiva

The main town of the western Alpujarras, Órgiva is a bit scruffier and considerably larger than neighbouring villages, although it shares the moniker 'Gateway to Las Alpujarras' with Lanjarón. A hippie scene has long been fertile here – the alternative life-style tipi village of 'Beneficio' is nearby and its inhabitants regularly come into town to sell their wares or busk at Órgiva's Thursday market. British visitors might recognise the town from Chris Stewart's best-selling book, *Driving Over Lemons*.

🛏 Sleeping

Casa Rural Jazmín   GUESTHOUSE €€
(☎958 78 47 95; www.casaruraljazmin.com; Calle Ladera de la Ermita; r €53-70; P❋✉) A sanctuary in the upper town, Casa Jazmín is a French-run house with four rooms, each decorated in a different style (Asian and Alpujarran rooms are smaller; French and African, larger). There's a communal terrace and a pool set in a dense garden. On a cul-de-sac, it has space for parking, once you make it up the winding street.

🍴 Eating & Drinking

Tetería Baraka   INTERNATIONAL €€
(www.teteria-baraka.com; Calle Estación 12; mains €10-13; ☉noon-10.30pm Sat-Wed, 9am-4.30pm Thu) This place has a laid-back vibe and an eclectic menu that includes Moroccan dishes, tofu burgers, *shwarmas,* delicious brownies and natural juices. There are also preserves, spices and teas for sale, plus bakery items to take away. Located beside the municipal car park in the upper part of town.

La Almazara   INTERNATIONAL €€
(☎958 78 46 28; Avenida González Robles 53; mains €15-25; ☉1-4pm & 8pm-midnight Thu-Tue) Has inventive dishes and excellent pizza served in an orange grove all summer.

🛍 Shopping

A New Age atmosphere prevails, especially at the Thursday morning market held in the centre of town.

Angel Vera   CERAMICS
(Órgiva-Pampaneira) Situated 4km out of Órgiva, this workshop displays the exquisite ceramics and woodwork of Angel Vera, with vases, tables, lamps and ornamental plates included in the display. Ceramic workshops also available.

Tara   JEWELLERY
(Avenida González Robles 19; ☉9am-2pm & 5.30-8pm Mon-Sat) In keeping with Órgiva's hippy spirit, Tara sells ethnic clothes and jewelry with strong subcontinental influences. Joss sticks add a whiff of exoticism.

LAS ALPUJARRAS BUSES FROM GRANADA

TO	COST (€)	DURATION (HR)	FREQUENCY (DAILY)
Bérchules	9.50	3¾	2
Bubión	6.09	2¼	3
Cádiar	8.74	2¾	3
Capileira	6.13	2½	3
Lanjarón	4.28	1	9
Pampaneira	6.05	2	3
Pitres	6.80	2¾	3
Órgiva	5.12	1¾	9
Trevélez	7.98	3¼	3
Válor	10	3½	2
Yegen	9.83	3¼	2

SCENIC DRIVE: THE MOOR'S SIGH

A spectacular alternative to the A44 from the coast to Granada is the **Carretera del Suspiro del Moro**. Straight through, the drive takes about two hours, but you can stop for a good walk en route. From the N340 in Almuñécar, turn northwest out of the main roundabout (McDonald's is off to the south side), where a small sign points towards Otívar.

In Otívar, note your car's odometer reading. The road ascends sharply here, with breathtaking panoramas. Where it finally levels off, after 13km, the landscape is barren limestone studded with pine trees. Just over 16km from Otívar, the trailhead for **Sendero Río Verde** starts on the left side of the road. This trail descends nearly 400m into the deep valley of the Río Verde, with a good chance of sighting ibex as you go. The full loop is 7.4km (about 3½ hours), but requires walking back to your car along the road, so when you reach the Fuente de las Cabrerizas, a water pump near the bottom of the gorge, you may prefer to turn around and head back the way you came.

Back on your way, and descending the other side of the mountain, 43.5km from Otívar you'll see a road signed 'Suspiro del Moro' heading to the left. Follow this, and in five minutes you emerge in front of the Suspiro del Moro tourist restaurant, a modern marker of the pass where, legend has it, the emir of Granada, Boabdil, looked back and let out a last regretful sigh as he left the city in 1492. Follow the 'Granada' signs to continue to the city, 12km further.

Pampaneira

The lowest village in the gorge is also the most obviously tourist-driven. You'll quickly ascertain its specialty craft: coarsely-woven Alpujarran rugs which are hung outside practically every shop. Paths fan out from here, including the 9km local jaunt known as 'Sendero Pueblos de Poqueira'.

◎ Sights & Activities

O Sel Ling   MONASTERY
(☏ 958 34 31 34; www.oseling.com; ⊙ 3.30-6pm) Opposite Pampaneira village, 2km up the western side of the Poqueira gorge, you can just make out the stupa of the small stone Buddhist monastery, established in 1982 by a Tibetan monk. It makes a good destination for a hike.

Nevadensis   OUTDOORS
(☏ 958 76 31 27; www.nevadensis.com; Plaza de la Libertad; ⊙ 10am-2pm & 5-7pm Tue-Sat, to 3pm Sun & Mon) The Alpujarras most all-encompassing outdoor adventure specialists have an office in Pampaneira's main square, which effectively serves as a local tourist information point and includes a mini-museum documenting the region's ecology and geology. They offer a huge range of activities, from mountaineering courses to guided hikes and canyoning.

🛏 Sleeping

Estrella de las Nieves   HOTEL €€
(☏ 958 76 39 81; www.estrelladelasnieves.com; Calle Huerto 21; s/d €54/70; ℗ 🕸 ☒) Opened in 2010, this dazzling white complex just above the town has airy, light and modern rooms with terraces overlooking the rooftops and mountains. It also has pleasant gardens and the definite perks of a car park and pool. The hotel is located just outside the village on the A-4132, towards Lanjarón.

🍴 Eating & Drinking

Bodega El Lagar   ANDALUCIAN €
(Calle Silencio; raciónes €6-8) Located on one of the prettiest winding sidestreets, this tiny place sells local products, including preserves, and some funky clothing, plus has an attractive tucked-away terrace for trying *raciónes* like chicken and garlic. It doubles as a bodega too, so ask to taste the wine – it costs less than €3 a litre and is surprisingly fruity and palatable.

Café Europa   CAFE €
(☏ 958 76 30 65; Plaza de la Libertad 3; tapas €3; ⊙ 8am-10pm) Fine central perch opposite the church, where you can tune into the local grapevine over coffee, *tostadas,* sandwiches or cakes – or raise the stakes with wine and some simple (local) tapas.

🛍 Shopping

Abuela Ili Chocolates   CHOCOLATE

(www.abuelailichocolate.com; Plaza de la Libertad 1; ⊙10am-1.30pm & 5-8pm Mon-Fri, to 1.30pm Sat) First, you get to taste loads of samples here. Second, the chocolate is just fabulous. It is made on the premises and includes some wonderful and unusual sweet and savoury flavours, ranging from mango to mustard (yes, that's right!). There's a small museum explaining the process.

Bubión

Bubión, the quiet middle village, has a small museum and is bisected by the GR7 cross-continental footpath. There's a tangible feel of its Moorish roots in its narrow backstreets, with their arches, flat-roofed houses and gutters running down the middle of the thoroughfare.

◉ Sights

Casa Alpujarreña   MUSEUM

(Calle Real; admission €2; ⊙11am-2pm Sun-Thu, 11am-2pm & 5-7pm Sat & holidays) Located in the lower village beside the church, this folk museum set in a village house gives a glimpse of bygone Alpujarran life, both good and bad – a washboard is dedicated to the women of Bubión who have endured this 'cruel instrument'.

BARRANCO DE POQUEIRA

When seen from the bottom of the Poqueira gorge, the three villages of Pampaneira, Bubión and Capileira, 14km to 20km northeast of Órgiva, look like splatters of white paint flicked Jackson Pollock–style against the grey stone behind. They're the most beautiful villages of the Alpujarras, and the most visited. The Poqueira is famous for its multitude of artisan crafts; leather, weaving and tilework are all practiced using age-old methods. Then there is the unique cusine made using locally produced ham, jam, cheese, honey, mushrooms and grapes. Arrive with a shopping bag and fill up. Equally alluring are the hiking trails that link the villages, many of them perfectly doable in a day. The best-stocked tourist office is in Pampaneira. The bus to and from Granada stops in all three villages.

Eating

Teide   ANDALUCIAN €

(Carretera de Sierra Nevada; mains €7-9; ⊙10am-10.30pm Wed-Mon) A good restaurant on the main road frequented by a local clientele of characters who stop by for hearty *raciónes* of *jamón* and wine. The dishes are mainly Alpujarran, with a few international additions like onion soup and spaghetti with pesto.

Estación 4   INTERNATIONAL €

(Calle Estación 4; mains €7-12; ⊙6-11pm Tue-Fri, 1-4pm & 6.30-11pm Sat & Sun; 🖋) Wind your way down below the main road to find this superb and elegant restaurant, with its minimalist dining room and varied menu, including international bites like hummus and vegetarian croquettes, plus some wonderful innovative salads and more traditional local fare.

🛍 Shopping

Nade Taller del Telar   HOMEWARES

(www.tallerdeltelar.com; Calle Trinidad 11; ⊙11am-2.30pm & 5-8.30pm) For a glimpse of the past, visit the French-owned weaving workshop, with its historic enormous looms that come from the Albayzín in Granada. Nade only uses natural fabrics in her weaving, like alpaca wool, silk and mohair. The shawls are beautiful, starting at around €65, and well worth the investment.

She also produces some original wall hangings, as well as sofa throws and blankets.

Capileira

Capileira, the highest, largest and – arguably – prettiest village, sports the best stash of restaurants and accommodation options, and has a long tradition for producing top quality leather goods. It's also the departure point for high-altitude hikes up or around Mulhacén.

◉ Sights

Casa Museo Pedro Antonio de Alarcón   MUSEUM

(☑958 76 30 51; Calle Mentidero; admission €1; ⊙11.30am-2.30pm Tue-Sun) A modest dual-interest museum dedicated to local farming and living utensils, and the life and work of the Guadix-born novelist Pedro Antonio de Alarcón, whose 1872 book *La Alpujarra* detailed his travels in the region. It has recently been comprehensively renovated.

🛏 Sleeping

Refugio Poqueira REFUGE €

(☑958 34 33 49; www.refugiopoqueira.com; per person €17, breakfast €5, dinner €14) This modern, 87-bunk refuge has a restaurant and hot showers – a just reward after a day of trekking the Sierra Nevada. You get here by walking 4km from the Mirador de Trevélez (about one hour), or following the Río Mulhacén for 2.3km down from the road beneath the western side of Mulhacén, then veering 750m southeast along a path to the refuge.

Phone ahead, if possible. The refuge is open year-round.

Hotel Real de Poqueira HOTEL €€

(☑958 76 39 02; www.hotelpoqueira.com; Doctor Castillas 11; s/d €50/70; ❋🕿⛲) Located in an old house next to Capileira's lily-white church, this place is one of several Poqueira accommodations in the village all run by the same family. However, with its expansive lobby, flop-down couches and smart, boutique-like rooms, this one has the edge. It's not what you expect in a small Alpujarra village, which makes it all the more epiphanic.

🍴 Eating

⭐Taberna Restaurante La Tapa SPANISH, MOROCCAN €

(☑618 30 70 30; Calle Cubo 6; mains €9-12; ⊙noon-4pm & 8pm-midnight; 🎜) Las Alpujarras is a culinary micro-region with its own distinct flavours and, at La Tapa, they're skilfully melded with the area's Moorish past, creating dishes such as wild boar casserole and couscous in earthenware dishes. The place is tiny but textbook Alpujarran.

Bar El Tilo ANDALUCIAN €

(Plaza Calvario; raciónes €8; ⊙11.30am-11pm) Capileira's village tavern enjoys prime position on a lovely whitewashed square with a terrace. *Raciónes* such as *albóndigas* (meatballs in tomato sauce) are enormous. There are also cakes and pies made daily.

🛍 Shopping

J Brown ACCESSORIES

(www.jbrowntallerdepiel.com; Calle Doctor Castilla 7; ⊙10am-1.30pm & 5-8pm Mon-Fri, to 1.30pm Sat) Don't miss the excellent leatherwork here, including bags, belts and Western-style hats, all handmade at very reasonable prices. And J Brown is not a Brit, but José Manuel Moreno (*moreno* meaning 'brown' in Spanish) – you can watch him at work at the back of the shop.

L'ATELIER

Sitting ironically in the middle of a region where the main local dish, *plato alpujarreño*, is a carnivorous mélange of sausages, cured meats, fried eggs and potatoes, L'Atelier (☑958 85 75 01; www.atelier-mecina.com; Calle Alberca 21; mains €8-12; ⊙1-4pm & 7.30-10pm; 🎜), is a curious anomaly – and a welcome one if you don't eat meat. Set in a traditional house in the hamlet of Mecina Fondales in La Tahá this snug, candlelit restaurant presents globetrotting vegetarian and vegan dishes (tabbouleh, Moroccan tagine, miso soup included) and the results are exceptional. L'Atelier's reputation was cemented by French chef Jean-Claude Juston in the 1990s and, despite a recent change in ownership, it has lost none of its shine. L'Atelier also rents several rooms (which start from €55).

La Tahá

In the next valley east from Poqueira, life gets substantially more tourist-free. Still known by the Arabic term for the administrative districts into which the Islamic caliphate divided the Alpujarras, this region consists of the town of Pitres and its six outlying villages – Mecina, Capilerilla, Mecinilla, Fondales, Ferreirola and Atalbéitar – in the valley just below, all of Roman origin. Day-trippers are few, and the expat residents have nearly blended in with the scenery.

Ancient paths between the seven hamlets (marked with signposts labelled 'Sendero Local Pitres-Ferreirola') wend their way through woods and orchards, while the tinkle of running water provides the soundtrack. About 15 minutes' walk below Fondales, an old Moorish-era bridge spans the deep gorge of the Río Trevélez. Park at the top of the town and follow signs saying 'Camino de Órgiva' and 'Camino del Campuzano'.

If you're walking in on the GR7, you'll be deposited in Pitres' Plaza La Alpujarra where you can procure refreshments in **Bar La Taha** (Plaza La Alpujarra 5; ⊙noon-11pm). Across the square a signboard displays a quote and photo of Federico García Lorca, who visited in 1928.

A good accommodation option, situated in Ferreirola, is **Sierra y Mar** (☑958 76 61 71; www.sierraymar.com; Calle Albaicín, Ferreirola; s/d incl breakfast €42/65; 🅿🛜).

Trevélez

To gastronomes, Trevélez equals ham – or *jamón serrano* to be more precise – one of Spain's finest cured hams that matures perfectly in the village's rarified mountain air. To hikers it means a cobweb of high mountain trails including easy access to Mulhacén, mainland Spain's highest peak. To statisticians it is the second highest village in Spain after Valdelinares in Aragón.

The village, sited at 1486m on the almost treeless slopes of the Barranco de Trevélez, is divided into *alto* (high) and *bajo* (low) sections. The Alpujarra bus generally stops in both. The *alto* section is older and more labyrinthine, while *bajo* has the bulk of the tourist facilities.

🏃 Activities

Trevélez is a spaghetti junction of hiking paths. The GR-7 passes through town and it's also starting point for one of the longer ascents of Mulhacén via Siete Lagunas, which is possible in around 12 hours if you're mega-fit (you can descend via the Mirador de Trevélez to make a circuit).

An easier hike follows the Sendero Horcajo up the Trevélez river valley from the top of town. The ultimate goal is the Cortijo de la Meseta, a *refugio* where you can stay overnight. The full walk one way is 8.7km.

🛏 Sleeping

Hotel La Fragua HOTEL €
(☑958 85 86 26; www.hotellafragua.com; Calle San Antonio 4; s/d €38/50; 🅿🛜) The rooms at La Fragua are typical mountain-village style: pine-furnished, simple and clean. Some have balconies, and there's a large rooftop deck. Early-rising walking groups can be noisy, though. The hotel is at the top of town, a 200m walk (signposted) from the highest plaza. A second, more modern property nearby (doubles for €55) has a pool and great views.

La Fragua is closed early January to early February.

🍴 Eating & Drinking

Restaurante La Fragua ANDALUCIAN €
(Barrio Alto; mains €8-13; ⏱1-4pm & 8-10.30pm; 🛜) Located at the very top of the village – a deterrent unless you're staying at the neighbouring hotel – but worth the hike up for partridge in walnut sauce, and the fig ice cream. There are some superb salads here, as well, and great views from the glassed-in top-floor terrace.

Mesón Joaquín ANDALUCIAN €
(Carretera Laujar, Órgiva Km 22; mains €8-12; ⏱noon-4.30pm) Welcome to ham city! White-coated technicians slice up transparent sheets of the local product, and the trout comes from the wholesaler just behind – wrapped in ham, of course. Vegetarians be warned: scores of cured hams hang within head-butting distance from the restaurant's roof.

Café-Bar El Chorrillo CAFE
(Plaza de Francisco Abellón; ⏱8am-midnight) The Chorrillo has many lures. Salt-of-the-earth friendly service, damned good coffee and smoothies, churros and hot chocolate, and a location that's within bus-spotting distance of the bus stop. It's not fancy. That's the point!

🛍 Shopping

Jamones González FOOD
(www.jamonescanogonzalez.com; Calle Nueva; ⏱10am-1.30pm & 5-8pm Mon-Fri, to 1.30pm Sat) The place to come if you fancy buying some of the famed Trevélez cured ham to take home. Also sells other local gourmet products.

Eastern Alpujarras

Seven kilometres south of Trevélez, the A4132 crosses the Portichuelo de Cástaras pass and turns east into a harsher, barer landscape, yet still with oases of greenery around the villages. Significantly fewer tourists make it this far from Granada, and those who do are often on long, solitary walking excursions. Many of the pleasures here are in eating: fresh, local products are the focus at the casual restaurants and inns.

The following five villages are located on the GR-7 footpath. All but Mairena are served by Alsa buses shuttling to and from Granada.

BÉRCHULES

In a green valley back in the hills, this village is a walkers' waypoint. **Hotel Los Bérchules** (☑958 85 25 30; mains €10-14), at the crossroads at the bottom of the village, has an excellent restaurant, with such local specialities as rabbit in an almond sauce. **Cuatro Vientos** (☑958 76 90 39; Calle Carretera 4; tapas from €1.50; ☺8am-11pm Tue-Sun), is an absolutely no-frills bar next door full of flat-capped farmers grazing on slices of ham and cheese, and knocking back glasses of sherry. For hospitality and great views, **Hotel Los Bérchules** (☑958 85 25 30; www. hotelberchules.com; Carretera de Granada 20; s/d €42/62; P ⓻ ☎) is a good accommodation option.

MECINA BOMBARÓN

The larger of three Alpujarra Mecinas (there's one in La Tahá and another east of Válor), this white mountain village is unjustly overlooked by all but the most dedicated walkers. Located on the GR7, 7km west of Yegen and 5km east of Bérchules, the village was the birthplace and final refuge of Abén Aboo, the last leader of the Moors in Spain. His death in 1571 signaled the end of the Moorish rebellion and the beginning of their expulsion.

There's a 13th-century medieval bridge on the eastern side of the settlement, just below the GR7, that used to carry the 'camino real' on its route between Granada and Almería. For refueling try **Restaurante El Portón** (☑958 06 49 23; Calle Iglesia Vieja 15; mains €7-10; ☺7.30am-12.30am), where the *patatas al pobre* (fried potatoes, peppers and onions) never tasted so good.

YEGEN

East of Bérchules, the 400-strong village of Yegen is best known as the home of British writer Gerald Brenan, a peripheral Bloomsbury Group member whose *South from Granada* depicted life here in the 1920s. A plaque marks **Brenan's house**, just off the fountain plaza below the main road. Walkers can explore the dramatically eroded red landscape on the **Sendero Gerald Brenan**, a 1.9km loop (one hour) – look for a map of the route on the main plaza. On the eastern edge of the village, the excellent restaurant at **El Rincón de Yegen** (☑958 85 12 70; Calle de las Eras 2; mains €14-20; ☺1-4.30pm & 9-11pm Tue-Sun) offers treats such as pears in Contraviesa wine and hot chocolate.

On the road midway between Yegen and Mecina Bombarón, there's a public **swimming pool** with amazing views of the valley; it's open July to September.

VÁLOR

Válor, 5km northeast of Yegen, was the birthplace of Aben Humeya, a *morisco* (converted Muslim) who led a 1568 rebellion against Felipe II's repressive policies banning Arabic names, dress and even language. The two years of guerrilla war throughout the mountains ended only after Don Juan of Austria, Felipe's half-brother, was brought in to quash the insurrection and Aben Humeya was assassinated by his cousin Aben Aboo. To re-create the historical clash, Válor musters a large Moros y Cristianos (Moors and Christians) festival on 14 and 15 September, with colourfully costumed 'armies' battling it out.

The village is known for its olive oil, goats' cheese and partridge, all of which you can sample at the notable **Restaurante Aben Humeya** (☑958 85 18 10; Calle Los Bolos; mains €8-12; ☺1.30-3.30pm & 8-11pm Tue-Sun), downhill off the main road. Its menu features seasonal treats, such as local mushrooms, along with standards like baby kid in a garlic-spiked sauce and delicate *croquetas* (croquettes). For dessert, there's the deadly rich *tocino del cielo* (egg-yolk custard), or soft cheese with honey, washed down with *vino rosado* from Albuñol.

Reason alone to visit the Alpujarra village of Válor, **Los Arcos** (☑958 85 17 71; www.los arcosholidays.com; Plaza de la Iglesia 3; s/d €40/60; P ⓻) is a spacious, welcoming, down-to-earth place to convene, relax and meet the locals/owners – actually a British couple called Jill and David Drummie. Surrounded by easily accessible mountain splendour, it's the kind of B&B you'll wish you lived in yourself. The breakfasts are deliciously large – just the ticket if you're off hiking on the GR-7 – and there's an expansive terrace with a complimentary-drinks bar.

MAIRENA

Up a very winding road just 6km from Válor, Mairena feels much further away, with fine views from its elevated position. **Las Chimeneas** (☑958 76 03 52; www. alpujarra-tours.com; Calle Amargura 6; d incl breakfast €90; ✳ @ ☎), an insitution among walkers, is a guesthouse run by a British couple who are extremely well informed about local history, ecology and tradition. They can arrange hikes, cooking classes, children's activities and more. They also have fine taste: the expansive rooms have an antique yet uncluttered style, and the **restaurant** (☑958 76 00 89; mains €15-20; ☻7-11pm) serves excellent dinners using organic produce from the owners' *finca* (farm).

Just east of Mairena is easy access to the Sierra Nevada, via the A337 and the 2000m Puerto de la Ragua pass. The road then heads down to La Calahorra.

COSTA TROPICAL

Granada's cliff-lined, 80km-long coast has a hint of Italy's Amalfi about it, although it is definitively Spanish when you get down to the nitty-gritty, with Moorish relics, old-school tapas joints and some damn fine churros. It's warm climate – there's no real winter to speak of – lends it the name Costa Tropical. A sprinkling of attractive beach towns less colonised by expats than those on the Costa del Sol is linked by several daily buses to Granada, Málaga and Almería.

Salobreña

POP 12,000

Between the N340 and the sea, Salobreña's huddle of white houses rises on a crag, topped with an impressive Islamic castle. The dark-sand beach isn't breathtaking, but it is wide, and the distance from the centre of town (about 1km) has kept the place from getting overbuilt. It's a low-key place for most of the year but it jumps in August. The **tourist office** (☑958 61 03 14; Plaza de Goya; ☻9am-3pm Mon-Thu & Sat, 9am-3pm & 4.30-6.30pm Fri) is on a small roundabout near the eastern exit from the N340.

◎ Sights & Activities

About 1km from the centre of town along Avenida del Mediterráneo, Salobreña's long beach is divided by a rocky outcrop, El Peñón. **Playa de la Charca**, the eastern part, is grey sand; the western **Playa de la Guardia** is more pebbly. There are loads of restaurants, beachside *chiringuitos* (small open-air eateries) and bars, and a spot of nightlife, on and near the sand. **Restaurante El Peñón** (www.restauranteelpenon.es; Paseo Marítimo; mains €6-12; ☻noon-midnight Tue-Sun) is probably better for its position, almost on top of the waves, than for its av-

erage seafood – the setting is particularly dramatic at night.

Castillo Árabe   CASTLE
(Arab Castle; admission incl Museo Histórico €3; ☻10am-2pm & 6-9pm) At the top of the hill and visible from afar, the Castillo Árabe dates from the 12th century, though the site was fortified as early as the 10th century. The castle was a summer residence for the Granada emirs, but legend has it that Emir Muhammad IX had his three daughters – Zaida, Zoraida and Zorahaida – held captive here. Washington Irving relates the story in Tales of the Alhambra.

The inner *alcazaba*, a setting for cultural events, retains much of its Nasrid structure. You can walk along parts of the parapets and take in views over the surf and the sugarcane fields. A zigzagging walkway leads from the beach to the castle, and a town bus runs to the church.

Museo Histórico   MUSEUM
(Plaza del Ayuntamiento; admission incl Castillo Árabe €3; ☻10am-2pm & 6-9pm) The Museo Histórico is located close to the Castillo Árabe and below the Iglesia de Nuestra Señora del Rosario church, and has a striking 16th-century archway. The museum comprises two main exhibition halls – one concentrating on archaeological history, with exhibits dating from the Neolithic and Bronze ages; the second has more contemporary photos and artwork, as well as a model of the castle.

🛏 Sleeping

Hostal San Juan   HOTEL €
(☑958 61 17 29; www.hostalsanjuan.com; Calle Jardines 1; s/d €43/60, 3-person apt €70; ☻closed Nov-Feb; ✳@🛜) A lovely tiled and plant-filled patio-lounge welcomes you at this long-established *hostal* on a quiet street about 400m southwest of the tourist office. The rooms have wrought-iron bedsteads and red-and-white bathroom tiling, and many can accommodate families, as can two apartments with kitchenettes. A large rooftop terrace takes in the sunset.

🍴 Eating

La Bodega   ANDALUCIAN €€
(Plaza de Goya; menú €9, mains €17-24; ☻1-4pm & 8-11pm) It's not all fish, fish and more fish at the beach: Salobreña has two very good restaurants that also look inland for inspiration. La Bodega, near the tourist office,

conjures country life, with farm tools on the walls and hanging meats, and you can mix a bit of the sea (excellent clams) with a steak and a glug of sherry from the barrel.

Mesón de la Villa ANDALUCIAN €€
(Plaza Francisco Ramírez de Madrid; mains €11-16; ⊙ closed Wed; 🔊) Hidden away on a quiet palm-filled plaza, locals come here for standards like broad beans with ham served in a warm, candlelit room – ideal if you're in town before the full heat of summer arrives. There are plenty of vegetarian dishes, including a rare eight-plus salad choice.

⊙ Getting There & Away

Alsa (Alsina Graells; 🖃 958 61 25 21; www.alsa. es) runs buses to Almuñécar (€1.17, 15 minutes, 17 daily), to Granada (€6.72, 1¼ hour, nine daily), to Nerja (€4.04, one hour, 12 daily) and to Málaga (€8.56, two hours, five daily). There are also buses to Almería (€10.19, three hours, two daily) and one at 5pm (except Sunday) to Órgiva (€3.28, one hour).

The buses stop just off Plaza de Goya.

The number 1 local bus (€1.10) runs a circular route through town and up to the Castillo Árabe roughly every hour 9am to 1.35pm and 4pm to 6.45pm Monday to Friday, and 9am to 1.35pm Saturday. If you are heading for the beaches, catch the number 2 local bus from the centre of town near the tourist office (€1.10, hourly).

Almuñécar & La Herradura

POP 27,195

Dedicated to beach fun, Almuñécar is not too expensive, a little rough around the edges and very relaxed. Many of the tourists on its pebbly beaches are Spanish, and its old city centre is a scenic maze below a 16th-century castle, albeit surrounded by dreary high-rises. The next-door village of La Herradura handles some of the overflow, but maintains a more castaway feel as it caters to a younger crowd of windsurfers. The N340 runs across the northern part of both towns.

⊙ Sights & Activities

Almuñécar's beachfront is divided by a rocky outcrop, the Peñón del Santo, with **Playa de San Cristóbal** – the best beach (grey sand and small pebbles) – stretching to its west, and **Playa Puerta del Mar** to the east, backed by a strip of cool cafes.

Castillo de San Miguel CASTLE
(Santa Adela Explanada; adult/child €2.35/1.60; ⊙ 10am-1.30pm & 4-6.30pm Tue-Sat, 10.30am-1pm Sun) At the top of a hill overlooking the sea, the Castillo de San Miguel was built by the conquering Christians over Islamic and Roman fortifications. The hot, circuitous climb up to the entrance rewards with excellent views and an informative little **museum**. Don't forget to peer into the dungeon at the skeleton, a reproduction of human remains discovered here.

Museo Arqueológico MUSEUM
(Calle San Joaquín, Almuñécar; adult/child €2.35/1.60; ⊙ 10am-1.30pm & 4-6.30pm Tue-Sat, 10.30am-1pm Sun) The Museo Arqueológico is set in 1st-century underground stone cellars called the Cueva de Siete Palacios, built when the Romans called the port town Sexi. The museum displays finds from local Phoenician, Roman and Islamic sites plus a 3500-year-old Egyptian amphora.

Parque Ornitológico Loro-Sexi AVIARY
(adult/child €4/2; ⊙ 10.30am-2pm & 6-9pm; 🔊) Just behind the Peñón del Santo this is a tropical bird aviary full of squawking parrots. Entry price is rather steep for what you get.

Parque Botánico El Majuelo PARK
(⊙ 9am-10pm) **FREE** A ramshackle park built around the remains of a Carthaginian and Roman fish-salting workshop, where the sauce called *garum* was produced and then shipped to kitchens across the empire. The park hosts the international **Jazz en la Costa** (www.jazzgranada.es) festival in mid-July.

🛏 Sleeping

Hotel Casablanca HOTEL €
(🖃 958 63 55 75; www.hotelcasablancaalmunecar. com; Plaza de San Cristóbal 4; s/d €40/48) Materialising close to the beach in the town of Almuñécar, the distinctive terracotta arches of the Hotel Casablanca really could have sprung from Casablanca. The place is furnished in distinctive Al-Andalus style, with sea views from some rooms. There's a ground-floor restaurant.

🍴 Eating

Plaza Kelibia in Almuñécar is a good start for tapas.

⭐ La Italiana Cafe CAFE €
(🖃 958 88 23 12; www.laitaliancafe.com; Hurtado de Mendoza 5; pizza & pasta €8-9; ⊙ 8am-10pm;

WORTH A TRIP

WATERSPORTS IN LA HERRADURA

If you're craving a more remote beach scene than Almuñécar, or more activity, consider heading 7km west to the small, horseshoe-shaped bay at La Herradura, where a younger demographic of windsurfers and paragliders congregate. **Windsurf La Herradura** (☎958 64 01 43; www.windsurflaherradura.com; Paseo Andrés Segovia 34) is one good operator for these, as well as less extreme water sports, including kayaking.

While the western Mediterranean, with its shallow, sandy coastal waters, is of limited interest for aspiring divers, the eastern Med, more specifically the Costa Tropical around La Herradura, is a different kettle of fish. Here you'll find a varied seabed of sea grass, sand and rock flecked with caves, crevices and passages. Local dive operator **Buceo La Herradura** (☎958 82 70 83; www.buceolaherradura.com; Puerto Marina del Este; immersion with equipment €47) keep a boat moored at the marina from where it's a five- to 10-minute journey out to various dive sites.

When you return, you can enjoy the seafood in one of the many *chiringuitos* on La Herradura's beach.

☎) Weirdly, considering its name and pizza/ pasta menu, La Italiana is *the* place to go for local Almuñécar pastries such as *torta de al-hajú* and *cazuela mohina*. Enjoy them with a cappuccino surrounded by ceiling frescoes and elaborately gilded pillars and mirrors.

La Ventura   ANDALUCIAN €€
(☎958 88 23 78; Calle Alta del Mar 18; mains €12-20; ⊙1-4pm & 8-11.30pm) A bit of a flamenco secret in Almuñécar and all the better for it, Ventura is best visited on Thursday and Sunday evenings when music and dance accompanies soild gold food that never veers far from local tradition: think fish salads and meat stews. A five-course meal is offered to coincide with the shows (9pm) for a reasonable €25.

Pepe Dígame   SEAFOOD €€
(☎958 34 93 15; Plaza San Cristóbal; mains €9.50-15; ⊙8am-10pm) One of those beachfront fish-biased restaurants where you can loll around all afternoon with a bottle of wine

as the kids throw pebbles into the sea and the fishermen sail back from a hard day at the 'office'.

ℹ Information

Main Tourist Office (www.almunecar.info; Avenida Europa; ⊙10am-2pm & 6-9pm) A few blocks back from Playa de San Cristóbal on the east side, in a pink neo-Moorish mansion.

Information Kiosk (Paseo del Altillo; ⊙10am-1.30pm & 6.30-9pm) Just north of the bus station near the N340 roundabout.

ℹ Getting There & Away

The **Almuñécar bus station** (☎958 63 01 40; Avenida Juan Carlos I 1) is just south of the N340. Buses go to Almería (€11.83, 3½ hours, at least five daily), Málaga (€7.44, 1¾ hours, 10 daily), Granada (€8.36, 1½ hours, nine daily), La Herradura (€1.17, 10 minutes, 16 daily), Nerja (€2.92, 30 minutes, 16 daily) and Salobreña (€1.33, 15 minutes, 16 daily). A bus goes to Órgiva (€4.69, 1¼ hours, one daily) at 4.45pm Monday to Saturday.

Almería Province

POP 701,688

Includes ➡

Almería 288
Desierto de
Tabernas 294
Níjar 295
Laujar de Andarax . . . 297
Parque Natural de
Cabo de Gata-Níjar . . . 298
Mojácar 303
Los Vélez 307

Best Places to Eat

➡ 4 Nudos (p301)

➡ Restaurante La Villa (p303)

➡ Casa Joaquín (p292)

➡ Mesón El Molino (p308)

➡ Casa Puga (p292)

➡ Tito's (p305)

Best Places to Stay

➡ El Jardín de los Sueños (p303)

➡ Plaza Vieja Hotel & Lounge (p291)

➡ MC San José (p301)

➡ Cortijo de la Alberca (p295)

Why Go?

One of Almería's main draws is the weather: 3000 hours of sunshine a year. It is also famous for being the greenhouse of Europe, a top growing area for fruit and vegetables sold throughout the EU. The downside of this agriculture-driven prosperity is a blight of plastic greenhouses in parts of the province but, turning a blind eye to them, Almería has plenty of appeal. Topping the list are the stunning coastline, beaches and volcanic, desert-like landscape of the Parque Natural de Cabo de Gata-Níjar. Up the eastern coast, the good-time resort of Mojácar has a great summer beach scene. Inland, you can visit the spectacular Sorbas caves and the Wild West film sets in the Tabernas Desert, and venture up to the green, mountainous Los Vélez region. But definitely don't skip Almería city, a vivacious Mediterranean-side capital with impressive monuments, excellent museums and superb tapas bars.

Driving Distances

	Almería	Mojácar	Vélez Rubio	Níjar
Mojácar	81			
Vélez Rubio	138	74		
Níjar	33	54	108	
San José	38	77	131	26

Almería Province Highlights

1 Kicking back on the rugged sandy beaches of the **Parque Natural de Cabo de Gata-Níjar** (p300)

2 Enjoying the great tapas bars, museums and historic monuments of **Almería** (p288)

3 Going underground in the otherworldly **Cuevas de Sorbas** (p295), a fascinating cave complex

4 Soaking up a sunny beach-bar afternoon, and gazing over sweeping vistas from the quaint old *pueblo*, at **Mojácar** (p303)

5 Lasso-twirling with the cowboys at the Wild West sets of **Desierto de Tabernas** (p294)

6 Exploring the green, mountainous, remote **Los Vélez** (p307) district

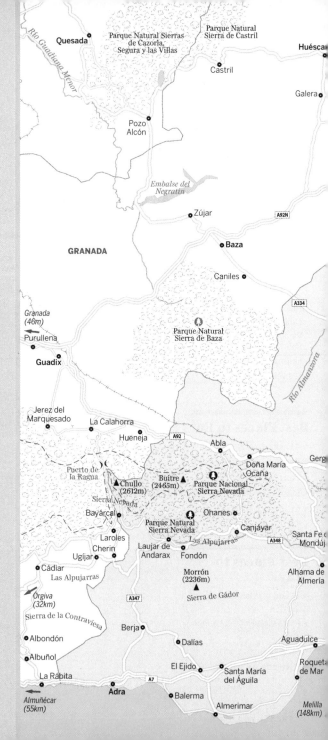

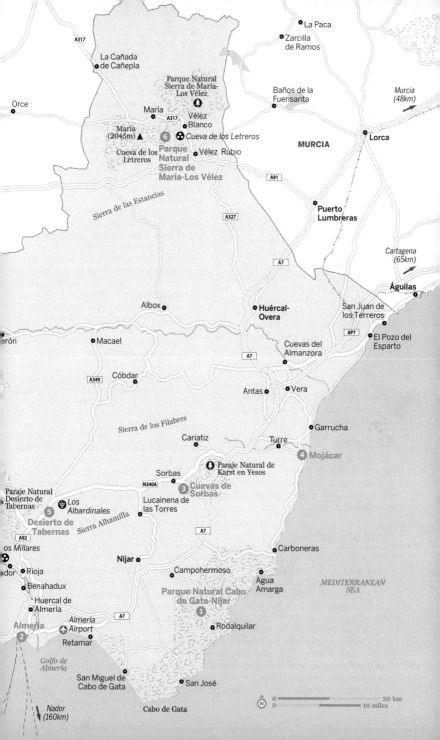

ALMERÍA

POP 165,000

Almería has come a long way. What was a couple of decades ago basically a tough port city, with its glory days buried firmly in the past, is today the increasingly polished, energetic and visitor-friendly capital of Andalucía's second-wealthiest province. Its cultural attractions are ever-growing and the tapas-bar scene in its spruced-up old centre rivals the best.

History

Founded in AD 955 by the Córdoba caliph Abd ar-Rahman III, Almería quickly became the largest, richest port in Moorish Spain and the headquarters of the Omayyad fleet. Its streets thronged with merchants from Egypt, Syria, France and Italy come to buy silk, glass, marble and glazed ceramics from all around Al-Andalus. It lost its trading supremacy during a Christian occupation from 1147 to 1157 but remained a significant Moorish city until finally conquered by the Catholic Monarchs in 1489. Almería then suffered a rapid decline and a 1658 census counted only 500 inhabitants, thanks to devastating earthquakes, the expulsion of Andalucía's Muslim population and attacks by Barbary pirates. In the late 20th century Almería's fortunes took a serious upswing, thanks to agriculture- and tourism-engendered prosperity in the surrounding region.

◉ Sights

Almería's main sights are the Alcazaba and the cathedral, both of which can be explored in a morning, but there are plenty of interesting additional distractions in the city's meandering streets.

★ **Alcazaba** FORTRESS

(Calle Almanzor; ⊘9am-7.30pm Tue-Sat Apr–mid-Jun, to 3.30pm Tue-Sat mid-Jun–mid-Sep, to 5.30pm Tue-Sat mid-Sep–Mar, to 3.30pm Sun all year) `FREE` A looming fortification with great curtain-like walls rising from the cliffs, the Alcazaba was founded in the mid-10th century and was one of the most powerful Moorish fortresses in Spain. It lacks the intricate decoration of Granada's Alhambra, but is nonetheless a compelling monument. Allow about 1½ hours to see everything. Pick up a guide leaflet in one of several languages at the kiosk, just inside the four-arch entrance gate.

The Alcazaba is divided into three distinct *recintos* (compounds). The lowest, the **Primer Recinto**, was residential, with houses, streets, wells, baths and other necessities – now replaced by lush gardens and water channels. From the battlements you can see the **Muralla de Jayrán**, a fortified wall built in the 11th century to defend the outlying northern and eastern parts of the city, as well as stunning city and coastal views.

In the **Segundo Recinto** you'll find the ruins of the Muslim rulers' palace, built by the *taifa* ruler Almotacín (r 1051–91), under whom medieval Almería reached its peak, plus a chapel, the **Ermita de San Juan**, that was originally a mosque. The highest section, the **Tercer Recinto**, is a citadel added by the Catholic Monarchs.

★ **Catedral de la Encarnación** CATHEDRAL

(Plaza de la Catedral; admission €5, free Mon morning; ⊘10am-1.30pm & 4-5pm Mon-Fri, to 1.30pm Sat) Cathedral or fortress? Almería's unusually weighty, six-towered cathedral, begun in 1525, was conceived both as a place of worship and

---

THE OLD MEDINA

It's intriguing to wander round the maze-like Almedina neighbourhood between the Alcazaba and the sea. This was the area occupied by the original Almería – a walled medina (city), bounded by the Alcazaba on the north, the sea on the south, and what are now Calle de la Reina and Avenida del Mar on the east and west. At its heart was the city's main mosque – whose mihrab (niche indicating the direction of Mecca) survives inside the **Iglesia de San Juan** (Calle San Juan; ⊘open for mass 8pm Apr-Sep, 7pm Oct-Mar, except Tue & Fri) – with the commercial area of markets and warehouses spread around it. Calle de la Almedina still traces the line of the old main street running diagonally across the medina. Some of the small houses along the medina's narrow streets are in ruins, while others are recently restored as efforts are made to revive this inner-city area. An excellent place to stop is **Tetería Almedina** (p293) teahouse. Also worth seeking out is the **Plaza de Pavía market** (⊘9am-2pm Mon-Sat), at its liveliest on Saturdays, with a rowdy mix of produce, cheap shoes and churros (delicious, fat, tubular doughnuts).

HEAVENLY HAMMAMS

Almería has two superb *hammams* (Arab baths). The sumptuous **Hammam Aire de Almería** (www.airedealmeria.com; Plaza de la Constitución 5; 1½hr session incl 15min aromatherapy €23; ☺10am-10pm), attached to **Plaza Vieja Hotel & Lounge** (p291), has a wonderful setting in a historic building on the graceful Plaza de la Constitución. This luxurious and spacious *hammam* exudes a feeling of tranquillity throughout its marble and warm-brick interior. It offers three baths: the *frigidarium* (16°C), the *tepidarium* (36°C) and the *caldarium* (40°C), as well as aromatherapy and other massages. Reservations are advised.

The smaller **Hammam Almeraya** (www.almeraya.info; Calle Perea 9; 1½hr session incl aromatherapy €16; ☺4-10pm Wed-Mon) has hot and cold baths, a 'Turkish' steam bath, and beautiful marble and tiled surroundings. It also offers massages, plus the relaxing **Tetería Almeraya** (pot of tea €2.50-9.50; ☺9am-2pm & 4pm-midnight, closed Tue evening & Sat & Sun morning), a teahouse with cocktails, plus all the teas you can think of. Reservations required.

as a refuge for the population from frequent pirate raids from North Africa. Basically a Gothic/Renaissance building, it had baroque and neoclassical features added in the 18th century. You enter from Calle Velázquez via a fine cloister carved from pale stone. The vast, impressive interior has a beautiful ceiling with sinuous Gothic ribbing and is trimmed in jasper, marble and carved walnut.

On the outside of the building, check out the cute stone lions around the northwest tower and the exuberant Sol de Portocarrero, a 16th-century relief of the sun, now serving as the city's symbol, on the cathedral's eastern end.

Museo de la Guitarra   MUSEUM
(🖉950 27 43 58; Ronda del Beato Diego Ventaja; admission €3; ☺10.30am-1.30pm Tue-Sun, 6-9pm Fri & Sat Jun-Sep, 10am-1pm Tue-Sun, 5-8pm Fri & Sat Oct-May) It's worth establishing two important facts before you enter this absorbing, recently opened interactive museum. First: the word 'guitar' is derived from the Andalucian-Arabic word *qitara,* hinting at its Spanish roots. Second: all modern acoustic guitars owe a huge debt to Almerían guitar-maker Antonio de Torres (1817–92), to whom this museum is dedicated. The museum itself is a minor masterpiece that details the history of the guitar and pays homage to Torres' part in it.

An interactive zone allows you to strum electric and acoustic instruments, quizzes test your musical knowledge, and a fascinating film shows how guitars are made.

Refugios de la Guerra Civil   HISTORIC SITE
(Civil War Shelters; 🖉reservations 950 26 86 96; Plaza de Manuel Pérez García; tour €3; ☺guided tours 10.30am & noon Tue-Sun, 6pm & 7.30pm Fri & Sat Jun-Sep, 10am & 11.30am Tue-Sun, 5pm & 6.30pm Fri & Sat Oct-May) During the civil war, Almería was the Republicans' last holdout province in Andalucía, and was repeatedly and mercilessly bombed. The attacks prompted a group of engineers to design and build the Refugios, a 4.5km-long network of concrete shelters under the city. Visits – by 1¼-hour guided tour, available in English as well as Spanish – take you through 1km of the tunnels including the re-created operating theatre and storerooms. Advance reservations essential.

Museo de Almería   MUSEUM
(Museo Arqueológico; Calle Azorín; ☺9am-3.30pm Tue-Sun mid-Jun–mid-Sep, to 7.30pm Tue-Sat, to 3.30pm Sun mid-Sep–mid-Jun) **FREE** This modern museum focuses chiefly on two prehistoric Almerían cultures of major importance – Los Millares (3200–2250 BC; probably the Iberian Peninsula's first metalworking culture), and El Argar (2250–1550 BC), which ushered in the Bronze Age. The numerous well-displayed finds from these sites are accompanied by excellent explanatory displays in English as well as Spanish.

Even if ancient pots and bones normally make you yawn, don't skip this – it's a rare example of multimedia technology deployed to excellent effect, touched with a Spanish flair for the macabre.

Centro Andaluz de la Fotografía   GALLERY
(Andalucian Photography Centre; www.centro andaluzdelafotografia.es; Calle Pintor Díaz Molina 9; ☺11am-2pm & 5.30-9.30pm) **FREE** Anyone

Almería

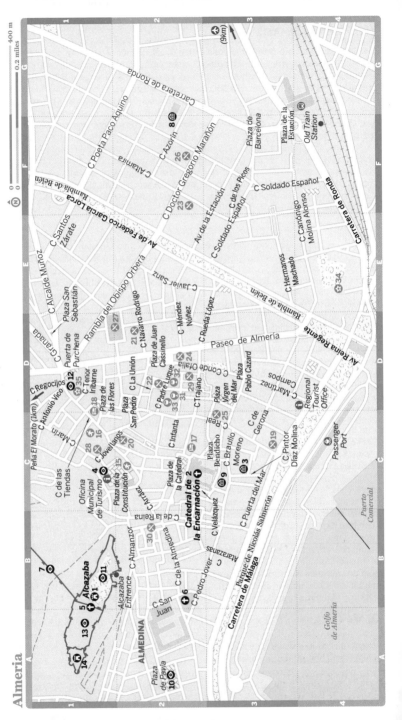

0   400 m
0   0.2 miles

Carretera de Ronda

(9km)

C Poeta Paco Aquino

C Azorín

8

26

C Altamira

C Doctor Gregorio Marañón

Plaza de Barcelona

Plaza de la Estación

Old Train Station

C de los Picos

C Soldado Español

23

Av de la Estación

C Soldado Español

C Canónigo Molina Alonso

C Hermanos Machado

C Santos Zárate

Rambla de Belén

C Alcalde Muñoz

Plaza San Sebastián

Rambla del Obispo Orberá

C Javier Sanz

Carretera de Ronda

34

C Granada

Puerta de Purchena

27

21

C Navarro Rodrigo

C Méndez Núñez

C Rueda López

Paseo de Almería

Av Reina Regente

Rambla de Belén

C Regocijos

12

35

C Tenor Iribarne

18

Plaza de las Flores

C La Unión

22

Plaza de Juan Cassinello

C Conde Ofalia

24

29

31

Plaza Virgen del Mar

Plaza Pablo Cazard

C de Gerona

Regional Tourist Office

Martínez Campos

Peña El Morato (1km)

C Antonio Vico

C Martín

28

C Jovellanos

16

20

15

C Padre Luque

32

33

C Trajano

25

C Real

C Braulio Moreno

19

C Pintor Díaz Molina

Passenger Port

Oficina Municipal de Turismo

4

Plaza de la Constitución

Plaza San Pedro

C Infanta

17

Plaza Bendicho

9

3

C de las Tiendas

C Gabriel

C de la Reina

Plaza de la Catedral

Catedral de la Encarnación 2

C Velázquez

Puerto Comercial

C Almanzor

C de la Almedina

Atarazanas

C Puerta del Mar

C Nicolás Salmerón

30

ALMEDINA

Alcazaba Entrance

Alcazaba

7

1

11

5

13

14

C de la Almedina

C San Juan

6

C Pedro Jover

Carretera de Málaga

Plaza de Pavía

10

Golfo de Almería

Almería

⊙ Top Sights
1 Alcazaba...B1
2 Catedral de la Encarnación C2

⊙ Sights
3 Centro Andaluz de la Fotografía..........C3
4 Centro de Interpretación
    Patrimonial.......................................C1
5 Ermita de San Juan B1
6 Iglesia de San Juan..............................B2
7 Muralla de Jayrán B1
8 Museo de Almería................................F2
9 Museo de la Guitarra...........................C3
10 Plaza de Pavía Market.........................A2
11 Primer Recinto B1
12 Refugios de la Guerra Civil D1
13 Segundo Recinto..................................A1
14 Tercer Recinto......................................A1

⊙ Activities, Courses & Tours
Hammam Aire de Almería ....(see 18)
15 Hammam Almeraya C1

⊙ Sleeping
16 Hotel Catedral C2
17 Hotel Nuevo Torreluz D1
18 Plaza Vieja Hotel & Lounge C2

⊗ Eating
19 Casa Joaquín C3
20 Casa Puga...C2
21 El Quinto Toro D2
22 Entrefinos...D2
23 Habana Cristal F2
24 La Coquette..D2
25 La Mala...C3
26 Lamarca F2
27 Mercado Central...................................D2
28 Nuestra Tierra......................................C1
29 Taberna Postigo D2
30 Tetería Almedina..................................B2

⊙ Drinking & Nightlife
31 La Campanilla D2
32 La Chica de Ayer D2
33 New Georgia...D2
Tetería Almeraya.........................(see 15)

⊙ Entertainment
34 Clasijazz...E4
35 Peña El Taranto D1

remotely interested in photography should visit this excellent centre, which puts on top-class exhibitions of work by international photographers. They vary dramatically in theme but are invariably edgy and thought-provoking.

Centro de Interpretación Patrimonial
INTERPRETATION CENTRE
(Plaza de la Constitución; ⊙10am-2pm Tue-Sun, 5-8pm Fri & Sat) FREE Three floors of clear historical exhibits and information, in English and Spanish, plus a panoramic roof terrace. Invaluable for setting the city's sights in context.

✦ Festivals & Events

Feria de Almería
FAIR
Ten days and nights of live music, bullfights, fairground rides, exhibitions and full-on partying in the second half of August.

🛏 Sleeping

Hotel Nuevo Torreluz
HOTEL €
(☑950 23 43 99; www.torreluz.com; Plaza de las Flores 10; r €50-63; ❈⊛) An updated four-star hotel enjoying a superb location on a small square in the historic centre. Rooms are on the small side but well equipped and com-

fortable, with elegant grey-and-silver colour schemes and high-pressure showers. The hotel runs a trio of cafes and restaurants around the square.

★ Plaza Vieja Hotel & Lounge
BOUTIQUE HOTEL €€
(☑950 28 20 96; www.plazaviejahl.com; Plaza de la Constitución 4; s €71-89, d €87-109; ❈⊛) This stylish spot is perfectly situated on beautiful Plaza de la Constitución, just steps from some of the city's top tapas bars. Part of the plush Hammam Aire de Almería (p289) set-up, the rooms here are spacious and modern with high ceilings, soft natural colours and vast photo-walls of local sights such as the Cabo de Gata.

Hotel Catedral
BOUTIQUE HOTEL €€
(☑950 27 81 78; www.hotelcatedral.net; Plaza de la Catedral 8; r €76-150; ❈@⊛) Cosied up to the cathedral and built with the same warm honey-coloured stone, the hotel building dates from 1850. It has been sensitively restored, combining clean contemporary lines with Gothic arches and an *artesonado* ceiling in the restaurant. Rooms are large, with luxury touches, and the roof terrace, with Jacuzzi, has heady cathedral views.

✕ Eating

For the highest concentration of the city's renowned tapas bars (p292), head for the area between Plaza de la Constitución and Paseo de Almería.

La Coquette   CAFE €

(Paseo de Almería 34; coffee & pastry from €2.60, ice cream from €1.60; ⊙ 8.30am-9pm; 🛜🛗) Owner Tesni has imported a classic French patisserie to Almería, selling cakes, quiches, croissants, crêpes and fruit-filled tarts. She also sells creamily authentic Italian *gelati*. The pavement tables are nicely shaded and shielded from street noise by glass panelling.

Habana Cristal   CAFE €

(Calle Altamira 60; coffee & tostada €3-5; ⊙ 7am-11pm Mon-Thu, 7am-1am Fri, 8am-1am Sat, 8am-11pm Sun) Senior señoras with *mucho* hairspray crowd into one of Almería's most emblematic cafes, where everyone ought to come for breakfast or an exotic coffee (such as the *vienés* with Tia Maria and cream) and cake, or an evening cocktail. There's a large outside terrace.

★ Casa Joaquín   SEAFOOD €€

(✆ 950 26 43 59; Calle Real 111; raciónes €10-21; ⊙ 1.30-3.30pm & 8.30-11pm Mon-Fri, to 4.30pm Sat, closed Sep) Reserve one of the few tables if you're really serious about your seafood. If you don't mind standing, you can jostle at the bar of this nearly century-old bodega famous for the freshness of its ingredients and their perfect, simple, traditional preparation.

There is no menu but you won't go wrong if you order the juicy local *quisquillas* or

---

TAPAS TOURS

The streets between Paseo de Almería and Plaza de la Constitución are packed with busy and atmospheric tapas bars. Like Granada, Almería maintains the tradition of free tapas with a drink. But it does its neighbour one better: here, all tapas are *a elegir*, meaning you choose what you want from a list. Portions are generous, and for the hungry, or to share between more than one person, almost everywhere offers *raciónes* and *medias-raciónes* (full- and half-sized plates of tapas items).

Casa Puga (www.barcasapuga.es; Calle Jovellanos 7; wine & tapa €2.80; ⊙ noon-4pm & 8pm-midnight Mon-Sat, closed Wed evening) The undisputed tapas champ (since it opened in 1870) is Casa Puga; make it an early stop, as it fills up fast. Shelves of ancient wine bottles, and walls plastered with everything from lottery tickets to ancient maps, are the backdrop for a tiny cooking station that churns out saucers of tasty stews and griddled meats, fish, mushrooms and shrimps.

Nuestra Tierra (Calle Jovellanos 16; wine & tapa €2.80; ⊙ 7.30am-noon Mon, 7.30am-4pm & 8pm-midnight Wed-Fri, noon-4pm & 8pm-midnight Sat, noon-4pm Sun) This tiny spot, with just five tables and a teensy bar, prepares really tasty little platters from local Almería ingredients. It's well worth getting their grilled octopus, or the ham, egg and spring onion in a bread roll, or a dozen other treats.

El Quinto Toro (Calle Juan Leal 6; drink & tapa €2.50; ⊙ noon-4pm & 8pm-midnight Mon-Sat) The 'Fifth Bull' rivals Casa Puga in traditional atmosphere, with the obligatory bull's head over the bar. Treats include anchovies with Roquefort cheese and rich *albóndigas* (meatballs) in a wine sauce.

La Mala (Calle Real 69; beer & tapa €2.50, tortillas €8-12; ⊙ noon-5pm & 8.30pm-1am Mon-Sat) Rock music and great *tortillas* (omelettes) are the successful recipe at this gaudily painted street-corner bar, where the crowd regularly spills into the street. Now's your chance to try an octopus or gorgonzola-and-mushroom omelette.

Entrefinos (Calle Padre Alfonso Torres 9; tapa & drink €3-5; ⊙ 1-4pm & 8pm-midnight) Lively Entrefinos re-creates a traditional bodega ambience with its high wood-beam ceiling, tall wooden tables and blackboard menus. The tapas, such as Angus-beef sirloin or crispfried John Dory, are a cut above the ordinary.

Taberna Postigo (Calle Guzmán; drink & tapa €2.20-3; ⊙ 11am-5pm & 7pm-1am Tue-Thu & Sun, to 3pm Fri & Sat) A major appeal of this friendly tavern is that the sprawl of tables is shaded by rows of leafy trees. Tapas *a la brasa* (grilled over hot coals) are favourites, as is the bacon with *pimientos* (peppers).

gambas rojas (types of shrimp) cooked *a la plancha* (grilled on a hotplate), or fried *calamares* (squid) or *lenguado* (sole).

Tetería Almedina
MOROCCAN €€

(http://teteriaalmedina.com; Calle Paz 2, off Calle de la Almedina; pot tea €2-7, mains €10-15; ⊗ noon-11pm or later Tue-Sun; 🗷) This lovely little cafe, in the oldest part of the city below the Alcazaba, serves tasty tagines, couscous dishes, salads and other Moroccan favourites, plus a fascinating range of teas, infusions and sweets, in an atmosphere redolent of a Moroccan teahouse.

It's run by a group dedicated to revitalising the old city, with its many Moroccan immigrants, and reviving the culture of Al-Andalus. There's usually flamenco, North African or other live music at 10pm Saturday.

Lamarca
ANDALUCIAN, DELI €€

(Calle Doctor Gregorio Marañón 33; raciónes €7-14; ⊗ 1.30-4pm & 8pm-midnight Mon-Sat, to 4pm Sun) What started as a humble ham shop has morphed into a funky deli-cum-restaurant group with several branches around Almería. Head to the back dining room to sample ham, sausages, cheeses and wines from all over Spain, in tapas sizes or *raciónes* to share, under a ceiling of hanging hams. There are salads and egg dishes too, for the less carnivorous.

Mercado Central
MARKET

(Circunvalación Ulpiano Díaz; ⊗ 9am-3pm Mon-Sat) Almería's central market is in a grand 1890s building near the top of Paseo de Almería and was aesthetically renovated in 2012. Go early to see squid so fresh they're still changing colour, as well as a profusion of vegetables from the surrounding greenhouses, including some very odd-looking varieties of tomato.

🍸 Drinking & Nightlife

The old-town tapas bars are many people's chosen drinking spots. The epicentre of 18-to-35 nightlife is the Cuatro Calles area around the intersection of Calles Real, Trajano and Eduardo Pérez. Within a couple of blocks you'll find a few dozen pubs and small clubs dedicated to good music and good times, with free admission. Wander round after about 11.30pm on Friday or Saturday to see who's going where. One spot with particular character is the New Georgia (Calle Padre Luque 17; ⊗ 4pm-3am), playing jazz, soul, blues and rock 'n' roll, with live

bands at midnight every Saturday. La Chica de Ayer (Calle San Pedro 1; ⊗ 4pm-3am) and the larger La Campanilla (Calle San Pedro 6; ⊗ 4pm-3am) spin commercial Spanish pop and rock, and some Latin rhythms for a good-time crowd who come here for the cocktails and dancing.

☆ Entertainment

Check www.almeriacultura.com for listings of upcoming flamenco, jazz, classical and other concerts. The atmospheric Tetería Almedina has regular flamenco or other music on Saturday nights.

Peña El Taranto
FLAMENCO

(🗷 950 23 50 57; www.eltaranto.com; Calle Tenor Iribarne) This is Almería's top flamenco club, where local guitar star Tomatito has been known to stroke the strings. There's usually live music, song and dance at about 10pm Thursday to Saturday. Visitors are welcome if there is space (admission is free, with drinks and tapas available).

Clasijazz
JAZZ

(http://clasijazz.com; Calle Maestro Serrano 9; admission nonmembers €2-25) Thriving music club Clasijazz has an excellent program of four or five events weekly ranging from jazz to classical to jam sessions, in a strikingly designed contemporary space.

ℹ️ Information

Oficina Municipal de Turismo (🗷 950 21 05 38; www.turismodeandalucia.org; Plaza de la Constitución; ⊗ 10am-3pm Mon-Fri, to 2pm Sat & Sun)

Regional Tourist Office (🗷 950 17 52 20; www.andalucia.org; Parque de Nicolás Salmerón; ⊗ 9am-7.30pm Mon-Fri, 9.30am-3pm Sat & Sun)

ℹ️ Getting There & Away

AIR
Almería's small **airport** (🗷 902 40 47 04; www.aena.es) is 10km east of the city centre. **EasyJet** (www.easyjet.com), **Ryanair** (www.ryanair.com), **Monarch Airlines** (www.monarch.co.uk) and **Thomas Cook Airlines** (www.thomascookairlines.com) fly direct from various English airports (Ryanair also flies from Dublin and Brussels); **Iberia** (www.iberia.com) and **Vueling** (www.vueling.com) serve Spanish destinations.

BOAT
Acciona Trasmediterránea (🗷 902 45 46 45; www.trasmediterranea.es) sails from the **passenger port** (Ctra de Málaga) to Nador (Morocco;

WORTH A TRIP

LOS ALBARDINALES

East of Tabernas, the terrain gets a little less arid – lush enough to support extensive olive groves producing large quantities of olive oil – including those of organic oil maker **Los Albardinales** (☑ 950 61 17 07; www.losarbardinales. com; Ctra N340A Km 474; mains €12-20; ☺ 8am-7pm Fri-Wed; P) 🖉 , a little more than 2km past the town. Visitors can tour the modern facilities to see how the oil is pressed and bottled, as well as a restored 1920s oil plant. You can also enjoy lunch or dinner at the restaurant, which emphasises quality local artisanal food, including organic wines. A shop is stocked with the oil, as well as organic wines, soaps, vinegars and other local products.

six hours) and Melilla (8½ hours) at least once daily, and Ghazaouet (Algeria; nine hours) at least once weekly. One-way passenger fares are €45, €38 and €92 respectively, and for two adults with a car €215, €181 and €560.

BUS

Buses and trains share the **Estación Intermodal** (☑ 950 26 20 98; Plaza de la Estación) just east of the centre. **Alsa** (☑ 902 42 22 42; www.alsa. es) provides most of the intercity bus services.

TO	FARE (€)	DURATION	FREQUENCY
Córdoba	29	5hr	1 daily
Guadix	17	2¼hr	2 daily
Granada	14-18	2-4hr	7 daily
Jaén	20	3-5hr	2 daily
Madrid	29	7hr	5 daily
Málaga	19-22	3-4½hr	7 daily
Murcia	20	3-4½hr	5 daily
Seville	37-45	5½-9hr	3 daily

TRAIN

Trains operated by **Renfe** (www.renfe.com) run from the **Estación Intermodal** (☑ 950 26 20 98; Plaza de la Estación), including direct to Granada (€20, 2½ hours, four daily), Seville (€41, 5½ hours, four daily) and Madrid (€46, 6½ hours, two daily).

ℹ️ Getting Around

TO/FROM THE AIRPORT
City bus 22 (www.surbus.com; €1.05, 30 minutes) runs from the airport to the Estación Inter-

modal every 70 minutes from 7.25am to 2.25pm and 4.35pm to 10.25pm, and from the Estación Intermodal to the airport every 70 minutes from 6.45am to 2.55pm and 5.05pm to 9.45pm. Taxis between airport and city centre cost about €15.

CAR
The A7/E15 runs a large ring around Almería; the easiest access to the centre is along the seafront (Carretera de Málaga) from the west, and the AL12 (Autovía del Aeropuerto) from the east.

PARKING
Underground car parks dotted around the central area cost about €16 per 24 hours.

TAXI
Catch a taxi at ranks on Paseo de Almería, or call ☑ 950 22 61 61 or ☑ 950 25 11 11.

NORTH OF ALMERÍA

Desierto de Tabernas

North of the city is a stretch of barren landscape that looks as if it has been transplanted from the Mojave desert – dun-coloured hills scattered with tufts of tussocky scrub. In the 1960s Clint Eastwood, Lee Van Cleef, Claudia Cardinale and other stars strode these badlands on location for the many 'spaghetti westerns' (so called because of their Italian producers and/or directors) that were filmed here – notably Sergio Leone's 'Dollars Trilogy' (*A Fistful of Dollars*, 1964; *For a Few Dollars More*, 1965; and *The Good, the Bad and the Ugly*, 1966) and *Once Upon a Time in the West* (1968). 'Western town' film sets here have since been turned into Wild West theme parks as well as continuing to be used for film-making. They make a fun day out, especially with kids.

◉ Sights

Oasys Mini Hollywood THEME PARK
(☑ 902 53 35 32; www.oasysparquetematico. com; Ctra N340A Km 464.5; adult/child €22/13; ☺ 10am-7.30pm Jun & Sep, to 9pm Jul & Aug, to 6pm Oct-May, closed Mon-Fri Nov-Mar; P🖈) This is the best-known and most expensive of the Wild West parks and provides some good family entertainment. The set itself is in decent condition, and the well-kept zoo has grown to a considerable size with some 800 animals at last count, including lions, giraffes, tigers and hippos. Children usually enjoy the 20-minute shoot-outs (resulting in

an unceremonious hanging), while adults may prefer the clichéd can-can show (or at least the beer) in the saloon.

There are also two pools (open about June to September) and a few restaurants and cafes (think overpriced burgers and chips), all adding up to a few hours of family fun. It's 27km from Almería. Take sunscreen and a hat: there is little shade.

Fort Bravo THEME PARK
(Texas Hollywood; ☎ 902 07 08 14; www.fortbravo.es; Ctra N340A Km 468.5; adult/child €18/10; ⏰ 9am-8pm Apr-Oct, to 7pm Nov-Mar; P) This place has a certain dusty charm. It stages daily Wild West and can-can shows, and has a summer pool and a saloon where David Beckham and other football stars once shot a Pepsi ad. Buggy rides, horse treks and overnight stays in log cabins are also available. Fort Bravo is 1km off the N340A, signposted 31km from Almería.

Níjar

POP 2900

The small town of Níjar, in the foothills of the Sierra Alhamilla, northeast of Almería, is known for producing some of Andalucía's most attractive glazed pottery and is a good place to find other crafts too. At the top of Avenida Federico García Lorca, the road bends and leads up into the heart of old Níjar. Here delightful Plaza La Glorieta is surrounded by trees and overlooked by the church of Santa María de la Anunciación. Further on still is tranquil Plaza del Mercado, where the Oficina Municipal de Turismo (☎ 950 61 22 43; Plaza del Mercado; ⏰ 10am-2pm & 4-8pm Mon-Sat) contains a small museum dedicated to the all-important theme of water. From here you can work your way up to the Atalaya, a ruined lookout tower visible above the village, whose panoramas encompass the whole valley below.

🛏 Sleeping

⭐ **Cortijo de la Alberca** RURAL HOTEL €€
(☎ 678 841248; www.cortijolaalberca.com; Camino de Huebro; s €50, d €65-95, r Aug €90-120; P 🛜 ❄) You'll get a friendly welcome at this charming spot just up the valley above Níjar. The adobe-walled rooms are comfy, spacious and rustic in style, with Moroccan lamps and mirrors, wood-and-cane ceilings and some antique traditional doors and windows. Terrific breakfasts and dinners are served at the original 250-year-old farmhouse.

SORBAS

The **Cuevas de Sorbas** (☎ 950 36 47 04; www.cuevasdesorbas.com; basic tour adult/child €15/11; ⏰ tours 10am-1pm & 4-6pm, afternoons 3-7pm Jul & Aug; P 🚻), 2km east of the town of Sorbas, are part of the vast network of underground galleries and tunnels of the Sorbas gypsum karst, a geologically unique area created by water eroding a layer of the soft mineral gypsum that was laid down as the sea retreated 5 million years ago. Gypsum erosion is normally quite rapid, but the lack of rain in Almería has slowed the process dramatically, resulting in the survival of this rare and spectacular cave network.

Several tours are available on which you can see glittering gypsum crystals, tranquil ponds, stalactites, stalagmites and dark otherworldly tunnels. The basic tour, suitable for everyone from children to seniors, lasts about 1½ hours. Tours need to be reserved at least one day ahead; English-, French- and German-speaking guides are available.

Sorbas is 60km northeast of Almería and 36km west of Mojácar. Buses run from Almería to Sorbas (€4.75, one hour) three times Monday to Friday, twice on Saturday and once on Sunday. Returning, there are three daily Monday to Saturday and two on Sunday.

English-run and combining the feel of a warren-like old Spanish farmhouse and a cosy English home, **Almond Reef** (☎ 950 36 90 97; www.almondreef.co.uk; Los Josefos, Cariatiz; incl breakfast s/d/f/ste €35/56/70/90; P 🛜 ❄) is a friendly retreat in a tiny hamlet that makes a good base for cyclists, walkers, motorcyclists and birdwatchers. As well as B&B, dinner is available and there are self-catering options too.

Take the Cariatiz turning off the N340A 8km northeast of Sorbas, and follow 'Todas Direcciones' and 'Ecomuseo Cariatiz' signs till you reach the square with the Ecomuseo. Almond Reef is 300m up the road from here.

Follow 'Huebro' signs through Níjar: the signed turning to the Cortijo is 900m up from the village.

Each room has tea- and coffee-making equipment and a terrace with views down the valley.

✗ Eating & Drinking

La Glorieta   SPANISH €€
(Plaza La Glorieta 5; mains €7-18, menú €10; ⊙7.30am-11pm) Enjoy a peaceful view from the terrace overlooking this delightful leafy square. Choices include a long list of tapas, plus a reasonable daily menu. Locals pack the place out – always a good sign.

🔒 Shopping

Avenida Lorca is lined with shops selling pottery, woven rugs, esparto-grass baskets and the local *higo chumbo* liquor, produced from the prickly pear cactus – though not all these goods are made in Níjar. For the workshops or showrooms of local potters, head down Calle Las Eras off the top of Avenida Lorca into the **Barrio Alfarero** (Potters' Quarter).

★**La Tienda de los Milagros**   CERAMICS
(www.latiendadelosmilagros.com; Callejón del Artesano 1; ⊙10am-10pm) This is the workshop of British ceramicist Matthew Weir and his Spanish wife Isabel Hernández, who produces artistic *jarapa* (cotton rag) rugs. As well as quality ceramics, Matthew makes woodblock prints and works with stoneware and porcelain. The workshop is just off Calle Las Eras, about 300m down from Avenica Lorca.

ℹ Getting There & Away

BUS
Níjar is served by five buses from Almería (€1.95, one to 1½ hours) Monday to Friday, three on Saturday and two on Sunday.

CAR
Níjar is 4km north of the A7, 30km northeast of Almería. There are parking bays all the way up Avenida Lorca.

LAS ALPUJARRAS DE ALMERÍA

The Almerían part of Las Alpujarras (the Sierra Nevada's southern foothills and valleys) is a lot less visited than its Granada counterpart, and admittedly less spectacular – but it's still a very pretty part of the world. White villages, clustered around large churches that were mostly once mosques, are strung along the valley of the Río Andarax between the mountains of the Sierra Nevada to the north and Sierra de Gádor to the south. Approaching from Almería city, the landscape is at first pretty barren, but it gradually becomes more lush, with lemon and orange orchards and vineyards producing plenty of Almerían wine.

Los Millares   ARCHAEOLOGICAL SITE
(⊙10am-2pm Wed-Sun; **P**) **FREE** The historical importance of Los Millares, where what was probably Spain's first metalworking culture emerged nearly 5000 years ago, is

---

TWO WAYS TO GROW A TOMATO

In Almería's unprotected flatlands, plastic-covered *invernaderos* (greenhouses) sprawl like some kind of extra-terrestrial colony. West of Almería city, the entire 35km-long coastal plain from Roquetas de Mar to Adra is coated in grey-white plastic and seems like a hallucination when you first set eyes on it. Ecological effects and issues over exploitation of immigrant labour notwithstanding, the vegetables grown here have brought wealth to a previously dirt-poor corner of Spain: Almería exports more than €2 billion of agricultural produce a year and produces, among other things, 30% of Europe's tomatoes.

Meanwhile, mountain-dwellers lament the spoiled views over the valleys and stick with the complex system of terraced gardens and irrigation channels installed by the Moors a millennium ago. No room for hypermodern agriculture here – the old way is the only way to eke a living out of the steep mountainsides.

But the real test is, how do the tomatoes taste? In summer, mountain-grown, sun-ripened tomatoes are delectable. But surprisingly, the *tomate Raf*, a greenish heirloom variety with a segmented surface, does very well in the hothouses – and ripens in winter, through to March or April. It's the province's pride and you should look for it on Almería menus or at markets. It's sweeter and with a denser texture than most regular tomatoes. Expect to pay at least €6 a kilo – if the price is lower, it's not the real Raf.

OFF THE BEATEN TRACK

OHANES

Detour off the A348 at Km 105 on to the winding route up to Ohanes, a tiny village specialising in *vino rosado* (rosé wine). While that's as good a reason to visit as any, it's really the drive here and down that's remarkable. On the 9km road up, you wind past stark red rock until you finally curve around a ridge into the upper part of the Ohanes valley. Here the scenery changes completely, to green terraces and flourishing vineyards. To explore the village, park near the top and walk down. When leaving, follow the road round to the west side of the valley where you'll enjoy the best views of the village and its amazing terrace-field systems. About 1.25km past the last village houses, you should fork left (downhill). This route to the valley is shorter than the ascent, but slightly more nerve-racking, dwindling to one lane as it zigzags down through the fields. It comes out just west of Canjáyar.

greater than the spectacle of its site today, but history and archaeology fans will enjoy a visit to the site above the Río Andarax, 20km from Almería city. Outlines of defensive walls remain, as do ruined stone houses and some reconstructions of distinctive domed graves.

A small on-site interpretation centre sheds light on the site's history, as does Almería's Museo de Almería (p289), which has plentiful exhibits on Los Millares' culture. The well-signposted site is 1km off the A348, 3km before Alhama de Almería.

Laujar de Andarax

POP 1562 / ELEV 918M

The pleasant 'capital' of the Almería Alpujarras is where Boabdil, the last emir of Granada, settled briefly after losing Granada. It was also the headquarters of Aben Humeya, the first leader of the 1568–70 *morisco* uprising. Today the vineyards around town produce a great deal of Almería's wine. Laujar is a friendly spot with a handsome three-tiered town hall crowned by a distinctive belfry, and the 17th-century brick Iglesia de la Encarnación, with a minaret-like tower and lavish golden altar, nearby.

Sights & Activities

El Nacimiento Waterfalls WATERFALL

(P) Just east of Laujar's main plaza, a signposted road heads 1.5km north to El Nacimiento, a pretty series of waterfalls in a deep valley, with a couple of restaurants nearby. On weekends, it's packed with families out for a barbecue.

Bodega Valle de Laujar WINERY

(www.bodegasvallelaujar.es; Ctra AL5402; 8am-2pm & 3.30-7pm; P) FREE This established bodega is a good choice for tasting local wines (free) and watching the bottling operations. Plenty of wine and other Alpujarras products (jams, cheeses, sausages, honey) are for sale, too. It's on the western access road into Laujar from the A348.

Cortijo El Cura WINERY

(www.cortijoelcura.com; 9am-7pm; P) A rare organic vineyard, family-run El Cura produces some prize-winning wines from autochthonous Alpujarras grapes: tastings and winery visits are free for small numbers of visitors. It has a beautiful old farmhouse setting, 800m south of the A348. Look for the signs 3km west of Laujar.

Sendero del Aguadero WALKING

The Sendero del Aguadero (PRA37) is a lovely path up through woodlands of alder, pine and chestnut. The whole trail is a circular route of 13km (about five hours), climbing and descending more than 600m, but you can double back whenever you like. Look out for wild boar and hoopoes (black-and-white birds with elaborate orange crests).

The path is around 1km from El Nacimiento waterfalls (p297).

Sleeping

Hotel Almirez HOTEL €

(950 51 35 14; www.hotelalmirez.es; Ctra AL5402; s/d €39/50; P) Colourful pot plants prettify this friendly place on Laujar's western access road from the A348. Rooms are plain but spotless, each with a terrace taking in lovely mountain views, and the hotel follows eco-friendly practices with electricity, water and its surrounding land.

Management is a good source of information on things to do in the Alpujarras, and the restaurant is a great option for a meal.

✕ Eating & Drinking

Fonda Nuevo Andarax ANDALUCIAN €
(Calle Villaespesa 43; mains €8-15, menú €10; ⊙8am-6pm, lunch 1-4pm) A popular restaurant and bar (with rooms) 300m west of the Plaza Mayor, with good valley panoramas from its bright dining room. You can go for *raciónes* (platefuls) of local *embutidos* (sausages and cured meats) or tortillas, or try one of the home-style *potajes* (soup-cum-stews) or assorted meats *a la brasa* (grilled).

Restaurante Almirez ANDALUCIAN €€
(Ctra AL5402, Hotel Almirez; mains €10-18; ⊙8am-11pm) This hotel restaurant serves hearty fare specialising in local Alpujarran ingredients and dishes, including *potajes*, plenty of meats, game such as quail and partridge, sausages, cheeses and salads. Good local wine too. It's on Laujar's western approach road from the A348.

ℹ Information

Centro de Visitantes Laujar de Andarax
(☑958 98 02 46; ⊙10am-2pm Thu-Sun, 6-8pm Fri-Sun Apr-Sep, 4-6pm Fri-Sun Oct-Mar) Good for information on walks in the area and general information on the Sierra Nevada national and natural parks. It's on Laujar's western access road, 1.5km from the town centre.

ℹ Getting There & Away

BUS

Four buses run from Almería to Laujar (€6.27, two to 2½ hours) Monday to Friday, and two on Saturday and Sunday. To continue to the Granada Alpujarras, you need to change buses in Berja and Ugíjar – only practical if you start on the 7.50am bus (Monday to Friday only) from Laujar to Berja.

COSTA DE ALMERÍA

Parque Natural de Cabo de Gata-Níjar

Some of Spain's most flawless and least crowded sandy beaches are strung like pearls between the dramatic cliffs of the Cabo de Gata promontory, southeast of Almería. With less than 200mm of rain in an average year, this is the driest place in Europe, yet more than 1000 varieties of animal and plant thrive in the arid, salty environment. A 340-sq-km area of coast and hinterland, plus a mile-wide strip of sea, are protected as the Parque Natural de Cabo de Gata-Níjar. The stark terrain, a product of volcanic activity more than 7 million years ago, is studded with agave plants and other desert succulents, and has only a few small settlements of whitewashed, flat-roofed houses and a scattering of abandoned or renovated farmsteads. The largest village is San José, a second home for many Almería city folk. The park is also a bonanza of bizarre rock formations, with an intriguing mining history, and is part of the European Geoparks (www.europeangeoparks.org) network.

There is plenty to do on Cabo de Gata besides just enjoying the beaches and walking. Diving, snorkelling, kayaking, sailing, cycling, horse riding, and 4WD and boat tours are all popular. A host of operators offers these activities from the coastal villages during Easter and from July to September, though only a few carry on year-round.

Cabo de Gata cape stands at the southwest point of the promontory: its name (from *ágata,* the Spanish for agate) may also refer to the entire promontory, from Retamar in the west to Agua Amarga in the east, or to the village of San Miguel de Cabo de Gata on the west coast.

⟳ Tours

El Cabo a Fondo BOAT TOUR
(☑637 449170; www.elcaboafondo.com; 1hr tour adult/child €20/15; ☒) Some of the most spectacular views of the Cabo de Gata coast are from the sea, and you'll get this perspective on Cabo a Fondo's outings starting from La Isleta del Moro, Las Negras or La Fabriquilla. Trips run up to eight times daily and are offered year-round, weather permitting (minimum numbers may be required in low seasons). Reserving ahead is essential.

ℹ Information

Centro de Interpretación Las Amoladeras
(Ctra Retamar-Pujaire Km 7; ⊙10am-3pm Thu-Sun) The park's main visitor centre, on the main road from Almería 2km west of Ruescas.

Centro de Información (www.cabodegata-nijar. com; Avenida San José 27, San José; ⊙10am-2pm & 5-8pm Apr-Oct, to 2pm Nov-Mar) Park information centre and local-products shop.

ℹ Getting There & Away

BUS

Alsa (☑902 42 22 42; www.alsa.es) Runs six daily buses from Almería to San Miguel de Cabo de Gata (€2.90, one hour), and one (except

Parque Natural de Cabo de Gata-Níjar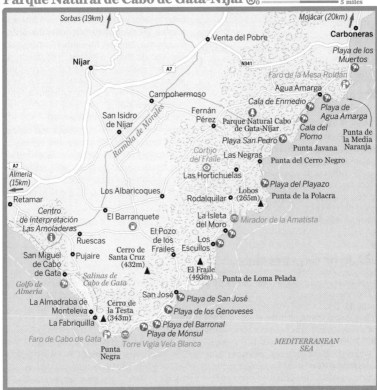

Sunday) to Las Negras (€2.90, 1¼ hours) and Rodalquilar (€2.90, 1½ hours).

Autocares Bernardo (☑ 950 25 04 22; www. autocaresbernardo.com) Runs buses between Almería and San José (€2.90, 1¼ hours, three Monday to Saturday, two on Sunday).

Autocares Frahermar (☑ 950 26 64 11; www. frahermar.com) Runs between Almería and Agua Amarga (€5.50, 1¼ hours) once daily except Tuesday and Thursday; service increases to once or twice every day in July and August.

TAXI

Autotaxi San José (☑ 950 38 95 50, 608 056255)

San Miguel de Cabo de Gata & Around

◉ Sights

Salinas de Cabo de Gata   SALT FLATS
(ℙ) Southeast of drab San Miguel de Cabo de Gata village, some of Spain's last surviv-ing sea-salt-extraction lagoons draw flocks of migrating flamingos and other water birds from spring to autumn: by late August there can be 1000 flamingos here. Birdwatching hides are placed at a few strategic points.

Salt is no longer collected from the la-goons but sea water is still let into them for the sake of the birds, via a channel at La Fabriquilla, at the south end of the lagoons.

Faro de Cabo de Gata   LIGHTHOUSE
(ℙ) At the southwest point of the promon-tory, this lighthouse overlooks the jagged volcanic reefs of the Arrecife de las Sirenas (Reef of the Mermaids), named after the monk seals that used to lounge here. The view into the water is fantastically clear. A side road runs 3km up to the **Torre Vigía Vela Blanca**, an 18th-century watchtower with wonderful views in both directions along the coast.

From the Torre the road is blocked to motor vehicles, but walkers and cyclists can continue 5km down to Playa de Mónsul and, beyond that, San José.

San José

San José is Parque Natural de Cabo de Gata-Níjar's main tourist centre and has the largest choice of restaurants.

🏃 Activities

Deportes Medialuna KAYAKING, CYCLING
(📞 950 38 04 62; www.deportesmedialuna.com; Calle del Puerto 7; rentals kayak/SUP per hour from €7/10, mountain bike per half-day/day €8/13; ⏲ 10am-2pm & 5-8pm Mon-Sat, to 2pm Sun) This locally run outfit operates year-round. It offers kayak and mountain-bike rental and guided trips, and SUP (stand-up paddle) rental and tuition, plus boat trips from June to September.

Diving & Snorkelling

The clean, clear water around Cabo de Gata's coast encourages a good range of fish and marine plants, and the diving and snorkelling here is rivalled in southern Spain only by Cabo de Palos in Murcia. The posidonia seagrass meadows are proof of water cleanliness, and along with caves, rocks and canyons they provide a habitat for many marine animals, including eagle rays, sunfish, moray and conger eels, grouper, angelfish and barracuda. You'll need a wetsuit year-round; the water is cold! There are dive centres in San José, La Isleta del Moro, Rodalquilar, Las Negras, Agua Amarga and Carboneras. A highlight for experienced divers is the wreck *El Vapor,* 1.8km off the Faro de Cabo de Gata.

CABO DE GATA BEACHES

Cabo de Gata's best beaches are along the south and east coasts, and some of the most beautiful and popular are southwest of San José. A gravel/earth road signposted 'Playas' and/or 'Genoveses/Mónsul' runs to them from San José. However, from about the start of July to mid-September, the road is closed to cars once the beach car parks (€5) fill up, typically by about 10am, but a bus (one way/return €1.50/2) runs from town from 9am to 7pm.

The first beach you reach is **Playa de los Genoveses** (Ⓟ), a 1km stretch of sand where the Genoese navy landed in 1147 in the Christian attack on Almería. Popular **Playa de Mónsul** (Ⓟ; you may recognise the rock overhang from *Indiana Jones and the Last Crusade*) is 2.5km past the Genoveses turn-off. You can walk to several more secluded beaches. Tracks behind the large dune at Mónsul's east end lead down to nudist **Playa del Barronal** (600m from the road). If you bear left just before Playa del Barronal, and work your way over a little pass just left of the highest hillock, you'll come down to El Lance del Perro. This beach, with striking basalt rock formations, is the first of four gorgeous, isolated, little beaches called the **Calas del Barronal**. Tides permitting, you can walk round the foot of the cliffs from one to the next.

A little west of Playa de Mónsul, paths lead from the road to two other less-frequented beaches, **Cala de la Media Luna** and **Cala Carbón**.

San José has a wide but busy sandy beach of its own, and to the northeast there are reasonable beaches at Los Escullos and La Isleta del Moro. These are convenient if you prefer less of a wilderness experience – there are restaurants and bars steps away. But much finer is **Playa del Playazo** (Ⓟ), a 400m broad, sandy strip between two headlands, one of which is topped by an 18th-century gun battery: it's 3.5km east of Rodalquilar (the last 2km along a drivable track from the main road), or 2.5km south from Las Negras by a coastal footpath.

Las Negras village is fronted by a part-sandy, part-stony beach, but there's a sandier one, **Playa San Pedro**, 3km northeast, between dramatic headlands. San Pedro hamlet is inhabited by a small floating bohemian population hanging out in tents, abandoned buildings and the odd cave. It's only accessible on foot or by inflatable boat (€10 return) from Las Negras. Boat frequencies depend on demand and weather.

Agua Amarga, a boho-chic beach getaway beloved of Spanish urbanites and Scandinavian sun-seekers, is fronted by a broad, sandy and popular beach. A 1.5km waymarked walk over a small hill to the southwest brings you to pretty little **Cala de Enmedio**, a beach enclosed between striking eroded rocks.

WALKING THE CABO DE GATA COAST

A network of roads and trails leads about 50km right around the coast from San Miguel de Cabo de Gata to Agua Amarga. The full hike requires three days and should be attempted only in spring or, better, autumn (when the sea is warm), as the summer heat is fierce and there is no shade. But you can embark on sections of the walk for a day or afternoon, and some of the beaches you'll pass are otherwise inaccessible.

From San José it's a fine 9km walk of about 2½ hours, passing some of the best beaches, southwest to the **Torre Vigía Vela Blanca**, an old lookout tower with superb panoramas. Northeast from San José to the tiny beach settlement of **Los Escullos**, it's a fairly level 8km walk with some good views, skirting the ancient volcano **El Fraile**, partly on old mining roads.

Another good stretch is from Rodalquilar along the valley to **Playa del Playazo**, then up the coast along scenic cliff edges to **Las Negras** (6km from Rodalquilar). It's another 3km to the real prize: **Playa San Pedro**, inaccessible by road, with its abandoned village that supports a small crew of boho-travellers. You can also drive to Las Negras, then walk to Playa San Pedro from there.

Isub DIVING, SNORKELLING
(☎950 38 00 04; www.isubsanjose.com; Calle Babor 8, San José; ⊙8.30am-2pm & 4-7.30pm Mon-Sat, to 2pm Sun Mar-Dec) Certified as a Five Star Dive Centre/Resort by the international scuba training organisation PADI, Isub offers a full range of diving courses, including baptism dives for beginners (€75), dive trips for qualified divers (€30 to €40 excluding equipment rental), snorkelling outings (€25 to €30) and equipment rental.

Sleeping

Most hotels in San José offer deep discounts outside the peak seasons of Semana Santa, July and August.

Aloha Playa HOSTAL €€
(☎950 61 10 50; www.pensionaloha.com; Calle Cala Higuera; r €80-85; ⊙closed Dec-Feb; ❄📶🏊) White walls, firm beds, sparkling bathrooms and reasonable prices make the Aloha an appealing choice to start with. Throw in the large pool at the back and the moderately priced restaurant with a broad menu, and it's one of the best deals in San José. It's 150m down the side street beside the tourist office.

La Posada de Paco HOTEL €€
(☎950 38 00 10; www.laposadadepaco.com; Avenida de San José 12; d €78-112; ⊙closed approx Nov-Feb; P❄📶🏊) Spacious, gleamingly bright rooms and a sunny feel give contemporarily styled Paco's an edge over most of its competitors. Rooms have their own terraces, some with sea views, and the hotel is equipped with a small pool and spa and a breakfast cafe.

★**MC San José** HOTEL €€€
(☎950 61 11 11; www.hotelesmcsanjose.com; Calle El Faro 2; incl breakfast s €129-142, d €154-215; ⊙closed early Nov-Feb; ❄@📶🏊) The MC offers the best of both hotel worlds: it has a chic contemporary design in gleaming whites and greys, and plenty of stylish details, but it also has the kind of hospitality that only comes from being run by a local family.

It features a rear sun-terrace area with a small pool, a comfy bodega area for tasting Almería wines, and a restaurant serving Mediterranean dishes with a contemporary touch.

Eating

The restaurants along San José's marina (north end of the beach) stay open through the afternoon in summer.

★**4 Nudos** SEAFOOD €€
(☎620 938160; www.cuatronudossanjose.com; Puerto Deportivo; mains €12-20; ⊙9am-midnight Apr-Oct, 11am-8pm Tue-Fri, 9am-5pm & 7pm-midnight Sat & Sun Nov-Mar, closed 2nd-half Jan) A cut above your average San José eatery, the 'Four Knots' is serious about its food but not too serious to be enjoyable. Friendly service complements terrific fresh fish and seafood – with exotica such as swordfish ceviche or tuna tataki alongside more classical preparations – and good Spanish wines.

It's set at the far end of the marina, overlooking the boats, with a roof terrace open from about June to September. Reservations advised except at the quietest times.

Casa Miguel   SEAFOOD €€

(☎950 38 03 29; www.restaurantecasamiguel. es; Avenida de San José 43-45; mains €11-18; ⊙1-4.30pm & 7.30-11pm Tue-Sun) Service and food are reliably good at this long-standing San José favourite with outdoor seating. Skip the pallid paella, however, in favour of the rich *arroz negro* (mixed seafood and rice, black from squid ink) or a *fritura* (mixed fried fish and shellfish). Or pick and mix with the daily fish specials.

El Pozo de los Frailes

✖️ Eating

La Gallineta   CONTEMPORARY SPANISH €€

(☎950 38 05 01; El Pozo de los Frailes; mains €10-26; ⊙1.30-3.30pm & 8.30-11pm Apr–mid-Oct, closed Mon except Jul & Aug) A small elegant restaurant in a former village shop 4km north of San José, La Gallineta is where urban escapees come for inventive, freshly made dishes with local ingredients and an international twist. Try a seafood dish or one of the speciality rice dishes (which must be ordered ahead if you want them in the evening).

You should book two or three days ahead at Easter or in July and August.

La Isleta del Moro

✖️ Eating

Casa Café de la Loma   MEDITERRANEAN, BASQUE €€

(☎950 38 98 31; www.casacafelaloma.com; La Isleta del Moro; mains €10-30; ⊙7pm-1am early Jul–end Aug; ✈️) A Mediterranean heaven with great sea views, this old *cortijo* (farmstead) runs a summer-only restaurant. The menu covers fresh fish and local meats but also plenty of creative salads and other vegetarian dishes, and there are regular jazz and flamenco concerts in the garden, by candlelight. Look for the turn-off from the main road just north of La Isleta del Moro.

Rodalquilar

The village of Rodalquilar, in the centre of the valley, was not long ago a ghost town, with just a few residents hanging on among the shells of a gold-mining industry abandoned in the 1960s. Since the 1990s it has come back to life as the headquarters of the parque natural and a holiday spot with bohemian-chic touches. Many buildings have been renovated, the main street is dotted with restaurants and shops, and there are numerous rural hotels and holiday homes in and around the village.

To get here, follow the road northeast of La Isleta del Moro. The road climbs to the breathtaking viewpoint **Mirador de la Amatista** (ℙ), before heading down into the Rodalquilar valley. The valley is an old volcanic caldera and it's here, among the time-worn lava, that the complexity of Cabo de Gata's flora is most evident, especially after the very brief spring rains, when delicate plants, some with a lifespan of only a few days, flourish.

⦿ Sights

★**Gold Mines**   RUINS

There is something very evocative about the old gold mines, which were at their peak of activity in the mid-20th century; a fascinating bit of industrial wreckage in a barren red-rock landscape. Stop first at **La Casa de los Volcanes** (⊙10am-2pm Thu-Sat; ℙ) FREE at the top of the village, a museum with excellent displays on the mines and the geology of Cabo de Gata. Behind the museum you can walk up among the abandoned crushing towers and decantation tanks from the 1950s.

The gravel road continues through the hills behind, pocked with abandoned mines and the ruined miners' hamlet of San Diego. It's dangerous to enter any of these, but the **Sendero Cerro del Cinto** walking trail, starting just below the Casa de los Volcanes, is an 11km circuit through this dramatic post-industrial landscape.

Jardín Botánico El Albardinal   GARDENS

(Calle Fundición; ⊙9am-2pm Tue-Fri, 10am-2pm & 4-6pm Sat & Sun; ℙ) FREE Rodalquilar's vast botanical garden behind the church is dedicated to the vegetation of semiarid eastern Andalucía. It's well planned, with every plant, tree and shrub identified. There is also a charming traditional *huerta* (vegetable garden), complete with scarecrow.

El Cortijo del Fraile   HISTORIC BUILDING

(ℙ) This abandoned farmstead on a windswept plain 6km northwest of Rodalquilar was the scene of the tragic true-life love-and-revenge story that inspired Federico García Lorca's best-known play, *Blood Wedding*. In 1928, in what's known as El Crimen de Níjar (Níjar Crime), a woman due to be married here disappeared with another man, who was then shot dead by the brother of the jilted groom. The romantically ruined 18th-century buildings are now fenced off but maintain a suitably doom-laden aura.

To get here take the road uphill from the Casa de los Volcanes (p302), go left at a fork after 3.2km, and turn right after a further 800m at a crossroads of tracks.

🛏 Sleeping

⭐ **El Jardín de los Sueños** BOUTIQUE HOTEL €€
(☑950 38 98 43, 669 184118; www.eljardindelos-suenos.es; Calle Los Gorriones; incl breakfast d €98, ste €118-140; 🅿❄🛜⚐) Just off the highway opposite Rodalquilar, this expanded old farmhouse is surrounded by a beautiful garden of dry-climate plants and fruit trees – some of which contribute to the substantial breakfasts. It's full of character and charm, very comfortable, and open all year. Bright colours, original art, tea/coffee equipment, private terraces, the occasional chandelier and the absence of TVs distinguish the rooms.

Suites with sky-lit bathtubs are worth the extra euros.

Agua Amarga

🛏 Sleeping

MiKasa BOUTIQUE HOTEL €€€
(☑950 13 80 73; www.mikasasuites.com; Carretera Carboneras 20; d incl breakfast €150-220; 🅿❄🛜⚐) MiKasa is the luxurious romantic-getaway option, and a delight with stunning pink Galician marble and lovely rooms. All rooms differ: one has a large circular bath, another a view of the sea, another a large private terrace. The hotel has two pools, a fancy spa and a beach bar, and the top-class Restaurante La Villa (p303) is next door.

Room rates drop deeply outside August.

🍴 Eating

⭐ **Restaurante**
La Villa MEDITERRANEAN FUSION €€€
(☑950 13 80 90; Carretera Carboneras 18, Agua Amarga; mains €19-24; ⊗8.30pm-last customer Jul & Aug, 8pm-last customer Wed-Sun Mar-Jun & Sep-Jan, 2-5pm Sat & Sun Mar-May & Sep-Jan) Next door to Agua Amarga's top hotel, La Villa is a sophisticated restaurant with a romantically lit dining room and pretty outside terrace. The dishes try just hard enough to be original, but stop short of being slaves

to drizzle and tower building. Reservations advised.

Try the seafood crêpes in brandy sauce, or bacon-wrapped beef tenderloin in Dijon sauce – and the gourmet black-Angus burgers are a big hit too.

Mojácar

POP 6337

There are two Mojácars: old Mojácar Pueblo, a jumble of white cube houses daubed over a hilltop 2km inland and dating back to at least Moorish times, and young Mojácar Playa, a low-rise modern resort spread out 7km along a broad sandy beach. As recently as the 1960s, the *pueblo* (village) was decaying and almost abandoned. A savvy mayor, Jacinto Alarcón, lured artists and others with bargain property offers, which set a distinct bohemian tone that is still palpable, despite an overlay of more generic tourism. In the picturesque *pueblo's* winding streets, there are mellow bars, galleries and intriguing small shops.

◉ Sights

The main sight is the very pretty *pueblo*, dotted with cute little plazas, bars and cafes. To reach the *pueblo* from Mojácar Playa, turn inland by the roundabout by the Parque Comercial, a large shopping centre towards the north end of the *playa* (beach); regular buses connect the two.

El Mirador del Castillo VIEWPOINT
A byproduct of Mojácar's revival as an arts colony, the villa called El Mirador del Castillo occupies the very top of the hill. Today it's a hotel and cafe-bar (both open Easter to October), and a mirador (lookout) to end all miradors, with panoramas stretching from the sea to a landscape studded with volcanic cones just like the one Mojácar occupies.

The cafe-bar provides sustenance after the hike up, along with a jazz soundtrack and plenty of space to relax over a coffee or *tapa*.

Beaches
Stretching some 7km, Mojácar Playa has enough sand for everyone, plus some excellent beach bars and restaurants opening right onto the sands. The broadest sands are at the south end, which also has a pleasant wide promenade.

Beyond the far south end of the main beach there's a 1.25km rocky stretch followed by 1.25km of sand ending at the **Castillo de Macenas** (🅿), an 18th-century watchtower (the main road loops inland then returns to the coast here). From the Castillo an unpaved road runs 3km south along the coast passing several small coves, some of which have nudist beaches. Along the way you can climb up the Torre Pirulico (P), a 13th-century watchtower.

✨ Festivals & Events

Moros y Cristianos HISTORICAL
(☉weekend nearest 10 Jun) Locals don costumes in dances, processions and other festivities to reenact the Christian conquest.

Noche de San Juan SUMMER SOLSTICE
(☉23 Jun) Basically a big beach party on beaches around Spain to mark the summer solstice. Expect bonfires, dancing and drinking from dusk until dawn.

🛏 Sleeping

Hostal El Olívar HOSTAL €
(☑950 47 20 02; www.hostalelolivar.es; Calle Estación Nueva 11, Mojácar Pueblo; s/d incl breakfast €38/59; ❋@🛜) A stylish and welcoming addition to the Mojácar Pueblo options, the Olívar has contemporary, pretty rooms with up-to-date bathrooms and tea/coffee sets. Some overlook a plaza, others the countryside. Breakfast is generous and you can take it on a panoramic terrace, when the weather is decent.

Hostal Arco Plaza HOSTAL €
(☑950 47 27 77; www.hostalarcoplaza.es; Plaza Nueva, Mojácar Pueblo; r €35; ❋🛜) In the centre of the *pueblo,* good-value, well-run Arco Plaza has sky-blue rooms with wrought-iron beds and white sheets. Many of them look over Plaza Nueva and the valley below, and there's a wide roof terrace with broad vistas. The plaza can be noisy in the evening but quietens down after midnight.

El Mirador del Castillo RURAL HOTEL €€
(☑694 454768; www.elmiradordelcastillo.com; Plaza Mirador del Castillo; r €69-120, ste €136; ☉Easter-Oct; ❋🛜🏊) Up at the tip-top of Mojácar's hill, this delightful small hotel, formerly a private villa, offers colourful, characterful rooms with superb views and rustic-style dark-wood furniture. Private terraces lead into the central garden and pool.

Hotel El Puntazo HOTEL €€
(☑950 47 82 65; www.hotelelpuntazo.com; Paseo del Mediterráneo 257, Mojácar Playa; d/apt/ste €90/139/151; P❋🛜🏊) A medium-sized hotel across the road from the beach, 1.7km south of the Parque Comercial, El Puntazo doesn't win prizes for aesthetic originality, but it's a well-run family business that provides all the necessaries for a comfortable stay. Apartments and suites are large and bright; the best have big sunny terraces. Discounts of 40% or more are available outside the mid-July-to-end-August high season.

🍴 Eating & Drinking

Both *pueblo* and *playa* have a good range of eateries serving varied cuisines, though some close from about November to March. In summer, especially August, Mojácar nightlife is hopping, with a number of friendly, lively bars tucked into small houses in the *pueblo,* while the *playa's* beach bars are in full swing.

MOJÁCAR'S HISTORIC FOUNTAIN

Near the foot of Mojácar Pueblo, **Fuente Pública** (Public Fountain, Moorish Fountain; Calle La Fuente) is a village landmark. Locals and visitors still fill containers with the water that tumbles out of 13 spouts into marble troughs and tinkles along a courtyard below colourful plants. A plaque tells us that in 1488 this was where the Catholic Monarchs' envoy met Mojácar's last Moorish mayor, Alavez, to negotiate the village's surrender.

As the plaque records, Alavez pleaded for his people to be allowed to stay in Mojácar with these poignant words: 'When the people of my race have lived more than 700 years in Spain, you say to us "You are foreigners, go back to the sea". In Africa...they will doubtless say to us, like you – and certainly with more reason than you – "You are foreigners: return across the sea by which you came and go back to your own land" '. History tells that the Catholic Monarchs agreed to Alavez' request for the Muslims to stay, then expelled them from Mojácar as soon as they had possession of its keys. The village was repopulated with Christian families from Murcia.

Mojácar Pueblo

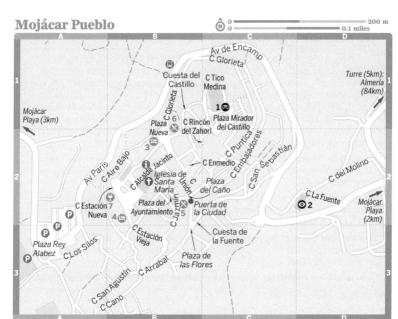

Mojácar Playa (3km)

Turre (5km); Almería (84km)

Mojácar Playa (2km)

La Taberna ANDALUCIAN €

(Plaza del Caño, Mojácar Pueblo; raciónes €6-12; ⊙noon-midnight, closed Wed Sep-Jun; ⚑) A big choice of both typical and original platters – meaty, fishy or veggie – gets everyone cramming into this thriving little restaurant inside a warren of intimate rooms, full of chatter and belly-full diners. It's beside an evocative old Moorish archway, the Puerta de la Ciudad.

★**Tito's** INTERNATIONAL FUSION €€

(☏950 61 50 30; Paseo del Mediterráneo 2, Playa de las Ventanicas; mains €10-15; ⊙10am-9pm Apr-Oct, to midnight late Jun–Aug; ☎) Warm-hearted ex-Californian Tito (see p306) creates the perfect laid-back atmosphere at this popular, cane-canopied hang-out on the southern beach promenade. It does terrific cocktails with fresh fruit and, from 1pm to 4.30pm (and 7pm to midnight from late June to August), some of the best food in town – carefully composed treats such as brie and almond salad with honey-mustard sauce or Galician mussels in white wine.

There's great Sunday-afternoon live music too. Right next door, the Mexican-style Tito's Cantina (www.facebook.com/lacantina. mojacar; mains €7-12; ⊙1-4pm Mar & Oct–mid-Jan, 7pm-midnight Mar–mid-Jan; ᴘ❀⚑) ⚑ serves

Mojácar Pueblo

⊙ **Sights**
1 El Mirador del Castillo C1
2 Fuente Pública D2

🛏 **Sleeping**
  El Mirador del Castillo ....(see 1)
3 Hostal Arco Plaza B2
4 Hostal El Olívar...................................B2

🍴 **Eating**
5 La Taberna...B2
6 Pulcinella B1

🍷 **Drinking & Nightlife**
7 El Loro Azul..B2

up fine enchiladas, quesadillas, fajitas, tacos and guacamole, and has a huge selection of tequilas and Mexican beers to make sure you are in suitable *ay caramba* mood.

Neptuno ANDALUCIAN €€

(www.neptunomojacar.com; Playa del Descargador; mains €8-19, menú €10-12; ⊙10am-5pm & 7pm-midnight, closed evenings Sun-Thu Oct-May; ⚑) Of the many *chiringuitos* (beach restaurants), Neptuno, 500m north of the Parque Comercial, is consistently one of the busiest and best regarded, especially for its

LOCAL KNOWLEDGE

TITO DEL AMO

Tito del Amo arrived in Mojácar from Los Angeles in 1964 as a young hippy looking for somewhere to feel part of a community, and bought a house the day he arrived, for US$3000. Mojácar Pueblo had only a few hundred inhabitants and Mojácar Playa didn't exist. Tito was one of the first foreigners to settle here. He turned an old inn into his now famous beach bar Tito's (p305) in the 1980s, helping to perpetuate the bohemian-artistic side of Mojácar life that had drawn him here. He recently featured in a documentary film, *Disney a través del espejo (Disney Through the Looking Glass)*, about Walt Disney, who Tito (along with many locals) believes was born in Mojácar and subsequently adopted in the USA.

Why did you choose Mojácar? When I came here in the '60s, there were just three cars in the village (remember I came from LA!), then there was the hilltop, the light, the clean air and the coastal setting. I couldn't resist.

Your favourite place? Aside from La Coquette (p292), which has simply the best French pastries and Italian ice cream in the province, I also enjoy Agua Amarga and the beautiful Cabo de Gata natural park.

Where do you like to go on your day off? I love the rugged rural scenery and just enjoy the simple pleasure of taking long walks in the surrounding countryside, especially the foothills near the coast.

If you didn't live in Mojácar, where else would you choose to live in Andalucía, and why? I could live in Granada too, for several reasons, but if only to be near the Alhambra!

---

wood-fire sardine feasts. It offers plenty of choice in fish, meat and rice dishes.

Pulcinella   ITALIAN €€
(www.pulcinellamojacar.com; Plaza Nueva, Mojácar Pueblo; mains €8-13; ⊙noon-4pm & 7-11pm, closed Thu Nov-Mar; ⊅⊞) Good Italian food and even better views from the terrace. There's plenty of pizza choice including the vegetarian Green Peace variety with lots of greens, plus pastas and some meat dishes including down-to-earth grilled chicken. Its recently opened beach branch, **Pulcinella Playa** (Paseo del Mediterráneo 62; mains €8-13; ⊙noon-4pm & 7-11pm), is by the Parque Comercial roundabout.

El Loro Azul   MUSIC BAR
(Plaza Frontón, Mojácar Pueblo; ⊙6pm-2am Wed-Mon, to 3am or 4am Fri & Sat) Tucked into one of the *pueblo's* quirky old houses, the convivial 'Blue Parrot' mixes great mojitos to a jazz, soul, blues and rock 'n' roll soundtrack for an international crowd.

Aku Aku   BEACH BAR
(www.facebook.com/mojacar.akuaku; Paseo del Mediterráneo 30, Mojácar Playa; ⊙10am-1am or later Apr-Oct) Aku Aku opens right onto the sands 2km south of the Parque Comercial. It's a fine spot to enjoy free jazz and flamenco concerts at 11pm on Fridays, Saturdays and Sundays in July and August.

ⓘ Information

Oficina Municipal de Turismo (☑902 57 51 30; www.mojacar.es; Plaza Frontón, Mojácar Pueblo; ⊙10am-2pm & 5-8pm Mon-Sat, to 2pm Sun)

ⓘ Getting There & Around

BUS

Buses to other towns and cities stop at various spots around the Parque Comercial roundabout. **Alsa** (☑902 42 22 42; www.alsa.es) runs two to four buses daily to/from Cuevas del Almanzora (€1.59, 35 minutes), Almería (€7.69, 1¼ hours, none on Sunday), Granada (€21, 4½ hours) and Murcia (€12, 2½ to three hours). For Granada and Murcia, it's necessary to buy tickets beforehand at **Hotel Simón** (☑950 47 87 69; Calle La Fuente 38, Mojácar Pueblo; ☏) or at **Mojácar Tour** (☑950 47 57 57; Centro Comercial Montemar, Avenida de Andalucía), 200m from the Parque Comercial roundabout.

A local bus (€1.20) runs a circuit from Mojácar Pueblo down along the full length of the beach and back again, roughly every half-hour from 9am to 11.30pm, June to September, till 9pm October to May.

CAR

Follow the main road through the *pueblo* to reach two large parking lots on the far edge.

TAXI

Taxis wait in the *pueblo's* Plaza Nueva, or call ☑950 88 81 11.

LOS VÉLEZ

The beautiful landscape of the remote Los Vélez district, in the northernmost part of Almería, is greener and more forested than most of the province. Three small towns – Vélez Rubio, Vélez Blanco and María – nestle in the shadow of the stark Sierra de María range, part of the Parque Natural Sierra María-Los Vélez, which offers some good walks and the famed rock art of the Cueva de los Letreros.

Vélez Rubio is the largest town, with an enormous 18th-century baroque church at its heart, but Vélez Blanco has more charm with its scramble of houses with red-tile roofs and handsome wrought-iron balconies presided over by a dramatic castle. At 1070m, it's often up above the clouds. On Wednesday mornings you can browse the lively street market on the central Calle Corredera.

On the way up from the coast, it's worth stopping at Cuevas del Almanzora, a busy agricultural town with a large castle containing surprising art treasures, and an unusual cave museum.

Sights

Cuevas del Almanzora

Castillo del Marqués de los Vélez CASTLE
(Plaza de la Libertad; Campoy museum & Goya gallery €2, other parts free; ⌚7.30am-2pm Tue-Sat Jul & Aug, 9.30am-1.30pm & 5-7pm Tue-Sat, 10am-1.30pm Sun Sep-Jun; P) The imposing 16th-century castle of the Fajardo family presides over the old part of Cuevas del Almanzora, housing a small archaeology museum devoted to the El Argar Bronze Age culture, a gallery of Goya lithographs and the Museo Antonio Manuel Campoy. This last exhibits a large and fascinating selection of paintings and sculpture, mainly by Spanish painters (including Picasso, Miró and Tàpies), from the collection of one of Spain's greatest art critics.

Cueva Museo MUSEUM
(admission €1; ⌚9.30am-1.30pm Tue-Sat year-round, 5-7pm Tue-Sat, 10am-1.30pm Sun Sep-Jun; P) People have lived in caves in and around Cuevas del Almanzora for thousands of years. Contemporary cave-homes are not open to the public, but if you want to see a relatively comfortable dwelling from the mid-20th century, head round the corner from the town's castle to the Cueva Museo. This cave housed a family with eight children up until the 1960s.

The helpful attendant was born in a cave herself so can tell you everything you want to know about cave life – providing you speak some Spanish, that is.

Vélez Blanco

Castillo de Vélez Blanco CASTLE
(⌚10am-2pm & 5-8pm Wed-Sun Apr-Sep, to 2pm & 4-6pm Oct-Mar; P) FREE The Disneyesque castle rising on a pinnacle high above Vélez Blanco's tiled roofs confronts the great sphinx-like butte La Muela (The Molar Tooth) across the valley as if in a bizarre duel. From the outside, the 16th-century castle is pure Reconquista fortress. But the inside is pure Renaissance palace – or was until 1904, when the carved marble arcades, columns, doorways, window-frames, statues and friezes were sold off by the impoverished owners.

American millionaire George Blumenthal ended up with the entire marble patio and later donated it to the Metropolitan Museum of Art in New York, where it is on permanent display. There is an ongoing project to make a copy of the patio and reinstall it.

PARQUE NATURAL SIERRA DE MARÍA-LOS VÉLEZ

If you go walking in the mountains of this natural park, a refuge for many birds of prey, you may well have the trails to yourself. A visit in spring or autumn is best, as shade is hard to come by on some trails. The **Centro de Visitantes Almacén del Trigo** (p308) in Vélez Blanco has information on walking trails: a good circular one is the 13km **Sendero Solana de Maimón**, which circles the Sierra de Maimón hills southwest of the town.

Off the A317, just west of the tiny upland town of María, is the **Jardín Botánico Umbría de la Virgen** (⌚10am-2pm Tue-Sun, to 4pm Oct-Apr) FREE. This botanical garden highlights the unique flora of the region, and you can combine it with a walk round the fairly easy **Sendero Umbría de la Virgen** path (3km, about 1¾ hours), which begins and ends here.

Cueva de los Letreros   ARCHAEOLOGICAL SITE
(guided visits €2; ☺ guided visits noon Sun year-round, 4.30pm Wed, Sat & Sun Sep-Jun, 7pm Wed, Sat & Sun Jul-Aug; P) Of several World Heritage–listed cave-painting sites in the area, this Stone Age ceremonial site on a hillside near Vélez Blanco is the star. The reddish drawings, made some time before 5500 BC, show, among other things, animals, a large horned figure dubbed El Hechicero (The Witchdoctor), a set of interconnected triangles that may be a kind of family tree, and Almería's favourite symbol the *indalo*, a stick person whose outspread arms are connected by an arc (possibly a bow).

Today the *indalo* is seen all over Almería, on walls and pendants, and as the province's official symbol. Some believe it's a lucky charm that wards off evil, and there's enough evidence of its use in earlier centuries (and millennia) for ethnologists to surmise it may be one of the longest continually used symbols in human culture.

The Cueva de los Letreros is 1km off the A317, opposite the entrance to Pinar del Rey camping complex, less than 1km down from Vélez Blanco towards Vélez Rubio. It's securely fenced, so you need to join one of the guided visits to get a close look. These go from the Pinar del Rey entrance: be there 10 minutes before the starting time.

🛏 Sleeping

El Palacil   APARTMENT €€
(✆ 950 41 50 43; www.elpalacil.com; Calle Molino Cantarería; d €65; P ❄ ☀) Beside a running stream and pond with geese and ducks, El Palacil offers attractive apartments with kitchen and sitting room for up to six people, with touches of old country style in the wooden furnishings and ceilings. There's a decent restaurant too, with pizzas and salads as well as good grilled meats and seafood.

🍴 Eating

★ **Mesón El Molino**   SPANISH €€
(✆ 950 41 50 70; Calle Curtidores 1; mains €10-22, menú €25-30; ☺ 1-4.30pm daily, 8-11pm Fri & Sat) Tucked away up a narrow lane near the centre of Vélez Blanco, this grand, old-fashioned restaurant places a real emphasis on top-quality ingredients, proudly displayed in the lobby: aged beef, perfect tomatoes, obscure cheeses and, of course, luscious hams. It's hearty country fare at its best, with a good wine list too.

❶ Information

Centro de Visitantes Almacén del Trigo
(✆ 950 41 53 54; Avenida Marqués de Los Vélez, Vélez Blanco; ☺ 10am-2pm Thu-Sun year-round, 6-8pm Sat Apr-Sep, 4-6pm Sat Oct-Mar) Useful information and exhibits on the Parque Natural Sierra de María-Los Vélez.

❶ Getting There & Away

BUS
During school terms, **Alsa** (✆ 902 42 22 42; www.alsa.es) runs one afternoon bus from Almería to Vélez Rubio (€15, two to three hours), Vélez Blanco (€15, two to three hours) and María (€16, 2¼ to 3¼ hours), stopping at Mojácar en route except Sundays. The return service starts from María at 6am (6.30pm on Sundays). From Vélez Rubio (Calle de la Amistad at the round-about by Hotel Zurich), Alsa runs buses to Granada (€14, two to three hours, four daily): Hotel Zurich sells tickets.

Understand Andalucía

ANDALUCÍA TODAY 310

The economic wounds from the Global Financial Crisis run deep, but the Andalucian spirit and resilience still shine through.

HISTORY 312

Battling religions, ideologies, cultures and armies, Andalucía is where Europe meets Africa – and the collision has rarely been dull.

ANDALUCIAN ARCHITECTURE 325

Andalucía is home to some of Europe's finest churches, forts and palaces. Read about what inspired architects to build them.

LANDSCAPE & WILDLIFE 332

Andalucía's dramatic, well-protected landscapes are home to spectacular species such as the Iberian lynx, ibex and imperial eagle.

FLAMENCO 338

More than just music, flamenco is a way of life – and an intrinsically Andalucian one at that.

ANDALUCIAN ARTS 344

From Velázquez to Lorca, Andalucian arts are full of creative magic.

BULLFIGHTING. 348

Some see it as tragedy, others as theatre – whatever your view, bullfighting is intrinsically entwined with Andalucian culture.

ANDALUCIAN KITCHEN 351

Goodbye France, hello Spain! In case you hadn't noticed, balmy Iberia now leads the way in global cuisine.

Andalucía Today

In the worst economic crisis that most Spaniards can remember, Andalucía has been hit especially hard. Many people are angry. But despondent? Never. It can be hard to reconcile the warmth and colour of the Andalucian atmosphere with the gloom and doom of the news stories. The music still plays, the fiestas go on. With their gregarious nature, enjoyment of the good things and their optimism, Andalucians still have plenty of fight left in them.

Best on Film

Marshland (2014) Alberto Rodríguez' suspenseful tale of detectives investigating murders in the Guadalquivir delta scooped 10 Goyas (the Spanish 'Oscars').

The Disappearance of García Lorca (Marcos Zurinaga; 1997) Journalist investigates the death of the great Spanish playwright (played by Andy García).

Zindagi Na Milego Dobara (Zoya Akhlar; 2011) This Bollywood tale inspired a miniboom in Indian tourism to Spain; it includes a full song-and-dance routine set in the village of Alájar; starring Hrithik Roshan and Katrina Kaif.

South from Granada (Fernando Colomo; 2003) Touching screen rendition of Gerald Brenan's classic book.

Best in Print

South from Granada (Gerald Brenan; 1957) Village life in Las Alpujarras in the 1920s.

The Ornament of the World (María Rosa Menocal; 2002) Examines the tolerance and sophistication of Moorish Andalucía.

Andalus (Jason Webster; 2004) Webster's adventurous travels uncover the modern legacy of the Moorish era.

Driving Over Lemons (Chris Stewart; 1999) An anecdotal bestseller about life on a small Alpujarras farm.

Boom & Bust

In 2007, Andalucía had never had it so good. A decade-long boom in construction and property prices, massive EU funds for agriculture and a constant flow of tourists saw unemployment down to 12%, the lowest in memory. Rows and rows of shiny new cars were parked outside shiny new shopping-cum-entertainment complexes. Instead of Andalucians emigrating for jobs – a time-honoured tradition in what has long been one of Spain's poorest regions – hundreds of thousands of immigrants were coming to work in Andalucía.

Then the bubble burst. Credit was crunched, property prices dived, construction ground to a halt. Unemployment doubled in two years and kept on going up. Businesses closed, homes were repossessed, half-built buildings stood silent, charities handed out ever more food to the hungry, Spanish banks were bailed out by the European Union (EU), *la crisis* became a way of life. A wave of anger at corruption and the political and financial elite spread across the country, spearheaded by a protest movement known as Los Indignados (The Indignant Ones). By 2013, 36% of the Andalucian workforce was jobless, with unemployment among 16-to-24-year-olds at a staggering 64%. People were talking of a 'lost generation', and once again Andalucians were leaving home – to Germany, Britain, Latin America – to find jobs. Many were university graduates who found no market for their skills in a region notoriously lacking in industry and where employers of all kinds were feeling the squeeze.

In 2013, with an austerity-minded Partido Popular (PP; People's Party) government now in office in Madrid, the politicians started talking about signs of recovery. Few people took any notice, and if they did, it was usually to comment that they didn't believe anything the corrupt *casta* (political-financial governing 'caste') had to say. But in 2014 the Spanish and Andalucian GDPs both grew by more than 1% after five years of decline, and unemployment figures were marginally down. It looked like Andalucía had turned a corner, though it would be a very long time, if ever, before anything like the heady mid-2000s came round again.

The Shake-Up

But the political landscape had changed. Ever since democracy was restored in the 1970s, Spain had effectively had a two-party system dominated by the left-of-centre Partido Socialista Obrero Español (PSOE; Spanish Socialist Worker Party) and the right-of-centre PP and its predecessors. In Andalucía it was the PSOE who had always held sway in the regional parliament, the Junta de Andalucía. But now two brand-new national forces spawned by the popular protest movements of *la crisis* had burst on the scene: the radical Podemos ('We Can'), campaigning to rein in big business and corruption and reduce poverty, and the anti-corruption but pro-business, antibureaucracy Ciudadanos (Citizens). In the Junta de Andalucía elections in March 2015, these two parties won 24% of the Andalucian vote and gained enough seats to stop the PSOE, for the first time ever, from forming a government. At the time of writing a re-run of the election was on the cards, since the old and new parties were too far apart in their demands for any kind of alliance to be negotiated.

One Way Forward

Through all the turmoil, tourism (one of the two mainstays of Andalucía's economy, along with agriculture) held up surprisingly well – in 2014 the number of foreign tourists arriving in Andalucía reached 8.5 million. Indeed the crisis may even have helped Andalucian tourism because more Spaniards took holidays in Spain. Andalucía has been careful to give attention to this key industry: its historic cities and seaside towns are being made more attractive, its hotels more elegant; its monuments spruced up, its museums modernised; its restaurants are serving ever-tastier food, and its tourism personnel and information services are more professional than ever before. The city of Málaga, which has long been a cultural poor cousin to the Sevilles and Granadas, is enjoying a spell in the limelight thanks to classy new museums and a big leap forward in its gastronomic scene. To the benefit of Andalucians and their visitors, tourism is one field where Andalucía's future looks bright indeed.

POPULATION: **8.4 MILLION**

AREA: **87,268 SQ KM**

UNEMPLOYMENT: **34%**

HIGHEST PEAK: **MULHACÉN (3479M)**

ALHAMBRA VISITORS: **2.4 MILLION (2014)**

IBERIAN LYNX POPULATION: **300–320**

if Andalucía were 100 people

92 would be Spanish **1** would be Moroccan
2 would be Sth American **1** would be Romanian
1 would be British **3** would be Other

belief systems
(% of population)

17
No religion

79
Roman Catholic

2
Muslim

1
Protestant Christian

2
Other

population per sq km

ANDALUCÍA   SPAIN   UK

≈ 95 people

History

From a beacon of culture in medieval Europe to the hub of a transcontinental empire, from a destitute backwater to a booming tourism destination – Andalucía has seen it all. Set at a meeting point of continents and oceans, it has been swayed by diverse cross-currents yielding a culture unique in the world. From Islamic palaces to Christian cathedrals to the rhythms of the flamenco guitar, Andalucía cherishes its heritage, and to travel here is to sense the past in the fabric of the present at every turn.

Andalucía's Early Innovators

Prehistoric Andalucians, especially in the east, introduced important technological advances to the Iberian Peninsula, perhaps thanks to contacts with more advanced societies elsewhere around the Mediterranean.

The Neolithic or New Stone Age reached Spain from Egypt and Mesopotamia around 6000 BC, bringing the revolution of agriculture – the plough, crops, domesticated livestock – and with it pottery, textiles and villages. The Cueva de los Letreros near Vélez Blanco in Almería province, with paintings of animals and human and mythological figures, is among the finest of numerous rock-art sites from this period, scattered up the Mediterranean side of Spain. Some 3500 years later the people of Los Millares, near Almería, learned how to smelt and shape local copper deposits and became Spain's first metalworking culture. Around the same time, people near Antequera were constructing Spain's most impressive dolmens (megalithic tombs, made of large rocks covered in earth), during the same era as the megalithic age in France, Britain and Ireland.

About 1900 BC the people of El Argar (Almería province) learned to make bronze, an alloy of copper and tin that is stronger than copper – ushering in the Bronze Age on the Iberian Peninsula.

Earlier, Andalucía may have been home to the last Neanderthal humans. Excavations at Gorham's Cave in Gibraltar show that Neanderthals were probably still hanging on there until at least 26,000 BC. Neanderthals had begun their terminal decline around 35,000 BC as a result of climate change and the arrival of Europe's first *Homo sapiens*,

Prehistoric Andalucía

Cueva de la Pileta, near Ronda

Dolmen de Menga and Dolmen de Viera, Antequera

Los Millares, Almería province

Orce, Granada province

Cueva de Ardales

TIMELINE

c 18,000 BC	1000–800 BC	700–600 BC
Palaeolithic hunter-gatherers paint quarry such as aurochs, stags, horses and fish in the Cueva de la Pileta (near Ronda), Cueva de Ardales and Cueva de Nerja.	Olives, grapevines and donkeys arrive in Andalucía with Phoenician traders, who establish coastal colonies such as Gadir (Cádiz) and Onuba (Huelva).	Iron replaces bronze as the most important metal around the lower Guadalquivir valley. The Tartessos culture that develops here is later mythologised as a source of fabulous wealth.

probably from North Africa. Like 21st-century tourists, early European *Homo sapiens* gravitated to Andalucía's relatively warm climate, which permitted varied fauna and thick forests to develop, and made hunting and gathering somewhat easier. Between 20,000 and 16,000 years ago they left impressive rock paintings of some of the animals they hunted in Andalucian caves, such as the Cueva de Ardales, Cueva de la Pileta (near Ronda) and Cueva de Nerja.

Traders & Invaders

As history dawned, Andalucía's rich resources and settled societies attracted seafaring traders from around the Mediterranean. Later, the traders were replaced by invaders as imperialistic states emerged in the Mediterranean and sought not just to tap local wealth but also to exert political control. All these newcomers – Phoenicians, Greeks, Carthaginians, Romans and Visigoths – left indelible marks on Andalucian life and identity.

Phoenicians, Greeks & Tartessos

By about 1000 BC, a flourishing culture rich in agriculture, animals and metals arose in western Andalucía. This attracted Phoenician traders (from present-day Lebanon), who arrived to exchange perfumes, ivory, jewellery, oil, wine and textiles for Andalucian silver and bronze. The Phoenicians set up coastal trading settlements at places such as Cádiz, Huelva and Almuñécar. In the 7th century BC Greeks arrived too, trading much the same goods. The Phoenicians and Greeks brought with them the potter's wheel, writing and three quintessential elements of the Andalucian landscape: the olive tree, the vine and the donkey.

The Phoenician- and Greek-influenced culture of western Andalucía in the 8th and 7th centuries BC is known as the Tartessos culture. The Tartessians developed advanced methods of working gold, but it was iron that replaced bronze as the most important metal. Tartessos was described centuries later by Greek, Roman and biblical writers as the source of fabulous riches. Whether it was a city or just a region no one knows. Some argue that it was a trading settlement near Huelva; others believe it may lie beneath the lower Guadalquivir marshes.

Carthage & Rome

A former Phoenician colony in modern Tunisia, Carthage came to dominate trade around the western Mediterranean from the 6th century BC. Unhappily for the Carthaginians, the next new Mediterranean power was Rome. Carthage lost to Rome in the First Punic War (264–241 BC), which was fought for control of Sicily. Later, Carthage occupied southern Spain, and the Second Punic War (218–201 BC) saw Carthaginian

Ancient Andalucía
....
Museo Arque-ológico, Seville
....
Museo de Huelva
....
Museo de la Ciu-dad, Carmona
....
Museo de Cádiz
....
Museo Arque-ológico, Almuñécar

Roman Andalucía
....
Itálica, Santiponce, near Seville
....
Baelo Claudia, Bolonia
....
Necrópolis Ro-mana, Carmona
....
Museo de la Ciu-dad de Antequera
....
Roman Amphithea-tre, Málaga
....
Museo Arque-ológico, Córdoba
....
Museo Histórico Municipal, Écija

HISTORY TRADERS & INVADERS

206 BC	100 BC–300	AD 98–138	AD 552
Roman legions under General Scipio Africanus defeat the army of Carthage at Ilipa, near Seville. Itálica, the first Roman town in Spain, is founded near the battlefield.	Andalucía becomes one of the wealthiest, most civilised areas of the Roman Empire, with Corduba (Córdoba) its most important city. Christianity arrives in the 3rd century AD.	The Roman Empire is ruled by two successive emperors from Itálica in Andalucía: Trajan (AD 98–117) and Hadrian (AD 117–138).	Byzantium, capital of the eastern Roman Empire, conquers Andalucía. The Visigoths, a Christian Germanic people now controlling the Iberian Peninsula, drive the Byzantines out in 622.

general Hannibal march his elephants over the Alps from Spain to threaten Rome. But the Romans opened a second front by sending legions to Spain, and their victory at Ilipa near modern Seville in 206 BC gave them control of the Iberian Peninsula. The first Roman town in Spain, Itálica, was founded near the battlefield soon afterwards.

As the Roman empire went from strength to strength, Andalucía became one of its most civilised and wealthiest areas. Rome imported Andalucian crops, metals, fish and *garum* (a spicy seasoning derived from fish, made in factories whose remains can be seen at Bolonia and Almuñécar). Rome brought the Iberian Peninsula aqueducts, temples, theatres, amphitheatres, baths, Christianity, a sizeable Jewish population (Jews spread throughout Mediterranean areas of the empire) – and the peninsula's main languages (Castilian Spanish, Portuguese, Catalan and Galician are all directly descended from the colloquial Latin spoken by Roman colonists).

The Visigoths

When the Huns erupted into Europe from Asia in the late 4th century AD, displaced Germanic peoples moved westwards across the crumbling Roman empire. One group, the Visigoths, took over the Iberian Peninsula in the 6th century, with Toledo, in central Spain, as their capital. The long-haired Visigoths, numbering about 200,000, were, like their relatively sophisticated Hispano-Roman subjects, Christian, but their rule was undermined by strife among their own nobility. Andalucía was an outpost of the Byzantine empire from 552 to 622 but then came under Visigothic sway.

Heartland of Islamic Spain

Andalucía was under Islamic rule, wholly or partly, for nearly eight centuries from 711 to 1492 – a time span much longer than the five centuries that have passed since 1492. For much of those eight centuries Andalucía was the most cultured and economically advanced region in a Europe that for most part was going through its 'dark ages'. The Islamic centuries left a deep imprint that still permeates Andalucian life and a legacy of unique monuments – Granada's Alhambra palace, Córdoba's great Mezquita (Mosque) and Seville's Alcázar palace give us a glimpse into the splendours of the age and are, for many visitors, the essential Andalucian cultural experience.

Arabs carried Islam through the Middle East and North Africa following the death of the prophet Mohammed in 632. Legend has it they were ushered on to the Iberian Peninsula by the sexual exploits of the last Visigothic king, Roderic. Chronicles relate how Roderic seduced young Florinda, the daughter of Julian, the Visigothic governor of Ceuta

Moorish Andalucía

Alhambra, Granada

Mezquita, Córdoba

Albayzín, Granada

Madinat al-Zahra, Córdoba

Giralda, Seville

Castillo de Gibralfaro, Málaga

Alcazaba, Almería

Mezquita, Almonaster la Real

Bobastro

711	756–929	785	929–1031
Muslim forces from North Africa thrash the Visigothic army near the Río Guadalete in Cádiz province. Within a few years, the Muslims overrun almost the whole Iberian Peninsula.	The Muslim emirate of Córdoba, under the Omayyad dynasty founded by Abd ar-Rahman I, rules over most of the Iberian Peninsula. The name Al-Andalus is given to Muslim-controlled areas.	The Mezquita (Mosque) of Córdoba, one of the world's wonders of Islamic architecture, opens for prayer.	The caliphate of Córdoba: ruler Abd ar-Rahman III declares himself caliph in 929; Al-Andalus attains its greatest power; and Córdoba becomes Western Europe's biggest city.

PATH OF KNOWLEDGE

Al-Andalus was an important conduit of classical Greek and Roman learning into Christian Europe, where it would exert a profound effect on the Renaissance. The Arabs had absorbed the philosophy of Aristotle, the mathematics of Pythagoras, the astronomy of Ptolemy and the medicine of Hippocrates during their conquests in the eastern Mediterranean and Middle East. Al-Andalus was one of the few places where Islamic and Christian worlds met, enabling this knowledge to find its way northward.

in North Africa, and how Julian sought revenge by approaching the Muslims with a plan to invade Spain. In reality, Roderic's rivals may just have been seeking support in the endless struggle for the Visigothic throne.

In 711 Tariq ibn Ziyad, the Muslim governor of Tangier, landed at Gibraltar with around 10,000 men, mostly Berbers (indigenous North Africans). Roderic's army was decimated, probably near the Río Guadalete in Cádiz province, and he is thought to have drowned as he fled. Within a few years, the Muslims had taken over the whole Iberian Peninsula except for small areas in the Asturian mountains in the far north. The name given to these territories was Al-Andalus. From this comes the modern name of the region that was always the Islamic heartland on the peninsula – Andalucía.

Al-Andalus' frontiers shifted constantly as the Christians strove to regain territory, but until the 11th century the small Christian states developing in northern Spain were too weak to pose much of a threat to Al-Andalus.

In the main cities, the Muslims built beautiful palaces, mosques and gardens, opened universities and established public bathhouses and bustling *zocos* (markets). The Moorish (as it's often known) society of Al-Andalus was a mixed bag. The ruling class was composed of various Arab groups prone to factional friction. Below them was a larger group of Berbers, some of whom rebelled on numerous occasions. Jews and Christians had freedom of worship, but Christians had to pay a special tax, so most either converted to Islam or left for the Christian north. Christians living in Muslim territory were known as Mozarabs (*mozárabes* in Spanish); those who adopted Islam were *muwallads (muladíes)*. Before long, Arab, Berber and local blood merged, and many Spaniards today are partly descended from medieval Muslims.

Most if not all of Córdoba's Omayyad rulers had Spanish mothers – concubine slaves from the north. Caliph Abd ar-Rahman III is said to have had red hair and blue eyes, and to have been the grandson of a Basque princess.

The Cordoban Emirate & Caliphate

The first centre of Islamic culture and power in Spain was the old Roman provincial capital Córdoba. In 750 the Omayyad dynasty of caliphs in

1091–1140	1160–73	1212	1227–48
The strict Muslim rulers of Morocco, the Almoravids, conquer Al-Andalus and rule it as a colony. Their power crumbles in the 1140s.	The Almoravids' successors in Morocco, the Almohads, in turn take over Al-Andalus, making Seville their capital and promoting arts and learning.	The armies of three northern Spanish Christian kingdoms, Castilla, Aragón and Navarra, defeat a large Almohad force at Las Navas de Tolosa in northeastern Andalucía – the beginning of the end for Al-Andalus.	Castilla's King Fernando III (El Santo, the Saint) conquers the west and north of Andalucía, culminating in the capture of Seville in 1248.

Damascus, supreme rulers of the Muslim world, was overthrown by a group of revolutionaries, the Abbasids, who shifted the caliphate to Baghdad. One of the Omayyad family, Abd ar-Rahman, escaped the slaughter and somehow made his way to Morocco and then to Córdoba, where in 756 he set himself up as an independent emir (prince). Abd ar-Rahman I's Omayyad dynasty more or less unified Al-Andalus for more than 250 years.

In 929 Abd ar-Rahman I's descendant Abd ar-Rahman III (r 912–961) gave himself the title caliph to assert his authority in the face of the Fatimids, a growing Muslim power in North Africa. Thus he launched the caliphate of Córdoba, which at its peak encompassed three quarters of the Iberian Peninsula and some of North Africa. Córdoba became the biggest, most dazzling and cultured city in Western Europe. Astronomy, medicine, mathematics, philosophy, history and botany flourished, and Abd ar-Rahman III's court was frequented by Jewish, Arabian and Christian scholars.

Later in the 10th century, the fearsome Cordoban general Al-Mansur (or Almanzor) terrorised the Christian north with 50-odd *razzias* (forays) in 20 years. In 997 he destroyed the cathedral at Santiago de Compostela in northwestern Spain – home of the cult of Santiago Matamoros (St James the Moor-Slayer), a key inspiration to Christian warriors. But after Al-Mansur's death, the caliphate disintegrated into dozens of *taifas* (small kingdoms), ruled by local potentates (often Berber generals).

Moorish Spain Reads

Moorish Spain (Richard Fletcher; 1992)

The Ornament of the World (Maria Rosa Menocal; 2002)

Andalus (Jason Webster; 2004)

IN ISLAMIC FOOTSTEPS

The medieval Islamic era left a profound stamp on Andalucía, and great architectural monuments such as Granada's Alhambra and Córdoba's Mezquita are the stars of this Islamic heritage. The characteristic tangled, narrow street layouts of many towns and villages also date from this period, as do the Andalucian predilections for fountains, running water and decorative plants. Flamenco music, though brought to its modern forms by Roma people in more recent times, has clear influences from medieval Andalucian Islamic music. The Muslims developed Spain's Hispano-Roman agricultural base by improving irrigation and introducing new fruits and crops, many of which are still widely grown, often on the same irrigated terraces created by the Moors. The Spanish language still contains many common words of Arabic origin, including the names of some of those new crops – *naranja* (orange), *azúcar* (sugar) and *arroz* (rice). Nowadays you can get a taste of Moorish life in luxurious *hammams* – bathhouses with the characteristic three pools of cold, warm and hot water – and Middle Eastern–style *teterías* (teahouses) that have opened in several Andalucian cities.

1249–1492	1250–80	1350–69	January 1492
The emirate of Granada, ruled by the Nasrid dynasty from the lavish Alhambra palace, sees the final flowering of medieval Muslim culture on the Iberian Peninsula.	Fernando III's son Alfonso X of Castilla, known as El Sabio (the Learned), makes Seville one of his several capitals and launches a cultural revival there.	Castilian king Pedro I 'El Cruel' creates the most magnificent section of Seville's Alcázar palace, but reputedly has a dozen relatives and friends murdered in his efforts to keep the throne.	After a 10-year war Granada falls to the armies of Castilla and Aragón, which are now united through the marriage of their rulers Isabel and Fernando, the 'Catholic Monarchs'.

The Almoravids & Almohads

Seville, in the wealthy lower Guadalquivir valley, emerged as the strongest *taifa* in Andalucía in the 1040s. By 1078 the writ of its Abbadid dynasty ran all the way from southern Portugal to Murcia (southeast Spain), restoring a measure of peace and prosperity to the south.

Meanwhile, the northern Christian states were starting to raise their game. When one of them, Castilla, captured Toledo in 1085, a scared Seville begged for help from the Almoravids, a strict Muslim sect of Saharan Berbers who had conquered Morocco. The Almoravids came, defeated Castilla's Alfonso VI, and ended up taking over Al-Andalus too, ruling it from Marrakesh as a colony and persecuting Jews and Christians. But the charms of Al-Andalus seemed to relax the Almoravids' austere grip: revolts spread across the territory from 1143 and within a few years it had again split into *taifas*.

In Morocco, the Almoravids were displaced by another strict Muslim Berber sect, the Almohads, who in turn took over Al-Andalus by 1173. Al-Andalus was by now considerably reduced from its 10th-century heyday: the frontier ran from south of Lisbon to north of Valencia. The Almohads made Seville capital of their whole realm and revived arts and learning in Al-Andalus.

In 1195, the Almohad ruler Yusuf Yakub al-Mansur thrashed Castilla's army at Alarcos, south of Toledo, but this only spurred other Christian kingdoms to join forces with Castilla against him. In 1212 the combined armies of Castilla, Aragón and Navarra routed the Almohads at Las Navas de Tolosa, north of Jaén, a victory that opened the gates of Andalucía. With the Almohad state riven by a succession dispute after 1224, Castilla, Aragón and two other Christian kingdoms, Portugal and León, expanded southwards down the Iberian Peninsula. Castilla's Fernando III took strategic Baeza (near Jaén) in 1227, Córdoba in 1236, and Seville, after a two-year siege, in 1248.

The Nasrid Emirate of Granada

The Granada emirate was a wedge of territory carved out of the disintegrating Almohad realm by Mohammed ibn Yusuf ibn Nasr, from whom it's known as the Nasrid emirate. Comprising essentially the modern provinces of Granada, Málaga and Almería, it held out for nearly 250 years as the last Muslim state on the Iberian Peninsula.

The Nasrids ruled from the lavish Alhambra palace in Granada, which witnessed the final flowering of Islamic culture in Spain. Their emirate reached its peak in the 14th century under emirs Yusuf I and Mohammed V, authors of the Alhambra's greatest splendours. The Nasrids' final downfall was precipitated by two things: one was Emir Abu al-Hasan's refusal in 1476 to pay any further tribute to Castilla; the other was the

HISTORY HEARTLAND OF ISLAMIC SPAIN

Jewish Andalucía

Centro de Interpretación Judería de Sevilla

....

Palacio de los Olvidados, Granada

....

Sinagoga del Agua, Úbeda

....

Casa de Sefarad, Córdoba

....

Sinagoga, Córdoba

....

Museo Sefardí, Granada

April 1492	August 1492	1500	1503
Under the influence of Grand Inquisitor Tomás de Torquemada, Isabel and Fernando expel from Spain all Jews who refuse Christian baptism. Some 200,000 Jews leave for other Mediterranean destinations.	Christopher Columbus, funded by Isabel and Fernando, sails from Palos de la Frontera and after 70 days finds the Bahamas, opening up a whole new hemisphere of opportunity for Spain.	Persecution of Muslims in the former Granada emirate sparks rebellion. Afterwards, Muslims are compelled to adopt Christianity or leave. Most, an estimated 300,000, undergo baptism.	Seville is granted a monopoly on Spanish trade with the Americas and becomes the cosmopolitan hub of world trade, with its population jumping from 40,000 to 150,000 by 1600.

unification in 1479 of Castilla and Aragón, Spain's biggest Christian states, through the marriage of their monarchs Isabel and Fernando. The Catholic Monarchs (Reyes Católicos), as the pair are known, launched the final crusade of the Reconquista (Christian Reconquest) against Granada in 1482.

Harem jealousies and other feuds among Granada's rulers degenerated into a civil war that allowed the Christians to push across the emirate. They captured Málaga in 1487, and Granada itself, after an eight-month siege, on 2 January 1492.

The surrender terms were fairly generous to the last emir, Boabdil, who received the Alpujarras valleys, south of Granada, as a personal fiefdom. He stayed only a year, however, before departing to Africa. The Muslims were promised respect for their religion, culture and property, but this didn't last long.

Christians in Control

The Catholic Monarchs, pious Isabel and machiavellian Fernando, united Spain under one rule for the first time since Roman days – a task completed when Fernando annexed Navarra in 1512, eight years after Isabel's death.

The relatively uniform culture of modern Andalucía has its roots in the early centuries of Christian rule. In their zeal to establish Christianity in the conquered territories, Andalucía's new rulers enforced increasingly severe measures that ended with the expulsion of two of the three religious groups that had cohabited in Al-Andalus.

In areas that fell under Christian control in the 13th century, Muslims who stayed on (Mudéjars) initially faced no reprisals. But in 1264 the Mudéjars of Jerez de la Frontera rose up against new taxes and rules that required them to celebrate Christian feasts and live in ghettos. After a five-month siege they were expelled to Granada or North Africa, along with the Mudéjars of Seville, Córdoba and Arcos.

Large tracts of southern Spain were handed to nobility and knights who had played important roles in the Reconquista. These landowners turned much of their vast estates over to sheep, and by 1300 rural Christian Andalucía was almost empty. The nobility's preoccupation with wool and politics allowed Jews and foreigners, especially Genoese, to dominate Castilian commerce and finance.

Fernando III's son Alfonso X (r 1252–84) made Seville one of Castilla's capitals and launched something of a cultural revival there, gathering scholars around him, particularly Jews, who could translate ancient texts into Castilian Spanish. But rivalry within the royal family, and challenges from the nobility, plagued the Castilian monarchy right through till the late 15th century when the Catholic Monarchs took things in hand.

Persecution of the Jews

After the Black Death and several bad harvests in the 14th century, discontent found its scapegoat in the Jews, who were subjected to pogroms

1568–70	1590–1680	17th century	19th century
Persecution of the *moriscos* (converted Muslims) leads to a two-year revolt centred on the Alpujarras valleys, south of Granada. *Moriscos* are eventually thrown out of Spain altogether by Felipe III between 1609–14.	Seville plays a leading part in Spain's artistic Siglo de Oro (Golden Age), as a base for artists such as Velázquez, Zurbarán and Murillo and sculptors such as Martínez Montañés.	The boom engendered by American trade fizzles out as silver shipments slump, and epidemics and bad harvests kill 300,000 Andalucians.	Andalucía sinks into economic depression, with landless labourers and their families making up three-quarters of the population.

around Christian Spain in the 1390s. As a result, many Jews converted to Christianity (they became known as *conversos*); others found refuge in Muslim Granada. In the 1480s the *conversos* became the main target of the new Spanish Inquisition, founded by the Catholic Monarchs, which accused many *conversos* of continuing to practise Judaism in secret.

In 1492 Isabel and Fernando ordered the expulsion of every Jew who refused Christian baptism. Around 50,000 to 100,000 converted, but some 200,000 left for other Mediterranean destinations – the Sephardic (Iberian Peninsula Jewish) diaspora. A talented middle class was decimated.

Morisco Revolts & Expulsion

The task of converting the Muslims of Granada to Christianity was handed to Cardinal Cisneros, overseer of the Inquisition. He carried out forced mass baptisms, burnt Islamic books and banned the Arabic language. As Muslims found their land being expropriated too, a revolt in Las Alpujarras in 1500 spread right across the former Granada emirate. Afterwards, Muslims were ordered to convert to Christianity or leave. Most converted, becoming known as *moriscos* (converted Muslims), but after the fanatically Catholic King Felipe II (r 1556–98) forbade the Arabic language, Arabic names and *morisco* dress in 1567, a new Alpujarras revolt spread across southern Andalucía and took two years to put down. The *moriscos* were then deported to western Andalucía and more northerly parts of Spain, before being expelled altogether from Spain by Felipe III between 1609 and 1614.

Seville & the Americas: Boom & Bust

If Islamic Andalucía's golden age was the 10th-century Cordoban caliphate, its Christian counterpart was 16th-century Seville.

In April 1492 the Catholic Monarchs granted the Genoese sailor Christopher Columbus (Cristóbal Colón to Spaniards) funds for a voyage across the Atlantic in search of a new trade route to the Orient. Columbus found the Americas instead – and opened up a whole new hemisphere of opportunity for Spain, especially for the river port of Seville.

During the reign of Carlos I (r 1516–56), the first of Spain's new Habsburg dynasty, the ruthless but brilliant conquerors Hernán Cortés and Francisco Pizarro subdued the Aztec and Inca empires respectively with small bands of adventurers, and other Spanish conquerors and colonists occupied further vast tracts of the American mainland. The new colonies sent huge quantities of silver, gold and other treasure back to Spain, where the crown was entitled to one-fifth of the bullion (the *quinto real*, or royal fifth).

The Spanish Inquisition was established by the Catholic Monarchs in 1478. Of the estimated 12,000 deaths for which it was responsible in its three centuries of existence, 2000 took place in the 1480s.

HISTORY SEVILLE & THE AMERICAS: BOOM & BUST

The American Adventure

Lugares Colombinos, near Huelva

Columbus' Tomb, Seville Cathedral

Archivo de Indias, Seville

Patio de la Montería, Alcázar, Seville

1805	1810–12	1850s	1873
In the Napoleonic Wars, Spanish sea power is terminated when a combined Spanish–French navy is defeated by the British fleet, under Admiral Nelson, off Cabo de Trafalgar, south of Cádiz.	With most of Spain under Napoleonic occupation, Cádiz survives a two-year siege. In 1812 the Cádiz parliament adopts Spain's first constitution, 'La Pepa', proclaiming sovereignty of the people.	Almería guitar maker Antonio Torres invents the modern acoustic guitar by enlarging the instrument's two bulges and placing the bridge centrally over the lower one, to give extra carrying power.	During Spain's chaotic, short-lived First Republic, numerous cities and towns declare themselves independent states. Seville and the nearby town of Utrera even declare war on each other.

Seville became the hub of world trade, a cosmopolitan melting pot of money-seekers, and remained the major city in Spain until late in the 17th century, even though a small country town called Madrid was named the national capital in 1561. The prosperity was shared to some extent by Cádiz, and less so by inland cities such as Jaén, Córdoba and Granada.

But Spain never developed any strategy for utilising the American windfall, spending too much on European wars and opulent palaces, cathedrals and monasteries, while wasting any chance of becoming an early industrial power. Grain had to be imported while sheep and cattle roamed the countryside. The ensuing centuries of neglect and economic mismanagement would turn Andalucía into a backwater, a condition from which it didn't start to emerge until the 1960s.

In the 17th century, silver shipments from the Americas shrank disastrously and the lower Río Guadalquivir, Seville's lifeline to the Atlantic, became increasingly silted up. In 1717 control of commerce with the Americas was transferred to the seaport of Cádiz, which enjoyed its heyday in the 18th century.

The Battle of Trafalgar (1805), in which Spanish sea power was defeated by Admiral Nelson's British fleet, is named after a small headland, Cabo de Trafalgar, in the town Los Caños de Meca, off which it was fought. A plaque commemorating those who died was erected on the bicentenary in 2005.

The Great 19th-Century Wealth Gap

The 18th century saw a few economic advances in Andalucía such as the construction of a new road from Madrid to Seville and Cádiz, the opening up of new land for wheat and barley and the arrival of new settlers from elsewhere in Spain, who boosted Andalucía's population to about 1.8 million by 1787. But Spain's loss of its American colonies in the early

LA PEPA

One of the few places to hold out against the French forces that occupied Spain during the Napoleonic Wars was Cádiz, which withstood a two-year siege from 1810 to 1812. During the siege, the Cortes de Cádiz, a Spanish parliament, convened in the city and on 19 March 1812 it promulgated Spain's first-ever constitution, the Constitución de Cádiz. This was a notably liberal document for its time and it decreed, among other things, universal male suffrage, a constitutional monarchy and freedom of the press. It didn't last long, being abolished by King Fernando VII on his restoration in 1814, but it remained a touchstone for Spaniards of liberal leanings – and was celebrated with fanfare on its bicentenary in 2012.

Spaniards call the Cádiz Constitution 'La Pepa' – the explanation being that the day of its promulgation, 19 March, is also the Día de San José (St Joseph's Day). None the wiser? The affectionate form of the Spanish name José is Pepe, and since the word *constitución* is of feminine gender, the Cádiz Constitution takes the feminine version of Pepe – so *¡Viva La Pepa!*

1891–1919	1923–30	1931–36	1933–36
Impoverished Andalucian rural workers launch waves of anarchist strikes and revolts. The powerful anarchist union, the CNT, is founded in Seville in 1910 and gains 93,000 members in Andalucía by 1919.	General Miguel Primo de Rivera, from the Andalucian town of Jerez de la Frontera, rules Spain in a moderate military dictatorship. He is dismissed by King Alfonso XIII in 1930.	The Second Republic: the king goes into exile and Spain is ruled first by the left, then the right, then the left again, with political violence spiralling.	Granada-born Federico García Lorca writes *Blood Wedding*, *Yerma* and *The House of Bernarda Alba* – his three tragedies rank as probably the greatest achievements of Andalucian literature.

19th century was desperate news for the thriving port of Cádiz, which had been totally reliant on trade with them, and as the 19th century wore on, Andalucía declined into one of Europe's most backward, socially polarised regions.

The Disentailments of 1836 and 1855, in which church and municipal lands were auctioned off to reduce the national debt, were a disaster for the peasants, who lost grazing lands. At one social extreme were the few bourgeoisie and rich aristocratic landowners; at the other, a very large number of impoverished *jornaleros* – landless agricultural day labourers who were without work for a good half of the year. Illiteracy, disease and hunger were rife.

Andalucian peasants began to stage uprisings, always brutally quashed. Russian Mikhail Bakunin gained a big following, with his anarchist ideas of strikes, sabotage and revolts as the path to spontaneous revolution and a free society, governed by voluntary cooperation. The powerful anarchist union, the Confederación Nacional del Trabajo (CNT; National Labour Confederation), was founded in Seville in 1910.

Andalucía has long been the home of the controversial activity of bullfighting. Spain's first official bullfighting school, the Escuela de Tauromaquia de Sevilla, was established in Seville by King Fernando VII in the 1830s.

The Civil War

The polarisation that gripped Andalucian society and politics in the 19th century was mirrored in Spain at large. As the 20th century progressed, divisions deepened and a large-scale conflagration looked increasingly inevitable. It came with the devastating Spanish Civil War of 1936–39.

The Prelude: Dictatorship & Republic

In 1923 an eccentric Andalucian general from Jerez de la Frontera, Miguel Primo de Rivera, launched a comparatively moderate military dictatorship with the cooperation of the big socialist union, the Unión General de Trabajadores (UGT; General Union of Workers). Primo was unseated in 1930 as a result of an economic downturn and discontent in the army. When Spain's burgeoning republican movement scored sweeping victories in local elections in 1931, King Alfonso XIII departed for exile in Italy.

The ensuing Second Republic (1931–36) was a tumultuous period of growing confrontation between left and right. National elections in 1931 brought in a mixed government including socialists, centrists and republicans, but the next elections in 1933 were won by the right. By 1934 violence was spiralling out of control, and the left, including the emerging communists, was calling increasingly for revolution. In the February 1936 elections a left-wing coalition narrowly defeated the right-wing National Front. Violence continued on both sides of the political spectrum, the anarchist CNT had over a million members and the peasants were on the verge of revolution.

In republican-held areas during the civil war, anarchists, communists or socialists ran many towns and cities. Social revolution followed. In Andalucía this was often anarchist-led, with private property abolished and churches and convents wrecked. Large estates were occupied by peasants and around 100 agrarian communes were established.

17 July 1936	1936–37	1936–39	1939–75
The Spanish garrison at Melilla (North Africa) revolts against the government, starting the Spanish Civil War. The plot is led by five 'Nationalist' generals, including Francisco Franco.	Western Andalucía falls early in the civil war to the Nationalists, who also take Málaga, with Italian help, in February 1937. Massacres are carried out by both Nationalists and republicans.	Helped by Nazi Germany and fascist Italy, Franco leads the Nationalists to civil-war victory. Much of eastern Andalucía remains in republican hands until the end of the war.	The Franco dictatorship: his opponents continue to be killed and jailed after the civil war; no political opposition is tolerated; the Catholic Church gains a privileged position in society.

But when the revolt came, on 17 July 1936, it came from the other end of the political spectrum. On that day the Spanish military garrison at Melilla in North Africa revolted against the leftist government, followed the next day by some garrisons on the mainland. The leaders of the plot were five generals. The Spanish Civil War had begun.

The War

The civil war split communities, families and friends. Both sides committed atrocious massacres and reprisals, especially in the early weeks. The rebels, who called themselves Nationalists, shot or hanged tens of thousands of supporters of the republic. Republicans did likewise to those they considered Nationalist sympathisers, including some 7000 priests, monks and nuns.

The basic battle lines were drawn very early. Cities whose military garrisons backed the rebels (most did) often fell immediately into Nationalist hands, as happened at Cádiz, Córdoba and Jerez. Seville was in Nationalist hands within three days and Granada within a few more. The Nationalists killed an estimated 4000 people in and around Granada after they took the city, including the great writer Federico García Lorca. There was slaughter in republican-held areas, too. An estimated 2500 were murdered in anarchist-controlled Málaga. The Nationalists then executed thousands in reprisals when they and their fascist Italian allies took the city in February 1937. Eastern Andalucía remained in republican hands until the end of the war.

By late 1936 General Francisco Franco emerged as the undisputed Nationalist leader, calling himself Generalísimo (Supreme General). The republicans had the support of some Soviet planes, tanks, artillery and advisers, and 25,000 or so French soldiers fought with them, along with a similar number of other foreigners in the International Brigades – but the scales of the war were tipped in the Nationalists' favour by weapons, planes and 92,000 troops from Nazi Germany and fascist Italy.

The republican government moved from besieged Madrid to Valencia in late 1936, then to Barcelona in 1937. In 1938 Franco swept eastwards, isolating Barcelona, and the USSR withdrew from the war. The Nationalists took Barcelona in January 1939 and Madrid in March. Franco declared the war won on 1 April 1939.

Franco's Spain

After the civil war, instead of reconciliation, more blood-letting ensued and an estimated 100,000 Spaniards were killed or died in prison. Franco ruled absolutely. He was commander of the army and leader of the sole political party, the Movimiento Nacional (National Movement). Army

---

A few communists and republicans continued their struggle after the civil war in small guerrilla units in Andalucía's mountains and elsewhere. *Between Two Fires* (2011) by David Baird is a fascinating document of the struggle between the guerrillas and the Guardia Civil (Civil Guard) around Frigiliana in 1940–50.

Civil War Reads

For Whom the Bell Tolls (Ernest Hemingway; 1940)

The Spanish Holocaust (Paul Preston; 2012)

The Spanish Civil War (Hugh Thomas; 1961)

1950–60	1969	1975–78	1982–96
Some 1.5 million Andalucians leave to find work elsewhere in Spain or Europe. New mass tourism on Andalucía's Costa del Sol helps to stimulate some economic recovery.	Andalucía's first national park, the Parque Nacional de Doñana, is declared. By the early 21st century, environmentally protected areas cover 20% of Andalucian territory, the biggest such program in Spain.	Following Franco's death, King Juan Carlos I and Prime Minister Adolfo Suárez engineer a transition to democracy. The 1978 constitution makes Spain a parliamentary monarchy with no official religion.	Sevillano Felipe González, of the left-of-centre Partido Socialista Obrero Español (PSOE), enjoys 14 years as Spain's prime minister, presiding over an economic boom after Spain joins the EU in 1986.

THE DUKES & DUCHESSES OF MEDINA SIDONIA

The Andalucian family that once owned more of Spain than any other family traces its lineage back to the Reconquista hero Alonso Pérez de Guzmán, legendary for his heroism while defending Tarifa in 1294. Guzmán and his descendants amassed vast landholdings in western Andalucía, and the title Duque de Medina Sidonia was conferred on one descendant, Juan Alonso de Guzmán, in 1445. By the early 16th century it was possible to travel right across the provinces of Huelva, Sevilla and Cádiz without leaving Medina Sidonia land.

In 1588 the seventh Duque de Medina Sidonia was appointed by Felipe II to command the Spanish Armada to invade England, despite his tendency towards seasickness and his lack of naval experience. Contrary to popular legend, the duke was neither incompetent nor a coward: the Armada's disastrous defeat is now put down chiefly to a flawed strategy ordered by the king.

The 15th duke's wife, María, Duchess of Alba, reputedly had a fling with the artist Goya and is widely thought to be the subject of Goya's scandalous nude portrait *La Maja Desnuda*.

But few of the dukes' careers match the colour of that of the 21st of the line, Duquesa Luisa Isabel Álvarez de Toledo, who died in 2008. Dubbed the 'Red Duchess', Duquesa Luisa was a committed republican who spent time in jail and exile during the Franco dictatorship, gave away Medina Sidonia estates to agricultural cooperatives and fell out with her three children. On her deathbed she married, under Spain's recently introduced same-sex marriage laws, her long-time companion and administrator of the huge family archive in Sanlúcar de Barrameda, Liliana Dahlmann.

garrisons were maintained outside every large city, strikes and divorce were banned and church weddings became compulsory.

Spain stayed out of WWII, but afterwards suffered a UN-sponsored trade boycott that helped turn the late 1940s into the *años de hambre* (years of hunger) – particularly in poor areas such as Andalucía where, at times, peasants subsisted on soup made from wild herbs.

In an effort to relieve Andalucian poverty, mass foreign tourism was launched on the Costa del Sol in the late 1950s. But 1.5 million hungry people still left Andalucía in the 1950s and '60s to look for work in Madrid, northern Spain and other countries. By the 1970s many Andalucian villages still lacked electricity, reliable water supplies and paved roads, and the education system was pathetically inadequate. Today a surprising number of rural Andalucians over 50 are still illiterate.

> By most estimates, about 350,000 Spaniards died in the civil war, although some writers put the figure as high as 500,000.

1982	1992	1996–2004	2000–10
Under Spain's new regional autonomy system, Andalucía gets its own parliament. Over the next 10 years, PSOE government at national and regional level eliminates the worst of Andalucian poverty.	Hundreds of thousands of people visit Expo '92 in Seville, and the superfast AVE (Alta Velocidad Española) Madrid–Seville rail link opens. Andalucian roads get a major upgrade, too.	Spain is governed by the right-of-centre Partido Popular (PP). Andalucian unemployment nearly halves (to 16%) thanks to a construction boom, tourism and industrial growth, and EU subsidies.	Hundreds of thousands of northern and eastern Europeans, Africans and Latin Americans migrate to Andalucía. Some are sun-seekers, more are job-seekers. The official foreign population grows to a record 700,000.

The New Democracy

Spain, and Andalucía, have come a very long way in the four decades since Franco died. Democracy has taken root, society has been liberalised beyond recognition, and living standards, despite the knock they have taken since the 2008 credit crisis, have climbed. High-speed trains, fast highways, shiny shopping malls, one-child families, gay marriage, thinly populated churches and heavily populated universities are just a few of the things that would amaze 1970s Andalucians today if they had been away for 40 years.

Franco's chosen successor, Alfonso XIII's grandson Prince Juan Carlos, took the throne two days after Franco's death in 1975. Much of the credit for Spain's transition to democracy goes to Juan Carlos and his prime minister, Adolfo Suárez. A new, two-chamber parliamentary system was introduced, and political parties, trade unions and strikes were all legalised. Spain enjoyed a rapid social liberation: contraceptives, homosexuality and divorce were legalised, adultery was decriminalised and a wave of hedonism was unleashed.

In 1982 Spain made a final break with the Franco era by voting the left-of-centre Partido Socialista Obrero Español (PSOE; Spanish Socialist Worker Party) into power. The PSOE's leader, Felipe González, a young lawyer from Seville, was to be prime minister for 14 years, and his party's young, educated leadership included several other Andalucians. The PSOE made improvements in education, launched a national health system and basked in an economic boom after Spain joined the European Community (now the EU) in 1986.

The PSOE also dominated Andalucía's regional government in Seville, inaugurated in 1982. PSOE government eradicated the worst of Andalucian poverty in the 1980s and early 1990s with grants, community works schemes and a relatively generous dole system. It also gave Andalucía Spain's biggest network of environmentally protected areas.

The PSOE lost power nationally in 1996 to the centre-right Partido Popular (PP; People's Party), which presided over eight years of economic progress. Andalucía benefited from steady growth in tourism and industry, massive EU subsidies for agriculture and a long construction boom, with its unemployment rate almost halving in the PP years to 16% (still the highest in Spain). The economic sun continued to shine after the PSOE regained power in 2004, until everything fell apart in 2008 when the global economic crisis hit Europe.

2003	2004	2008–14	2014
The Museo Picasso opens in Málaga, which joins Barcelona, Paris and New York as cities with major collections of the art of Pablo Picasso, born in Málaga in 1881.	The PSOE wins the Spanish national and Andalucian regional elections, days after the Madrid train bombings by Islamic extremists, which kill 191 people and injure 1800.	Andalucía is savaged by economic recession; unemployment leaps from 14% to 36%. The PP returns to power nationally in 2011 with an austerity program to tackle the crisis.	King Juan Carlos abdicates, with his health and the monarchy's popularity declining, making way for his son, Felipe VI.

Andalucian Architecture

From the noble Renaissance palaces of Úbeda and Baeza to the finely carved stucco-work that beautifies the Alhambra, Andalucía's architecture is a study in grace, skilled workmanship and unique cultural interchange. Hybridisation is almost a hobby here. Browse the region's towns and cities, and you'll see mosques converted into churches, Moorish arches held up by Roman columns, and minarets refashioned as belfries. Spared the carpet bombing that plagued other European cities in WWII, most of Andalucía's historic buildings are remarkably well preserved.

Moorish Factor

Architecturally speaking, Spain – and in particular Andalucía – is different from the rest of Europe. The reason? The Moorish factor. The conquering Christian armies may have disposed of Al-Andalus' emirs and government by 1492, but, tellingly, they didn't have the heart to flatten its most iconic buildings. Córdoba's Mezquita still stands, as does Seville's Giralda, and numerous other noble citadels. As a result, Andalucía's architecture is a story of layers, hybrids and Christian–Moorish intermixing. Even today, 500 years since the fall of Granada, the impact of Islam is never far from the surface. In villages across the region, and in the heart of cities such as Granada's Albayzín, intricate tangles of streets are redolent of North African medinas. Similarly, the Islamic love of ornate, scented gardens – hidden inner sanctums that safeguarded residents from prying eyes – can be seen in patios, courtyards and the carefully manicured greenery that embellishes Andalucía's Moorish-influenced houses and palaces. The resulting picture is as inspiring as it is complicated. Indeed, one could argue that European architectural design reached its highpoint in the 1350s in a palace complex at the foot of the Sierra Nevada called the Alhambra.

In more recent times, architects have often sought to emulate the glories of the Moors by regularly revisiting Islamic form and vision. One of the more spectacular results can be seen in Seville's Plaza de España constructed in the 1920s.

> **Islamic Fortresses**
>
> Alcazaba, Almería
>
> Torre del Oro, Seville
>
> Alcazaba, Antequera
>
> Alhambra, Granada
>
> Castillo de Gibralfaro, Málaga
>
> Castillo de los Guzmán, Tarifa

Islamic Architecture

The period of Islam's architectural dominance began with the Omayyads, the Moorish invaders who kick-started eight centuries of Islamic rule in 711 and ushered in an era which bequeathed the region, more than anywhere else in Europe, with a strong sense of the exotic. Elaborate monuments on an unprecedented scale – Granada's Alhambra and Córdoba's Mezquita, for example, which stand like bookends to Islam's reign – were the means by which the Islamic rulers of Al-Andalus brought architectural sophistication to Europe. They remain the most visible legacy of Andalucía's Islamic past.

HORSESHOE ARCH

The Visigoths are usually classified as Europe's forgotten civilisation, inbetweeners who had the historical misfortune of following the more flamboyant Romans. But these erstwhile rulers of an empire larger than the Córdoba caliphate did leave behind one indelible legacy: the horseshoe arch. So called because of their shape (a departure from the earlier semicircle arch), these stylistic arches were recognised and adapted by the Omayyads, who had found them adorning various Visigoth churches, most notably in Córdoba. The Mezquita in Córdoba displays the best early incarnations of horseshoe arches, but the style endured to become the hallmark of Spanish Islamic architecture, passed down through Almorávid, Almohad, Nasrid and Mudéjar architects employed by the Christians.

Omayyads

The Omayyads of Damascus had been overthrown by the revolutionary Abbasids in 750, forcing their leader Abu'l-Mutarrif Abd ar-Rahman bin Muawiya to escape to Morocco and then Spain. In 756 he set himself up as an independent emir, Abd ar-Rahman I, in Córdoba, launching a dynasty that lasted until 1009 and made Al-Andalus, at the western extremity of the Islamic world, the last outpost of Omayyad culture. But it was Abd ar-Rahman I's successor, Al Hakim II (r 961–76), who would leave the Omayyads' most enduring architectural mark in Andalucía.

Mezquita of Córdoba

Abd ar-Rahman I was responsible for founding Córdoba's Mezquita in AD 784, a building that was – and indeed still is – the epitome of Islamic architecture's grace and pleasing unity of form. This sense of harmony – perhaps the Mezquita's most enduring miracle – is all the more remarkable given the significant alterations carried out over the centuries. Zealous Christian architects darkened the original light-filled interior by building thick outer walls, and in the middle of the 16th century an incongruous Christian cathedral was plonked right in the middle of the former mosque.

The Mezquita at Almonaster La Real in Huelva province is like a miniature version of Córdoba's Mezquita, with rows of arches forming five naves, the central one leading to a semicircular mihrab.

In its original form, the Mezquita was a square split into two rectangular halves: a covered prayer hall, and an open courtyard where the faithful performed their ritual ablutions before entering the prayer hall. This early structure drew on the essential elements of Omayyad architecture. It maintained, for example, the 'basilical' plan of some early Islamic buildings by having a central 'nave' of arches, broader than the others, leading to the mihrab, the niche indicating the direction of Mecca (and thus of prayer) that is key to the layout of any mosque. But the Mezquita's prayer hall broke away from the verticality of earlier landmark Omayyad buildings, such as the Great Mosque of Damascus and the Dome of the Rock in Jerusalem. Instead, it created a broad horizontal space that evoked the yards of desert homes that formed the original Islamic prayer spaces. It also conjured visions of palm groves with mesmerising lines of two-tier, red-and-white-striped arches in the prayer hall.

As Córdoba grew into its role as the increasingly sophisticated capital of Al-Andalus, each emir was desperate to leave his personal stamp on Al-Andalus' landmark building. Later enlargements extended the lines of arches to cover an area of nearly 120 sq metres, making it one of the biggest of all mosques. These arcades afford ever-changing perspectives, vistas disappearing into infinity and interplays of light and rhythm that rank among the Mezquita's most arresting features.

For all its 8th-century origins and the later extensions, the Mezquita's golden age was the 10th century. It was then, particularly during the 960s under the reign of Al-Hakim II, that the Mezquita came to be considered the highpoint of the splendid 10th-century 'caliphal' phase of Spanish Islamic architecture. Al-Hakim II created a magnificent new mihrab, decorated with superb Byzantine mosaics that imitate those of the Great Mosque of Damascus. In front of the mihrab Al-Hakim II added a new royal prayer enclosure, the *maksura*; its multiple interwoven arches and lavishly decorated domes were much more intricate and technically advanced than anything previously seen in Europe. The *maksura* formed part of a second axis to the building, an aisle running along in front of the wall containing the mihrab – known as the qibla wall because it indicates the qibla, the direction of Mecca. This transverse axis creates the T-plan that features strongly in many mosques. In its 'final' 10th-century form the Mezquita's roof was supported by 1293 columns.

Almoravids & Almohads

As the centuries wore on, power shifted as competing North African dynasties turned their attention to the glittering prize of Al-Andalus. Some, such as the Almoravids – a Berber dynasty from Morocco from the late 11th to mid-12th centuries – yielded few notable buildings in Spain. But the second wave of Moroccan Berbers to conquer Al-Andalus, the Almohads, more than made up for the Almoravids' lack of architectural imagination.

Late in the 12th century, the Almohads made a priority of building huge Friday mosques in the main cities of their empire, with Seville especially benefiting from their attention. The design of the mosques was simple and purist, with large prayer halls conforming to the T-plan of the Córdoba Mezquita, but the Almohads introduced some important and beautiful decorative innovations. The bays where the naves meet the qibla wall were surmounted by cupolas or stucco *muqarnas* (stalactite or honeycomb vaulting composed of hundreds or thousands of tiny cells or niches), an architectural style with its origins in Iran or Syria. On walls, large brick panels with designs of interwoven lozenges were created. Tall, square, richly decorated minarets were another Almohad trademark.

Seville's cathedral, the city's Great Mosque in Islamic times, is where Almohad architecture is most stunningly on show. The Giralda, the minaret of the Seville mosque, is the masterpiece of surviving Almohad buildings in Spain, with its beautiful brick panels. The mosque's prayer hall was demolished in the 15th century to make way for the city's cathedral, but its ablutions courtyard, Patio de los Naranjos, and its northern gate, the handsome Puerta del Perdón, survive.

MADINAT AL-ZAHRA

The Córdoban caliphate's 'brilliant city', the Madinat al-Zahra was as architecturally lavish as it was ephemeral. The pet project of Abd ar-Rahman III, it was conceived as the caliphate's new capital in AD 936 and laid out from scratch 5km west of the city of Córdoba. Named after his favourite wife, Az-Zahra, Rahman planned his retreat as a royal residence, palace and seat of government, set away from the hubbub of the city in the same manner as the Abbasid royal city of Samarra, north of Baghdad. Its chief architect was Abd ar-Rahman III's son, Al-Hakim II, who later embellished the Córdoba Mezquita so superbly. In contrast to Middle Eastern palaces, where the typical reception hall was a domed *iwan* (hall opening to a forecourt), Madinat al-Zahra's reception halls had a 'basilical' plan, each with three or more parallel naves – similar to mosque architecture. Although it was wrecked during the collapse of the Córdoba caliphate less than a century after it was built, the remaining imposing horseshoe arches, exquisite stucco work and extensive gardens suggest that it was a large and lavish place.

With defence a primary preoccupation due to Christian advances in the north, the Almohads went on a fortress-building spree in the 12th and early 13th centuries. Cities with bolstered defences included Córdoba, Seville and Jerez de la Frontera. Seville's primary Almohad creation – aside from its mosque – was the river-guarding Torre del Oro, still standing to this day. Another survivor is Jerez's Alcázar – the tall, austere brick building is based on an unusual octagonal plan inscribed within a square; inside its walls the former Almohad mosque was turned into a church, while its minaret became a bell-tower. Less heralded Almohad-era creations are Tarifa's Castillo de los Guzmán and the city walls of historic Niebla in Huelva province.

Nasrids

With the armies of the Reconquista (Christian reconquest) continuing their seemingly inexorable march southwards, the last emirate of Islamic Al-Andalus, the Nasrid emirate of Granada (1249–1492), could have been forgiven for having its mind on nonarchitectural matters. But in a recurring theme that resonates down through Andalucian history, it was the architecture that emerged from this period that best captured the spirit of the age. The Alhambra is at once an expansive fortification that reflected uncertain times and an extraordinary palace of last-days opulence.

Alhambra

Granada's magnificent palace-fortress, the Alhambra, is the only surviving large medieval Islamic palace complex in the world. It's a palace-city in the tradition of Madinat al-Zahra but it's also a fortress, with 2km of walls, 23 towers and a fort-within-a-fort, the Alcazaba. Within the Alhambra's walls were seven separate palaces, mosques, garrisons, houses, offices, baths, a summer residence (the Generalife) and exquisite gardens.

The Alhambra's designers were supremely gifted landscape architects, integrating nature and buildings through the use of pools, running water, meticulously clipped trees and bushes, windows framing vistas, carefully placed lookout points, interplays between light and shadow, and contrasts between heat and cool. The juxtaposition of fountains, pools and gardens with domed reception halls reached a degree of perfection suggestive of the paradise described in the Quran. In keeping with the Alhambra's partial role as a sybarite's delight, many of its defensive towers also functioned as miniature summer palaces.

A huge variety of densely ornamented arches adorns the Alhambra. The Nasrid architects refined existing decorative techniques to new heights of delicacy, elegance and harmony. Their media included sculp-

ANDALUCÍA'S FORMAL GARDENS

Paradise, according to Islamic tradition, is a garden. It's an idea that architects took to heart in Al-Andalus, surrounding some of Andalucía's loveliest buildings with abundant greenery, colour, fragrances and the tinkle of water.

Generalife gardens, Alhambra, Granada Landscaping of near-perfect sophistication.

Alcázar gardens, Seville A classic Islamic palace pleasure garden.

Gardens of the Alcázar de los Reyes Cristianos, Córdoba Lush terrace with abundant water.

Parque de María Luisa, Seville Sprawling greenery in the heart of Seville.

Palacio de Viana, Córdoba Formal gardens with an emphasis on symmetry.

tured stucco, marble panels, carved and inlaid wood, epigraphy (with endlessly repeated inscriptions of 'There is no God but Allah') and colourful tiles. Plaited star patterns in tile mosaic have since covered walls the length and breadth of the Islamic world, and Nasrid Granada is the dominant artistic influence in the Maghrib (northwest Africa) even today.

Mudéjars & Mozarabics

The days of Islam's rulers may have been numbered in Al-Andalus, but Islam's architectural legacy lived on, even in areas under Christian rule. Gifted Muslim artisans were frequently employed by Christian rulers and the term Mudéjar – from the Arabic *mudayan* (domesticated) – which was given to Muslims who stayed on in areas reconquered by the Christians, came to stick as an architectural label.

One hallmark of Mudéjar style is geometric decorative designs in brick or stucco, often further embellished with tiles. Elaborately carved timber ceilings are also a mark of the Mudéjar hand. *Artesonado* is the word used to describe ceilings with interlaced beams leaving regular spaces for decorative insertions. True Mudéjar *artesonados* generally bear floral or simple geometric patterns.

You'll find Mudéjar or part-Mudéjar churches and monasteries all over Andalucía (Mudéjar is often found side by side with the Christian Gothic style). Andalucía's classic Mudéjar building is the exotic Palacio de Don Pedro, built in the 14th century inside the Alcázar of Seville for the Christian King Pedro I of Castilla. Pedro's friend, Mohammed V, the Muslim emir of Granada, sent many of his best artisans to work on Pedro's palace, and, as a result, the Palacio de Don Pedro is effectively a Nasrid building, and one of the best of its kind. Nowhere is this more evident than in the beautiful Patio de las Doncellas at its heart, with its sunken garden surrounded by exquisite arches, tiling and plasterwork.

The term Mozarabic, from *musta'rib* (Arabised), refers to Christians who lived, or had lived, in Muslim-controlled territories in the Iberian Peninsula. Mozarabic architecture was, unsurprisingly, much influenced by Islamic styles and includes, for instance, the horseshoe arch. The majority of Mozarabic architecture is found in northern Spain: the only significant remaining Mozarabic structure in Andalucía is the rock-cut church at Bobastro.

Christian Architecture

The churches and monasteries built by the Christian conquerors, and the palaces and mansions of their nobility, are a superb part of Andalucía's heritage. But there is, as always, a uniquely Andalucian twist: after the Christian reconquest of Andalucía (1227–1492), many Islamic buildings were simply repurposed for Christian ends. Many Andalucian churches occupy converted mosques (most famously at Córdoba), many church towers began life as minarets, and the zigzagging streets of many an old town – such as Granada's Albayzín district – originated in labyrinthine Islamic-era street plans.

Andalucian Gothic

Christian architecture reached northern and western Andalucía with the Reconquista during the 13th century. The prevailing architectural style throughout much of Christian Europe at the time was Gothic, with its distinctive pointed arches, ribbed vaults, flying buttresses and fancy window tracery. Dozens of Gothic or part-Gothic churches, castles and mansions are dotted throughout Andalucía. Some of these buildings combine Gothic with Mudéjar style, while others have Gothic mixed with later styles and so have ended up as a stylistic hotchpotch.

Although strongly associated with Andalucía, Mudéjar architecture originated in Castile and Aragón during the 12th and 13th centuries. The best Andalucian Mudéjar buildings are in Seville.

Roman Footprints

Itálica
••••••••••••••••••••
Baelo Claudia
••••••••••••••••••••
Calzada Romana (Roman road), Benaocaz-Ubrique
••••••••••••••••••••
Puente Romano, Córdoba
••••••••••••••••••••
Roman Amphitheatre, Málaga
••••••••••••••••••••
Teatro Romano, Cádiz

The final flourish of Spanish Gothic was Isabelline Gothic, from the time of Queen Isabel la Católica. Isabelline Gothic features sinuously curved arches and tracery, and facades with lacelike ornament and low-relief sculptures (including lots of heraldic shields).

Clean Lines of the Renaissance

The Renaissance in architecture was an Italian-originated return to classical ideals of harmony and proportion, dominated by columns and shapes such as the square, circle and triangle. Many Andalucian Renaissance buildings feature elegant interior courtyards lined by two tiers of wide, rounded arcades. Whereas the Gothic period left its most striking mark upon public Christian architecture, the Renaissance period was an era in which the gentry built themselves gorgeous urban palaces with delightful patios surrounded by harmonious arched galleries.

Spanish Renaissance architecture had three phases. First came plateresque, taking its name from the Spanish for silversmith, *platero,* because it was primarily a decorative genre, with effects resembling those of silverware. Round-arched portals were framed by classical columns and stone sculpture. Next came a more purist style, while the last and plainest phase was Herreresque, after Juan de Herrera (1530–97), creator of the austere palace-monastery complex of El Escorial, near Madrid, and Seville's Archivo de Indias.

All three phases of Renaissance architecture were spanned in Jaén province by the legendary master architect Andrés de Vandelvira (1509–75), who gave the town of Úbeda one of the finest ensembles of Renaissance buildings in Spain. Vandelvira was much influenced by Burgos-born Diego de Siloé (1495–1563), who was primarily responsible for the cathedrals of Granada, Málaga and Guadix.

Alonso Cano (1601–67) was a sculptor, architect and painter from Granada whose creative talents were as vivid as his famous temper. He's sometimes called the Spanish Michelangelo, and his most celebrated work is the elaborate baroque facade of Granada's cathedral.

Baroque Backlash

An inevitable reaction to the Renaissance sobriety that preceded it came in the colours and dramatic sense of motion of baroque. This style really seemed to catch the Andalucian imagination, and Andalucía was one of the places where baroque blossomed most brilliantly, reaching its peak of elaboration in the 18th century.

Baroque style was at root classical, but it specialised in ornamental facades crammed with decoration, and interiors chock-full of ornate stucco sculpture and gilt paint. Retables – the large, sculptural altarpieces that adorn many Spanish churches to illustrate Christian stories and teachings – reached extremes of gilded extravagance. The most hyperbolic baroque work is termed *churrigueresco* after a Barcelona family of sculptors and architects named Churriguera.

Before full-blown baroque there was a kind of transitional stage, exemplified by more sober works such as Alonso Cano's 17th-century facade for Granada's cathedral.

Seville has probably more baroque churches per square kilometre than any city in the world. However, the church at Granada's Monasterio de La Cartuja, by Francisco Hurtado Izquierdo (1669–1725), is one of the most lavish baroque creations in all Spain, with its multicoloured marble, golden capitals and profuse sculpture. Hurtado's followers also adorned the small town of Priego de Córdoba with seven or eight baroque churches.

Modern Andalucian Architecture

In the 19th century, Andalucía acquired some neo-Gothic and neo-baroque architecture, but most prevalent were neo-Mudéjar and neo-Islamic styles, harking back to an age that was now catching the fancy of the Romantic movement. Mansions such as the Palacio de Orleans y Borbon in Sanlúcar de Barrameda, and public buildings ranging from train stations in Seville to markets in Málaga and Tarifa, were constructed in colourful imitation of past Islamic architectural styles. For the 1929 Exposición Iberoamericana, fancy buildings in almost every past Andalucian style were concocted in Seville, chief among them the gaudy Plaza de España ensemble by local architect Aníbal González.

During the Franco dictatorship, drab Soviet-style blocks of workers' housing were erected in many cities, while Andalucía's decades-long tourism boom spawned, for the most part, architecture that ranged from the forgettable to the kind of concrete eyesores you wish you could forget. The dawn of the 21st century has sparked a little more imagination, most notably in Seville where a trio of big architectural projects – the Metropol Parasol, the Cajasol tower and the Pabellon de la Navegación – has added culture *and* controversy to the urban framework.

On a much smaller scale, Andalucía's architects and builders have demonstrated greater flair in restoring older edifices to serve as hotels, museums or other public buildings. Projects such as Málaga's Museo Picasso and Jaén's Palacio de Villardompardo are both 16th-century urban palaces turned into top-class modern museums.

Landscape & Wildlife

Andalucía is better known internationally for its history and culture than its wilderness. The fact that nearly 20% of the land is environmentally protected comes as a surprise to many visitors, who end up wishing they'd planned their trips with more natural attractions in mind. Icons to rival the Alhambra include the snowcapped Sierra Nevada and the precious wetlands of Doñana, both national parks. These stellar landmarks are backed up by a supporting cast of 80 more protected areas.

Landscape

Andalucía has mountains in abundance, from the relatively low hills of the geographically distinct Sierra Morena to the heights of the Sierra Nevada. The former, which rarely surpasses 1000m, rolls across the north of Andalucía like the last outpost of rugged southern Spain before it yields to the sweeping flat lands and empty horizons of central Spain's high *meseta* (plateau). It's more beautiful than dramatic, divided between evergreen oak woodlands, scrub, rough grazing pasture and scattered old stone villages.

Closer to the coast, the Cordillera Bética was pushed up by the pressure of the African tectonic plate on the Iberian subplate 15 to 20 million years ago. This band of jagged mountains widens out from its beginnings in southwest Andalucía to a breadth of 125km or so in the east. The 75km-long Sierra Nevada southeast of Granada, with a series of 3000m-plus peaks (including 3479m-high Mulhacén, the highest mountain on mainland Spain), forms a subchain of the Cordillera Bética. The cordillera then continues east from Andalucía across Spain's Murcia and Valencia regions, before re-emerging from the Mediterranean as the Balearic Islands of Ibiza and Mallorca. Much of it is composed of limestone, yielding some wonderful karstic rock formations.

Apart from the coastal plain, which varies in width from 50km in the far west to virtually nothing in parts of Granada and Almería provinces, the fertile valley of the 660km-long Río Guadalquivir is Andalucía's other major geographical landmark. Andalucía's longest river rises in the Cazorla mountains of Jaén province, flows westward through Córdoba and Seville, and enters the Atlantic at Sanlúcar de Barrameda. Before entering the ocean, the river splits into a marshy delta known as Las Marismas del Guadalquivir, which includes the Parque Nacional de Doñana.

Andalucía's Main Parks & Protected Areas

Andalucía has the biggest environmental-protection program in Spain. More than 90 areas, covering some 17,000 sq km, have been set aside, amounting to 20% of Andalucian territory, and more than 60% of the total protected area in Spain.

Parque Nacional de Doñana

Millions of birds and the Iberian lynx give the park its fame (Doñana is one of the endangered cat's last footholds). Its habitat range is as-

---

Andalucía contains both Spain's wettest region (Grazalema in Cádiz province, with up to 200cm annually) and its driest (the Desierto de Tabernas in Almería province, with a mere 14cm annually).

The mountain La Veleta, in the Sierra Nevada, sports Europe's highest paved road, which climbs to within 10m of its summit at 3380m.

PARKS & PROTECTED AREAS

Andalucía's protected areas fall into two main categories:

➡ *Parques nacionales* (national parks) are areas of exceptional importance for their fauna, flora, geomorphology or landscape, and their conservation is considered to be in the national interest. These are the most strictly controlled protected areas and may include reserve areas closed to the public, or restricted areas that can only be visited with permission. Spain has just 14 *parques nacionales,* and two of them – Doñana and Sierra Nevada – are in Andalucía.

➡ *Parques naturales* (natural parks) are intended to protect cultural heritage as well as nature, and to promote economic development that's compatible with conservation. Many include roads, networks of walking trails, villages and even small towns, with accommodation often available within the park. Like national parks, they may include areas that can only be visited with permission. There are 24 *parques naturales* in Andalucía; they account for most of its protected territory and include nearly all of its most spectacular country.

Other types of protected areas in Andalucía include *parajes naturales* (natural areas; there are 31 of these) and *reservas naturales* (nature reserves, numbering 29). These are generally smaller, little-inhabited areas, with much the same goals as natural parks. There are also 37 *monumentos naturales* (natural monuments), protecting specific features such as waterfalls, forests or dunes.

tonishing – wetlands, dunes, beaches and woodlands at the mouth of the Guadalquivir – and supports deer and wild boar. It is best explored by 4WD.

Parque Nacional Sierra Nevada

Spectacular high-mountain wilderness dominates here. The Sierra Nevada's high peaks are often snowcapped, even as the rest of Andalucía bakes in the sweltering heat. This *parque nacional* is best explored on foot: along its many trails you'll see ibex (around 5000 inhabit the park) and high-altitude plants you won't find elsewhere.

Parque Natural Sierra de Andújar

A medium-sized park in the Sierra Morena in the northwest of Jaén province, Andújar is notable for its rare mammals. It contains Andalucía's largest population of Iberian lynx and its last remaining colony of wolves; their survival is thanks, in part, to the fact that the park contains the largest expanse of natural vegetation in the Sierra Morena.

Parque Natural de Cabo de Gata-Níjar

Flamingo colonies, volcanic cliffs and sandy beaches make for a combination unlike any other protected area in Andalucía. One of the region's driest corners, the park showcases a semidesert terrain, and promises a range of activities, including swimming, birdwatching, walking, horse riding, diving and snorkelling.

Parque Natural Los Alcornocales

Some of the most extensive examples of the distinctive southern Spanish phenomenon of *alcornocal*es (cork-oak forests) carpet the rolling hill country of this park in Cádiz province, north of Algeciras. It's one of Andalucía's lesser-known protected areas, ensuring that its extensive hiking trails are rarely overwhelmed.

Doñana, established in 1969, was Spain's sixth national park, out of 15; the Sierra Nevada, established in 1999, was the 12th.

Parque Natural Sierra de Grazalema

Ibex, griffon vultures and other species occupy this beautiful, damp, hilly region that is notable for its vast sweeps of Mediterranean woodlands and stands of Spanish firs. Archetypal white Andalucian villages serve as gateways to fantastic hiking trails, but you can also climb, canyon, paraglide and go caving to your heart's content.

Parque Natural Sierra de las Nieves

Spectacular vistas and deep valleys characterise this mountain region buried deep in the interior of Málaga province. With two iconic examples of Andalucian flora (stands of Spanish firs) and fauna (ibex), as well as other species, the park is an ideal choice for those looking to hike through the Andalucian wilds.

El Parque Natural Sierras de Cazorla, Segura y las Villas is the largest protected area in Spain and the second largest in Europe.

Parque Natural Sierra Norte

Spring wildflowers carpet the rolling Sierra Morena country of this northern Andalucian park, but its appeal extends further, to ancient villages and expansive panoramas. There's no better way to explore this remote country than hiking or horse riding from village to village.

Parque Natural Sierras de Cazorla, Segura y las Villas

Abundant, easily visible wildlife, craggy mountains, deep valleys and thick forests – it's difficult to overestimate the charms of this beautiful park, Spain's largest (2099 sq km). Red and fallow deer, wild boar, mouflon and ibex provide the wildlife interest. Hike or explore on horseback or by 4WD.

Paraje Natural Torcal de Antequera

Striking limestone formations are what most visitors remember about this mountainous natural area close to Antequera in Málaga province. It contains some of the strangest landforms in Andalucía and has a handful of walking trails. Not surprisingly, given the terrain, it also draws climbers from across Europe.

Wildlife

Andalucía is a haven for wildlife that no longer exists elsewhere, and wildlife enthusiasts, if they know where to look, are unlikely to return home disappointed. A terrific source of up-to-date information on An-

RAREST TREE

Sometimes known as Andalucía's 'national tree', the endangered Spanish fir (Abies pinsapo) is the proverbial lynx of the arboreal world. This elegant survivor of the last ice age clings on today in only two main enclaves in Andalucía: Parque Natural Sierra de Grazalema and, more abundantly, Parque Natural Sierra de las Nieves, together covering a total area of around 4000 hectares. An equally small tract exists in Morocco's Rif Mountains.

The distinctive conically shaped Spanish fir grows to about 25m in height and inhabits mountainous areas at an altitude between roughly 900m and 1800m. Despite its historical durability, the tree wasn't properly 'discovered' and logged in a botanical sense until the 1830s by a Swiss scientist named Pierre Boissier.

Threats to the Spanish fir are numerous. Fire, farming, poor forest management, climate change and invasive species have all played a part in reducing its numbers. In the 1960s its reach was down to just 700 hectares, although prudent environmentalism in recent years has seen coverage increase. To protect the trees in the popular Parque Natural Sierra de Grazalema, access to walking trails where they grow is either controlled by a permit system or restricted altogether during periods of high fire risk.

dalucian fauna and flora is the English-language Iberianature (www.iberianature.com).

Signature Mammals

Many large mammal species that once roamed across Western Europe are now confined to small, isolated populations surrounded by an ever-expanding sea of humanity. That they survive at all in Andalucía is thanks to the region's varied, often untamed terrain, but even here they remain at serious risk.

Andalucía's most celebrated mammal, and one of its most endangered, is the Iberian lynx. The animal's numbers have recovered in the last decade and, with patience and a bit of luck, it's no longer impossible to see one in the wild.

Wolves *(lobos)* are even rarer – an estimated 50 or so survive in the Sierra Morena, mostly in Jaén province's Parque Natural Sierra de Andújar. Cut off from the rest of Europe's wolves – around 2000 survive in Spain – the wolf was, in 1986, declared in danger of extinction in Andalucía. In an effort to protect it from hunters and farmers, farmers are now awarded compensation if their animals are attacked by wolves. The wolf population has nonetheless sunk to levels that are probably fatally low.

Hunting throughout the 20th century is a primary reason why lynx and wolf populations have declined so alarmingly. In order to satisfy rural Andalucians' passion for hunting, and to provide an alternative prey to endangered species, the Andalucian government has introduced the mouflon *(muflón),* a wild sheep that's relatively plentiful, especially in the Parque Natural Sierras de Cazorla, Segura y las Villas.

In no apparent danger of extinction, and one of the region's most easily viewed mammals, is the ibex *(cabra montés),* a stocky wild mountain goat whose males have distinctive long horns. Around 37,000 ibex live in Andalucía, with the largest populations found in the Sierra Nevada; Parque Natural Sierras de Cazorla, Segura y las Villas; Sierras de Tejeda y Almijara; and Sierra de las Nieves. The ibex spends its summer hopping with amazing agility around high-altitude precipices; it descends to lower elevations in winter.

One of Spain's most unusual wildlife-watching experiences is the sight of Barbary apes, the only wild primates in Europe, clambering Gibraltar's heights.

Just as the sight of Barbary apes can seem like an apparition of Africa on European soil, whales *(ballenas)* and dolphins *(delfines)* are more often associated with the open waters of the Atlantic than the Mediterranean. Even so, the Bahía de Algeciras and Strait of Gibraltar harbour plenty of common, striped and bottlenose dolphins, as well as some pilot, killer and even sperm whales.

More common, less iconic mammals abound. Although some are nocturnal, those you may come across once you leave behind well-trodden trails include wild boar *(jabalí),* red deer *(ciervo),* roe deer *(corzo),* fallow deer *(gamo),* genet *(gineta),* Egyptian mongoose *(meloncillo),* red squirrel *(ardilla),* badger *(tejón)* and otter *(nutria).*

Endangered Lynx

The Iberian (or pardel) lynx *(lince ibérico* to Spaniards; *Lynx pardina* to scientists) is the most endangered cat species in the world. The species once ranged across southern Europe (the Hispanic Legions of the Roman Empire wore breastplates adorned with the Iberian lynx) and a century ago there were still 100,000 Iberian lynx left in the wild. Now there are around 320 in Andalucía, confined to two main areas: Doñana national and natural parks, and the Sierra Morena in northern Jaén province.

LANDSCAPE & WILDLIFE WILDLIFE

Common Tree Species

Holm oak

Cork oak

Spanish fir

Eucalyptus

Poplar

Olive

So plentiful was the lynx until 1966 that the Spanish government classed it as 'vermin', encouraging hunters to declare open season on the cat. By 1973, the species was officially protected. But this has, until recently, done little to slow the lynx's precipitous decline, prompting fears that it would soon be the first cat species to become extinct since the sabre-toothed tiger, 10,000 years ago. Until 2007, when the Spanish government confirmed the presence of 15 Iberian lynx in the Montes de Toledo region of Castilla-La Mancha, the only proven breeding populations were in two areas of Andalucía: one is the eastern Sierra Morena, with perhaps 200 to 220 adult lynx; the other is the Parque Nacional de Doñana, with around 100 to 110 adult lynx.

A falling rabbit population, caused by disease and hunting, has played a significant role in the lynx's demise, but human beings are the primary offenders. Of all lynx deaths since 2000, almost 80% were caused directly by humans through a loss of habitat due to new farmland, roads, dams and pine or eucalyptus plantations; illegal traps and snares set for other animals (especially foxes and wolves); and road accidents (33 lynx were run over in the area around the Parque Nacional de Doñana from 1995 to 2006).

But there are tentative signs that the lynx may have turned the corner. An in-captivity breeding program was set up at El Acebuche in Parque Nacional de Doñana in 1992 and it has proved an extraordinary success: 18 lynx were born in the first four months of 2009 alone. Live film of lynxes in the breeding program is displayed on a screen at the Parque Nacional de Doñana's El Acebuche visitor centre, though the breeding centre itself is closed to the public. There are also breeding centres elsewhere in Andalucía, including at Jerez de la Frontera's zoo and in the Sierra de Andújar, Jaén province. Lynx conservation passed a milestone in 2015, when the animal was taken off the 'critically endangered list' thanks to a steady increase in its distribution and overall numbers in the last half decade.

Birdwatcher's Paradise

Andalucía is something of a last refuge for large mammal species, and serves a similar purpose for several highly endangered raptor species. When it comes to migratory bird species, however, Andalucía is a veritable superhighway.

For many in the birdwatching fraternity, raptors are the most loved birds of the avian world. Andalucía has 13 resident raptor species, as well as a handful of summer visitors from Africa. Glowering in the almost-sinister manner of its kind, Europe's biggest bird, the rare and endangered black vulture *(buitre negro)* has established a stronghold in the Sierra Morena, with around 230 pairs scattered from Huelva's Sierra Pelada to Jaén's Sierra de Andújar. As probably the world's biggest population of black vultures, survival here is critical to the viability of the species.

Also emblematic and extremely rare is the Spanish imperial eagle *(águila imperial ibérica)*, found in no other country. Its total numbers have increased from about 50 pairs in the 1960s to some 200 pairs today, helped by an active government protection plan operative since 1960. About 50 pairs are in Andalucía – mostly in the Sierra Morena, with about eight pairs in the Doñana area. Poisoned bait put out by farmers or hunters is the imperial's greatest enemy.

The bearded vulture or lammergeier *(quebrantahuesos)*, with its majestic 2m-plus wingspan, disappeared from Andalucía – its last refuge in Spain except for the Pyrenees – in 1986. But all, it seems, is not lost. A breeding centre has been established in the Parque Natural Sierras de Cazorla, Segura y las Villas and, as a first step, three young bearded vultures were released into the wild in 2006. As of 2012, about 20 bearded vultures had successfully adapted to life in the wild.

Other large birds of prey in Andalucía include the golden eagle *(águila real)*, the griffon vulture *(buitre leonado)* and the Egyptian vulture *(alimoche)*, all found in mountain regions.

If Andalucía's raptors lend gravitas to birdwatching here, the waterbirds that visit Andalucía add a scale rarely seen in Europe. Andalucía is a haven for waterbirds, mainly thanks to extensive wetlands along the Atlantic coast, such as those at the mouths of the Guadalquivir and Odiel rivers. Hundreds of thousands of migratory birds, including an estimated 80% of Western Europe's wild ducks, winter in the Doñana wetlands, and many more call in during spring and autumn migrations.

Laguna de Fuente de Piedra, near Antequera, sees as many as 20,000 greater flamingo *(flamenco)* pairs rearing chicks in spring and summer. This beautiful pink bird can also be seen in several other places, including Cabo de Gata, Doñana and the Paraje Natural Marismas del Odiel; the last has extensive wetlands that serve as a haven for other waterbirds.

The large, ungainly white stork *(cigüeña blanca)*, actually black and white, nests from spring to summer on electricity pylons, trees and towers (sometimes right in the middle of towns) across western Andalucía; the Dehesa de Abajo is home to a large woodland colony.

For more information on Andalucía's bird life, check out the website of SEO/BirdLife (www.seo.org).

Flamenco

Reflective but uplifting, raw but layered, pure yet loaded with historical and emotional complexity, flamenco is far more than just a musical genre – it's a culture unto itself. Some cite the importance of Spain's Roma in flamenco's embryonic development, others emphasise the key role of the Moors, Jews or even Byzantines; almost all agree that the circumstances that sparked its genesis were unique. Flamenco, proudly and unequivocally a product of Andalucía, couldn't have happened anywhere else.

Basics

One of the beauties of flamenco is its lack of straightforwardness – online searches and historical sleuthing usually throw up more questions than answers. A handful of basic points offer some clarity. First, flamenco is an expressive art, incorporating more than just music. In the early days it was a realistic reflection of the lives of those who sang it – the oppressed – and they carried it with them everywhere: in the fields, at work, at home and in their famed *juergas* (Roma parties). Second, it is very much a 'live' spectacle and – for purists at least – a necessarily spontaneous one. The preserve of the nomadic Roma until the 19th century, performances were never rehearsed or theatrical, and the best ones still aren't. Third, flamenco hinges on the interaction between its four basic elements: the *cante* (song), the *baile* (dance), the *toque* (guitar), and an oft-forgotten fourth element known as the *jaleo* (handclaps, shouts and audience participation/appreciation). The *cante* sits centre stage, as the guide. In its earliest incarnations, flamenco didn't have regular dancers, and guitars weren't added until the 19th century. Some flamenco forms, such as *martinetes* and *carceleras*, remain voice only. In traditional flamenco performances, players warm up slowly, tuning their guitars and clearing their throats while the gathered crowd talk among themselves. It is up to the dancers and musicians to grab the audience's attention and gradually lure them in.

Best Cultural Centres

Palacio de los Olvidados, Granada

Casa de la Memoria, Seville

Casa del Arte Flamenco, Granada

Flamenco Palos (Musical Forms)

The purist expression of flamenco is known as *cante jondo* (literally 'deep song'), a primitive collection of *palos* that includes *soleares* (quintessential flamenco *palo* with a strong, strict rhythm), *siguiriyas* (tragic and expressive flamenco *palo*), *tientos*, *martinetes* and *carceleras*. *Cante jondo* is considered to be the main building block of flamenco and good singers – whose gravelly, operatic voices can sound like a cross between Tom Waits and Pavarotti – are required to sing as if their lives depended upon it, and leave a piece of their soul in every stanza. The raw emotion and almost religious absorption of these powerful performers can be rather unnerving to the uninitiated. The aim is to inspire *duende* – the musical spirit that reaches out and touches your soul during an ecstatic live performance. But *duende* can be elusive. The poet Federico García Lorca, in his many commentaries on the subject, often alluded to its intangibility. Thus, it is up to the singer to summon it up, amalgamating yearning, superstition, anguish and fervour into a force that is both intimate and transcendental.

The other main grouping of flamenco songs is called *cantes chicos* (little songs), *palos* that are more light-hearted and accessible derivatives of *cante jondo*. Popular *cantes chicos* are the upbeat *alegrías* from Cádiz, descended from sailor's jigs; the fast but tongue-in-cheek *bulerías* from Jerez; and the ubiquitous tangos made popular by the great Sevillana singer La Niña de los Peines.

A third, more nebulous, group of *palos* (sometimes called *cantes andaluzes*) exists outside of what most aficionados would call 'pure' flamenco. This consists mainly of fandangos which are descended from Spanish folk music, with each region broadcasting their own variation. The most famous are the strident Fandangos de Huelva, enthusiastically danced during the religious pilgrimage Romería del Rocío. *Verdiales*, an ancient Arabic-style song/dance, are a type of fandango from Málaga, a province that also concocted the freer and easier (and undanced) *malagueñas*. *Granainas* are an ornamental and introspective fandango offshoot from Granada with no set rhythm; *tarantas* are an earthier, sparser version of the form from the mining communities of the Levante (Almería).

Other, hard-to-classify, *cantes* are *farrucas*, folk dances thought to have originated in Galicia, and *sevillanas*, a quintessential Andalucian fiesta dance best seen at Seville's annual Feria de Abril. A more recent subgenre of flamenco are the *ida y vuelta* (return) *palos*, musical forms that have been sugar-frosted with influences from Latin America before being 'returned' to Spain. The most widely circulated are the *guajira* and *rumba palos* from Cuba and the *columbianas* from Colombia.

The *sevillana palo* doesn't actually originate in Seville. Rather it is a long-standing folk dance, originally called a *seguidilla*, thought to hail from the Castile region. Since the mid-19th century it has been the de rigueur dance at Seville's Feria de Abril.

Historical Roots

The origins of flamenco are intriguingly vague. The long-time preserve of marginalised and culturally oppressed people (most of whom were illiterate), it was neither written about nor eulogised in its early days. Instead, the music was passed through bloodlines by word of mouth. No published testimonies exist before 1840.

The genesis of the art as we now know it was ignited in Andalucía sometime in the early 15th century, among disparate groups of Roma, Jews, Moors and ordinary Spaniards. Anthropological evidence suggests that the nomadic Roma had begun a 400-year-long western migration from the Indian subcontinent in the 11th century, settling all over Europe, with a southern contingent reaching Andalucía in the early 1400s. The Roma brought with them a dynamic form of musical expression – a way of performing that encouraged embellishment, virtuosity and improvisation – and they blended this rich musicality with the songs and melodies of the regions where they settled. In Andalucía, they found natural allies among the Jews and Moors recently disenfranchised by the Reconquista (Christian reconquest). The collision of these three distinct cultures and the subsequent marinating of their music and culture over three or four centuries resulted in what we now know as *cante jondo*, or pure flamenco.

A Tale of Three Cities

Flamenco is a world music these days, its power and influence enjoyed by theatre-goers in Bógota and dancers in New York. But it is in the music's Andalucian heartland – the region that conceived, shaped and popularised it – where you'll hear it at its purest and best.

Saetas are religious laments that are often included under the name 'flamenco'. You'll still hear them sung unaccompanied from upper-floor balconies during Semana Santa processions as the float passes beneath.

The Ortegas are one of the great Roma families. It's produced such flamenco singers as El Fillo (Francisco Ortega Vargas) and El Caracol ('The Snail'; Manuel Ortega Juárez), as well as legendary bullfighters such as Joselito 'El Gallo' ('The Rooster'; José Gómez Ortega)

FLAMENCO LEGENDS

El Planeta (1785–1850) Legendary Roma blacksmith who purportedly invented many unaccompanied *cantes* (songs).

El Fillo (1829–78) Protégée of El Planeta and famed for his gravelly voice, dubbed the *voz afillá*.

Silverio Franconetti (1831–89) Non-Roma who met El Fillo in Morón de la Frontera. Became an accomplished singer and set up Spain's most famous *café cantante* in Seville.

Antonio Chacón (1869–1929) Non-Roma singer with a powerful voice. Hired by Franconetti to sing in his Seville *café cantante* in the 1890s.

Ramón Montoya (1880–1949) Accompanist to Chacón from 1922 onwards – he put the guitar centre stage in flamenco.

La Niña de los Peines (1890–1969) Dynamic Roma singer from Seville who sang with Chacón and provided a vital link between the golden age and the 1950s revivalists.

El Caracol (1909–73) Discovered at age 12 at the Concurso de Cante Jondo in 1922. Went on to become one of the greatest, yet most self-destructive, flamenco singers of all time.

Camarón de la Isla (1950–92) Performed in a club owned by El Caracol; this modern flamenco 'god' from San Fernando (La Isla) lived fast, died young and dabbled in bold experimentation.

Paco de Lucía (1947–2014) Guitar phenomenon from Algeciras who became Camarón's main accompanist, and successfully crossed over into jazz and classical music.

The music's documented history begins in the early 19th century and is essentially a tale of three cities in western Andalucía: Seville, Cádiz and Jerez, and their respective Roma neighbourhoods. Jerez has often been coined the 'cradle of flamenco', primarily because its densely packed Roma quarters of Santiago and San Miguel have produced so many great artists. Today, the city is home to Andalucía's main flamenco centre/school and hosts two major festivals: Festival de Jerez (in February) and Fiestas de Ontoñō (in September). Flamenco in Cádiz grew up in the Santa María neighbourhood, wedged romantically against the crashing ocean; while in Seville its font was the riverside Roma district of Triana. Draw a line between these three cities and you'll capture a handful of other towns with strong flamenco traditions, mainly in Sevilla province.

The first real flamenco singer of note was the mysteriously named El Planeta (Antonio Monge Rivero), a Roma blacksmith born in either Jerez or Cádiz around 1785. El Planeta wasn't a performer in the modern sense, but he soon became well known for his passionate singing voice, which rang eloquently out of his forge and gave birth – allegedly – to such early flamenco *palos* as *martinetes* and *livianas*. El Planeta sits at the head of a flamenco family tree of interrelated singers, musicians and dancers, which has carried on to the present day. His immediate heir was El Fillo (Francisco Ortega Vargas), whose naturally gravelly voice became the standard to which all others were compared.

Best Festivals

Festival de Jerez, Jerez de la Frontera

Bienal de Flamenco, Seville

Potaje Gitano de Utrera, Utrera

Golden Age

Flamenco's so-called 'golden age' began in the late 1840s and lasted until around 1915. In the space of 70 years, the music metamorphosed from an esoteric Roma art practised spontaneously at raucous *juergas*, into a professional and increasingly popular form of public entertainment that merged *cante jondo* with other forms of Spanish folkloric music.

It was during this fertile epoch that the modern musical forms took shape. Other innovations included the more complex choreography of flamenco dance and the emergence of the guitar as the de rigueur accompanying instrument.

The catalysts for change were the famous *cafés cantantes* that took root in many Spanish cities, especially in Andalucía. The first cafe opened in Seville in 1842, and the establishments gradually spread, reaching their apex in the 1880s with prestigious venues such as the Café Silverio in Seville. Decorated with mirrors, bullfighting posters, gilded stages, and tables where patrons could enjoy alcoholic beverages, the cafes were the engine rooms of a dramatic musical cross-fertilisation not dissimilar to the blues-country fusion that later spat out rock and roll. Presiding over this conflation was Silverio Franconetti, proprietor of Seville's Café Silverio and soulful inheritor of El Fillo's *voz afillá* (hoarse, cracked voice in the style of the singer El Fillo). Yet, despite his Roma blood and lifelong penchant for *siguiriyas* and *soleares*, Franconetti couldn't stop the bastardisation of the music he loved as it fled from the *juergas* into the cafes, substituting tragic harshness for tuneful palatability. Unwittingly, he had created the catalyst for flamenco's jump from music of the Roma to popular property.

Best Peñas

Peña de la Platería, Granada

Peña Flamenca La Perla, Cádiz

Peña Juan Breva, Málaga

FLAMENCO SLIDE INTO DECADENCE

Slide into Decadence

In 1920 pure flamenco, threatened by changing public tastes and impending political crises, was an endangered species. Fearing oblivion,

---

FLAMENCO TRIANGLE

Six cities located within a rough nodule of land in southwest Andalucía make up the so-called flamenco triangle.

Seville Thanks to its size and cultural importance, Seville played a vital role in flamenco's early evolution. Much of the music's inspiration came from the gritty Roma neighbourhood of Triana, famous for its sad laments known as *soleares*. Seville was also the main breeding ground of the *café cantante* scene that popularised flamenco during the late 19th century.

Morón de la Frontera Many flamenco legends passed through Morón in the 19th century, but it wasn't until the 1960s that the town became influential, establishing its annual Gazpacho festival and opening the pioneering Espartero Flamenco School under the auspices of American flamencologist Donn E Pohren. Morón is still famed for its eloquent guitarists, in particular Juan de Gastor.

Utrera Utrera's annual Potaje festival was started by a local Roma brotherhood in 1957 and is one of the oldest flamenco festivals in Spain. The town has long been home to many notable flamenco families, including sisters Fernanda and Bernanda de Utrera, who found fame singing haunting *soleares* in the 1960s.

Lebrija The city on the edge of the marshes was the birthplace in 1863 of the pioneering Roma singer El Pinini, an early exponent of upbeat *cantiñas* and head of the influential Pena clan who later migrated to Utrera. Its annual flamenco festival, the Carocolá, conceived in 1966, is named for its *carocoles* (snails), served as a food accompaniment.

Jerez de la Frontera Nowhere epitomises flamenco like Jerez, a city with two proudly traditional Roma neighbourhoods that between them have produced a steady stream of legendary singers. The city also invented its own unique flamenco musical form – the fast, buoyant *bulerías*.

Cádiz Jerez' near neighbour was another early flamenco innovator, its sailor's *jotas* (jigs) evolving into *alegrías*, one of flamenco's more joyous musical subgenres. The city's Roma neighbourhood, the Barrio Santa María, is a maze of narrow streets patrolled by troubadours and seagulls.

Andalucian aesthetes Federico Lorca and Manuel de Falla organised a competition in Granada in 1922 to try to save the art – the Concurso de Cante Jondo. But with the civil war approaching, the die was cast. The music entered an era known as *ópera flamenco*, when *cante jondo* was diluted further by folk music, greater commercialisation and imported foreign influences from Latin America. The controversial figure of the moment was Pepe Marchena (1903–76), flamenco's first well-paid superstar who broke with tradition by singing lighter fandangos and *cantes de ida y vuelta*, often backed by an orchestra. Purists were understandably leery, while others saw it as the natural evolution of a music that had leapt suddenly into the public domain. Just below the radar, *cante jondo* survived, in part because it was still performed by Roma singers such as Manuel Torre and La Niña de los Peines, the greatest male and female voices of their age.

Translated Stage Names

Camarón de la Isla – Shrimp from the Island

El Caracol – The Snail

La Niña de los Peines – Girl of the Combs

Tomatito – Little Tomato

Rebirth

By the 1950s, the re-evaluation of *cante jondo* fell to Antonio Mairena (1909–83), an impassioned Roma *cantaor* (singer) from Seville province and the first real flamencologist to historically decipher the art. Mairena insisted on singing only old forms of *palos,* such as *siguiriyas* and *martinetes*, many of which he rescued from almost certain extinction. Through his stubborn refusal to pamper to commercial tastes, he provided a lifeline between the golden age and the revival that was to come.

By the 1960s, nascent *tablaos* – nightclubs staging professional flamenco shows – had filled the vacuum left by the closure of the *cafés cantantes* in the 1920s. Some *tablaos,* particularly those in the new

---

CONCURSO DE CANTE JONDO, 1922

On an ethereal summer's evening in June 1922, a little-known Andalucian poet named Federico García Lorca stood in the Plaza de Aljibes in Granada's Alhambra and welcomed 4000 guests to the Concurso de Cante Jondo (competition of 'deep song'), a flamenco singing contest he had organised in collusion with the distinguished Spanish classical composer Manuel de Falla.

Between them, Spain's two great avant-garde thinkers had struggled relentlessly in their bid to elevate flamenco – and in particular *cante jondo* – into a serious art form, a dynamic cultural genre of half-forgotten Andalucian folkloric traditions that was being asphyxiated by a growing penchant for watered-down forms of flamenco 'opera'.

Amassed inside the atmospheric confines of the Alhambra were an impressive array of intellectuals, writers, performers, musicians and flamenco purists. One 72-year-old *cantaor* (singer) named Tio Bermúdez had walked 100km from his home village to be there, and stunned the audience with his interpretations of old-style *siguiriyas*. Another, an old blind woman of Roma stock exhaustively hunted down by Lorca, sang an unaccompanied *liviana*, a flamenco form long thought to be dead. A 12-year-old boy named Manolo Ortega, aka 'El Caracol' ('The Snail'), so impressed the judges that he walked off with first prize. Gathered beneath the cypress trees in a courtyard filled with the aroma of jasmine and lavender, young men swapped guitar *falsetas* (riffs), ladies stood up and danced *soleares*, while others listened to the virtuosity of established stars such as Ramón Montoya and Manuel Torre. The complex – observers later reported – seemed to be alive with a magical energy.

Whether the *concurso* ultimately 'saved' flamenco is open to debate. While the music gained some short-lived prestige, and sporadic recordings and revivals ensued, its golden age was well and truly over. An era of decadence followed, hastened by the onset of the civil war and the repressive Franco dictatorship that followed. Flamenco's modern rebirth ultimately had to wait for a second *concurso* in Córdoba in 1956, and the subsequent rise of more ground-breaking innovators over a decade later.

resort towns on the coast, were fake and insipid, while others played a role in re-establishing *cante jondo* alongside the newer forms of *palos*. Flamenco's ultimate revival was spearheaded, however, not by venues but by the exciting performers who frequented them. Two in particular stood out. Paco de Lucía from Algeciras was a guitarist so precocious that by age 14 he had absorbed everything any living musician could teach. His muse and foil was Camerón de la Isla, a Roma singer from San Fernando (La Isla), who by the early 1970s had attained the kind of godlike status normally reserved for rock stars and bullfighters. Between them, Camerón and Lucía took flamenco to a different level, injecting it with out-of-the box innovations (such as electric guitars and keyboards) while, at the same time, carefully safeguarding its purity. Suddenly the rest of the world was sitting up and taking notice.

Modern Flamenco

In the 1970s musicians began mixing flamenco with jazz, rock, blues, rap and other genres. The purists loathed these changes, but this *nuevo* flamenco (new flamenco) greatly broadened flamenco's appeal. The seminal recording was a 1977 flamenco-folk-rock album, *Veneno* (Poison), by the group of the same name centred on Kiko Veneno and Raimundo Amador, both from Seville.

The group Ketama, whose key members were all from Granada's Montoya flamenco family, were crucial in bringing flamenco to a younger audience in the 1980s and '90s, mixing the music with African, Cuban, Brazilian and other rhythms. Wide-ranging in their search for complementary sounds, Ketama's *Songhai* (1987) and *Songhai II* (1995) – collaborations with Malian *kora* (harp) player Toumani Diabaté – were among the group's best albums. In 2002 the album *Dame la mano* shocked purists by crossing flamenco with rap. The group split soon after.

Flamenco today is as popular as it has ever been and probably more innovative. While established singers such as Enrique Morente, José Menese and Carmen Linares remain at the top of the profession, new generations continue to increase flamenco's audience. Among the most popular are José Mercé from Jerez, whose exciting album *Lío* (Entanglement; 2002) was a big seller, and El Barrio, a 21st-century urban poet from Cádiz. Other artists include Cádiz' Niña Pastori, who arrived in the late 1990s singing jazz- and Latin-influenced flamenco. Her albums, such as *Entre dos puertos* (Between Two Ports; 1997), *María* (2002) and *Joyas prestadas* (Borrowed Jewels; 2006), are great listening.

Flamenco dance has reached its most adventurous horizons in the person of Joaquín Cortés, born in Córdoba in 1969. Cortés fuses flamenco with contemporary dance, ballet and jazz, to music at rock-concert amplification. He tours frequently both in Spain and all over the world with spectacular solo or ensemble shows.

On the guitar, modern virtuosos include Manolo Sanlúcar from Cádiz, Tomatito from Almería (who used to accompany El Camarón de la Isla) and Vicente Amigo from Córdoba; they accompany today's top singers or perform solo.

FLAMENCO MODERN FLAMENCO

Best Tablaos

Tablao El Arenal, Seville

Jardines de Zoraya, Granada

El Palacio Andaluz, Seville

Home Town Flamenco Musical Forms

Alegrías – Cádiz

Bulerías – Jerez de la Frontera

Soleares – Seville

Tarantos – Almería

Fandangos – Huelva

Granaínas – Granada

Rondeñas – Ronda

Verdiales – Málaga

Andalucian Arts

For significant parts of Spanish history, Andalucía has stood at the forefront of the nation's artistic and cultural life. There has been no single high point. Instead, halcyon eras have come and gone, often ebbing and flowing with the power of Spain in world affairs. Though all the arts are well represented in Andalucía, the region has produced a particularly rich seam of talented painters, including two of the most influential masters to ever grace the world stage: Diego Velázquez and Pablo Picasso.

Córdoba Caliphate

Today Córdoba is a journeyman city of just over 300,000 people, famous for its ancient Mezquita and left-leaning political inclinations. However, 1000 years ago, it was the most populous and culturally vibrant city in Europe, possibly the world. The Córdoba of the 8th to 11th centuries was an intellectual powerhouse, replete with libraries, schools and a university that competed with the rival caliphate of Damascus to promote the global spread of ideas. Emir Abd ar-Rahman II (r 822–52) was a strong patron of the arts who maintained a close relationship with the influential Arabic poet and musician, Ziryab; Abd ar-Rahman III (r 912–61) filled his city Madinat al-Zahra with the finest Islamic art, crafts and mosaics, much of it copied from Byzantium artists; while Al-Hakim II (r 961–76) was an avid reader who collected and catalogued hundreds of thousands of books. Many of the great works of Greek philosophy were later translated and reinterpreted in medieval Córdoba by scholarly polymaths such as Averroës (1126–98), Maimonides (1135–1204) and Ibn Tufail (1105–85), who dabbled in both the sciences and the arts.

Though Córdoba's influence declined after its reconquest by the Christians in 1236, the invaders from the north subtly absorbed many of the city's work and ideas. It was partly through this intellectual inheritance that Western Europe attained the know-how and inspiration that sparked the Renaissance, a movement that took shape in Italy two centuries later.

Other artists may get more credit, but Andalucian painter Francisco Pacheco (1564–1644), from Sanlúcar de Barrameda, was teacher and mentor to numerous greats, including Diego Velázquez (who married his daughter) and Francisco Zurbarán.

Nasrid Flowering

The Nasrid emirate established in Granada in 1232 was more of a defensive entity than an outward-looking culture-spreader in the mould of Córdoba. However, its foppish rulers were vociferous appreciators of the arts, in particular poetry. Several of the emirate's sultans became acclaimed poets, most notably Yusuf III (1408–17), whose yearning, romantic verse acted as a prelude to the Byronic reawakening of poetry 400 years later. The highpoint of the Granadian flowering came during the illustrious reigns of Yusuf I (1333–54) and Muhammad V (1354–91), the two great builders of the Alhambra. Both sultans established literary circles in their courts. Yusuf employed Arabic poet and historian, Ibn al-Khatib (1313–75), whose verse was set to music and whose lyrical poems remain inscribed on the walls of Alhambra's palaces and fountains. Muhammad V installed al-Khatib as his *vizier* (political advisor), a position that stoked much political controversy at the time and possibly cost al-Khatib his life. In 1375, al-Khatib's student and fellow poet Ibn Zamrak (1333–93) hired assassins to kill him. Ibn Zamrak subsequently became court poet to Muhammad V, during an era when poetry and cultural exchange with Morocco and Egypt had created a healthy cross-continental flow of ideas.

Golden Century

For a brief but glittering 50 years during Spain's Siglo de Oro (Golden Century), ignited in 1492, Andalucian painters pretty much defined world art. The mantle rested on the shoulders of three Seville-based giants. Bartolomé Murillo (1617–82) was a baroque master with a delicate touch and a penchant for documentary and religious painting. Francisco de Zurbarán (1598–1664) was a more restrained exponent of the Italian art of *chiaroscuro* (the technique of contrasting light and dark elements in a painting to create a dramatic effect), born in Extremadura but intrinsically linked to the Seville school. Diego Velázquez (1599–1660) was the so-called artist's artist, whose exacting methods and subtle use of colour and tone opened up the doors to impressionism and ultimately made him an aesthetic guru. Velázquez's most celebrated work, *Las Meninas,* is a revolutionary masterpiece of illusion in which the artist depicts himself contemplating his invisible subjects, the King and Queen of Spain, whose faces appear reflected in a mirror. Three centuries after his death, an enamoured Picasso made 58 abstract attempts to reinterpret the great work.

Both Velázquez and Zurbarán were employed by the royal court of Philip IV, while Murillo was favoured by the Catholic Church. Murillo painted several works for Seville cathedral, but is best known for his interpretation of the Virgin Mary's Immaculate Conception, executed in 1650 and now displayed in Madrid's El Prado. Velázquez and Zurbarán tackled the same topic in 1618 and 1630, respectively.

Preceding the artistic revolution, and in the days when flamenco was still an esoteric Roma art, Spanish music, soaking up contemporary Italian traditions, gained wider European recognition through Renaissance composers such as Francisco Guerrero (1528–99). Guerrero, the main choir master at Seville cathedral, composed sacred and secular music heavy with conservative and Gregorian traditions. His mantle was carried on by his assistant Alonso Lobo (1555–1617), from Osuna, whose

ANDALUCIAN ARTS GOLDEN CENTURY

Byron first visited Andalucía in 1809. Inspired by the experience, he wrote his mock-epic poetic masterpiece *Don Juan,* based on the famous Spanish fictional hero, in the early 1820s.

IMMACULATE CONCEPTIONS

Spend more than an hour in a baroque art gallery in Andalucía and you'll almost certainly encounter a painting honouring the *Inmaculada Concepción* (Immaculate Conception). A longstanding devotional cult in Spain, the rendering of this holy image, depicting an adolescent Virgin Mary looking heavenwards, with 12 stars above her head and a moon beneath her feet, reflects the Catholic belief that Mary was born free of original sin.

Debate about the doctrine emerged in 1613 in Seville, when a Dominican friar denounced it from the pulpit, prompting a backlash from the Jesuits who were enthusiastically supported by the Spanish Crown. The Spanish kings subsequently used the leading painters of the day to spread their propagandist message about the 'Conception', using potent religious iconography. The rules of how to paint the image were first codified by Francisco Pacheco in 1649, in his book *Arte de la Pintura* (The Art of Painting). A fervent royalist and believer in Catholic doctrine, Pacheco was also a teacher to future masters Diego Velázquez and Alonso Cano, and was key in ensuring the iconography was widely adopted. A rare early attempt at the *Inmaculada* by Velázquez can be seen in Seville's Hospital de los Venerables Sacerdotes. Later baroque masters, including Zurbarán and Murillo, were equally enamoured with the *Inmaculada,* with Murillo painting it at least a dozen times. One of his finest renditions (perhaps the greatest *Inmaculada* ever painted) hangs in a converted chapel in Seville's Museo de Bellas Artes.

devout works – including hymns, masses and psalms – helped cement Seville as a fermenting ground for sacred music.

A contemporary of Miguel de Cervantes, but active primarily in the poetic sphere, Luís de Góngora (1561–1627), from Córdoba, was a baroque wordsmith, as famous for his life-long feud with writing rival (and contemporary) Francisco de Quevedo as for his effortless lyricism. He was ground-breaking enough to have a genre of writing named after him: Gongorismo, a style that stood the test of time and was enthusiastically revived by Federico Lorca and the Generación de '27 three centuries after the master's demise.

Generation of '98

The Andalucian art scene dimmed in the 18th and 19th centuries as Spain lost its overseas empire and position as a global power. Just as the decline looked to be terminal after Spain's humiliation in the Spanish-American war in 1898, a wake-up call was sounded by a group of critical writers known as the Generación de '98. The circle, led by Seville-born social realist poet Antonio Machado (1875–1939) chided the nation for being asleep, adrift in a sea of mediocrity, and their critical works, flecked with rebellion and realism, aimed to offset the cultural malaise and re-establish the nation's literary prominence. Around the same time, classical music found a cohesive Iberian voice in a group of four Spanish composers, two of whom were from Andalucía. Both Manuel de Falla (1876–1946) from Cádiz and Joaquín Turina (1882–1949) from Seville used influences absorbed from the Parisian impressionists, Debussy and Ravel, to craft operas, songs and chamber music that resonated with echoes of Andalucian folklore. Falla, in particular, was fascinated by flamenco; along with poet Federico García Lorca he organised the Concurso de Cante Jondo in 1922.

Generation of '27

From time to time, exceptional circumstances prompt the flowering of exceptional artistic movements. Post-war rigidity in the US led to the rise of the hedonistic Beat poets. In early-20th-century London, the Bloomsbury Set reacted noisily against so-called Victorian values. Spain's great blossoming took place in the small window of serenity between the end of WWI and the onset of the Spanish Civil War. In 1927 in Seville, a key group of 10 Spanish poets came together to mark the 300th anniversary of the death of lyrical baroque master Luís de Góngora. The meeting had a strong southern bias. Of the 10, six were born in Andalucía, including the peerless Federico García Lorca (from Granada), the romantic-turned-polemicist poet Rafael Alberti (from El Puerto de Santa María), and the surrealist wordsmith Vicente Aleixandre (from Seville).

Julio Romero de Torres (1874–1930) was a realist artist from Córdoba born a few years before Picasso, who consequently often fell into the shadow of the Cubist master. He embraced realism and is known for his haunting studies of Spanish women.

Unlike the more pessimistic Generación de '98, which had criticised the conformism of Spain after the restoration of the monarchy in 1874, the 27ers were less damning of what had gone before in their exploration of classic themes such as love, death, destiny and the beauty of images. Obsessed by the work of Góngora, they espoused wider poetic expressionism and free verse, combining elements of the new surrealism with echoes from Spain's ancient folkloric tradition (in particular, flamenco). The movement was ultimately shattered and dispersed by the Civil War, an event that killed Lorca and sent many of the others into a long exile.

The last surviving member of the Generación de '27, Francisco Ayala from Granada died in 2009 aged 103. Ayala spent many years in exile in Argentina and Puerto Rico after his father and brother were murdered by Nationalists in the Civil War.

PICASSO RECLAIMED

Ironically for a boy given multiple names at birth, Picasso became famous for signing his paintings with just one. Born in Málaga in 1881 to an artist father, Don José Ruíz y Blasco (also Málaga-born), the young Pablo lived in the city until he was 10. In 1891 he moved with his family to A Coruña in the Galicia region and then, in 1895, to Barcelona where he ultimately established his artistic reputation. Since he never returned permanently to Málaga, Picasso's connection with Andalucía has often been understated; you'll find better expositions of his art in Barcelona and Paris. But with Málaga undergoing a cultural reawakening in the late 1990s, the city has taken steps to reclaim him. The Picasso Foundation was established in 1988 in his Casa Natal (birth house) in Plaza de la Merced and, in 2003, after 50 years of on-off planning, the Museo Picasso Málaga was opened in a 16th-century palace to honour its most famous native son.

Lorca – Man of Many Talents

Andalucia's (and Spain's) greatest writer, Federico García Lorca, is best known for his poems and plays and – more tragically – his senseless murder at the hands of Spanish fascists at the start of the Civil War. But Lorca's talents went far beyond verse. The Granada-born writer was an accomplished pianist, an actor with a rural theatre troupe, a director of his own and other people's plays, and a deft cultural organiser (he was instrumental in conceiving the Concurso de Cante Jondo, along with classical composer Manuel de Falla, in 1922). In collusion with Falla, Lorca also co-composed an unfinished opera, *Lola, la Comedianta;* inspired by another friend, Salvador Dalí, he demonstrated his skill for art – his drawings and paintings were published in books and displayed at exhibitions. Lorca once even drafted a surrealistic film screenplay titled *Viaje a la Luna* (A Trip to the Moon; not filmed until 1998).

Dead by the age of 38, Lorca's achievements were squeezed into a fertile two decades between the years 1918 and 1936, when he was shot and slung into an unmarked grave just outside Granada. Not surprisingly, his legacy is massive and regularly refuelled by the seemingly eternal search for his remains. They are thought to lie somewhere near the village of Viznar, beneath the pastoral Vega he loved so dearly.

The 2008 British-Spanish film *Little Ashes* (*Cenicitas*) is based on longstanding rumours of a 1920s love affair between Federico García Lorca and Salvador Dalí.

Twentieth Century & Beyond

The huge task for 20th- and 21st-century Andalucian writers and artists has been escaping the shadow left by Picasso and Lorca. Heading the post-Franco literary generation is Antonio Muñoz Molina, a novelist and essayist from Úbeda best known for his book *Sefarad* (2003), an exploration of the Jewish experience – from their expulsion from Spain to the Holocaust. António Soler from Málaga added another new voice with his novel *El Camino de los Ingleses* (The Way of the English; 2004) tracking a group of friends' summer of transition from adolescence to adulthood. The book was made into a film starring Antonio Banderas. One of Andalucía finest contemporary writers is Jaén-born Salvador Compán, a specialist in short novellas, the most recent of which, *Palabras insensatas que tú comprenderás* (Foolish Words That You Will Understand) was published in 2012.

In the art world, Madrid's identity-searching *Movida* movement (the post-Franco cultural awakening) included gay pop artists Enrique Naya and José Carrero from Cádiz. Operating jointly under the name Costus, their Madrid apartment/studio became a metaphoric G-spot for the *Movida*'s main protagonists, including film director Pedro Almodóvar, who featured it in his cult movie *Pepi, Luci, Bom y Otras Chicas del Montón* (Pepi, Luci, Bom and Other Girls on the Heap; 1980).

Bullfighting

There is no more controversial issue in Spain than bullfighting. Already banned in two of the country's autonomous communities (Catalonia and the Canary Islands), the opposition to this divisive but historically complex practice has grown considerably in recent years, though it's unlikely Andalucía will cave in any time soon. Spain's southernmost region is where modern bullfighting was invented and it has produced the lion's share of the nation's legendary matadors.

For & Against

Supporters of bullfighting emphasise its historical legacy and high-profile place in Spanish culture. Some advocates go further claiming that *corridas* (bullfights) are less cruel than slaughterhouses; fighting bulls, they argue, live longer in better conditions than domestic beasts. For its opponents, however, bullfighting is intolerably cruel, an unashamed blood sport and a blight on Spain's conscience in these supposedly more enlightened times. The antibullfighting lobby is bigger and more influential in parts of northern Spain. Spanish antibullfighting organisations include the Barcelona-based Asociación para la Defensa de los Derechos del Animal (Association for the Defence of Animal Rights; www.addaong.org). The British-based League Against Cruel Sports (www.league.org.uk), established in 1924, also campaigns against bullfighting. For information about creative protests against bullfighting, visit www.runningofthenudes.com.

An *espontáneo* is a spectator at a bullfight who illegally jumps into the ring and attempts to fight the bull. Famous matador 'El Cordobés' controversially launched his career this way. Ironically, years later, one of his own fights was interrupted by a less lucky *espontáneo* who was fatally gored.

History

Culturally speaking, bullfighting shares many similarities with flamenco: its roots are foggy, the practice is distinctively Spanish (and Andalucian) in nature and the inherent skills have traditionally been passed down through bloodlines in various dynasties or families.

Some historical testimonies suggest it was Roman emperor Claudius who introduced bullfighting to Spain. However, it was the Moors who refined what was then an unregulated spectacle by adding ritualistic moves and employing the use of horses. The practice was largely the preserve of the horse-riding nobility until the early 1700s, when an Andalucian from Ronda named Francisco Romero got down from his mount, feinted a few times with a cape and killed the bull with a sword to end the *corrida*. Francisco's methods quickly gained popularity and he became the first professional bullfighter and head of a famous Ronda-Romero dynasty. Francisco's son Juan Romero evolved bullfighting further by adding the *cuadrilla* (bullfighting team). Despite his dangerous profession, Juan allegedly lived until the age of 102. Third in line, Pedro (Francisco's grandson) remains the most celebrated bullfighter of all time, with more than 5000 bulls slain in a 60-year career. Pedro introduced theatrics to bullfighting and established it as a serious pursuit. His methods remained commonplace for nearly a century.

Bullfighting's 'golden age' came in the 1910s when it was transformed from an ostentatious 'circus act' into a breathtaking show of aesthet-

HISTORIC BULLRINGS

There are close to 70 bullfighting rings in Andalucía. The season runs from Easter Sunday to October. The cities with the strongest traditions are Seville and Ronda.

Seville Home to La Maestranza, the so-called 'Catedral del Toreo' (Cathedral of Bullfighting) and the oldest bullfighting venue in the world, dating from 1761. The biggest program runs in tandem with the Feria de Abril.

Ronda The neoclassical Plaza de Toros de Ronda was built in 1784 and was frequented by Pedro Romero and, later, the Ordóñez clan. The Corrida Goyesca festival is held here in September. It is the world's largest ring by size at 66m in diameter.

El Puerto de Santa María A Cádiz-province town with a big bullfighting legacy and a 15,000-capacity ring dating from 1880.

Antequera Surrounded by parkland, Antequera's bullring was rebuilt in 1984 to its original 1848 design. It has a museum on-site.

Málaga The famous Malagueta opened in 1878 and was built in neo-Mudéjar style. It holds 14,000 spectators.

Córdoba The Plaza de los Califas, built in 1965, has Andalucía's largest seating capacity with room for nearly 17,000 spectators.

Osuna This small bullring dating from 1904 gained new fame in 2014 when scenes from the TV series *Game of Thrones* (season five) were filmed there.

ics and technicality with a miniscule margin for error. The change was prompted by a famous rivalry between two matadors: Juan Belmonte and Joselito 'El Gallo.' Regarded as the two greatest bullfighters in history, they were born within three years of each other in Sevilla province.

Juan Belmonte (1892–1962) had deformed legs. Unable to move like a classic matador, he elected to stand bolt upright and motionless in the ring until the bull was nearly upon him. He once quipped that he went into the ring like a 'mathematician proving a theorem'. This startling new technique kept the audience's hearts in their mouths and resulted in Belmonte getting gored more than 20 times; yet he lived. His rival Joselito (1895–1920) wasn't so lucky. Joselito was a child prodigy who adapted Belmonte's close-quarter methods. The two quickly became rivals and their duels with the *muleta* (the red cloth waved by the matador) between 1912 and 1920 are unlikely to be replicated. Joselito was fatally gored in 1920, a sacrificial 'death in the afternoon' that Hemingway – who went on to become a good friend of Belmonte – later wrote about in his famous book.

Doused in tradition, the essence of bullfighting has changed little since Joselito's demise. Manolete (1917–47), a notoriously serious bullfighter from Córdoba, added some of the short, close passes with the *muleta* that are now common in modern bullfighting, while his fellow Cordoban 'El Cordobés' combined flamboyance inside the ring with equally flamboyant antics outside it. Perhaps the greatest rivalry since the 1910s was between *madrileño* (inhabitant of Madrid) Luís Miguel Dominguín and Ronda stalwart Antonio Ordóñez, catalogued once again by Hemingway over the 'dangerous summer' of 1959.

Juan Carlos I, the former Spanish king, was once quoted as saying: 'the day the EU bans bullfighting is the day that Spain leaves the EU.'

The Fight

Bullfights usually begin at about 6pm and, as a rule, three different matadors will fight two bulls each. Each fight takes about 15 minutes.

After entering the arena, the bull is first moved about by junior bullfighters, known as *peones,* wielding great capes. The colourfully attired matador then puts in an initial appearance and makes *faenas* (moves) with the bull, such as pivoting before its horns. The more closely and calmly the matador works with the bull, the greater the crowd's appreciation. The matador leaves the stage to the *banderilleros,* who attempt to goad the bull into action by plunging a pair of *banderillas* (short prods with harpoon-style ends) into his withers. Next, the horseback *picadors* take over; they shove a lance into the withers, greatly weakening the bull. The matador then returns for the final session. When the bull seems tired out and unlikely to give a lot more, the matador chooses the moment for the kill. Facing the animal head-on, the matador aims to sink a sword cleanly into its neck for an instant kill – the *estocada.*

A skilful, daring performance followed by a clean kill will have the crowd on its feet; the crowd will wave handkerchiefs in appeal to the fight president to award the matador an ear of the animal.

Andalucian Kitchen

While other parts of Spain form constellations of Michelin stars and run kitchens that look more like chemistry labs than homely hearths, Andalucía revels in simple cuisine. The coast produces fish, the mountains nurture meat (including melt-in-your-mouth cured hams) and the ubiquitous olive groves provide the region's staple ingredient – olive oil. The twist in Andalucian cooking lies in its palpable Moorish inflections. The Moors pioneered the cultivation of rice and citrus fruits, and brought in pungent spices like cinnamon, nutmeg, coriander and saffron.

Fruits of the Sea

That old legend about the Costa del Sol megaresorts once being nothing more than a collection of fishing villages is largely true. Seafood is a way of life all along the Andalucian coast. It is a tradition forged in the days when Andalucía was one of Spain's poorest regions, and fishing fleets almost literally kept the region afloat. Fishing is now the preserve of big business, and the smaller fleets are something of an endangered species, surviving most often in nostalgic reminiscences in waterfront bars. But the spirit of the former age lives on, and the region's daily catch – from both the Mediterranean and Atlantic – is eagerly awaited by restaurant chefs, hungry patrons and *abuelas* (grandmothers) alike.

Andalucians eat fish in a variety of ways, but they are, above all, famous for their *pescaito frito* (fried fish). A particular specialty of Cádiz, El Puerto de Santa María and the Costa de la Luz (although you'll also find it in Granada), fried fish Andalucian-style is an art form with more subtlety than first appears. Just about anything that emerges from the sea is rolled in chickpea and wheat flour, shaken to remove the surplus, then deep-fried ever so briefly in olive oil, just long enough to form a light, golden crust that seals the essential goodness of the fish within. There are few products of the sea that don't get the deep-fry treatment, but the more common ones include *chipirones* or *chopitos* (baby squid), *cazón en adobo* (dogfish or shark that feed on shellfish, producing a strong, almost sweet flavour) and *tortilla de camarones*, a delicious, crispy frittata embedded with tiny shrimps.

Other choices you'll encounter again and again include: *boquerones* (anchovies), served either fried or marinated in garlic, olive oil and vinegar; *sardinas a la plancha* (grilled sardines); *gambas* (prawns) and *langostinos* (king prawns) served grilled, fried or cold with a bowl of fresh mayonnaise, with the most sought-after coming from Sanlúcar de Barrameda; *chanquetes* (similar to whitebait and served deep-fried), a speciality of Málaga; *ostras* (oysters); *pezespada* (swordfish); and *salmonetes* (red mullet). Stocks of *atún* (tuna) are rapidly depleting, but remain a favourite along the Costa de la Luz, especially in Barbate and Zahara de los Atunes.

At last count, there were nine Michelin-starred restaurants in Andalucía; only two – Dani García Restaurante in Marbella and Aponiente in El Puerto de Santa María – get two stars.

Prized bluefin tuna are still caught on the Costa de la Luz using the ancient *almadraba* method that utilises stretched, mazelike nets anchored to the sea floor. The technique has been employed for 3000 years and was pioneered by the Phoenicians.

Fruits of the Land

Coastal Andalucía is not alone in its devotion to the local produce. Andalucians from the interior make the grand (but by no means unfounded) claim to anyone who will listen that the olive and *jamón* (cured ham) – those mainstays of the Spanish table – produced here are the finest in all of Spain.

But *jamón* is not the only meat that Andalucians get excited about. Throughout the bullfighting season (around May to September), bars and restaurants proudly announce '*hay rabo de toro*', which roughly translates as, 'yes, we have bull's tail'.

Andalucians also love cheese, and although most are imported from elsewhere in Spain, there are exceptions. Typical Andalucian cheeses include Grazalema, from the mountains of Cádiz, made from ewes' milk and similar to Manchego; Málaga, a goats' cheese preserved in olive oil; and Cádiz, a strong, fresh goats' cheese made in the countryside around Cádiz.

Tejeringos are extralong churros (fried crunchy doughnuts) that have been wrapped into a spiral shape.

The region also produces what are arguably the finest fruits and vegetables in Spain, due to its generous climate. That's not to say that vegetables dominate most restaurant menus across this most carnivorous of regions – they're there, but usually in the background. The fantastic produce is eaten in season and generally bought fresh in open-air morning markets. Almería province, east of Málaga, is Europe's winter garden, with kilometres of plastic-covered hothouses of intensively grown vegetables.

Jamón

There is no greater taste-bud-teasing prospect than a few wafer-thin, succulent slices of *jamón*. Nearly every bar and restaurant in Andalucía has at least one *jamón* on the go at any one time, strapped into a cradlelike frame called a *jamónera*. More often, they have several hams, the skin and hooves still attached, hanging from the walls or ceiling.

Unlike Italian prosciutto, Spanish *jamón* is a bold, deep red, well marbled with buttery fat. At its best, it smells like the forest and the field. Like wines and olive oil, Spanish *jamón* is subject to a strict series of classifications. *Jamón serrano,* which accounts for around 90% of cured ham in Spain, refers to *jamón* made from white-coated pigs introduced to Spain in the 1950s. Once salted and semidried by the cold, dry winds of the Spanish sierra, most now go through a similar process of around a year's curing and drying in a climate-controlled shed.

Jamón ibérico, also called *pata negra* (black leg), is more expensive and comes from a black-coated pig indigenous to the Iberian peninsula

ORIGIN OF TAPAS

There are many stories concerning the origins of tapas. One holds that in the 13th century, doctors to King Alfonso X advised him to accompany his small sips of wine between meals with small morsels of food. So enamoured was the monarch with the idea that he passed a law requiring all bars in Castilla to follow suit. Another version attributes tapas to bar owners who placed a saucer with a piece of bread on top of a sherry glass either to deter flies or prevent the punter from drinking on an empty stomach and getting too tipsy. As for the name, *tapa* (which means 'lid') is said to have attained widespread usage in the early 20th century, when King Alfonso XIII stopped at a beachside bar in Cádiz province. When a strong gust of wind blew sand in the king's direction, a quick-witted waiter rushed to place a slice of *jamón* (cured ham) atop the king's glass of sherry. The king so much enjoyed the idea (and the *jamón*) that, wind or no wind, he ordered another – and the name stuck.

and a descendant of the wild boar. Gastronomically, its star appeal is its ability to infiltrate fat into the muscle tissue, thus producing an especially well-marbled meat. Considered to be the best *jamón* of all is the *jamón ibérico* of Jabugo, in Andalucía's Huelva province, which comes from pigs free-ranging in the Sierra Morena oak forests. The best Jabugo hams are graded from one to five *jotas* (Js). *Cinco jotas* (JJJJJ) hams come from pigs that have never eaten anything but acorns (*bellotas*). If the pig gains at least 50% of its body weight during the acorn-eating season, it can be classified as *jamón ibérico de bellota,* the most sought-after designation for *jamón.*

Other much sought-after products from the pig include: *morcilla,* a blood sausage with rice or onions, best eaten lightly grilled; chorizo, a spicy pork sausage with paprika; and *lomo,* another cured pork sausage.

Olive Oil

Spain is the world's largest olive-oil producer and Andalucía's statistics are impressive: there are over 100 million olive trees in Andalucía; it is the world's biggest producer of olive oil; a remarkable 17% of the world's olive oil originates in Jaén province, which produces more olive oil than Greece; and Jaén's more than 4500 sq km of olive trees are, it is sometimes claimed, the world's largest human-made forest. The seemingly endless olive groves of Córdoba, Jaén and Sevilla were originally planted by the Romans, but the production of *az-zait* (juice of the olive) – from which the modern generic word for olive oil, *aceite,* is derived – was further developed by the Muslims. Both olives and olive oil continue to be staples of the Andalucian kitchen.

Olive-oil production is almost as complicated as that of wine, with a range of designations to indicate quality. The best olive oils are those classified as 'virgin' (which must meet 40 criteria for quality and purity) and 'extra virgin' (the best olive oil, with acidity levels no higher than 1%). Accredited olive-oil-producing regions receive Denominación de Origen (DO; a designation that indicates the unique geographic origins, production processes and quality of the product). Those in Andalucía include Baena and Priego de Córdoba in Córdoba, and Sierra de Segura and Sierra Mágina in Jaén.

The most common type of olive is the full-flavoured and (sometimes) vaguely spicy *picual,* which dominates the olive groves of Jaén province and accounts for 50% of all Spanish olive production. It takes its name from its pointed *pico* (tip) and is considered ideal for olive oil due to its high proportion of vegetable fat, natural antioxidants and polyphenol;

Spain produces 45% of the world's olive oil and is also responsible for 20% of world consumption.

the latter ensures that the oil keeps well and maintains its essential qualities at a high cooking temperature. Another important type of olive is the *hojiblanca*, which is grown predominantly around Málaga and Sevilla provinces. Its oil, which keeps for less time and should be stored in a cool dark place, is said to have a taste and aroma reminiscent of fruits, grasses and nuts.

Cold Soups

One of the most important influences over Andalucian chefs has always been the region's climate, and the perfect antidote to Andalucía's baking summers is *gazpacho andaluz* (Andalucian gazpacho). This cold soup appears in many manifestations, but its base is almost always a blended mix of tomatoes, peppers, cucumber, garlic, breadcrumbs, oil and (sherry) vinegar. Aside from climate, history played a significant role in its popularity here: it's a legacy of the New World, when Columbus brought back tomatoes and peppers from his travels. The basis for gazpacho developed in Andalucía among the *jornaleros* (agricultural day labourers), who were given rations of oil and (often stale) bread, which they soaked in water to form the basis of a soup, adding the oil, garlic and whatever fresh vegetables were at hand. All ingredients were pounded using a mortar and pestle, and a refreshing and nourishing dish was made. Gazpacho is sometimes served in a jug with ice cubes, and with side dishes of chopped raw vegetables such as cucumber and onion.

A thicker version of gazpacho is *salmorejo cordobés*, a cold tomato-based soup from Córdoba where soaked bread is essential; it's served with bits of *jamón* and crumbled egg. *Ajo blanco* is a white gazpacho, a North African legacy, made with almonds, garlic and grapes instead of tomatoes.

Drinks

Wine

Vino production in Andalucía was introduced by the Phoenicians, possibly as early as 1100 BC. The Roman colonisers who followed were famous imbibers of wine, while the Moors, whose holy book, the Quran, preached abstinence from alcohol, continued to grow grapes and enjoy furtive tipples. Andalucía's wine economy skyrocketed in the 16th century, spearheaded by a new British penchant for sherry.

The Montilla-Morales region in southern Córdoba province produces a wine that is similar to sherry, though isn't fortified by the addition of brandy; the *fino* variety is the most acclaimed. Málaga province knocks out sweet, velvety Málaga Dulce, a drink that pleased palates from Virgil to the ladies of Victorian England, until the vines were blighted around the beginning of the 20th century. Today the Málaga area is Andalucía's smallest wine region for yield. You can sample Málaga wine straight from the barrel in some of the city's numerous bars.

Almost every village throughout Andalucía has its own basic wine, known simply as *mosto*. Eight areas in the region produce distinctive, good, non-DO wines that can be sampled locally: Aljarafe and Los Palacios (Sevilla province); Bailén, Lopera and Torreperogil (Jaén province); Costa Albondón (Granada province); Laujar de Andarax (Almería province); and Villaviciosa (Córdoba province).

Wine not only accompanies meals but is also a popular bar drink – and it's cheap: a bottle costing €5 in a supermarket or €12 in a restaurant will be a decent wine. *Vino de mesa* (table wine) may cost less than €1.50 a litre in shops. You can order wine by the *copa* (glass) in bars and restaurants: the *vino de la casa* (house wine) may come from a barrel for

Food & Wine Websites

www.spaingourmetour.com

www.andalucia.com/gastronomy

www.sherry.org

www.winesfromspain.org

about €1. For quality wines, visitors to Andalucía have traditionally opted to play away with Rioja (from the Basque region), but new winemakers in regions such as Las Alpujarras have begun experimenting with tempranillo, pinot noir and cabernet sauvignon grapes to produce some fine blends.

Sherry

Sherry, Andalucía's celebrated fortified wine, is produced in the towns of Jerez de la Frontera, El Puerto de Santa María and Sanlúcar de Barrameda, which make up the 'sherry triangle' of Cádiz province. These unique wines are produced by a combination of climate, chalky soils that soak up the sun but retain moisture and a special maturing process called the *solera* process.

The main distinction in sherry is between *fino* (dry and straw-coloured) and *oloroso* (sweet and dark, with a strong bouquet). An *amontillado* is an amber, moderately dry *fino* with a nutty flavour and a higher alcohol content. An *oloroso* combined with a sweet wine results in a cream sherry. A *manzanilla* is a chamomile-coloured *fino* produced in Sanlúcar de Barrameda; its delicate flavour is reckoned to come from sea breezes wafting into the bodegas.

Beer

Andalucians love their beer, though you'll rarely see them knocking back pints. The most common way to order a *cerveza* (beer) is to ask for a *caña* (a small draught beer; 250mL) or a *tubo* (a larger draught beer; about 300mL), which come in a straight glass. If you just ask for a *cerveza* you may get bottled beer, which tends to be more expensive. A small bottle (250mL) is called a *botellín* or a *quinto*; a bigger one (330mL) is a *tercio*. San Miguel, Cruzcampo and Alhambra are all decent Andalucian beers.

Brewpubs and microbreweries, where small-batch beers are produced using experimental recipes, are a new but growing phenomenon in

According to legend, the white Pedro Ximénez grape was brought to Andalucía in the luggage of German/Flemish soldier Peter Siemens in the mid-16th century from the Netherlands. Translated into Spanish, 'Peter Siemens' became 'Pedro Ximénez', today the moniker of Andalucíás finest sweet dessert sherry.

ANDALUCIAN KITCHEN DRINKS

WINE REGIONS

Andalucía has six *Denominaciónes de Origens* (DOs; appellations) for its wines.

Málaga Málaga province's long winemaking tradition has had its peaks and troughs, but is currently enjoying something of a renaissance. The region is known for its sweet dessert wines made from Moscatel and Pedro Ximénez grapes. With a high sugar content, the wines are dark, full-bodied and pair well with dried fruit, chocolate and local pâtés.

Sierras de Málaga An offshoot of the Málaga DO formed in 2001, this region produces the standard sweet wines, along with some lighter whites such as chardonnay and sauvignon blanc containing lower alcohol per volume (below 15%).

Jerez-Xerez-Sherry The legendary sherry region was Spain's first DO in 1933, and uses mainly Palomino grapes to make some of the world's oldest wines. Varietals span from dry *fino* to sweet Pedro Ximénez.

Manzanilla Sanlúcar de Barrameda Although it uses the same grapes as Jerez, Sanlúcar's coastal microclimate produces a more delicate, suave sherry with a faint salty essence known as Manzanilla.

Condado de Huelva The white wines in this understated DO are primarily made from Zalema grapes, which produce fresh, light, if unspectacular, wines that go well with seafood.

Montilla-Moriles This DO in southern Córdoba province centers on the town of Montilla and produces sweet dessert wines closely related to sherry using Pedro Ximénez and Moscatel (Muscat) grapes.

Andalucía. You'll find pioneers of the genre at Cervezas Taifa in Seville and Cervezas Califa in Córdoba, serving various IPAs, stouts and pilsner lagers.

Coffee & Tea

Andalucians generally take their coffee strong, short and hot. In true Mediterranean style, takeaways aren't common and there is rarely any size differential beyond the standard 5–6 fl oz cup. A *café con leche* is half-milk, half-coffee (something like cafe latte); a *cortado* is espresso with a dribble of milk (like an Italian macchiato); and *solo* is a straight, black espresso. Ask for it *en vaso* if you want it in a glass and *sombra* or *manchado* if you want lots of milk.

Tea is best procured in *teterías* (Moorish-style teahouses; see p245). *Teterías* are legion in Granada, but have also spread to other cities in recent years, most notably Málaga – and to a lesser extent Jerez, Cádiz and Almería. Long tea menus contain numerous perfumed or spiced varietals. The tea is poured from ornate silver pots into small glasses, Moroccan-style.

Survival Guide

DIRECTORY A–Z ... 358

Accommodation........358

Customs
Regulations............360

Discount Cards........360

Electricity 360

Food 360

Gay & Lesbian
Travellers..............360

Health.................361

Insurance..............361

Internet Access........361

Language Courses......361

Legal Matters 362

Maps..................362

Money.................363

Opening Hours 363

Post...................363

Public Holidays........364

Safe Travel............364

Telephone 364

Time 365

Toilets.................365

Tourist Information 365

Travellers
with Disabilities 365

Visas..................365

Women Travellers.......366

TRANSPORT 367

GETTING THERE
& AWAY...............367

Entering the Region.....367

Air 367

Land 368

Sea 369

GETTING AROUND......369

Bicycle 369

Boat 369

Bus 369

Car & Motorcycle.......370

Taxi 371

Train 371

LANGUAGE 373

Glossary...............378

Directory A–Z

Accommodation

Accommodation in Andalucía, like the rest of Spain, is incredibly varied. You can enjoy historical immersion by staying in a sympathetically restored former monastery or palace, or join the backpacker brigade in a cheap but comfortable hostel. In between you can run the price gamut from economical, no-frills family-run *hostales* to fancy boutique hotels. The state-run *parador* chain is a nationwide collection of luxury hotels which usually inhabit old historic buildings. Boutique hotels are on the rise in Andalucía and they often cleverly combine historic features with dynamic modern design accents. Seville and Granada have plenty of accommodation options to choose from, but a number of the smaller *pueblos blancos* (white towns) also offer some spectacular places to stay.

Guesthouses are more common in rural areas (where they are often called *casas rurales*); these days, they are sometimes foreign-owned and run. In smaller towns you're more likely to encounter *hostales*, which often offer excellent value for money. Similar to *hostales* in price and nature are *pensiones* (pensions) and *posadas* (inns). These places sometimes also offer apartments and/or family rooms.

Some hotels allow young children to stay in rooms with their parents for no extra charge if they share a bed. An additional bed usually costs €15 to €30. Always specify beforehand when booking.

Hostels & Hostales

In Spain, it is important to make a distinction between hostels and *hostales*. Hostels offer standard backpacker accommodation with dorm beds, kitchen facilities, communal lounges, shared bathrooms and bags of local information on hand for budget travellers. Prices vary according to room size and, to a lesser extent, season, but start at around €16 for a shared dorm room. Dorms can have four, six, eight or 10 beds, and many hostels offer double rooms and/or family rooms as well, usually with shared bathrooms. *Hostales* are small family-run hotels where basic but adequate facilities are provided in single, double or triple rooms rather than dorms. Double rooms rarely go for more than €60. Travellers can usually expect private bathrooms and more personal service.

In Andalucía, hostels are normally confined to the main cities such as Seville, Granada and Málaga, although there are a handful of Hostelling International (HI) hostels in smaller villages such as El Bosque (in the Parque Natural Sierra de Grazalema), Cortes de la Frontera and Cazorla. The privately run **Oasis Hostels** (www.hosteloasis.com) is an excellent non-HI bet. It runs hostels in Granada and Málaga, as well as two in Seville (one of which is in an old palace). All are centrally located and offer heaps of hidden freebies such as tapas tours, drink vouchers, bike hire and pancake breakfasts. Casa Caracol (p113) in Cádiz is another superfriendly private place in the old Santa María quar-

---

ACCOMMODATION PRICING

The following is a guide to our pricing system. Unless stated otherwise, prices are for a double room with private bathroom in high season.

€ less than €65

€€ €65 to €140

€€€ more than €140

ter. **Melting Pot** (Map p144; ☑956 68 29 06; www.melting-pothostels.com; Calle Turriano Gracil 5; dm/d incl breakfast from €13/35; [P][@][⟨⟩]) in Tarifa is a mega-laid-back option of equal quality.

For more information on hostels or to make online bookings, see www.hostel-world.com or www.hostel-bookers.com.

Camping Grounds

Andalucía has approximately 150 camping grounds accommodating both caravans and tents. Cádiz province leads the way with 32 facilities, while Seville province has a select five. Rural areas offer the most idyllic camping spots. Highlights include the Costa de la Luz with more than 20 camping grounds, the areas abutting the Parque Nacional de Doñana marshes, the steep Las Alpujarras valleys in the

Sierra Nevada, the Cazorla mountains and the Cabo de Gata coastline. Camping grounds in Spain are graded first class, second class or third class, and facilities are generally very good. Even a third-class camping ground will have hot showers, electrical hook-ups and a cafe; top-notch places, meanwhile, often have minimarkets and swimming pools.

Camping grounds normally charge separately per adult, child and car. Average prices are rarely higher than €7.50, €5 and €6 respectively. Many facilities also rent cabins or bungalows

from approximately €50 a night depending on size and season.

The **Federación Española de Clubes Campistas** (FECC; www.guiacamping-fecc.com) is Spain's main camping club. Its website is an excellent information resource; from it you can access the websites of individual campgrounds, and most allow you to make reservations online and provide further contact info. It also publishes an annual *Guía Camping*, available in bookshops in Spain.

PARADORES: HISTORIC LUXURY

The state-run *parador* hotels were founded by King Alfonso XIII in the 1920s. There are 16 of them in Andalucía, all rated either three or four stars. Prices range from €100 to €370, but check the www.parador.es website for significant discounts. Occupying some astounding locations, these are possibly the best accommodation options around if you're up for a splurge. The following all occupy fine historical buildings:

Parador de Arcos de la Frontera (Map p132; ☑956 70 05 00; www.parador.es; Plaza del Cabildo; r €100-170; [❄][@][⟨⟩]) Andalucía's smallest *parador* inhabits a former palace (the Casa del Corregidor) in Arcos de la Frontera's main square. The clifftop views are stunning.

Parador de Granada (Map p254; ☑958 22 14 40; www.parador.es; Calle Real de la Alhambra; r €335; [P][❄][@][⟨⟩]) Andalucía's and Spain's most celebrated (and expensive) *parador* is encased in a 15th-century convent inside the walls of the Alhambra, Granada.

Parador Castillo de Santa Catalina (☑953 23 00 00; www.parador.es; Cerro de Santa Catalina; r €169; [P][❄][@][⟨⟩][≋]) Medieval-style hotel built in the 1960s on the site of a 13th-century Christian castle. It sits atop a hill overlooking the city of Jaén and the surrounding Sierra Morena.

Parador Málaga Gibralfaro (Map p162; ☑952 22 19 02; www.parador.es; Castillo de Gibralfaro; r incl breakfast €130-155; [P][❄][⟨⟩][≋]) On a hill next to the 14th-century Castillo de Gibralfaro and adjacent Alcazaba, this *parador* overlooks the whole spread of Málaga's city centre.

Parador de Ronda (Map p180; ☑952 87 75 00; www.parador.es; Plaza de España; r €160-171; [P][❄][@][⟨⟩][≋]) Encased in the former town hall next to Ronda's gaping gorge and location of a real-life civil-war massacre, fictionalised by Hemingway in *For Whom the Bell Tolls*.

Parador Condestable Dávalos (Map p233; ☑953 75 03 45; www.parador.es; Plaza Vázquez de Molina; r €188; [P][❄][⟨⟩]) A luxury *parador* in one of Úbeda's trademark 16th-century Renaissance palaces.

Self-Catering Apartments & Casas Rurales

Self-catering apartments and houses are relatively easy to procure in Andalucía and are particularly popular in coastal resort areas. Basic one-bedroom apartments start at around €30 per night, while a luxury pad with a swimming pool somewhere like Marbella will set you back up to €400 a night for four people.

Casas rurales are usually old renovated farmhouses run as B&Bs or as more independent short-term holiday lets. They exist predominantly in smaller towns and villages. Prices for double rooms run from €50 to €100 though many people opt for longer term bookings, thus saving money.

The agencies listed here all deal with online bookings. In the peak summer months (June to August) and around holiday periods (Semana Santa and Easter) it is best to book at least a month in advance.

Apartments Spain (www. apartments-spain.com) Budget-oriented apartments and rentals throughout Spain.

Atlas Rural (www.atlasrural. com) All forms of rural accommodation in Spain from small *casas rurales* to *paradores*.

Customs Regulations

Duty-free allowances for travellers entering Spain from outside the EU include 2L of wine (or 1L of wine and 1L of spirits), and 200 cigarettes or 50 cigars or 250g of tobacco.

There are no restrictions on the import of duty-paid items into Spain from other EU countries for personal use. You *can* buy VAT-free articles at airport shops when travelling between EU countries.

Discount Cards

At museums, never hesitate to ask if there are discounts for students, young people, children, families or seniors.

➡ Senior cards pffer reduced prices for people over 60, 63 or 65 (depending on the place) at various museums and attractions (sometimes restricted to EU citizens) and occasionally on transport.

➡ Student cards offer discounts (usually half the normal fee) for students. You will need some kind of identification (eg an International Student Identity Card; www.isic.org) to prove student status. Not accepted everywhere.

➡ Travel, sights and youth-hostel discounts are available to travellers under 26 with the European Youth Card (www.euro26.org), known as Carnet Joven in Spain. The International Youth Travel Card (IYTC; www.istc.org) offers similar benefits.

Electricity

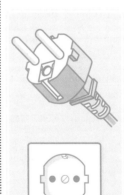

220V/230V/50Hz

240V/50Hz

Food

See the Eat Like a Local (p30) and Andalucian Kitchen (p351) chapters for information on the region's food.

Gay & Lesbian Travellers

Spain is one of the most progressive countries in the world for LGBTI travellers. Gay people have been able to serve openly in the Spanish military since 1979, antidiscrimination laws were introduced in the 1990s and Spain became the third country in the world to legalise same-sex marriage nationwide in 2005.

Andalucía's liveliest gay scene is in Torremolinos, closely followed by Málaga, Seville and Granada, but there are gay- and lesbian-friendly bars and clubs in all major cities. Some cities produce special leaflets and maps advertising gay-specific sights. Ask at tourist information offices.

Websites such as www. travelgayeurope.com and www.patroc.com have helpful listings of gay and gay-friendly accommodation, bars, clubs, beaches, cruising areas, health clubs and associations. Patroc has special sections for the cities of Seville and Granada.

The **Federación Andaluza Arco Iris** (✆951 38 39 62; www.federacionarcoiris. blogspot.com) is an organisation based in Málaga that campaigns for equal opportunities for LGBTI people.

Health

For emergency treatment, go straight to the *urgencias* (casualty) section of the nearest hospital, or call ✆061 for an ambulance.

Good health care is readily available and *farmacias* (pharmacies) offer valuable advice and sell over-the-counter medication. In Spain, a system of *farmacias de guardia* (duty pharmacies) operates so that each district has one open all the time. When a pharmacy is closed, it posts the name of the nearest open one on the door.

Tap water is generally safe to drink in Spain, but in the city of Málaga many people prefer to play it safe by drinking bottled water. Do not drink water from rivers or lakes as it may contain harmful bacteria.

Insurance
Medical Insurance

If you're an EU citizen, or a citizen of Norway, Iceland or Switzerland, the free **EHIC** (European Health Insurance Card; ✆UK 0845 606 2030;

www.ehic.org.uk/internet/home.do) covers you for most medical care in Spain, including maternity care and care for chronic illnesses such as diabetes (though not for emergency repatriation). However, you will normally have to pay for medicine bought from pharmacies, even if prescribed, and perhaps for some tests and procedures. The EHIC does not cover private medical consultations and treatment in Spain; this includes nearly all dentists, and some of the better clinics and surgeries. For more information on applying for an EHIC from your home country follow the appropriate link on the European Commission website (http://ec.europa.eu/social/). Non-EU citizens should find out if there is a reciprocal arrangement for free medical care between their country and Spain.

Travel Insurance

A travel-insurance policy to cover theft, loss and medical problems is a good idea. Travel agents will be able to make recommendations. Check the small print: some policies specifically exclude 'dangerous activities', which can include scuba diving, motorcycling or even trekking. Strongly consider a policy that covers you for the worst possible scenario, such as an accident requiring an ambulance or emergency flight home. Find out in advance if your insurance plan will make payments to doctors or hospitals directly, rather than you having to pay on the spot and claim later. The

former option is generally preferable, as it doesn't leave you out of pocket. If you have to claim later, make sure you keep all documentation.

Buy travel insurance as early as possible. If you buy it in the week before you leave home, you may find, for example, that you are not covered for delays to your trip caused by strikes.

Paying for your airline ticket with a credit card often provides limited travel-accident insurance, and you may be able to reclaim payment if the operator doesn't deliver.

Worldwide travel insurance is available at www.lonelyplanet.com/travel-insurance. You can buy, extend and claim online anytime.

Internet Access

Wi-fi is almost universally available at hotels, as well as in some cafes, restaurants and airports; generally (but not always) it's free. Connection speed often varies from room to room in hotels (and coverage sometimes is restricted to the hotel lobby), so always ask when you check in or make your reservation. Some tourist offices may have a list of wi-fi hot spots in their area.

Language Courses

Privately run language schools are scattered all over Spain and many of them are excellent. But, with most courses requiring a minimum of one week's study, it's important to find the right location. Seville is a beautiful city in which to linger for a week or two and has an abundance of top-notch language schools. If you'd prefer a slightly smaller city with instant access to history and beaches, try Cádiz where a couple of good schools are located in the old quarter. For a more rural experience in a diminutive hilltop town close to the coast, you can't beat Vejer de la Frontera.

The best schools running language courses include:

CLIC (Map p58; ☏954 50 21 31; www.clic.es; Calle Albareda 19) Schools in Seville and Cádiz.

Escuela Delengua (Map p262; ☏958 20 45 35; www.delengua.es; Calderería Vieja 20; 2-week course €260) Centre in student-heavy city of Granada.

K2 Internacional (Map p114; ☏956 21 26 46; www.k2internacional.com; Plaza Mentidero 19) School in Cádiz.

La Janda (☏956 44 70 60; www.lajanda.org; Calle José Castrillón 22; per 20hr week €180) Family-run school in Vejer de la Frontera.

Legal Matters

➡ Spain's once-liberal drug laws were severely tightened in 1992. The only legal drug is cannabis, and then only for personal use – which means very small amounts. Public consumption of any drug is illegal. It would be very unwise to smoke cannabis in hotel rooms or guesthouses. Travellers entering Spain from Morocco, especially with a vehicle, should be prepared for intensive drug searches.

➡ Spain's drink-driving laws are relatively strict: the blood-alcohol limit is 0.05%, or 0.01% for new drivers.

➡ Under the Spanish constitution, anyone who is arrested must be informed immediately, in a manner understandable to them, of their rights and the grounds for the arrest. Arrested people are entitled to the assistance of a lawyer (and, where required, an interpreter) during police inquiries or judicial investigations. For many foreign nationalities, including British citizens, the police are also obliged to inform an arrested person's consulate immediately. Arrested people may not be compelled to make a statement. Within 72 hours of arrest, the person must be brought before a judge or released.

Police

Spain has three main types of police:

Policía Nacional (National Police; ☏091) Covers cities and bigger towns, sometimes forming special squads dealing with drugs, terrorism and the like. A further contingent is to be found shuffling paper in bunkerlike police stations called *comisarías*.

Policía Local (Local Police; ☏092) Also known as Policía Municipal, are controlled by city and town halls and deal mainly with minor matters such as parking, traffic and by-laws. They wear blue-and-white uniforms.

Guardia Civil (Civil Guard; ☏062) The responsibilities of the green-uniformed Guardia Civil include roads, the countryside, villages and international borders.

If you need to go to the police (for example, if you're the victim of petty theft), any of them will do, but your best bet is to approach the Policía Nacional or Policía Local.

Maps

Michelin's 1:400,000 *Andalucía* (No 578) is excellent for overall planning and touring, with an edition published each year. It's widely available in and outside Andalucía; look for it at petrol stations and bookshops.

Maps provided by tourist offices are often adequate for finding your way around cities and towns. For something more comprehensive, most cities are covered by one of the Spanish series such as Telstar, Escudo de Oro, Alpina or Everest, all with street indexes; they're available in bookshops. Be sure to check the publication dates.

Local availability of maps is patchy, so it's a good idea to try to obtain them in advance. **Stanfords** (www.stanfords.co.uk) has a good range of Spain maps and you can order them online.

Walking Maps

If you're going to do any walking in Andalucía you should arm yourself with the best possible maps, especially as trail markings can be patchy.

Spain's **Centro Nacional de Información Geográfica** (CNIG; www.cnig.es), the publishing arm of the Instituto Geográfico Nacional (IGN), produced a useful *Mapa Guía* series of national and natural parks, mostly at 1:50,000 or 1:100,000, in the 1990s. The CNIG also covers about three-quarters of Andalucía in its 1:25,000 *Mapa Topográfico Nacional* maps, most of which are up to date. Both the CNIG and the **SGE** (Army Geographic

Service; ☏915 12 66 00, ext 6630; Darío Gazapo 8, Madrid; ⊙9am-1.30pm) publish 1:50,000 series: the SGE's, called *Serie L*, tends to be more up to date (most of its Andalucía maps have been revised since the mid-1990s). CNIG maps may be labelled CNIG, IGN or both.

The CNIG website lists where you can buy CNIG maps (click on 'Información y Venta') or you can buy online. There are sales offices in Andalucía's eight provincial capitals, including Seville, Granada and Málaga.

Good commercially published series, all usually accompanied by guide booklets, come from **Editorial Alpina** (www.editorialalpina. com), **Editorial Penibética** (www.penibetica.com) and Britain's **Discovery Walking Guides** (www.walking. demon.co.uk).

The **Junta de Andalucía** (www.juntadeandalucia. es), Andalucía's regional government, also publishes a range of Andalucía maps, including a *Mapa Guía* series of natural and national parks. These have been published recently and are widely available, although are perhaps better for vehicle touring than for walking, with a scale of 1:75,000. The covers are predominantly green, as opposed to the CNIG *Mapas Guías* that are mainly red or pink. Other Junta maps include 1:10,000 and 1:20,000 maps covering the whole of Andalucía – they are good maps but there are few sales outlets for them.

Money

The most convenient way to bring your money is in the form of a debit or credit card, with some extra cash in case of an emergency.

ATMs

Many credit and debit cards can be used for withdrawing money from *cajeros automáticos* (ATMs) that display the relevant symbols such as Visa, MasterCard, Cirrus etc. There is usually a charge (around 1.5% to 2%) on ATM cash withdrawals abroad.

Cash

Most banks and building societies will exchange major foreign currencies and offer the best rates. Ask about commissions and take your passport.

Credit & Debit Cards

You can get by very well in Andalucía with a credit or debit card enabling you to make purchases directly and withdraw cash euros from ATMs.

Not every establishment accepts payment by card, but most do. You should be able to make payments by card in midrange and top-end accommodation and restaurants, and larger shops, but you cannot depend on it elsewhere. When you pay by card, you will be asked for ID such as your passport. Don't forget to memorise your PIN numbers as you may have to key these in as you pay, and do keep a note of phone numbers to call for reporting a lost or stolen card.

American Express (Amex) cards are much less widely accepted than Visa and MasterCard.

Taxes & Refunds

In Spain, value-added tax (VAT) is known as IVA (ee-ba; *impuesto sobre el valor añadido*). Visitors are entitled to a refund of the 21% IVA on purchases costing more than €90.16 from any shop, if they are taking them out of the EU within three months. Ask the shop for a cash-back (or similar) refund form showing the price and IVA paid for each item, and identifying the vendor and purchaser. Present the refund form to the customs booth for IVA refunds at the airport, port or border when you leave the EU.

Tipping

Spanish law requires menu prices to include the service charge, and tipping is a matter of personal choice – most people leave some small change if they're satisfied, and 5% is usually plenty. Porters will generally be happy with €1. Taxi drivers don't have to be tipped but a little rounding up won't go amiss.

Opening Hours

Opening hours have some local and seasonal variations.

Banks 8.30am to 2pm Monday to Friday, 9am to 1pm Saturday

Cafes 8am to 11pm

Night-time bars and clubs 10pm to 4am

Post offices 8.30am to 8.30pm Monday to Friday, 9am to 1.30pm Saturday

Restaurants 1pm to 4pm and 8pm to midnight

Shops 9am to 1.30pm and 5pm to 9pm Monday to Saturday

Supermarkets 9am to 9pm Monday to Saturday

Gibraltar businesses don't take a siesta. Restaurants tend to open 8am to 8pm and shops 10am to 6pm; most shops close after lunch on Saturday and reopen Monday morning.

Post

Postage stamps are sold at *estancos* (tobacconist shops with 'Tabacos' in yellow letters on a maroon background), as well as at *oficinas de correos* (post offices; www.correos.es). It's quite safe to post mail in the yellow street *buzones* (postboxes) as well as at post offices. Mail to or from other Western European countries normally arrives within a week; to or from North America within 10 days; and to or from Australia and New Zealand within two weeks.

Public Holidays

Everywhere in Spain has 14 official holidays a year – some are holidays nationwide, some only in one village. The list of holidays in each place may change from year to year. If a holiday date falls on a weekend, sometimes the holiday is moved to the Monday or replaced with another at a different time. If a holiday falls on the second day following a weekend, many Spaniards take the intervening day off too, a practice known as making a *puente* (bridge).

The two main periods when Spaniards go on holiday are Semana Santa (Holy Week, leading up to Easter Sunday) and the six weeks from mid-July to the end of August. At these times accommodation in resorts can be scarce and transport heavily booked.

There are usually nine official national holidays:

Año Nuevo (New Year's Day) 1 January

Viernes Santo (Good Friday) 25 March 2016, 14 April 2017

Fiesta del Trabajo (Labour Day) 1 May

La Asunción (Feast of the Assumption) 15 August

Fiesta Nacional de España (National Day) 12 October

Todos los Santos (All Saints' Day) 1 November

Día de la Constitución (Constitution Day) 6 December

La Inmaculada Concepción (Feast of the Immaculate Conception) 8 December

Navidad (Christmas) 25 December

In addition, regional governments normally set three holidays, and local councils a further two. The three regional holidays in Andalucía are usually the following:

Epifanía (Epiphany) or **Día de los Reyes Magos** (Three Kings' Day) 6 January

Día de Andalucía (Andalucía Day) 28 February

Jueves Santo (Holy Thursday) Easter

The following are often selected as local holidays by town halls:

Corpus Christi Around two months after Easter

Día de San Juan Bautista (Feast of St John the Baptist, King Juan Carlos II's saint's day) 24 June

Día de Santiago Apóstol (Feast of St James the Apostle, Spain's patron saint) 25 July

Safe Travel

Most visitors to Andalucía never feel remotely threatened, but a sufficient number have unpleasant experiences to warrant an alert. The main thing to be wary of is petty theft (which may of course not seem so petty if your passport, cash, travellers cheques, credit card and camera go missing). Be careful but don't be paranoid.

Telephone

The reasonably widespread blue payphones are easy to use for international and domestic calls. They accept coins, *tarjetas telefónicas* (phonecards) issued by the national phone-company Telefónica and, in some cases, various credit cards. Calling from your computer using an internet-based service such as Skype is generally the cheapest option.

Mobile Phones

Spain uses GSM 900/1800, which is compatible with the rest of Europe and Australia but not with the North American system unless you have a GSM/GPRS-compatible phone (some AT&T and T-Mobile cell phones may work), or the system used in Japan. From those countries, you will need to travel with a tri-band or quadric-band phone.

You can buy SIM cards and prepaid time in Spain for your mobile phone, provided you own a GSM, dual- or tri-band cellular phone. This only works if your national phone hasn't been code-blocked; check before leaving home. Only consider a full contract if you plan to live in Spain for a while.

All the Spanish mobile-phone companies (Telefónica's MoviStar, Orange and Vodafone) offer *prepagado* (prepaid) accounts for mobiles. The SIM card costs from €10, to which you add some prepaid phone time. Phone outlets are scattered across the country. You can then top up in their shops or by buying cards in outlets, such as *estancos* (tobacconists) and news-stands. Pepephone (www.pepephone.com) is another option.

If you plan on using your own phone while in Spain, check with your mobile provider for information on roaming charges, especially if you're using a phone from outside the EU.

Phone Codes & Useful Numbers

Spain has no telephone area codes. Every phone number has nine digits and for any call within Spain you just dial all those nine digits. The first digit of all Spanish fixed-phone numbers is 9. Numbers beginning with 6, 7 or 8 are mobile phones. Phone numbers in Gibraltar have eight digits.

Calls to Spanish numbers starting with 900 are free. Numbers starting with 901 to 906 are pay-per-minute numbers and charges vary. For a rundown on these numbers, visit www.andalucia.com/travel/telephone/numbers.htm.

Some useful numbers:

International access code ☏00

Spain country code ☏34

Phonecards

Cut-rate prepaid phonecards can be good value for international calls. They can be bought from *estancos*, small grocery stores, *locutorios* (private call centres) and news-stands in the main cities and tourist resorts. If possible, try to compare rates. Many of the private operators offer better deals than those offered by Telefónica. *Locutorios* that specialise in cut-rate overseas calls have popped up all over the place in bigger cities.

Time

➡ Mainland Spain is on GMT/UTC plus one hour during winter, and GMT/UTC plus two hours during the country's daylight-saving period, which runs from the last Sunday in March to the last Sunday in October.

➡ Most Western European countries have the same time as Spain year-round, the major exceptions being Britain, Ireland and Portugal. Add one hour to these three countries' times to get Spanish time.

➡ Spanish time is normally US eastern time plus six hours, and US Pacific time plus nine hours.

➡ In the Australian winter subtract eight hours from Sydney time to get Spanish time; in the summer subtract 10 hours (the difference is nine hours for a few weeks in March).

➡ Morocco is on GMT/UTC year-round, so is two hours behind Spain during Spanish daylight-saving time, and one hour behind at other times of the year.

Toilets

Public toilets are almost nonexistent; many (but not all) tourist offices are an exception. It's OK to wander into many bars and cafes to use the toilet, although you're usually expected to order something while there. It's worth carrying some toilet paper with you as many toilets lack it.

Tourist Information

All cities and many smaller towns and villages in Andalucía have at least one *oficina de turismo* (tourist office). Staff are generally knowledgeable and increasingly well versed in foreign languages; they can help with everything from town maps and guided tours to opening hours for major sights and, sometimes, bus timetables. Offices are usually well stocked with printed material. Opening hours vary widely.

Tourist offices in Andalucía may be operated by the local town hall, by local district organisations, by the government of whichever province you're in, or by the regional government, the Junta de Andalucía. There may also be more than one tourist office in larger cities: in general, regional tourist offices offer information both on the city and the wider region, while municipal tourist offices deal just with the city and immediate surrounds. The Junta de Andalucía's environmental department, the Consejería de Medio Ambiente, also has visitor centres located in many of the environmentally protected areas (*parques naturales* and so on). Many present interesting displays on local flora and fauna and carry information on hiking routes.

Many tourist offices have Bluetooth information points which allow you to download town maps, guided tours and events listings directly to your mobile phone.

Travellers with Disabilities

Wheelchair accessibility in Andalucía is improving as new buildings (including hotels) meet regulations requiring them to have wheelchair access. Many midrange and top-end hotels are now adapting rooms and creating better access for wheelchair users; accessibility is poorer at some budget accommodation options.

If you call a taxi and ask for a 'eurotaxi', you should be sent one adapted for wheelchair users.

International organisations can usually offer advice (sometimes including Andalucía-specific info).

Accessible Travel & Leisure (☑01452-729739; www.accessibletravel.co.uk) Claims to be the biggest UK travel agent dealing with travel for people with a disability, and encourages independent travel.

Mobility International (☑541-343 1284; www.miusa.org; 132 E Broadway, Suite 343, Eugene, USA) Advises disabled travelers on mobility issues and runs an educational exchange program.

Visas

Spain is one of 26 member countries of the Schengen Convention, under which 22 EU countries (all but Bulgaria, Croatia, Cyprus, Ireland, Romania and the UK) plus Iceland, Norway, Liechtenstein and Switzerland have abolished checks at common borders. Bulgaria, Croatia, Cyprus and Romania are all legally obliged to become a part of the Schengen Area in the near future.

The visa situation for entering Spain is as follows:

➡ For citizens or residents of EU and Schengen countries, no visa is required.

➡ For citizens or residents of Australia, Canada, Israel, Japan, New Zealand and the USA, no visa is required for tourist visits of up to 90 days.

➡ For other countries, check with a Spanish embassy or consulate.

➡ To work or study in Spain a special visa may be required; contact a Spanish embassy or consulate before travel.

➡ Remember that Gibraltar is not part of Schengen and if you do not have permission to enter the UK, you may not enter Gibraltar.

Women Travellers

Women travellers in Spain will rarely experience harassment, although you may find yourself subjected to stares, catcalls and comments from time to time. Skimpy clothes are the norm in many coastal resorts, but people tend to dress more modestly elsewhere. Although most places you'll visit are safe, think twice about going alone to isolated stretches of beach or country, or down empty city streets at night. Some women travellers have reported feeling more comfortable at the front of public transport. Remember the word for help (socorro) in case you need to use it.

Each province's national police headquarters has a special Servicio de Atención a la Mujer (SAM; literally 'Service of Attention to Women'). The national **Comisión para la Investigación de Malos Tratos a Mujeres** (Commission for Investigation into Abuse of Women; ☑emergency 900 10 00 09; www.malostratos.org; ⊘9am-9pm) maintains an emergency line for victims of physical abuse anywhere in Spain. In Andalucía the **Instituto Andaluz de la Mujer** (☑900 20 09 99; ⊘24hr) also offers help.

Transport

GETTING THERE & AWAY

Andalucía is a top European holiday destination and is well linked to the rest of Spain and Europe by air, rail and road. Regular hydrofoils and car ferries run to and from Morocco, and there are also ferry links to Algeria. Flights, tours and rail tickets can be booked online at lonelyplanet.com/bookings.

Entering the Region

Immigration and customs checks usually involve a minimum of fuss, although there are exceptions. Spanish customs look for contraband duty-free products designed for illegal resale in Spain, in particular from people arriving from Morocco. Expect long delays at this border, especially in summer.

Air

Getting to Andalucía by air from the rest of Europe is easy. Dozens of regular and charter airlines fly into the region's five airports from elsewhere in Europe, especially the UK, and a couple also fly from the UK to Gibraltar. Andalucía's busiest airport, Málaga, also has flights from Morocco. The region is well connected by domestic flights to other Spanish cities. From outside Europe, you'll normally need to change planes en route, usually at Madrid or Barcelona or in another European country. A couple of charters connect Málaga with Montreal in Canada and, seasonally, with JFK in New York.

High season is generally mid-June to mid-September, although flights can also be fully booked (and prices higher) during Semana Santa (Holy Week; the week leading up to Easter Sunday).

Airports

Málaga Airport (AGP; ☎952 04 88 38; www.aena.es) is the main international airport in Andalucía and Spain's fourth busiest, with almost 60 airlines connecting the city to Spain, Europe and further afield.

Seville (SVQ; ☎954 44 90 00; www.aena.es), **Granada** (GRX; ☎958 24 52 07; www.aena.es), **Jerez de la Frontera** (☎956 15 00 00; www.aena.es) and **Almería** (☎902 40 47 04; www.aena.es) also have connections to other Spanish and European cities, although apart from flights to and from Seville, the choices are far more limited. To see which airlines fly into the airport you're hoping to start your journey in, visit www.aena.es, choose the airport from the pull-down menu on the left, then click on 'Airlines' for a full list. The website also has detailed information on facilities at each airport.

CLIMATE CHANGE & TRAVEL

Every form of transport that relies on carbon-based fuel generates CO_2, the main cause of human-induced climate change. Modern travel is dependent on aeroplanes, which might use less fuel per kilometre per person than most cars but travel much greater distances. The altitude at which aircraft emit gases (including CO_2) and particles also contributes to their climate change impact. Many websites offer 'carbon calculators' that allow people to estimate the carbon emissions generated by their journey and, for those who wish to do so, to offset the impact of the greenhouse gases emitted with contributions to portfolios of climate-friendly initiatives throughout the world. Lonely Planet offsets the carbon footprint of all staff and author travel.

Gibraltar airport (GIB; ✈20073026) also receives a small number of flights direct from the UK.

Land
Border Crossings

If you're coming from Morocco, journey times are increased by a couple of hours by border formalities, which are notoriously strict at the ferry departure and arrivals terminals. There are usually long queues at customs on both sides of the Strait of Gibraltar.

Bus

Andalucía is well connected by bus with the rest of Spain. Although there are direct bus services from many European countries, it rarely works out cheaper than flying and takes a whole lot longer.

Places from where taking a bus may work out to be more economical include Lisbon and Morocco. **Alsa** (www.alsa.es) has regular daily services to Seville from Lisbon (seven hours). Alsa also runs several weekly buses between Moroccan cities such as Casablanca, Marrakesh and Fès, and Andalucian destinations such as Seville, Marbella, Málaga, Granada, Jerez de la Frontera and Almería, via the Algeciras–Tangier ferries. As an indication of time, the Málaga–Marrakesh trip takes 19 to 20 hours.

Buses run to most Andalucian cities and medium-sized towns from elsewhere in Spain, with the largest selection leaving from Madrid's **Estación Sur de Autobuses** (www.estacionautobuses-madrid.com). The trip from Madrid to Seville, Granada or Málaga takes around six hours. There are also services down the Mediterranean coast from Barcelona, Valencia and Alicante to Almería, Granada, Jaén, Córdoba, Seville, Málaga and the Costa del Sol. The best bus companies serving Andalucía from other parts of Spain are Alsa and **Secorbus/Socibus** (✆902 22 92 92; www.socibus.es).

Car & Motorcycle

Drivers can reach Andalucía from just about anywhere in Spain in a single day on the country's good-quality highways. The main routes run down the centre of the country from Madrid and along the Mediterranean coast from Barcelona. Popular vehicle ferries run from the UK to Bilbao and Santander in northern Spain, from where you can drive to Andalucía via Madrid. Ferry routes also connect Andalucía with Tangier and Nador in Morocco and with Ceuta and Melilla, the Spanish enclaves on the Moroccan coast.

The main highway from Madrid to Andalucía is the A4/AP4 to Córdoba, Seville and Cádiz. For Jaén, Granada, Almería or Málaga, turn off at Bailén. In the east, the AP7/A7 leads all the way down the Mediterranean side of Spain from La Jonquera on the French border as far as Algeciras.

If you just want to drive once you get to Andalucía, it usually works out cheaper (and quicker) to fly and hire a car there. In the UK, further information on driving in Europe is available from the AA (www.theaa.com).

Train

Renfe (www.renfe.es) is the excellent national Spanish train system which runs services in Andalucía. It has benefited from massive investment in recent years, meaning journeys are fast, efficient and comfortable.

IN SPAIN

The fastest train to Andalucía is the 280km/h Alta Velocidad Española (AVE) from Madrid, operated by Renfe. These trains connect Madrid to Córdoba (one way from €62.10, 1¾ hours), Seville (from €75.50, around 2½ hours) and Málaga (from €79.50, 2½ hours) in not much more time than travelling by plane. Multigauge Alvia trains also run direct between Madrid and Cádiz three or four times daily. From most other parts of Spain you can reach Andalucía by train in one day, usually with a connection in Madrid or Barcelona.

Most long-distance trains have *preferente* (1st-class) and *turista* (2nd-class) carriages. They go under various names indicating standards of comfort and time of travel:

➡ **Daytime trains** Consist of AVEs on the Madrid–Seville and Madrid–Córdoba–Malaga routes, Alvia on the Madrid–Cádiz and Huelva routes, and Altaria on the Madrid–Granada and Ronda–Algerciras routes.

➡ **Overnight trains** Comfortable Trenhotels (with seats, couchettes and sleeping compartments) run between Barcelona and Granada.

Buy your ticket in advance as trains can get fully booked, especially in July and August. You can do so in English by phone and online. Phone-booked tickets must be collected and paid for at a Renfe ticket office within 72 hours of booking and more than 24 hours before the train's departure. Internet tickets can be paid for online. The first time tickets are purchased online by credit card, they must be picked up at a Renfe ticket office at least one hour before the train's departure; subsequent tickets with the same card can be printed online.

There are some discounts available on fares:

➡ Return fares on long-distance trains are 20% less than two one-way fares.

➡ Children aged under four years travel free (except for high-speed trains where they pay the four- to 13-year-old rate).

➡ Children aged four to 13 get 40% off the cost of seats and couchettes.

➜ The European Youth Card (www.euro26.org) gives 20% or 25% off long-distance and regional train fares.

OUTSIDE SPAIN

If you're coming from elsewhere in Europe and can afford to take at least a day to arrive, there are rail routes to Andalucía, always involving a change of train. The best routing is through Barcelona Sants station (roughly 5½ hours from Málaga and Seville), where you can catch direct trains to Paris. In Paris there are connections onto Amsterdam, the UK and Germany. Alternatively, take a train from Barcelona to Geneva (changing in Valence) where there are connections to Italy. For more details on these and other routes, check **The Man in Seat 61** (www.seat61.com)

Sea

You can sail to Andalucía from the Moroccan ports of Tangier and Nador, as well as Ceuta or Melilla (Spanish enclaves on the Moroccan coast), and Oran and Ghazaouet (in Algeria). The routes are: Melilla–Almería, Nador–Almería, Oran–Almería, Ghazaouet–Almería, Melilla–Málaga, Tangier–Gibraltar, Tangier–Algeciras, Ceuta–Algeciras and Tangier–Tarifa.

All routes usually take vehicles as well as passengers and the most frequent sailings are to/from Algeciras. Usually, at least 18 sailings a day ply the routes between Algeciras and Tangier (1½ hours) and nine between Algeciras and Ceuta (one hour). Extra services are added at busy times, especially during the peak summer period (mid-June to mid-September) when hundreds of thousands of Moroccan workers return home from Europe for holidays. If you're taking a car, book well ahead for July, August or Easter travel, and expect long queues and customs formalities.

The following are the main ferry companies; there's little price difference between them.

Acciona/Trasmediterránea (www.trasmediterranea.es)

Inter Shipping (www.intershipping.es)

FRS (www.frs.es)

If you're coming from the UK, **Brittany Ferries** (www.brittanyferries.com) operates a twice-weekly car ferry from Plymouth or Portsmouth to Santander (24 hours, March to November) and another twice-weekly ferry from Portsmouth to Bilbao (30 hours). From Bilbao and Santander, there are long-distance road, bus and rail connections to Andalucía.

GETTING AROUND

Andalucía has excellent road and bus networks. Having your own vehicle enables you to make the most of your time as bus services to smaller villages rarely operate more than once a day and there are often no services on weekends. Train services are similarly excellent, although they're not much use for getting around Cádiz or Huelva provinces.

Bicycle

Andalucía is good biking territory, with wonderful scenery and varied terrain. While some mountain roads (such as those through the Sierra de Grazalema or Sierra Nevada) are best left to professional cyclists, there aren't too many corners of Andalucía that keen and reasonably fit cyclists can't reach. Plenty of lightly trafficked country roads, mostly in decent condition, enable riders to avoid the busy main highways. Road biking here is as safe as anywhere in Europe provided you make allowances for some drivers' love of speed. Day rides and touring by bike are particularly enjoyable in spring and autumn, avoiding weather extremes.

➜ It's often possible to take your bike on a bus (you'll usually just be asked to remove the front wheel).

➜ You can take bikes on overnight sleeper trains (not long-distance daytime trains), and on most regional and suburban trains; check at the train station for any special conditions before buying tickets.

➜ Bicycles are available for hire in main cities, coastal resorts and inland towns and villages that attract tourism. They're often *bicis todo terreno* (mountain bikes). Prices range from €10 to €20 a day. Seville is easily the region's most cycle-friendly city.

➜ Bike lanes on main roads are rare, but cyclists are permitted to ride in groups up to two abreast.

➜ Helmets are obligatory outside built-up areas.

Boat

There is a regular catamaran service between Cádiz and El Puerto de Santa María.

Bus

Buses in Andalucía are mostly modern, comfortable and inexpensive, and run almost everywhere – including along some unlikely mountain roads – to connect remote villages with their nearest towns. The bigger cities are linked to each other by frequent daily services. On the quieter routes, services may be reduced (or nonexistent) on Saturday and Sunday.

➜ Alsa's luxurious 'Supra' buses have wi-fi, free drinks and snacks, toilets and single seats available.

→ Larger towns and cities usually have one main *estación de autobuses* (bus station) where all out-of-town buses stop. In smaller places, buses tend to operate from a particular street or square, which may be unmarked. Ask around; locals generally know where to go.

→ During Semana Santa (Holy Week) and July and August it's advisable to buy most bus tickets a day in advance.

→ On a few routes, a return ticket is cheaper than two singles.

→ Travellers aged under 26 should ask about discounts on intercity routes.

→ Buses on main intercity routes average around 70km/h, and cost around €1.20 per 14km.

Car & Motorcycle

Andalucía's excellent road network and inexpensive rental cars make driving an attractive and practical way of getting around.

Bringing Your Own Vehicle

Bringing your own car to Andalucía is possible. Roads are generally good, although driving and finding parking in cities can be tiresome. Petrol (around €1.30 to €1.42 per litre in Spain) is widely available. In the event of break-downs, every small town and many villages will have a garage with mechanics on-site.

If the car is from the UK or Ireland, remember to adjust the headlights for driving in mainland Europe (motor-accessory shops sell stick-on strips which deflect the beams in the required direction).

Driving Licences & Documentation

All EU countries' licences (pink or pink and green) are accepted in Spain. Licences from other countries are supposed to be accompanied by an International Driving Permit, but in practice your national licence will suffice for renting cars or dealing with traffic police. The International Driving Permit, valid for 12 months, is available from automobile clubs in your country.

When driving a private vehicle in Europe, proof of ownership (a Vehicle Registration Document for UK-registered vehicles), driving licence, roadworthiness certificate (MOT), and either an insurance certificate or a Green Card should always be carried. Also ask your insurer for a European Accident Statement form, which can greatly simplify matters in the event of an accident.

Hire

If you plan to hire a car in Andalucía, it's a good idea to organise it before you leave home. As a rule, local firms at Málaga Airport or on the Costa del Sol offer the cheapest deals. You can normally get a four-door, air-con, economy-class car from local agencies for around €150 a week in August or €120 a week in January. Many local firms offer internet booking and have a desk in or just outside the airport. In general, rentals away from the holiday *costas* (coasts) are more expensive.

Well-established local firms with branches at Andalucian airports and/or major rail stations (such as Málaga and Seville) include the following:

Centauro (☑902 10 41 03; www.centauro.net)

Crown Car (☑952 17 64 86; www.crowncarhire.com)

Helle Hollis (☑952 24 55 44, UK 0871 222 7245; www.hellehollis.com)

Niza Cars (☑952 23 61 79; www.nizacars.es)

Pepecar.com (☑807 41 42 43; www.pepecar.com)

Major international rental companies are also usually available:

Avis (☑902 13 55 31; www.avis.com)

MAIN BUS COMPANIES

COMPANY	WEBSITE	TELEPHONE	MAIN DESTINATIONS
Alsa	www.alsa.es	☑902 42 22 42	Almería, Córdoba, Granada, Jaén, Málaga, Seville
Casal	www.autocarescasal.com	☑954 99 92 90	Carmona, Seville
Comes	www.tgcomes.es	☑902 19 92 08	Algeciras, Cádiz, Granada, Jerez, Málaga, Ronda, Seville
Damas	www.damas-sa.es	☑959 25 69 00	Ayamonte, Huelva, Seville
Los Amarillos	www.losamarillos.es	☑902 21 03 17	Cádiz, Jerez, Málaga, Ronda, Seville
Portillo	www.ctsa-portillo.com	☑902 14 31 44	Algeciras, Costa del Sol, Málaga, Ronda
Transportes Ureña	www.urena-sa.com	☑957 40 45 58	Córdoba, Jaén, Seville

Enterprise (☎902 10 01 01; www.enterprise.es)

Europcar (☎913 43 45 12; www.europcar.com)

Hertz (☎917 49 90 69; www. hertz.es)

To rent a car you need to be aged at least 21 (23 with some companies) and to have held a driving licence for a minimum of one year (sometimes two years). Under-25s have to pay extra charges with many firms.

Insurance

Third-party motor insurance is a minimum requirement throughout Europe. If you live in the EU, your existing motor insurance will probably provide automatic third-party cover throughout the EU if you're travelling in your own vehicle. Check with your insurer if you will also be covered for medical or hospital expenses or accidental damage to your vehicle. You might have to pay an extra premium if you want the same protection abroad as you have at home. A European breakdown-assistance policy is a good investment, providing services such as roadside assistance, towing, emergency repairs and 24-hour telephone assistance in English.

If you're renting a vehicle in Andalucía, the routine insurance provided may not go beyond basic third-party requirements. For cover against theft or damage to the vehicle, or injury or death to driver or passengers, you may need to request extra coverage. Always read the fine print and don't be afraid to ask.

Parking

Street parking can be hard to find in larger cities during working hours (about 9am to 2pm Monday to Saturday and 5pm to 8pm Monday to Friday). You'll often have to use underground or multistorey car parks, which are common enough in cities, and well-enough signposted, but not cheap (typically around €1 per hour or €10 to €15 for 24 hours). City hotels with their own parking usually charge for the right to use it, at similar or slightly cheaper rates to underground car parks.

Blue lines along the side of the street usually mean you must pay at a nearby meter to park during working hours (typically around €0.50 to €1 an hour). Yellow lines mean no parking. A sign with a red line through a blue backdrop also indicates that parking is prohibited. It's not sensible to park in prohibited zones, even if other drivers have (you risk your car being towed and paying at least €60 to have it released).

Road Rules

➡ As elsewhere in continental Europe, drive on the right and overtake on the left (although the latter is just as often honoured in the breach).

➡ The minimum driving age is 18 years.

➡ Rear seat belts, if fitted, must be worn and children under three must sit in child safety seats.

➡ The blood-alcohol limit is 0.05% (0.01% for drivers with a licence less than two years old) and breath-testing is carried out on occasion.

➡ The police can – and do – carry out spot checks on drivers so it pays to have all your papers in order. Nonresident foreigners may be fined on the spot for traffic offences. You can appeal in writing (in any language) to the Jefatura Provincial de Tráfico (Provincial Traffic Headquarters); if your appeal is upheld, you'll get your money back, but don't hold your breath for a favourable result. Contact details for each province's traffic headquarters are on the Dirección General de Tráfico website (www.dgt.es). Click on 'Trámites y Multas', then 'Direcciones y Teléfonos', then 'Jefaturas', then select the province you're in.

➡ The speed limit is 50km/h in built-up areas, between 80km/h and 100km/h outside built-up areas, and 120km/h on *autopistas* (toll highways) and *autovías* (toll-free highways).

➡ In Spain it's compulsory to carry two warning triangles (to be placed 100m in front of and 100m behind your vehicle if you have to stop on the carriageway), and a reflective jacket, which must be donned if you get out of your vehicle on the carriageway or hard shoulder outside built-up areas.

➡ It's illegal to use hand-held mobile phones while driving.

Taxi

Taxis are plentiful in larger places, and most villages have a taxi or two. Fares are reasonable – a typical 2km to 3km ride should cost about €3.50 to €4.50, with airport runs costing a bit extra. Inter-city runs are around €0.60 per kilometre. You don't have to tip taxi drivers, but rounding up the change is always appreciated.

Train

Renfe (Red Nacional de los Ferrocarriles Españoles, Spanish National Railways; ☎902 24 02 02; www.renfe.es) has an extensive and efficient rail system in Andalucía linking most of the main cities and many smaller places. Trains are at least as convenient, quick and inexpensive as buses on many routes.

➡ High-speed AVE trains run between Córdoba and Málaga, Córdoba and Seville, and Seville and Málaga.

➡ Generally, more-frequent services between Andalucian destinations are provided by the cheaper (but slower)

Train Routes

one-class *regional* and *cercanía* trains. *Regionales*, some of which are known as Andalucía Exprés, run between Andalucian cities, stopping at many towns en route. *Cercanías* are commuter trains that link Seville, Málaga and Cádiz with their suburbs and nearby towns.

➡ Train tickets can be booked online with Renfe, which also lists full up-to-date timetables.

➡ Reservations are necessary on high-speed AVE trains, but less important on shorter, slower routes.

➡ Regional trains average around 75km/h, for a cost of around €1 per 15km.

➡ Return fares on many routes operated by Renfe (but not its *cercanía* services) are 20% less than two one-way fares.

Language

Spanish (*español*) – also called Castilian (*castellano*) – is spoken throughout Andalucia.

Most Spanish sounds are pronounced the same as their English counterparts. If you read our coloured pronunciation guides as if they were English, you'll be understood. Note that the kh is a throaty sound (like the 'ch' in Scottish *loch*), r is strongly rolled, ly is pronounced as the 'lli' in 'million' and ny as the 'ni' in 'onion'. If you travel outside the region, you'll also notice that the 'lisped' th sound, which is typical of the pronunciation in the rest of Spain, is pronounced as s in Andalucia. In our pronunciation guides, the stressed syllables are in italics.

Where necessary in this chapter, masculine and feminine forms are marked as 'm/f', while polite and informal options are indicated by the abbreviations 'pol' and 'inf'.

BASICS

Hello.	*Hola.*	o·la
Goodbye.	*Adiós.*	a·dyos
How are you?	*¿Qué tal?*	ke tal
Fine, thanks.	*Bien, gracias.*	byen gra·syas
Excuse me.	*Perdón.*	per·don
Sorry.	*Lo siento.*	lo syen·to
Yes.	*Sí.*	see
No.	*No.*	no
Please.	*Por favor.*	por fa·vor
Thank you.	*Gracias.*	gra·syas

WANT MORE?

For in-depth language information and handy phrases, check out Lonely Planet's *Spanish Phrasebook*. You'll find it at **shop.lonelyplanet.com**, or you can buy Lonely Planet's iPhone phrasebooks at the Apple App Store.

You're welcome.	*De nada.*	de na·da
My name is ...		
Me llamo ...		me lya·mo ...
What's your name?		
¿Cómo se llama Usted?		ko·mo se lya·ma oo·ste (pol)
¿Cómo te llamas?		ko·mo te lya·mas (inf)
Do you speak English?		
¿Habla inglés?		a·bla een·gles (pol)
¿Hablas inglés?		a·blas een·gles (inf)
I don't understand.		
No entiendo.		no en·tyen·do

ACCOMMODATION

hotel	*hotel*	o·tel
guesthouse	*pensión*	pen·syon
youth hostel	*albergue juvenil*	al·ber·ge khoo·ve·neel
I'd like a ... room.	*Quisiera una habitación ...*	kee·sye·ra oo·na a·bee·ta·syon ...
single	*individual*	een·dee·vee·dwal
double	*doble*	do·ble
air-con	*aire acondicionado*	ai·re a·kon·dee·syo·na·do
bathroom	*baño*	ba·nyo
bed	*cama*	ka·ma
window	*ventana*	ven·ta·na

How much is it per night/person?
¿Cuánto cuesta por noche/persona? kwan·to kwes·ta por no·che/per·so·na

Does it include breakfast?
¿Incluye el desayuno? een·kloo·ye el de·sa·yoo·no

DIRECTIONS

Where's ...?
¿Dónde está ...? don·de es·ta ...

KEY PATTERNS

To get by in Spanish, mix and match these simple patterns with words of your choice:

When's (the next flight)?
¿Cuándo sale   kwan·do sa·le
(el próximo vuelo)?   (el prok·see·mo vwe·lo)

Where's (the station)?
¿Dónde está   don·de es·ta
(la estación)?   (la es·ta·syon)

Where can I (buy a ticket)?
¿Dónde puedo   don·de pwe·do
(comprar   (kom·prar
un billete)?   oon bee·lye·te)

Do you have (a map)?
¿Tiene (un mapa)?   tye·ne (oon ma·pa)

Is there (a toilet)?
¿Hay (servicios)?   ai (ser·vee·syos)

I'd like (a coffee).
Quisiera (un café).   kee·sye·ra (oon ka·fe)

I'd like (to hire a car).
Quisiera (alquilar   kee·sye·ra (al·kee·lar
un coche).   oon ko·che)

Can I (enter)?
¿Se puede (entrar)?   se pwe·de (en·trar)

Can you please (help me)?
¿Puede (ayudarme),   pwe·de (a·yoo·dar·me)
por favor?   por fa·vor

Do I have to (get a visa)?
¿Necesito   ne·se·see·to
(obtener   (ob·te·ner
un visado)?   oon vee·sa·do)

What's the address?
¿Cuál es la dirección?   kwal es la dee·rek·syon

Can you please write it down?
¿Puede escribirlo,   pwe·de es·kree·beer·lo
por favor?   por fa·vor

Can you show me (on the map)?
¿Me lo puede indicar   me lo pwe·de een·dee·kar
(en el mapa)?   (en el ma·pa)

at the corner	en la esquina	en la es·kee·na
at the traffic lights	en el semáforo	en el se·ma·fo·ro
behind ...	detrás de ...	de·tras de ...
far away	lejos	le·khos
in front of ...	enfrente de ...	en·fren·te de ...
left	izquierda	ees·kyer·da
near	cerca	ser·ka
next to ...	al lado de ...	al la·do de ...
opposite ...	frente a ...	fren·te a ...
right	derecha	de·re·cha
straight ahead	todo recto	to·do rek·to

EATING & DRINKING

What would you recommend?
¿Qué recomienda?   ke re·ko·myen·da

What's in that dish?
¿Que lleva ese plato?   ke lye·va e·se pla·to

I don't eat ...
No como ...   no ko·mo ...

Cheers!
¡Salud!   sa·loo

That was delicious!
¡Estaba buenísimo!   es·ta·ba bwe·nee·see·mo

Please bring us the bill.
Por favor, nos trae   por fa·vor nos tra·e
la cuenta.   la kwen·ta

I'd like to book a table for ...	Quisiera reservar una mesa para ...	kee·sye·ra re·ser·var oo·na me·sa pa·ra ...
(eight) o'clock	las (ocho)	las (o·cho)
(two) people	(dos) personas	(dos) per·so·nas

Key Words

appetisers	aperitivos	a·pe·ree·tee·vos
bar	bar	bar
bottle	botella	bo·te·lya
bowl	bol	bol
breakfast	desayuno	de·sa·yoo·no
cafe	café	ka·fe
(too) cold	(muy) frío	(mooy) free·o
dinner	cena	se·na
food	comida	ko·mee·da
fork	tenedor	te·ne·dor
glass	vaso	va·so
highchair	trona	tro·na
hot (warm)	caliente	ka·lyen·te
knife	cuchillo	koo·chee·lyo
lunch	comida	ko·mee·da
main course	segundo plato	se·goon·do pla·to
market	mercado	mer·ka·do
(children's) menu	menú (infantil)	me·noo (een·fan·teel)
plate	plato	pla·to
restaurant	restaurante	res·tow·ran·te
spoon	cuchara	koo·cha·ra
supermarket	supermercado	soo·per·mer·ka·do
vegetarian food	comida vegetariana	ko·mee·da ve·khe·ta·rya·na

SIGNS

Abierto	Open
Cerrado	Closed
Entrada	Entrance
Hombres	Men
Mujeres	Women
Prohibido	Prohibited
Salida	Exit
Servicios/Aseos	Toilets

with	con	kon
without	sin	seen

Meat & Fish

beef	carne de vaca	kar·ne de va·ka
chicken	pollo	po·lyo
cod	bacalao	ba·ka·la·o
duck	pato	pa·to
lamb	cordero	kor·de·ro
lobster	langosta	lan·gos·ta
pork	cerdo	ser·do
prawns	camarones	ka·ma·ro·nes
salmon	salmón	sal·mon
tuna	atún	a·toon
turkey	pavo	pa·vo
veal	ternera	ter·ne·ra

Fruit & Vegetables

apple	manzana	man·sa·na
apricot	albaricoque	al·ba·ree·ko·ke
artichoke	alcachofa	al·ka·cho·fa
asparagus	espárragos	es·pa·ra·gos
banana	plátano	pla·ta·no
beans	judías	khoo·dee·as
beetroot	remolacha	re·mo·la·cha
cabbage	col	kol
(red/green) capsicum	pimiento (rojo/verde)	pee·myen·to (ro·kho/ver·de)
carrot	zanahoria	sa·na·o·rya
celery	apio	a·pyo
cherry	cereza	se·re·sa
corn	maíz	ma·ees
cucumber	pepino	pe·pee·no
fruit	fruta	froo·ta
grape	uvas	oo·vas
lemon	limón	lee·mon

lentils	lentejas	len·te·khas
lettuce	lechuga	le·choo·ga
mushroom	champiñón	cham·pee·nyon
nuts	nueces	nwe·ses
onion	cebolla	se·bo·lya
orange	naranja	na·ran·kha
peach	melocotón	me·lo·ko·ton
peas	guisantes	gee·san·tes
pineapple	piña	pee·nya
plum	ciruela	seer·we·la
potato	patata	pa·ta·ta
pumpkin	calabaza	ka·la·ba·sa
spinach	espinacas	es·pee·na·kas
strawberry	fresa	fre·sa
tomato	tomate	to·ma·te
vegetable	verdura	ver·doo·ra
watermelon	sandía	san·dee·a

Other

bread	pan	pan
butter	mantequilla	man·te·kee·lya
cheese	queso	ke·so
egg	huevo	we·vo
honey	miel	myel
jam	mermelada	mer·me·la·da
oil	aceite	a·sey·te
pepper	pimienta	pee·myen·ta
rice	arroz	a·ros
salt	sal	sal
sugar	azúcar	a·soo·kar
vinegar	vinagre	vee·na·gre

Drinks

beer	cerveza	ser·ve·sa
coffee	café	ka·fe
(orange) juice	zumo (de naranja)	soo·mo (de na·ran·kha)
milk	leche	le·che
red wine	vino tinto	vee·no teen·to
tea	té	te
(mineral) water	agua (mineral)	a·gwa (mee·ne·ral)
white wine	vino blanco	vee·no blan·ko

EMERGENCIES

Help!	¡Socorro!	so·ko·ro
Go away!	¡Vete!	ve·te

QUESTION WORDS

How?	¿Cómo?	ko·mo
What?	¿Qué?	ke
When?	¿Cuándo?	kwan·do
Where?	¿Dónde?	don·de
Who?	¿Quién?	kyen
Why?	¿Por qué?	por ke

Call ...!	¡Llame a ...!	lya·me a ...
a doctor	un médico	oon me·dee·ko
the police	la policía	la po·lee·see·a

I'm lost.
Estoy perdido/a.   es·toy per·dee·do/a (m/f)

I'm ill.
Estoy enfermo/a.   es·toy en·fer·mo/a (m/f)

It hurts here.
Me duele aquí.   me dwe·le a·kee

I'm allergic to (antibiotics).
Soy alérgico/a a   soy a·ler·khee·ko/a a
(los antibióticos).   (los an·tee·byo·tee·kos) (m/f)

Where are the toilets?
¿Dónde están los   don·de es·tan los
servicios?   ser·vee·syos

SHOPPING & SERVICES

I'd like to buy ...
Quisiera comprar ...   kee·sye·ra kom·prar ...

I'm just looking.
Sólo estoy mirando.   so·lo es·toy mee·ran·do

Can I look at it?
¿Puedo verlo?   pwe·do ver·lo

I don't like it.
No me gusta.   no me goos·ta

How much is it?
¿Cuánto cuesta?   kwan·to kwes·ta

That's too expensive.
Es muy caro.   es mooy ka·ro

Can you lower the price?
¿Podría bajar un   po·dree·a ba·khar oon
poco el precio?   po·ko el pre·syo

There's a mistake in the bill.
Hay un error en   ai oon e·ror en
la cuenta.   la kwen·ta

ATM	cajero automático	ka·khe·ro ow·to·ma·tee·ko
credit card	tarjeta de crédito	tar·khe·ta de kre·dee·to
internet cafe	cibercafé	see·ber·ka·fe
post office	correos	ko·re·os
tourist office	oficina de turismo	o·fee·see·na de too·rees·mo

TIME & DATES

What time is it?	¿Qué hora es?	ke o·ra es
It's (10) o'clock.	Son (las diez).	son (las dyes)
Half past (one).	Es (la una) y media.	es (la oo·na) ee me·dya
At what time?	¿A qué hora?	a ke o·ra
At ...	A la(s) ...	a la(s) ...

morning	mañana	ma·nya·na
afternoon	tarde	tar·de
evening	noche	no·che
yesterday	ayer	a·yer
today	hoy	oy
tomorrow	mañana	ma·nya·na

Monday	lunes	loo·nes
Tuesday	martes	mar·tes
Wednesday	miércoles	myer·ko·les
Thursday	jueves	khwe·bes
Friday	viernes	vyer·nes
Saturday	sábado	sa·ba·do
Sunday	domingo	do·meen·go

January	enero	e·ne·ro
February	febrero	fe·bre·ro
March	marzo	mar·so
April	abril	a·breel
May	mayo	ma·yo
June	junio	khoo·nyo
July	julio	khoo·lyo
August	agosto	a·gos·to
September	septiembre	sep·tyem·bre
October	octubre	ok·too·bre
November	noviembre	no·vyem·bre
December	diciembre	dee·syem·bre

TRANSPORT

Public Transport

boat	barco	bar·ko
bus	autobús	ow·to·boos
plane	avión	a·vyon
train	tren	tren
tram	tranvía	tran·vee·a
first	primer	pree·mer
last	último	ool·tee·mo
next	próximo	prok·see·mo

I want to go to (Córdoba).
Quisiera ir a (Córdoba). kee·*sye*·ra eer a (*kor*·do·ba)

At what time does it arrive/leave?
¿A qué hora llega/sale? a ke o·ra *lye*·ga/*sa*·le

Is it a direct route?
¿Es un viaje directo? es oon *vya*·khe dee·*rek*·to

Does it stop at (Granada)?
¿Para en (Granada)? *pa*·ra en (gra·*na*·da)

Which stop is this?
¿Cuál es esta parada? kwal es *es*·ta pa·*ra*·da

Please tell me when we get to (Seville).
¿Puede avisarme pwe·de a·vee·*sar*·me
cuando lleguemos kwan·do lye·*ge*·mos
a (Sevilla)? a (se·*vee*·lya)

I want to get off here.
Quiero bajarme aquí. kye·ro ba·*khar*·me a·*kee*

a ... ticket	*un billete de ...*	oon bee·*lye*·te de ...
1st-class	*primera clase*	pree·*me*·ra *kla*·se
2nd-class	*segunda clase*	se·*goon*·da *kla*·se
one-way	*ida*	ee·da
return	*ida y vuelta*	ee·da ee *vwel*·ta
aisle/window seat	*asiento de pasillo/ ventana*	a·*syen*·to de pa·*see*·lyo/ ven·*ta*·na
bus/train station	*estación de autobuses/ trenes*	es·ta·*syon* de ow·to·*boo*·ses/ *tre*·nes
cancelled	*cancelado*	kan·se·*la*·do
delayed	*retrasado*	re·tra·*sa*·do
platform	*plataforma*	pla·ta·*for*·ma
ticket office	*taquilla*	ta·*kee*·lya
timetable	*horario*	o·*ra*·ryo

Driving & Cycling

I'd like to hire a ...	*Quisiera alquilar ...*	kee·*sye*·ra al·kee·*lar* ...
4WD	*un todo-terreno*	oon to·do·te·*re*·no
bicycle	*una bicicleta*	oo·na bee·see·*kle*·ta
car	*un coche*	oon *ko*·che
motorcycle	*una moto*	oo·na *mo*·to
child seat	*asiento de seguridad para niños*	a·*syen*·to de se·goo·ree·*da* pa·ra *nee*·nyos
diesel	*gasóleo*	ga·so·le·o

NUMBERS

1	*uno*	*oo*·no
2	*dos*	dos
3	*tres*	tres
4	*cuatro*	*kwa*·tro
5	*cinco*	*seen*·ko
6	*seis*	seys
7	*siete*	*sye*·te
8	*ocho*	*o*·cho
9	*nueve*	*nwe*·ve
10	*diez*	dyes
20	*veinte*	*veyn*·te
30	*treinta*	*treyn*·ta
40	*cuarenta*	kwa·*ren*·ta
50	*cincuenta*	seen·*kwen*·ta
60	*sesenta*	se·*sen*·ta
70	*setenta*	se·*ten*·ta
80	*ochenta*	o·*chen*·ta
90	*noventa*	no·*ven*·ta
100	*cien*	syen
1000	*mil*	meel

helmet	*casco*	*kas*·ko
mechanic	*mecánico*	me·*ka*·nee·ko
petrol	*gasolina*	ga·so·*lee*·na
service station	*gasolinera*	ga·so·lee·*ne*·ra

How much is it per day/hour?
¿Cuánto cuesta por kwan·to *kwes*·ta por
día/hora? *dee*·a/o·ra

Is this the road to (Malaga)?
¿Se va a (Málaga) se va a (*ma*·la·ga)
por esta carretera? por *es*·ta ka·re·*te*·ra

(How long) Can I park here?
¿(Por cuánto tiempo) (por *kwan*·to *tyem*·po)
Puedo aparcar aquí? pwe·do a·par·*kar* a·*kee*

The car has broken down (at Cádiz).
El coche se ha averiado el *ko*·che se a a·ve·*rya*·do
(en Cádiz). (en *ka*·dees)

I have a flat tyre.
Tengo un pinchazo. *ten*·go oon peen·*cha*·so

I've run out of petrol.
Me he quedado sin me e ke·*da*·do seen
gasolina. ga·so·*lee*·na

Are there cycling paths?
¿Hay carril bicicleta? ai ka·*reel* bee·see·*kle*·ta

Is there bicycle parking?
¿Hay aparcamiento ai a·par·ka·*myen*·to
de bicicletas? de bee·see·*kle*·tas

GLOSSARY

alameda – *paseo* lined (or originally lined) with *álamo* (poplar) trees
alcázar – Islamic-era fortress
artesonado – ceiling with interlaced beams leaving regular spaces for decorative insertions
autopista – toll highway
autovía – toll-free dual carriageway
AVE – Alta Velocidad Española; the high-speed train between Madrid and Seville
ayuntamiento – city or town hall
azulejo – tile

bahía – bay
bailaor/a – flamenco dancer
bandolero – bandit
barrio – district or quarter (of a town or city)
bodega – winery, wine bar or wine cellar
buceo – scuba diving
bulería – upbeat type of flamenco song
buzón – postbox

cajero automático – automated teller machine (ATM)
calle – street
callejón – lane
cambio – currency exchange
campiña – countryside (usually flat or rolling cultivated countryside)
campo – countryside, field
cantaor/a – flamenco singer
cante jondo – 'deep song', the essence of flamenco
capilla – chapel
capilla mayor – chapel containing the high altar of a church
carnaval – carnival; a pre-Lent period of fancy-dress parades and merrymaking
carretera – road, highway
carta – menu
casa rural – a village house or farmhouse with rooms to let
casco – literally 'helmet'; used to refer to the old part of a city (*casco antiguo*)
castellano – Castilian; the language also called Spanish

castillo – castle
caza – hunting
centro comercial – shopping centre
cercanía – suburban train
cerro – hill
cervecería – beer bar
chiringuito – small, often makeshift bar or eatery, usually in the open air
Churrigueresque – ornate style of baroque architecture named after the brothers Alberto and José Churriguera
cofradía – see *hermandad*
colegiata – collegiate church, a combined church and college
comedor – dining room
comisaría – station of the Policía Nacional (National Police)
converso – Jew who converted to Christianity in medieval Spain
cordillera – mountain chain
coro – choir (part of a church, usually in the middle)
corrida de toros – bullfight
cortes – parliament
cortijo – country property
costa – coast
coto – area where hunting rights are reserved for a specific group of people
cruce – cross
cuenta – bill (check)
cuesta – sloping land, road or street
custodia – monstrance (receptacle for the consecrated Host)

dehesa – woodland pastures with evergreen oaks
Denominación de Origen (DO) – a designation that indicates the unique geographical origins, production processes and quality of wines, olive oil and other products
duende – the spirit or magic possessed by great flamenco performers
duque – duke
duquesa – duchess

embalse – reservoir
ermita – hermitage or chapel

escalada – climbing
estación de autobuses – bus station
estación de esquí – ski station or resort
estación de ferrocarril – train station
estación marítima – passenger port
estanco – tobacconist
estrella – literally 'star'; also class of overnight train with seats, couchettes and sleeping compartments

farmacia – pharmacy
faro – lighthouse
feria – fair; can refer to trade fairs as well as to city, town or village fairs
ferrocarril – railway
fiesta – festival, public holiday or party
finca – country property, farm
flamenco – means flamingo and Flemish as well as flamenco music and dance
frontera – frontier
fuente – fountain, spring

gitano – the Spanish word for Roma people
Guardia Civil – Civil Guard; police responsible for roads, the countryside, villages and international borders. They wear green uniforms. See also *Policía Local, Policía Nacional*.

hammam – Arabic-style bathhouse
hermandad – brotherhood (which may include women), in particular one that takes part in religious processions; also *cofradía*
hospedaje – guesthouse
hostal – simple guesthouse or small place offering budget hotel-like accommodation

infanta – daughter of a monarch but not first in line to the throne
infante – son of a monarch but not first in line to the throne

jardín – garden
judería – Jewish barrio in medieval Spain
Junta de Andalucía – executive government of Andalucía

lavandería – laundry
librería – bookshop
lidia – the modern art of bullfighting on foot
lucio – pond or pool in the Doñana *marismas* (wetlands)

madrugada/madrugá – the 'early hours', from around 3am to dawn; a pretty lively time in some Spanish cities
marismas – wetlands, marshes
marisquería – seafood eatery
marqués – marquis
medina – Arabic word for town or inner city
mercadillo – flea market
mercado – market
mezquita – mosque
mihrab – prayer niche in a mosque indicating the direction of Mecca
mirador – lookout point
morisco – Muslim converted to Christianity in medieval Spain
moro – 'Moor' or Muslim (usually in a medieval context)
movida – the late-night bar and club scene that emerged in Spanish cities and towns after Franco's death; a *zona de movida* or *zona de marcha* is an area of a town where people gather to drink and have a good time
mozárabe – Mozarab; Christian living under Islamic rule in medieval Spain
Mudéjar – Muslim living under Christian rule in medieval Spain; also refers to their decorative style of architecture
muelle – wharf, pier
muladí – Muwallad; Christian who converted to Islam, in medieval Spain

nazareno – penitent taking part in Semana Santa processions
nieve – snow
nuevo – new

oficina de correos – post office
oficina de turismo – tourist office
olivo – olive tree

palacio – palace
palo – literally 'stick'; also refers to the categories of flamenco song
panadería – bakery
papelería – stationery shop
parador – one of the Paradores Nacionales, a state-owned chain of luxurious hotels, often in historic buildings
paraje natural – natural area
parque nacional – national park
parque natural – natural park
paseo – avenue or parklike strip; walk or stroll
paso – literally 'step'; also the platform an image is carried on in a religious procession
peña – a club; usually for supporters of a football club or flamenco enthusiasts (*peña flamenca*), but sometimes a dining club
pensión – guesthouse
pescadería – fish shop
picadero – riding stable
pícaro – dice trickster and card sharp, rogue, low-life scoundrel
pinsapar – forest of *pinsapo*
pinsapo – Spanish fir
piscina – swimming pool
plateresque – early phase of Renaissance architecture noted for its decorative facades
playa – beach
plaza de toros – bullring
Policía Local – Local Police; also known as Policía Municipal. Controlled by city and town halls, they deal mainly with minor matters such as parking, traffic and bylaws. They wear blue-and-white

uniforms. See also *Guardia Civil, Policía Nacional.*
Policía Municipal – Municipal Police; see *Policía Local*
Policía Nacional – National Police; responsible for cities and bigger towns, some of them forming special squads dealing with drugs, terrorism and the like.
preferente – 1st-class carriage on a long-distance train
provincia – province; Spain is divided into 50 of them
pueblo – village, town
puente – bridge
puerta – gate, door
puerto – port, mountain pass
puerto deportivo – marina
puerto pesquero – fishing port
punta – point

rambla – stream
Reconquista – the Christian reconquest of the Iberian Peninsula from the Muslims (8th to 15th centuries)
refugio – shelter or refuge, especially a mountain refuge with basic accommodation for hikers
regional – train running between Andalucian cities
reja – grille; especially a wrought-iron one over a window or dividing a chapel from the rest of a church
Renfe – Red Nacional de los Ferrocarriles Españoles; Spain's national rail network
reserva – reservation, or reserve (eg nature reserve)
reserva nacional de caza – national hunting reserve
reserva natural – nature reserve
retablo – retable (altarpiece)
ría – estuary
río – river
romería – festive pilgrimage or procession
ronda – ring road

sacristía – sacristy, the part of a church in which vestments, sacred objects and other valuables are kept
salina – salt lagoon

Semana Santa – Holy Week; the week leading up to Easter Sunday

sendero – path or track

sevillana – a popular Andalucian dance

sierra – mountain range

Siglo de Oro – Spain's cultural 'Golden Century', beginning in the 16th century and ending in the 17th century

taberna – tavern

tablao – flamenco show

taifa – one of the small kingdoms into which the Muslim-ruled parts of Spain were divided during parts of the 11th and 12th centuries

taquilla – ticket window

taracea – marquetry

tarjeta de crédito – credit card

tarjeta telefónica – phone-card

teléfono móvil – mobile telephone

terraza – terrace; often means an area with outdoor tables at a bar, cafe or restaurant

tetería – Middle Eastern–style teahouse with low seats around low tables

tienda – shop, tent

tocaor/a – flamenco guitarist

torre – tower

trenhotel – sleek, expensive, sleeping car–only train

turismo – means both tourism and saloon car; *el turismo* can also mean the tourist office

turista – second-class carriage on a long-distance train

valle – valley

zoco – large market in Muslim cities

Behind the Scenes

SEND US YOUR FEEDBACK

We love to hear from travellers – your comments keep us on our toes and help make our books better. Our well-travelled team reads every word on what you loved or loathed about this book. Although we cannot reply individually to your submissions, we always guarantee that your feedback goes straight to the appropriate authors, in time for the next edition. Each person who sends us information is thanked in the next edition – the most useful submissions are rewarded with a selection of digital PDF chapters.

Visit **lonelyplanet.com/contact** to submit your updates and suggestions or to ask for help. Our award-winning website also features inspirational travel stories, news and discussions.

Note: We may edit, reproduce and incorporate your comments in Lonely Planet products such as guidebooks, websites and digital products, so let us know if you don't want your comments reproduced or your name acknowledged. For a copy of our privacy policy visit lonelyplanet.com/privacy.

OUR READERS

Many thanks to the travellers who used the last edition and wrote to us with helpful hints, useful advice and interesting anecdotes:

Nancy Barker, Dianne & Virgil Bodeen, Richard Dinkeldein, Laura Gravina, David Hutcheson, Anne Jovaras, Bernard Jovaras, John Kearins, Tim Kuemmerle, Graham Newton, Juhana Rantavuori, Derek Sime, Gary Stocker, Jacques Tribier

AUTHOR THANKS

Isabella Noble

A huge *gracias* to all the *andaluces* (and *guiris*) who helped me out on the road. A big thank you to Annie and Pepi in Vejer for fantastic foodie tips, to Antonio for the good times in Écija and to Tessa for being the ultimate Gibraltar insider. Special thanks to Papi and Jacky, my favourite research assistants and roadtripping companions, and to my fabulous co-authors. As always, thanks to Susan Forsyth, for starting the Tarifa trend.

John Noble

Special thanks to Izzy for sharing the whole experience, to Tito for good conversation and a fascinating film, and to all the so-welcoming *andaluces* who helped me along the way.

Josephine Quintero

Josephine would like to extend a mighty grand *gracias* to the numerous staff at the various tourist offices. She would also like to thank Robin Chapman for joining her in all that dining and wining research, as well as Jorge Guzman, a valuable contact in Málaga along with all her Spanish *malagueño* friends who provided endless advice and tips. Finally she would like to thank Destination Editor Lorna Parkes and everyone else involved in the title at Lonely Planet.

Brendan Sainsbury

Thanks to all the untold bus drivers, chefs, hotel receptionists, tour guides and flamenco singers who helped me in this research.

ACKNOWLEDGMENTS

Climate map data adapted from Peel MC, Finlayson BL & McMahon TA (2007) 'Updated World Map of the Köppen-Geiger Climate Classification', *Hydrology and Earth System Sciences*, 11, 1633–44.

Illustrations pp52-3, 200-1 & 252-3 by Javier Zarracina.

Cover photograph: Plaza de España, Parque de María Luisa, Seville, Alan Copson / AWL ©.

THIS BOOK

This 8th edition of Lonely Planet's *Andalucía* guidebook was researched and written by Isabella Noble, John Noble, Josephine Quintero and Brendan Sainsbury. The 7th edition was written by Brendan Sainsbury, Josephine Quintero and Daniel C Schechter, and the 6th was written by Anthony Ham, Stuart Butler, Vesna Maric, John Noble and Zora O'Neill.

This guidebook was produced by the following:

Destination Editors
Jo Cooke, Lorna Parkes

Product Editor
Elizabeth Jones

Senior Cartographer
Anthony Phelan

Book Designer
Cam Ashley

Assisting Editors
Imogen Bannister, Kellie Langdon, Bella Li, Charlotte Orr, Victoria Smith, Gabrielle Stefanos, Ross Taylor, Tracy Whitmey

Cartographers
Piotr Czajkowski, Julie Dodkins

Cover Researcher
Naomi Parker

Thanks to Sasha Baskett, Daniel Corbett, Brendan Dempsey, Ryan Evans, Anna Harris, Andi Jones, Kate Mathews, Claire Naylor, Karyn Noble, Darren O'Connell, Martine Power, Jessica Rose, Diana Saengkham, Dianne Schallmeiner, Ellie Simpson, Angela Tinson

Index

A
accommodation 358-60, *see also individual locations*
language 373
activities 23-5, 36-40, 82, *see also individual activities & locations*
Agua Amarga 303
air travel 367-8
airports 367-8
Alájar 96-7
Alcalá la Real 226
Alcaracejos 217
Alcázar (Seville) 56-7, 59
Alfarnate 190
Alfarnatejo 190
Algeciras 149
Alhambra 9, 250-5, 328-9, **252-3**, **254**, **8-9**, **252-3**
Almería 288-94, **290**
  accommodation 291
  drinking & nightlife 293
  entertainment 293
  festivals & events 291
  food 292-3
  history 288
  sights 288-9, 291
  tapas 292
  travel to/from 293-4
  travel within 294
Almería province 46, 285-308, **286-7**
  accommodation 285
  car travel 285
  food 33, 285
  highlights 286-7
Almodóvar del Río 216
Almohads 327-8
Almonaster la Real 98
Almoravids 327
Almuñécar 283-4

Map Pages **000**
Photo Pages **000**

animals rights 348
Antequera 185-8
apes 153, 335
Aracena 20, 93-5, **94**
archaeological sites
  Acinipo 184-5
  Baelo Claudia 148
  Casa del Obispo 109
  Cueva de la Pileta 184
  Cueva de los Letreros 308
  Dolmen de Menga 186
  Dolmen de Viera 186
  Dolmen del Romeral 186
  Itálica 98
  Los Millares 296-7
  Madinat al-Zahra 205-6, 327
  Necrópolis Romana 99, 101
  Teatro Romano (Cádiz) 109
  Templo Romano (Córdoba) 204-5
architecture 21, 231, 325-31
  books 330
Arcos de la Frontera 131-3, 135, **132**
Ardales 185
area codes 364
Arroyo Frío 240
art galleries, *see* museums & galleries
arts 15, 22, 51, 266, 344-7
ATMs 363
Ayamonte 87

B
Baelo Claudia 148
Baena 211
Baeza 16, 227-31, **228**, **16**
Barbary apes 153, 335
Baroque architecture 330-1
Barranco de Poqueira 278
bathrooms 365
beaches 14, 21, 84
  Cabo de Gata 300, **13**
  Cala Carbón 300

Cala de Enmedio 300
Cala de la Media Luna 300
Calas del Barronal 300
El Palmar 141
El Puerto de Santa María 128
Flecha del Rompido 86
Isla Canela 87
Isla Cristina 86-7
La Carihuela 171
Los Caños de Meca 141
Matalascañas 87
Mojácar Playa 303-4
Playa Burriana 193
Playa Calahonda 193
Playa Central 86
Playa Chica 143
Playa de la Caleta 112
Playa de la Charca 282
Playa de la Gaviota 86
Playa de la Guardia 282
Playa de la Malagueta 163
Playa de la Muralla 128
Playa de la Puntilla 128
Playa de la Rada 175
Playa de la Victoria 113
Playa de las Cortinas 141
Playa de los Genoveses 300
Playa de los Lances 143
Playa de Mónsul 300
Playa de Pedregalejo 163
Playa de San Cristóbal 283
Playa de Santa Catalina 128
Playa de Valdelagrana 128
Playa de Valdevaqueros 143
Playa del Barronal 300
Playa del Cañuelo 193
Playa del Faro 141
Playa del Playazo 300, 301
Playa el Palo 163
Playa Fuentebravía 128
Playa Puerta del Mar 283

Playa San Pedro 300, 301
Playamar 171
Punta del Moral 87
Punta Paloma 143
Tarifa 143
Zahara de los Atunes 142, **15**
beer 355-6
Belalcázar 217
Benalmádena 170-2
Benaoján 184
Bérchules 281
bicycle travel, *see* cycling
birds 336-7
birdwatching 38, 336-7
  Centro de Fauna Silvestre Collado del Almendral 240-1
  Centro de Visitantes José Antonio Valverde 89
  El Rocío 90, 91
  Gaucín 185
  Gibraltar 154
  Laguna de Fuente de Piedra 189
  Parque Natural Sierra de Andújar 226-7
  Peñón de Zaframagón 138
  Sierra Nevada 275
boat travel 369
bodegas
  El Puerto de Santa María 127, 128
  Jerez de la Frontera 120-1
  Laujar de Andarax 297
  Montilla 212
  Sanlúcar de Barrameda 130
Bolonia 148
books 310, *see also* literature
  architecture 330
  food 353
  history 316, 322
  wine 353
border crossings 150, 149, 368

Bubión 278
budget 19
bullfighting 182, 321, 348-50
bullrings 349
Plaza de Toros (El Puerto de Santa María) 127
Plaza de Toros (Mijas) 177
Plaza de Toros (Ronda) 179
Plaza de Toros de la Real Maestranza 64
bus travel 19, 368, 369-70
business hours 363
butterflies 171

C
Cabo de Gata 13, 298-303, **299**, **13**
Cabo de Trafalgar 141
Cádiz 13, 109, 112-18, 320, **114-15**, **13**
accommodation 113
activities 112-13
courses 113
drinking & nightlife 117
entertainment 117-18
festivals & events 112
food 113, 116-17
internet resources 118
sights 109, 112
travel to/from 118
travel within 118
Cádiz province 45, 108-50, **110-11**
accommodation 108
beaches 108
car travel 108
food 32
highlights 110-11
Calle Sierpes 65
Caminito del Rey 20, 187
camping grounds 359
Cano, Alonso 330
Capileira 278-9
Capilla Real 257
car hire 370-1
car travel 19, 368, 370-1, see also driving tours
language 377
Carmona 99-102, **100**
Carnaval 23, 112
Carretera del Suspiro del Moro 277

Map Pages **000**
Photo Pages **000**

casa rurales 360
Castaño del Robledo 97-8
castles & forts 42, see also palaces & mansions
Alcazaba (Almería) 288
Alcazaba (Antequera) 186
Alcazaba (Granada) 254
Alcazaba (Guadix) 271
Alcazaba (Málaga) 157, 160
Alcázar (Jerez de la Frontera) 119
Alcázar (Seville) 56-7, 59
Alcázar de la Puerta de Sevilla 99
Alcázar de los Reyes Cristianos 202-3
Alhambra 9, 250-5, 328-9, **252-3**, **254**, **8-9**, **252-3**
Castillo Árabe (Constantina) 107
Castillo Árabe (Olvera) 138
Castillo Árabe (Salobreña) 282
Castillo de Albánchez 232
Castillo de Almodóvar 216
Castillo de Aracena 93
Castillo de Gibralfaro 160
Castillo de Guzmán 143
Castillo de Jimena 148
Castillo de la Calahorra 272
Castillo de la Yedra 237
Castillo de las Almadrabas 142
Castillo de los Duques 132
Castillo de los Guzmán 91
Castillo de los Sotomayor 217
Castillo de Miramontes 217
Castillo de Priego de Córdoba 214
Castillo de San Jorge 66
Castillo de San Marcos 125-6
Castillo de San Miguel 283
Castillo de San Sebastián 112
Castillo de Santa Catalina (Cádiz) 112
Castillo de Santa Catalina (Jaén) 222-3

Castillo de Santiago 130
Castillo de Segura 243
Castillo de Vejer de la Frontera 139-40
Castillo de Vélez Blanco 307
Castillo de Zuheros 212
Castillo del Marqués de los Vélez 307
Fortaleza de la Mota 226
Moorish Castle (Gibraltar) 153
cathedrals, see churches & cathedrals
caves 42
Barriada de las Cuevas 271
Cueva de la Pileta 184
Cueva de los Letreros 308
Cueva de los Murciélagos 213
Cueva de Nerja 192
Cuevas de Sorbas 295
Cuevas del Almanzora 307
Gruta de las Maravillas 93
Guadix 271
Sacromonte 260
St Michael's Cave 153
Cazalla de la Sierra 105, 107
Cazorla 237-8
cell phones 364
Centro Lorca 20, 270
ceramics 236
children, travel with 41-3
Costa del Sol 171
Seville 71
Christian architecture 329-31, see also churches & cathedrals
Christian art 345
churches & cathedrals 329-31
Basílica de La Macarena 68
Basílica Menor de Santa María de la Asunción 132-3
Basílica San Juan de Díos 259
Capilla de los Benavides 229
Catedral de Baeza 227-8
Catedral de Cádiz 109
Catedral de Granada 257
Catedral de Guadix 271
Catedral de la Asunción 222

Catedral de la Encarnación 288-9
Catedral de la Sierra 217
Catedral de Málaga 157
Catedral de San Salvador 119
Catedral de Sevilla 9, 50-6, **52-3**, **9**, **52-3**
Colegiata de Santa María de la Asunción 102
Colegiata de Santa María la Mayor (Antequera) 186
Colegiata del Salvador 256
Ermita de Nuestra Señora Reina de los Ángeles 96
Ermita del Rocío 90
Iglesia de la Asunción 242
Iglesia de la Aurora 214
Iglesia de la Santa Cruz 228
Iglesia de Nuestra Señora de la O 129
Iglesia de San Francisco 214
Iglesia de San Jorge 85
Iglesia de San Juan (Almería) 288
Iglesia de San Juan (Écija) 104
Iglesia de San Martín (Almonaster la Real) 98
Iglesia de San Martín (Niebla) 91
Iglesia de San Mateo 143
Iglesia de San Pablo-Santo Domingo 104
Iglesia de San Pedro 133
Iglesia de Santa Ana 256
Iglesia de Santa María (Cazorla) 237
Iglesia de Santa María (Écija) 104
Iglesia de Santa María de Granada 91
Iglesia de Santa María de la Alhambra 254
Iglesia de Santa María de los Reales Alcázares 234
Iglesia de Santa María de Mesa 136
Iglesia de Santa María La Mayor 179
Iglesia del Carmen 187
Iglesia del Divino Salvador 139
Iglesia Nuestra Señora de Gracia 271

Iglesia Parroquial Nuestra Señora de la Encarnación 138
Iglesia Prioral de Nuestra Señora del Mayor Dolor 93
Iglesia Prioral de Santa María de la Asunción 99
Parroquia de la Asunción 214
Parroquia de Nuestra Señora de la O 67
Parroquia de Santa Ana 67
Parroquia Mayor de Santa Cruz 104
Parroquia del Divino Salvador 65
Sacra Capilla de El Salvador 232
Santa Iglesia Catedral de Córdoba 202
Santuario de la Virgen de la Cabeza 226
Santuario de Nuestra Señora de la Cinta 82
Seville cathedral 9, 50-6, **52-3**, **9**, **52-3**
churros 31
cinema 347, see also films
Civil War 321-2
climate 18, 23-5
coffee 356
cold soups 354
Colón, Cristóbal, see Columbus, Christopher
Columbus, Christopher 50-1, 84, 85, 319
Comares 190
Cómpeta 190-1
Concurso de Cante Jondo 342
Constantina 107
convents
Convento de San Francisco 254
Convento de Santa Clara (Carmona) 99
Córdoba 198-211, **204**
accommodation 207-8
drinking 209
entertainment 209
festivals & events 206
food 208-9
history 198
patios 202
shopping 209
sights 198-206
tourist information 210
travel to/from 210
travel within 210-11

Córdoba province 45, 195-218, **196-7**
accommodation 195
car travel 195
food 32, 195
highlights 196-7
Costa de la Luz 14, 86-7, 139-50, **15**
Costa del Sol 170-8
Costa Tropical 282-4
courses
cooking 31, 69, 140
flamenco 69
language 69, 113, 140, 361-2
credit cards 363
Cueva de la Pileta 184
Cueva de los Letreros 308
Cueva de Nerja 192
Cuevas de Sorbas 295
Cuevas del Almanzora 307
currency 18, 150
customs regulations 360
cycling 37, 369, see also vías verdes (greenways)

D

dance 338-43, see also flamenco
debit cards 363
del Amo, Tito 305, 306
Desfiladero de Despeñaperros 225-6
Desierto de Tabernas 294-5
disabilities, travellers with 365
discount cards 360
diving 37-8
Cabo de Gata 300-1
La Herradura 284
Nerja 193
Tarifa 143
Dolmen de Menga 186
Dolmen de Viera 186
Dolmen del Romeral 186
dolphin-watching 145, 154
drinks 354-6
language 374-5
driving licences 370
driving tours, see also car travel
Sierra Norte de Sevilla 106, **106**
white towns 134, **134**
Duque de Medina Sidonia 323

E

eagles 336
Écija 103-5
economy 310-11
El Altiplano 271-2
El Burgo 183
El Chorro 185, 187
El Fraile 301
El Palmar 141
El Pedroso 107
El Pozo de los Fraires 302
El Puerto de Santa María 125-9, **126**
El Rinconcillo 266
El Rocío 90-2
El Yelmo 242
electricity 150, 360
Embalse del Conde del Guadalhorce 185
Embalse del Tranco 240
emergencies 19
language 375
Estepona 175-7
events, see festivals & events
exchange rates 19

F

Feria de Abril 23, 70, **2**
Feria del Caballo 24, 122, **24**
Fernández, Alejo 51
ferry travel 369
Festival de Jerez 23, 122
festivals & events 23-5
Bienal de Flamenco 25, 70
Bluescazorla 238
Carnaval 23, 112
Carreras de Caballos 130
Corpus Christi 25, 181
Cruces de Mayo 206
Día de la Cruz 261
Día de los Reyes Magos 23
Feria de Abril 23, 70, **2**
Feria de Baeza 229
Feria de Fuengirola 173
Feria de la Manzanilla 130
Feria de la Tapa 25
Feria de la Virgen de la Luz 145
Feria de Málaga 25, 163-4
Feria de Mayo 206
Feria de Pedro Romero 25, 181
Feria de Primavera y Fiestas del Vino Fino 127

Feria de San Miguel 133
Feria del Caballo 24, 122, **24**
Feria del Corpus Cristi 260-1
Festival de Jerez 23, 122
Festival de la Guitarra de Córdoba 206
Festival Internacional de la Guitarra 25
Festival Internacional del Aire 242
Festival Internacional de Música y Danza (Granada) 261
Festival Internacional de Música y Danza Ciudad de Úbeda 235
Festividad Virgen del Carmen 127
Fiesta de los Patios de Córdoba 24-5, 206
Fiesta Mayor de Verdiales 25, 163
Fiestas Colombinas 82
Fiestas de Otoño 25
Jazz en la Costa 283
Moros y Cristianos 304
Moto GP 24
Motorcycle Grand Prix 122
Noche de San Juan 193, 304
Noche del Vino 190
Real Feria de Agosto 187
Romería de la Virgen de la Cabeza 226
Romería del Rocío 24, 90, 130
Semana Santa (Antequera) 187
Semana Santa (Arcos de la Frontera) 133
Semana Santa (Baeza) 229
Semana Santa (Córdoba) 206
Semana Santa (Granada) 260
Semana Santa (Jaén) 224
Semana Santa (Málaga) 163
Semana Santa (Seville) 17, 23, 69-70, **17**, **24**
Semana Santa (Úbeda) 235
Velada de Nuestra Señora de la Oliva 140
Virgen del Carmen 193
films 310, see also cinema

flamenco 12, 62-3, 338-43, **12**, **62-3**
  Almería 293
  Cádiz 117, 341
  Córdoba 203-4
  courses 69
  El Puerto de Santa María 128
  festivals 70, 340
  Granada 268
  Jerez de la Frontera 119, 124, 341
  Lebrija 341
  Málaga 169
  Morón de la Frontera 341
  museums 64, 160, 203-4
  Seville 48, 76-7, 341
  Utrera 341
  Vejer de la Frontera 141
flamingos 337
Flecha del Rompido 86
food 21, 41-2, 165, 351-5, 361, **35**, see also individual locations
  books 353
  churros 31
  cooking courses 31, 69, 140
  gazpacho 354, **35**
  internet resources 354
  jamón (ham) 280, 352-3
  language 374-5
  olive oil 211, 230, 294, 353-4
  seafood 351
  tapas 13, 34, 168, 265, 292, 352, **13**
  tomatoes 296
forts, see castles & forts
fountains
  Fuente de los Leones 227
  Fuente del Rey 214
  Fuente Pública 304
Franco, General Francisco 322-3
Frigiliana 191
Fuengirola 172-3

G
Game of Thrones filming locations
  Alcázar 56-7, 59
  Osuna 103
gardens, see parks & gardens

Gaucín 185
gay travellers 360-1
gazpacho 354, **35**
Generación de '27 346
Generación de '98 346
geography 332
Gibraltar 45, 108, 150-5, **151, 152**
  accommodation 154
  activities 153-4
  food 154-5
  history 151
  shopping 155
  sights 151-3
  travel to/from 155
  travel within 155
Giralda (Seville) 56
Golden Century art 345-6
Góngora, Luís de 346
GR7 (Sendero de Gran Recorrido 7) footpath 146, 275
GR240 footpath 275
GR247 footpath 20, 241
Granada 247, 250-70, **254**, **258-9, 262-3, 5**
  accommodation 261-3
  activities 260
  drinking & nightlife 267-8
  entertainment 268
  festivals & events 260-1
  food 263-7
  history 247
  shopping 269
  sights 250-60
  street art 256
  tapas 265
  teterías (teahouses) 267
  tourist information 269
  tours 260
  travel to/from 269-70
  travel within 270
Granada province 46, 246-84, **248-9**
  flamenco 246
  food 32, 246
  highlights 248-9
  travel seasons 246
Grazalema 135-6
Greek settlement 313
Guadix 271-2

H
hammams 244-5, **245**
  Aire Baños Árabes 61, 64
  Hammam Al-Andalus (Málaga) 163

Hammam Andalusí (Jerez de la Frontera) 122
Hammam de Al Andalus (Granada) 260, **244**
hang-gliding 39-40
health 361
Hedionda sulphur baths 176
hiking 21, 36-7
  Alá   jar-Castaño del Robledo 96
  Aracena 93
  Cabo de Gata 301
  Cahorros Altos 273
  Caminito del Rey 187
  Camino de los Charcones 137
  Cañón de Bailón 213
  Castaño del Robledo-Galaroza Loop 97
  Cerro de San Cristóbal 98
  El Calvario-Corazón de Jesús 135
  El Torreón 138
  Garganta Verde 136, 137
  GR7 146, 275
  GR240 275
  GR247 20, 241
  Las Alpujarras 275
  Las Laderas-Camino Viejo Loop 105
  Linares de la Sierra 93
  maps 362-3
  Mediterranean Steps (Gibraltar) 153
  Mijas 177
  Mulhacén 273, 275
  Paraje Natural Torcal de Antequera 189
  Parque Nacional de Doñana 89
  Parque Natural de la Breña y Marismas del Barbate 141-2
  Parque Natural Los Alcornocales 148, 149-50
  Parque Natural Sierra de Hornachuelos 216-17
  Parque Natural Sierra de las Nieves 183
  Parque Natural Sierra de María-Los Vélez 307
  Parque Natural Sierra Norte de Sevilla 105
  Parque Natural Sierras de Cazorla, Segura y Las Villas 240
  Raya Real 89

Sendero Botánico 216
Sendero Cerro del Cinto 302
Sendero Charco de la Boca 89
Sendero de Ermitas y Monasterios 237
Sendero de Gran Recorrido 7 (GR7) 146, 275
Sendero de Los Ángeles 216
Sendero del Acantilado 141-2
Sendero del Aguadero 297
Sendero del Arroyo de las Cañas 107
Sendero del Gilillo 237
Sendero del Guaitenejo 185
Sendero del Pinsapar 137
Sendero Gerald Brenan 281
Sendero Guadalora 216-17
Sendero Lagunas del Acebuche 89
Sendero Los Castañares 107
Sendero Río Borosa 241
Sendero Río Hozgarganta 148-50
Sendero Río Verde 277
Sendero Salto del Cabrero 137
Sendero Subida al Picacho 148
Sendero Umbría de la Virgen 307
Sierra de Grazalema 137-8
Sierra Nevada 273, 275
Sulayr 275
Trevélez 280
Veleta 273, 275
Vía Verde de la Sierra 138
Vía Verde de la Sierra Norte 105
Vía Verde de la Subbética 213
Vía Verde del Aceite 223-4
hilltop towns 22
history 312-24
  books 316, 322
  Islamic Spain 314-18
  prehistoric Andalucía 312-13
  Reconquista 317-19

Spanish Civil War 321-2
Spanish Inquisition 319
traders & invaders
  313-14
holidays 364
Hornos 242
horse riding 38-9, **2**
  Aracena 93
  Cómpeta 190
  Lanjarón 275
  Parque Nacional de
    Doñana 89
  Tarifa 143
horses 121, 122
hostales 358-9
hostels 358-9
Huelva 82-4, **83**
Huelva province 44, 79,
  82-98, **80-1**
  accommodation 79
  activities 82
  car travel 79
  food 31-2, 79
  highlights 80-1
  internet resources 82

I
Iberian lynx 226, 311, 335,
  335-6, **14**
ibex 335
immigration 367
insurance 361, 371
internet access 361
internet resources 19
Isla Cristina 86-7
Islamic architecture 325-9,
  see also castles & forts;
  mosques; palaces &
  mansions
Islamic culture 314-18,
  344-5
Itálica 98
itineraries 26-9, *see*
  also driving tours

J
Jaén 222-5, **223**
Jaén province 46, 219-43,
  220-1
  accommodation 219
  car travel 219, 232
  food 32, 219
  highlights 220-1
jamón (ham) 280, 352-3
Jerez de la Frontera 119-25,
  120-1
  accommodation 122
  activities 121-2
  drinking & nightlife 124-5

entertainment 124, 125
festivals & events 122
food 122-4
sights 119-21
travel to/from 125
travel within 125
Jewish culture 316, 317
Jimena de la Frontera
  148-50
Jiménez, Juan Ramón 86

K
kitesurfing 16, 39, 144-5,
  17, **39**

L
La Axarquía 189-91
La Herradura 283-4
La Isleta del Moro 302
La Pepa 320
La Rábida 84
La Tahá 279-80
La Vega 271-2
Laguna de Fuente de
  Piedra 189
language courses 69, 113,
  140, 361-2
languages 18, 373-80
Lanjarón 275-6
Las Alpujarras 12, 272-3,
  275-82, 296-8, **274**
Laujar de Andarax 297-8
legal matters 362
lesbian travellers 360-1
Linares de la Sierra 95-6
literature 266, 270, 346-7
Lorca, Federico Garcia 266,
  270, 346, 347
Los Cahorros 273
Los Caños de Meca 141-2
Los Escullos 301
Los Pedroches 217
Los Tresmiles 273, 275
Los Vélez 307-8
Lugares Colombinos 84-6
lynx 226, 311, 335, 335-6,
  14

M
macaques 153, 335
Madinat al-Zahra 205-
  6, 327
Mairena 281-2
Málaga 15, 157, 160-70,
  162, **166-7**, **15**
  accommodation 164
  activities 163
  drinking & nightlife 167-8

entertainment 169
festivals & events 163-4
food 164-7
history 157
shopping 169
sights 157, 160-1, 163
travel to/from 169-70
travel within 170
Málaga province 45, 156-
  94, **158-9**
  accommodation 156
  car travel 156
  food 32, 156
  highlights 158-9
mansions, *see* palaces &
  mansions
maps 362-3
Marbella 173-5
markets
  Almería 288, 293
  Córdoba 205
  Málaga 161
  Tarifa 143
Matalascañas 87
measures 362
Mecina Bombarón 281
Mezquita (Córdoba) 10, 20,
  198-202, 326-7, **200-1**,
  11, **200-1**
Mijas 177-8
Minas de Riotinto 92-3
mining 92-3, 302
mobile phones 364
Moguer 85-6
Mojácar 303-6, **305**
Molina, Antonio Muñoz 347
monasteries
  Conjunto Monumental
    de la Cartuja 68
  Iglesía y Monasterio de
    Santiago 271
  Monasterio de la
    Encarnación 102
  Monasterio de la Rábida
    84
  Monasterio de
    Montesión 237
  Monasterio de San
    Isidoro del Campo
    98-9
  Monasterio de San
    Jerónimo 259-60, **22**
  Monasterio de Santa
    Clara 85
  O Sel Ling 277
money 18, 19, 150, 360,
  363
Montilla wines 212
Morocco, travel to/from
  149, 368, 369

mosques 326-7
  Alcázar (Jerez de la
    Frontera) 119
  Mezquita (Almonaster la
    Real) 98, 326
  Mezquita (Córdoba) 10,
    20, 198-202, 326-7,
    200-1, **11**, **200-1**
motorcycle travel 368, 370-1
mouflon 335
Mozarabies 329
Mudéjars 329
Muelle de las Carabelas 84
Mulhacén 273, 275
Murillo, Bartolomé Esteban
  51
Museo Picasso Málaga 15,
  157, 160, **15**
museums & galleries 42
  Archivo de Indias 61
  Archivo-Museo San Juan
    de Dios 256
  Baños Arabes 181
  Carmen Museo Max
    Moreau 256-7
  Casa Alpujarreña 278
  Casa de Pilatos 65
  Casa de Sefarad 203
  Casa del Obispo 109
  Casa Museo Arte
    Andalusí 234
  Casa Museo de Mijas 177
  Casa Museo Manuel de
    Falla 255
  Casa Museo Martín
    Alonso Pinzón 85
  Casa Museo Pedro
    Antonio de Alarcón 278
  Casa Museo Zenobia y
    Juan Ramón Jiménez
    86
  Centre Pompidou Málaga
    20, 160-1
  Centro Andaluz de la
    Fotografía 289, 291
  Centro Cerámica Triana
    66
  Centro de Arte
    Contemporáneo de
    Málaga 161
  Centro de Arte
    Contemporáneo de
    Mijas 177
  Centro de Interpretación
    Cuevas de Guadix 271
  Centro de Interpretación
    Judería de Sevilla 61
  Centro de Interpretación
    Olivar y Aceite 20
  Centro de la
    Interpretación
    Mudéjar 69

museums & galleries
continued
Centro Flamenco
Fosforito 203-4
Centro José Guerrero
257
Centro Lorca 270
Centro Velázquez 61
Colección Arte Garó 175
Conjunto Monumental
de la Cartuja 68
Cueva Museo 307
El Pabellon de la
Navegación 68
Fundación Rafael Alberti
126
Fundación Rodríguez-
Acosta 255
Gibraltar Museum 152
Hospital de la
Caridad 64
Hospital de los
Venerables
Sacerdotes 61
Huerta de San Vicente
270
La Casa de los Volcanes
302
La Cilla 138
Metropol Parasol 65
Military Heritage Centre
153
Museo Antiquarium 65
Museo Arqueológico
(Almuñécar) 283
Museo Arqueológico
(Córdoba) 204
Museo Arqueológico
(Estepona) 175
Museo Arqueológico
(Jerez de la Frontera)
119
Museo Arqueológico
(Seville) 67
Museo Automovilístico
Málaga 161, 163
Museo Batalla de las
Navas de Tolosa 226
Museo Carmen Thyssen
160
Museo Casa Natal
Federico García Lorca
270
Museo Conventual de las
Descalzas 186
Museo Cuevas del
Sacromonte 260
Museo de Almería 289

Museo de Arte Flamenco
160
Museo de Artes y
Costumbres Populares
(Jaén) 222
Museo de Artes y
Costumbres Populares
(Seville) 67
Museo de Artesanía
Textil 135
Museo de Bellas Artes
(Granada) 254
Museo de Bellas Artes
(Seville) 64-5
Museo de Cádiz 112
Museo de Huelva 82
Museo de Málaga 160
Museo de Nerja 192-3
Museo de Osuna 102
Museo de Ronda 179
Museo de la Alhambra
254
Museo de la Ciudad de
Carmona 99
Museo de la Ciudad de
Antequera 186
Museo de la Guitarra
289
Museo de las Cortes de
Cádiz 112
Museo de San Juan de la
Cruz 234
Museo del Baile
Flamenco 64
Museo del Bandolero
179, 181
Museo del Carnaval 86
Museo del Grabado
Español 174
Museo del Jamón 93
Museo del Vidrio y
Cristal 160
Museo Histórico
(Salobreña) 282
Museo Histórico
Municipal (Écija) 104
Museo Histórico
Municipal (Priego de
Córdoba) 215
Museo Internacional de
Arte Naïf 222
Museo Julio Romero de
Torres 204
Museo Lara 179
Museo Minero 92
Museo Naval 85
Museo Picasso Málaga
15, 157, 160, **15**
Museo Ralli 174-5
Museo Ruso de Málaga
20, 161
Museo Sefardi 255

Palacio de la Condesa de
Lebrija 65
Palacio de los Olvidados
20, 256
Palacio de Viana 205
Plaza de Toros de la Real
Maestranza 64
Torre de la Calahorra
203
Torre del Oro 64

N
Nacimiento del
Guadalquivir 240
Nasrids 328-9
national parks & nature
reserves 332-4, *see
also* parks & gardens
Centro de Fauna
Silvestre Collado del
Almendral 240-1
Paraje Natural Torcal de
Antequera 188-9, 334
Parque Dunar 87
Parque Nacional de
Doñana 14, 87-90, 130,
332-3
Parque Nacional Sierra
Nevada 273-5, 333
Parque Natural de Cabo
de Gata-Níjar 298-303,
333, **299**, **13**
Parque Natural de
Despeñaperros
225-6
Parque Natural de
Doñana 88
Parque Natural de la
Breña y Marismas del
Barbate 141-2
Parque Natural Los
Alcornocales
148-50, 333
Parque Natural Sierra de
Andújar 226-7, 333
Parque Natural Sierra de
Cardeña y
Montoro 217
Parque Natural Sierra de
Grazalema 137-8, 334
Parque Natural Sierra de
Hornachuelos 216-18
Parque Natural Sierra de
las Nieves 183, 334
Parque Natural Sierra de
María-Los Vélez 307
Parque Natural Sierra
Norte 334
Parque Natural Sierra
Norte de Sevilla 105-7
Parque Natural Sierras
de Cazorla, Segura y
las Villas 239-43, 334

Parque Natural Sierras
Subbéticas 211-16
Upper Rock Nature
Reserve 153
nature reserves, *see*
national parks & nature
reserves; parks &
gardens
Necrópolis Romana 99, 101
Nelson, Horatio Lord 152
Nerja 191-4, **192**
newspapers 362
Niebla 91
Níjar 295-6

O
Ohanes 297
olive oil 211, 230, 294,
353-4
Olvera 138-9, **22**
Omayyads 326
opening hours 363
Órgiva 276
Osuna 102-3
outdoor activities
23-5, 36-40, 82, *see
also individual
activities & locations*

P
palaces & mansions, *see
also* castles & forts
Alcazaba (Almería) 288
Alcazaba (Málaga)
157, 160
Alcázar (Jerez de la
Frontera) 119
Alcázar (Seville) 56-7, 59
Alcázar de los Reyes
Cristianos 202-3
Alhambra 9, 250-5,
328-9, **252-3**, **254**,
8-9, **252-3**
Casa de Pilatos 65
Casa del Mayorazgo 139
Castillo de Zuheros 212
Palacio de Dar-al-Horra
256
Palacio de Govantes y
Herdara 102
Palacio de Jabalquinto
228
Palacio de la Condesa de
Lebrija 65
Palacio de los Cepeda
102
Palacio de los Duques de
Medina Sidonia 129
Palacio de Los
Marqueses de la
Algaba 69

Palacio de Orleans y Borbón 129
Palacio de Peñaflor 104
Palacio de Vázquez de Molina 232
Palacio de Viana 205
Palacio de Villardompardo 222
Palacio del Deán Ortega 232
Palacio Marqués de la Gomera 102
Palacio Vela de los Cobos 234
Palos de la Frontera 84-5
Pampaneira 277-8
paradores 359
paragliding 39-40, 284
Paraje Natural Torcal de Antequera 188-9
parking 371
parks & gardens 328, *see also* national parks & nature reserves
  Alameda Botanic Gardens 152
  Casa del Rey Moro 179
  Jardín Botánico El Albardinal 302
  Jardín Botánico Umbría de la Virgen 307
  Jardín Micológico 'La Trufa' 215
  Orchidarium 175
  Parque Botánico El Majuelo 283
  Parque de María Luisa 66-7
Paseo de España 161
Parque de María Luisa 66-7
Parque Nacional de Doñana 14, 87-90, 130, 332-3
Parque Natural de Cabo de Gata-Níjar 298-303, 333, **299**, **13**
Parque Natural Los Alcornocales 148-50, 333
Parque Natural Sierra de Andújar 226-7, 333
Parque Natural Sierra de Grazalema 137-8, 334
Parque Natural Sierra de Hornachuelos 216-18
Parque Natural Sierra de las Nieves 183, 334
Parque Natural Sierra de María-Los Vélez 307
Parque Natural Sierra Norte de Sevilla 105-7

Parque Natural Sierras de Cazorla, Segura y las Villas 239-43, 334
Parque Natural Sierras Subbéticas 211-16
passports 367
Peña de Arias Montano 96
Peña de Hierro 92
peñas 63, 341
Peñón de Zaframagón 138
Phoenician settlement 313
phonecards 364-5
Picasso, Pablo 157, 347
planning
  Andalucía basics 18-19
  Andalucía's regions 44-6
  budgeting 19
  calendar of events 23-5
  children, travel with 41-3
  food 30-5
  internet resources 19
  itineraries 26-9
  outdoor activities 36-40
  repeat visitors 20
  travel seasons 18, 23-5
Plaza de San Francisco 65
poetry 270, 346-7
police 362
politics 310-11
population 311
Portugal, travel to/from 87
postal services 363
pottery 236
Pradollano 273
Priego de Córdoba 214-16
public holidays 364

R
radio 362
Real Escuela Andaluza del Arte Ecuestre 121
religion 311
Renaissance architecture 330
Río Guadalquivir 332
Río Madera 243
Rio Tinto company 82, 92
road rules 371
rock climbing 40, 185
Rodalquilar 302-3
Roman settlement 313-14
Romería del Rocío 90
Ronda 10, 178-84, **180**, **10**
  accommodation 181-2
  drinking & nightlife 183
  entertainment 184
  festivals & events 181
  food 182-3
  sights 178-9, 181

travel to/from 184
travel within 184
Ronda la Vieja 184-5
Royal Andalucian School of Equestrian Art 121

S
Sacromonte 260
safety 364
Salinas de Cabo de Gata 299
Salobreña 282-3
San José 300-2
San Miguel de Cabo de Gata 299-300
Sanlúcar de Barrameda 129-31
Santa Elena 225-6
Santa Eufemia 217
Santiponce 98-9
seafood 351
Segura de la Sierra 242-3
Semana Santa
  Antequera 187
  Arcos de la Frontera 133
  Baeza 229
  Córdoba 206
  Granada 260
  Jaén 224
  Málaga 163
  Seville 17, 23, 69-70, **17**, **24**
  Úbeda 235
Sendero de Gran Recorrido 7 (GR7) 146, 275
senior travellers 360
Serranía de Ronda 184-5
Sevilla province 44, 79, 98-107, **80-1**
  accommodation 79
  activities 82
  car travel 79
  food 31, 79
  highlights 80-1
  internet resources 82
Seville (Sevilla) 44, 48-61, 64-78, **49**, **54-5**, **58**, **60**
  accommodation 70-2
  activities 61, 64, 66-7, 68
  bicycle travel 66
  children, travel with 71
  courses 69
  drinking & nightlife 75-6
  entertainment 76-7
  festivals & events 17, 23, 69-70, **17**, **24**
  flamenco 48
  food 48, 72-5

highlights 49
history 50
shopping 77
sights 50-7, 59, 61, 64-9
tourist information 77-8
tours 69
travel seasons 48
travel to/from 78
travel within 78
Seville cathedral 9, 50-6, **52-3**, **9**, **52-3**
sheep 335
sherry 10, 33, 130, 355, **11**, *see also* bodegas
  festivals 127
  food pairings 33
  history 129
Sherry Triangle 118-31
Sierra de Aracena 95-8, **96**
Sierra de Cazorla 239-43, **239**
Sierra Nevada 12, 272-5, 332, **274**, **12**
siesta 33
Siglo de Oro (Golden Century) 345-6
skiing 40, 273
snorkelling 37-8, 300-1
snowboarding 40, 273
Sorbas 295
spaghetti westerns 294
Spanish Civil War 321-2
Spanish fir 334
spas, *see* hammams
storks 337
surfing 39, 141, 142
synagogues
  Sinagoga de Córdoba 203
  Sinagoga del Agua 234

T
tabancos 123
tablaos 63, 343
tapas 13, 34, 168, 265, 292, 352, **13**
Tarifa 16, 142-7, **144**, **17**, **39**
  accommodation 145-6
  activities 143-5
  drinking & nightlife 147
  festivals & events 145
  food 146-7
  sights 143
  travel to/from 147
taxes 363
taxis 371
tea 356, see also *teterías* (teahouses)
telephone services 150, 364-5

teterías (teahouses) 244-5, 267, 293, 356, **244, 245**
theatres
  Gran Teatro Falla 117
  Sevilla de Ópera 76
  Teatro Cervantes 169
  Teatro Villamarta 125
theme parks 42
  Fort Bravo 295
  Isla Mágica 68
  Oasys Mini Hollywood 294-5
  Tivoli World 171
time 365
tinto de verano 169
tipping 363
toilets 365
tomatoes 296
Torrecilla 183
Torremolinos 170-2
Torres, Julio Romero de 346
tourist information 365
towers
  Torre de la Calahorra 203
  Torre del Tajo 141
  Torre Pirulico 304
  Torre Tavira 109, 112
Trafalgar Cemetery 152
train tours 92-3
train travel 19, 368-9, 371-2, **372**

travel to/from Andalucía 367-9
travel within Andalucía 369-72
trees 334, 336
trekking, *see* hiking
Trevélez 280
Triana 66-7

U
Úbeda 16, 231-7, **233**
  accommodation 235
  drinking & nightlife 236
  festivals & events 235
  food 235-6
  pottery 236
  shopping 236
  sights 232, 234
  travel to/from 236-7
  travel within 236-7
unemployment 310-11
Upper Rock Nature Reserve 153

V
Válor 281
Vandelvira, Andrés de 231, 330
vegetarian travellers 32
Vejer de la Frontera 20, 139-41, **16**
Velázquez, Diego 51, 345
Veleta 273, 275

Vélez Blanco 307-8
Vélez Málaga 189
vías verdes (greenways) 37
  Vía Verde de la Sierra 138
  Vía Verde de la Sierra Norte 105
  Vía Verde de la Subbética 213
  Vía Verde del Aceite 223-4
Villanueva de Córdoba 217
visas 150, 365-6
Visigoths 314, 326
vultures 336-7

W
walking, *see* hiking
weather 18, 23-5
websites 19
weights 362
whale-watching 145
white towns 16, 131-9
  Arcos de la Frontera 131-3, 135
  driving tour 134, **134**
  Grazalema 135-6
  Olvera 138-9
  Vejer de la Frontera 20, 139-41, **16**
  Zahara de la Sierra 136
wildlife 43, 334-7

wildlife-watching 38, 88-9, *see also* birdwatching, dolphin-watching, *individual animals*
  Centro de Fauna Silvestre Collado del Almendral 240-1
  Parque Natural Sierra de Andújar 226-7
windsurfing 39, 144-5, 284
wine 179, 212, 353, 354-5, *see also* bodegas
wolves 335
women travellers 366
WWII 153, 323

Y
Yegen 281

Z
Zahara de la Sierra 136
Zahara de los Atunes 142, **15**
ziplining 174
zoos
  Biopark 172
  Oasys Mini Hollywood 294
  Parque Ornitológico Loro-Sexi 283
Zuheros 211-14
Zurbarán, Francisco de 345

Map Legend

Sights

- Beach
- Bird Sanctuary
- Buddhist
- Castle/Palace
- Christian
- Confucian
- Hindu
- Islamic
- Jain
- Jewish
- Monument
- Museum/Gallery/Historic Building
- Ruin
- Shinto
- Sikh
- Taoist
- Winery/Vineyard
- Zoo/Wildlife Sanctuary
- Other Sight

Activities, Courses & Tours

- Bodysurfing
- Diving
- Canoeing/Kayaking
- Course/Tour
- Sento Hot Baths/Onsen
- Skiing
- Snorkelling
- Surfing
- Swimming/Pool
- Walking
- Windsurfing
- Other Activity

Sleeping

- Sleeping
- Camping

Eating

- Eating

Drinking & Nightlife

- Drinking & Nightlife
- Cafe

Entertainment

- Entertainment

Shopping

- Shopping

Information

- Bank
- Embassy/Consulate
- Hospital/Medical
- Internet
- Police
- Post Office
- Telephone
- Toilet
- Tourist Information
- Other Information

Geographic

- Beach
- Gate
- Hut/Shelter
- Lighthouse
- Lookout
- Mountain/Volcano
- Oasis
- Park
- Pass
- Picnic Area
- Waterfall

Population

- Capital (National)
- Capital (State/Province)
- City/Large Town
- Town/Village

Transport

- Airport
- Border crossing
- Bus
- Cable car/Funicular
- Cycling
- Ferry
- Metro station
- Monorail
- Parking
- Petrol station
- S-Bahn/S-train/Subway station
- Taxi
- T-bane/Tunnelbana station
- Train station/Railway
- Tram
- Tube station
- U-Bahn/Underground station
- Other Transport

Note: Not all symbols displayed above appear on the maps in this book

Routes

- Tollway
- Freeway
- Primary
- Secondary
- Tertiary
- Lane
- Unsealed road
- Road under construction
- Plaza/Mall
- Steps
- Tunnel
- Pedestrian overpass
- Walking Tour
- Walking Tour detour
- Path/Walking Trail

Boundaries

- International
- State/Province
- Disputed
- Regional/Suburb
- Marine Park
- Cliff
- Wall

Hydrography

- River, Creek
- Intermittent River
- Canal
- Water
- Dry/Salt/Intermittent Lake
- Reef

Areas

- Airport/Runway
- Beach/Desert
- Cemetery (Christian)
- Cemetery (Other)
- Glacier
- Mudflat
- Park/Forest
- Sight (Building)
- Sportsground
- Swamp/Mangrove

OUR STORY

A beat-up old car, a few dollars in the pocket and a sense of adventure. In 1972 that's all Tony and Maureen Wheeler needed for the trip of a lifetime – across Europe and Asia overland to Australia. It took several months, and at the end – broke but inspired – they sat at their kitchen table writing and stapling together their first travel guide, *Across Asia on the Cheap*. Within a week they'd sold 1500 copies. Lonely Planet was born.

Today, Lonely Planet has offices in Franklin, London, Melbourne, Oakland, Beijing and Delhi, with more than 600 staff and writers. We share Tony's belief that 'a great guidebook should do three things: inform, educate and amuse'.

OUR WRITERS

Isabella Noble

Huelva & Sevilla Provinces, Cádiz Province & Gibraltar English/Australian on paper but Spanish at heart, Isabella grew up in a Málaga mountain village and later lived in Cádiz province. Adventures this edition included exploring Vejer's magic, hiking Grazalema's Garganta Verde, getting lost in Cádiz Carnaval and sipping *tintos* on bleach-blonde beaches in Tarifa, one of her favourite places in the world. For now, she lives in London and writes on Spain, India and beyond for a number of publications. Isabella also wrote the Outdoor Activities chapter. Find her on Twitter/Instagram @isabellamnoble.

Read more about Isabella at:
http://auth.lonelyplanet.com/profiles/isabellanoble

John Noble

Córdoba Province, Jaén Province, Almería Province John, originally from England's Ribble Valley, has lived in an Andalucian mountain village since 1995. He has explored Andalucía from end to end, playing a part in all eight editions of this guidebook. The highlight of research for this edition was going to the Sierra de Andújar to look for wildlife and quite coincidentally getting mixed up in the enormous once-a-year festivities of the Romería de la Virgen de la Cabeza. John also wrote the Andalucía Today and History chapters.

Read more about John at:
http://auth.lonelyplanet.com/profiles/ewoodrover

Josephine Quintero

Málaga Province Josephine has lived in a small village just outside Málaga since 1992. As well as continually 'discovering' the Costa capital, Josephine loves strolling along the beachside promenades throughout the coastal resorts. A highlight this trip was discovering a Roman sulphur spring that has escaped being commercialised and enjoying inspirational art during an open studio weekend in the picturesque mountainside village of Gaucín. Josephine also wrote the Travel with Children chapter.

Read more about Josephine at:
http://auth.lonelyplanet.com/profiles/josephinequintero

Brendan Sainsbury

Seville, Granada Province Originally from Hampshire, England, Brendan first went to Spain on an Interrail ticket in the 1980s. He went back as a travel guide several years later and met his wife-to-be in a small village in rural Andalucía in 2003. He has been writing books for Lonely Planet for a decade, including four previous editions of the *Spain* and *Andalucía* guidebooks. Brendan loves Granada, the writing of Federico Lorca, cycling along *via verdes* and attending as many flamenco shows as his research allows. Brendan also wrote the Plan Your Trip, Understand and Survival Guide sections.

Read more about Brendan at:
http://auth.lonelyplanet.com/profiles/brendansainsbury

Published by Lonely Planet Publications Pty Ltd
ABN 36 005 607 983
8th edition – Jan 2016
ISBN 978 1 74321 387 2
© Lonely Planet 2016   Photographs © as indicated 2016
10 9 8 7 6 5 4 3 2 1
Printed in China

Although the authors and Lonely Planet have taken all reasonable care in preparing this book, we make no warranty about the accuracy or completeness of its content and, to the maximum extent permitted, disclaim all liability arising from its use.